The Modern Gang Reader

Third Edition

Arlen Egley Jr.
National Youth Gang Center

Cheryl L. Maxson
University of California–Irvine

Jody Miller
University of Missouri–St. Louis

Malcolm W. Klein
University of Southern California

New York   Oxford
OXFORD UNIVERSITY PRESS

Oxford University Press, Inc., publishes works that further Oxford University's
objective of excellence in research, scholarship, and education.

Oxford   New York
Auckland   Cape Town   Dar es Salaam   Hong Kong   Karachi
Kuala Lumpur   Madrid   Melbourne   Mexico City   Nairobi
New Delhi   Shanghai   Taipei   Toronto

With offices in
Argentina   Austria   Brazil   Chile   Czech Republic   France   Greece
Guatemala   Hungary   Italy   Japan   Poland   Portugal   Singapore
South Korea   Switzerland   Thailand   Turkey   Ukraine   Vietnam

Published by Oxford University Press, Inc.
198 Madison Avenue, New York, New York 10016
http://www.oup.com

ISBN 978-0-19-533066-3

Printing number: 9 8 7 6 5 4 3 2 1

Printed in the United States of America
on acid-free paper

Contents

Section I: DEFINING AND UNDERSTANDING GANGS

---

* New to the Third Edition

Section II: DISTRIBUTION AND STRUCTURES OF GANGS

* New to the Third Edition

Section III: RACE, ETHNICITY, AND GENDER IN GANGS

Section IV: GANGS, VIOLENCE, AND DRUGS

---

* New to the Third Edition

Section V: PROGRAMS AND POLICIES

* New to the Third Edition

About the Editors

Arlen Egley Jr. is currently the senior analyst for the National Youth Gang Survey and has published journal articles and book chapters on gangs. **Cheryl L. Maxson, Jody Miller,** and **Malcolm W. Klein** have each published extensively on the subject of gangs, and are recognized as among the leading researchers in the field. ✦

Introduction

Gang activity continues to be a widespread and serious problem in the United States. In addition to numerous (typically larger) cities across the nation with chronic gang problems, in the past 15 years many new cities and towns have reported experiencing gang problems. For most of these areas gangs come and go rather quickly, but for others they have become all too familiar, all too stable. And with each new "discovery" of a gang problem there comes a whole host of stereotypes, misconceptions, and fallacies proclaimed, circulated, and recirculated in the general public. What is known about gangs from systematic, impartial research is all too often unheeded and neglected.

Our intention for this book is to expose the reader to some of the most salient, contemporary issues surrounding gangs. Within that broad intention, we have opted for satisfying quality and readability rather than always seeking the most detailed; we have sought articles that best represent a larger category of material, articles that contribute to a *pattern* of information, and articles that present different or even opposing views on various topics.

As we began preparations for the third edition of *The Modern Gang Reader*, we quickly realized that many new and important pieces on gangs had been published since the last edition. The process of arriving at a third edition, we knew, would be met with some difficulty. First, we invited an additional editor who has been involved in recent gang research and publication and who is currently the senior survey analyst of the largest ongoing study of gang activity across the United States. Second, each of us reviewed the wealth of information published since the last edition and then presented our selections to the other editors. Owing to the quality of recently published material, we did not immediately agree on but a few articles. It took many rounds to decide which articles to include, which ultimately led us to the painful job of deciding which articles from the previous edition to

remove. While there are certainly many justified arguments about the inclusion or continuance of certain articles that have been omitted in this edition, our ultimate goal was, as always, to present the reader with a collection of articles that fit together as an ensemble, a comprehensive exposure to the varied and important research topics regarding gangs. Some topics are entirely new—stemming from largely unprecedented research designs and/or agendas—while others have seen increased research attention and refinement. The end result, we believe, is a highly accessible, readable, and expansive book representing the current knowledge of gang research.

The format of this book is quite straightforward. Section I begins with a discussion of definitional issues regarding gangs—where any discussion of gangs should begin—and proceeds with a brief overview of the history of gang research, a macro-level framework from which to understand the emergence of gangs, and the social variables and processes that contribute to individuals' joining and leaving the gang. Section II includes recent gang trends as depicted by a large sample of law enforcement agencies, the variability of gang structure and behavior across the United States, a comparison of U.S. gangs to their cross-national counterparts, and an overview of prison gangs. Section III offers an inspection of gangs across racial/ethnic and gender lines and, while noting important differences along these dimensions, demonstrates that on the whole gangs exhibit far more similarities than is generally believed. Section IV gets to the heart of what interests most people about gangs—their antisocial behavior—and specifically concentrates on two behaviors often associated with gangs—violence and drugs. What one *does* about gangs is the most complex issue of all. Thus, the fifth and final section presents articles covering the many different responses to gangs. These include prevention strategies that target the general population, intervention strategies that attempt to provide services to current gang members, and suppression strategies that are perhaps best exemplified by law enforcement procedures to crack down on gangs and deter their criminal behavior.

Despite the programs and policies and laws, we are left with the sad but inescapable conclusion that despite many genuine efforts to develop gang intervention and control programs, we have not come far. We have learned far more about what to avoid than what can be done positively. Equally sadly, little of what has been learned has been incorporated into prevention and control programs.

To understand why this is so, it may be helpful to review several points in this introduction. Although covered in various ways in the readings we have selected for the volume, the following points can be highlighted as background to what follows.

1. Street Gangs and Others

"Gang" is an ambiguous term, subject to changing usages over time. Most, though not all, of this book is concerned with modern *street* gangs, not with the Mafia, prison gangs, terrorist groups, supremacist groups, motorcycle clubs, or the many thousands of other youth groups that are occasionally delinquent. Even with those exclusions, street gangs come in bewildering varieties. They can be as small as a dozen or so members, they may number several hundred members, or they may be unusual federations of several thousand members. They are primarily but not exclusively male (ratios of males to females are described as ranging from almost 1 to 1 to 10 to 1 or more; there are some all-female gangs, but these are few). Perhaps 85 percent of street gangs consist primarily of racial and ethnic minorities—black, Hispanic, Asian—and can be found in large urban centers, in suburbs, and in isolated towns and cities. Street gang members can range in age from pre-teens to adults in their 30s, with the average age between 16 and the early 20s in most gangs, though this varies by gender. They are usually territorial (both in the sense of living in relatively circumscribed areas and in the sense of having strong neighborhood loyalties). While most of the members' waking hours are spent on normal, even dull activities, street gang members more than most young people evidence an orientation toward antisocial behavior—various forms of delinquent and criminal behavior. In most cases, they are generalists rather than specialists in crime; that is, the crime patterns are versatile, ranging from the most minor forms of vandalism and petty theft to less common serious violent offenses. Yet it is the violence that has captured public attention and engendered the kinds of suppressive official responses described in several parts of Section V.

Not all gangs are street gangs. The recent emergence of drug distribution gangs, for instance, has fueled much of the outcry against street gangs because the two gang forms have mistakenly been taken as synonymous. They are not. There has been some similar confusion of prison gangs and street gangs as well (see Chapter 13), while others have hoped to include white racist groups like the Skinheads in the same category as the more traditional street gangs (see Chapter 9). Every such attempt to overgeneralize yields not only conceptual confusion, but also control programs more likely to fail for bringing to bear on one gang form the beliefs about another. Category-specific kinds of intervention are needed.

2. Gangs Then and Now

A "classical" period of gang research that built upon the original work of Frederic Thrasher in 1930s' Chicago flourished in the 1950s and 1960s in New York, Boston, Chicago, and Los Angeles. In those days, most street gangs studied were of the traditional or vertical type, each consisting of several age-specific subgroups and often one or two auxiliary girls' groups. They ranged in size from 50 to 200 members and in ages of 11 or 12 to the early 20s. Highly territorial and violent far more in talk than in actions, these gangs were black and Hispanic, but also white in the earlier years—Irish, German, Polish, Italian, and so on.

Located principally in lower- and working-class sections of major metropolitan areas, these youthful gangs fought among and between themselves, and committed a wide variety of delinquent offenses of a principally nonserious type. They were significant features of their inner-city communities, but with a few exceptions they were not the sources of fear and terror one is accustomed to hearing of now.

Things have changed. Instead of a few

score gang-involved communities, we now have a few thousand reporting gang problems. The variety of gang structures has grown, making generalizations more difficult. Many older young adults are now involved and firearms are readily available, yielding a far more apparent violent aspect to many gangs: around 1,500 people have been killed in gang incidents in each of the cities of Los Angeles and Chicago since the turn of the twenty-first century. Ethnic patterns have changed as well, with most street gangs being of minority status, adding to mainstream society's disdain for gang members. Partly because of gang proliferation and increased violence levels, but also reflective of more conservative political times, the official approach to gangs has swung from prevention and social intervention to law enforcement control programs and "crackdown" legislation. In reading the various selections in this volume, readers should note the years of original publication in order to set each piece in its proper place.

3. Sources of Gang Knowledge

The selections in this book come from a wide assortment of sources and methodological approaches. Each contains its own strengths and limitations and, as such, we remind our readers of the obvious truth that no one method can claim fairly to be the best. Each has its problems, and we would argue for a pluralistic approach.

Ethnographic field research, usually concentrating on one or only a few gangs, seldom yields tested generalizations—gangs differ, communities differ, and researcher perspectives differ. Ethnographic research with a comparative focus has been especially fruitful in recent years, avoiding some, but not all, of these limitations. Further, crime statistics of a reliable sort are seldom collected in such studies. Yet from such close-at-hand research, one tends to get at the perspective of the gang member that is simply not otherwise available. Ethnographers "know" gangs in a way that survey researchers and analysts of official crime data cannot hope to achieve.

By the same token, those who rely on youth or adult surveys—interviews or questionnaires—are subject to two highly suspect sets of reporters, the gang members and those who process them (such as the police and service providers). Their perspec-

tives are sometimes self-serving and often unverifiable. On the other hand, surveys can yield systematic information on a wider population of gangs and can take into account the expertise of people who have worked extensively with gangs. A combination of ethnography and survey techniques is perhaps the best antidote.

Those who rely principally on official records—police, court, corrections—have other problems. The records contain a minimum of verifiable data about individual gang members, and far less about gang structures. The criminal records include only a small portion of actual offenses committed, and are disproportionately about the more serious offenses. Yet in no other way can so much gang crime data be gathered, nor data on large numbers of gangs across many communities. And, we have discovered, it is usually only the police who have an overview of gangs in their city; community residents and agency officials are knowledgeable—when they are—only about groups very close by.

It is well to be skeptical about any one source of gang knowledge, and about any one piece of gang description as being applicable to gangs generally. We urge caution, and we urge comprehensive review and respect for what can emerge from many sources. This volume reflects this viewpoint.

4. Group Contexts

So far, we have said little about gang theories. They abound, but unfortunately tend not to be very comprehensive. We find no specific theory of gangs to be satisfactory, and no general theory to be adequate to many specific instances. Further, how one sees gangs is very dependent on the context one employs.

A. Deviance

Gangs and gang behavior are socially deviant, but so are many other things. Within the relatively disadvantaged neighborhoods that spawn gangs, one may well find drug sales and use, homelessness, alcoholism, high dropout rates at school, prostitution and gambling, high rates of non-marital cohabitation and teenage pregnancy, high rates of public health problems, and so on. In other words, gangs don't appear in *gang* neighborhoods, but most often in *problem-prone* neighborhoods where gang involvement is one among many patterns of social deviance. For many gang writers, then, the gang is not the problem: the nature of the community and how it came to be that way is the problem. Gangs, like other social problems, are the byproducts of their communities, and perhaps it is the source of community ills that is the appropriate target of intervention.

B. Racism

As noted above, most gangs are composed of racial and ethnic minorities. This is not a random pattern; it is no accident. Gangs emerge in minority communities, usually those overwhelmed by poverty, unemployment, and low levels of social services, because the dominant society permits such communities to exist. Inadvertent or institutional racism—the racism of social neglect—is hard for many to face, and harder yet to combat. Yet the gangs we describe are a product of these forms of racism. Blame does not inhere in the gangs alone, and many gang researchers find modern gangs more blameless because they reflect an often insensitive white America.

C. Youth

As one reads media and other reports of gang activity, it is easy to form stereotypes of marauding bands, sophisticated automatic weapons, innocent victims, terrorized neighborhoods, and outmanned police handcuffed by restrictive judicial rulings. These are, in fact, occasional facets of the gang problem—very occasional. We lose sight of the humdrum life of most gang members, of their dislocation from much of mainstream America, and of the fact that so many spend their prime gang years as adolescents in trouble, not adult hoods ripping off society. One need not condone criminal behavior in order to appreciate that these are youth—*our* youth—whose futures in many instances are salvageable if we have the patience to apply the knowledge available to us and the persistence to continue supporting the research on gang youth that will yield better prevention and intervention tools.

D. Social Psychology

Of several intellectual traditions that can be brought to bear on gang issues, social psychology seems a particularly pertinent one. Gangs are groups, and a great deal of work has been carried out by social psychol-

ogists on group structure and function. Consider just these well-researched concepts: group size, leadership, cohesiveness, group norms and values, conformity, peer pressure, intergroup relations, role-modeling, morale, rumor transmission, and communication patterns. Each has a well-documented knowledge base, and each can be applied to the understanding of gang processes. A number of gang researchers—fewer than might be hoped—have placed gangs in this intellectual context and have successfully analyzed a number of common gang patterns as well as some of the reasons gangs have been so resistant to attempts at social intervention and control.

E. Organizational Behavior

In addition to their own group organization features, gangs are affected by social organizations whose study comprises another highly relevant intellectual context. Families, school, community agencies, city and state legislation bodies, police, courts, and corrections personnel are all members of informal and formal organizations. As such, these people interact with gangs as organizational representatives both motivated by and constrained by organizational values and norms, bureaucratic procedures, special interests, political pressures, conflicting ideologies and perspectives, self-protection, and inertia.

Gangs develop, flourish, and languish in the contexts of these organizations. Some gang researchers have described the likely effect on gangs of existing and alternative organizational milieus, finding that such analyses help to refocus attention on nongang factors that can exacerbate the gang situation. Again, the clear implication is that blame and credit do not belong to the gangs alone.

F. Community Structures

Finally, there is a need to consider the macro-structure of gang-involved communities. From Thrasher on, gang researchers have rather uniformly been sensitive to the level of structure and organization of communities as contributors to gang development and absorbers of gang activity. Socially well-organized neighborhoods can include gangs, but more commonly it is neighborhoods in transition (ethnic, economic, etc.) and structurally disadvantaged neighborhoods that have most often been described as gang-prone.

Thus, a number of gang researchers have concentrated on ways that reorganizing and activating communities can reduce the level of gang tension and reintegrate gang members into mainstream activities. Here, the gang is at most a secondary target of intervention, and the level of a community's social capacity is the primary target.

Each of these contexts—deviance, racism, youth, social psychology, organization, and community structure—provides a perspective from which to understand gangs. As such, each is deliberately included among the papers in this volume. Keepings one's eye on the perspective from which an author seems to be working aids interpretation of the positions taken, and provides the basis for healthy skepticism in judging the validity of the work in question. In other words, we urge our readers to be interpretive, not just to be recorders of the works presented here.

We end with one other cautionary note. As one considers the articles included in this volume and other gang-related writings as well, one should keep in mind that the gang problem is often *used* for other, usually political, purposes. Gangs have become social and political footballs, kicked around in the public arena to justify ideologies, organizational build-ups, legislative reforms, and budgetary enhancements. Each time one sees or hears of a new proposal to "deal with the gang problem," it seems fair to question the extent to which that proposal is designed to address gangs, and the extent to which it addresses the proposer's needs. Experience in the gang world fosters a mildly cynical outlook. ◆

Section I

Defining and Understanding Gangs

Chapter 1
Defining and Researching Gangs

Robert J. Bursik Jr.
and Harold G. Grasmick

Our understanding of the nature and extent of gang behavior, and our beliefs about the actions we should take to respond to it, is highly dependent on how gang is defined and the methods used to gather information about a gang. Bursik and Grasmick draw from the extensive gang literature to illustrate both process-based and delinquency-based approaches to gang definitions. In their methodological review, they describe the inherent limitations of each major method and warn that the gang literature must be approached with an eye to these limitations. The editors of this volume share their concern and urge readers to consider the definitional stances and methodological strategies adopted by each researcher. The representativeness of the study sample, reliability of informants, and adequacy of comparison groups are critical elements of the context of gang research and the information it produces.

Peggy Sanday (1990) has provided a detailed description of the dynamics that led to a gang rape alleged to have been committed by members of a fairly well-organized, cohesive group of older adolescents in Philadelphia. Prior to this particular incident, the XYZs (a fictitious name) had already developed a widespread reputation in the neighborhood for problematic behavior. Women commonly reported that they had been verbally harassed by members of the gang who hung around drinking beer on

Reprinted from: Robert J. Bursik Jr. and Harold G. Grasmick, *Neighborhoods and Crime: The Dimensions of Effective Community Control.* Copyright © 1993 by Lexington Books. Reprinted by permission.

benches along the primary street in the area. Since these benches were situated in front of their clubhouse, the group made it clear that this was their "turf" to do with as they pleased.

Although all the members of this gang were enrolled in school, the group allocated some degree of special status to those who performed poorly. One of the judges involved in the rape case noted that a statement that the XYZs had offered into evidence was "ungrammatical . . . replete with misspellings . . . garbled and incomprehensible" (Forer 1990:xvii). As Sanday has reported, new members of the community were commonly warned about the group, and women were urged to consider the potential dangers of attending the parties that were regularly thrown by the gang.

To many, this short description has all the hallmarks of classic, popular descriptions of a gang, that is, a group of inner-city adolescents, a concern with turf, harassment of local residents, an organizational structure, some degree of solidarity, and mutual participation in serious forms of illegal behavior. Sanday notes (p. 71) that during her two interviews with one of the people implicated in the gang rape, "[H]is dislike for what I was doing and his sense of superiority to people like me were expressed throughout. . . ." In general, we would guess that most readers would not consider this to be a group with which they would like to interact on a regular basis. However, we have left one very important piece of information out of our short summary of Sanday's study: these were all members of a prominent fraternity at a prestigious, upper-middle-class university; the neighborhood in question was a campus community in Philadelphia.

Perhaps some readers think that this is an inappropriate example of gang activity, for public images of such behavior usually do not include the activities of fairly affluent fraternity members at highly respected colleges. Yet consider the influential definition of a gang provided by Klein (1971:13): any identifiable group of youngsters who (a) are generally perceived as a distinct aggregation by others in their neighborhood, (b) recognize themselves as a denotable group (almost invariably with a group name), and (c) have been involved in a sufficient number of delinquent incidents to call forth a consistent negative response from neighborhood residents and/or law enforcement agencies.

As anyone familiar with campus life is aware, all fraternities easily qualify under the first two conditions; each has a unique name, and highly visible, relatively arcane symbols (i.e., Greek letters) are used to signify membership in such groups. The third condition is the one that would disqualify many (and perhaps most) fraternities. Yet Sanday's ethnographic material clearly shows that the "XYZ" fraternity had a "dangerous" reputation on campus, and we would be surprised to find many college campuses without at least one such house. Nevertheless, despite the fact that the XYZs clearly qualified as a gang under Klein's definition and the fact that one of the judges described the similarities of this case to those involving more traditional gang members as "striking" (Forer 1990:xvi), there is no indication that Philadelphia's long-established Gang Crimes Unit had any involvement in the case.

Thus, we come to the heart of the problem: exactly how are we to define a gang? Without a generally accepted definition of the concept, it is impossible to make any kind of informed judgment concerning the nature and extent of gang behavior, much less changes that have occurred over time. Some criminologists would certainly include the XYZ case in the computation of rates of gang crimes;[1] others would object strongly to such a classification.

Likewise, what are we to make of the fact that many small, stable, rural communities have recently claimed to be the site of gang behavior? For example, a Knight-Ridder newspaper item (Wallace 1991) describes the case of Frederick, Oklahoma (population 5,200), where the local police chief believes that violent, drug-dealing gangs are staking out territory in the community. The primary basis for his conclusion is the existence of some "Bloods" graffiti in the area, a number of auto thefts, cases of shoplifting and intimidation, reports of drug dealing, and warning notes (this time from the Crips) that have been left on cars.

It is clear that one of the gravest mistakes that a community can make is to deny the existence of a gang-related problem until a series of serious incidents force the issue. Columbus, Ohio, for example, denied that it had any type of problem until members of the mayor's family were brutally attacked by people claiming gang affiliation (Huff 1989:530–531). Therefore, the situation in Frederick might be seen as an outcome of the expansion of gang-controlled drug markets that had been widely discussed (U.S. General Accounting Office 1989). However, while the concern of the Frederick police chief certainly is understandable, a healthy degree of skepticism is warranted concerning the large number of communities who suddenly have discovered a "gang problem" in their midst. Grasmick was recently told by a high school teacher from Oklahoma City (which does have a documented gang problem), that once particular symbols (such as certain forms of dress or graffiti) became associated with gang membership in his school, they quickly became adopted by many nongang adolescents as a sign of personal rebellion.[2] Therefore, the incidents that were reported in Frederick (including the graffiti) may not be gang-related in any respect other than they represent the efforts of local youths to adopt symbols that are guaranteed to elicit a horrified reaction from the adults in their community.

There are other dynamics that also must be considered when evaluating the extent to which an area is characterized by gang activity. Many concerned communities have invited law enforcement personnel to speak to local leaders about whether they have a gang problem and, if so, what they should do about it. One of the central themes that usually emerges is that without proper action on the part of the community, it is likely to be overrun with gang-related problems in a relatively short period of time. Such messages are quickly picked up by the local media and spread to the general public. Hagedorn (1988:30), for example, reports that the elites and the media of Milwaukee adopted an image of gang behavior that was promoted by the Chicago Gang Crimes Unit and reinforced by "scary slide shows of murders and a display of gang weapons that would make the U.S. Army run for cover." During these presentations, Milwaukee was warned that if the city failed to act "in a hard line manner," Milwaukee's gangs would be like those in Chicago within five years or less. We find this passage to be especially interesting in that one member of Oklahoma City's Gang Crimes Unit has worked especially hard to promote the image of impending gang danger across the state. . . .

Finally, it must be noted that since access to some federally funded law enforcement programs is more likely if a gang problem can be demonstrated in a community, some agencies may have vested interests in the "discovery" of gang activity. It is impossible to determine the extent to which the apparent diffusion of gang behavior reflects such economic considerations. However, such dynamics have been suggested as an explanation of why police estimates of the number of gangs in Phoenix increased from 5 or 6 to over 100 in a very short period of time (Zatz 1987).

It certainly has not been our intention in this section to downplay the seriousness of some gang activities or to imply that most communities are exaggerating the problems they face. Rather, we have attempted to emphasize that without a precise and parsimonious understanding of what constitutes a gang and gang behavior, it is often difficult to separate fact from mythology. Unfortunately, several factors make it very difficult to arrive at such an understanding.

Crime and Delinquency as Group Phenomena

There are very few issues concerning which criminologists usually feel confident enough to make strong declarative statements. However, the group nature of delinquency is certainly one of those issues. One of the most influential findings of the Shaw and McKay research [1931] was that almost 90 percent of the delinquent events reflected in the juvenile court records of Cook County involved two or more participants (Shaw et al. 1929:7–8). The group orientation was strongly reinforced several years later when Edwin Sutherland (1934) began to develop his influential theory of differential association, which emphasized the small-group dynamics associated with the learning of delinquent and criminal behavior. More recent work has noted some important offense-specific differences in the rates of group offending. In addition, a large proportion of offenders do not engage in illegal behavior strictly in group situations (see the review of Reiss 1988). Nevertheless, the presumed group nature of illegal behavior is a generally uncontested part of criminological lore.

There have been several important criticisms of the group hypothesis. The differential association perspective suggests that the most important sources of information concerning the techniques, motivations, and justifications for illegal behavior are intimate personal groups (see Sutherland's [1934] propositions 3 and 4). Given the apparent group nature of crime and delinquency, the intimate nature of these groups might suggest that offenses occur primarily within aggregations with temporal histories, fairly developed sets of relationships among the members, and relatively high levels of cohesiveness and solidarity. However, Klein (1969) has argued that the existence of two or more offenders in a single incident does not in itself guarantee that the event represents the outcome of such group dynamics. He criticizes in particular the influence that the Shaw and McKay findings have had on the discipline, for they were based on official records in which it is impossible to determine the actual group dynamics that may have been involved.

Klein illustrates this problem with several hypothetical examples, including one in which a relatively large number of strangers are attending a party and they happen to purchase marijuana from one of the other attendees. If the police happen to bust the party and make multiple arrests for possession, the arrest reports would most likely note that several people were involved in the incident. However, they would not constitute a group in any sociological sense of the word. Rather, these people were simply "contiguous individuals" (Klein 1969:67) who were engaged in the same behavior in the same location. Because of such conceptual ambiguities, some researchers now utilize alternative phrases (such as "co-offending"; Reiss 1988) to refer to events in which more than one person was involved but in which the existence of group dynamics is not clear.[3]

Klein certainly is not arguing that group dynamics are unrelated to criminal and delinquency behavior. Rather, he is emphasizing the need to recognize the basic distinction between the sociological notions of aggregate and group processes. In that respect, some unknown percentage of illegal behavior may be more validly viewed as a form of collective behavior in which an aggregate of relative strangers respond to a particular stimulus; this aggregate may have a very limited prior history and may disband after that particular response. There is a large body of literature that indicates that persons are more likely to engage in illegal behavior if their closest friends are involved in such behavior (see Elliott et al. 1985). However, there also is evidence that many delinquent behaviors occur in the company of individuals to whom a person has relatively weak associational bonds. Martin Gold (1970:83–94) has likened this situation to a "pickup game" of basketball in which the roster of players depends on who happens to be on the playground at the same time. That is, those present may define an opportunity as suitable for basketball (delinquency), and once the game is concluded, many of them go their separate ways. While certain interesting dynamics are involved in the definition of the situation, they have a relatively short-term relevance to the participants. These are not typically the kinds of processes that sociologists attribute to groups. As a result, some criminologists have raised important questions concerning the extent to which group solidarity is reflected in the illegal behavior of co-offenders (see Morash 1983).

Much of the confusion that has arisen in the gang literature, as well as in the public's perception of gang behavior, is due to the often interchangeable use of the words "group" and "gang" (see the criticism of Klein and Maxson 1989). For example, while Walter Miller (1980) delineates twenty different types of "law-violating youth groups," he only considers three of these to represent gangs (see Table 1.1). If the general pattern of relationships among co-offenders is much more fluid than is usually assumed, perhaps the primary distinction between group and gang crime and delinquency pertains to the internal dynamics of the aggregate that may result in a criminal event. For example, Bernard Cohen (1969:66) considers delinquent groups to represent relatively small cliques that coalesce sporadically without apparent reason and spontaneously violate the law. Cohen considers such groups to be ephemeral, with no elaborate organizational structure, name, or sense of turf. Gangs, on the other hand, are highly developed aggregates with relatively large memberships. As opposed to delinquent groups, gangs have elaborate organizations, names, senses of corporate identity, and identifications with particular territories. A similar typology has been developed by Irving Spergel (1984). The viability of such distinctions will be examined in the next section.

Table 1.1
Types and Subtypes of
Law-Violating Youth Groups

1	Turf gangs
2	Regularly associating disruptive local groups/crowds
3	Solidary disruptive local cliques
4	Casual disruptive local cliques
5	Gain-oriented gangs/extended networks
6	Looting groups/crowds
7	Established gain-oriented cliques/limited networks
7.1	Burglary rings
7.2	Robbery bands
7.3	Larceny cliques and networks
7.4	Extortion cliques
7.5	Drug-dealing cliques and networks
7.6	Fraudulent gain cliques
8	Casual gain-oriented cliques
9	Fighting gangs
10	Assaultive cliques and crowds
10.1	Assaultive affiliation cliques
10.2	Assaultive public-gathering crowds
11	Recurrently active assaultive cliques
12	Casual assaultive cliques

Reprinted from Miller (1980) by permission of the editors.

Defining Gang Delinquency

John Hagedorn (1988) has identified two primary ways in which the gang has been defined within the criminological literature. The first, and oldest, approach has emphasized the processes that give rise to such groups. Albert Cohen (1955), for example, defines gangs in terms of collective reactions to problems of social status, while Richard Cloward and Lloyd Ohlin (1960) focus on the interaction between legitimate and illegitimate opportunity structures. However, we feel that the most important processual definition for understanding the relationship between neighborhood dynamics and gang behavior is that of Frederic Thrasher (1927), who defines a gang as "an interstitial group originally formed spontaneously and then integrated through conflict. . . . The result of this collective behavior is the development of tradition, unreflective internal structure, esprit de corps, solidarity, morale, group awareness, and attachment to a local territory" (p. 46).

Several aspects of Thrasher's definition are worth noting. First, "interstitial" has a dual connotation. Thrasher uses it in one sense to represent the period of life when one is neither a child nor an adult; gangs therefore are a reflection of the period of adjustment between childhood and maturity (p. 32). For this reason, Thrasher argues that such groups are relatively short-lived and that adult gangs or members are relatively rare.[4] Yet this does not mean that gangs are characterized by age homogeneity. Rather, as older members age out of the group, younger members join, leading to a set of loosely connected, age-based cliques within the gang.

Thrasher also used the term "interstitial" to refer to neighborhoods located between Chicago's central business district and "the better residential areas" (p. 6). Since these were areas characterized by neighborhood deterioration and residential turnover (p. 46), Thrasher's model is clearly a variation of the social disorganization approach. . . . The systemic implications of his approach are clearly evident in his discussion (p. 33) of the failure of "directing and controlling customs and institutions to function efficiently in the boy's experience." The spirit of this aspect of Thrasher's processual definition is evident in Spergel's (1984:201) more recent definition of integrated gangs as a reflection of the inability of primary and secondary community institutions to provide mechanisms of opportunity or control.

Second, Thrasher's emphasis on "spontaneous formation" reflects his argument that all childhood play groups represent potential forms of gangs (see pp. 23–26). Since such groups usually arise on the basis of interaction and familiarity, they tend to form around particular residential locations in a neighborhood where youths are likely to come into contact with one another. Thus, street corner groups represent the basic building block upon which Thrasher develops his thesis. The key determinant of the transition into a gang is contact with other groups (either other play groups or adults) who express disapproval or opposition to the playgroup. For example, Hagedorn (1988:57–60) observes that fierce rivalries developed among the many breakdancing groups that arose during the early 1980s in Milwaukee; gangs sometimes emerged as a result of the fights that often broke out after competitions. Such conflict can produce an awareness of the distinction between "us" and "them" and the development of a sense of solidarity among group members. The existence of a street corner group therefore can serve as a source of protection from other groups in the neighborhood (see Spergel 1984:202).

Finally, note that delinquent or criminal activities are not mentioned in Thrasher's definition. While he certainly recognized that such activities may be facilitated by gang membership, he emphasized the variability that existed in the 1,313 groups that he identified as gangs: some are good, some are bad. Thrasher's approach emphasizes the social dynamics that may lead to cohesion among a play group and the resulting development of a gang. The relationship of gangs to delinquency is therefore a key analytical issue.

Although such process-based definitions of the gang continue to appear in the literature, Hagedorn (1988:57) notes that most current research is no longer characterized by a focus on how gangs arise within particular community contexts and how they function within those social environments. Rather, he argues that the fundamental question has become "why gang members are delinquent." The definition of Klein (1971) presented earlier in this chapter, with its criterion that the number of delinquencies committed by the group has called forth some type of negative response, represents a commonly used example of such an approach. The implications of this shift in focus are much more important than they may first appear, for illegal behavior is considered to be a definitional aspect of gang activity, whereas for Thrasher it was an empirical question.

Even more so than was the case with processual definitions, there is an enormous variety of delinquency-based definitions which have become the basis for different policies, laws, and strategies. One of the most interesting attempts to produce a definition with a broad consensual base is that of Walter Miller (1975, 1980), who asked a national sample of youth service agency staff members to respond to the questions: "What is your conception of a gang? Exactly how would you define it?" His final definition is based on the responses of 309 respondents representing 121 youth serving agencies in 26 areas of the country (Miller 1980:120), including police officers, prosecutors, defenders, educators, city council members, state legislators, ex-prisoners, and past and present members of gangs and groups (1980:117).

Of the 1,400 definitional characteristics

that were provided by his sample, Miller reports that there were six items with which at least 85 percent of the respondents agreed (1980:121): a youth gang is a self-formed association of peers, bound together by mutual interests, with identifiable leadership, well-developed lines of authority, and other organizational features, who act in concert to achieve a specific purpose or purposes, which generally include the conduct of illegal activity and control over a particular territory, facility, or type of enterprise.

Such delinquency-based definitions have been criticized for several reasons. Klein and Maxson (1989:205) call Miller's approach "discouraging" and argue that to define a concept on the basis of the results of a "vote" does not make it inherently more definitive or valid than other approaches. Yet their criticisms are not aimed solely at Miller, for they note that the definitional task is "difficult and arbitrary" and an "inherently unsatisfying task." The continued existence of a great variety of delinquency-based definitions (see Spergel 1990) suggests that consensus does not exist for any particular conceptualization (although the definition provided in Klein 1971 has been particularly influential). Ruth Horowitz (1990:43) notes that the variation in locally used definitions may be useful for understanding how the relationships among criminal justice personnel, the community, the gang, and the individual gang member are defined. Nevertheless, the lack of a standard, nationwide definition of a gang makes estimates that have been made concerning the number of youth gangs in the United States or comparisons that have been made over time or between communities relatively meaningless (Spergel 1990:180).

Some contemporary researchers have expressed a more general discomfort with all definitions that assume generalizable groups structures and processes or that equate crime with gang behavior (see Hagedorn 1988; Fagan 1989:643). Merry Morash (1983:310) argues that these approaches developed due to a growing reliance on definitions used by law enforcement and social work personnel. Since many of these agencies classify groups as gangs if violent or criminal activity is a major activity, gangs are by definition heavily involved in illegal behavior and Thrasher's question concerning the relationship between gang membership and delinquency becomes tautological (see Short 1990:160).

To illustrate the implications of such definitional assumptions, Morash created a scale of "gang likeness" based on an adaptation of Miller's definition.[5] While her analysis presents evidence that the gang-likeness variable has a significant effect on delinquency, more general peer group processes, such as the delinquent behavior of one's friends, are of much greater importance. Overall, she concludes (p. 325) that membership in a stereotyped gang is not a sufficient condition to stimulate serious delinquency. This seems to provide an important contradiction to the finding of many studies that gang members are involved in significantly higher levels of crime and drug use (see Fagan 1989). However, Klein and Maxson (1989:204) take issue with Morash's findings, noting that adolescent church or school groups could have qualified as gangs using her criteria.

Other characteristics of gangs that might be the subject of empirical investigation are also embedded into definitions such as that developed by Miller. For example, while some of the informants in Hagedorn's (1988) study reported that their gangs had fairly specialized and formalized ranks, others insisted that the structure was very informal; a few even stated that their gangs had no recognized leader (p. 92). Likewise, Joan Moore (1978:44) reports that the historical circumstances that set the context for the development of each of the age-based cliques (*klikas*) in Los Angeles Chicano gangs has resulted in significant differences among groupings in the same gang, each of which may have its own organizational structure (see also Keiser 1969:15).

We find the arguments of Hagedorn and Morash very persuasive, for those characteristics that are assumed by researchers such as Miller to be defining features of gangs actually exhibit a great deal of variation among groups who have been identified as gangs. Rather than taking these characteristics for granted, it would seem to be much more theoretically fruitful to examine the processes that give rise to such group variation. Perhaps one of the reasons why the Klein (1971) definition has been extremely popular is that the three criteria are extremely flexible and are relevant to a wide range of gang types.

Nevertheless, we are uncomfortable with

the delinquent behavior criterion, for it makes a possible outcome of gang activity one of the defining characteristics. Klein and Maxson (1989:204) defend their position by noting that "to think of modern street gangs independent of their criminal involvement is to ignore the very factor that makes them qualitatively different from other groups of young people."[6] Despite our own misgivings concerning the presumed equivalence of gang activity and crime, there is no question that the major criterion used by many audiences in the definition of gang is the group's participation in illegal behavior (Spergel 1990:179).

Methods of Gang Research

. . . Easily the longest tradition of gang research is based on some variant of ethnographic fieldwork with gang members (or the combination of such research with supplementary forms of data collection). The work of Thrasher (1927) is exemplary in this respect. Although we know very little concerning how he actually collected his data (see Short 1963:xviii), it is clear that it represented primarily a combination of personal observation and documents that were supplemented by court records and census materials. Over the course of his seven-year study, he amassed enough material to identify 1,313 Chicago gangs.

While Bookin and Horowitz (1983) noted that fieldwork techniques had a declining popularity in sociology and predicted that they would rarely be used in future research, Horowitz (1990:37) recently has retracted that statement, for they certainly represent one of the major forms of data collection used in the study of gangs.[7] Unfortunately, ethnographers no longer have the resources at their disposal to conduct such a "census" of gangs as that of Thrasher. Therefore, the modern emphasis has been on the depth of data, rather than the breadth. Generally this is not considered a problem in fieldwork, for such research is much more concerned with the identification and analysis of process and meaning than with the ability to generalize findings to some larger population. Nevertheless, it must be emphasized that the representativeness of the gangs that have been described is not clear. Many times the gangs have been chosen on the basis of their notoriety within a community (see Keiser 1969; Muehlbauer

and Dodder 1983), because of chance circumstances that bring a gang to the attention of a researcher, such as the prior participation of gang members in social service projects (Short and Strodtbeck 1965; Klein 1971; Hagedorn 1988; Harris 1988), or because of their location in particular communities upon which researchers have elected to focus (Klein 1971; Moore 1978; Horowitz 1983; Campbell 1984; Sullivan 1989; Jankowski 1991).

There are special difficulties in conducting fieldwork with gangs that do not arise in many other fields of inquiry. First, and most obviously, while most researchers are highly educated, middle-class persons, many gang members are not. It takes a skilled ethnographer to overcome the initial hostility that is often inherent to interactions with gang members (see the descriptions provided by Horowitz 1983:Chapter 1; Moore 1978:Appendix A; Hagedorn 1988:32–33). In addition to this inherent suspicion, many researchers have noted that gang members are notoriously unreliable as informants (Spergel 1990:175); Klein (1971:18) feels that "the only thing worse than the young reporter's description of a gang incident is his [sic] acceptance of the gang participant's statement about it." This problem was forcibly driven home to the first author of this book during a conversation with a friend who formerly had been a central member of one of Chicago's most notorious fighting gangs. He described with great pleasure how during times of boredom, members of his group would have an informal competition to see who could convincingly tell the most outrageous story to a social worker who had been assigned to work with the group. Therefore, the collection of valid data through fieldwork with gangs is only possible after an extended period of contact during which trust is established.

There is also a more subtle problem in the reliability of data drawn from fieldwork with gangs. An important concern in all ethnographic studies is the degree to which the presence of the researcher has a significant effect on the nature of the dynamics that are observed. For example, some of the most important studies of gang dynamics (such as that of Short and Strodtbeck 1965) have relied to a significant degree on the observations of "detached workers," that is, social service personnel who have been assigned to work with gangs in their natural settings. As Klein (1971:151) notes, those procedures that are often used to maximize contact with gangs (such as group counseling sessions or attendance at club meetings) may in fact increase group cohesiveness, which may lead to an increase in gang delinquency. In addition, the assignment of a group worker may increase the local reputation of a gang, which in turn may attract new members. Thus, the presence of a fieldworker can result in a set of group dynamics and activities that would not have occurred otherwise.

Despite these problems, ethnographic work has provided some of the most important insights that criminologists have about gangs, and much of the richest data has been obtained under situations that may have seemed doomed to failure (see Horowitz 1983). However, as we have noted, there are problems in the generalizability of such data. A second approach to gang research has attempted to overcome this limitation by incorporating surveys into the study design. While this often has been done in conjunction with ongoing fieldwork (such as Short and Strodtbeck 1965; Joe and Robinson 1980), this is not necessarily the case (Giordano 1978; Bowker et al. 1980; Morash 1983; Fagan 1989; Curry and Spergel 1991).

Many of the same problems concerning trust and hostility that characterize fieldwork studies also are present in survey-based study designs. However, two other issues make gang survey research especially problematic. The first is the sampling frame itself, that is, the population of gang members from which the respondents should be selected. Obviously, there is no "official" listing of all gang members in an area, but even if one existed, the ongoing flux in gang membership would make a list obsolete almost immediately (Short and Strodtbeck 1965:10). The police in many communities have compiled lists of suspected gang members, but these tend to be very inaccurate. Klein (1971:19) tells the story of how he examined the files kept by the police concerning the members of a particular gang. Whereas he had the names of over 100 members, the police had less than 20 and much of their information concerning addresses and offense histories was extremely dated. One solution is to administer surveys to those people who have been identified as gang members through fieldwork (see Short

and Strodtbeck 1965). Another is to interview people known to be gang members, ask them for the names of other people who should be interviewed, and continue to build the sample of respondents through such a "snowball" approach (see Fagan 1989).

While such techniques can potentially collect a great deal of useful information concerning the characteristics and behavior of gang members, it is often desirable to compare the distributions of these variables to those found among youths not involved in gang activity.[8] However, the selection of an appropriate comparison group is very difficult. The sample survey data examined in the 1989 paper of Jeffrey Fagan, for example, included only the responses of gang members, and he was only able to draw comparisons with nongang youths by comparing his findings with other published research. While Short and Strodtbeck (1965) did include nongang youths in their sample, all these respondents were affiliated in some manner with youth-serving agencies (p. 5). Therefore, the degree to which these youths are representative of nongang youths in general is not clear.

Several attempts have been made to identify gang membership and make the relevant comparisons on the basis of more broadly administered surveys (Morash 1983; Rand 1987; Spergel and Curry 1988; Curry and Spergel 1991). The validity of the information that has been collected on the basis of such study designs depends on two crucial considerations. First, how likely is it that youths involved in gangs will be represented in the sample? Some researchers have tried to maximize this possibility by drawing all or part of their sample from those youths residing in correctional facilities (Bowker et al. 1980; Morash 1983). Such approaches would tend to overrepresent those youths with extensive or especially violent offense histories. Other sampling designs are likely to underrepresent active gang members. Spergel and Curry (1988) and Curry and Spergel (1991), for example, surveyed all male students in the sixth through eighth grades at four schools in Chicago. Likewise, Fagan (1990) supplemented the gang data noted earlier with information collected from a sample of high school students residing in the same three neighborhoods and a snowball sample of dropouts. However, school-based samples are especially prone to errors in studies of delinquency since the most active delinquents may be those youths who are most likely to be truant during the time of administration. In general, it is extremely difficult to draw a representative sample of gang members.

The second consideration reflects the identification of respondents as gang members. Some surveys have simply asked the respondents if they belong to a gang (Rand 1987; Johnstone 1981). While John Johnstone presents some evidence (p. 362) to suggest that the adolescents in his sample interpreted the term "gang" consistently, he does note problems with such an assumption. Other researchers assume the existence of a continuum along which a youth group is more or less like a particular operational definition of a gang (Morash 1983; Spergel and Curry 1988; Curry and Spergel 1991). We have already noted Klein and Maxson's (1989) criticism of the scale developed by Morash for its apparent inability to differentiate among dramatically different types of youth groups. The Spergel and Curry scale is a much narrower approach to the measurement of gangs and includes such items as the flashing of gang signs, the wearing of colors, and attacking (or being attacked) in a gang-related incident. One of their most important findings is that the indicators of gang involvement scaled differently for Hispanics and African Americans, which highlights our argument that the search for a broadly relevant uniform definition of gangs may be relatively fruitless. In addition, contrary to the findings of Morash, they present evidence of a strong relationship between gang involvement and serious delinquency.

Overall, the use of surveys is no guarantee that the results of a study are any more reliable than those produced through more traditional fieldwork approaches. Rather, results are especially sensitive to the nature of the sampling design, the selection and wording of the indicators of gang membership, and the relevance of those indicators to the populations under consideration.

The final technique that has been used to collect data on gangs is based on information that has been collected by law enforcement agencies. While sometimes this information is used to supplement that derived through fieldwork or survey designs, much of the current knowledge concerning

gangs is the result of studies that have been based primarily on such data (Miller 1975; Spergel 1984, 1986; Curry and Spergel 1988; Klein and Maxson 1989; Maxson et al., 1985). Bernard Cohen (1969) has argued that the Philadelphia Gang Crimes Unit uses sociologically sophisticated definitions of gang and nongang activities in its classification of criminal events. However the official classification of an offender as a gang member generally is not systematic and may not be based on reliable criteria (Klein and Maxson 1989:206).

In addition to the problem of identifying gang membership based on the information included in official records, there is an equally difficult problem in the classification of illegal events as gang-related. For example, suppose a member of a gang is arrested for the armed robbery of a convenience store. On the basis of the description of the event provided in the arrest report, it may be impossible to determine whether it was committed due to gang membership. Unfortunately, there are no national standards for the identification of a crime as gang-related. For example, the Los Angeles Police and Sheriff's Departments designate a homicide as gang-related "if either the assailant or the victim is a gang member or, failing clear identification, elements of the event, such as motive, garb, characteristic gang behavior, or attribution by witnesses, indicate the likelihood of gang involvement" (Klein and Maxson 1989:206–207). However, the Chicago Police Department uses a much more restrictive definition that is based on the evidence of "gang function or motivation" (Curry and Spergel 1988:384). Maxson and Klein (1990) note that a reclassification of the Los Angeles data on the basis of the Chicago criterion leads to a significant reduction in the estimated rate of gang homicide and question whether the massive efforts of gang control and suppression that have characterized Los Angeles would have developed if this alternative definition had been used to gauge the extent of the problem.

The existence of such definitional inconsistencies makes it very difficult to make any kind of reliable comparisons between jurisdictions concerning the level of gang activity. However, definitions may also be characterized by inconsistencies even within the same jurisdiction. For example, Curry and Spergel (1988:385) note that prior to 1986, arson, theft, burglary, and vice offenses (including those that were drug-related) were not included in the gang crime reporting system. Such changes make it nearly impossible to examine the trends in many forms of gang behavior in Chicago over time, including the changing nature of drug use and distribution that has received so much attention in other parts of the country.

Overall, the inherent limitations of the dominant forms of data collection on gangs are very serious. Therefore, in many respects, we simply cannot be as confident of our knowledge concerning gangs as we are in other areas of criminology. However, despite these problems of measurement, certain patterns have emerged in a sufficient number of studies and locations to provide at least a minimal degree of confidence in those empirical regularities. This is especially the case in gang research that has emphasized the neighborhood dynamics related to such behavior.

Notes

1. For example, our colleague John Cochran has referred to certain fraternities on the University of Oklahoma campus as "syndicates of rape," which has made him a very popular figure in the Letters to the Editor department of the school newspaper.

2. Interestingly, at least in that high school, this meant that the dominant gang continually revised its preferred style of dress to maintain a symbolic separation between it and the general school population.

3. The careful reader will note that this problem is very similar to the compositional effect–group effect issue that was discussed in Chapter 2 in respect to neighborhoods. [Editors' note: See Chapter 2 of Bursik and Grasmick, *Neighborhoods and Crime: The Dimensions of Effective Community Control.* New York: Lexington Books, 1993.]

4. A very similar argument concerning the role of gangs in adolescent development has been presented by Bloch and Niederhoffer (1958).

5. Items included in the final scale reflected whether or not the group meets outside the home, if youths are typically members for four or more years, if the group usually meets in the same place, if the group comes from just one part of the neighborhood, if the group has a name, if the group contains older and younger kids, if the respondent meets with the group at least four days a week, and if the respondent takes part in several activities with the group.

6. Spergel (1990) notes that many gang researchers who once believed that gang behavior was not especially serious or lethal (such as Miller and Klein) now have come to the position that such groups are responsible for a large number of homicides and are active participants in widespread narcotics trafficking (see, for example, Miller 1975; Klein and Maxson 1985, 1989).

7. We use the term "fieldwork" in a very broad sense to refer to qualitative study designs that involve some degree of interaction between the researcher and the gang member. They can range from intensive observation conducted by the researcher over extended periods (as in Horowitz 1983; Campbell 1984; Sullivan 1989; Jankowski 1991), through the reports provided by social service workers who deal with a particular gang on a regular basis (as in Short and Strodtbeck 1965; Klein 1971; or Moore 1985), to sets of intensive, unstructured interviews with respondents identified as gang members (as in Vigil 1988 or Hagedorn 1988). Many studies have combined two or more of these techniques into a single research design.

8. In fact, the availability of such information is absolutely essential to the development of processual approaches to gangs.

References

Bloch, Herbert A., and Arthur Niederhoffer (1958). *The Gang: A Study in Adolescent Behavior.* New York: Philosophical Library.

Bookin, Hedy, and Ruth Horowitz (1983). "The End of the Youth Gang: Fad or Fact?" *Criminology* 21:585–602.

Bowker, Lee H., Helen Shimata Gross, and Malcolm W. Klein (1980). "Female Participation in Delinquent Gang Activities." *Adolescence* 59:509–519.

Campbell, Ann (1984). *The Girls in the Gang.* Oxford: Basil Blackwell.

Cloward, Richard A., and Lloyd Ohlin (1960). *Delinquency and Opportunity.* New York: Free Press.

Cohen, Albert K. (1955). *Delinquent Boys.* Glencoe, IL: The Free Press.

Cohen, Bernard (1969). "The Delinquency of Gangs and Spontaneous Groups." Pp. 61–111 in *Delinquency: Selected Studies,* edited by Thorsten Sellin and Marvin E. Wolfgang. New York: Wiley.

Curry, G. David, and Irving A. Spergel (1988). "Gang Homicide, Delinquency, and Community." *Criminology* 26:381–405.

———. (1991). *Youth Gang Involvement and Delinquency: A Report to the National Youth*

Gang Intervention and Suppression Research and Development Project. Washington, DC: Office of Juvenile Justice and Delinquency Prevention.

Elliott, Delbert S., David Huizinga, and Suzanne S. Ageton (1985). *Explaining Delinquency and Drug Use.* Beverly Hills, CA: Sage.

Fagan, Jeffrey (1989). "The Social Organization of Drug Use and Drug Dealing Among Urban Gangs." *Criminology* 27:633–669.

———— (1990). "Social Processes of Delinquency and Drug Use Among Urban Gangs." Pp. 183–219 in *Gangs in America,* edited by C. Ronald Huff. Newbury Park, CA: Sage.

Forer, Lois G. (1990). "Foreword." Pp. xiii–xxv in *Fraternity Gang Rape: Sex, Brotherhood, and Privilege on Campus,* by Peggy Sanday. New York: New York University Press.

Giordano, Peggy C. (1978). "Girls, Guys, and Gangs: The Changing Social Context of Female Delinquency." *Journal of Criminal Law and Criminology* 69:126–132.

Gold, Martin (1970). *Delinquent Behavior in an American City.* Belmont, CA: Brooks-Cole.

Hagedorn, John M. (1988). *People and Folks: Gangs, Crime, and the Underclass in a Rustbelt City.* Chicago: Lakeview Press.

Harris, Mary G. (1988). *Las Cholas: Latino Girls and Gangs.* New York: AMS Press.

Horowitz, Ruth (1983). *Honor and the American Dream.* New Brunswick, NJ: Rutgers University Press.

———— (1990). "Sociological Perspectives on Gangs: Conflicting Definitions and Concepts." Pp. 37–54 in *Gangs in America,* edited by C. Ronald Huff. Newbury Park, CA: Sage.

Huff, C. Ronald (1989). "Youth Gangs and Public Policy." *Crime and Delinquency* 35:524–537.

Jankowski, Martin Sanchez (1991). *Islands in the Street: Gangs and American Urban Society.* Berkeley: University of California Press.

Joe, Delbert, and Norman Robinson (1980). "Chinatown's Immigrant Gangs: The New Young Warrior Class." *Criminology* 18:337–345.

Johnstone, John W. C. (1981). "Youth Gangs and Black Suburbs." *Pacific Sociological Review* 24:355–375.

Keiser, R. Lincoln (1969). *The Vice Lords: Warriors of the Streets.* New York: Holt, Rinehart and Winston.

Klein, Malcolm W. (1969). "On Group Context of Delinquency." *Sociology and Social Research* 54:63–71.

———— (1971). *Street Gangs and Street Workers.* Englewood Cliffs, NJ: Prentice Hall.

Klein, Malcolm W., and Cheryl L. Maxson (1985). " 'Rock' Sales in South Los Angeles." *Sociology and Social Research* 69:561–565.

———— (1989). "Street Gang Violence." Pp. 198–234 in *Violent Crime, Violent Criminals,* edited by Neil A. Weiner and Marvin E. Wolfgang. Newbury Park, CA: Sage.

Maxson, Cheryl L., Margaret A. Gordon, and Malcolm W. Klein (1985). "Differences Between Gang and Nongang Homicides." *Criminology* 23:209–222.

Maxson, Cheryl L., and Malcolm W. Klein (1990). "Street Gang Violence: Twice as Great or Half as Great?" Pp. 71–100 in *Gangs in America,* edited by C. Ronald Huff. Newbury Park, CA: Sage.

Miller, Walter B. (1975). *Violence by Youth Gangs as a Crime Problem in Major American Cities.* National Institute for Juvenile Justice and Delinquency Prevention, U.S. Justice Department. Washington, DC: U.S. Government Printing Office.

———— (1980). "Gangs, Groups, and Serious Youth Crime." Pp. 115–138 in *Critical Issues in Juvenile Delinquency,* edited by David Schichor and Delos H. Kelly. Lexington, MA: D.C. Heath.

Moore, Joan W. (1978) *Homeboys.* Philadelphia: Temple University Press.

———— (1985). "Isolation and Stigmatization in the Development of an Underclass: The Case of Chicano Gangs in East Los Angeles." *Social Problems* 33:1–12.

Morash, Merry (1983). "Gangs, Groups, and Delinquency." *British Journal of Criminology* 23:309–335.

Muehlbauer, Gene, and Laura Dodder (1983). *The Losers: Gang Delinquency in an American Suburb.* New York: Praeger.

Rand, Alicia (1987). "Transitional Life Events and Desistance from Delinquency and Crime." Pp. 134–162 in *From Boy to Man, from Delinquency to Crime,* by Marvin E. Wolfgang, Terence P. Thornberry, and Robert M. Figlio. Chicago: University of Chicago Press.

Reiss, Albert J., Jr. (1988). "Co-Offending and Criminal Careers." Pp. 117–170 in *Crime and Justice: A Review of Research.* Vol. 10, edited by Michael Tonry and Norval Morris. Chicago: University of Chicago Press.

Sanday, Peggy (1990). *Fraternity Gang Rape: Sex, Brotherhood, and Privilege on Campus.* New York: New York University Press.

Shaw, Clifford R., and Henry D. McKay (1931). *Social Factors in Juvenile Delinquency.* National Commission on Law Observation and Enforcement, No. 13, Report on the Causes of Crime, Volume II. Washington, DC: U.S. Government Printing Office.

Shaw, Clifford R., Frederick M. Zorbaugh, Henry D. McKay, and Leonard S. Cottrell (1929). *Delinquency Areas.* Chicago: University of Chicago Press.

Short, James F., Jr. (1963). "Introduction to the Abridged Edition." Pp. xv–liii in *The Gang,* by Frederic Thrasher. Chicago: University of Chicago Press.

——— (1990). *Delinquency and Society*. Englewood Cliffs, NJ: Prentice Hall.

Short, James F., Jr., and Fred L. Strodtbeck (1965). *Group Process and Gang Delinquency*. Chicago: University of Chicago Press.

Spergel, Irving A. (1984). "Violent Gangs in Chicago: In Search of Social Policy." *Social Service Review* 58:199–226.

——— (1986). "Violent Gangs in Chicago: A Local Community Approach." *Social Service Review* 60:94–131.

——— (1990). "Youth Gangs: Continuity and Change." Pp. 171–275 in *Crime and Justice: A Review of Research*. Volume 12, edited by Michael Tonry and Norval Morris. Chicago: University of Chicago Press.

Spergel, Irving A., and G. David Curry (1988). "Socialization to Gangs: Preliminary Baseline Report." School of Social Service Administration, University of Chicago.

Sullivan, Mercer L. (1989). *Getting Paid: Youth Crime and Work in the Inner City*. Ithaca, NY: Cornell University Press.

Sutherland, Edwin H. (1934). *Principles of Criminology*, Second Edition. Philadelphia: J. B. Lippincott.

Thrasher, Frederic M. (1927). *The Gang*. Chicago: University of Chicago Press.

United States General Accounting Office (1989). *Nontraditional Organized Crime*. Washington, DC: U.S. Government Printing Office.

Vigil, James D. (1988). *Barrio Gangs: Street Life and Identity in Southern California*. Austin: University of Texas Press.

Wallace, Linda S. (1991). "Big-City Terror Stalks Small-Town America." *Knight-Ridder Newspaper Service*, December 26.

Zatz, Marjorie S. (1987). "Chicano Youth Gangs and Crime: The Creation of a Moral Panic." *Contemporary Crises* 11:129–158. ◆

Chapter 2
The History of Gang Research

*Scott H. Decker
and Barrik Van Winkle*

In this introductory section of their book Life in the Gang, *Decker and Van Winkle provide an overview of the history of research and theory concerning street gangs. Gangs were a topic of serious concern in the early part of the twentieth century, then again in the middle decades, and again beginning in the late 1980s and into the 1990s. Gang research falls in and out of favor depending upon the particular theoretical framework dominant within criminology at a given time—for instance, gang research fell out of favor in the late 1970s and 1980s, when individuals—rather than groups—were of primary interest to criminologists. Although the specific theoretical premises differ among early gang researchers, there are recurrent themes outlined by Decker and Van Winkle: poverty, economic instability, population changes and migration patterns, the geographic isolation of urban youth and consequent lack of access to legitimate social institutions, and the ways in which gangs fill these voids for some youths.*

Early Gang Studies

The themes of immigration, urbanization, ethnicity, and poverty are most evident in examinations of gangs in the 1890s and at the turn of the century. The majority of such accounts were journalistic in nature. Faced with waves of immigrants from western Europe, New York found itself with a considerable level of gang activity in the late 1890s, much of it involving Irish immigrants. According to Riis (1892, 1902) young Irish (and later Italian) immigrants found integration into the economy to be difficult. Lacking activities to occupy their time, they formed gangs to provide for social and material needs. His descriptions of the gang focused on the myriad social conditions faced by the children of immigrants: poverty, poor education, poor housing, dirt and the lack of wholesome activities. Gang life was a natural outcome for such youth:

> So trained for the responsibility of citizenship, robbed of home and of childhood, with every prop knocked from under him, all the elements that make for strength and character trodden out in the making of the boy, all the high ambition of youth caricatured by the slum and become base passions,—so equipped he comes into the business of life. As a "kid" he hunted with the pack in the street. As a young man he trains with the gang, because it furnishes the means of gratifying his inordinate vanity; that is the slum's counterfeit of self-esteem. (Riis 1902, pp. 236–237)

The response to such problems was rather straightforward; occupy the time of these individuals and they will cease to be involved in gang activity. Activities such as athletics were recommended as "safety-valves" (Riis 1892, p. 131) for youthful energies.

The role of immigration in gang formation provided an important foundation for later examinations of gangs. Asbury (1928) studied gangs in New York City, especially in the Five Points area populated largely by recent Irish immigrants yet to move out of the economic underclass. He provided encyclopedic descriptions of the variety of gangs and their activities. The primary activities for these gangs were fighting, with each other as well as rival gangs. Asbury was careful to make the distinction between those who grow up in a gang and criminals who organize to perform illegal acts more effectively. He highlighted with considerable detail the colorful names used by these gangs, names that included the Roach Guards, Pug Uglies, Shirt Tails, and Dead Rabbits. It is an important historical footnote that red and blue, the colors adopted by the contemporary Bloods and Crips respectively, were the colors used by the Irish gangs of New York City in the 1920s. The Roach Guards used blue as their color, and the Dead Rabbits used red as their symbol.

This underscores one feature common to most American gangs throughout history, the use of symbols to identify members. Asbury also described numerous small gangs with affiliations to a larger gang, suggesting that most gang activity was concentrated around the neighborhood among a small group of friends well-known to each other.

Thrasher's Study of Gangs

Thrasher's pioneering work appeared in 1927, the first serious academic treatment of gangs. Working within the sociological paradigm of the Chicago School, Thrasher gave gangs a cultural and ecological context. Using the concepts of culture and neighborhood ecology, he sought to explain gang transmission (the intergenerational character of gangs in neighborhoods and subcultures) as part of a process of collective behavior. Gangs in Chicago were found primarily in interstitial areas. These areas were characterized by three consistent ecological features: (1) deteriorating neighborhoods, (2) shifting populations, and (3) mobility and disorganization of the slum. The "ganging process" was dynamic and produced organizations that were constantly undergoing change. In this context, Thrasher saw gangs as

> . . . the spontaneous effort of boys to create a society for themselves where none adequate to their needs exists. What boys get out of such association that they do not get otherwise under the conditions that adult society imposes is the thrill and zest of participation in common interest, more especially in corporate action, in hunting, capture, conflict, flight, and escape. Conflict with other gangs and the world about them furnishes the occasion for many of their exciting group activities. (1927, p. 37)

Thrasher found considerable variation in the definition of gangs but also noted that gangs played a variety of functions, further complicating efforts to define them in precise ways. In his view, gangs originated from the spontaneous group activity of adolescents and were strengthened by conflict. This process consists of three stages. In its earliest stage, the gang is diffuse, little leadership exists, and the gang may be short lived. Some gangs progress to the next stage, where they become solidified. Conflict with other gangs plays a notable role in this process, helping to define group boundaries and strengthen the ties between members, uniting them in the face of a common threat. The final step in the evolution of the gang occurs when it becomes conventionalized and members assume legitimate roles in society. For those groups that fail to make this transition, delinquent or criminal activity becomes the dominant focus of the group. Among Thrasher's great strengths is his description of the process by which groups form, solidify, and disintegrate. He portrayed the relationship between gangs and other forms of social organization in a figure that traces the natural history of the gang. Most notable about this figure are the poignant reminders that social associations characterize most adolescent activities, and the majority of activities are law abiding.

Activities within the gang, according to Thrasher, were diverse and motivated by typical youthful concerns, such as thrills and excitement. A number of predatory activities were observed, with stealing being the most common. Many gangs were characterized by Thrasher as conflict groups that developed out of disputes and flourished in the presence of threats from rival groups. Fighting was the preeminent activity, and clashes with members of one's own gang were as likely as those with members of rival gangs. For gang members, violence served both to unite them and to speed the adaptation of the gang to its environment. In this way, violence played an especially important function in the integration of members into the group. The threat presented by rival gangs served to intensify solidarity within the gang, especially for new members. Despite their involvement in criminal or delinquent activity, most gang members were assimilated into legitimate social activities, most often athletics.

Gangs are isolated from mainstream society both by geography and lack of access to legitimate institutional roles. This isolation contributes to the within-group solidarity so critical to Thrasher's account of gangs, but it also plays another role. It helps to explain the lack of integration into the economic, educational, and social structure of cities and serves to prevent many gang members from giving up their gang affiliations for activities of a more law abiding nature. The isolated nature of the gang also allows it to enforce its rules (such as they may be) in a manner largely unimpeded by other institutions. Order is maintained through informal mechanisms as well, particularly "collective representations" (p. 297) such as symbols, signs, and group argot. The power of the collective is seen in its role in "mutual excitation" (p. 299), promoting behavior among gang members that they would not normally engage in. Despite the attention given to the larger collective of the gang, Thrasher notes the importance of subgroups within the gang.

> The two- and three-boy relationship is often much more important to the individual boy than his relationship to the gang. In such cases a boy would doubtless forego the gang before he would give up his special pal or pair of pals. (p. 322)

It is important to note that these subgroups exist in all parts of the city, regardless of whether they are affiliated with larger gangs.

Despite the fact that Thrasher's observations of gangs are nearly seventy years old, and that the demographic characteristics of cities have changed profoundly since then, many of his conclusions have important implications for the contemporary study of gangs. The central questions he addressed—gang transmission, growth of gangs, sources of cohesion among gang members, the role of threats, the importance of collective behavior, distinguishing adolescent group behavior from gang behavior, and most importantly the role of culture in understanding gangs—remain important today. And many of his observations, especially about the role of structural variables and group process within gangs, remain critical issues for the contemporary study of gangs.

Gangs in the Sixties

The advent of the Depression and World War II induced a decline in gangs and the attention paid to them. However, the conclusion of World War II brought rapid social change to American cities, as the American economy struggled to adapt to peacetime. At the same time, northern cities experienced a massive migration of southern blacks moving to the "promised land" (Lerman 1991) of jobs and greater opportunity. In many ways, this migration mirrored earlier waves of European immigrants who had moved to the industrial cities of the northeast and Midwest seeking employment. And like many of their European counterparts

who came before them, southern blacks often found their new homes to be less than hospitable places.

Theory Development

Gangs began to reemerge in cities in the 1950s and spawned a new generation of gang research, theory, and policy. Attention paid to gangs by criminologists in the 1950s and 1960s yielded important theoretical insights and policy recommendations. Building on the theoretical traditions of Emile Durkheim and Robert Merton, Albert Cohen (1955) developed the theory of status frustration to explain the process by which boys become involved in delinquent activities and gangs. Because they are judged by middle-class standards that many are ill equipped to meet, working-class and lower-class boys develop frustrations about achieving status goals. As a means of resolving these status concerns, they turn to delinquent activities and to the group affiliation of the gang. Richard Cloward and Lloyd Ohlin (1960) also built on the Mertonian tradition of emphasizing the role of shared cultural success goals and institutional means of achieving those goals. Rather than emphasizing status concerns, they focused on the blocked opportunities for achieving legitimate success faced by most working-class and lower-class boys. Because the opportunities for success were differentially distributed by neighborhood, some boys found that they lacked the access to achieving the goals society defined as important. The result was three forms of adaptations; conflict gangs, property gangs, or retreatist gangs. The adaptations resulted from the level of available opportunities and the extent to which boys were integrated in the neighborhood.

Not all commentators on gangs and youth delinquency concurred with the premise that a single set of cultural values permeated American society. For the theories of Cohen and Cloward and Ohlin, it is critical that this be the case, because the commitment to a common set of values causes status frustration (for Cohen) or blocked opportunities (for Cloward and Ohlin) and leads to delinquency. Walter Miller (1958) theorized that a far different set of values permeated lower-class culture, values that naturally lead to increased levels of delinquent and gang involvement. For Miller, six "focal concerns" defined life for lower-class boys: fate, autonomy, smartness, toughness, excitement, and trouble. Commitment to these values, as opposed to those of the dominant culture, need not be explained by lack of access to legitimate success roles. Lower-class boys learned these values as a consequence of living in their own neighborhoods where such values were dominant. Miller's approach emphasized the role of a subculture in the creation and maintenance of delinquent groups and gangs.

An important development in theory and research occurred with the appearance of Lewis Yablonsky's (1962) work on the violent gang. Drawing on Thrasher, he identified three types of gangs—delinquent gangs, violent gangs, and social gangs—indicating that the violent gang was the most persistent and problematic for society. Not unexpectedly, the role of violence looms large in every aspect of this gang. The violent gang forms in response to threats against safety, and thus represents a form of protection for its members. It has a loose structure and little formal character; for example, leaders in this gang "emerge" and membership within gang subgroups in many cases is more important than the larger gang. Violence, the defining event for members of these types of gangs, can arise over seemingly senseless matters but most often occurs in response to perceived threats against gang territory. Membership fulfills a number of needs; most importantly, it meets the psychological needs of boys incapable of finding such fulfillment in the larger society. Because of its lack of organization, Yablonsky identifies the violent gang as a "near group" (p. 272); a "collective structure" situated somewhere between totally disorganized aggregates (like mobs) and well-organized aggregates (like delinquent or social gangs).

Action Research

Much criminological work takes place in a policy vacuum; that is, the research is seldom closely coordinated with ongoing policy or programmatic initiatives. A remarkable exception to this is found in the work of four researchers: Spergel (1966), Klein (1971), and Short and Strodtbeck (1974). Each of these projects evaluated a gang intervention program that was premised on theories about gangs and gang behavior. And in each, the researchers used the evaluation to revisit theories about gangs

and delinquency, an occasion too rare in our field. We examine each of these because they helped to set the tone for the gang research that was to follow.

While Spergel, Klein, and Short and Strodtbeck all examined active gang and delinquency prevention programs, Spergel's work was most concerned with the practical matters of working with gangs. He analyzed the approach to gang intervention that had become popular, the detached worker. At its heart, detached street work is problem-oriented, group social work, an approach with a long history, especially in Chicago, where the Chicago Area Projects had used it for some time. In part, this approach depended on the social structure of the neighborhood or community in which it operated. Spergel argued that successful work with gang members depended on an understanding of four factors: (1) the delinquent subculture (beliefs, norms and values) within the neighborhood, (2) the delinquent group itself, (3) the individual delinquent, and (4) the agency worker. Spergel highlighted the role of delinquency theory, particularly that of Cloward and Ohlin, and argued that street work *practice* must be determined by *theoretical explanations* of delinquent groups. Spergel's work had a prescriptive orientation, offering program and intervention suggestions for street workers addressing gang and delinquent behavior.

Klein (1971) assumed both a more theoretical and analytic approach to dealing with gangs, though his analysis emerged from the "action context" of evaluating gang intervention programs. Two programs, the Group Guidance Project and the Ladino Hills Project (which operated from 1962 through 1968) formed the basis of his analysis. He notes the programmatic efforts of Mobilization for Youth in New York, the Los Angeles Youth Project, the Chicago Area Projects, and Youth for Service in San Francisco. Each of these projects held many features in common, especially the detached worker approach that took programming into the community and encouraged street workers to fully involve themselves in the gang and gang activities. Klein's theoretical antecedents include Cohen, Cloward and Ohlin, Miller, and Bloch and Niederhoffer.

Klein arrived at the unsettling conclusion that the Group Guidance Project may have increased delinquency among gang members. Specifically, he found that delinquency increased among gang members who received the most services and that solidarity among gang members seemed to increase as a result of the attention paid to the gang by street workers. This led Klein to the conclusion that gang intervention programs may have the latent consequence of contributing to the attractiveness of gangs, thereby enhancing their solidarity and promoting more violence. He paid considerable attention to issues of gang structure, particularly solidarity among gang members. He concluded that most characteristics of gang structure were difficult to differentiate from other features of adolescent street culture and that members of gangs shared most in common with other (nongang) adolescents. His conclusions that gangs and gang members contained large variation within their respective ranks reinforced his earlier observation that gangs were not monolithic.

Klein's views of leadership and the sources of cohesion within gangs were consistent with his definition of gangs and gang membership. In his view, leadership was largely age related and was not so much a specific office as it was a mixture of functions. This reinforced the notion that gangs resembled other features of youth culture (disorganized, spontaneous, short-term) more than they did more formal adult structures. Further support for this contention was found in the consistent report by gang members that their primary activity was "hanging out" with other members on the street. And their delinquency was described as "cafeteria style" (p. 125) rather than a purposive, well-organized specialization. Cohesiveness, the force that keeps gangs together, was more a product of external than internal sources. That is, the bonds of gang membership do not become stronger in response to internal mechanisms (meetings, codes, signs, activities) but rather as a response to external pressures. In general, Klein found that few gang goals existed outside of those generated by external pressures, and the few internal gang norms that did exist were weak and transient. The external sources of cohesion were structural (poverty, unemployment, and weak family socialization) but also included pressures that resulted from interaction with other gangs as well as members of one's own gang. In particular, the threat of violence from another gang increased solidarity within the gang. One ef-

fect of this is that most victims of gang violence were other gang members. Of particular concern to Klein was the role membership interaction played in strengthening gang cohesiveness. The more gang members met and the more important their gang was perceived to be in the community, the stronger the bonds were between gang members. Against this backdrop, Klein saw the intervention of detached workers and gang programs enhancing gang cohesiveness, making the dissolution of the gang a greater challenge.

The Ladino Hills Project gave Klein the opportunity to build on findings from the Group Guidance Project. A specific effort was made to avoid increasing gang solidarity, an outcome that would make the gang more attractive, increase membership, and expand delinquent activities. A working premise of this approach was that programmatic "attention" paid to gangs by such institutions as the police, social workers, and the schools had the latent consequence of making the gang more attractive and should be avoided. In addition, organized gang events were discouraged. The results were encouraging in many respects, as gang cohesiveness declined during the project. Despite this, the rate of delinquency increased, particularly for more serious crimes. However, the amount of delinquency overall declined, a decline that was concentrated among "companionship" offenses. The withdrawal of adults from gang activities diminished both gang cohesion and delinquency.

Short and Strodtbeck (1974) began their analysis with a premise similar to Klein's, specifically that the War on Poverty may have increased gang solidarity. Based on research in Chicago, their conclusions are similar to those of Klein, particularly with regard to gang structure, cohesion, and activities. Short and Strodtbeck adopted an approach consistent with the poverty area research of Shaw and McKay and the group delinquency perspective found in the theories of Cohen, Cloward and Ohlin, and Thrasher. They found, however, that it was difficult to locate gangs that correspond to those described in most theories. This led them to examine in greater depth the *processes* and *values* that lead to gang delinquency. Indeed, they use the concept of values to link the social status (especially social class) of gang members to their illegitimate behavior.

Short and Strodtbeck paint a picture of gangs, gang members, and gang activities remarkably similar to that drawn earlier by Klein. Like their Los Angeles counterparts, gang members in Chicago reported that the activity that consumed the greatest amount of their time was "hanging out" on the street. Short and Strodtbeck found five specific indices of gang activity: (1) conflict, (2) institutional social activities, (3) sexual behavior, hanging out, and selling alcohol, (4) homosexuality, fathering illegitimate children, and common-law marriages, and (5) involvement in minor car-related crimes, conflict, and alcohol use. They observed that these behaviors are not greatly dissimilar from the more routine activities of adolescent males. Stated differently, these analysts were unable to find activities that consistently differentiated gang members from their nongang peers. Gangs had a shifting membership and structure, with allegiances vacillating over time. Leadership seldom had power and generally was incapable of exacting discipline from members. Concomitantly, few strong group norms laid claims on the behavior of individual gang members.

Status plays a central role in Short and Strodtbeck's explanation of gang formation and activities. Threats to the status of the gang were particularly important, and conflict emerged from disputes about the reputation of the gang. But status threats also operate at the individual level for Short and Strodtbeck. They regard threats, especially to individual status, as fundamental to understanding the origin of gangs. Three systems external to the gang provide the major sources of (and threats to) individual status: (1) adult institutions such as school and jobs, (2) community institutions in the areas that generate gangs, especially street culture, and (3) gang culture. In the course of maintaining relationships with each of these systems, gang members experience threats to their status as individuals. For Short and Strodtbeck, the gang emerges as a collective solution to status threats posed by these relationships. This solution, however, is of short duration.

As America attempted to deal with demands by racial and ethnic minorities for an increased share of economic and social justice, attention to the gangs of the 1950s and early 1960s waned. Gangs faded from public concern in the sixties, replaced by broader concerns over race, increasing crime, and urban unrest. Perhaps the decline in interest over gangs confirmed what Klein and Short and Strodtbeck had reported; gangs had little permanence and stability and, if left alone, may well fade away. Whether the attention paid to other problems caused the decline in gangs, or whether gangs simply faded from the urban scene remains an open question. Regardless of the explanation, social scientists, social workers, policymakers, and the public turned their attention to other matters. This may reflect a change in the funding priorities of the federal government, as resources for studying youth gangs were no longer available (Horowitz 1983).

References

Asbury, Herbert. 1928. *The Gangs of New York*. Garden City, NJ: Alfred Knopf.

Cloward, Richard and Lloyd Ohlin. 1960. *Delinquency and Opportunity*. Glencoe, IL: Free Press.

Cohen, Albert. 1955. *Delinquent Boys*. Glencoe, IL: Free Press.

Horowitz, Ruth. 1983. *Honor and the American Dream: Culture and Identity in a Chicano Community*. New Brunswick, NJ: Rutgers University Press.

Klein, Malcolm W. 1971. *Street Gangs and Street Workers*. Englewood Cliffs, NJ: Prentice Hall.

Lerman, Nicholas. 1991. *The Promised Land: The Great Black Migration and How It Changed America*. New York: Vintage Press.

Miller, Walter B. 1958. "Lower Class Culture as a Generating Milieu of Gang Delinquency." *Journal of Social Issues*, Volume 14: 5–19.

Riis, Jacob A. 1892 (1971). *The Children of the Poor*. New York: Arne Press.

———. 1902. *The Battle with the Slum*. Montclair, NJ: Patterson Smith.

Short, James F., Jr. and Fred L. Strodtbeck. 1974. *Group Process and Gang Delinquency*. Chicago: University of Chicago Press.

Spergel, Irving. 1966. *Street Gang Work: Theory and Practice*. Reading, MA: Addison-Wesley.

Thrasher, Frederick. 1927. *The Gang*. Chicago: University of Chicago Press.

Yablonsky, Lewis. 1962 (1973). *The Violent Gang*. Baltimore: Penguin. ✦

Chapter 3
A Multiple Marginality Framework of Gangs

James Diego Vigil

Here and abroad, issues of migration and immigration seem directly related to street-gang presence. Race, ethnicity, and nationality constantly suffuse discussion of gang formation. As these factors become reflected in poverty, inadequate housing, overcrowded schools, and questionable law enforcement practices, author Vigil (pronounced Veeheel) describes an overall pattern of "multiple marginality" for minority youth. This is the author's framework for understanding street-gang formation and persistence in a large, multi-ethnic region like the Los Angeles area. The weakness of "normal" social-control systems leaves the gang to develop cultural norms and perspectives around its marginal status.

In the second half of the nineteenth century, young immigrant men of Irish, Italian, German, and Polish origin gathered on the street corners of their respective neighborhoods to confront together the rigors of their new life in the industrialized cities of the eastern United States. They were often given colorful names by their society—one early Irish group was known as the Plug Uglies. What were these early gangs like, and how do they compare to today's gangs?

For the most part, they were Irish, joining together in the face of poverty,

Reprinted from *A Rainbow of Gangs: Street Cultures in the Mega-City* by James Diego Vigil, pp. 3–15, 17–178, 188–192. Copyright © 2002. By permission of the University of Texas Press.

squalid conditions, and great prejudice. In general they were older than the gang members of today, although a considerable number were in their late teens. The products of unhealthy slums and malnutrition, . . . [the gangs] were considerably larger than those of today, numbering in the hundreds; one gang claimed 1,200 members. . . . The weapons the gangs used were deadly and imaginative. Some were fortunate enough to own pistols and muskets, but the usual weapons were knives and brickbats and bludgeons. For close work, there were brass knuckles, ice picks, pikes and other interesting paraphernalia.[1]

Today, at the beginning of a new century, the names of gangs are still colorful, though self-chosen—Nip 14, Crips, Maravilla, the Businessmen. Today, too, the processes young immigrants go through in dealing with life in a new country are essentially the same as in the past, and gangs continue to be a byproduct of migration, though migrants today come from more places throughout the world into more areas of this country. Unfortunately, one way the gang scene has changed, dangerously, is in the greater use of drugs and guns during the second half of the twentieth century.[2]

The fact is that throughout the twentieth century the outcome of the acculturation process proved to be a negative one for many individuals, and thus also negative for U.S. society at large. In the early decades of the century, writers and researchers looked at the problems involved in the process of adapting to U.S. culture and produced compelling portraits of those who were struggling through it.[3] Not much recent research, however, has taken another look at the lives of those who fall out of the system. This [article] seeks to do so by providing an in-depth, multicultural portrait of the contemporary gangs that dominate the street corners of Los Angeles, a city that has seen an extraordinary influx of peoples from all over the world. They have had to find their way in a local society that itself is undergoing great change, which makes them an especially rich source of information on the problems of acculturation at this point in time.

Los Angeles is a model of urban diversity, a growing megalopolis stretching in all directions from the city center. It is a place full of different languages and cultural traditions, but also one filled with ethnic and racial tensions that threaten to erupt at any time, as they did during the 1992 Rodney King riots. Relatively new as major cities go, in the first half of the twentieth century Los Angeles experienced rapid economic growth which led to expansion into suburban areas. When civil unrest threatened white work-ing- and middle-class families in the 1960s, that expansion accelerated as many of them moved into the suburbs. At the same time the city was undergoing these demographic shifts, it also was experiencing changes in its labor market and structure.[4] Both inter-nal migration (from small towns and vari-ous regions of the country) and large-scale immigration from foreign countries in-creased exponentially. Los Angeles was no longer primarily a white working- and middle-class American city but a new global metropolis.

These dramatic social transformations strained the city's infrastructure and institu-tional support system. Housing became a problem for many, especially in older neigh-borhoods like Pico-Union, where Central Americans made their home. Up to a dozen persons crammed into apartment units meant for two or three, so that as many as one hundred people might be living in a sin-gle four-story building. Schools built for seven hundred students were expected to hold twice that number, and the needs of the large and growing number of non-English-speaking students could not be quickly and smoothly accommodated; bilingual pro-grams were in place but greatly under-funded and overwhelmed. Long gone were the days when the Los Angeles Police De-partment, the city's "finest," enjoyed the wholehearted support and admiration in-spired by *Dragnet*, the popular television po-lice drama set in Los Angeles. For decades black and Chicano leaders had been railing against unfair and disrespectful treatment of the people in the mostly low-income com-munities they represented.[5] As more and more new people, including thousands of political refugees, flooded into the city, police-community relations worsened, de-spite an increase in the number of minority and female officers in the department.

Los Angeles is more than a model of the mega-city; it is the prototypical mega-city with problems, problems that to some de-gree are also afflicting other urban centers worldwide. These cities have generated or are in the process of generating mega-gangs, mostly within their poor communi-ties. This subcultural process unfolds in like manner from place to place, although as it does the unique history and culture of each place leaves its stamp.

It is unavoidably clear that gangs consti-tute one of the most important urban youth issues in the United States today.[6] Recent es-timates place the number of gangs nation-wide at 30,533 and the number of gang members at 815,896.[7] The Los Angeles area tops the list with close to 8,000 gangs and 200,000 gang members.[8] These figures are for males only; female gang members are many fewer in number (from 4 to 10 percent of all Los Angeles gang members),[9] but their significance is considerable, for studies show that nationwide a high percentage of all incarcerated females belong to gangs.[10] Furthermore, the arrest rates of young women recently have increased at a faster pace than for nongang males,[11] and the types of offenses committed by them are be-coming more serious and violent.

Since the early 1980s, drug trafficking and abuse, gang violence (often tied to drugs), and all sorts of other criminal activi-ties have increased markedly across the United States.[12] In Los Angeles County, gang homicides have recently gone down, but in the 1982–1991 period they climbed from 205 to 700,[13] and by the middle of the 1990s they nearly topped 1,000. As U.S. soci-ety attempted to keep up with the crime problem during that period, the prison pop-ulation tripled.[14] In Los Angeles, the use of gang injunctions, battering rams, special-ized gang law-enforcement units, and harsher penalties such as "three strikes" at-test to a pervasive law and order preoccupa-tion in dealing with youth in minority areas.

Street gangs do emerge primarily in low-income ethnic minority neighborhoods. Some of the Los Angeles gangs can be traced as far back as the 1930s. Initially no more than small bands of wayward children in East Los Angeles Chicano communities, these "boy gangs" metamorphosed over the decades into a deeply rooted gang subcul-ture characterized by a collection of gangs fashioned within the communities of vari-ous ethnic groups.[15] Social neglect, os-tracism, economic marginalization, and cultural repression were largely responsible for the endurance of the subculture. When the economic structure of the city changed and largescale immigration swept into the city from the 1960s forward, gang forma-tion accelerated. No ethnic community has been immune to the problem, although the Chicano, African American, Vietnamese, and Central American communities have been especially affected.

Looking at these four ethnic groups com-paratively, as I do here, is important for a number of reasons.[16] Besides revealing ob-vious differences between groups—their time of arrival in the city, their destination within it, types of intragroup variations, and so forth—the comparative approach can tell us a great deal about gang dynam-ics and street life. Ethnicity plays an im-portant role when cultural groups live in close contact and their physical or cultural characteristics are used to create social boundaries.[17] In Los Angeles, as elsewhere in the United States, ethnic minorities whose physical characteristics most clearly distinguish them from the white majority are most readily subjected to prejudice and discrimination.

As we shall see, the gang experience is shaped by the way in which the particular history and culture of each ethnic group and family interact with the overriding eco-nomic and psychological forces in the larger society.[18] Time, place, and gender are cen-tral to this dynamic. For example, on the one hand, criminal justice practices are less gender-biased today: females who engage in deviant gang behavior are no longer per-ceived as immoral or mentally disturbed, but delinquent.[19] On the other hand, tradi-tional mores of an immigrant culture can come into conflict with those of the host so-ciety: expectations concerning the role of the female can be quite different within the home than they are outside it.

Basically, the street gang is an outcome of marginalization, that is, the relegation of certain persons or groups to the fringes of society, where social and economic condi-tions result in powerlessness. This process occurs on multiple levels as a product of pressures and forces in play over a long period of time. The phrase "multiple mar-ginality" reflects the complexities and per-sistence of these forces.[20] Macrohistorical and macrostructural forces—those that occur at the broader levels of society—lead to economic insecurity and lack of oppor-tunity, fragmented institutions of social control, poverty, and psychological and emotional barriers among large segments of

the ethnic minority communities in Los Angeles. These are communities whose members face inadequate living conditions, stressful personal and family changes, and racism and cultural repression in schools.

Again, consider the pressures and strains in the lives of females, which are especially pronounced. They must contend with major forces from without and from within their own ethnic group and social class that deepen their experiencing of marginali-zation: exacerbated sexism (such as male dominance and exploitation), family fric-tion related to the conflict between tradi-tional cultural attitudes toward females and those of the general society, barriers to achieving economic well-being, and child-bearing and childcare burdens. For them the marginalization processes are doubly compounded, since the protection and su-pervision traditionally afforded girls in a family's country of origin is lessened and they frequently become vulnerable to physi-cal and sexual abuse and exploitation, often within their own families.[21]

Daily strains from many directions take their toll and strip minority peoples of their coping skills. Being left out of mainstream society in so many ways and in so many places relegates these urban youths to the margins of society in practically every sense. This positioning leaves them with few op-tions or resources to better their lives. Often, they seek a place where they are not marginalized—and find it in the streets. Thus, a result of multiple marginalization has been the emergence of street gangs and the generation of gang members. The same kinds of pressures and forces that push male youth into gangs also apply to females.[22]

Society and the criminal justice system have so far not fashioned adequate re-sponses to curtail gang growth. Families, schools, and law enforcement merit special scrutiny in this regard for two main reasons. First, they are the primary agents of social control in society. Second, they are uniquely adaptive and responsive to the concerns of society. Although each of these institutions has made its separate contribution to the gang problem, it is their joint actions (or in-actions) that make the problem worse. It is in the vacuum of their collective failure that street socialization has taken over and rooted the quasi-institution of the street gang.

Figure 3.1
Framework of Multiple Marginality "Act and React"

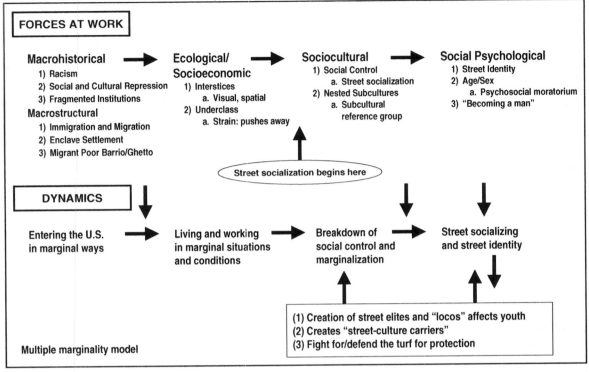

Families

Family life and parenting practices play the initial role in the socialization of a child. It is within the family that individuals form their first significant relationships, and family training first guides and directs them onto a conventional path of participation in society. In short, parents are the primary caretakers who introduce the child to the world. They gradually expand the child's social space (i.e., from the cradle to the bedroom to the home to the neighborhood) to include other, non-kin influences. Disruptions in family life place stress on parenting practices and duties. In poverty-ridden, ethnic minority communities, these disruptions often result in abbreviated or curtailed supervision and direction of household children.[23] Female gang members are often twice affected, since they generally become single parents—"stroller queens," in the words of one flippant observer. Despite the alarming statistics, however, it must be noted that some of these women successfully navigate a life of poverty, mature out of gangs, and become strong and committed mothers.

Schools

Clearly, educational institutions serve as society's primary arena for turning out citizens and trained members of the workforce. In the United States, schools are next in importance to the family in providing structure and meaning to children's lives and acting as an agency for social control. As a child grows up, schools eventually assume the responsibilities of the family for the bulk of each child's daytime activities.

The members of the ethnic groups included here have come mostly from an immigrant background, and so the U.S. system of formal education is new to them.[24] The shift in care and supervision of a child from family to school, into the hands of non-kin, can be particularly troublesome for those who have migrated to Los Angeles from small communities where they enjoyed extensive kinship networks (which serve to provide what has been called social capital). If stressed parents, now without these networks, are already crippled in socializing their children, then sending them to school under the charge of schoolteachers compounds the problem.

Low-income and ethnic minorities have

historically suffered negative, damaging experiences in the educational system. Research shows that standard school policies such as tracking by ability group and the use of standardized tests as the ultimate measure of educational performance and ability have worked against minority students. These students often attend segregated, underfunded, inferior schools, where they encounter cultural insensitivity and an ethnocentric curriculum.[25]

The motivation and strategies for seeking a higher status begin in the family but are formally forged in the educational system and process. In complex societies, schools serve as the mechanism for youths to translate their aspirations into conventional, constructive goals. In terms of reaching for a higher status, many low-income children exhibit a gap between aspirations and expectations. Even though they might have high hopes, they are led (often unaware) to see their goals as outside of their world, exceeding their grasp. Being pragmatic, they assume they won't realize their dreams.[26]

Law Enforcement

The acceptance of the "rightness" of the central social value system is pivotal to social control and citizenship, for individuals are obviously more likely to break the rules if they do not believe in the rules and regulations. Social order depends on the personal internalization of the values of society (the "ought-tos") and of patterned behavior that adheres to the norms of society (the blueprints for action). The latter are first and primarily inculcated by parents, followed by schools, and reinforced early on by peers, especially during the passage from childhood to adulthood.

Youths who are weakly (or not at all) tethered to home and school have weakened ties to society's conventional institutions and values. Because of this deficit, members of law enforcement—the street social-control specialists—often step in as the controlling authority of last resort for our youth. Law enforcement and the criminal justice apparatus serve as the sanctioning source for individuals who consistently fail to conform. When they enter the picture, it is clear that society has not only failed to properly integrate its low-income members but additionally, as we will shortly note, is making it easier for them to become street socialized.

Street Socialization

Multiple forces working jointly lead to children spending more time on the streets, under the purview and guidance of a multiple-aged peer group.[27] In various Los Angeles ethnic communities, this group often takes the form of the street gang. For girls as well as boys, the street becomes a haven and gang life is romanticized, even though it often ultimately brings them trouble and, for girls, additional victimization.[28] What established gangs in the neighborhood have to offer is nurture, protection, friendship, emotional support, and other ministrations for unattended, unchaperoned resident youth. In other words, street socialization fills the voids left by inadequate parenting and schooling, especially inadequate familial care and supervision. This street-based process molds the youth to conform to the ways of the street. On the streets, the person acquires the models and means for new norms, values, and attitudes.

Macrostructural forces have all too often warped or blocked the educational trajectories of minority children, especially the most marginalized gang youth segments of the population.[29] Dropout rates for ethnic minorities, especially for Latinos and African Americans, are notoriously high, and the children most affected are the street-based ones[30]: In some South Central Los Angeles high schools, the rates are as high as 79 percent.[31] Once out of school, the students drop into gangs and commit to the gang's values and norms.

Street socialization alienates youths from what is learned in the schools, while societal discrimination and economic injustice further erode allegiance to conventional commitments. Boys and girls from these backgrounds are regularly truant from school and organize "ditching parties," a practice that reinforces "we-ness" among street peers.[32] (Ditching parties are get-togethers, often to share drinks or drugs, by adolescents who are "ditching," i.e., illicitly not attending school.) With such a weak educational foundation, coupled with family voids, it is no wonder that a conventional path to a higher status escapes the purview of most gang members. Generally poor job prospects exacerbate the situation for minority youth who already have family and school difficulties.

Through the marginalization and street

socialization of urban youth and the creation of a street gang subculture, with values and norms of its own, the street gang becomes a subsociety. Once this subsociety has been created to meet the needs of its creators, it persists and becomes an urban fixture in certain neighborhoods, compelling future generations of youth to join it or otherwise come to terms with it. In these ways, at home and in schools, urban youth acquire a gang-oriented set of rules and regulations.

Gang norms perpetuate a state of male dominance, and females, with few exceptions, largely follow these rules and regulations. Once a member of a gang, a girl or young woman gains status recognition mostly from other homegirls and only occasionally from homeboys. Generally speaking, female street gangs are auxiliaries to the male set. The few autonomous or mixed gangs that exist do not last as long as the auxiliaries, even though the female members continue their street life and associations in another context. Of the few examples cited in the literature, one black female gang in San Francisco was reported to have separated from the males when they discovered that as drug traffickers they could keep all the profits for themselves.[33]

To complicate matters, most of the experiences gang youth have with law enforcement are hostile and antagonistic. For example, special gang units sometimes fan the flames of conflict between rival gangs, police seek and arrest undocumented youths and turn them over to immigration authorities for deportation, and prison guards single out incarcerated gang members for special treatment. Overall, ethnic minority youths, gang or nongang, resent the "dissing" (disrespect) meted out by patrol officers. These experiences further undermine the recognition and acceptance of the dominant value system, for once youths have begun to reject the law and its underlying values, they often develop a resistance orientation and take a defiant and destructive stance.[34]

Toward a More Complete Understanding of Gangs

Although family, schools, and law enforcement are the key elements of social control in any industrialized, urban society and largely responsible for street socialization developments, they are also accessible and open to human intervention and alteration. Throughout the last half century or more, our society has attempted to aid and assist struggling families, introduced innovative schooling programs intended to spark learning among the less fortunate, and sought to correct and improve law enforcement strategies and techniques designed to increase conformity. Our leaders and policymakers who think they are heeding the concerns of the citizenry initiate many of these formulas for change and improvement in each institution. However, political leaders and policymakers typically miss the point in assessing the issue of urban gangs, failing to recognize the importance of formulating strategies based on the characteristics of a low-income population of long-term duration.[35]

Adaptation and integration into the city for many racially distinct and culturally different newcomers usually entails starting off on the bottom rung of the ladder. However, some groups have had the rungs above them sawed off, in effect. Most of them are therefore unable to move up as quickly or smoothly as, say, white ethnics of the nineteenth century. Some particularly talented or assertive individuals manage to stretch past gaps in the rungs to make their way up the metaphorical ladder, but others cannot escape the conditions they find themselves in. The persistent pattern of inferior living situations and substandard working conditions that they confront results in major family stresses and strains, deep-rooted schooling barriers and difficulties, and hostile and negative relations and interactions with law enforcement personnel. From this context the street culture and subsociety has emerged.

Structural causes must therefore be at the forefront of any serious discussions on what causes gangs and creates gang members, which is why the multiple marginality framework begins with ecological and economic factors that are at the root of the breakdown of social control.[36] Those who set policy have lapsed into facile answers, thus allowing ideological arguments (e.g., moral evaluations) to cloud the debate on how to guide our approach to this problem. Often, perspectives and decisions on policy make for a triangulation approach that gives equal weight to every or any side. To help guide our thinking on policy, it is imperative that we examine more closely the multiple factors that affect the youths from various ethnic backgrounds who join gangs.

A cross-cultural, comparative look will sharpen our understanding of the similarities and differences among gang youths in various ethnic groups. We will learn more about how ethnic customs and habits play out when other forces begin to dominate the socialization routines of each group, especially during adolescence. When street socialization takes over, a remarkably similar street orientation and culture emerges for each group, irrespective of ethnic traditions, and, with only slightly greater variation, regardless of gender. Moreover, a comparative examination will afford us a broad, historical approach to how and why social control was disrupted, when and where groups and individuals became social outcasts, and what political forces overshadowed the process. By looking at different groups and isolating the key issues that collectively shape gang behavior and attitudes, we might better generate strategies and approaches to help alleviate and resolve the worst effects of gang life. If nothing else, we can begin to put to rest the contemporary politically tainted dialogue that interferes with a balanced consideration of the problem. Society needs objective investigations and evidence, not "moral panic"[37]—in short, facts, not fears.

Ideally, the solution to the gang problem is linked to resolving all problems arising directly or indirectly from the tremendous social and economic inequalities in our society. Clearly, causes built into the social system are crucial to understanding gangs and gang members, even though not all poverty-stricken children join gangs.[38] But poverty areas generate most gang members, and the poorest of the poor are often more marginalized and thus more subject to street socialization and joining gangs, an indication that even within poverty populations there is internal variation.[39]

As the economic and social system prevalent in the United States increasingly becomes dominant around the globe, gangs likewise are becoming a worldwide phenomenon, typically linked to the migration of large numbers of people to cities.[40] The adaptation to cities by already poor people, sometimes made poorer in the transition, too often results in marginalization processes. Studies worldwide indicate that the migration of former peasants and rural workers often carries with it a series of living and working disruptions that strongly undermine traditional social control institutions,[41] as it has for the youths focused on in this comparative study. Thus, many children in these situations are forced to grow up on the streets. To eliminate this marginalization process and the resultant street socialization would require massive changes in our way of life at the macrostructural level.

However, if we focus on the intermediate (meso and micro) levels of social control, such as families, schools, and law enforcement, we can do something for the proximate future. To pull off even this will require a great engagement and involvement and a retooling of the connections among these agents. Put another way, if we are powerless to address changes at the macro level, then we certainly can and must muster the resources to work at them at the intermediary or micro level. . . .

Notes

1. Haskins 1974: 31.
2. Moore 1998; Maxson, Klein, and Cunningham 1993; Curry and Decker 1998; Huff 1996; Yablonsky 1997; Canada 1995.
3. Researchers and writers who recorded compelling portraits of immigrant Polish, German, Irish, and Italian youths include Ashbury 1927, Thrasher 1927, and Yablonsky 1997.
4. Oliver, Johnson, and Farrell 1993; *Los Angeles Times*, May 12, 1992; Wilson 1987; Johnson and Oliver 1991, 1992; Hagedorn 1988.
5. Escobar 1998.
6. Klein 1995a; Decker and Van Winkle 1996; Boyle 1995; see Klein 1995a, 1971, and Bursik and Grasmick 1993 for definitions of gangs.
7. OJJDP 1996.
8. Klein 1995b.
9. Curry 1995; Campbell 1990.
10. Giordano 1978.
11. OJJDP 1996.
12. Decker and Van Winkle 1994; Padilla 1993; Canada 1995; Currie 1993.
13. Katz 1991.
14. Scheer 1995, 2000; *MacTalk* 1999; Jacobs 1977.
15. Bogardus 1926; Moore 1978; Vigil 1988.
16. Montemayor 2000.

17. Melville 1994.
18. McAdoo 1993.
19. Campbell 1990.
20. Vigil 1988; Vigil and Yun 1998.
21. Moore and Hagedorn 2001; Moore 1991.
22. Quicker 1983; Chesney-Lind and Sheldon 1992.
23. Hernandez 1998.
24. African Americans approximate this dynamic in their rural South to urban North and West migration (Frazier 1966), and thus the U.S. system of formal education, while not new to them, has been kept out of their reach.
25. Orfield 1988; Suzuki and Valencia 1997; Valencia 1991; Moreno 1999; Clark 1983; Kozol 1992; Oakes 1985.
26. Buriel 1984.
27. Vigil 1993.
28. Moore, Vigil, and Levy 1995.
29. Vigil 1999.
30. Fields 1991; Presidential Advisory Commission 1999.
31. Kawachi 1997.
32. Campbell 1990.
33. Lauderback et al. 1992.
34. See Willis 1977 for a discussion of the similar development of an oppositional culture by the British laboring class.
35. Wilson 1987; Moore and Vigil 1993; Farley 1987.
36. Vigil 2002.
37. Jackson and Rudman 1993; Zatz 1987.
38. Spergel and Curry 1998; Klein 1995b.
39. Vigil 1996; Hazlehurst and Hazlehurst 1998.
40. Hazlehurst and Hazlehurst 1998; Hecht 1998.
41. Szanton Blanc 1995.

References

Ashbury, H. 1927. *The Gangs of New York*. Garden City, N.Y.: Garden City Publishing.

Bogardus, E. 1926. *The City Boy and His Problems*. Los Angeles: House of Ralston, Rotary Club of Los Angeles.

Boyle, Gregory J. September 29, 1995. "Victimizers Call Us to Compassion, Too." *Los Angeles Times*, B4.

Buriel, R. 1984. "Integration with Traditional Mexican American Culture and Sociocultural Adjustment." In *Chicano Psychology*, 2nd ed., edited by J. L. Martinez and R. Mendoza, 253–271. New York: Academic Press.

Bursik, R. J., Jr., and H. G. Grasmick. 1993. *Neighborhoods and Crime*. New York: Lexington.

Campbell, Anne. 1990. "Female Participation in Gangs." In *Gangs in America*, edited by C.

Ronald Huff, 163–182. Thousand Oaks, Calif.: Sage Publications.

Canada, G. 1995. *Fist, Sticks, Knives, Guns*. Boston: Beacon.

Chesney-Lind, Meda, and Randall G. Sheldon. 1992. *Girls: Delinquency and Juvenile Justice*. Pacific Grove, Calif.: Brooks/Cole Publishing.

Clark, Reginald. 1983. *Family Life and School Achievement: Why Poor Black Children Succeed or Fail*. Chicago: University of Chicago Press.

Currie, Elliot. 1993. *Reckoning: Drugs, the Cities, and the American Future*. New York: Hill and Wang.

Curry, G. D. November 1995. "Responding to Female Gang Involvement." Paper presented at the American Society of Criminology annual meeting.

Curry, G. D., and S. H. Decker. 1998. *Confronting Gangs: Crime and Community*. Los Angeles, Calif.: Roxbury Publishing.

Decker, Scott, and B. Van Winkle. 1994. "Slinging Dope: The Role of Gangs and Gang Members in Drug Sales." *Justice Quarterly* 11(4): 583–604.

———. 1996. *Life in the Gang: Family, Friends, and Violence*. New York: Cambridge University Press.

Escobar, E. 1998. *Race, Police, and the Making of a Political Identity: Police-Chicano Relations in Los Angeles, 1900–1945*. Berkeley: University of California Press.

Farley, J. E. 1987. "Disproportionate Black and Hispanic Unemployment in U.S. Metropolitan Areas." *American Journal of Economics and Sociology* 46(2): 129–150.

Fields, C. June 1991. "Hispanic Pipeline." *Change Magazine*, 30–36.

Frazier, E. F. 1966. *The Negro Family in the United States*. Rev. ed., abr. Chicago: University of Chicago Press.

Giordano, Peggy C. 1978. "Girls, Guys and Gangs: The Changing Social Context of Female Delinquency." *Journal of Criminal Law and Criminology* 69(1): 126–132.

Hagedorn, J. M., with Perry Macon. 1988. *People and Folks: Gangs, Crime and the Underclass in a Rust-belt City*. Chicago: Lake View Press.

Haskins, J. 1974. *Street Gangs: Yesterday and Today*. New York: Hastings House.

Hazlehurst, K., and C. Hazlehurst, eds. 1998. *Gangs and Youth Subcultures: International Explorations*. New Brunswick, N.J.: Transaction Publishers.

Hecht, T. 1998. *At Home in the Street: Street Children of Northeast Brazil*. New York: Cambridge University Press.

Hernandez, Arturo. 1998. *Peace in the Streets: Breaking the Cycle of Gang Violence*. Washington, D.C.: Child Welfare League of America.

Huff, C. R., ed. 1996. *Gangs in America*, 2d ed. Thousand Oaks, Calif.: Sage Publications.

Jackson, P., and C. Rudman. 1993. "Moral Panics and the Response to Gangs in California." In *Gangs: The Origins and Impact of Contemporary Youth Gangs in the United States*, edited by S. Cummings and D. J. Monti, 257–276. Albany: State University of New York Press.

Jacobs, J. 1977. *Statesville: The Penitentiary in Mass Society*. Chicago: University of Chicago Press.

Johnson, J., and M. Oliver. 1991. "Economic Restructuring and Black Male Joblessness in U.S. Metropolitan Areas." *Urban Geography* 12(6): 542–562.

———. 1992. "Structural Changes in the U.S. Economy and Black Male Joblessness: A Reassessment." In *Urban Labor Markets and Job Opportunity*, edited by G. Peterson and W. Vroman, 113–147. Washington, D.C.: Urban Institute Press.

Katz, Jesse. December 8, 1991. "Gang Killings in L.A. County Top a Record 700." *Los Angeles Times*, A1, 23.

Kawachi, J. A. 1997. "A Holistic Approach Toward Dropout Prevention Policies for Minority Youth in the United States." Paper submitted to the Honors 196 seminar "Urban Poverty and Public Policy," University of California, Los Angeles.

Klein, M. 1971. *Street Gangs and Street Workers*. Englewood Cliffs, N.J.: Prentice-Hall.

———. 1995a. *The American Street Gang*. New York: Oxford University Press.

———. September 19, 1995b. "Deference to Gangs Makes Them Kings of the Roost." *Los Angeles Times*, B3.

Kozol, Jonathan. 1992. *Savage Inequalities: Children in America's Schools*. New York: HarperPerennial.

Lauderback, David, Joy Hanson, and Dan Waldorf. 1992. " 'Sisters Are Doin' It for Themselves': A Black Female Gang in San Francisco." *Gang Journal* 1: 57–72.

Los Angeles Times. May 12, 1992. *Understanding the Riots: Los Angeles Before and After the Rodney King Case*. Insert, Sunday edition.

MacTalk [newsletter]. September 1999. "Prison Guards—A Major Force in California." *MacTalk* 8(9): 3.

Maxson, C. L., M. W. Klein, and L. C. Cunningham. 1993. *Street Gangs and Drug Sales*. Report to the National Institute of Justice. Washington, D.C.: National Institute of Justice, Office of Justice Programs, U.S. Department of Justice.

McAdoo, Harriet Pipes. 1993. *Family Ethnicity*. Thousand Oaks, Calif.: Sage Publications.

Melville, M. 1994. "Hispanic Ethnicity, Race and Class." In *Handbook of Hispanic Cultures in the United States: Anthropology*, edited by T. Weaver, 85–106. Houston: Arte Público Press.

Montemayor, Raymond. 2000. *Adolescent Diversity in Ethnic, Economic, and Cultural Contexts*. Thousand Oaks, Calif.: Sage Publications.

Moore, J. W. 1978. *Homeboys*. Philadelphia: Temple University Press.

———. 1991. *Going Down to the Barrio: Homeboys and Homegirls in Change*. Philadelphia: Temple University Press.

———. 1998. "Understanding Youth Street Gangs: Economic Restructuring and the Urban Underclass." In *Cross-Cultural Perspectives on Youth and Violence*, edited by M. Watts, 17–35. Stamford, Conn.: JAI Press.

Moore, J. W, and J. Hagedorn. 2001. *Female Gangs: A Focus on Research*. Washington, D.C.: Office of Juvenile Justice and Delinquency Prevention, U.S. Department of Justice.

Moore, J. W, and J. D. Vigil. 1993. "Barrios in Transition." In *In the Barrios: Latinos and the Underclass Debate*, edited by J. Moore and R. Pinderhughes, 27–49. New York: Russell Sage Foundation.

Moore, J. W., J. D. Vigil, and J. Levy. 1995. "Huisas of the Street: Chicana Gang Members." *Latino Studies* 6(1): 27–48.

Moreno, J. E, ed. 1999. *The Elusive Quest for Equality*. Cambridge: Harvard Educational Review, Harvard University Press.

Oakes, J. 1985. *Keeping Track: How Schools Structure Inequality*. New Haven, Conn.: Yale University Press.

OJJDP (Office of Juvenile Justice and Delinquency Prevention). June 1996. *Female Offenders in the Juvenile Justice System: Statistic Summary*. Washington, D.C.: U.S. Department of Justice.

Oliver, M. L., J. H. Johnson, and W. C. Farrell. 1993. "Anatomy of a Rebellion: A Political-Economic Analysis." In *Reading Rodney King/Reading Urban Uprising*, edited by R. G. Gooding-Williams, 117–141. New York: Routledge.

Orfield, G. 1988. "Exclusion of the Majority: Shrinking College Access and Public Policy in Metropolitan Los Angeles." *Urban Review* 20: 147–163.

Padilla, F. 1993. *The Gang as an American Enterprise*. New Brunswick, N.J.: Rutgers University Press.

Presidential Advisory Commission on Educational Excellence for Hispanic Americans. 1999. *Our Nation on the Fault Line: Hispanic American Education*. Prepared by Richard A. Figueroa and Sonia Hernandez. Washington, D.C.: The Commission.

Quicker, John C. 1983. *Homegirls: Characterizing Chicana Gangs*. San Pedro, Calif.: International Universities Press.

Scheer, R. August 27, 1995. "New National Monument: The Jailhouse." *Los Angeles Times*, B3.

———. March 7, 2000. "We Locked 'Em Up, Threw Away the Key." *Los Angeles Times*, B7.

Spergel, I. A., and G. D. Curry. 1998. "The National Youth Gang Survey: A Research and Development Process." In *The Modern Gang Reader*, edited by M. W. Klein, C. L. Maxson, and J. Miller, 254–265. Los Angeles: Roxbury Publishing.

Suzuki, Lisa, and Richard Valencia. 1997. "Race, Ethnicity and Measured Intelligence: Educational Implication." *American Psychologist* 52(10): 42–56.

Szanton Blanc, C., with contributors. 1995. *Urban Children in Distress: Global Predicaments and Innovative Strategies.* Florence, Italy: UNICEF.

Thrasher, F. 1927. *The Gang.* Chicago: University of Chicago Press.

Valencia, R. 1991. *Chicano School Failure and Success: Research and Policy Agendas for the 1990s.* London: Falmer Press.

Vigil, J. D. 1988. *Barrio Gangs: Street Life and Identity in Southern California.* Austin: University of Texas Press.

———. 1993. "The Established Gang." In *Gangs: The Origins and the Impact of Contemporary Youth Gangs in the United States*, edited by S. Cummings and D. Monti, 95–112. Albany: State University of New York Press.

———. 1996. "Understanding Life in an East Los Angeles Public Housing Project: A Focus on Gang and Non-Gang Families." Working paper, Center for the Study of Urban Poverty, University of California, Los Angeles.

———. 1999. "Streets and Schools: How Educators Can Help Chicano Marginalized Gang Youth." *Harvard Educational Review* 69(3): 270–288.

———. 2002. "Community Dynamics and the Rise of Street Gangs." In *Latinos! Remaking America*, edited by M. Suarez-Orozco. Berkeley: University of California Press; Cambridge, Mass.: Harvard University Press.

Vigil, J. D., and S. C. Yun. 1998. "Vietnamese Youth Gangs in the Context of Multiple Marginality and the Los Angeles Youth Gang Phenomenon." In *Gangs and Youth Subcultures: International Explorations*, edited by K. Hazlehurst and C. Hazlehurst, 117–139. New Brunswick, N.J.: Transaction Publishers.

Willis, P. E. 1977. *Learning to Labour.* Farnborough, England: Saxon House.

Wilson, W. J. 1987. *The Truly Disadvantaged.* Chicago: University of Chicago Press.

Yablonsky, Lewis. 1997. *Gangsters: Fifty Years of Madness, Drugs, and Death on the Streets of America.* New York: New York University Press.

Zatz, M. S. 1987. "Chicano Youth Gangs and Crime: The Creation of a Moral Panic." *Contemporary Crises* 11: 129–158. ✦

Chapter 4
The Antecedents of Gang Membership

Terence P. Thornberry,
Marvin D. Krohn,
Alan J. Lizotte, Carolyn A.
Smith, and Kimberly Tobin

The issue of what puts youth at risk of joining gangs is best studied using longitudinal methods in which youth are studied over a long period of time. The authors of this chapter applied this technique to a large sample of youth in one city, and included questions about gang membership. By looking at factors before as well as during periods of gang membership, they were able to study some causes of joining gangs as well as derive hints about which factors might help to prevent such joining. Using seven broad categories of variables, the authors establish which are the best single predictors. Even more important, they show that it is the accumulation of single risk factors that provides the best prediction of who will join gangs. It is interesting to note, nonetheless, that even among youth most at risk, there are many who avoid or resist gang joining. Certainly, we need more research on how such individual youth accomplish this resistance.

A Risk Factor Approach

. . . Risk factors are "individual or environmental hazards that increase an individual's vulnerability to negative developmental out-

comes" (Small and Luster, 1994: 182; see also Farrington, 2000; Werner and Smith, 1982). Consistent with the multidimensionality of the life-course approach, risk factor models assume that there are multiple, and often overlapping, risk factors in an individual's background that lead to adverse outcomes. In the terms of developmental psychopathology, outcomes are characterized by equifinality, or multiple pathways to the same outcome (Cicchetti and Rogosch, 1996). Furthermore, this approach assumes that *cumulative risk*, that is, risk that occurs in many different life domains, is most strongly related to adversity (Werner and Smith, 1982).

Identifying risk factors, especially those that occur early in the life course, has several theoretical and practical advantages (Farrington, 2000). Theoretically, identifying factors that increase risk suggests fruitful areas for exploration in more formal causal analyses. It also helps in isolating variables that mediate or translate increased vulnerability into actually experiencing the outcome. Practically, knowledge of risk factors helps structure the design of intervention programs by identifying "at-risk" youth for whom prevention and treatment efforts are most warranted. Also, the identification of the most salient risk factors suggests substantive areas for intervention efforts. Alleviating antecedent variables that are associated with increased risk for a particular outcome may also reduce the probability that the person will experience the outcome. Moreover, identifying the cluster or constellation of risk factors associated with a particular outcome is helpful to clinicians because they deal with the entire individual and all of his or her presenting problems.

Despite these advantages, there have been surprisingly few examinations of risk factors for gang membership. Prior studies in this area are primarily correlational in design and compare gang members to non-members in terms of attributes measured during periods of active gang membership. In these studies temporal order is not established and it is therefore not clear whether the factors identified are antecedent risk factors for gang membership, co-occurring problems, or consequences of being in a gang. Because most prior studies do not establish proper temporal order, they suggest, rather than identify, risk factors for gang

Reprinted from: Terence P. Thornberry, Marvin D. Krohn, Alan J. Lizotte, Carolyn A. Smith, and Kimberly Tobin, *Gangs and Delinquency in Developmental Perspective*, pp. 56–76. Copyright © by Cambridge University Press. Reprinted with the permission of Cambridge University Press.

membership. In this section we first review the results of these studies and then review in more detail the few studies that more properly assess risk factors for gang membership.

Correlational Studies

Consistent with the basic tenet of a risk factor approach—that there are likely to be multiple rather than single pathways to adverse outcomes—prior research has examined correlates of gang membership in a variety of domains. Howell (1997: 124) has categorized risk factors into five groups: community, family, school, peer, and individual characteristics. We further divide Howell's category of individual characteristics into a prior problem behavior category and other individual characteristics. We also subdivide the family category into family sociodemographic characteristics and parent-child relationship factor.

Area Characteristics. Several studies have found that living in socially disorganized areas is related to gang membership (Bowker and Klein, 1983; Curry and Spergel, 1992; Moore, 1978, 1991; Short, 1990). These findings are consistent with the general observation that gangs themselves tend to cluster in high-crime, socially disorganized neighborhoods (e.g., Fagan, 1996; Short and Strodtbeck, 1965; Vigil, 1988). Not surprisingly, youths who reside in those same neighborhoods are at increased risk for gang membership. These findings are also consistent with research results that suggest that the availability of drugs (Curry and Spergel, 1992; Hill et al., 1995) and the presence of gangs (Curry and Spergel, 1992; Nirdorf, 1988) in the neighborhood also increase the risk for gang membership.

Other studies, however, do not link area characteristics with an increased risk of gang membership. For example, in a study by Bjerregaard and Smith (1993) using the Rochester data, social disorganization and neighborhood poverty are not significantly related to the risk of gang membership. Fagan (1990) also found no significant association between gang membership and social integration, neighborhood integration, or neighborhood violence. Similarly, Winfree, Backstrom, and Mays (1994) found that urban residence does not differentiate gang members from nonmembers.

Family Sociodemographic Characteris-tics. Several studies have examined sociodemographic characteristics as risk factors for gang membership. Very little research in the gang literature examines race or ethnicity as a predictor of gang membership, because most studies are conducted within racially homogeneous gangs. Among the studies that do exist, the comparison is generally between white subjects and either African American or Hispanic youths. By and large, Hispanic and African American subjects are more likely to be gang members than are white subjects (Esbensen and Huizinga, 1993; Hill et al., 1999; Schwartz, 1989; Winfree et al., 1994).

Some studies have found that low family socioeconomic status or poverty is related to gang membership (Bowker and Klein, 1983; Moore, 1991; Schwartz, 1989). Structural characteristics of families have also been examined with varying results. Bowker and Klein (1983) and Vigil (1988) found that coming from single-parent families increases the risk of joining gangs, whereas LeBlanc and Lanctôt (1998), in a study comparing gang members and nonmembers in a Quebec sample restricted to adjudicated boys, did not.

Parent-Child Relations. In addition to concerns about family structure, many studies have examined family processes and parent-child relationships as risk factors for gang involvement. In general, poor family management strategies increase the risk for gang membership by adolescents (LeBlanc and Lanctôt, 1998; Moore, 1991; Vigil, 1988). More specifically, low family involvement (Friedman, Mann, and Friedman, 1975; LeBlanc and Lanctôt, 1998), inappropriate parental discipline (Winfree et al., 1994), low parental control or monitoring (Bowker and Klein, 1983; Campbell, 1990; LeBlanc and Lanctôt, 1998; Moore, 1991), poor affective relationships between parent and child (Campbell, 1990; Moore, 1991), and parental conflict (LeBlanc and Lanctôt, 1998) put youths at risk for becoming gang members. These family-based risk factors are quite consistent with those generally observed as increasing risk for involvement in delinquency (see Hawkins, Catalano, and Miller, 1992; Loeber and Stouthamer-Loeber, 1986).

School Factors. Failure in the educational arena can also be a major source of risk for gang membership. Bowker and Klein (1983) reported that female students who have low educational expectations are at increased risk for gang membership, a finding also observed by Bjerregaard and Smith (1993) for females but not males. Gang membership is more likely among adolescents whose parents have low educational expectations for them (Schwartz, 1989). Poor school performance and low commitment to and involvement in school are correlated with gang membership (LeBlanc and Lanctôt, 1998). In a related vein, gang membership is associated with educational frustration (Curry and Spergel, 1992) and stress (LeBlanc and Lanctôt, 1998).

Teachers also play a role in predicting the likelihood of gang membership. Gang members, as compared with nonmembers, are more likely to experience negative labeling by teachers (Esbensen, Huizinga, and Weiher, 1993) and are less likely to have a teacher as a positive role model (Schwartz, 1989; Wang, 1994), although LeBlanc and Lanctôt (1998) did not find low attachment to teachers to be related to gang membership.

Low school self-esteem (Curry and Spergel, 1992; Schwartz, 1989) and educational marginality (Bjerregaard and Smith, 1993) increase the risk for gang membership. Two studies have suggested that school stress resulting from factors such as getting into trouble in school or getting poor grades is related to gang membership (Cohen et al., 1994; Shelden, Snodgrass, and Snodgrass, 1992).

Peer Relationships. Several studies have found that adolescents who associate with deviant peers are more likely to join gangs, especially peers who are themselves gang members (Curry and Spergel, 1992; Nirdorf, 1988; Winfree et al., 1994). Gang membership has been shown to be related to precocious sexual activity (Bjerregaard and Smith, 1993; LeBlanc and Lanctôt, 1998) and also, in the case of young women, dating older males, especially older gang males who are involved in deviant activity (Bowker and Klein, 1983).

Having friends who are involved in delinquency is strongly related to being a gang member (Bjerregaard and Lizotte, 1995; Bjerregaard and Smith, 1993; Bowker and Klein, 1983; Curry and Spergel, 1992; Esbensen et al., 1993; Fagan, 1990; LeBlanc and Lanctôt, 1998; Nirdorf, 1988; Winfree et

al., 1994). The relationship between deviant peers and gang membership is perhaps the strongest one observed in this literature. Because delinquent gangs are in many ways a specific version of a delinquent peer group, the finding is not surprising. Relatedly, loitering or "hanging out" with peers in unsupervised peer groups is also related to gang membership (LeBlanc and Lanctôt, 1998).

Individual Characteristics. Gang members have been characterized as being personally maladjusted, although findings in this area are rather inconsistent (see Bjerregaard and Smith, 1993, for a review). With regard to self-esteem, a number of studies found that low self-esteem increases the likelihood of gang membership (Cartwright, Tomson, and Schwartz, 1975; Rice, 1963; Schwartz, 1989; Wang, 1994). In contrast, Bjerregaard and Smith (1993), Bowker and Klein (1983), and Esbensen et al. (1993) did not find self-esteem to be related to gang membership. We have little information on the effect of stressful or negative life events as a risk factor for joining a gang except for the studies cited earlier relating to school stress and family stress.

The individual's attitudes also play a role in increasing the risk of gang membership. Winfree et al. (1994) found that progang attitudes are associated with gang membership and Esbensen et al. (1993) found that gang members have a higher tolerance for deviance and higher levels of normlessness (see also Fagan, 1990). LeBlanc and Lanctôt (1998) reported that deviant beliefs and techniques of neutralization are related to gang membership and also that gang members have significantly poorer scores than nonmembers on 10 of their 13 personality scales, including orientation to tough and adult-type behaviors, aggression, repression, denial, neuroticism, and extroversion.

Prior Deviance. Finally, several studies have found that adolescents who are already involved in deviant and problem behaviors are more likely to join gangs than are adolescents who are not involved in those behaviors. For example, gang membership has been shown to be related to alcohol and drug use (Bjerregaard and Smith, 1993; Cohen et al., 1994; LeBlanc and Lanctôt, 1998; Thornberry et al., 1993), violence (Friedman et al., 1975; LeBlanc and Lanctôt, 1998), being an illegal gun owner (Bjerregaard and Lizotte, 1995), and general delinquency (Curry and Spergel, 1992; Esbensen and Huizinga, 1993; LeBlanc and Lanctôt, 1998; Nirdorf, 1988). In addition, official contact with the juvenile justice system has been shown to be related to gang membership (Cohen et al., 1994; LeBlanc and Lanctôt, 1998).

Risk Factor Studies

Recently a few longitudinal studies have begun to investigate the impact of *prior* attributes and characteristics that may increase the risk of subsequent gang membership. That is, they have begun to assess more properly a risk factor model for gang membership.

Using data from the Seattle Social Development Project, Hill et al. (1999) examined risk factors measured at ages 10–12 as predictors of gang membership between ages 13 and 18. Risk factors were drawn from five domains: neighborhood, family, school, peers, and individual characteristics. They found that "[21] of the 25 constructs measured at ages 10–12 predicted joining a gang at ages 13 to 18. Predictors of gang membership were found in all of the measured domains" (Hill et al., 1999: 308). Within each of these domains the most potent risk factors are neighborhood youth in trouble and availability of marijuana; family structure, especially living with one parent and other adults or with no parents; low achievement in elementary school or being identified as learning disabled; association with deviant peers; prior involvement in marijuana use or violence; and externalizing problem behaviors. Hill et al. also found that having multiple risk factors greatly increases the chances of joining a gang.

Bjerregaard and Lizotte (1995) used the Rochester data to look specifically at the impact of earlier delinquency and gun ownership on the likelihood of being a gang member. They found that prior involvement in serious delinquency and street delinquency, but not more general forms of delinquency, increases the likelihood of later gang membership. They also found that owning guns for protection, but not for sporting purposes, increases the chances of joining a gang.

Lahey et al. (1999) examined predictors of first gang entry for the males in the Pittsburgh Youth Study. Their study was restricted to African American males because of the small number of white male gang members available for analysis. In bivariate relationships, gang membership is predicted by prior conduct disorder behaviors, self-reported delinquency, and associations with delinquent peers. Gang membership is not bivariately related to household income, household structure, neighborhood crime level, or parental supervision, however.

Summary

Overall, we have a good deal of information from prior studies that can inform a risk factor model. It appears that gang membership is a product of numerous risk factors from multiple developmental domains and that gang members are likely to have serious deficits in many developmental areas. Because of the cross-sectional nature of most of these studies, however, we do not have a clear, well-replicated understanding of which antecedent conditions increase risk for later gang membership. In addition, a risk factor model requires a general, representative sample that includes both individuals who experience the outcome (i.e., gang membership) and those who do not experience it. Unfortunately, there are relatively few gang studies (e.g., Hill et al., 1999; Lahey et al., 1999) that have both of these design features—that is, a representative sample that follows both gang members and comparison nonmembers across time. We now capitalize on the longitudinal design of the Rochester study to help fill this gap in our knowledge.

Measurement

The key variable in this analysis is gang membership . . . , measured by a self-report item contained in our interviews. Unfortunately for this analysis, at Wave 2 we asked the respondents if they had *ever* been a gang member, but not the age at which they joined the gang. Thus, for subjects who were in a gang at Wave 2 proper temporal order cannot be established between Wave 1 risk factors and *later* gang membership. We therefore limit this analysis to respondents who joined a gang at Wave 3 or after. Starting at the Wave 3 interview, we asked the respondents whether they were a gang member at any time during the six-month interval since the previous interview. Because of this, we can establish proper temporal order between earlier risk factors, measured at either Wave 2 or prior to Wave 2, and later gang membership. Thus, the primary dependent variable in this chapter is joining a gang at any time between Waves 3 and 9.

Based on the domains previously identified, and consistent with a general ecological framework (Bronfenbrenner, 1979), risk factors for gang membership are grouped into seven domains: area characteristics, family sociodemographic characteristics, parent-child relations, school factors, peer relationships, individual characteristics, and early delinquency. . . . Briefly, area risk factors include racial composition, census-tract-level poverty, and arrest rate, as well as family perceptions of neighborhood disorganization and violence. Sociodemographic characteristics of families include economic disadvantage, race/ethnicity, and the composition of households. Measures of parent-child relations include attachment, involvement, supervision, positive parenting, child maltreatment, and family hostility. School factors include lack of school commitment, aspirations and achievement, and lack of attachment to teachers. Peer risk factors include peer delinquency, early dating, precocious sexual activity, and unsupervised time with friends. Individual factors include stressful or negative life events and various indicators of psychopathology such as high levels of externalizing behavior, low self-esteem, depressive symptoms, and delinquent beliefs. Prior delinquency includes early general delinquency, violent delinquency, drug use, and age of onset of delinquency.

Because of the nature of the analysis to follow, especially the examination of cumulative risk, we dichotomize all the risk factor variables. Many are already dichotomies, for example, race/ethnicity and whether or not there is a history of child maltreatment. Continuous variables were divided at their median, so variables such as attachment to parents or commitment to school represent respondents who are above or below the midway point on the variable. Dichotomizing all the variables creates a common metric for the logistic regressions reported here and provides a rather intuitive interpretation for the odds ratios that are presented. Also, dichotomies are helpful in determining whether a respondent has a particular risk factor, a necessary step in assessing cumulative risk. . . .

Results

Bivariate Analysis

The first step in the analysis is an examination of bivariate relationships between early risk factors and subsequent gang membership. Because gang membership is a dichotomous variable, we use odds ratios from bivariate logistic regressions to estimate the strength of the associations. Odds ratios of less than 1 indicate that the risk factor is associated with a *reduced* likelihood of gang membership, whereas odds ratios greater than 1 indicate that the likelihood of gang membership is *increased* when this factor is present. For example, an odds ratio of .8 indicates that respondents who possess the particular attribute indicated by the predictor variable have a likelihood of gang membership that is 80% of that of those who do not have the attribute. On the other hand, an odds ratio of 1.3 indicates that those with the risk factor have a likelihood of gang membership that is 30% higher than those without the risk factor. An odds ratio of 2.0 indicates that the likelihood of gang membership is 100% higher or, in other words, is twice as high. An odds ratio of 1 indicates no relationship between the two variables. To examine whether the same risk factors predict gang membership for boys and girls, we do separate analyses by gender (see Table 4.1).

Male Gang Membership. For males, 25 of the 40 Wave 2 risk factors are significantly related to subsequent gang membership in the expected direction. Each domain contains a number of significant relationships indicating that diverse areas of the lives of these adolescents have the potential to put a youth at risk for joining a gang.

The objective indicators of area characteristics are more important predictors of gang membership than are the subjective perceptions of what neighborhoods are like. Respondents who live in neighborhoods that have a higher proportion of African Americans, poorer residents, and a higher arrest rate are more likely to become gang members. On the other hand, among indicators based on parental perceptions of problems in the neighborhood, only neighborhood drug use significantly increases

Table 4.1
*Bivariate Odds Ratios Between Risk Factors
and Joining a Gang Between Waves 3 and 9*

	Males	Females
Area Characteristics		
Percentage African American	1.59*	0.81
Percentage in Poverty	1.88**	1.40
Community Arrest Rate	1.79**	1.14
Neighborhood Disorganization	0.95	2.56*
Neighborhood Violence	0.86	1.64
Neighborhood Drug Use	1.51*	1.87
Neighborhood Integration	0.71	1.97
Family Sociodemographic Characteristics		
African American	2.28**	2.06
Hispanic	1.19	0.50
Parent Education	0.53**	0.96
Family Disadvantage	1.39	1.90
Poverty Level Income	1.91**	1.40
Lives with Both Biological Parents	0.47**	0.50
Family Transitions	1.42	1.46
Parent-Child Relations		
Attachment to Parent	1.02	0.80
Attachment to Child	0.69*	1.36
Parental Involvement	0.94	1.29
Parental Supervision	0.53**	1.01
Positive Parenting	1.10	3.07
Report of Child Maltreatment	1.78*	1.77
Family Hostility	0.77	1.21
School Factors		
Commitment to School	0.64*	0.80
Attachment to Teacher	0.48**	0.24**
College Aspirations	1.09	0.30**
Subject's College Expectations	0.70	0.12**
Parent's College Expectations for Subject	0.64*	0.43*
Math Score	0.41**	0.65
Peer Relationships		
Delinquent Peers	1.97**	2.02
Early Dating	2.82**	2.91*
Precocious Sexual Activity	1.58*	1.66
Unsupervised Time with Friends	1.41	1.35
Individual Characteristics		
Negative Life Events	3.25**	1.28
Depression	1.71**	1.13
Self-Esteem	0.82	0.93
Externalizing Behaviors	1.98**	2.24*
Delinquent Beliefs	2.15**	4.27**
Early Delinquency		
General Delinquency	3.26**	2.82*
Violent Delinquency	4.19**	1.44
Drug Use	2.49**	2.57
Age of Onset of General Delinquency	0.78	0.35

Note: To preserve temporal order, risk factors are measured either at Wave 2 or prior to Wave 2. Because of missing data, the n's vary across these measures, ranging from 488 to 534 for the males and from 169 to 183 for the females. The only exception is age of onset, which can be calculated for offenders (n = 340 for males and n = 96 for females).

*p < .05 (one-tailed test). **p < .01 (one-tailed test).

the likelihood of males becoming gang members.

The risk of joining a gang is significantly related to four demographic characteristics. Being African American, having a parent with less education, living in a family with an income below the poverty level, and living in homes where both biological parents are not present increase the risk of joining a gang. The combined results from the area and family domains confirm the results of many previous gang studies and indicate that socioeconomic disadvantage is an important risk factor for gang membership.

The quality of the relationship between parents and children also contributes to the risk of joining a gang. In families where parents are less attached to their sons and do not supervise them very well, the odds that the child will become a gang member increase. Also, if there is an official record of child maltreatment, the boy's chances of being a gang member are increased.

Both objective and subjective measures of school problems significantly increase the risk that males will join gangs. Low commitment to school, weak attachment to teacher, and lower parental expectations that their son will go to college are significantly related to gang membership. Those respondents who scored lower on a standardized math test also are significantly more likely to join a gang.

Three of the four measures in the peer domain significantly increase the risk that youth will join gangs. Having friends who are involved in delinquent behavior increases the risk for gang membership. Also, males who are involved in precocious sexual activity and who begin dating at an early age are more likely to become gang members.

Among the individual characteristics, experiencing negative life events has a substantial impact on the risk of gang membership, increasing the odds of joining a gang threefold. Mental health problems such as having depressive symptoms and externalizing problem behaviors also play an important role. Attitudes that are favorable to delinquent behavior increase the odds that males will become gang members. Only self-esteem is not significantly related to gang membership.

Finally, involvement in prior illegal activity increases the likelihood of later gang membership. As might be expected, this is particularly true for violence; those who

self-report violence above the median value at Wave 1 are four times as likely to become gang members as are those who self-report less violence. Early age of onset of delinquency is not significantly related to gang membership, however.

In summary, a wide band of factors from different domains of the adolescent's life appear to come together to influence the chances of becoming a gang member for these young males. These range from the contextual impact of poor neighborhoods and family hardship to the more personally experienced stress of negative life events and proximity to deviant peers.

Although many risk factors are significantly related to later gang membership, fewer factors appear to have a strong effect based on the size of the odds ratios (OR) presented in Table 4.1. The following variables at least double (OR > 2.0) or cut in half (OR < .50) the odds of being a gang member: being African American; not living with both parents; low attachment to teachers; low math scores; early dating; experiencing negative life events; delinquent beliefs; and prior delinquency, violence, and drug use.

Female Gang Membership. . . . [T]he temporal distribution of gang membership is highly skewed for the female respondents; most joined a gang by Wave 2 and only 18 joined at Wave 3 or after. Consequently, the number of female gang members available for this analysis is quite low and that reduces statistical power. Hence, we can expect fewer risk factors to be significant predictors of gang membership for females as compared with males. Indeed, only 9 of the 40 potential risk factors are statistically significant.

For the females, none of the objective neighborhood characteristics is statistically significant, which is in direct contrast to what we found for males. Of the perceptual measures, only parental perception of neighborhood disorganization significantly increases the odds of females becoming gang members.

Among the sociodemographic characteristics, none of the measures is statistically significant. The size and direction of most of the coefficients are, however, consistent with what was found for males. It would appear that coming from a disadvantaged family background increases the odds of gang membership for females, as it did for males.

The odds of joining a gang are not significantly affected by any of the parent-child relations variables, although several of these variables were important for the males.

School variables appear to be the most important domain for predicting female gang membership. In particular, being attached to teachers and having aspirations to attend college decrease the odds of females joining gangs. Relatedly, both the parent's and the adolescent's lowered expectations about attending college are significantly related to increasing the odds of gang membership.

Early dating is the only peer variable that significantly increases the odds of joining a gang for the females; females who begin dating boys at an early age are more likely to be gang members than those who wait till an older age. Although the odds ratios are not statistically significant for precocious sexual activity and having delinquent peers, they are in the expected direction and of approximately the same magnitude as those observed for the males.

Among the individual characteristics, only externalizing behaviors and delinquent beliefs are statistically significant. Perhaps most surprising is the relatively small effect that experiencing negative life events has in increasing the odds of female gang membership. Negative life events are very important for males but appear to have little impact for females, a finding that is consistent with the general literature on gender differences in the effects of childhood and adolescent stress (e.g., Bolger et al., 1995; Emery and O'Leary, 1982).

Interestingly, prior participation in violence and drug use does not significantly increase the odds of joining a gang, perhaps because of the lower rate of female involvement in violence and drug use at these ages. The significant effect for general delinquency indicates that participation in any type of delinquency is important in predicting female gang membership rather than participation in a particular type.

Statements concerning the effect of risk factors on female gang membership cannot be as definitive as they were for males because of the smaller number of females in our sample and especially the smaller number of female gang members in this analysis. However, living in a socially disorganized neighborhood, school-related variables, early dating, externalizing behaviors, having delinquent beliefs, and prior general delinquency appear to be important factors in increasing the odds that females will join gangs. Although not as clear-cut as the situation for males, it also appears that female gang members have multiple risk factors in multiple domains, an analytic issue we return to later in this chapter. . . .

Cumulative Risk

One of the basic premises of a life-course approach is that risk accumulates, and, as a consequence, exposure to risk in multiple domains of development greatly increases the person's vulnerability to adverse outcomes (see Garmezy, 1995; Rutter, 1987; Werner and Smith, 1982). In other words, while experiencing risk in one domain (e.g., family *or* school) increases the odds of adverse outcomes, experiencing risk in multiple domains (e.g., family *and* school) should have an even larger impact on behavior. To test this hypothesis we examine two models of cumulative risk, a variable-based model and a domain-based model.

Variable-Based Model. In the variable-based model we simply count the number of risk factors that each person experienced at Wave 2. The risk factors are those listed in the bivariate table (Table 4.1). In this analysis some of the variables are reverse coded so that a score of 1 always indicates risk. For example, coding for commitment to school is reversed, with those scoring below the median (i.e., having low commitment) receiving a score of one. Overall, scores could range from 0 to 40. For this analysis the respondents are grouped into four categories, those experiencing 10 or fewer risk factors, 11–15 risk factors, 16–20 risk factors, and 21 or more.[1] The results are presented in Figure 4.1, for males and females separately. Recall that to preserve temporal order, this analysis is limited to those who first joined a gang at Wave 3 or after. The total prevalence of gang membership at these waves is 19.7% for the males and 11.9% for the females.

There is a strong positive relationship between experiencing multiple risks and the chances of becoming a gang member. For the male subjects, only 1 (0.7%) of those with 10 or fewer risk factors joined a gang. For those with 11–15 risk factors in their background 13.0% were gang members, and that percentage increased to 23.4% for those with 16–20 risk factors and to 43.5% for those with 21 or more risk factors. Clearly, a

Figure 4.1
*Cumulative Risk for Gang Membership, Variable-Based Model
(top n is for males, bottom n is for females)*

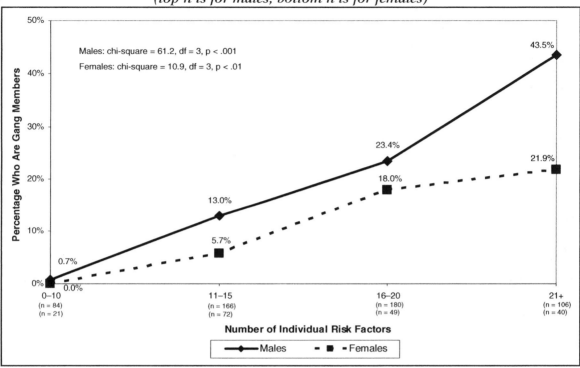

strong relationship exists between accumulated risk and the likelihood of joining a gang.

The data for the female respondents paint much the same picture. None of the females with fewer than 10 risk factors reported being a gang member. As risk accumulates, however, the prevalence of gang membership increases to 5.7%, to 18.0%, and finally to 21.9% for those with 21 or more risk factors.

These patterns suggest that youths can experience some degree of risk—here fewer than 10 risk factors—and still be quite resilient to the lure of gang membership. As risk accumulates, however, the chances of joining a gang increase sharply. Youths experiencing many risk factors are far more likely to join a gang than are their counterparts.[2]

Domain-Based Model. The results in Figure 4.1 suggest that youths experiencing risk in multiple developmental domains are at increased risk for gang membership. Because the model is variable-based, however, it is possible that risk only accumulated in a few domains and not across multiple domains. For example, under the scoring procedure in Figure 4.1, a respondent who was a very poor student could receive a score of six, without experiencing risk in any other domain. This possibility, generated by the richness of measurement that is available, is not very consistent with the notion of multidimensionality, which is concerned with the consequences of different pathways or arenas of development on producing different outcomes. To examine the issue of multidimensionality more exactly, we now switch to a domain-based model of risk.

The domain-based measure is created in a two-step process. We first determined if the respondent experienced higher than average risk in each domain—for example, area characteristics or family sociodemographic characteristics. To do so, we calculated the median number of risk factors experienced by the subjects in each domain and then classified each subject as being above or below the median in that domain. Second, we then counted the number of domains in which the respondent was above the median. With seven domains, scores could range from 0 to 7 (see Table 4.1). The

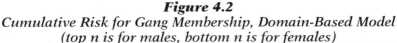

Figure 4.2
Cumulative Risk for Gang Membership, Domain-Based Model
(top n is for males, bottom n is for females)

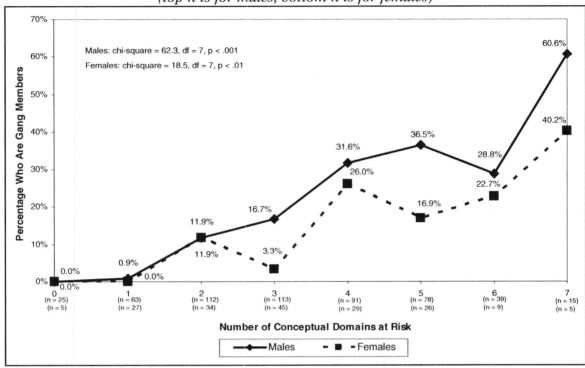

results are presented in Figure 4.2 for male and female respondents separately.

Here we see an even stronger relationship between cumulative risk and the chances of becoming a gang member. Of the males who did not experience risk in any of these seven domains, none became a gang member. Of those who experienced risk in only one domain, only 0.9% joined a gang. After that point the prevalence of gang membership increases rather steadily from 11.9% of those who were above average on two domains to 36.5% of those experiencing risk in five of the seven domains. There is then a slight decrease—to 28.8%—for those experiencing risk in six of the seven domains. For the 15 youths who were above average in all seven domains, however, the prevalence of gang membership reaches a peak at 60.6%, a high rate compared with a total prevalence of gang membership (at Waves 3 to 9) of about 20% for the males.

The pattern of results for female respondents is similar, although somewhat more erratic because of the smaller sample sizes. None of the young girls who avoid risk or have risk in a single domain becomes a gang member. Risk in a few domains increases

the chances of gang membership and the prevalence of gang membership increases to about 20% for those who experience risk in between four and six domains. At the end of the distribution, of those experiencing risk in all seven domains, 40.2% report being a gang member.

Summary. Overall, the results for the cumulative risk analysis are quite consistent with the basic hypothesis of the multidimensionality of risk. As risk accumulates, the chances of gang membership increase dramatically. Youth are quite resilient—at least in terms of the chances of joining a gang—in light of low levels of risk. As risk accumulates, however, the likelihood of joining a gang increases substantially, a pattern observed for both males and females. For example, 43.5% of the male and 21.9% of the female respondents were gang members if they experienced 21 or more risk factors, as compared with average rates of gang membership of 19.7% for the males and 11.9% for the females. In the domain-based approach, 60.6% of the male and 40.2% of the female respondents were gang members if they experienced risk in all seven domains.

Substantively, it is interesting that the impact of cumulative risk is stronger in the domain-based approach. Consistent with a life-course model, it indicates that non-redundant disadvantages that cumulate across different domains or ecological contexts appear to generate a greater chance of adverse outcomes than do more redundant disadvantages, accumulated in one or two domains. This finding also highlights the difficulties we face in trying to intervene with individual gang members, because they are likely to experience disadvantage in multiple developmental domains.

Conclusion

The results of our examination of risk factors for gang membership are quite consistent with the multidimensionality of a life-course perspective. It does not appear that gang membership is associated with a single developmental domain; on the contrary, gang members have multiple disadvantages in multiple domains of their development. Whereas the impact of individual risk factors is rather modest, their cumulative impact is quite large. It appears that youth can tolerate lower levels of risk, or risk in a few domains, and still avoid an increased likelihood of joining a gang. As risk increases, however, so too does the likelihood of joining a gang. Indeed, in the highest category of cumulative risk the chances of joining a gang are generally more than twice as high as the mean prevalence at these ages.

In terms of individual risk factors, we saw that many more individual variables are significant for the males than for the females. This difference may be an artifact of the smaller number of female gang members and attenuated statistical power, a possibility supported in the cumulative risk factor analysis where sample size is less important. In that case, the results are quite similar for both the males and the females. Overall, the results suggest that social disadvantage, poor performance in school, early dating, externalizing behaviors, prior delinquency, and delinquent beliefs increase the chances of a youth subsequently joining a gang. These findings, based on analyses where proper temporal order is preserved, are consistent with those from prior cross-sectional research.

Although accumulated disadvantage in these areas increases the chances of later gang membership, it does not guarantee it. Indeed, even at the highest level of risk (see Figures 4.1 and 4.2), many adolescents are not gang members. Despite the accumulated level of disadvantage in their backgrounds, there appear to be protective processes that help them avoid this outcome. Identifying the processes that do so is a significant challenge for future research as that information could be particularly helpful to intervention efforts.

Notes

1. Without grouping, the substantive results are the same but the pattern is not as smooth because of the uneven number of cases across the distribution.

2. The analysis just presented counts all the risk factors listed in Table 4.1, including those that are statistically significantly related to gang membership and those that are not. The inclusion of the nonsignificant variables may mute the impact of cumulative risk. We therefore repeated the analysis, including only the significant variables. The pattern is identical to that in Figure 4.1. For example, of the males in the highest category, 16–21 significant risk factors, 43% were gang members.

References

Bjerregaard, Beth, and Alan J. Lizotte. (1995). Gun ownership and gang membership. *Journal of Criminal Law and Criminology* 86:37–58.

Bjerregaard, Beth, and Carolyn A. Smith. (1993). Gender differences in gang participation, delinquency, and substance use. *Journal of Quantitative Criminology* 9:329–355.

Bolger, Kerry E., Charlotte J. Patterson, William W. Thompson, and Janis B. Kupersmidt. (1995). Psychosocial adjustment among children experiencing persistent and intermittent family economic hardship. *Child Development* 66:1107–1129.

Bowker, Lee H., and Malcolm W. Klein. (1983). The etiology of female juvenile delinquency and gang membership: A test of psychological and social structural explanations. *Adolescence* 18:739–751.

Bronfenbrenner, Uri. (1979). *The Ecology of Human Development: Experiments by Nature and Design.* Cambridge, MA: Harvard University Press.

Campbell, Anne. (1990). Female participation in gangs. Pp. 163–182 in C. Ronald Huff (Ed.), *Gangs in America.* Newbury Park, CA: Sage.

Cartwright, Desmond S., Barbara Tomson, and Hershey Schwartz. (1975). *Gang Delinquency.* Monterey, CA: Brooks/Cole.

Cicchetti, Dante, and Fred A. Rogosch. (1996). Equifinality and multifinality in developmental psychopathology. *Development and Psychopathology* 8:597–600.

Cohen, Marcia I., Katherine Williams, Alan M. Bekelman, and Scott Crosse. (1994). Evaluation of the National Youth Gang Drug Prevention Program. Pp. 266–275 in Malcolm W. Klein, Cheryl L. Maxson, and Jody Miller (Eds.), *The Modern Gang Reader*. Los Angeles: Roxbury.

Curry, G. David, and Irving A. Spergel. (1992). Gang involvement and delinquency among Hispanic and African-American adolescent males. *Journal of Research in Crime and Delinquency* 29:273–291.

Emery, Robert E., and K. Daniel O'Leary. (1982). Children's perceptions of marital discord and behavior problems of boys and girls. *Journal of Abnormal Child Psychology* 10:11–24.

Esbensen, Finn-Aage, and David Huizinga. (1993). Gangs, drugs, and delinquency in a survey of urban youth. *Criminology* 4:565–589.

Esbensen, Finn-Aage, David Huizinga, and Anne W. Weiher. (1993). Gang and non-gang youth: Differences in explanatory factors. *Journal of Contemporary Criminal Justice* 9:94–116.

Fagan, Jeffrey. (1990). Social processes of delinquency and drug use among urban gangs. Pp. 183–219 in C. Ronald Huff (Ed.), *Gangs in America*. Newbury Park, CA: Sage.

———. (1996). Gangs, drugs, and neighborhood change. Pp. 39–74 in C. Ronald Huff (Ed.), *Gangs in America* (2nd ed.). Thousand Oaks, CA: Sage.

Farrington, David P. (2000). Explaining and preventing crime: The globalization of knowledge. The American Society of Criminology 1999 presidential address. *Criminology* 38:1–24.

Friedman, C. Jack, Fredrica Mann, and Alfred S. Friedman. (1975). A profile of juvenile street gang members. *Adolescence* 10:563–607.

Garmezy, Norman. (1995). Stress resistant children: The search for protective factors. Pp. 213–233 in J. E. Stevenson (Ed.), *Aspects of Current Child Psychiatry Research*. Oxford: Pergamon.

Hawkins, J. David, Richard F. Catalano, and Janet Y. Miller. (1992). Risk and protective factors for alcohol and other drug problems in adolescence and early adulthood: Implications for substance abuse prevention. *Psychological Bulletin* 112:64–105.

Hill, Karl G., J. David Hawkins, Richard E. Catalano, Eugene Maguin, and Richard Kosterman. (1995). The role of gang membership in delinquency, substance use, and violent offending. Paper presented at the annual meeting of the American Society of Criminology, Boston, November 17.

Hill, Karl G., James C. Howell, J. David Haw-

kins, and Sara R. Battin-Pearson. (1999). Childhood risk factors for adolescent gang membership: Results from the Seattle Social Development Project. *Journal of Research in Crime and Delinquency* 36:300–322.

Howell, James C. (1997). *Juvenile Justice and Youth Violence*. Thousand Oaks, CA: Sage.

Lahey, Benjamin B., Rachel A. Gordon, Rolf Loeber, Magda Stouthamer-Loeber, and David P. Farrington. (1999). Boys who join gangs: A prospective study of predictors of first gang entry. *Journal of Abnormal Child Psychology* 27:261–276.

LeBlanc, Marc, and Nadine Lanctôt. (1998). Social and psychological characteristics of gang members according to the gang structure and its subcultural and ethnic makeup. *Journal of Gang Research* 5:15–28.

Loeber, Rolf, and Magda Stouthamer-Loeber. (1986). Family factors as correlates and predictors of juvenile conduct problems and delinquency. Pp. 29–149 in Michael H. Tonry and Norval Morris (Eds.), *Crime and Justice: An Annual Review of Research* (Vol. 7). Chicago: University of Chicago Press.

Moore, Joan W. (1978). *Homeboys*. Philadelphia: Temple University Press.

———. (1991). *Going Down to the Barrio: Homeboys and Homegirls in Change*. Philadelphia: Temple University Press.

Nirdorf, B. J. (1988). *Gang Alternative and Prevention Program: Program Policy and Procedure Handbook*. Los Angeles: County of Los Angeles Probation Department.

Rice, Robert. (1963, October 19). A reporter at large: Persian queens. *New Yorker* 39:139ff.

Rutter, Michael. (1987). Psychosocial resilience and protective mechanisms. *American Journal of Orthopsychiatry* 57:316–331.

Schwartz, Audrey J. (1989). Middle-class educational values among Latino gang members in East Los Angeles County high schools. *Urban Education* 24:323–342.

Shelden, Randall G., Ted Snodgrass, and Pam Snodgrass. (1992). Comparing gang and non-gang offenders: Some tentative findings. *Gang Journal* 1:73–85.

Short, James F., Jr. (1990). New wine in old bottles? Change and continuity in American gangs. Pp. 223–239 in C. Ronald Huff (Ed.), *Gangs in America*. Newbury Park, CA: Sage.

Short, James F., Jr., and Fred L. Strodtbeck. (1965). *Group Process and Gang Delinquency*. Chicago: University of Chicago Press.

Small, Stephen A., and Tom Luster. (1994). Adolescent sexual activity: An ecological risk-factor approach. *Journal of Marriage and the Family*, 56, 181–192.

Thornberry, Terence P., Marvin D. Krohn, Alan J. Lizotte, and Deborah Chard-Wierschem. (1993). The role of juvenile gangs in facilitating delinquent behavior. *Journal of Research in Crime and Delinquency* 30:55–87.

Vigil, James Diego. (1988). *Barrio Gangs: Street Life and Identity in Southern California.* Austin: University of Texas Press.

Wang, Alvin Y. (1994). Pride and prejudice in high school gang members. *Adolescence* 29:279–291.

Werner, Emmy E., and Ruth S. Smith. (1982). *Vulnerable but Invincible: A Longitudinal Study of Resilient Children and Youth.* New York: McGraw-Hill.

Winfree, L. Thomas, Jr., Teresa Vigil Backstrom, and G. Larry Mays. (1994). Social learning theory, self-reported delinquency, and youth gangs: A new twist on a general theory of crime and delinquency. *Youth and Society* 26:147–177. ✦

Chapter 5
Getting Into Gangs

Jody Miller

Like the prior chapters, Miller's concern here
is with issues of joining gangs. However,
there are two important contrasts. Her work
involves personal interviews on a cross-
sectional basis rather than longitudinal, and
she is concerned here with female gang membership only. Comparing gang to non-gang
youth to clarify the risks leading to gang
membership, Miller finds neighborhood peer
networks and family problems to be the most
proximate risks. Using both surveys and in-
depth interviews to get at these issues, as well
as a two-city comparison, lends further validity to the findings. Note that, as in the previous chapter, it is the accumulation of risk
factors that best predicts gang membership.

Gang membership doesn't happen overnight. Research shows that youths typically
hang out with gang members for some
time—often as much as a year—before making a commitment to join.[1] Moreover, there
are pushes and pulls even earlier in life that
increase the likelihood that young people
will associate with gangs in the first place.
The goal of this chapter is to explore girls'
pathways into gangs by painting a picture of
the broader contexts and precipitating
events that lead young women to spend time
with gang members and to join gangs.

On the whole, cities like Columbus and
St. Louis have not had gang problems long
enough to have intergenerational gang involvement within families. Consequently
gangs remain concentrated among adolescents and young adults. The young women
in this study typically began hanging out
with gang members when they were quite
young—around age twelve on average—and
they joined at an average age of thirteen. In
fact, 69 percent of the girls in the sample described joining their gangs before they
turned fourteen. . . . In considering girls'
motives for joining gangs, it is important to
keep their youthfulness in mind.

Three themes emerged in my research
with regard to the life contexts that contribute to girls' gang involvement, at least among
the kinds of gang girls in my sample. What's
notable is that they emerged independently,
both in the surveys—as factors distinguishing gang from nongang girls—and in the in-
depth interviews, as contexts that young
women attributed to their becoming gang-
involved. First were girls' neighborhood
contexts, and their exposure to gangs via
both neighborhood peer and other friendship networks. A second theme that emerged
for some young women was the existence of
serious family problems, such as violence
and drug abuse, which led them to avoid
home, contributed to their weak supervision, and pushed them to attempt to meet
social and emotional needs elsewhere.
Finally, many young women described the
strong influence that gang-involved family
members—particularly older siblings in Columbus and siblings and cousins in St.
Louis—had on their decisions to join.

While each young woman revealed her
own trajectory into gang life, there were
many common circumstances across girls'
stories. In fact, the three themes noted
above rarely stood alone in young women's
stories of how they came to join their gangs.
Instead they were overlapping in girls' accounts. As each told of individual life experiences, most recounted complex pathways
into gangs that involved, in varying ways,
the themes I've just described. Before I delve
into each of these themes in greater detail, it
is important to have a clear picture of the
extent of their interrelationships, and how
they differed for gang and nongang girls.

. . . Figure 5.1 illustrates how young
women accounted for their gang involvement. Girls were classified as having neighborhood exposure to gangs when they said
there was a lot of gang activity in their
neighborhood, or they reported gang members living on their street. Gang-involved
family members included girls with a sib-

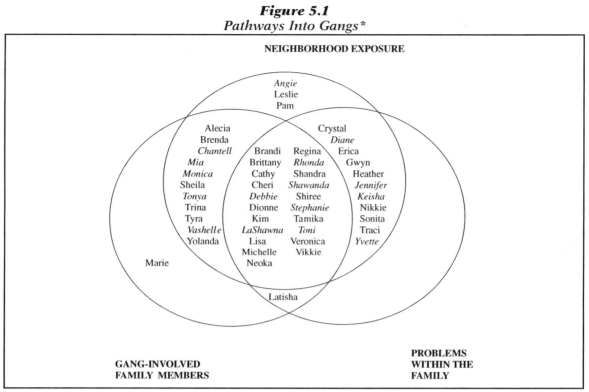

Figure 5.1
Pathways Into Gangs*

NEIGHBORHOOD EXPOSURE

Angie
Leslie
Pam

Alecia
Brenda
Chantell
Mia
Monica
Sheila
Tonya
Trina
Tyra
Vashelle
Yolanda

Brandi   Regina
Brittany *Rhonda*
Cathy   Shandra
Cheri   *Shawanda*
Debbie   Shiree
Dionne   *Stephanie*
Kim   Tamika
LaShawna *Toni*
Lisa   Veronica
Michelle Vikkie
Neoka

Crystal
Diane
Erica
Gwyn
Heather
Jennifer
Keisha
Nikkie
Sonita
Traci
Yvette

Marie

Latisha

GANG-INVOLVED
FAMILY MEMBERS

PROBLEMS
WITHIN THE
FAMILY

*Girls whose names are italicized report regular involvement in serious delinquency.

ling in a gang, with multiple family members, in gangs, or girls who described another family member (e.g., a cousin or aunt) as having a decided influence on their decision to join. Girls with family problems included those with three or more of the following: violence between adults in the home, having been abused, drug or alcohol abuse in the family, or family members in jail. Four additional girls who did not report three of these were also categorized as such because of their discussions of the impact of family problems. These included Heather, who was sexually abused by multiple members of her family; Rhonda and Latisha, who reported frequent abuse and witnessed physical violence among adults in the family; and Jennifer, whose parents were killed in a car crash, the loss of whom she felt was a turning point in her life.

What's striking about Figure 5.1 is the extent to which young women reported multiple dimensions of these risk factors. Taken individually, a majority of girls fit within each category: 96 percent described living in neighborhoods with gangs (of these, 69 percent explicitly described their neighborhood and peer networks as factors in their deci-

sions to join). Likewise, 71 percent recognized family problems as contributing factors, and 71 percent had siblings or multiple family members in gangs, or described the influence of gang-involved family members on their decisions to join. In all, 90 percent of the gang members in the study report two or more dimensions of these risk factors, and fully 44 percent fit within the overlap of all three categories. . . . In Figure 5.1, the names of young women involved in ongoing serious delinquency are italicized. It is notable that only a third of the gang members were involved in serious offending. The majority of girls, despite their gang involvement, were not. . . .

Figure 5.2 provides a similar picture of nongang girls' exposure to the risk factors highlighted by gang girls. Nongang girls were classified using the same survey criteria as gang girls. . . . Young women listed outside the diagram met none of these criteria, though they nonetheless had some exposure to gangs. Several things are notable in comparing Figures 5.1 and 5.2. First, while the vast majority of gang girls (90 percent) fit in overlapping categories, only a third of the nongang girls experienced multiple of these

Figure 5.2
Nongang Girls' Exposure to Risk Factors for Gangs*

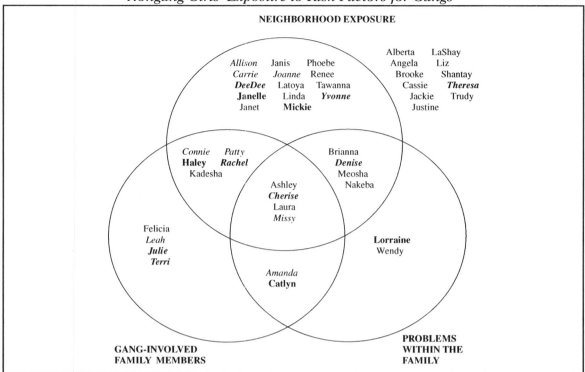

*Girls whose names are italicized report half or more of their friends are gang members; girls whose names appear in boldface have considered joining gangs.

risk factors for gangs, and only four nongang girls (9 percent, versus 44 percent of gang girls) reported all three dimensions. These data will be broken down individually in Tables 5.1 and 5.3. Those contexts most likely to be shared between gang and nongang girls were neighborhoods that exposed them to gangs, which 59 percent of nongang girls reported. However, only 26 percent of the nongang girls reported serious family problems, compared to 71 percent of gang girls. Likewise, 71 percent of gang members reported significant gang-involved family members, while only a third of the nongang girls had gang members in their immediate family or multiple gang members in their extended family. Thus, while the majority of nongang girls had gangs around them, most didn't have other experiences that could tip the scales in favor of gang involvement. . . .

Neighborhood Contexts and Networks

Scholars long have recognized factors such as neighborhood characteristics, pov-

erty, and limited opportunities as being associated with the extent and nature of gangs in communities.[2] Recent studies of female gang involvement likewise have made the connection between these factors and young women's participation in gangs.[3] In fact, many scholars have pointed to the gang as a means for inner city youths—male and female—to adapt to the oppressive living conditions imposed by their environments. According to Karen Joe and Meda Chesney-Lind, "the gang assists young women and men in coping with their lives in chaotic, violent, and economically marginalized communities."[4] . . .

In both [Columbus and St. Louis] there is substantial racial inequality, but on the whole Columbus is more socioeconomically stable than St. Louis. But what about the neighborhoods of the girls in my sample? . . . In both cities, the vast majority of girls in the study lived in neighborhoods that were economically worse off and more racially segregated than the city as a whole. Their neighborhoods had substantially lower median incomes and higher rates of poverty and unemployment than the citywide averages. . . . [Y]oung women in St. Louis were drawn from more [racially] segregated and economically devastated neighborhoods, on average, than young women in Columbus. In fact, two-thirds of the gang members in St. Louis lived in neighborhoods that were 80 percent or more African-American. . . .

Living in these neighborhoods means living in places with substantial amounts of crime.[5] In recent times, it often also means living in neighborhoods with street gangs. It goes without saying that in order to join a gang a young woman must have some exposure to gangs—at least the one she's joining. It's useful, then, to examine girls' descriptions of the extent of gang activity in their neighborhoods, but also the meanings they attribute to it. An important component of this is the extent to which they view gangs in the neighborhood as having facilitated or contributed to their decisions to join.

Table 5.1 illustrates girls' characterizations of the extent of gang activity in their neighborhoods. In both Columbus and St. Louis, the vast majority of young women described some exposure to gangs in their neighborhoods. . . . My interest here . . . is the extent and proximity of gang activity in girls' neighborhoods. As Table 5.1 shows, gang members were significantly more likely than nongang girls to report "a lot" of gang activity in their neighborhoods, and to note that there were other gang members who lived on their street.[6] While the vast majority of the gang members . . . described gang activity in their neighborhoods in these terms, just over half of the nongang girls did so. While all of the girls in the study could be characterized as at risk for problem behaviors and detrimental life consequences, only half of them had joined gangs. It appears then, that coupled with other factors, living in neighborhoods with gangs in close proximity increases the likelihood that young women will choose to become gang-involved themselves.

Documenting the existence of gang activity in girls' neighborhoods provides one piece of the puzzle. But what meanings do gang-involved girls attribute to gangs in their neighborhoods, and to what extent do they perceive neighborhood gangs as having had an impact on their decision to join? Because one goal of my study was to try to come away with an understanding of gang life from girls' points of view, this is an im-

Table 5.1
Exposure to Gangs

	Gang Members (N=48)	Nongang (N=46)
There is a lot of talk about gangs around the neighborhood	38 (80%)	31 (67%)
There is a lot of gang activity around the neighborhood	40 (83%)	25 (54%)*
There are other gang members living on the same street	39 (81%)	21 (46%)*
There are rival gangs close by	35 (73%)	26 (57%)

* p < .05

portant line of inquiry. Other scholars have suggested that gangs can function to alleviate the boredom experienced by inner-city youths, who have few options for recreation or entertainment. John Quicker summarizes, "to be in a gang is to be part of something. It means having a place to go, friends to talk with, and parties to attend. It means recognition and respected status."[7] In addition, many scholars talk about the protective functions of gangs.[8] A number of the young women in my study had been victims of crime, prior to as well as after joining gangs. Many articulated a specifically gendered sense of protection that they saw resulting from being in gangs that were predominantly male. . . .

Not surprisingly, the majority of the gang girls suggested that their decision to become gang-involved stemmed in part from exposure to gangs through their neighborhood peer networks. Most often, they described a process in which they began to hang out with older gang-involved kids around the neighborhood as they reached adolescence, and these associations eventually led them to want to join. For instance, Angie was fifteen when we spoke, and had joined her gang at age eleven. She described how changes in her neighborhood shaped her desire to become a gang member:

> It's like, our neighborhood started changing a little bit, people started movin' in and out, and I was associating with the people who moved in and out, you know, and I was just, then, they was, a lot of 'em was in gangs, or things like that, and I wanted to be in a gang.

Because she was so young when she joined, it was a couple of years before she became actively involved. Instead, it appears that the older members thought it was cute that a young girl from the neighborhood wanted to be a member, but had few expectations for her participation. She explained:

> They was just like, "Hey, you wanna be a member?" I was like, one day, and I was like, "Yeah, yeah! I wanna be one, I wanna be one, I wanna be one!" Then they put me in and I was in, but then I, and as the years went by that's when I started really gettin' involved wid 'em, but then [at that time] I didn't, I didn't see them that much.

Chantell also described her neighborhood context as the overriding factor leading to her gang membership. She was fourteen when we spoke, and became gang-involved at age twelve. Chantell lived with her mother, grandmother, and siblings in a neighborhood where gangs were "just like everywhere." She described her childhood as one in which she grew up with gangs. She explained, "when I was little, I mean when I was young, I grew up around 'em. Just grew up around 'em, basically. Then when you grow up around 'em and you see 'em so much, until you want to get initiated."

At the time she decided to join, many of Chantell's neighborhood friends also were joining, as well as her older sister. "It was like a lot of gang-banging, I mean, it was just like, people were just like gettin' in it and having fun." Though she was somewhat torn about joining—"like wondering should I or shouldn't I, stuff like that, or what would happen if I did, or if I didn't"—eventually she decided to go ahead. "I was around 'em so much, the things they did I did," she explained, "so I said, since I grew up with 'em, I'm already hanging out with 'em, couldn't be no difference, so."

Chantell's comments about seeing other young people "gettin' in it and having fun" was echoed by a number of young women who described joining gangs in part because of their desire to belong to a neighborhood group, fit in, and have fun. This was especially the case for girls who joined quite young. Crystal joined at age twelve, noting, "you see other people doing it and you just think it's cool." And Nikkie, who also joined at twelve, explained, "if you ain't in it you just be . . . you just be feelin' left out. You be like, 'oh they all in a gang and I'm just sittin' here.'" As a result, she said, "I was like, 'I

wanna get in it.' And I got in it." Latisha joined at twelve and explained, "it's fun. That's why I joined, 'cause it was fun and I seen what they was doing and I thought it was fun and it was cool or whatever." Likewise Pam joined at thirteen, and noted:

> They just [were] having fun, going to parties, kickin' it, staying out all night, new clothes, new shoes, selling drugs and all that. I wanted to be like that too. I wanted to wear name brand shoes, name brand clothes, I wanted my hair done and everything just like that so that's what I done.

In addition, residential instability appeared to be a factor shaping the influence of neighborhood gangs on girls' decision making. Over half of the gang members in the sample (52 percent in both cities) described having moved within the year prior to our interview, and two-thirds had moved within the previous two years. In comparison, 28 percent of the nongang girls had moved in the last year, and 48 percent within the previous two years. Moreover, these figures do not include such things as running away from home or spending time in detention or placement facilities—experiences that a large number of girls reported and that are indicative of further residential instability. While this instability is likely related to other family and economic problems that may be linked to risks for gang involvement, it is also the case that, upon arrival in a new environment, becoming involved with a local gang provides young women with a means of fitting in with a new crowd and becoming known. As Shawanda described, "I just needed some friends, [joining the gang] was a quick way to make me a friend." In fact, several girls explicitly described joining gangs upon moving to new places, and others decided to join when they met gang members in residential facilities.

For instance, Traci had only recently moved to Columbus when we spoke, and likewise had recently joined her gang. She explained that moving to a new city, she "wanted to be like other people." At the same time she began noticing "all these blue scarves and red scarves and stuff," she got to know the neighbor in the apartment above hers—a young man who was a member of a neighborhood Crips set. Shortly thereafter she joined the gang and began going out with the young man. Traci felt that joining the gang was a way both to make friends, and to fit into her new environment. La-Shawna was sent to Columbus to live with relatives when she was thirteen, and had been gang-involved since age twelve in the large city where she previously lived. In Columbus she became gang-involved when she "hooked up with" another gang member in a residential facility, where her knowledge of "big-city" gangs provided her with status and reputation.

A handful of young women, mostly in Columbus, described becoming gang-involved as a result of friends' involvement, rather than through neighborhood peer networks. Jennifer, Leslie, and Heather joined their gangs after a close friend introduced them to other gang members. For instance, Heather said of her decision to join: "I [was] at my friend Chad's house and they [gang members] had just came over 'cause they was friends with Chad's, and we just started talkin' and hangin' out and then they started talkin' about a gang and it's like that, I just got in there." Likewise, Jennifer joined her gang after her best friend introduced her to the OG ("Original Gangster," e.g., leader). She explained, "my friend was already in it and she would come over and she'd talk about all the, how it's real, it's just real cool to be in and everything like that." Once Jennifer met the OG, she began spending time with the other gang members, and eventually was allowed to join.[9]

Leslie had run away from home, and became friends with a gang girl she met at a local shelter for teen runaways. She returned home, but later "ran away with my friend. And she took me down there and introduced me to [the gang]." Leslie talked to the OG, who "told me that I would, it was an easy way to be protected and, um, I wouldn't have any problems. I wouldn't have to worry about money, food, clothing, a place to stay, 'cause I'da have all that because I was in the gang." At the point we interviewed, Leslie was pregnant and planning to sever her ties to the gang. Her outlook on it was decidedly negative. Of her initial conversation with the OG and decision to join, she surmised, "it was a bunch of lies . . . and I fell into the trap and believed him."

JM: And why do you say it was a lie now?

LESLIE: Because I was almost in the gang for about a year and a half. And,

just bein' in there, you didn't go anywhere. You, um, you really didn't, I mean, succeed in anything 'cause the stuff that you were doin' was wrong. And, half, that's why half of 'em, half the guys are in here [the detention center] now, it has to do with some kind of gang-related somethin'.

. . . Young women in St. Louis were more likely to describe their neighborhood gangs as wary of outsiders, and thus new people—unless they were the relatives or friends of youths in the neighborhood—were less able to quickly assimilate into the local gang as girls in Columbus described.[10] Pam, for instance, joined her neighborhood gang when she was thirteen. She said, "I grew up with some of them, went to school with some of them, and by me knowing them I just knew the other ones 'cause they used to be around." Much like Chantell, Pam joined because she'd "been knowing them anyway all my life for real." But she described a gang with somewhat tighter boundaries than what Chantell had described. Pam explained that for someone to join her gang:

They just got to be known or something. You can't just be no anybody. They got to know you or they been knowing you or they grew up with you or something like that or you family. Other than that, they just don't put you in there like that. . . . 'Cause anybody that is in the gang, everybody grew up together for real. It's just not like no anybody, like they gonna get anybody. You want to be in this gang? It ain't like that. You got to know a person, you got to grow up around it or be around it.

Tyra articulated much the same beliefs as Pam, noting, "If you ain't in our streets or nothin', live on our streets, you ain't joining nothin'." She said she joined her gang because "I grew up in that neighborhood with them." Moreover, Tyra suggested that part of the nature of gangs in St. Louis is attributable to how dangerous many neighborhoods are. She explained: "Growing up on the North Side [of St. Louis], you got to be like that 'cause everywhere you look, you turn around and somebody is getting killed. I don't care what nobody say, I think the North Side worse than any side."

Very few of the young women described getting involved with their gangs because their boyfriend was a member. In fact, only three girls—Rhonda, Marie and Stephanie—described this as a specific motivating factor. This is not to suggest that young women didn't have boyfriends, including within their gangs. For instance, Traci became gang-involved at around the same time her gang-involved neighbor became her boyfriend. But she didn't attribute her desire or decision to join the gang as having to do with him. Instead she said, "I just wanted to join, I don't know why, when I moved out here [to Columbus] I just *had* to join a gang." It is significant that only a handful of girls described a relationship with a boyfriend as a factor influencing their decision to join a gang, with most describing broader neighborhood peer networks as having greater importance. This finding challenges some long-held beliefs about young women in gangs, but also is in keeping with other research which suggests that, despite being overlooked by many scholars, girls' friendships are an important factor for explaining both their gang involvement and their delinquency.[11]

While neighborhood and friendship networks help answer the question of how and why girls come to join gangs, these remain only a partial explanation. In fact, as Figure 5.1 illustrates, often there are other precipitating factors to consider. Many young women described problems in their family lives that led them to spend time away from home, out on the streets, and with gang members. In addition, like their relationships with friends in the neighborhood, having gang-involved family members was significantly related to girls' gang involvement in both Columbus and St. Louis. In the next section, I will discuss further the impact of family problems on girls' gang involvement; then I will return to the issue of gang-involved family members.

Family Problems as Precipitating Circumstances

The family has long been considered crucial for understanding delinquency and gang behavior among girls.[12] Problems such as weak supervision, lack of attachment to parents, family violence, and drug and alcohol abuse by family members all have been suggested as contributing to the likelihood that girls will join gangs.[13] My study provides additional support for these conclusions, based on comparative findings from

survey interviews, and from young women's accounts of why they joined gangs.

As Table 5.2 illustrates, gang members were significantly more likely to come from homes with numerous problems than were the young women who were not in gangs. Gang girls were significantly more likely to have witnessed physical violence between adults in their homes, and to describe having been abused by adult family members. In addition, gang members were much more likely to report that there was regular drug use in their homes. Most important, gang members were significantly more likely to describe experiencing *multiple* family problems—with 60 percent describing three or more of the five problems listed in Table 5.2, and 44 percent reporting that four or more of these problems existed in their families. In fact, only *three* gang members—Angie, Brenda, and Chantell—said there were none of these problems in their families, compared to nine (20 percent) of the nongang girls.

In addition, a number of gang girls had been sexually abused or raped in the context of their families.[14] In all, 25 (52 percent) of the gang members in my study reported having been sexually assaulted, and described a total of 35 instances of sexual assault. Of these 35 incidents, 23 of them (66 percent) were committed by family members or men whom young women were exposed to through their families. Eight of these assaults were committed by immediate family members (e.g., girls' fathers, brothers, and in one case her mother). Eight were committed by extended family (e.g., girls' cousins, grandfathers, uncles), and seven were committed by individuals that

Table 5.2
Problems Within the Family

	Gang Members (N=48)	Nongang (N=46)
Witness to Physical Violence Between Adults	27 (56%)	12 (26%)*
Abused by Family Member	22 (46%)	12 (26%)*
Regular Alcohol Use in Home	27 (56%)	17 (37%)
Regular Drug Use in Home	28 (58%)	8 (17%)*
Family Member in Prison/Jail	35 (73%)	31 (67%)
Three + Family Problems	29 (60%)	11 (24%)*
Four + Family Problems	21 (44%)	6 (13%)*

* $p < .05$

young women came into contact with through their families. For instance, Tamika was raped by her stepfather's brother, Vikkie by her mother's boyfriend's friend, Yolanda by her uncle's friend, and Brittany by her aunt's boyfriend. While fewer nongang girls had been sexually assaulted (10 of 46, or 22 percent), like the gang girls, two-thirds of these assaults (eight of twelve) occurred in the context of the family.

For many young women, home was not a particularly safe place. Turning to young women's descriptions of their decision to join a gang, it is not surprising that the majority (though by no means all) noted family problems as contributing factors. The ways in which family problems facilitated girls' gang involvement were varied, but they shared a common thread—young women began spending time away from home as a result of difficulties or dangers there, and consequently sought to get away, and to meet their social and emotional needs elsewhere. Often young women specifically said that their relationships with primary caregivers were problematic in some way. A number of researchers have suggested that "the gang can serve as a surrogate extended family for adolescents who do not see their own families as meeting their needs for belonging, nurturance, and acceptance."[15] Regardless of whether gangs actually fulfill these roles in young women's lives, it is clear that many young women believe that the gang will do so when they become involved. . . .

The most common family-related themes described by young women as contributing to their gang involvement were drug addiction and abuse.[16] While 58 percent of the gang members described regular drug use in their homes, ten girls (21 percent) explicitly discussed the impact of their mothers' crack or heroin addiction. Drug-addicted parents, while not necessarily described as abusive, often were quite neglectful, leaving girls feeling abandoned and unloved, but also not providing necessary supervision over their time and activities. Moreover, given the intense degradation of many drug-addicted women on the streets, these particular young women likely dealt with the trauma of having knowledge of or even witnessing their mother's involvement in such situations.[17]

Keisha was fourteen when we spoke, and had joined her gang the previous year. She described her neighborhood as "nothin' but Folks and Crips," and attributed her decision to become a gang member to her sense of abandonment resulting from her mother's drug addiction. She explained: "My family wasn't there for me. My mom smokin' crack and she act like she didn't wanna be part of my life, so I just chose the negative family, you know what I'm saying?" Likewise, Crystal described joining her gang at a time when she was "fighting with my mama 'cause she was on drugs."

Shandra got to know members of her gang "walking to school, back and forth to school and I would see them in the mornings and after school and after awhile I just [started] hanging around smoking weed and just kicking it with them." She elaborated:

> Right around the time that I started hanging with them I had just got put out of school and had tried to kill myself not too long before that 'cause I was just, you know, I had run away from home and I was just dealing with a lot of stuff. 'Cause my mother is on drugs real bad, and her and her boyfriend used to be fighting all the time and I just, I don't know, I guess I just didn't want to be around that. So I chose to be around the gang.

Shandra said after she "just used to kick it with them [gang members] so much, one day I just woke up and I just say I wanna be one of them, and then I told them and then they jumped me in the 'hood." She was twelve when she joined her gang. Shandra's mother knew she had become gang-involved, "because I started coming in late and I be high when I came in, I started dressing like a gang member, wearing all stars and khakis and stuff like that." But she explained, her mother "didn't really say nothing about it." At the time, Shandra said she "felt close to" the other gang members, and "bond[ed] with them like they [my] family." When she first joined, she continued, the gang was so "important for me that I did anything I could to get respect from the OGs and just, you know, be down for [the gang]. It was important because I wanted to feel, I guess accepted to the gang, accepted in the gang."

In addition to their belief that joining a gang would fill emotional voids, a number of these young women said that a lack of supervision attributable to their mothers' addiction also was a contributing factor. Veronica, for example, joined her gang when she was "gettin' ready to be twelve," after her older brothers had joined. She said the gang was "right there in my neighborhood . . . then I seen that my brothers, 'cause I seen my brothers get put in. So then I said I wanna be put in." At the time, she explained, "I was just doin' what I wanted to 'cause when I found out my mom was doin' drugs and stuff. So she wasn't never in the house, so she didn't know."

Likewise, Yvette explained, "My mama, she on drugs, [we] used to fight and stuff. Me and her don't get along . . . [and] my father, he just ain't been around." Yvette said because of her mother's drug habit, when she was growing up her mother often "made me stay out late and stuff like that." Eventually Yvette "just started hanging out with" gang members in her neighborhood, whom she described as also being unsupervised. "I just hung around with some people that can do what they want to do, stay out late, whatever, go home when they want to go home, I'm hanging out with them." She said "it was like, I wasn't going to school a lot so I got with them. We was having so much fun. Most of them didn't go to school so I felt like I didn't need to go to school. . . . I had fun with the gang so I became one of them." Though her mother was unhappy and threatened Yvette when she found out about her gang involvement, Yvette said, "it was like too late for her to try and change me."

Another theme that emerged in some girls' discussions of how they became gang involved was the impact of being physically or sexually abused by family members. In most of these cases, violence and victimization in the family precipitated girls' decisions to avoid home, and several girls described running away from home and living for extended periods with friends—often exposing them to gangs. In a few cases, being placed outside the home as a consequence of abuse also had the unintended consequence of exposing girls to gangs and gang members. Erica's story is a case in point.

Erica was seventeen when we spoke, and had joined her gang when she was fifteen. She lived with her father and stepmother for most of her childhood, until her father and uncle raped her at the age of eleven, whereupon she was removed from the home. Since that time she had been shuffled back and forth between foster homes, group homes, and residential facilities, and had lit-tle contact with her family because they turned their backs on her. Erica explained, "I didn't have *no* family. Because of the incidents with my dad and my uncle. After that, they just deserted me and I didn't, I had nothin' else." Though she said her step-mother was the primary person who raised her, their relationship was severely damaged by the rape. "She doesn't, she doesn't believe it. I mean, even after he [dad] pleaded guilty she still doesn't believe it."

Erica's childhood up to that point had been filled with violence. Her father was physically abusive toward her stepmother, herself, and her siblings, and as a young child, Erica had witnessed her biological mother being raped. Both her father and stepmother had spent time in jail, and there was heavy alcohol and drug use in the home as she was growing up. As a result, she described herself as a physically aggressive child. She explained, "in elementary school before I even knew anything about gangs, I'd just get in a lot of fights." In fact, her nickname in elementary school was "Iron Mike," in recognition of her Tyson-like characteristics. Her initial contact with gangs came when she was fourteen and living in a foster home. During her stay there, she met a group of kids and began spending time with them:

> I didn't know 'em, but I just started talkin' to 'em. And, they always wore them blue rags and black rags and all that. And, I asked them, I said, "well you part of a gang?" And they tell me what they're a part of. So, it was like, everywhere I went, I was with them. I was never by myself. If they went out to [a] club I went with them. If they did anything, I was with them. And, um, we went down to some club one night and it was like a whole bunch of 'em got together and um, I asked to join.

Erica said she joined the gang "just to be in somethin'," and so that it could be "like a family to me since I don't really have one of my own." She felt that being in the gang allowed her to develop meaningful relationships. She explained, "people trust me and I trust them. It's like that bond that we have that some of us don't have outside of that. Or didn't have at all. That we have inside of that gang, or that set." Nonetheless, . . . Erica expressed some ambivalence about being in a gang, because it involved antisocial attitudes and behaviors that she didn't see as being part of who she really was, particularly as she neared adulthood. Her decision to join, though, was in part a search for belonging and attachment.

Likewise, Brittany described a terribly violent family life. She lived in a household with extended family—twelve people in all—including her mother, grandmother, stepfather, and an adolescent uncle who was physically abusive. Her aunt's boyfriend had sexually assaulted her at the age of five, but family members didn't believe her. Though she didn't know her father, who was in jail, she had early memories of him physically abusing her mother. Moreover, she felt very disconnected and unloved by her family, and also described being isolated at school: "I didn't have no friends, used to always get teased . . . my grades started going down, I started getting real depressed, started skipping school, smoking weed after school and stuff." Brittany saw the gang as a means of finding love. She explained: "I felt that my family didn't care for me . . . that when I was on the streets I felt that I got more love than when I was in the house so I felt that that's where my love was, on the streets, so that's where I stayed." And though she did not admit to doing so herself, Brittany noted, "my best friend got initiated [into the gang] by having sex with twelve boys."

Other young women also focused on a myriad of family factors in explaining their gang involvement. Diane's experiences are exemplary of how family problems could compound in a way that ultimately leads to gang involvement. When we spoke Diane was fifteen, and among the most deeply entrenched gang members in the sample. She had joined her gang at eleven, but was only ten when she began hanging out with members, including the seventeen-year-old young man who lived next door:

> I think I was about ten and a half years old and we started hanging out over there, over at his house and all his friends would come over and I just got into, just hangin' out, just becomin' friends with everybody that was there. And then I started smokin' weed and doin' all that stuff and then when I turned eleven it was like, well, 'cause they seen me get in fights and they seen how my attitude was and they said, "Well I think that you would be, you would be a true, a very true Lady Crip."

The time she spent with the gang, and her decision to join, were predictable results of her life history up to that point. As a young child, the family moved around a lot because her father was on the run from the law. Her father dealt drugs out of their home, and had a steady stream of friends and clients moving in and out of the place. Exposed to crime and drugs at an early age, Diane tried marijuana for the first time at age nine. She noted, "I was just growin' up watchin' that stuff." Her life changed dramatically when she was ten and her father was sent to prison, leaving her care to her drug-addicted mother. Diane explained:

> We didn't have very much money at all. Like, my mom was on welfare. My dad had just gone to jail. My dad had just gone to prison for four years. . . . My mom was on drugs. My, see my dad, always sellin' acid, quaaludes, cocaine and my mom was on, just smokin' marijuana and doin' crack. Back then she was just real drugged out, had a lot of problems and it was just me and my little brother and my little sister and that's all that was goin' on, besides me goin' to school and comin' home to seein' my mom do whatever, hit the pipe, and goin' next door and hangin' out.

Diane remained very dedicated to her gang and fellow members, noting passionately, "I *love* my cousins [fellow Crips]. I *love* 'em." This was in large part because of what they provided her when she felt she had little else. She elaborated, "that neighborhood's not a good neighborhood anyway, so. I had nothin' to look forward to, but these people they helped me out, you know? I mean, I was a young kid on my own. . . . I was just a little girl, my dad's gone and my mom's on drugs." Diane's father had been released from prison when we spoke, but was locked up again—as was Diane—for an armed robbery they had committed together. Ironically, her close bond with her father, and the knowledge she'd gained from him about how to commit crime, had resulted in a great deal of status for her among her gang peers. She noted, "my dad is just so cool. Everybody, everybody in my little clique, even people that aren't in my set, just my regular friends, they all love my dad."

As these young women's stories illustrate, a multitude of problems within families can increase young women's risk for gang involvement. This occurs through girls' attempts to avoid home, to meet social and emotional needs, as a result of ineffective supervision over their activities and, in cases like Diane's, by showing young women through example that criminal lifestyles are appropriate. These problems are exacerbated when young women live in neighborhoods with gangs, which provide a readily available alternative to life at home. Moreover, older gang members appear "cool," and their seemingly carefree lifestyle and reputed familial-like bonds to one another are an appealing draw for young girls with so many troubles at home.

Gang Involvement Among Family Members

Some girls who lack close relationships with their primary caregivers can turn to siblings or extended family members to maintain a sense of belonging and attachment. However, if these family members are gang-involved, it is likely that girls will choose to join gangs themselves. Moreover, even when relationships with parents or other adults are strong, having adolescent gang members in the family often heightens the appeal of gangs.[18] As Table 5.3 illustrates, gang members were significantly more likely than nongang girls to report family members in gangs. Most importantly, gang members were much more likely to have siblings in gangs, and were more likely to have two or more gang-involved family members.

These relationships were actually somewhat different in the two sites—with the relationship between girls' gang membership and that of her family being most marked in St. Louis. In Columbus, gang girls were not significantly more likely than nongang girls to have a family member in a gang—57 percent of gang members had family in gangs, versus 48 percent of nongang girls. By comparison, all but one of the gang members in

Table 5.3
Gang Membership Among Family Members

	Gang Members (N=48)	Nongang (N=46)
Gang Member(s) in Family	38 (79%)	25 (54%)*
Sibling(s) in Gang	24 (50%)	8 (17%)*
Multiple Gang Members in Family	29 (60%)	13 (28%)*

* p < .05

St. Louis (96 percent) reported having at least one gang-involved family member. In fact, a greater percentage of nongang girls in St. Louis (62 percent) described having a family member in a gang than did gang members in Columbus (57 percent). Moreover, St. Louis gang members were the only group for whom a majority reported having more than one gang-involved family member. In all, 21 St. Louis gang members (78 percent) described having multiple gang members in the family, compared to 38 percent of Columbus gang members, 29 percent of nongang girls in St. Louis, and 28 percent of nongang girls in Columbus.

However, gang members in both cities were significantly more likely to report a gang-involved sibling than nongang girls. In all, 52 percent of St. Louis gang members and 48 percent of Columbus gang members had siblings in gangs, compared to 19 and 16 percent of the nongang girls in these cities, respectively. In St. Louis, nine gang girls reported brothers in gangs, and ten reported sisters; in Columbus, eight gang girls had brothers in gangs and three had gang-involved sisters. Overall, 35 percent of the gang members had brothers who were gang members, and 27 percent had sisters in gangs. In addition, four gang members— two in each city—described having parents who had been in gangs.

Turning to young women's accounts of how they became gang-involved and the role family members played, there also are notable differences between the two sites. In Columbus, all of the young women who described the influence of a family member mentioned a sibling or siblings. In St. Louis, on the other hand, eight girls pointed to siblings, while twelve identified a cousin and/or aunt who prompted their decision to join. Gang girls in St. Louis also were more likely to talk about the influence of *female* family members, be they sisters, aunts or cousins. Perhaps as a consequence . . . , gang girls in St. Louis were more likely to talk about the importance of their friendships with other girls in the gang, while most gang girls in Columbus identified more with young men.

In general, the greater influence of extended family members on girls' gang involvement in St. Louis was striking. The likely explanation lies in the socioeconomic differences between the two cities and their effects on the strength of extended family networks. As I noted above, the young women in Columbus tended to live in neighborhoods with higher than average rates of poverty and racial segregation than the city as a whole. However the neighborhoods of girls in Columbus were somewhat better on social and economic indicators than the neighborhoods of girls in St. Louis. Moreover, while there are pockets of concentrated poverty in Columbus, St. Louis exhibits much larger geographic areas blighted by intense poverty, racial isolation, and population loss, resulting in large numbers of vacant lots and abandoned buildings in many of the poorest neighborhoods.

So how might these differences relate to the tendency for St. Louis gang members to say that extended family networks, rather than immediate family, drew them into gangs, while this simply was not the case in Columbus? I would suggest that the answer may lie in families' responses to entrenched poverty conditions. Research has shown that African American families living in poverty often rely to a great degree on extended family for economic, social, and emotional support.[19] Given the more detrimental economic conditions in St. Louis, it may be that extended family networks are stronger there than in Columbus. This would help explain why St. Louis gang members seemed to spend more time with their relatives outside the immediate family, and consequently, why those relatives had a stronger influence on girls' decision-making with regard to gangs. Regardless of which family members have an impact, it is clear that having family members who are in gangs increases the likelihood that girls will perceive gangs as an appropriate option for themselves as well.

More often than not, young women who joined gangs to be with or like their older siblings did so in the context of the types of family problems noted earlier. Veronica, who I discussed above, was a case in point. Her mother's drug addiction left her and her siblings unsupervised; when her older brothers began hanging out with the neighborhood gang, she followed suit. In fact, she went on to tell me, "then my *little* brother wanted to get put in it. And he was like only about six [laughs]. They told him no."

Similarly, Lisa was thirteen when we spoke, and only recently had joined her gang. Her brother Mike had been a member of a Folks gang for several years, and when the family relocated to another area of Columbus, he decided to start his own set of the gang in their new neighborhood. Lisa was among its members. Prior to Mike starting his own set, Lisa hadn't considered joining, but nonetheless said she "claimed [Folks] because that's what my brother was so I wanted to be like that too." Their mother had died when Lisa was eleven, and she described their father as physically abusive and distant. She felt very close to her brother, and said her desire to be with him was her primary reason for joining his gang.

Several weeks before Lisa joined, her brother's girlfriend Trish—who was also Lisa's best friend—was initiated. Lisa explained, "One day Trish was like, 'Well you wanna be true?' And I was like, 'Yeah.' And they was like, 'All right.' And they took me behind the railroad tracks and kicked the shit outta me and I was in it [laughs]." Lisa was initiated into the gang on the same day as her boyfriend and another male friend of theirs. A primary concern for her was to make a good impression on her brother. She explained:

> The boys was scared. They was like, "Man, I don't know, I don't know." And then I was like, I just looked at my brother. Then I looked at my friend and I looked at them boys and I was like, "I'll go first." So I just did it, I think . . . why I did it then is just to be, I don't know. Just to show them, my brother, that I was stronger than them boys.

Although she enjoyed what she described as the "fun and games" that she had with her brother and the other gang members, Lisa was actually ambivalent about being in a gang. She told me, "Right now I wish, I kinda wish I never got into it but I'm already in it so, like, um, I just, I don't know. I don't think I'm gonna be that heavy as my brother is, like all the time, you know, yeah, yeah." Lisa was especially concerned for her brother, who took his gang involvement quite seriously, which she perceived as putting his physical safety at risk. She explained, "My brother, when he was little, he was a little geeky little kid that wore glasses. But now he's like, you know, and I don't understand it but uh, I wish he was still a little kid that wore glasses." Nonetheless, she felt being in the gang allowed her to spend time with him. She surmised, "We all just hang out all the time. We just are always together. If you see me you see my brother. If you see my brother you see his girlfriend. If you see me you see my boyfriend. I mean, it's just like that."

In fact, a number of young women described joining their gangs in order to be around and meet the approval of their older brothers regardless of whether—like Lisa and Veronica—they had family problems at home. When Tonya was younger, she said she noticed "my brother just started wearing red all the time, all the time." She continued, "then after school . . . he just kept going outside. All these dudes and girls used to have fun, selling drugs and having money and stuff. And then I just wanted to do it. I thought it would be fun so I joined. I tried to join and then my brother let me join." Tonya said her initiation into the gang involved "just a couple of my brother's friends, he didn't let nobody really [cause me] pain for real, like really beat me up. They was just beating me up so I would have to fight back. I had some bruises, busted lip, in another minute it was gone, it was cool." What wasn't gone was Tonya's belief that "I had gained my brother's respect and stuff." Only thirteen at the time, she said "in the beginning I was like a little shortie. I didn't sell drugs, I didn't run around shooting or none of that." Her involvement increased, though, when she began "going out with one of my brother's friends," who provided her with drugs, which, she said, was "how I started selling dope."

Monica was also thirteen when she joined her brothers' gang. She had four older brothers, between the ages of 20 and 28 at the time she joined, all of whom were members of the same Crips set. Sixteen at the time we spoke, she remained the youngest member of her gang, and said she joined because she "wanted to be like" her older brothers. Monica described that she "always followed them around," and explained, "all four of my brothers were in so I was like, 'all right, I wanna be in a gang.' So I used to ride around with them all the time. And then my brother asked me, he said, 'Do you wanna be down or what?' . . . And I was like, 'Fine, I'll do it.' So I did." Perhaps because of the adult role models in her family, and because she "grew up around it," Monica, like Diane, was one of the most committed—and consequently delinquent—gang members. She told me, "I'm down for real, I'm down for life." Diane's strong gang commitment resulted from gang members filling a care-giving niche unavailable to her from her family while her father was in jail. In contrast, Monica's commitment was the result of her close bonds to her family.

A number of the young women in St. Louis, as I noted above, described the influence of extended family members—most often cousins, but sometimes also aunts. All of these young women talked about spending quite a bit of their time at their relatives' homes, sometimes but not always when they lived in the same neighborhoods. Trina joined her gang when she was eleven; both her cousins and aunts were members, and she described "just being around over there, being around all of them" growing up. Trina said her aunts and cousins had dressed her in gang colors from the time she was young, and she surmised, "I just grew up into it."

Likewise, Shiree described her gang as "a family thing," and Alecia also said her gang involvement was "like a family thing." Alecia explained, "my auntie first moved on [the street] where I live now . . . [and] I started visiting my cousin." The gang evolved from "everyone that was growing up in that 'hood. . . . I seen all my relatives, not my father and mother, but you know, all my relatives in it and then I came over just like that." She said "It ain't like they talked me into it or nothing." But eventually she and her mother and siblings moved to the same block, further solidifying her gang affiliation.

Vashelle said she joined her gang "because my family, all of my cousins, my relatives, they was Bloods already and then I moved over there because my cousin was staying over there so I just started claiming [the gang]." While in general Vashelle believed that girls joined gangs for "little stuff, they want a family or something," she argued that these were not her own motives. She explained, "It's just something I wanted to do because my cousin was in it so I wanted to be hanging around. . . . I ain't no follower. It's something I wanted to do and by them doing it was just more influence on me."

In some cases conflict in girls' immediate families increased the time they spent with relatives. Vickie began spending time with a gang-involved cousin when she became frustrated at home and "just wanted to get out of the house." She explained, "My mama always wanted me to baby-sit. I got tired of doing that. She always yell and stuff, she come home from work and start yelling. Like that kind of stuff and I got tired of hearing that. I need somebody to hang out with where I wouldn't be home half of the time." She turned to her cousin and "just started hanging out with him." The members of his gang, she said, "was like, 'you gonna do something [to join]?' I was like, I just gotta do what I gotta do," and so she joined.

As the preceding stories have illustrated, in some cases girls' trajectories into gangs are more heavily influenced by neighborhood dynamics, in others by severe family problems, and in still others by close ties to gang-involved family members. Dionne is perhaps the best illustration of how all of the factors I've described thus far—neighborhood context, family problems, and gang-involved family members—can come together to fuel girls' gang involvement. Dionne grew up in a housing project with gangs, where she had four male cousins who were members. She had been physically and sexually abused repeatedly by her mother's boyfriend, who was also her father's brother.[20] She explained:

> When [I] was little my uncle tried to have sex with me and stuff. I was like eight or seven, you know, and I told my mama in her sleep. I told my mama what happened, I woke her up out of sleep. You know she told me, she say, I'll get him when I wake up. For real, when she woke up, he ain't do nuttin' but tell her, "Aw, she lyin'. She just wants some attention." You know, and she hit me 'cause, you know, she thinkin' I'm just sayin' somethin'. I was mad though, and he thought he could take advantage by keep on doin' it.

There was also drug and alcohol abuse in the home, her mother had spent time in jail, and her mother and mother's boyfriend were violent toward one another. Dionne noted, "my mama, you know, me and my mama didn't get along. . . . My uncle [her mother's boyfriend], you know, we didn't get along. It was like, you know, he couldn't stand me, I don't know why. . . . He told me to my face, 'I hate you,' he say, 'I hope you die.'" Consequently, Dionne said "I used to like goin' to school, 'cause to get away from home." Eventually she began running away and spending time on the streets around her housing project with her cousins and other gang members. "I just started hangin' with 'em and doin' what they did then, and they,

it was like, they, you know, was used to me hangin' around." When she was eleven, one of her cousins tattooed the gang's name and her nickname on her forearm. Dionne was drunk when her cousin tattooed her, but she said that afterwards the tattoo "made me feel big and stuff, you know?" While she was abused and felt neglected and disparaged at home, Dionne said being with the gang "be kinda fun, you know, bein' around all your little friends, just chillin' or somethin'." . . .

Conclusion

This chapter has illustrated the range of circumstances that help pave girls' pathways into gangs. Notably, some of their discussions clearly parallel the discussions young men provide with regard to their decisions to join, particularly the strength of neighborhood peer networks. Young women join gangs because they perceive these groups as capable of meeting a variety of needs in their lives, both social and emotional, and sometimes economic as well. Previous research has suggested that a number of factors—among them socioeconomic context, family problems, and peer influences—contribute to girls' gang involvement. My research offers further support for these findings by comparing the experiences of gang and nongang girls, and also details in concrete ways the various trajectories through which some young women join gangs while others are able to avoid gang involvement.

My work suggests the strong influence of three overlapping factors—exposure to neighborhood gangs, problems within the family, and having gang-involved family members. The vast majority of gang girls described their decision to get into a gang as involving interactions between two or more of these factors. So for instance, girls who grew up in close proximity to gangs, particularly those with serious family problems, became aware of gangs and often chose these groups as a means of meeting social needs and avoiding home. In addition, my study found that (mostly adolescent) kinship networks had a strong relationship to girls' gang involvement. Girls with older siblings or relatives in gangs often looked up to those family members and, particularly but not always when there were other problems at home, sought to spend time with them on the streets and around their gangs. Notably, gang members in Columbus who said family members had an impact on their decision to join named siblings; in St. Louis they were more likely to mention cousins or other extended family members.

Finally, my research offers further support for the importance of family problems in facilitating many girls' gang involvement. Joan Moore's work found strong evidence, comparing male and female gang members, that young women recounted more cases of childhood abuse and neglect, and more frequently came from homes where wife abuse and other family problems were present.[21] My study fills in an additional piece of the puzzle by comparing female gang members with their nongang counterparts. Not only do female gang members come from more troubled families than their male counterparts, as Moore's work shows, but they also come from more troubled families than "at risk" girls who don't join gangs. Even among the handful of girls I interviewed who associated with gangs but didn't join, this appeared to be the case.

Moreover, my discussions with young women shed some light on how these family problems led to gang involvement. Often when relationships with primary caregivers were weak or ineffective, girls began spending time with the older adolescents who were hanging out on the street or around the neighborhood. For instance, drug-addicted parents led young women to feel neglected and abandoned, and did not provide needed supervision over their time and activities. For other young women, physical or sexual abuse or other conflicts in the household precipitated their spending time away from home. Given their likelihood of living in neighborhoods where gangs were present, and having older siblings or relatives in gangs, these groups were readily available for girls to hang out with and eventually, over time, step into.

Notes

1. See Decker and Van Winkle, *Life in the Gang,* chapter three.
2. See . . . Hagedorn, *People and Folks;* . . . Klein, *The American Street Gang;* Moore . . . *Going Down to the Barrio;* . . . Vigil, *Barrio Gangs.*
3. See Campbell, *The Girls in the Gang* and "Female Participation in Gangs"; Fishman, "The Vice Queens"; Joe and Chesney-Lind, " 'Just Every Mother's Angel' "; Quicker,

Homegirls. . . . Though not about young women in gangs, Baskin and Sommers also provide a useful account of how neighborhood and peer contexts facilitate women's involvement in violent crime. See their "Females' Initiation into Violent Street Crime."
4. Joe and Chesney-Lind, " 'Just Every Mother's Angel,' " p. 411.
5. See Bursik and Grasmick, *Neighborhoods and Crime;* Wilson, *The Truly Disadvantaged.*
6. Significance levels are based on Chi-Square tests. It's important to note here that while I use statistics to make comparisons throughout the book, my sample is purposive in nature and thus violates key assumptions regarding random or representative sampling. While technically statistical methods are inappropriate for my sample, I use these methods not in an attempt to generalize to a larger population, but to highlight the strength of the patterns I uncovered.
7. Quicker, *Homegirls,* p. 80. See also Joe and Chesney-Lind, " 'Just Every Mother's Angel.' "
8. See Decker, "Collective and Normative Features of Gang Violence"; Joe and Chesney-Lind, " 'Just Every Mother's Angel' "; Lauderback et al., " 'Sisters Are Doin' It For Themselves.' "
9. Jennifer was the only member of an all-female gang that I was able to interview in Columbus. She described the OG, who was in her mid-twenties and had started the gang several years before Jennifer joined, as very careful about who she allowed to join. This was not in keeping with the overall pattern in Columbus, where gangs tended to be fluid and loosely defined groups.
10. In their study of St. Louis gangs, Scott Decker and Barrik Van Winkle describe in similar ways the strength of neighborhood ties in the city, which they suggest have been quite longstanding—existing long before the recent re-emergence of gangs there. See their *Life in the Gang.*
11. See Bjerregaard and Smith, "Gender Differences in Gang Participation, Delinquency and Substance Use"; Bowker and Klein, "The Etiology of Female Juvenile Delinquency and Gang Membership"; Campbell, "On the Invisibility of the Female Delinquent Peer Group" and "Female Participation in Gangs." . . .
12. See Canter, "Family Correlates of Male and Female Delinquency"; Cernkovich and Giordano, "Family Relationships and Delinquency"; . . . Hagan et al., "Class in the Household"; Joe and Chesney-Lind, " 'Just Every Mother's Angel' "; Moore, *Going Down to the Barrio.* . . .
13. Joan Moore documented a myriad of factors within families that contribute to the like-

lihood of gang involvement for young women. These include the following: childhood abuse and neglect, wife abuse, having alcohol or drug addicts in the family, witnessing the arrest of family members, having a family member who is chronically ill, and experiencing a death in the family during childhood. Her conclusion, based on comparisons of male and female gang members, is that young women in particular are likely to come from families that are troubled. See Moore, *Going Down to the Barrio*. . . .

Joe and Chesney-Lind observed that the young women they spoke with sometimes had parents who worked long hours, or parents who were unemployed or underemployed—circumstances which they suggest affected girls' supervision and the quality of their family relationships. See their " 'Just Every Mother's Angel.' " Esbensen and Deschenes, in a multi-site study of risk factors for delinquency and gang behavior, found that lack of parental supervision was associated with gang membership for male and female gang members, but that maternal attachment was more predictive of gang membership for males than females. See Esbensen and Deschenes, "A Multi-Site Examination of Gang Membership". . . .

14. These are included in my measure of abuse in Table 5.2 when a family member committed the assault, but not when it was someone else the girl was exposed to through her family.

15. Huff, "Gangs in the United States"; but see Decker and Van Winkle, *Life in the Gang*.

16. There is a growing body of literature that supports the link between childhood maltreatment and youths' subsequent involvement in delinquency. See Smith and Thornberry, "The Relationship Between Childhood Maltreatment and Adolescent Involvement in Delinquency"; Widom, "Child Abuse, Neglect, and Violent Criminal Behavior."

17. See Bourgois and Dunlap, "Exorcising Sex-for-Crack"; Maher, *Sexed Work*.

18. Other research offers support for the relationship between girls' gang involvement and that of their family members. . . . See Moore, *Going Down to the Barrio;* Joe and Chesney-Lind, " 'Just Every Mother's Angel' "; Lauderback et al., " 'Sisters Are Doin' It For Themselves.' " Geoffrey Hunt made an important observation about gangs and "family" during my presentation of a paper based on this study at the 1998 meetings of the American Sociological Association. While scholars typically talk about the gang as a "surrogate" family for young people, in

fact there are many cases in which both "real" and "fictive" kin are members of girls' gangs. Thus, when young women speak of the familial nature of their gang relationships, they sometimes are literally speaking about their blood relatives.

19. See Collins, *Black Feminist Thought*. . . .

20. Fortunately, when Dionne was interviewed for this project she was no longer living in her mother and uncle's home. She was living with her father, whom she described as "always giving me attention," and was in counseling to cope with what had happened to her.

21. Moore, *Going Down to the Barrio*. See note 13 above for more details.

References

Baskin, Deborah R. and Ira B. Sommers. 1993. "Females' Initiation into Violent Street Crime." *Justice Quarterly* 10: 559–581.

Bjerregaard, Beth and Carolyn Smith. 1993. "Gender Differences in Gang Participation, Delinquency, and Substance Use." *Journal of Quantitative Criminology* 4: 329–355.

Bourgois, Philippe and Eloise Dunlap. 1993. "Exorcising Sex-for-Crack: An Ethnographic Perspective from Harlem." Pp. 97–132 in *Crack Pipe as Pimp: An Ethnographic Investigation of Sex-for-Crack Exchanges*, edited by Mitchell S. Ratner. New York: Lexington Books.

Bowker, Lee H. and Malcolm W. Klein. 1983. "The Etiology of Female Juvenile Delinquency and Gang Membership: A Test of Psychological and Social Structural Explanations." *Adolescence* 18: 739–751.

Bursik, Robert J. Jr. and Harold G. Grasmick. 1993. *Neighborhoods and Crime: The Dimensions of Effective Community Control*. New York: Lexington Books.

Campbell, Anne. 1984. *The Girls in the Gang*. New York: Basil Blackwell.

———. 1990. "Female Participation in Gangs." Pp. 163–182 in *Gangs in America*, edited by C. Ronald Huff. Newbury Park: Sage Publications.

———. 1990. "On the Invisibility of the Female Delinquent Peer Group." *Women & Criminal Justice* 2: 41–62.

Canter, Rachelle J. 1982. "Family Correlates of Male and Female Delinquency." *Criminology* 20: 149–167.

Cernkovich, S. A. and Peggy C. Giordano. 1987. "Family Relationships and Delinquency." *Criminology* 25: 295–319.

Collins, Patricia Hill. 1990. *Black Feminist Thought: Knowledge, Consciousness, and the Politics of Empowerment*. Boston: Unwin Hyman.

Decker, Scott H. 1996. "Collective and Normative

Features of Gang Violence." *Justice Quarterly* 13(2): 243–264.

Decker, Scott H. and Barrik Van Winkle. 1996. *Life in the Gang.* Cambridge: Cambridge University Press.

Esbensen, Finn-Aage and Elizabeth Piper Deschenes. 1998. "A Multi-Site Examination of Gang Membership: Does Gender Matter?" *Criminology* 36: 799–828.

Fishman, Laura T. 1995. "The Vice Queens: An Ethnographic Study of Black Female Gang Behavior." Pp. 83–92 in *The Modern Gang Reader,* edited by Malcolm W. Klein, Cheryl L. Maxson and Jody Miller. Los Angeles: Roxbury Publishing Company.

Hagan, John, John Simpson and A. R. Gillis. 1987. "Class in the Household: A Power-Control Theory of Gender and Delinquency." *American Journal of Sociology* 92: 788–816.

Hagedorn, John M. 1988. *People and Folks: Gangs, Crime and The Underclass in a Rustbelt City.* Chicago: Lake View Press.

Huff, C. Ronald. 1993. "Gangs in the United States." Pp. 3–20 in *The Gang Intervention Handbook,* edited by Arnold P. Goldstein and C. Ronald Huff. Champaign, IL: Research Press.

Joe, Karen A. and Meda Chesney-Lind. 1995. " 'Just Every Mother's Angel': An Analysis of Gender and Ethnic Variations in Youth Gang Membership." *Gender & Society* 9: 408–430.

Klein, Malcolm W. 1995. *The American Street Gang: Its Nature, Prevalence and Control.* New York: Oxford University Press.

Lauderback, David, Joy Hansen, and Dan Waldorf. 1992. " 'Sisters Are Doin' It For Themselves': A Black Female Gang in San Francisco." *The Gang Journal* 1: 57–70.

Maher, Lisa. 1997. *Sexed Work: Gender, Race and Resistance in a Brooklyn Drug Market.* Oxford: Clarendon Press.

Moore, Joan. 1991. *Going Down to the Barrio: Homeboys and Homegirls in Change.* Philadelphia: Temple University Press.

Quicker, John C. 1983. *Homegirls: Characterizing Chicana Gangs.* San Pedro, CA: International University Press.

Smith, Carolyn and Terence P. Thornberry. 1995. "The Relationship Between Childhood Maltreatment and Adolescent Involvement in Delinquency." *Criminology* 33: 451–479.

Vigil, James Diego. 1988. *Barrio Gangs: Street Life and Identity in Southern California.* Austin: University of Texas Press.

Widom, Cathy Spatz. 1989. "Child Abuse, Neglect, and Violent Criminal Behavior." *Criminology* 27: 251–271.

Wilson, William Julius. 1987. *The Truly Disadvantaged: The Inner City, the Underclass, and Public Policy.* Chicago: University of Chicago Press. ✦

Chapter 6
Leaving the Gang

Scott H. Decker
and Janet L. Lauritsen

The previous two chapters looked at why youth join gangs. Decker and Lauritsen provide the other bookend to this matter—why youth leave gangs. If they didn't, we'd have a nation overrun with gang members. Unlike many myths about the difficulties of escaping the gang life, the author's data reveal some complex processes that involve two patterns, the decision to quit and drifting into quitting. In neither case is quitting the gang as difficult as it is often portrayed. Violence, often seen as a defining characteristic of gang culture, paradoxically is often cited by the authors' gang respondents as a principal reason for leaving the gang life. Violence and its consequences on life and limb can be a powerful educator. Unfortunately, as the authors report, given the high death rate among their respondents, the lesson is often learned too late.

Early studies of gangs found that adult membership in gangs was a rare phenomenon, and more recent surveys of high-risk youth confirm the importance of studying gang membership as a transitory affiliation. For instance, Thrasher (1927/1963) argued that gangs were overwhelmingly composed of adolescent boys, and Thornberry, Krohn, Lizotte, and Chard-Wierschem (1993) and Esbensen and Huizinga (1993) found that the vast majority of youth who reported gang membership also reported that affiliation to be of short duration. Despite findings that leaving the gang appears to be associated with reductions in criminal involvement (e.g., Rand, 1987), most analyses of gang involvement focus on becoming a gang

Reprinted from: C. Ronald Huff (ed.), *Gangs in America III*, pp. 51–67. Copyright © 2002 by Sage Publications, Inc. Reprinted by permission of Sage Publications, Inc.

member rather than discontinuing those affiliations.

The more general topic of desistance from crime has also been given less attention than other aspects of criminal activity. Recently, however, interest in desistance processes has been renewed, spurred in part by the availability of longitudinal data sources describing individuals' lives (Sampson & Laub, 1993). The findings from this literature highlight the significance of social ties, such as marriage, employment, military service, and parenthood, and broader emotional and psychological processes of maturational reform. Using a phenomenological approach, Maruna (2001) describes the fluidity of the desistance process and encourages researchers to approach the study of "going straight" as a process rather than an outcome with discrete properties.

In this chapter, we describe how gang members in St. Louis leave their gangs, using data from a field study of gang and ex-gang members. We draw conclusions about these findings in the context of the existing research on gangs and the broader literature on desistance. Finally, we discuss the need to resolve complex definitional issues, and the need for additional information for theoretical and programmatic purposes.

What Is Known About Leaving the Gang?

In 1971, Klein noted that there had been no study of the progression of gang members to adulthood. Although Moore (1991) and Vigil (1988) have sketched out some of the details of this progression, it remains a topic about which too little is known. Sanchez-Jankowski (1991, p. 61) speculated that there were six ways gang members could exit from their gang: (a) age out, (b) die, (c) go to prison, (d) get jobs, (e) join other organizations, and (f) leave as the gang subdivides. His research found no systematic pattern in the way individual gang members left their gangs, and he underscored the diversity of reasons that individual gang members provided when asked how they came to disassociate themselves from the gang.

Additional insight about leaving the gang has been gleaned from studies of prison gangs. Based on a series of prisoner interviews, Skolnick (1988) reported that the only way to leave the gang was to "fade out" by gradually withdrawing from the activities of the group (p. 4). Despite this observation, he reported that prison gang members believed that membership was permanent—that is, they believed that gang members had no way out of their gang other than death. Similarly, Fong, Vogel, and Buentello (1995) studied data from the Texas prison system and found that inmates who left their prison gangs experienced greater consequences than those leaving street gangs, since the prison constituted a closed system in which gang members could not move, hide, or enmesh themselves in alternative networks. Nonetheless, Fong et al. reported that a substantial number of prison gang members left their gangs each year, generally without consequence.

Of course, findings based on prison gangs may not be generalizable to life outside the walls. Prison gangs often include the most hardened and criminally involved inmates, some of whom were gang members before their imprisonment, and there is evidence to suggest that the prison experience itself may increase solidarity among gang members (Fleisher & Decker, 2001). But even in such an extreme environment, leaving a gang may occur more often than has generally been assumed. Moreover, gang members themselves may be especially likely to overstate the consequences of leaving the gang.

Vigil (1988) presents one of the most detailed discussions of the process of exiting the gang. In his analysis of Chicano gangs in Los Angeles, he found that there was a "succession quality" to leaving the gang—that is, most gang members left the gang through a process not dissimilar to that which they used in entering the gang—a gradual series of steps and commitments. The social process underlying this transition is important to underscore. Most life changes do not occur in a sudden manner. Just as getting married or growing enmeshed in a job does not typically occur overnight, severing ties with friends in a gang is unlikely to occur instantaneously.

Unlike the findings from other research, Vigil reports that exiting the gang was frequently accompanied by the ritual of being "beaten out." This process involves either running a line or being in a circle to absorb the blows of fellow gang members to prove one's worth. Thus, in his research, leaving the gang also involved a symbolic process that announced to fellow gang members that the tie between the group and the individual had been severed.

Vigil also found that members who left the gang typically had developed increased ties to social institutions, most often prison, but also with jobs and family. He characterizes the process of leaving the gang as more difficult than joining, in part because leaving the group means rejecting one's friends and peers. He argues that because the gang provides a source of support and friendship, members do not leave until a suitable substitute has been found. Vigil emphasizes how difficult this may be for adolescents, for whom peer associations are particularly important.

Hagedorn (1994) conducted a series of interviews with Milwaukee gang members that consisted of 47 interviews in 1987 and 101 interviews in 1992. Most of the latter set of interviews was with adults (median age = 26), and 23 of these gang members had also been interviewed in 1987. From these interviews Hagedorn developed a four-category typology of adult gang members, based largely on their relationships to drug sales and employment in the legitimate economy. Two of these categories—"Legits" and "Homeboys"—are relevant for the current discussion.

Despite strong commitments to the goals of legitimate society, few of the African American and Latino gang members from the original sample had become Legits—that is, individuals who had reported that they left the gang, were not involved in drug sales, and were involved in jobs or school. The Legits were most easily classified as ex-gang members using their behaviors, attachments, and identification as criteria. However, identification of the gang member status of Homeboys was more difficult. The typical Homeboy was in his mid-20s, past the peak age of offending, and generally worked in the legitimate economy. But Homeboys often found themselves unable to fulfill their conventional aspirations and moved between the legitimate and the illegal economy quite frequently. Thus, Homeboys represented a middle category of gang member, falling somewhere between Legits and active gang members. As such, they reinforce the notion that leaving the gang is a gradual process, often involving increasing commitments to conventional institutions. What remains unclear, however, is whether the impetus to leave the gang is the result or the cause of conventional affiliations.

Much of the gang literature suggests that gang members age out of the gang (Horowitz, 1983; Klein, 1971), and recent research on high-risk youth confirms this description. Battin, Hill, Abbott, Catalano, and Hawkins (1998) and Thornberry, Lizotte, Krohn, Farnworth, and Jang (1994) note that gang membership among teenagers typically averages 2 years or less. Thus gang membership is most often short-lived, characterized as much by leaving as by joining. However, aging out does not appear to be uniformly experienced by all gang members. Horowitz (1983) reports that "peripheral" or "fringe" members found it easier to leave the gang than did "core" members, due to lesser involvement in gang activities and reduced dependence on the gang for social or instrumental support.

Individuals may encounter a variety of problems when leaving the gang, some of which stem from the gang itself, but many have their focus outside the gang. For instance, despite announcing a decision to leave the gang, ex-gang members may continue to be seen as gang members by their own gang, rival gangs, the police, and the community. Gang identities often remain fixed well after the decision to leave the gang has been made and acted on. Some acts committed while a gang member transcend the period of membership. For instance, the announcement of a decision to leave the gang would not necessarily reduce the incentive for rival gang members to redress a previous act of violence, nor would such information reduce the efforts of police to make arrests for criminal activities committed while a gang member. Past gang activity may also hinder an individual's ability to gain employment, making it more difficult for the labor market to produce conformity.

Under these conditions it is easy to imagine that some gang members may decide that leaving the gang is not worth the effort. After all, what incentive is there to leave the gang when it is the source of friendships and when past activities as a gang member cause others to continue to treat them as if they were still gang members? Even though adolescence is a period in life when many affiliations are tried and rejected, the dilemma surrounding gang membership is

that it has a more enduring external character than many other affiliations.

Our reading of the literature surrounding the process of leaving the gang found that most of this research is descriptive. We found no research designed to assess systematically the conditions under which members choose to leave the gang or the factors that account for the length of time one remains a gang member. However, gang members do report that they see themselves and others leaving for a variety of reasons and in numerous ways. These accounts can guide researchers' efforts in determining whether the decision to leave the gang is driven by individual characteristics, experiences within the gang, external ties such as investments in social institutions or attachments to prosocial persons, or some other set of unknown factors. In order to examine the significance of these factors, many definitional issues need to be addressed. These issues became apparent in our investigation of gang and ex-gang members in St. Louis.

The Data

To structure our investigation of leaving the gang, we rely on data from a 3-year field study of gangs in St. Louis conducted between October 1990 and September 1993, and follow-up data for approximately half of the sample through 1998. The city of St. Louis experienced dramatic economic and population losses similar to those that plagued many other midwestern industrialized cities in the 1970s and 1980s. Gangs in St. Louis grew in number and membership during the mid-1980s (Decker & Van Winkle, 1996).

For this project, *gangs* were defined as age-graded peer groups that exhibited permanence, engaged in criminal activity, and had symbolic representations of membership. A street ethnographer who verified membership and observed gang activity in neighborhoods made contacts with active and ex-gang members. This person, an ex-offender himself, had built a reputation as "solid" on the street through his work with the community and previous research work. Using snowball sampling procedures, initial field contacts were made and the sample was built to include more subjects (Biernacki & Waldorf, 1981; Decker & Van Winkle, 1996).

Individuals who admitted current or past

membership and agreed to an interview became part of our sample. Current and past membership was also verified by information from field observation or other subjects, and individuals were considered "ex-gang members" based on self-reports. Subjects had to have been ex-gang members for at least 3 months to be classified as such. We also sought to include family members of gang members in our interviews.

Three features distinguish this work from most studies of gangs. First, no criminal justice contacts were used to gain access to the members of the sample. Using criminal justice channels (police, courts, probation, and social service agencies) may result in a different type of subject than one found in the field. For example, police and criminal justice samples may be more involved in law breaking. Second, the gang members themselves told their story. Although an interview instrument was used, ample opportunity was provided in open-ended questions for the subjects to elaborate on questions and add new insights. Third, this was a field study of gangs, not conducted in the offices of a social service or youth agency. All participants in the study were initially contacted in the neighborhoods where they lived and acted out their gang activities. This enabled project personnel to observe a number of gang activities, including violent encounters between gangs. It is our belief that a sample recruited in this way enhances the validity of responses.

The data for this analysis consist of interviews with 99 active gang members and 24 ex-gang members. We look at data from both sets of subjects so that active members' perceptions of what leaving the gang would entail could be compared to the experiences of ex-members. As expected, the ex-gang members were somewhat older (mean = 19 years of age) than the currently active gang members (mean = 17). Twenty-two of the ex-gang members were black males and 2 were black females. The sample of active gang members included 4 white males, 7 black females, and 88 black males. Half of the ex-gang members had left the gang for a period of less than a year at the time of the interview.

The past gangs of ex-gang members were each classified according to the level of organization (Decker, Bynum, & Weisel, 1998). Eleven of the ex-gang members came from gangs with a "loose" organizational structure, lacking leadership and having few group goals and infrequent group associations. Five ex-members came from gangs with a high level of organization, and five came from gangs that were organized in moderate fashion.

Reasons for Leaving

Ex-Gang Member Reports

We begin by examining the reasons ex-members offered for leaving the gang, as well as the way in which they left their gangs. When asked why they left their gangs, the majority (16 ex-gang members, or two thirds of this group) offered a specific reason: They left because of the level of violence. Many of these individuals left because of personal experiences of violence.

EX003: Well, after I got shot, I got shot in my leg. You know how your life just flash? I was walking to my father's house, he stay on the westside. I was walking and then I saw, see I don't like the color red, I hate the color red, and it was like a whole corner full of Bloods. It was like, what's up, Blood? I said no. They said, "What you claim?" And then we had a fight and I hit a few of them. It was like ten of them and then I ran and then all I heard was pow, I was still running. I had on some white jogging pants and I saw blood running down the back of my leg and I just ran over to my father's house. It [the bullet] didn't go in, it was like grazing me. It just scared me cause I ended up being shot at. I had a gun put to my head before but I never been shot at.

INT:[1] Why did you quit being in the gang?

EX014: Because I was put in the hospital.

INT: You were hospitalized?

EX014: Yeah, for four days.

INT: What were you hospitalized for?

EX014: I got beat in the back of the head with a bat.

INT: By other gang members, some Bloods or something?

EX014: Hoover [Crips].

INT: Why did you get out?

EX011: Because I got to realizing it wasn't my type of life. I didn't want to live that type of life. One time, I got seriously stabbed and I was in the hospital for like three months.

INT: Where did you get it?

EX011: Right in my back. Close to the kidney. I was in the hospital for like three months. After I got out of the hospital, I tried to cope with it a little more, but I just faded away from it.

In other cases, the *threat or fear of personal violence* was offered by the individual as a reason for leaving the gang.

INT: Why did you quit?

EX001: Because we might get shot. Somebody in our hood got shot last night and the day before that. They killing for no reason.

EX013: I didn't want to die. Just one day I got out.

Some left because *family members were the victims of violence* or violence was threatened against family members. For these individuals, this single event was reported as the reason for leaving the gang.

INT: Why did you leave?

EX018: My cousin got shot.

The majority of ex-members who cited violence as the reason they left their gangs underscored the vicarious nature of violence that had occurred against other members of their gangs.

EX016: Yeah, that really came to me because when one of my friends got killed and you look at his face, it was hard. It could have been me. His parents were at the point. . . . It was just hard on me because the reason why he got in was because of me. It was hard for me to go up to his parents. At that point, I was saying that it wasn't my fault. When I really woke up was when my friend died because we got in there together. He said I'm gonna get in if you get in.

INT: Can you tell me why did you decide to leave the gang?

EX002: Because all my friends were getting killed that I used to hang with and because the 'hood I'm staying in there's a lot of Bloods, which I didn't want to be.

INT: Why did you leave?

EX009: Because people was dying. It wasn't about nothing to me no more.

INT: Why did you leave?

EX012: My best friend, he got killed. We was in the eighth grade together [and] freshman year.

The remaining eight individuals offered diverse reasons why they left their gangs. Three said that they had moved out of town, severing ties with the gangs in their former cities of residence. Two additional ex-members could not offer a reason why they left. Three individuals cited family ties, including caring for children or other obligations to family.

INT: Why did you quit?

EX021: Because I've got two children to live for.

INT: Why did you leave?

EX013: Because of my loved ones. I just couldn't keep neglecting them.

EX011: When I was in the gang I wasn't spending time with my daughter, I wasn't taking care of her, I wasn't doing, that's mainly why me and my baby's mother broke up because stuff I was getting in. She didn't want to be around me, the kind of person that I was then. Now, I have got me a job, I was getting locked up before.

In some of these cases, gang members reported a single event (especially violence) for leaving their gangs; in others an accumulation of events and attachments preceded the decision. Thus, a combination of maturational reform, aging, and proximity to violence produced the motivation for leaving the gang for a number of individuals. Similar to other studies (e.g., Hagedorn, 1994), we found that participation declined with age and was associated with involvement in activities in postadolescent stages of the life course (job, family, concern about one's future). Familial ties and victimization experiences were cited far more often than institutional affiliations as reasons to terminate ties to the gang.

Next, we describe the specific method or route by which ex-members left their gang. Once again, a single answer dominated the responses. Fifteen of the 24 ex-gang members (63%) told us that they simply quit their gangs and that this did not involve a specific method or technique. While others have noted gang rituals for leaving, this was not observed among St. Louis gang members. This may be due to the fact that the gangs were characterized by loose ties among members, few formal rules, few strong leaders, and little articulated structure. Also, subgroups within St. Louis gangs claimed stronger allegiances than did the larger gang (Decker & Van Winkle, 1996). It was in those subgroups that most illegal activity, especially drug sales, but also robberies and burglaries, took place. It is also possible that the strength of friendship ties within the subgroup protected ex-gang members from retaliation for leaving the gang. Perhaps ironically, the peer group that facilitated gang membership later served to mitigate the consequences of leaving the gang, particularly when an ex-member maintained associations with gang members after leaving.

EX001: I just quit. I stopped hanging out with them. There was about three of us that quit, we just stopped hanging out with them and everything.

INT: How did you leave? Did you have to announce something, did you get beat out?

EX008: Just stopped claiming.

INT: So when guys would ask you if you were claiming, you would say no, I'm out of that now?

EX008: Yeah.

INT: Did people respect that?

EX008: No.

INT: What did they do when you told them you weren't claiming any more?

EX008: Most of them started talking stuff. Once you in, you in it for life and all that stuff.

INT: How did you get out?

EX011: Some of them be funning saying they got to kill they mother but some of the stuff is true. How I really got out of it, I just got me a little job, stopped hanging out with them.

INT: How did you leave?

EX019: I just walked away.

INT: It was that easy? They didn't. . . .

EX019: No, they didn't fuck with me.

A small number of ex-gang members told us they were threatened after they left the gang.

INT: How did you leave?

EX016: I just stopped socializing with them. I was threatened to get killed after I left but it really didn't faze me.

Interestingly, only a small number of ex-members report having to fight a member to formally leave the gang.

EX004: If you want to get out you get beat down.

INT: So you get out the same way you get in?

EX004: Right. There's more dudes on you. About six dudes on you.

INT: How did you leave the gang?

EX024: Moved out of there.

INT: You had to beat up on other members to get out?

EX024: Yeah.

While this was reported to have happened to only a few ex-gang members, it was the predominant myth among gang members. As Klein (1971) and Decker and Van Winkle (1996) have noted, such myths among gangs have served to dominate the public's views of gangs. If so, these false perceptions should not serve as the basis of gang intervention policy.

A final group of five ex-members reported that they left their gangs by moving. One, who had moved to St. Louis from California, told us that one could never really leave the gang, but that moving out of state was the way he severed ties with his gang.

INT: When did you quit the gang?

EX006: I never did quit. You can never get out of the gang. Only way you can quit is to stop hanging around them or move to another state.

INT: How long [since] you moved from California?

EX006: Four years, really three and a half.

INT: So [the] gang consider[s] you in the gang until you die, right?

EX006: You can get out of the gang if you really wanted to. But in California you have to kill somebody to get out of the gang. You got to kill your mother or somebody like that to get out of it. I can't get out of it. I ain't killing my mother.

Overall, most members of our ex-gang sample indicated they left the gang because of concerns over violence targeted directly at them or at members of their gang. Many commentators (Klein, 1971; Sanchez-Jankowski, 1991; Short & Strodtbeck, 1965/1974; Vigil, 1988; Yablonsky, 1973) identify violence as a defining feature of gang life. A large body of research indicates that gang violence (real or mythic) provides much of the solidarity that keeps gangs together (Klein, 1971; Moore, 1978; Short & Strodtbeck, 1965/1974; Thrasher, 1927/1963; Vigil, 1988). Our findings suggest that violence may have contradictory consequences: The very activity that may keep gangs together appears to have provided the impetus for the majority of this sample to leave the gang. This paradox is certainly worth more detailed exploration.

Active Gang Member Reports

We now turn to data from the 99 active gang members—first to their reports during the 3-year field study, and then to the results of a follow-up search for these members approximately 5 years later. Some have argued that status as a gang member is a "master status," one that influences most behavior and is not shed easily (Sanchez-Jankowski, 1991). Active gang members have a stake in maintaining such a view of gang membership because the viability of their gang depends on the ability of active gang members to maintain the perception that leaving the gang is nearly impossible. This may, in part, explain the efforts of active gang members to foster the belief that drastic steps (such as killing your mother) are the only means by which individuals can leave the gang.

Although most active gang members strongly expressed the belief that one can never leave the gang, a majority of the active gang members knew individuals who had left their gang. Indeed, 55 of the 81 active gang members who responded to this question (68%) told us they knew individuals who had left. This apparent contradiction may be the result of close associations that remained beyond the gang identification. We also found that the reasons that individuals left the gang were essentially the same among gang and ex-gang members. In rank order, violence, family, and just stopping were the three categories identified most often by active gang members. Again, gang experiences and social processes, rather than institutional commitments, were the core reasons for leaving the gang.

Almost half of the active gang members who knew individuals who left their gang identified violence as the primary reason. Being shot or beaten up was the reason offered most frequently.

INT: Why did they decide to leave, do you know?

036: Got shot in the head.

INT: Why did he get out of it?

048: Cause he was getting beat up too much.

INT: Why did they leave the gang?

083: They got beat up bad.

Other gang members left because they knew members of their own gang who had been the victims of violence.

INT: How did they decide to leave?

004: One of they friends got killed.

INT: Why did they leave?

035: Death in they family.

INT: You mean somebody was killed?

035: Somebody that was real close to them and they figured they had to leave.

Often, the victims were relatives of a gang member, making the violence more salient to them.

INT: Do you know why he decided to leave?

075: One person left because his brother got shot so he just went out.

INT: His brother didn't die, did he?

075: Yeah, he did.

Or in other cases, gang members grew weary of threats against their families.

INT: Do you know why he decided to leave?

087: Same reason I left from where I was at.

INT: Too much heat and static?

087: Yeah, cause it would get so far as they will harass your family, like shoot your house up or something.

The second-largest category of active gang members who knew a fellow gang member who had left the gang identified family and job concerns as the primary reason for breaking ties with the gang.

INT: Do you know why he left?

093: This white boy Gary used to be with us, he use to be a Blood and stuff like that but he got this gal pregnant and he got his own house and he told us he didn't want to be in the gang any more.

INT: Do you know anybody who used to be in a gang but isn't any more?

021: My brother used to be in a gang but he don't claim no more.

INT: How come?

021: He was with the gang but he got serious with his girlfriend and got her pregnant and he said fuck that shit [the gang]. I'm just going to lay low with my gal, I ain't got time for that. He don't got time for that [gang] stuff.

037: My big brother [left the gang]. He was in the 38s. They say to get out of the 38s you got to kill your parents, kill one of your parents. My brother was making good grades, got him a scholarship and everything and he was like, I'm leaving this alone. They tried to make him kill my mother. He was like, you must be crazy, and I was on his side.

A number of gang members also told us they knew gang members who had simply stopped being in the gang.

INT: Are there people who used to be in your gang but aren't any more?

003: Well, we did have a few people who left but they had talked to us about it and said they didn't want to be in the gang any more. We said all right man, that's cool. We a gang; if you just want out, you want out, you out of here.

INT: Do you know why they decided to leave?

011: 'Cause it don't prove anything cause everybody splitting up slowly 'cause it don't really prove nothing. If we need their help they will come back and help.

INT: Do you know anybody who used to be in a gang but isn't any more?

086: Yeah.

INT: Do you know why they decided to leave?

086: They just stopped. They not in it but they still a gang member.

These observations confirm the view that leaving the gang is not a process that requires taking exceptional steps, and most ex-gang members report gradually severing the bonds between themselves and the gang. Indeed, in many instances active gang members saw the logic of such decisions made by their peers.

Active Gang Member Reports: Five Years Later

Perhaps the most striking finding we can report is the number of deaths that had occurred to the original sample of active gang members approximately 5 years after they were interviewed. The salience of violence for life in the gang has been reported for a variety of contexts (Decker & Van Winkle, 1996; Klein, 1995; Sanders, 1994), and our follow-up study of the initial sample reaffirms this view. The search for the original 99 gang members through December 1998 yielded 51 subjects, of whom 19 had died, 2 were in state prison, and 4 were in vocational rehabilitation (wheelchairs). While we could track only about half of the initial sample (51 out of 99), these grim outcomes occurred to approximately half of those who could be located (i.e., approximately one quarter of the initial sample). It is difficult to predict whether those who could not be found experienced similar fates.

Defining an Ex-Gang Member

These interviews also illustrate some of the difficulties in determining when gang membership ceases and how that may influence future interactions and affiliations with active gang members. What some subjects describe as a rather simple experience, in fact draws attention to important definitional issues. For instance, the last two subjects (011 and 086) indicate that ex-gang members could still be designated as gang members, because they report emotional ties (086) or see themselves as individuals who can be counted on for involvement in certain gang activities (011). We address this complexity below.

The answer to the question, "Is this subject still a gang member?" is explicitly tied to the definitions of both a *gang* and a *member,* and there is still considerable debate over these terms (see, e.g., Ball & Curry, 1995; Covey, Menard, & Franzese, 1992; Decker & Kempf, 1991). Most studies rely on self-report questions (e.g., "Are you a member of a street or youth gang?") and require that the group to which the youth belongs engage in some illegal activity (see, e.g., Esbensen & Huizinga, 1993). If we use these criteria for gang membership, it also seems reasonable to rely on self-reports for determining ex-gang member status as well.

Although each of the "ex-gang members" reported that he or she was no longer a member of a gang, a considerable proportion claimed that they continued to participate in both criminal and noncriminal activities with members of the gang, and others reported emotional ties to gang members. Using these two dimensions—activities and attachments—we display in Table 6.1 a typology for describing an ex-member's relationship with the gang.

Persons who fall into Category A are most easily classified as ex-gang members. These individuals no longer have attachments to members of their former gangs and no longer engage in activities (criminal or non-criminal) with those members. Ex-members who have moved to new towns, and those who report new families and jobs and no current ties to the gang, would be easily placed in this category. Ex-gang members who said that they no longer associated with members of their gangs but still had friendships that were strong enough to elicit "helping out" their old associates if there was "trouble" fall into Category B. Ex-gang members falling into Category C are those who no longer report emotional ties to the gang but still engage in activities with persons still in the gang. These ex-members seek out former associates for activities such as drug sales or hanging out, but they eschew the affiliation as a member of the gang and their relationships appear to be more instrumental. In the St. Louis data, these were individuals who most likely left

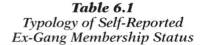

Table 6.1
Typology of Self-Reported
Ex-Gang Membership Status

		Emotional Ties With Members of Previous Gang Network	
		NO	YES
Engage in Activities With Members of Previous Gang Network	NO	A	B
	YES	C	D

for family or employment reasons and who no longer define themselves as gang members because their primary commitments lie elsewhere. Although an argument could be made that these individuals are still active gang members (despite their own protests), to do so would require changing the working definition of membership to include only activity and attachments, and to disregard self-reported status. Finally, we also uncovered ex-gang members who claimed to be involved in activities with their gang and committed to emotional aspects of the gang (Category D), yet no longer considered themselves to be gang members. The primary difference between these persons and those in Category C is the degree to which these friendships are valued.

As the above categories suggest, determining when a person is an "ex-gang member" was found to be more difficult than initially expected because self-described ex-gang members continue to report varying degrees of attachments and activities with others in the gang, and the process of disengagement is often gradual. This conceptual difficulty parallels some of the obstacles highlighted in the more general literature on recidivism. For instance, Maruna (2001) discusses the tendency for desistance to be viewed by criminologists as an event or voluntary decision in the lives of offenders. Yet few subjects who report that they no longer engage in criminal conduct made these decisions only once. Maruna reminds us that criminal behavior is sporadic, and as such "termination" or "desistance" takes place repeatedly (p. 23). He also reminds us that there is a vast difference between the decision to go straight and the actual process of doing so.

Conclusions

Leaving the gang is a more complex and variable process than suggested in previous research, and many parallels can be found in the research on desistance. In some instances, it appears that persons make an explicit decision to leave; others simply drift away. The St. Louis data suggest that the way in which individuals "leave" the gang may be related to the characteristics of both the group and the individual, but more likely reflects informal social processes than institutional involvement or incentives. Violent experiences also motivated some gang members to leave. A key area for gang research should be to investigate not only individual and group-level influences, but also to examine the role of potential "triggering events" in individual motivations and decision making. Unfortunately, these data do not permit us to determine what factors distinguish those who leave following violent experiences from those who stay.

Despite these complexities, do we have sufficient information for suggesting how the duration of gang membership might be shortened? One of the ironic findings noted above was that the majority of ex-gang members in this sample said that violence had played a role in their decision to leave the gang while at the same time the prior literature has found that violent events tend to strengthen group solidarity. Although our findings do not tell us how this process operates, they do suggest an opportunity for intervention. Seizing opportunities when gang members have been victimized by violence or have witnessed a close friend's victimization may offer promising avenues for reducing gang involvement.

Our findings suggest that the role of violence in discouraging membership or enhancing cohesion may have an important time dimension. In the short term, violence may cause some gang members to reflect on the risks of their participation in the gang and to question the viability of their membership. The extent to which they are physically separated from the gang will likely play a large role in determining how salient violent victimization will be for their decision to leave the gang. Over the longer term, enhanced by interaction with other gang members, violence can serve to enhance cohesion (Klein, 1971; Short & Strodtbeck, 1965/1974). The trick, then, is to intervene immediately following acts of violence, when gang members are separated from their gang, or at least when they are in small groups that are apart from the gang. Such opportunities are not likely to exist in the offices of social service agencies. Rather, they are likely to be found in hospital emergency rooms, at the police station, or in family settings. As Fearn, Decker, and Curry (2000) argue, gang intervention policies need to adopt strategies that address proximate and fundamental causes of gangs. Such intervention is likely to be successful to the extent that it (a) occurs very shortly after the victimization, and (b) occurs separate from the influence of the gang. Follow-up services may be necessary, particularly to counteract the socializing power of the gang in "reconstructing" the violence in a fashion that serves to reintegrate the gang member into the collective.

Note

1. INT stands for interviewer; the digit number stands for the number of the subject. Ex-gang members are denoted by EX before the subject number.

References

Ball, R., & Curry, G. D. (1995). The logic of definition in criminology: Purposes and methods for defining "gangs." *Criminology,* 33(2), 225–245.

Battin, S. R., Hill, K. G., Abbott, R. D., Catalano, R. R், & Hawkins, J. D. (1998). The contribution of gang membership to delinquency beyond delinquent friends. *Criminology,* 36(1), 93–115.

Biernacki, P., & Waldorf, D. (1981). Snowball sampling: Problems and techniques of chain referral sampling. *Sociological Methods and Research,* 10, 141–163.

Covey H. C., Menard, S., & Franzese, R. J. (1992). *Juvenile gangs.* Springfield, IL: Charles C Thomas.

Decker, S., & Kempf, K. (1991). Constructing gangs: The social definition of youth activities. *Criminal Justice Policy Review,* 5, 271–291.

Decker, S. H., & Van Winkle, B. (1996). *Life in the gang: Family, friends, and violence.* Cambridge, UK, & New York: Cambridge University Press.

Decker, S. H., Bynum, T., & Weisel, D. (1998). A tale of two cities: Gang as organized crime groups. *Justice Quarterly,* 15(3), 395–425.

Esbensen, F.-A. & Huizinga D. (1993). Gangs, drugs, and delinquency in a survey of urban youth. *Criminology,* 31(4), 565–589.

Fearn, N. E., Decker, S. H., & Curry, G. D. (2000). Public policy responses to gangs: Evaluating the outcomes. In J. Miller, C. L. Maxson, & M. W. Klein (Eds.) *The modern gang reader* (2nd ed., pp. 330–344). Los Angeles, CA: Roxbury.

Fleisher, M. S., & Decker, S. H. (2001). "Going home, staying home": Approaches to integrating prison gang members into the community. *Correctional Management Quarterly,* 5(1), 66–78.

Fong, R., Vogel, R., & Buentello, S. (1995). Blood-in, blood-out: The rationale behind defecting from prison gangs. *Gang Journal,* 2, 45–51.

Hagedorn, J. M. (1994). Homeboys, dope fiends, legits, and new jacks: Adult gang members, drugs, and work. *Criminology,* 32, 197–219.

Horowitz, R. (1983). *Honor and the American dream: Culture and identity in a Chicano community.* New Brunswick, NJ: Rutgers University Press.

Klein, M. W. (1971). *Street gangs and street workers.* Englewood Cliffs, NJ: Prentice Hall.

———. (1995). *The American street gang: Its nature, prevalence, and control.* New York: Oxford University Press.

Maruna, S. (2001). *Making good: How ex-convicts reform and rebuild their lives.* Washington DC: American Psychological Association.

Moore, J. W. (1978). *Homeboys: Gangs, drugs, and prison in the barrios of Los Angeles.* Philadelphia: Temple University Press.

———. (1991). *Going down to the barrio: Homeboys and homegirls in change.* Philadelphia: Temple University Press.

Rand, A. (1987). Transitional life events and desistance from delinquency and crime. In M. Wolfgang, T. Thornberry, & R. Figlio (Eds.), *From boy to man, from delinquency to crime* (pp. 134–162). Chicago: University of Chicago Press.

Sampson, R. J., & Laub, J. H. (1993). *Crime in the making: Pathways and turning points through life.* Cambridge, MA: Harvard University Press.

Sanchez-Jankowski, M. (1991). *Islands in the street: Gangs and American urban society.* Berkeley: University of California Press.

Sanders, W. B. (1994) *Gangbangs and drive-bys: Grounded culture and juvenile gang violence.* New York: Aldine de Gruyter.

Short, J. F., Jr., & Strodtbeck, F. L. (1965/1974). *Group process and gang delinquency.* Chicago: University of Chicago Press.

Skolnick, J. (1988). *The social structure of street drug dealing* (BCS Forum). Sacramento: State of California.

Thornberry, T. P., Krohn, M. D., Lizotte, A. J., & Chard-Wierschem, D. (1993). The role of juvenile gangs in facilitating delinquent behavior. *Journal of Research in Crime and Delinquency,* 30(1), 55–87.

Thornberry, T. P., Lizotte, A. J., Krohn, M. D., Farnworth, M., & Jang, S. J. (1994). Delinquent peers, beliefs, and delinquent behavior: A longitudinal test of interactional theory. *Criminology,* 32, 47–84.

Thrasher, F. M. (1963). *The gang: A study of 1,313 gangs in Chicago.* Chicago: University of Chicago Press. (Original work published 1927.)

Vigil, J. D. (1988). *Barrio gangs: Street life and identity in Southern California.* Austin: University of Texas Press.

Yablonsky, L. (1973). *The violent gang.* New York: Penguin. ✦

Section II

Distribution and Structures of Gangs

Chapter 7
Recent Patterns of Gang Problems in the United States

Results From the 1996–2002 National Youth Gang Survey

Arlen Egley Jr., James C. Howell, and Aline K. Major

Until the establishment of the National Youth Gang Center (NYGC), there was almost no valid way to assess the size and seriousness of America's gang problem, despite several surveys that seemed to demonstrate a major increase in street-gang prevalence. Despite the rather loose definition of gangs used in the continuing NYGC surveys over a seven-year period, the resulting data appear to be far superior to any from the earlier works. The proliferation of gangs is the most notable of all changes in the gang arena, and these data derive from a large, nationally representative sample of U.S. jurisdictions. In this chapter, the authors inform us of both the stability and variability of street-gang presence throughout the nation. Further, they illustrate how gang growth and prevalence are related to types of jurisdiction, large and small, urban and rural. Discussion of why gangs exist must account for patterns such as those in this chapter.

Introduction

Three significant changes in America's gang problem over the past 20 years have been noted: a greater degree of lethality as-

sociated with the availability of firearms; a greater amount of diversity in the structure and form of contemporary gangs; and an unprecedented spread of gang problems from large urban areas to many smaller cities and towns, as well as suburban and rural counties—areas atypically associated with gangs (Klein, 2002, p. 243). The wave of gang violence in the early to mid-1990s perhaps best exemplifies the first of these points. And in recent years, the emergence of a "hybrid gang culture"—gangs that do not follow the same rules or methods of operation as their predecessors—continues to redefine the boundaries of the form and behaviors of youth gangs (Howell, Moore, and Egley, 2002; Starbuck, Howell, and Lindquist, 2001).

Klein's third observation, the proliferation of gang problems across the United States, serves as the focal point of this article. While it is generally known that many new localities experienced the emergence of youth gang activity in the past two decades, this fact alone raises a whole new series of questions concerning the extent and pattern of this proliferation. In this chapter we explore the spread of youth gang problems across the United States using data obtained annually from a representative sample of law enforcement agencies from 1996 to 2002. We also discuss findings from previous national-level surveys that have provided a foundation of knowledge for understanding the scope of the current gang problem. The following are the relevant questions that we address:

- How extensive is the current youth gang problem?
- Is the likelihood of gang problems the same across all city sizes and county types?
- Where and how did the presence of gang problems vary in the mid- to late 1990s and early 2000s?
- What are the noticeable patterns of gang-problem emergence across cities?
- What characteristics distinguish jurisdictions that have and have not been persistently affected by gang problems in recent years?
- How many gang members have been identified by law enforcement, and how has this number changed over the years?

Reprinted by permission of Waveland Press, Inc. from Finn-Aage Esbensen, Stephen G. Tibetts, and Larry Gaines (eds.), *American Youth Gangs at the Millennium*, pp. 90–108. Long Grove, IL: Waveland Press, Inc., 2004. All rights reserved.

In addressing these questions, we hope to provide a more concrete and descriptive nationwide portrait of the current youth gang problem and the implication these findings have for the coming years.

Prior National-Level Youth Gang Surveys

National-level surveys measuring the scope of the gang problem were initiated around 30 years ago (see Curry and Decker, 2003, pp. 17–30; Howell, 1994). In this section we review earlier surveys and their continuing importance for current national survey efforts. No doubt the reader will notice that these surveys were conducted by a number of different researchers over intermittent years and with various sampling frames. This is largely due to the fact that various research agendas were the impetus for each different survey. The common thread throughout each, however, was the measurement of the presence and magnitude of gang-related problems across many different localities and communities. Due to the pioneering and sedulous work of this group of researchers, our understanding of the nature and extent of the nation's youth gang problem covers more than a quarter of a century.

The first series of efforts to study the nation's gang problem was undertaken by Walter Miller (1975). Six of the twelve cities selected for his initial study were identified as having a "gang problem" in 1975. Miller (1982) subsequently expanded the sample to include 36 metropolitan areas and revealed the widespread presence of gangs that, judging by media accounts, had seemingly disappeared from the nation's landscape. Based on reports from multiple sources across a wider range of cities, Miller estimated that during the late 1970s there were approximately 2,300 gangs with 98,000 members located in approximately 300 U.S. cities and towns. With the exception of cities in California, Miller noted a positive relationship between city population size and reported gang presence. He also calculated the relative proportion of police arrests in the largest gang-problem cities, estimating that 42 percent of all arrests of male youth for serious and violent crimes and about 23 percent of all homicide arrests were gang members. Because of the pervasiveness and seriousness of gang crime, Miller (1976,

1990) recommended a new federal initiative to systematically gather information on youth gangs nationwide. Miller has continued to compile a list of localities with gang problems, culminating in a recent report that finds that cities experiencing youth gang problems increased nearly tenfold between the 1970s and the late 1990s (Miller, 2001).

The next gang survey, conducted in the early 1980s (Needle and Stapleton, 1983), assessed law enforcement responses to youth gangs in 60 cities with populations over 100,000, of which 27 of them reported gang problems. In finding that the majority of police departments operated without written policies and procedures in dealing with youth gangs and with personnel who have little to no formal training in gang intervention techniques, the study authors offered numerous recommendations for improving police responses to youth gangs. Although it was limited in scope, this study established the need for law enforcement training and technical assistance in dealing with youth gangs.

Subsequent youth gang surveys were considerably broader in scope, beginning with the only national assessment of organized community agency and police efforts to combat gangs (Spergel, 1995; Spergel and Curry, 1990, 1993). This landmark 1988 study began with a universe of 101 cities in which the presence of gangs was suspected. Contacts with police, regarding the presence of gangs and the existence of an organized agency or community response, reduced the number to 74 cities. A total of 254 respondents were surveyed in the 45 cities (and 6 institutional sites) that were classified as "chronic" or "emerging" gang-problem cities. Thirty-five of these jurisdictions reported over 1,400 gangs and 120,500 gang members. Gang programs and strategies were examined in detail in the studied cities. This comprehensive study is best known for the foundation it laid for the most sustained federal gang program, the Comprehensive Gang Prevention, Intervention, and Suppression framework (Spergel, 1995; Spergel and Curry, 1990, 1993) that a number of communities continue to implement.

Klein, Maxson, and colleagues established ongoing contact with a number of law enforcement agencies in the 1980s and 1990s. A 1992 survey of law enforcement personnel in approximately 1,100 cities found that "gang member migration, although widespread, should not be viewed as the major culprit in the nationwide proliferation of gangs" (Maxson, 1998, p. 8). By the mid-1990s, Klein (1995a) concluded in his highly regarded book that there were approximately 9,000 gangs and 400,000 gang members in 800 to 1,100 cities in the United States.

Curry, Ball, and Fox (1994) surveyed police departments in 122 cities (including all 79 with populations over 200,000) in 1992. To be counted as having a "gang" problem, agencies had to "identify the group as a 'gang' that was involved in criminal activity and included youth in its membership" (p. 2). Overall, 110 of these agencies (including 72 of the 79 largest police departments) were identified as having a gang problem. Over 4,800 gangs and 249,000 gang members were reported. Additionally, one agency reported a "posse" problem and another reported a "crew" problem, which the authors argue corresponds to the operational definition of a "gang" problem (p. 10).

Curry and colleagues (Curry, Ball, and Decker, 1996a, 1996b) expanded their survey efforts in 1994 (covering the 1993 calendar year) to include all cities with populations over 150,000 and a random sample of 284 cities with populations between 25,000 and 150,000. Using the same measurement technique as before, 57 percent of these agencies were identified as having a "gang problem." Because this sample was representative of all cities over 25,000, the authors could estimate that over 750 cities had gang problems in 1993. A "conservative" nationwide estimate of over 8,600 gangs and 378,500 gang members was also provided (Curry, Ball, and Decker, 1996b, p. 29).

Three main gang survey developments led to federal support from the Office of Juvenile Justice and Delinquency Prevention for the annual national youth gang surveys of law enforcement that are reported in this chapter. Although it initially was rejected, Miller's (1990) recommendation later stimulated support for a sustained federal youth gang program of research, program development, and survey research. Spergel and Curry's national assessment of gang problems and responses to them increased federal interest in gaining a better under-

standing of problems youth gangs present and possible solutions. Lastly, the success of two surveys by Curry et al. (1994 and 1996b) and the quality of the gang information increased federal officials' confidence in the value of information on youth gangs that could be obtained in surveys of law enforcement agencies.

The 1996–2002 National Youth Gang Survey

Survey Sample

In 1994, the Office of Juvenile Justice and Delinquency Prevention (OJJDP) established the National Youth Gang Center (NYGC) to maintain and contribute to the body of critical knowledge about youth gangs and effective responses to them nationwide. Since 1995, NYGC has conducted the National Youth Gang Survey (NYGS). Taken from a nationally representative sample of law enforcement agencies, the NYGS annually assesses the presence and extent of the youth gang problem in jurisdictions throughout the United States. The 1996–2001 survey sample consisted of 3,018 police and sheriffs' departments. An updated sample of 2,563 agencies, based on newly updated information from the U.S. Census Bureau and the Federal Bureau of Investigation (FBI), was selected for the 2002 survey and will be used in subsequent surveys. Agencies included in the two nationally representative NYGS samples are as follows:

1996–2001 NYGS Sample (Former sample):

- All police departments serving cities with populations of 25,000 or more (n = 1,216).
- All suburban county police and sheriffs' departments (n = 661).
- A randomly selected sample of police departments serving cities with populations between 2,500 and 24,999 (n = 398).
- A randomly selected sample of rural county police and sheriffs' departments (n = 743).

2002 NYGS Sample (Current sample):

- All police departments serving cities with populations of 50,000 or more (n = 627).

- All suburban county police and sheriffs' departments (*n* = 745).
- A randomly selected sample of police departments serving cities with populations between 2,500 and 49,999 (*n* = 699).
- A randomly selected sample of rural county police and sheriffs' departments (*n* = 492).

Sixty-three percent of the agencies in the 2002 NYGS (current) sample were also surveyed from 1996 to 2001, permitting an ongoing longitudinal assessment of gang problems in a large number of jurisdictions. Annual NYGS response rates ranged from 84 to 92 percent across the survey years.

Measurement Issues

One of the most difficult issues encountered in gang research pertains to the definitional dilemma of what constitutes a "gang"—and by extension, a gang member and gang-related incident. A large-scale effort in the late 1980s was unsuccessful in obtaining a consensus among researchers and practitioners for a standardized definition of these concepts (Spergel and Bobrowski, 1989). A similar attempt in the mid-1990s by NYGC, consisting of professionals from local and federal law enforcement agencies, juvenile justice operational and planning agencies, and academia, suffered similar results. In the past ten years, at least 20 states have passed laws explicitly defining "gangs" and "gang members" (Howell, Moore, and Egley, 2002). Some do this to "enhance" or increase the severity of penalties for criminal offenses committed by gang members, while others are more interested in establishing procedures for intelligence gathering. While these codified definitions frequently share commonalities (e.g., identifiable group, pattern of criminal activity), there is also variation in other definitional components. For the purposes of the NYGS, a "youth gang" is defined for the law enforcement agency as:

> A group of youths or young adults in your jurisdiction that you or other responsible persons in your agency or community are willing to identify or classify as a "gang." DO NOT include motorcycle gangs, hate or ideology groups, prison gangs, or other exclusively adult gangs.

Thus, the NYGS measures youth gang activity as an identified problem by interested community agents. This approach is both less restrictive and self-determining, allowing for the observed variation across communities in gang definitions. Across survey years, questionnaire items have examined the characteristics emphasized by law enforcement in defining a gang. Respondents in the 1998 NYGS primarily emphasized involvement in group criminal activity, with varying degrees of emphasis placed on other definitional elements such as having a name, displaying common colors and other symbols, and protecting turf/territory (NYGC, 2000).

Other research has concentrated on evaluating procedures to identify youth gang members. Curry and Decker (2003) argue that the self-nomination technique—asking youth, "Are you now or have you been a gang member?"—is the most powerful and direct measure. To support their contention, the authors point out that support for the self-nomination method has been found across all methodological approaches, including youth surveys, field research, and secondary data analysis of police records. They note that "such convergence across [research] methods is rare indeed" (p. 6). Esbensen, Winfree, He, and Taylor (2001) investigated the impact of using increasingly restrictive definitions of gang membership from a large self-administered survey of middle-school youth and concluded that "the self-nomination technique is a particularly robust measure of gang membership capable of distinguishing gang from nongang youth" (p. 124).

Many law enforcement agencies report relying on self-admission in determining gang membership. In the 2002 NYGS, respondents were provided a list of five commonly used criteria to identify gang membership (e.g., arrested or associates with known gang members, tattoos or other symbols, identified by a reliable source). Sixty-one percent of all gang-problem respondents indicated the most frequently used method (alone or in combination with other factors) by their agency to identify and document individuals as gang members was that "the individual claims to be a gang member." Katz (2003) spent time observing the practices of a midwestern city's gang unit in 1996–97 and found that officers often looked for "other aggravating clues" even though the individual had already met the criteria specified by the department to record them as a gang member. He concludes that "there might be a great deal of underdocumentation that takes place by gang unit officers," cautioning, however, that it is difficult to surmise the extent of this as officers used a "substantial amount of discretion in the collection and documentation of gang-related data" (p. 510–511). In another study, Katz, Webb, and Schaefer (2000) investigated a large, southwestern city's gang-unit file and found that those individuals documented as gang members by the police were more criminally active than a matched sample of nongang youth offenders. The authors conclude these findings demonstrate both the importance of establishing criteria for documenting gang membership and the potential utility of gang intelligence lists.

Thus, law enforcement data represent one methodological avenue for viewing and understanding the nature and extent of local gang problems. Curry, Ball, and Decker (1996b) remind us, however, that a better empirical assessment of the extent of local

gang activity can be made by examining gang-related crime statistics rather than numbers of gangs and gang members. Unfortunately, as they also note, this statistic "is the one that has been most neglected in law enforcement record keeping" (p. 36), reflecting the importance of standardized definitions, recording procedures, and reporting practices.

Survey Findings

Prevalence of Youth Gang Problems Across Jurisdictions. Figure 7.1 displays the percent of city law enforcement agencies reporting youth gang problems by service population size from 1996 to 2002. All city law enforcement agencies with a service population above 250,000 affirmatively reported gang problems across all seven of the survey years. A large majority of city agencies in the next largest population group (i.e., 100,000–249,999) reported gang problems as well. For the remaining two population groups, reports of gang problems declined noticeably from 1996 to 2001. Of all city police departments with a service population above 2,500, over 90 percent serve a population below 50,000. Thus, the

Figure 7.1
City Law Enforcement Reports of Gang Problems, 1996–2002

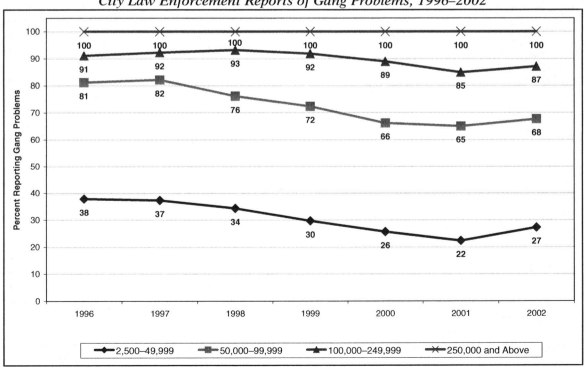

16 percent decline from 1996 to 2001 in reported gang problems for this group of agencies importantly influences the estimated number of jurisdictions with gang problems.

Figure 7.2 displays gang-problem trends for county law enforcement agencies by county type and reveals a high degree of similarity in the shape of their patterns. Nearly 60 percent of the suburban county law enforcement agencies reported gang problems in the first two survey years, and the statistic for this group declined steadily to just over one-third in 2001. For rural counties, around one-fourth reported gang problems in the first two surveys, and just over one in ten have reported gang problems in recent years.

Based on the most recent survey results, it is estimated that youth gangs were active in over 2,300 jurisdictions served by city law enforcement agencies with a service population above 2,500 and over 550 jurisdictions served by county law enforcement agencies in 2002. These findings are comparable to recent survey years (accounting for the assumed margin of error for the randomly sampled groups) and provide preliminary evidence that the overall number of jurisdic-

tions experiencing gang problems in a given year has stabilized. Figure 7.3 displays the more than 1,400 law enforcement agencies in the NYGS in the contiguous 48 states that reported gang problems in one or more years between 1999 and 2001.

In sum, three patterns are notable in the above examination of reported gang problems. First, prevalence rates of youth gang problems remained very high in the largest cities across the United States. All city agencies with a service population above 250,000 reported gang problems in all survey years, and so did an overwhelming majority of city agencies with a service population of 100,000–249,999. Second, and in stark contrast, reports of gang presence steadily declined in counties and smaller cities over initial survey years. For example, over one-third of the city agencies with a service population of 2,500–49,999 reported gang problems in the first three survey years. This number fell to around one in four in the last three survey years. Third, little change in gang-problem prevalence rates over recent survey years is observed for these counties and smaller cities. This apparent reversal in trend is one to closely observe in future NYGC surveys.

Figure 7.2
County Law Enforcement Reports of Gang Problems, 1996–2002

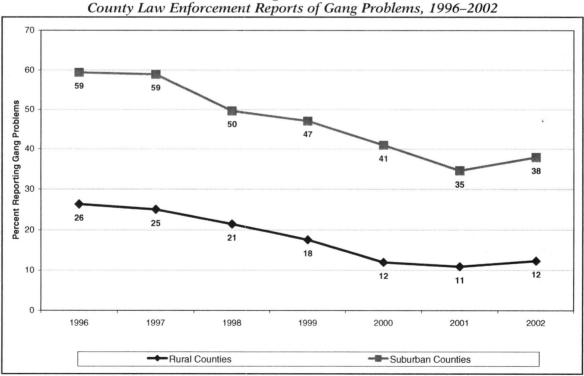

Figure 7.3
Jurisdictions in the Contiguous States Reporting Youth
Gang Problems in One or More Years, 1999–2001

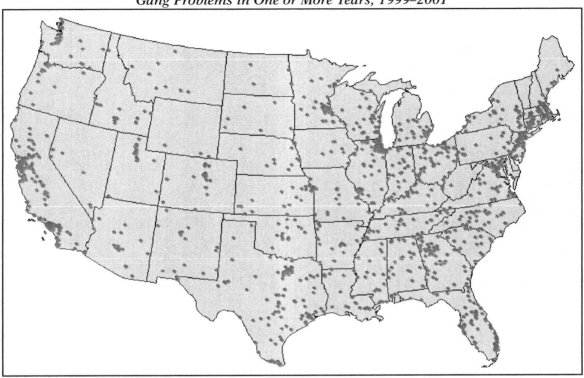

Proliferation of Youth Gang Problems.
Undoubtedly, part of the increase in estimated number of cities, towns, and counties
experiencing gang problems over the past
30 years can be attributed to an increasing
number of areas studied (i.e., breadth of
coverage). In this section, we provide evidence that an equal or greater part of this
increase can also be attributed to the proliferation of gang problems nationwide.

To gain insight into the timing of the
spread of gang problems across U.S. cities,
the 2000 NYGS asked respondents for the
approximate year when their current youth
gang problem began, more simply referred
to as "year of onset." Figure 7.4 shows the
cumulative percent[age] of cities by year of
onset for each of four population groups.
For example, among city law enforcement
with a service population of 50,000–99,999,
the year of gang-problem onset was reported as 2000 or before by 66 percent
(which, being the *total* cumulative percent[age], also reflects the percent[age]
reporting youth gang problems in 2000
for this population group). Comparatively,
nearly 40 percent of this group of agencies

reported both gang problems in 2000 and a
year of onset before 1991, and under 10 percent reported the year of onset before 1983.
Therefore, both the slope of the trajectory
and corresponding time period characterize
the growth of youth gang problems across
these cities.

Cities with larger population sizes (i.e.,
100,000 and above) experienced a much
higher and faster rate and earlier onset of
gang proliferation than all other cities. Approximately one-third of these cities reported gang problems before 1985, and an
additional 50 percent reported an onset of
gang problems in the following ten-year period (i.e., from 1985 to the mid-1990s), the
most sharply observed increase. These
patterns are increasingly less pronounced
across the remaining population groups,
suggesting a cascading pattern of gang proliferation from the larger to smaller populated areas. This is also reflected in the
average year of onset across population
groups, which was 1985 for cities with populations 100,000 and above, 1988 for cities
50,000–99,999, 1990 for cities 25,000–
49,999, and 1992 for cities below 25,000.

Figure 7.4
Patterns of Gang Proliferation in Cities Reporting Gang Activity in 2000

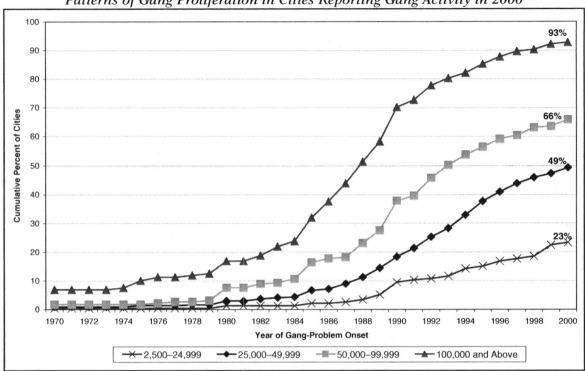

Patterns of Gang Problems Within Jurisdictions. The preceding two sections describe the nation's current gang problem by examining prevalence and proliferation rates across years. However, longitudinal data can offer a more revealing look into the dynamic nature of gang problems by examining within-jurisdiction patterns of gang presence across NYGS years. Data for this analysis pertain to the 1996–2001 NYGS where the same agencies were surveyed annually. One of three patterns are logically possible for each jurisdiction during this six-year period: (1) a persistent gang problem, as indicated by consistent reports of youth gang problems across all survey years; (2) a variable gang problem, as indicated by reported gang problems in at least one survey year and no gang problems in any other year[1]; and (3) absence of gang problems, as indicated by consistent reports of no youth gang problems in the jurisdiction. To examine within-jurisdiction patterns of gang problems, each agency's reporting record of gang presence was inspected and coded.[2]

Figure 7.5 displays gang-problem patterns for city law enforcement agencies by service population size. Within each population group, the percent[age] of agencies that reported persistent and variable gang problems are displayed. Not displayed are the percent[age] of agencies that did not report gang problems in any survey year between 1996 and 2001. For example, for city agencies with service populations between 50,000 and 99,999, over half (58 percent) reported persistent gang problems across survey years, and an additional 33 percent reported variable gang problems. Additionally, this indicates that 91 percent of these cities reported gang problems in at least one year between 1996 and 2001, while the remainder (9 percent) experienced no gang problems. A strong relationship between city population size and gang-problem pattern is clearly noticeable in Figure 7.5. As the size of the population group increases, so does the percent[age] of city agencies that report persistent gang problems. Variable gang problems are observed much more frequently in the smaller population groups. Nearly half of the agencies in the two smallest population groups reported a variable gang problem over the six-year period.

Figure 7.6 displays gang-problem patterns for county law enforcement agencies.

Figure 7.5
Gang-Problem Patterns Reported by City Law Enforcement, 1996–2001

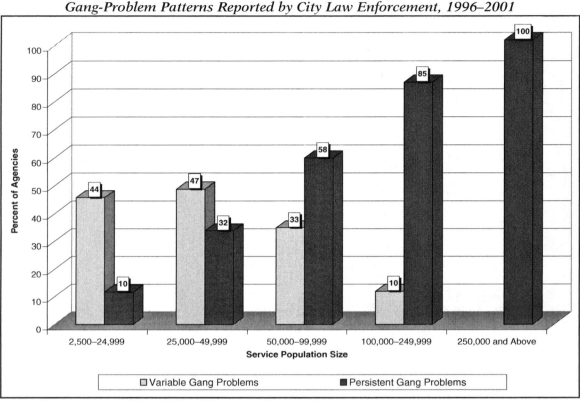

See text for description of "variable" and "persistent" gang problems.

Variable gang problems are more frequently observed in both county types. Forty-seven percent of the suburban counties experienced variable gang problems from 1996 to 2001, and just over one-fourth experienced persistent gang problems. For rural counties, these numbers are 37 percent and 4 percent, respectively.

Figure 7.7 looks more closely at selected characteristics of the city and county agencies that reported a variable gang problem from 1996 to 2001. Remarkably similar features are observed for both agency types. A large majority of agencies in the NYGS sample that reported variable gang problems have a service population below 50,000. Also, a large majority of the agencies reporting variable gang problems report both a relatively recent onset of gang activity and a relatively small number of gang members. These results mirror the comments of one gang researcher: "The bulk of the [gang] proliferation is proliferation of a *relatively small problem*" (Klein, 1995b, p. 233, emphasis added).

Overall, findings from the previous three

sections are consistent with Miller's prediction, based upon his documentation of gang-problem localities over a three-decade period (Miller, 2001), of a possible decreasing trend in the number of localities with gang problems into the late 1990s. Indicative of the cycle of gang proliferation, smaller cities and counties are at greater risk of being affected by gang problems during peak periods of gang activity in the larger areas. Diffusion of the gang culture has been cited as having a "major impact on gang proliferation" (Klein, 1995a, p. 205), along with a growing urban underclass associated with economic restructuring and deindustrialization (Moore, 1998). The cascading pattern of year of gang-problem onset across city sizes presented in Figure 7.4 is notably consistent with these assertions. As the cycle progressed, reports of gang problems began to recede to the larger populated areas, which are characterized by larger numbers of gang members. This cycle highlights the dynamic and sometimes transitory nature of gang problems across smaller jurisdictions. At the time of the 1996

Figure 7.6
Gang-Problem Patterns Reported by County Law Enforcement, 1996–2001

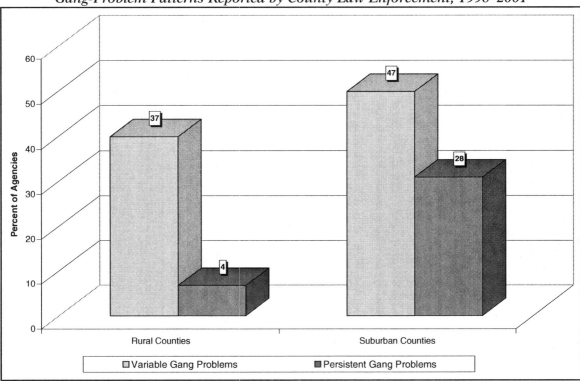

See text for description of "variable" and "persistent" gang problem.

NYGS, prevalence rates of gang problems were the highest observed in NYGS years and, as suggested by the year of gang-problem onset analysis, may have been even greater in the years immediately preceding 1996. Results from the 1996–2002 NYGS are consistent with (1) a relatively stable presence of gang problems across the larger areas, and (2) a recession phase in the cycle of gang proliferation from 1996 to 2001, where many of the more recently affected areas (e.g., smaller cities and counties) contributed only briefly and, comparatively speaking, only minimally to the overall gang problem.

Estimating the Number of Youth Gang Members. Estimating the number of gang members has previously been deemed to be particularly important because, in part, it "reflects individual youths who are either *potential* offenders or victims in gang-related violence" (Curry and Decker, 2003, pp. 28–29, emphasis in original). Research has consistently demonstrated that youth are significantly more criminally involved during periods of active gang membership, particularly in serious and violent offenses

(see, for example, Battin, Hill, Abbott, Catalano, and Hawkins, 1998; Esbensen and Huizinga, 1993; Thornberry, Krohn, Lizotte, Smith, and Tobin, 2003). This finding has been noted as "one of the most robust and consistent observations in criminological research" (Thornberry, 1998, p. 147). In this section we provide nationwide estimates of youth gang members from 1996 to 2002 based on reports from the nationally representative sample of law enforcement agencies in the NYGS.

Figure 7.8 displays "reasonable" estimates[3] of the number of gang members from 1996 through 2002. Approximately 731,500 gang members were estimated to be active in the United States in 2002, an increase of approximately 5 percent from the estimated number in 2001. The percent change in estimated number of gang members from 1996 to 2001 (the largest absolute difference between any two survey years) was –18 percent, while the percent[age] change in the estimated number of gang-problem jurisdictions between these two years was –38 percent. This difference in rates is largely the result of the decline in

Figure 7.7
Selected Characteristics of City and County Agencies
Reporting Variable Gang Problems, 1996–2001

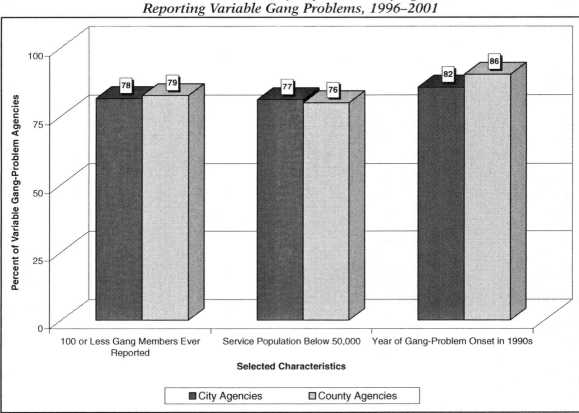

See text for description of "variable" gang problem.

proportion of smaller cities and counties reporting gang problems that also reported comparatively fewer gang members over the survey years from 1996 to 2001.

In 1998, just over 84 percent of all gang members were estimated to be in larger cities (i.e., populations 25,000 and above) and suburban counties, with the remainder in smaller cities (i.e., populations below 25,000) and rural counties. Since that time, this percentage has steadily risen to the point that approximately 90 percent of all gang members were estimated to be active in larger cities and suburban counties in 2001. This is, of course, in large part a product of the decline in number of smaller cities and rural counties reporting gang problems from 1996 to 2001. From 1998 to 2001, these two areas combined reported 43 percent fewer gang members, compared to 5 percent fewer members in larger cities and suburban counties. In fact, the estimated reduction in the *number* of gang members in smaller cities and rural counties over this four-year period is greater than the estimated reduction in the *number* of gang members in larger cities and suburban counties.

Conclusion and Discussion

Results from the 1996 to 2002 NYGS reveal the extensiveness of the current youth gang problem. The latest estimate finds that youth gangs were active in nearly 2,900 law enforcement jurisdictions across the United States in 2002. While the decline in number of areas reporting gang problems might initially appear encouraging, two observations temper this finding. First, among those areas accounting for the overwhelming majority of this decline (i.e., smaller cities and rural counties), fewer gang members were reported and few of these agencies experienced high levels of gang-related violence during their gang-problem periods (National Youth Gang Center, forthcoming). Most of these areas, then, contributed only

Figure 7.8
Estimated Number of Gang Members Based on Reports
by City and County Law Enforcement, 1996–2002

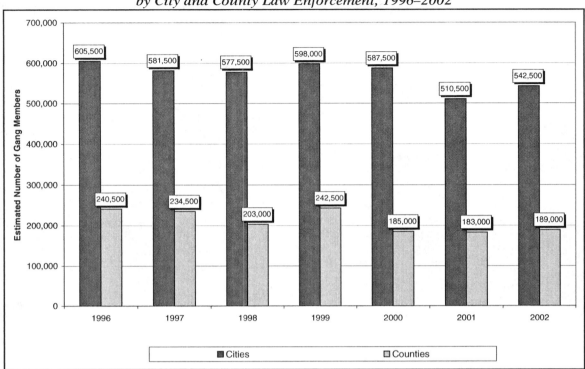

minimally to the overall gang problem. Second, in more recent surveys (i.e., 2000 to 2002), the overall estimated number of jurisdictions experiencing gang problems in a given year has more or less stabilized. These findings are reflective of the cyclical pattern of gang activity (Klein, 1995b). These cycles occur at multiple levels—within regions, cities, and neighborhoods—and all contribute to the portrait of our nation's gang problem.

Despite the variability of gang problems across the smaller populated areas in the past decade, the size of gang membership has remained formidable. In any given year of the NYGS, over one-half million gang members are estimated to be active in U.S. cities alone. These numbers are comparable to those found by Curry and colleagues (1994) almost a decade ago when gang problems, especially gang violence, were rising to unprecedented heights. They referred to the large number of gang members identified by law enforcement as "a sobering national statistic" (p. 36), a description that is no less accurate today.

In referring to the seeming re-emergence of gang activity in the 1970s, Miller (1982) remarked, "There is no new wave, but rather

a continuation of an old wave—a wave that strikes with great fury at one part of the shore, recedes, strikes again at another, ebbs away, strikes once more, and so on" (p. 7). His words were prophetic of the gang problem in the 1990s. How prophetic they will be in this decade will largely be the result of our efforts to proactively respond to our current youth gang problem.

Notes

1. This category comprises agencies that report patterns consistent with an emerging or desisting gang problem and agencies who report gang problems intermittently across survey years.

2. In order to increase confidence in properly interpreting each jurisdiction's pattern, certain classification restrictions were imposed. First, the agency must have responded to three or more surveys, and second, it must have responded to a recent survey (i.e., 2000 or 2001 NYGS). Ninety-two percent (n = 2,766) of the survey sample agencies were included in the analysis under these restrictions.

3. In previous national gang surveys of law enforcement, Curry, Ball, and Decker (1996b, p. 31) provide "more 'reasonable' estimates"

by using an estimation procedure which substitutes the 5 percent trimmed mean (a more robust measure of central tendency) for missing values. The estimates provided in Figure 7.8 are based on this approach, similarly providing "reasonable" estimates.

References

Battin, S. R., Hill, K. G., Abbott, R. D., Catalano, R. F., and Hawkins, J. D. (1998). The contribution of gang membership to delinquency beyond delinquent friends. *Criminology*, 36(1), 93–115.

Curry, G. D., Ball, R. A., and Decker, S. H. (1996a). *Update on Gang Crime and Law Enforcement Recordkeeping: Report of the 1994 NIJ Extended National Assessment Survey of Law Enforcement Anti-Gang Information Resources*. Research Report. National Criminal Justice Reference Service. Washington, DC: U.S. Department of Justice.

———. (1996b). Estimating the national scope of gang crime from law enforcement data. In C. R. Huff (Ed.), *Gangs in America* (pp. 21–36). Thousand Oaks, CA: Sage.

Curry, G. D., Ball, R. A., and Fox, R. J. (1994). Gang crime and law enforcement recordkeeping. *Research in Brief*. Washington, DC: U.S. Department of Justice, National Institute of Justice.

Curry, G. D., and Decker, S. H. (2003). *Confronting Gangs: Crime and Community* (2nd ed.). Los Angeles, CA: Roxbury.

Esbensen, F., and Huizinga, D. (1993). Gangs, drugs, and delinquency in a survey of urban youth. *Criminology*, 31(4), 565–589.

Esbensen, F., Winfree, L. T., He, N., and Taylor, T. J. (2001). Youth gangs and definitional issues: When is a gang a gang, and why does it matter? *Crime and Delinquency*, 47(1), 105–130.

Howell, J. C. (1994). Recent gang research: Programs and policy implications. *Crime and Delinquency*, 40(4), 495–515.

Howell, J. C., Moore, J. P., and Egley, A. Jr. (2002). The changing boundaries of youth gangs. In C. R. Huff (Ed.), *Gangs in America III* (pp. 3–18). Thousand Oaks, CA: Sage Publications.

Katz, C. M. (2003). Issues in the production and dissemination of gang statistics: An ethnographic study of a large midwestern gang unit. *Crime and Delinquency*, 49(3), 485–516.

Katz, C. M., Webb, V. J., and Schaefer, D. R. (2000). The validity of police gang intelligence lists: Examining differences in delinquency between documented gang members and nondocumented delinquent youth. *Police Quarterly*, 3(4), 413–437.

Klein, M. W. (1995a). *The American Street Gang*. New York: Oxford University Press.

———. (1995b). Street gang cycles. In J. Q. Wilson and J. Petersilia (Eds.), *Crime* (pp. 217–236). San Francisco, CA: Institute for Contemporary Studies Press.

———. (2002). Street gangs: A cross-national perspective. In C. R. Huff (Ed.), *Gangs in America III* (pp. 237–254). Thousand Oaks, CA: Sage Publications.

Maxson, C. L. (1998). Gang members on the move. *Juvenile Justice Bulletin*. Youth Gang Series. Washington, DC: U.S. Department of Justice, Office of Juvenile Justice and Delinquency Prevention.

Miller, W. B. (1975). *Violence by Youth Gangs and Youth Groups as a Crime Problem in Major American Cities*. Washington, DC: U.S. Department of Justice, Office of Juvenile Justice and Delinquency Prevention.

———. (1976). New federal initiatives re: serious collective youth crime. In *Hearings Before the Subcommittee to Investigate Juvenile Delinquency of the Committee on the Judiciary* (pp. 262–66), United States Senate, 95th Cong. 2d Sess., April 10 and 12.

———. (1982) (Reissued in 1992). *Crime by Youth Gangs and Groups in the United States*. Washington, DC: U.S. Department of Justice, Office of Juvenile Justice and Delinquency Prevention.

———. (1990). Why the United States has failed to solve its youth gang problem. In C. R. Huff (Ed.), *Gangs in America* (pp. 263–287). Newbury Park, CA: Sage.

———. (2001). *The Growth of Youth Gang Problems in the United States: 1970–1998*. Washington, DC: U.S. Department of Justice, Office of Juvenile Justice and Delinquency Prevention.

Moore, J. W. (1998). Understanding youth street gangs: Economic restructuring and the urban underclass. In M. W. Watts (Ed.), *Cross-Cultural Perspectives on Youth and Violence* (pp. 65–78). Stamford, CT: Jai Press.

National Youth Gang Center. (2000) *1998 National Youth Gang Survey*. Washington, DC: Office of Juvenile Justice and Delinquency Prevention.

National Youth Gang Center. (forthcoming). *National Youth Gang Survey: 1999–2001. Summary Report*. Tallahassee, FL: National Youth Gang Center.

Needle, J., and Stapleton, W. V. (1983). *Police Handling of Youth Gangs*. Washington, DC: U.S. Department of Justice, Office of Juvenile Justice and Delinquency Prevention.

Spergel, I. A. (1995). *The Youth Gang Problem*. New York, NY: Oxford University Press.

Spergel, I. A., and Bobrowski, L. (1989). *Minutes from the "Law Enforcement Youth Gang Definitional Conference: September 25, 1989."* Rockville, MD: Juvenile Justice Clearinghouse.

Spergel, I. A., and Curry, G. D. (1990). Strategies and perceived agency effectiveness in dealing with the youth gang problem. In C. R. Huff (Ed.), *Gangs in America* (pp. 288–309). Newbury Park, CA: Sage.

———. (1993). The National Youth Gang Survey: A research and development process. In A. Goldstein and C. R. Huff (Eds.), *The Gang Intervention Handbook* (pp. 359–400). Champaign, IL: Research Press.

Starbuck, D., Howell, J. C., and Lindquist, D. J. (2001). Hybrid and other modern gangs. *Juvenile Justice Bulletin.* Youth Gang Series. Washington, DC: U.S. Department of Justice, Office of Juvenile Justice and Delinquency Prevention.

Thornberry, T. P. (1998). Membership in youth gangs and involvement in serious and violent offending. In R. Loeber and D. P. Farrington (Eds.), *Serious and Violent Juvenile Offenders: Risk Factors and Successful Interventions* (pp. 147–166). Thousand Oaks, CA: Sage.

Thornberry, T. P., Krohn, M. D., Lizotte, A. J., Smith, C. A., and Tobin, K. (2003). *Gangs and Delinquency in Developmental Perspective.* New York, NY: Cambridge University Press. ✦

Chapter 8
The Evolution of Street Gangs

An Examination of Form and Variation

Deborah Lamm Weisel

"The" street gang doesn't exist, as the author of this chapter demonstrates. There are demonstrable types of street gangs, and even these can evolve from one form to another. Sometimes they merge, and sometimes they splinter. The stereotypic, media-driven image of large, highly organized street gangs akin to adult organized crime cartels are by far the exception. The author describes different gang types and their characteristics and suggests ways in which gang control programs need to take into account the differences between gang types.

Street gangs continue to be a pervasive problem in America's cities. They contribute to high rates of violent crime, instill fear in citizens, and engage in a range of troublesome behavior, from vandalism and graffiti to drug dealing and property crime. Problems related to gangs—especially those that are more organized, engage in serious criminal activity, or are violent—are a major concern. Although gangs have been around since at least the beginning of the 20th century, it is plausible that at least some of these organizations are changing, developing into criminal enterprises that may be similar in structure and criminal activity to traditional organized crime.

Much of the evidence that gangs may be metamorphosing into organized-crime-like enterprises is anecdotal, suggested by high-

Reprinted from: Winifred L. Reed and Scott H. Decker (eds.), *Responding to Gangs: Evaluation and Research*, pp. 25–65. Washington, DC: U.S. Department of Justice, National Institute of Justice, July 2002, NCJ 190351.

profile prosecutions, media coverage, or the actions of law enforcement agencies. Cases such as the 1987 conviction of members of Chicago's El Rukns on terrorism charges, which linked that gang with Libya's Moammar Gadhafi, raised concerns about the seriousness and possible transformation of contemporary gangs. Other high-profile cases, in which Federal RICO (Racketeer Influenced and Corrupt Organizations Act) charges were used to convict gang members, reinforced these concerns. Indeed, the Federal response to gangs bolstered the perception that gangs were becoming highly organized criminal enterprises. In 1991, the FBI created Operation Safe Streets, a program in which the bureau's 52 field offices participate in a series of multi-agency task forces targeting gangs and violent crime (Freeh 1999), in which 300 agents were reassigned from counterintelligence to violent crime investigations. The media coverage of and political reaction to gang violence contributed to perceptions that the gang problem was becoming increasingly serious (Jackson and Rudman 1993; Zatz 1987; McCorkle and Miethe 1998).

As a result of widespread evidence of rising gang violence and the incursion of gangs into middle America, numerous questions have been raised about gangs. In the 1990s, many gangs were widely described as rather disorganized groups (Klein 1995a; Spergel 1995). As Thrasher (1963 [1927]) pointed out, however, "under favorable conditions," gangs can undergo a "natural evolution" from a loosely organized group into a mature form.[1] How does this occur? As gangs become more prevalent, do they become more highly organized, taking on the features of formal organizations? Do gangs naturally become larger and develop greater labor and criminal specialization? While a large body of literature on organizational evolution suggests that successful organizations become larger and more formally organized over time (see, for example, Simmel 1902–3; Starbuck 1965; Greiner 1972; Kimberly, Miles, and Associates 1980; Staw and Cummings 1990), scant attention has been paid to the ways in which gangs change over time. These and other questions shaped this inquiry into the form and evolution of contemporary gangs.

This study was conducted to generate information about the different types of gangs and to document the changes occurring in them over time. The first part of the study was designed to identify and describe the different types of gangs through police sources, focusing on distinctions between the typical gang and the more serious gangs in a jurisdiction—violent gangs, drug-dealing gangs, and entrepreneurial or money-making gangs. The second part of this study was designed to examine highly organized gangs to determine how they are organized and shed light on their evolution over time.

Approach to Research

Two methods of research were used—a nationwide mail survey of police agencies, conducted in 1995, and structured, in-person interviews with gang members in four gangs in two cities, conducted in 1996 and 1997.

The aim of the survey, administered to 385 large municipal police agencies, was to identify the various types of gangs and highlight distinctions among them by organizational characteristics, demographic composition, criminal activities, and other factors. The survey drew from Fagan's (1989) typology of gangs: violent, drug-dealing, entrepreneurial, delinquent, or social—a typology based predominantly on the behavior of gang members.[2] Also examined were the evolution of gangs over time, including changing patterns of leadership, organizational characteristics, and gang duration.

In the field portion of the study, four highly organized criminal gangs in Chicago and San Diego were examined. "Organized" gangs are the exception, not the rule, among the universe of gangs in the United States. In the fieldwork, the organizational structure of these gangs was investigated and documented and changes in these gangs over time were identified, including their transformation or transition into groups or organizations resembling traditional organized crime groups. Differences and similarities between gangs within and across the two cities were highlighted.

By focusing on the most serious or organized gangs within jurisdictions, this study, in effect, ignores the most common or typical gangs. These more typical or prevalent gangs are no less important than the more organized gangs, and may be more troublesome for communities on a day-to-day

basis. Yet this research sought to understand how serious gangs operated and the extent to which typical gangs develop or evolve into more serious or mature gangs over time. Concentrating on a particular type of gang made it possible to gather specific information about individual gangs rather than being limited to collecting general information about a broader range of gangs. By focusing on the "most organized" gangs, the research team was able to home in on characteristics of specific gangs and examine how they have evolved in recent years. As Blau and Scott (1962: 224) note, large organizations did "not spring into existence full-blown but develop[ed] out of simpler ones." An examination of these mature gangs may therefore provide unique insight into the effect of organizational processes on an important subset of contemporary gangs. Thus, although an examination of four gangs limits the generalizability of findings to all gangs, the greater depth of the investigation makes it possible to arrive at reasoned judgments about the extent of organization likely among other, less organized gangs. In addition, by examining the dynamics of highly organized gangs, the study lays the groundwork for a reexamination of how law enforcement monitors and responds to criminal gangs and other criminal groups.

The mail survey was distributed to all law enforcement agencies serving populations of 100,000 or more and to a randomly selected third of all agencies serving populations between 50,000 and 100,000.[3] Responses were obtained from 82 percent of agencies serving large populations and 57 percent of agencies serving small populations—a total of 286 agencies.[4] This number represented 74 percent of all agencies surveyed.

Two cities—Chicago and San Diego—were selected for the field portion of the study. On their face, these two cities and their gang problems were quite different. Chicago, with a population of nearly 3 million, reported an estimated 130 gangs and 60,000 gang members in 1997.[5] Gangs have existed in Chicago since at least the beginning of the last century. In stark contrast, street gangs are a much more recent phenomenon in San Diego, although the roots of the city's gangs in its Latino car clubs date to the 1950s (see, for example, Pennell et al. 1994). San Diego had an estimated 65 gangs and nearly 5,000 gang members in 1997. The two cities also vary in demographics, economic conditions, urban geography, and in other important ways. In Klein's (1995a) terms, Chicago can be characterized as a "chronic" gang city, while San Diego is considered an "emerging" gang city. Gang crime has been estimated as linked to more than 50 percent of crime in Chicago, while reported gang involvement in crime is much lower in San Diego (National Drug Intelligence Center 1998). Indeed, the two cities were selected precisely because of these differences as well as the presumed differences in the nature and characteristics of their gangs.

Two gangs in each city were selected for study—a Hispanic and a black gang in each. The Black Gangster Disciples (BGDs) and the Latin Kings were selected in Chicago, and the Logan Calle Treinta/Red Steps and Lincoln Park Piru/Syndo Mob gangs in San Diego.[6] Like their home cities, the gangs also varied. The BGDs are one of the largest and most well-established gangs in the country. With an estimated membership of 10,000 to 30,000, this gang has been heavily involved in drug trafficking. It was established about 1974, although its roots are in the 1960s. The BGDs have been remarkably tenacious despite the conviction and death of key leaders. In the 1990s, they formed a prosocial group called Growth and Development, which shares the same initials as the gang, to further educational and economic objectives. The Latin Kings, with 3,000 to 15,000 members, are also an extremely large gang. This gang was established in the 1960s or 1970s, but its roots go back to the 1940s.

In San Diego, the gang known as Syndo Mob was a set of Lincoln Park Piru, a predominantly black gang formed in the early 1980s with an initial membership of 12 people. The organization was heavily involved in drug trafficking, but some 26 members were indicted on Federal charges, and by the late 1980s its ranks had been decimated. In the mid-1990s, the gang had approximately 165 members. In contrast to Syndo, the Logan gang factions of Calle Treinta and Red Steps are Hispanic. The roots of the Logan gang go back to the 1940s, while Calle Treinta and Red Steps were both established in the mid-1970s. Each set has approximately 200 members.

The gang members interviewed for this study were identified through probation and prison sources in each city. Researchers sought to identify gang members who were more intensively involved with the gang and hence presumably more knowledgeable about its organization and activities. Gang members were asked to participate in a semi-structured interview, assured of confidentiality, and paid $20 for participating. A total of 85 gang members were interviewed—26 Black Gangster Disciples, 18 Latin Kings, 20 from the Logan factions, and 21 from the Syndo Mob. Of the gang members interviewed, 61 percent (52) were contacted through the local probation department and the remainder were identified through prison records. The sample was opportunistic and is in no way random or representative.

Among the research issues this study examined were the nature of the organizational structure and criminal activity of the specific gangs and gang types. The study sought to determine the ways in which criminal gangs may be organizationally similar to traditional crime groups. The types of criminal activity in which these gangs engage and some of the organizational characteristics of these gangs were also examined.

Examining gangs both from the police perspective and from within the gang itself made it possible to compare and contrast these two (presumably quite divergent) points of view. Because police are concerned primarily with criminal activity, in many jurisdictions they tend to concentrate their attention on the most serious gangs and the most serious offenders in those gangs. Nonetheless, because local police deal with a wide range of behavior, from disorder, vandalism, and loitering to driveby shootings and drug dealing, they have a broad perspective on gang behavior.[7] In contrast, gang members tend to view their gang from a different perspective, focusing more on their gang's friendship networks than on its criminal activity.

The Police Perspective

Police agencies surveyed in this study were able to identify the various types of gangs that coexist in their communities and how these gangs differed in some important ways. When asked to categorize the most typical gang in their jurisdiction, police responded that the delinquent gang is most common. Forty-six percent of police respondents said that the typical gang in their jurisdiction is a delinquent gang consisting primarily of juveniles who engage in vandalism and other delinquent behavior, or a more socially oriented or "party" gang. Twenty-six percent of respondents reported drug-dealing gangs (or other entrepreneurial gangs) as the most typical in their jurisdiction, whereas 28 percent reported violent gangs as most typical.[8]

Overall, more police respondents described the typical gang in their jurisdiction as a loose-knit organization (45 percent) with no formal structure (47 percent), territorial (50 percent), and primarily oriented toward criminal purposes (60 percent). Respondents were divided in their view of the leadership structure of the typical gang: 30 percent said that their typical gang had no formal leadership, whereas 37 percent reported formal leadership as a component of the typical gang.

Police see important regional differences in gang structure and activities. As expected, the larger cities typically have more gangs, larger gangs, and gangs that have been in existence for longer periods of time. Consistent with that observation, these cities also tend to have gangs that are more involved in serious criminal activity, are more highly organized, and have a more identifiable leadership structure. Delinquent gangs, more common in smaller cities, tend to be more loosely organized, with ephemeral leadership; these gangs are newer and lack the historic roots of gangs established generations ago. Delinquent gangs were reported as most typical among Southeast and Midwest respondents (by 56 and 54 percent, respectively). In the Western States, violent gangs were most common, whereas income-generating gangs (including drug-dealing gangs) were reported most commonly in the Northeast (see Table 8.1). Despite the predominance of gang type by region, large numbers of respondents reported other types of gangs in the region. For example, 35 percent of respondents in the Northeast and 42 percent of respondents in the West reported delinquent gangs as most typical.

The distribution of number of gangs within jurisdictions was consistent with the findings for types of typical gang by size of jurisdiction; violent gangs were identified less frequently in small cities, and delinquent gangs were identified most frequently. In cities with populations of 100,000 or less, 13 percent of respondents classified their typical gang as violent while 66 percent of respondents in these cities classified their typical gang as delinquent. In large cities (with populations of 200,000 or more), 44 percent of respondents classified their typical gang as violent. Yet even a large proportion of respondents from large cities—nearly one-third (31 percent)—reported delinquent gangs as their most typical gang.

Police were asked a series of questions about the structure of more serious gangs in each jurisdiction—the violent, drug-dealing, and entrepreneurial gangs. Police respondents most often described serious gangs as lacking a clear or hierarchical organizational structure: More than half of respondents reported that their violent gangs and drug-dealing gangs (51 and 56 percent, respectively) had no clear organizational structure. A similar number reported that violent and drug-dealing gangs had no clear leadership. Entrepreneurial gangs were the type of gang the police viewed as most likely to feature a hierarchy: 36 percent said that entrepreneurial gangs in their jurisdictions had an organizational structure, and 41 percent said that these gangs had a clearly identifiable leadership.

Criminal Activity of Gangs

Klein's observations (1995a) about street gangs and the Youth Gang Survey's findings about youth gangs (Office of Juvenile Justice and Delinquency Prevention 1999) were confirmed by police, who reported a great deal of criminal versatility among their serious gangs.[9] Assaults, crack cocaine sales,

Table 8.1
Type of Typical Gang, by Region

Region	Violent Gangs (n = 132)	Income-Generating Gangs* (n = 74)	Delinquent Gangs (n = 80)
Northeast	11%	54%	35%
Southeast	18	26	56
Midwest	14	33	54
West	45	13	42
Total	28	26	46

* Includes drug-dealing gangs.
Source: Survey of police, 1995.

g.. iti, intimidation, vandalism, violence as a means of discipline, and violence as a means of retaliation were the most common criminal activities of gangs as reported by police respondents.[10] Each gang type tended to favor certain sorts of crimes. For example, entrepreneurial gangs were reported to have the highest involvement in motor vehicle theft and theft in general, whereas violent gangs had the highest involvement in assault, intimidation, graffiti, and vandalism. As expected, drug-dealing gangs were the most involved in selling crack, powder cocaine, marijuana, and other drugs, according to the police.

Yet police reported that most gangs, regardless of type, participated in many different types of crime (see Table 8.2). For example, entrepreneurial gangs frequently also sell crack cocaine, with 39 percent of police respondents reporting that these gangs often or very often engage in such activity. Similarly, violent gangs frequently commit burglary, with 36 percent of police respondents reporting high levels of participation. Police reported that all gang types mark their territories with graffiti, although the highest level of participation was associated with violent gangs (67 percent of respondents). Although drug-dealing is featured prominently in police estimates of gang activity, only one type of gang—drug-

dealing gangs—engages predominantly in this activity.

The breadth of criminal activity identified within the various gang types suggests that while police may characterize gangs as concentrating on a specific type of crime (such as drug dealing), gangs as criminal organizations (and their members) have great criminal versatility, participating in a range of crimes rather than specializing in a few crime types. Police responses in this study indicated a clear recognition of this criminal versatility.

From the police perspective, serious gangs are changing over time in ways that create more problems for police and the community: 78 percent of police respondents said serious gangs had grown larger in the past 3 years, while 72 percent said serious gangs had become more violent during that period. (The term "serious gang" combines gangs identified by respondents as violent, drug-dealing, and entrepreneurial gangs.) Police respondents said that serious gangs had grown larger in the past 3 years, both in size and in geographic coverage. Some of the growth had occurred through retention of older members who failed to leave the gang, effectively increasing the gang's size. Fifty-four percent of police respondents reported that the average age of members of serious gangs had increased.

Table 8.2
Criminal Activity, by Gang Type

	Percent of Police Who Report That Violent Gangs Commit the Offense Very Often or Often (n = 223)	Percent of Police Who Report That Drug-Dealing Gangs Commit the Offense Very Often or Often (n = 148)	Percent of Police Who Report That Entrepreneurial Gangs Commit the Offense Very Often or Often (n = 75)
Motor Vehicle Theft	25	25	44
Arson	1	1	1
Assault	87	69	57
Burglary	36	25	37
Driveby Shooting	42	49	32
Crack Sale	55	80	39
Powder Cocaine Sale	23	46	29
Marijuana Sale	35	54	33
Other Drug Sale	17	26	25
Graffiti	67	50	38
Home Invasion	10	11	27
Intimidation	81	72	74
Rape	7	4	8
Robbery	33	30	36
Shooting	37	41	38
Theft	49	37	52
Vandalism	57	38	37

Note: Reflects aggregation of police estimates of participation in criminal activity by a gang of that type in the jurisdiction.

Gangs had also expanded geographically over the past 3 years: 53 percent of police respondents said serious gangs had migrated into their community, and 43 percent reported that gangs in their city had expanded to other jurisdictions, including suburban communities. Serious gangs are also causing more problems for police, evolving into organizations that have some features of traditional organized crime. Seventy-two percent of police respondents reported that in the past 3 years serious gangs were using more sophisticated weapons, and 46 percent reported that gangs had developed links with other crime groups. A total of 19 percent of police respondents in the past 3 years said that gangs were committing more sophisticated crime, 17 percent reported that they were using more sophisticated technology, and 16 percent said they had acquired legitimate businesses.

Summary of Survey Findings

Police respondents portrayed a picture of gangs that reflected recognition of a wide array of sizes, organizational structures, and activities. Rather than characterizing all gangs in much the same way, police drew clear distinctions among different gangs and among different types of gangs in their jurisdictions. Notably, most police respondents did not appear to stereotype serious gangs as highly organized or highly specialized.

For this study, information from the police provided a context for examining the organizational evolution of serious gangs from a different perspective—through the eyes of gang members. Because of their institutional objectives, police tend to look at gangs from the perspective of their criminal behavior; examining gang structure, leadership, and noncriminal gang activities are of secondary importance. Yet understanding how gangs emerge, grow, and evolve over time has substantial implications for police in developing effective strategies in response to the gang problem.

The Perspective of Gang Members

In the second part of this study, the nature of four gangs and their changes over time were examined from the perspective of gang members. The gangs were the Syndo Mob/Lincoln Park Piru and Calle Treinta/Red Steps in San Diego and the Black Gang-

ster Disciples and Latin Kings in Cl Members of two of the gangs described their gang and its operations as disorganized. By measures of formal organization, two of the four gangs were found to be highly organized, but only one could be characterized as exhibiting features of traditional organized crime.

The gangs were examined with a view to determining whether they exhibited the characteristics of formal organizations or bureaucratic structures, including leadership, role differentiation, participation in formal meetings, compliance with formal rules and discipline, specialization, and goal orientation.[11] The two Chicago gangs were higher on every measure of organization than those in San Diego. Both Chicago gangs featured more formal and distinctive roles of leadership, more explicit (and even written) rules and clearer consequences for breaking them, more routinely held and purposeful meetings, and the collection of dues. Only in the Black Gangster Disciples were there high levels of relationships with neighborhood businesses (including ownership and control of these businesses), relationships with gangs in other cities across the country, formal contacts with prison gangs, and involvement in political activities. These features are also characteristic of organized crime.

Although some law enforcement agencies, such as the FBI, would characterize San Diego's Latin Kings as highly organized . . . , the gang members interviewed did not uniformly support that view. Some Latin Kings described some features of formal organizations, but most did not. This inconsistency between the study findings and the perspective of Federal law enforcement agencies is not unexpected. The FBI's focus is on economic enterprise where there is gang leadership; this view may exaggerate the role of older or more crime-involved gang members. Although leaders, adult members, and heavy crime involvement may be present within the gang, these features are unlikely to characterize the gang as a whole.

Unlike the Chicago gangs, the gangs examined in San Diego featured little formal leadership, and were described by the gang members interviewed as primarily friendship and kinship networks rather than criminal enterprises. Gangs in Chicago also included these traits of friendship and brotherhood, but they were subordinate to the objectives of economic opportunity and protection.

Many of the organizational differences between Chicago and San Diego gangs may be attributable to the vastly different size of the gangs and the respective gang population. Although Chicago is about twice as large as San Diego in population, it has nearly 12 times more gang members. Of the gangs studied, the largest Chicago gang is approximately 25 times larger than either San Diego gang. Even by the most conservative estimates of the number of BGD members, this exponential difference in size likely contributes to much of the organizational characteristics.

Criminal Activity of Gangs

Like the police respondents, gang members in both cities reported that their gang is extensively involved in a wide range of criminal activity. Indeed, gang members reported much greater participation of their gang in specific criminal activities than police attributed to specific serious gangs. In the interviews, gang members reported about two to three times as much criminal activity as did police.

The wide variety of criminal activity reported by gang members indicates little specialization of the gang as a criminal enterprise (see Table 8.3). Again, this finding is consistent with Klein's (1995a) depiction of gangs as criminally versatile. Assaults and drug sales were the activity most often reported, but most gang members said that their gangs were involved in

almost every criminal activity. In fact, the only exception was the Latin Kings' involvement in shootings: Only for this crime did less than a majority indicate their gang was involved.

Although the San Diego gangs were less formally organized, the members interviewed reported levels of criminal behavior as high as those reported by the Chicago gang members. In fact, for all but three crimes, gang members from San Diego reported even higher gang participation than Chicago gangs. Gang members from the two cities reported similar gang participation rates in assaults, driveby shootings, and crack sales.

The high levels of participation in a wide range of criminal behavior by all four gangs suggests that these gangs can be considered criminal generalists. Indeed, according to organizational theory, organizations operating in highly volatile environments are much more likely to be generalists than specialists (Katz and Kahn 1966; Meyer 1978). Generalist organizations can adapt more quickly to changing conditions and are more likely to survive than specialists because the latter must learn a new set of complex skills to create a new specialty (or "niche") under changing conditions. While organizational specialization may be sustained under conditions of short-term volatility, it will not be useful in the continuously volatile gang environment (Katz and Kahn 1966), in which there is ongoing competition with other gangs and a presumed high level of attention from police and other criminal justice organizations.[12] Such en-

Table 8.3
Gang Participation in Criminal Activity, by City and Crime

	Chicago		San Diego	
Crime	BGDs (n = 26)	Latin Kings (n = 18)	Calle Treinta/Red Steps (n = 20)	Lincoln Park/Syndo Mob (n = 21)
Assault	96%	94%	95%	95%
Auto Theft	69	77	85	86
Burglary	73	65	75	95
Driveby Shooting	84	94	75	100
Crack Sale	85	53	70	100
Cocaine Sale	89	75	85	86
Marijuana Sale	85	94	95	95
Graffiti	65	88	80	91
Robbery	77	82	80	91
Shooting	81	42	95	91
Theft	65	88	85	91
Vandalism	65	77	80	86

vironmental volatility would likely discourage specialization both within and among gangs.

Organizations can also be classified by the extent of specialization of their individual members. Like the gangs they belonged to, the members of all four gangs studied reported participating in a wide range of criminal activities, from vandalism to drug sales (see Table 8.4). When *group* criminal activities were compared with *individual* criminal activities (Tables 8.3 and 8.4), it was found that gang members participated substantially less in some of the gang's criminal activities than did the gang itself. This finding could reflect a respondent's reluctance to identify all of his individual criminal behavior,[13] but it also suggests that there are criminal activities in which some gang members participate but others do not.

All gang members reported participating in a wide range of criminal activities. A majority of all gang members reported that they had engaged in assaults (74 percent) and sold marijuana (68 percent). Nearly half had engaged in motor vehicle theft, theft, burglary, and vandalism.

The differences between the two cities in gang *member* participation in criminal activity were consistent with the differences in *gang* participation. Gang members in San Diego reported greater individual participation in almost all 11 crime types than did Chicago gang members. A large majority (90 percent) of San Diego gang members reported individual involvement in assault. San Diego gang members also reported greater involvement in assault and marijuana sales than gang members in Chicago.

When members' responses from each city were combined, it was found that gang members in Chicago were more involved in cocaine sales and shootings than were gang members from San Diego. Gangs in the two cities reported similar rates of involvement in motor vehicle theft.

The breadth of criminal activities reported by individuals helps confirm the notion that most gang members are criminal generalists much like the gangs to which they belong. Just as generalist organizations adapt more quickly to changing environmental conditions, generalist gang members are inherently easier to replace than specialists. Because they report involvement in fewer types of crime, the Chicago gangs and their members appear to be slightly more specialized than the San Diego gangs and gang members.

Goal Orientation

Centrality of goals is a key and defining feature of formal organization (Parsons 1987; Weber 1947; Blau and Scott 1962; Katz and Kahn 1966; Stinchcombe 1965; Lippitt 1982). Organizations are established to attain certain goals and are structured to maximize their attainment. It is widely recognized, however, that organizational goals may be vague, changing, numerous, contradictory, and not always closely linked with the organization's day-to-day activities. In some forms of organization, the goals of individuals and those of the organization are consistent, and the former may be thoroughly integrated into the latter (Popielarz and McPherson 1995; Scott 1993).

Among the features of formal organiza-

Table 8.4
Individual Participation by Gang Members in Criminal Activity, by City and Crime

| Crime | Chicago | | San Diego | |
	BGDs (n = 26)	Latin Kings (n = 18)	Calle Treinta/Red Steps (n = 20)	Lincoln Park/Syndo Mob (n = 21)
Motor Vehicle Theft	46%	47%	45%	48%
Assault	62	53	85	95
Burglary	30	41	35	62
Crack Sale	42	24	30	71
Cocaine Sale	52	41	45	29
Marijuana Sale	69	50	70	86
Graffiti	31	59	60	52
Robbery	31	29	40	67
Shooting	42	47	40	38
Theft	46	47	60	86
Vandalism	31	53	65	52

tion in the gangs Thrasher (1963 [1927]) studied, he recognized that they were directed toward goals. According to Klein (1995a), their *members*, on the contrary, typically have a "rather low focus on group goals" because these goals may come into conflict with the individual needs of gang members. "Gangs," says Klein, "are not committees, ball teams, task forces, production teams, or research teams. The members are drawn to one another to fulfill individual needs, many shared and some conflicting: they do not gather to achieve a common, agreed-upon end" (1995a: 80). Yet group rewards, Klein contends, are an important individual motivation for joining a gang. These include status, companionship, excitement, and protection. Among individual motivations, gang members routinely join for a sense of "belonging" or of "family." Material rewards associated with group crime are also a factor in promoting gang membership.

Among gang members studied here there was strong evidence of organizational goals and purposefulness focused on making money.[14] These economic objectives were often described in quite varied terms, and organizational goals were often embedded in broader descriptions of the purpose of the gang. Many gang members showed evidence of integrating or blending the larger organizational objectives with their own individual needs. Among San Diego gang members, moneymaking appeared incidental to the friendship and social networks. As San Diego gang members put it—

> We kick it together, smoke marijuana, maybe jack something. If we think we can make some money selling it, we will take it.

> Throughout the whole time [I've been in the gang] I was a party cat. . . . The one thing I did throughout the whole time was party. I always liked to party. Liked to have fun. If you are going to have fun you got to make your money. So you sell drugs or you do violent crimes to get money.

> We get together and have little picnics and things with the community. Sometimes we get together and set up moves to make on other gangs. When you go to other neighborhoods and they selling certain things we go and take theirs, we make moves. . . . We do more transactions, money transactions. We mainly making money. That is a main part of the gang, making the money. The riding on other neighborhoods and shooting and all that, that's part of the gang too but the main thing is getting our money.

> [We] smoke weed, sell dope, I would say that's about it that I know of. [We] have parties and stuff. . . . [We p]robably hang out, that's about it, make money.

In contrast, gang members from Chicago tended to describe their gangs as primarily focused on making money:

> Well, in my words, a gang ain't nothing but people come together to do crime and make money and be a family to each other. That's the original idea.

> A gang, nowadays, would be money making, make money.

> [A gang is] a bunch of brothers hooked up, trying to make money.

> [The gang is] really [about] making money, it's holding your own neighborhood so nobody can come into your neighborhood and try to take the bread out of your mouth.

But Chicago gang members also articulated the objectives of the gang in a broader way that emphasized the social and familial rewards of gang membership:

> A gang is a group of individuals bound together for a common purpose. [They are bound together] a lot of ways, socially, economically, emotionally sometimes.

> Basically [a gang is] a group of people with the same objectives, trying to reach for the same goals.

Gang members in Chicago and San Diego viewed their gangs as an opportunity for social interaction (including partying, "hanging out," getting women) and as a family, brotherhood, or support system. Gang members in both cities described the role of the gang as a means of protection from rivals, a means of survival, and a source of respect. Many gang members appear to seamlessly combine social interaction with making money: For San Diego gangs, social interaction, friendship, and self-protection

appeared to be the primary purpose, and moneymaking was incidental or opportunistic. Although the concept of gang as brotherhood or family was also extremely important to the Chicago gangs, making money was their central organizational objective or defining feature.

Organizational Transformation: Consolidation and Splintering

Perhaps the strongest evidence of the formal organizational character of the gangs studied was the organizational transformation each had experienced over time.[15] Like other organizations, gangs are seldom static entities. Although the temporary gangs described by Thrasher (1963 [1927]) typically disintegrated, the gangs in this study reflected patterns of consolidation (primarily through merger with, or acquisition of, smaller gangs), reorganization, and the splintering of larger gangs into spinoff gangs. Such findings are consistent with those of Thrasher, who noted that groups form and re-form over time.

Gang members' richly detailed descriptions of the organizational transformations that occurred in each of the gangs were evidence of both the tenacity and enduring nature of the gang and offered insights into its organizational growth or decline. One gang member described the merger that created the BGDs:

> [Black Gangster Disciple Nation, Black Gangsters, Disciples, and High Supreme Gangsters] actually was all brought together in 1981. Although you had the same members that came together, all these different gangs all came together under one name. It's like we'll take some of your doctrines, we'll take some of your doctrines to satiate everybody's upbringing, what they originally were, and bring them all together under one thing. . . . There was many different smaller organizations just in the process of being brought together. And then a couple of years later everybody was brought together under one law, under a one-people concept, all of us being the same thing.

Two other gang members told a similar story of merger and acquisition:

> Before I became a Black Disciple, I was a Rod; it was an extremely small organization and we converted over to GD's, to Black Gangster Disciples. . . . Disciples been around for ages. Like I said, in the

beginning there was Devil Disciples. But the GD organization has been in existence since 1971.

> They were attempting to form a conglomerate. . . . [I]t was three organizations that come together and formed one big organization.

Unlike the Chicago gangs, which showed evidence of mergers, gangs in San Diego appeared to exhibit a pattern of splintering through the division of larger gangs and the creation of new, spinoff gangs. Logan gang members described the evolution of their gang this way:

> Thirtieth Street was originally all of Logan. Then along came another 'hood called Logan Trece—another little gang. So they had to get permission from 30th to start their little gang. Give them a little part of Logan. So Red Steps came along and asked them too. So Red Steps and Logan Trece to gain some respect from other gangs, they had to start fighting and all that. So that's where it all started.

> There is two more [gangs] in Logan Heights. There is Red Steps and Trece Logan Heights. But back in the old days, it used to just be Logan. But as time went by, they started separating because of freeways getting built and boundaries started separating them apart. But they are still united though. Except there is always family disputes between the different family cliques.

Spergel (1990: 204) believes that the reason for splintering is "competition between cliques [within the gang]." Such competition, he wrote, "may be a central dynamic leading to the gang splitting into factions or separate gangs." It seems reasonable that external pressures—law enforcement, neighborhood dynamics, competition with other gangs—and other "pull" factors could also splinter the gang. These same dynamics could also lead small gangs to join forces to provide protection or to form economic alliances.

The notion of gang mergers is occasionally mentioned in the gang literature but has not been fully discussed. During the 2-year period in which Huff (1989) studied gangs in two Ohio cities, the number of gangs in Cleveland declined from 50 separately named gangs to 15 or 20; in Columbus, the number of gangs dropped from 20 to 15 during the course of the study. Mergers accounted for the reduction in the number of gangs, according to Huff, although some gangs dissolved and some groups originally identified as gangs may have actually been splinter groups rather than gangs. While mergers may result in larger gangs (that is, more gang members in a gang), such an increase in size does not necessarily take place. Mergers may serve only to offset attrition of gang members, resulting in no net increase in gang size.

As Monti (1993) noted, gang cliques and sets can combine and reassemble in different ways over time; a portion of the gangs he studied in St. Louis were "absorbed" into other gangs during a 2-year period. The growth of the Blackstone Rangers in Chicago was described by Sale (1971) as occurring through takeovers of existing gangs and "renovation" of cliques. The gang's original street clique clashed with rival gangs and then later combined with them. The result, after 10 years, was a much larger version of the Blackstone Rangers. The observation that the merger is an organizational feature of contemporary gangs and occurs over time is an accepted but poorly understood dimension of the organizational growth of gangs.

Similarly, there has been little discussion in the field of gang research of splintering, although there is recognition that cliques or subsets of gangs have a life of their own. Spergel et al. (1991) reported that internal competition within the gang may cause it to split into factions or form a separate gang. He also suggested that gangs might splinter and dissolve if more criminal opportunities become available to members through drug trafficking gangs or other criminal groups. According to Goldstein and Huff (1993), there is serious intragang rivalry between sets within the Bloods or the Crips in Los Angeles, especially when the profits of drug dealing are at issue. They note that there can be as much violence between different sets of the same gang as between rival gangs, a fact that may contribute to further splintering of the gang. Decker (1996) described how the rise of violence in larger gangs can result in the emergence of splinter gangs. Monti (1993) suggested that when gangs reach a certain size, they would split when friction occurred among members and remained unsettled. This splintering occurs because, when the gang is small, the gang

can exercise cohesion and control through face-to-face personal interactions (Kornhauser 1978), but large increases in the size of individual gangs appear to lead to breaches within gangs, resulting in more gangs in a jurisdiction.

The concepts of gang merger and splintering can be framed within organizational theory. Organizational theory holds that populations of organizations of a similar form and function tend to reach an equilibrium. Over time, some organizations die out and others form—some through schism, which occurs when subgroups break away to create a new organization. The process continues until the number of organizations is stable (Tucker et al. 1988; Hannan and Freeman 1987; Hannan and Carroll 1992). Historically, this phenomenon is driven by organizational creation and failure—two processes that are much more common than adaptation.

Summary of Gang Member Interviews

The gang members interviewed in this study provided richly textured descriptions of the character of their gangs. Framed in an organizational context, their narratives illuminate and clarify police observations about gang size, gang activities, and changes in gangs over time. The evidence from these interviews demonstrates that the four gangs studied have been in existence for many years and have experienced major organizational changes. Changes in gang name and size are the most observable indications of these organizational shifts. The generalist orientation of the gangs and their members may have contributed to their survival through periods of organizational upheaval and environmental uncertainty.

Unexpected Agreement

It might be expected that the views of police and gang members would be quite divergent on issues such as the nature of gang leadership and activities. This study, however, did not identify any major differences. In large part, police descriptions of gangs were not inconsistent with those of gang members. Indeed, the interviews with gang members tended to elaborate on police observations of the variation within and among gangs. For the most part, the police did not tend to stereotype gangs; they did not, for example, describe them as showing evidence of formal organization and hierarchy where this was not well established. Nor did the police tend to see role and organizational specialization within gangs. Instead, they recognized a wide range of gang types, identified different structures within different gangs, and described a wide range of behaviors of gangs and gang members. In the interviews, gang members confirmed and elaborated on these observations.

It is worth noting that both police and gang members indicated that the large and enduring gangs examined in this study exhibited *some* distinctive features of formal organizations. There was little evidence, however, that their structure is highly bureaucratic—an anomaly, according to organizational theory. Despite their large size and organizational longevity, of the four gangs examined, in only two was there evidence of the bureaucratic structure of large organizations (leadership, membership levels, regular meetings, specialization, and written rules). Only one gang exhibited the more elaborate features of traditional organized crime groups—relationships with other gangs nationwide (including prison gangs), incursion into legitimate businesses, and involvement in political activities (Decker, Bynum, and Weisel 1998). In all four gangs, however, there was some evidence of formal organization, such as organizational continuity and an orientation toward goals.

The gangs studied here appear to represent a fundamentally different form of organization, one that can be described as adaptive or organic rather than bureaucratic. These forms of organization have also been called "federations, networks, clusters, cross-functional teams, lattices, modules, matrices, almost anything but pyramids" (Bennis 1993).[16]

In stark contrast to the myriad literature on bureaucratic organizations, there have been few studies of organic organizations—and thus there is a dearth of descriptions of this form even among organizations such as legitimate businesses. An examination of the recognized features of the organic-adaptive model, however, suggests that the gangs studied here feature the attributes associated predominantly with this form of organization. These include an emphasis on individual goals concurrent with organizational goals, diffuse leadership, the active role of subgroups, a generalist orientation,

persistence in a volatile environment, and continuity despite the absence of hierarchy. Adaptive or organic organizations thrive in a volatile or changing environment, and organizations that survive under such conditions are more likely to maintain multipurpose and flexible structures, with flexible leadership and little differentiation among member roles (Meyer 1978; Burns and Stalker 1961).

Despite some evidence of bureaucratic features in the gangs studied, the results of the interviews with gang members make it difficult to support the hypothesis that these gangs have evolved into formal organizations mirroring traditional organized crime.[17] Although the Chicago gangs have some explicit features of formal organizations, on other dimensions, the evidence is less clear: Group and role specialization, for example, appear minimal.

Their organizational continuity and their expansion and membership growth suggest that these four groups can be considered successful organizations. They have endured and thrived at times when environmental exigencies might have logically selected against them. Their survival and growth have been punctuated by organizational changes—mergers, splintering, consolidation, and other organizational dynamics. These changes have been responsible for the gangs' growth to their current, large size.

The substantial organizational change these gangs experienced is consistent with organizational theories that see social organizations as not static but changing in important ways, adapting to changing environmental conditions. According to one widely held notion, organizations proceed through temporal and sequential stages of development, a process commonly known as the organizational life cycle. The gangs in this study—with their patterns of consolidation and fragmentation—showed clear evidence of such a process. According to Klein (1995a), the proliferation of gangs in the 1980s resulted from the establishment of many small, autonomous organizations. The result was that gangs were large in number but small in size. As Klein points out, however, "there are a lot of acorns out there that could become stable, traditional oaks" (p. 104). In other words, small, autonomous gangs can grow into stable, traditional, and much larger gangs, the latter, of course, being of far greater concern to the public and to police.

Life cycles of gangs suggest that smaller, socially oriented gangs can evolve into more serious gangs, often merging or aligning with larger or more organized gangs for protection. While transformation into large, networked gangs such as the BGDs is clearly an exception, for that gang, the merger and acquisition process was a major contribution to its growth. Of course, gangs are also growing larger for a number of reasons, among them that the age range is expanding, with members remaining in the gang longer and the gang retaining members who move outside the neighborhood.

Size will continue to be a major factor in predicting the extent of organization in a gang. The largest gang in this study showed the clearest evidence of bureaucratic organizational features, suggesting the need for a systematic process for counting gangs and their members and for close attention to changes that affect the number and size of gangs in a specific area or jurisdiction. Klein (1995b) describes the cyclical processes of the seasonal and epochal variations in gang activity (crime) through which gangs proceed. Many of these epochal cycles, Klein believes, are city-specific and may reflect upturns and downturns in subareas and neighborhoods within cities. This view, of course, suggests that cities or counties are the relevant population boundary for monitoring gang crime and changes in the size and number of gangs. As Klein (1995b) states, aggregate numbers of gangs, gang members, and gang crime tend to mask important changes in gangs that occur at smaller geographic levels.

Implications for Police Practice

For the police, monitoring the growth of individual gangs or of organizational changes taking place among or within gangs in a jurisdiction provides insights that can aid in developing effective responses to gang problems. Differences among gang types and among specific gangs—especially organizational differences such as patterns of leadership, membership age, size, duration, criminal involvement, and so forth—have significant law enforcement implications. Hierarchical or organized crime models that target gang leadership by using vertical prosecution and applying Federal statutes[18]

may be appropriate for law enforcement agencies or prosecutors that focus on the few gangs having particularly distinctive leadership patterns. This model is probably not useful for addressing the vast majority of the country's street gangs. Spergel (1990), for example, has warned against exaggerating the organized character of gangs. Such exaggeration may be a byproduct of an organized crime model that targets gang leadership, which tends to characterize *most* gangs by the troublesome features of a few gangs. Indeed, the present study indicates that street gangs do not necessarily progress into highly organized crime organizations. Organizational processes, however, may contribute to marked increases in gang size, influencing the structure, operations, and relationships of some gangs.

The criminal versatility of the gangs and gang members observed in this study suggests that law enforcement efforts that target particular criminal behavior will work primarily for highly specialized gangs. Most gangs are not. Even the most troublesome gangs in this study appeared to be highly adaptive generalists. Most research suggests that rather than employing generic antigang strategies, approaches to gang problems should be framed very narrowly to address identified problems of concern to communities and police (e.g., Sherman et al. 1998; Bureau of Justice Assistance 1997).

Gangs and gang-related problems vary. Indeed, Spergel's model requires that law enforcement agencies carefully assess *local* problems before implementing any antigang strategy. Because there have been few useful evaluations of such strategies, there is a need for rigorous evaluations, which could help move the country to more quickly identify the most effective methods for solving the various gang problems.

Police have tried a wide variety of measures to address the problem of gangs at the local level. They have employed situational crime prevention, for example, altering the flow of vehicular traffic to reduce gang-related violence[19]; enforcing antiloitering statutes to keep gangs from intimidating and menacing community members (Regini 1998); using civil injunctions to keep gang members out of areas where they cause trouble (Cameron and Skipper 1997; Gibeaut 1998; Regini 1998); setting up traffic checkpoints (Crawford 1998); carrying out aggressive curfew and truancy enforcement

(Fritsch, Caeti, and Taylor 1999); and cracking down on weapons violations, often using Federal laws that impose stiffer penalties. Some jurisdictions have used a technique known as "lever pulling," targeting specific chronic offenders with warrants, close supervision of probation conditions, and other measures.[20]

Many of these law enforcement approaches have been integrated into community or problem-oriented approaches to gangs. The approaches also include mediation, situational crime prevention, working with families, and other strategies (Sampson and Scott 2000; Bureau of Justice Assistance 1997). Klein (1997) warns that policing that involves only enforcement will solidify gangs by increasing cohesion among gang members. Policing strategies are most effective when teamed with intervention programs such as providing economic opportunities, job training, remedial education, and other services and community involvement (see, for example, Spergel 1995; Spergel et al. 1991). These diverse strategies may be necessary to deal with highly versatile and adaptive gangs.

At the turn of the 21st century, a wide variety of organizations fall under the umbrella category of "gangs." One type or size of criminal organization may differ from another only by a matter of degree. Howell and Decker (1999) distinguish between drug gangs and street gangs, and between youth gangs and adult criminal organizations. These distinctions (and others) will have the most value when employed at the local level. As Starbuck, Howell, and Lindquist (forthcoming) point out, their changing nature makes it increasingly difficult to categorize and characterize them. These authors describe the new gang form as a hybrid organization. Even 70 years ago, Thrasher (1963 [1927]) recognized that the distinctions between gangs and other criminal organizations crime were rather illusory. There is, according to Thrasher, "no hard and fast dividing line between predatory gang boys and criminal groups of younger and older adults. They merge into each other by imperceptible gradations." It is important to identify and monitor the inherent distinctions and similarities among different criminal organizations within jurisdictions, since these elements reflect local conditions, criminal opportunity, and other explanatory variables. Such an examination

will aid in building an accurate perception of local problems and will be useful in avoiding the stereotypes and overreaction that may lead to well-intentioned but misguided policies and practices. Just such a continued examination may aid in building a corpus of information that will offer greater insight into the form and structure—and inherent variation—of contemporary gangs.

Notes

1. Not all gangs "mature"; indeed, many disintegrate. Some gang researchers have described this maturation process. Knox (1994) characterizes gangs by their stage of development, from pre-gang to emergent gang, from crystallized gang to formalized gangs, suggesting that gangs move from one category to another as they grow larger and more like a formal organization. Thrasher described the transformation of gangs to a solidified form as a function of longevity, conflict, and the age of their members (1963 [1927]: 47–62).

2. Fagan (1989) examined gang participation in criminal activity and drugs, classifying gangs as party gangs, which engage in few nondrug criminal behaviors except vandalism; social gangs, which engage in few delinquent activities; delinquent gangs, which engage in violent and property crime but few drug sales; and organized gangs, which are extensively involved in the sale and use of drugs along with predatory crime. Other typologies of gangs based on police information have taken different approaches. For example, Maxson and Klein (1995) identified common structures for 59 gangs and looked at how offending was related to these structures. As these authors note, however, "police attend far more to gang crime than gang structure," leading the present study to focus on gang behaviors as an organizing characteristic.

3. Surveys were addressed to police chiefs, who were asked to have it completed by the person in the department most knowledgeable about gangs. As a result, respondents varied from police chiefs to investigations commanders to gang or youth unit supervisors. Since populations served by respondents varied from 50,000 to more than 3 million, it seemed appropriate that knowledgeable police respondents could be identified at different levels of different organizations. The technique of surveying the police chief is also used by the National Youth Gang Survey (see Office of Juvenile Justice and Delinquency Prevention 1999).

4. The higher response rate from larger police departments likely reflects the greater prevalence of gangs in large jurisdictions; smaller jurisdictions with few or no gangs were probably less likely to respond to the survey.

5. Estimates of numbers of gangs and gang members vary by source. City-level estimates were provided by the National Youth Gang Center based on annual surveys conducted in 1996–1999.

6. Federal and local law enforcement sources were used to identify the most organized gangs in each city. General gang history was provided by local police sources.

7. In contrast to local law enforcement, which focuses on the criminal *behavior* of individual gang members, Federal responses to gangs, such as the FBI's Safe Streets Task Force, appear to focus on the *structure* of gangs, especially leadership, using tools such as Racketeering Influenced and Corrupt Organizations (RICO) statutes to dismantle gangs. Indeed, the stated policy of the FBI is to address violent street gangs through long-term, proactive investigations by concentrating on criminal enterprise and conspiracy. See Freeh (1999) and the sidebar "The FBI's Enterprise Theory of Investigation" for a more detailed description of the FBI's work on gangs and organized crime.

8. Fagan (1989) notes that social gangs accounted for 28 percent of all gangs; party gangs accounted for 7 percent; serious delinquents constituted 37 percent; and "organization"-type gangs represented 28 percent of all gangs. These proportions varied, however, from one city to another. In Chicago, gangs were predominantly serious delinquents and organized gangs; in Los Angeles, gangs were social (38 percent) and serious delinquents (36 percent), whereas San Diego gangs consisted of more serious delinquents (39 percent) and organized gangs (31 percent).

9. Klein (1995a) called this versatility "cafeteria style" crime, a type in which gang members combine opportunistic crime with crime requiring more planning. It should be noted that participation of the gang in crime is different from participation of individual gang members in crime; the former term aggregates activities of gang members, the latter reflects individual behavior. Both concepts of criminal activity are examined in this study.

10. Although this study revealed higher levels of criminal versatility in serious gangs, the findings of this study are parallel with findings about criminal activity of youth gangs in the National Youth Gang Survey (Office of Juvenile Justice and Delinquency Prevention 1999). Police participants in the youth gang survey reported criminal versatility among gang members, with high involvement by youth gang members in aggravated assault, larceny/theft, motor vehicle theft, and burglary. Slightly more than one-fourth of all NYGS respondents reported high involvement by gang members in those crimes. If youth gangs evolved into the more serious criminal gangs examined in this study, one would anticipate substantial increases in assaults, robbery, theft, and burglary and some increase in motor vehicle theft.

11. An earlier report of the findings from this study described the extent to which these organizational characteristics were present in these four gangs (Decker, Bynum, and Weisel 1998).

12. One respondent described the volatile environment as follows: "Standing on the street corner and talking and sitting there getting high all day, you make plenty of money, I'm not gonna lie about that, but it gets tiresome always looking for the police too or looking for somebody that is gonna try to kill you for your money."

13. Taylor (1990) and Joe (1993) reported that older gang respondents minimized gang activity, and Goldstein (1991) noted that gang members may exaggerate or hide information. Although the gang members interviewed for this study appeared to have been mostly honest in their responses, it seems reasonable to assume that many would be disinclined to own up to the range of their own criminal activity.

14. Gang members were asked to define a gang, to describe the purpose of the gang (including why they joined the gang), and to describe what is good about being in a gang.

15. Gang members were asked to tell interviewers about the history of their gang.

16. Similar terms include negotiated order, federation, loosely coupled system, temporary system, organic-adaptive organization, coalition, external model, post-bureaucracy, colleague model, interactive organization, network, and blended or open organization.

17. As with contemporary gangs, there is a great deal of debate about the definition and degree of organization of organized crime. See Maltz (1985) and Kenney and Finckenauer (1995) for a discussion of this issue as it relates to organized crime.

18. Limitations of these strategies are described by Johnson, Webster, and Connors (1995) and Miethe and McCorkle (1997).

19. See Lasley (1998) for a discussion of Opera-

tion Cul de Sac, an example of a situational crime prevention tactic.

20. "Lever pulling" and RICO statutes were employed in a widely publicized reduction of violence program in Boston. See Kennedy (1997).

References

Bennis, Warren G. 1993. *Beyond Bureaucracy: Essays on the Development and Evolution of Human Organization*. San Francisco: Jossey-Bass.

Blau, Peter M., and W. Richard Scott. 1962. *Formal Organizations: A Comparative Approach*. San Francisco: Chandler Publishing Co.

Bureau of Justice Assistance. 1997. *Addressing Community Gang Problems: A Model for Problem Solving*. Washington, DC: U.S. Department of Justice, Bureau of Justice Assistance. NCJ 156059.

Burns, Tom, and G. M. Stalker. 1961. *The Management of Innovation*. London: Tavistock.

Cameron, Jeffrey R., and John Skipper. 1997. "The Civil Injunction: A Preemptive Strike Against Gangs," *FBI Law Enforcement Bulletin* 66(11): 12–15.

Crawford, Kimberly A. 1998. "Checkpoints: Fourth Amendment Implications of Limiting Access to High Crime Areas," *Law Enforcement Bulletin* 67(3): 27–32.

Decker, Scott. 1996. "Collective and Normative Features of Gang Violence," *Justice Quarterly* 13(2): 243–264.

Decker, Scott H., Timothy S. Bynum, and Deborah Lamm Weisel. 1998. "A Tale of Two Cities: Gangs as Organized Crime Groups," *Justice Quarterly* 15(3): 395–425.

Fagan, Jeffrey. 1989. "The Social Organization of Drug Use and Drug Dealing Among Urban Gangs," *Criminology* 27(4): 633–667.

Freeh, Louis J. 1999. "Ensuring Public Safety and National Security Under the Rule of Law: A Report to the American People on the Work of the FBI 1993–1998." Washington, DC: U.S. Department of Justice, Federal Bureau of Investigation.

Fritsch, E. J., T. J. Caeti, and R. W. Taylor. 1999. "Gang Suppression Through Saturation Patrol, Aggressive Curfew, and Truancy Enforcement: A Quasi-Experimental Test of the Dallas Anti-Gang Initiative," *Crime and Delinquency* 45(1): 122–139.

Gibeaut, John. 1998. "Gang Busters," *ABA Journal* 84(January): 64–68.

Goldstein, Arnold P. 1991. *Delinquent Gangs: A Psychological Perspective*. Champaign, IL: Research Press.

Goldstein, Arnold P. and C. Ronald Huff, eds. 1993. *The Gang Intervention Handbook*. Champaign, IL: Research Press.

Greiner, Larry E. 1972. "Evolution and Revolu-

tion as Organizations Grow," *Harvard Business Review* 50(July–August): 37–46.

Hannan, Michael T., and Glenn R. Carroll. 1992. *Dynamics of Organizational Populations: Density, Legitimation, and Competition*. New York: Oxford University Press.

Hannan, Michael T., and John Freeman. 1987. "The Ecology of Organizational Founding: American Labor Unions, 1836–1985," *American Journal of Sociology* 92(4): 910–43.

Howell, James C., and Scott H. Decker. 1999. "The Youth Gangs, Drugs and Violence Connection," *Juvenile Justice Bulletin* January. Washington, DC: U.S. Department of Justice, Office of Juvenile Justice and Delinquency Prevention.

Huff, C. Ronald. 1989. "Youth Gangs and Public Policy," *Crime and Delinquency* 35(4): 524–537.

Jackson, Patrick, with Cary Rudman. 1993. "Moral Panic and the Response to Gangs in California," in *Gangs: The Origins and Impact of Contemporary Youth Gangs in the United States*, ed. Scott Cummings and Daniel J. Monti. Albany: State University of New York Press: 257–275.

Joe, Karen. 1993. "Issues in Accessing and Studying Ethnic Youth Gangs," *Gang Journal* 1(2) : 25–36.

Johnson, Claire, Barbara Webster, and Edward Connors. 1995. *Prosecuting Gangs: A National Assessment*. Research in Brief. February. Washington, DC: U.S. Department of Justice, National Institute of Justice. NCJ 151785.

Katz, Daniel, and Robert L. Kahn. 1966. *The Social Psychology of Organizations*. New York: John Wiley and Sons.

Kennedy, David M. 1997. "Pulling Levers: Chronic Offenders, High-Crime Settings, and a Theory of Prevention," *Valparaiso University Law Review* 31(2): 449–484.

Kenney, Dennis Jay, and James O. Finckenauer. 1995. *Organized Crime in America*. Belmont, CA: Wadsworth Publishing Co.

Kimberly, John R., Robert H. Miles, and Associates, eds. 1980. *The Organizational Life Cycle: Issues in the Creation, Transformation, and Decline of Organizations*. San Francisco: Jossey-Bass.

Klein, Malcolm W. 1995a. *The American Street Gang: Its Nature, Prevalence and Control*. New York: Oxford University Press.

———. 1995b. "Street Gang Cycles," in *Crime*, ed. James Q. Wilson and Joan Petersilia. San Francisco: Institute for Contemporary Studies Press.

———. 1997. "The Problem of Street Gangs and Problem-Oriented Policing," in *Problem-Oriented Policing: Crime-Specific Problems Critical Issues and Making POP Work*, ed. Tara O'Connor Shelley and Anne C. Grant. Washington, DC: Police Executive Research Forum: 57–88.

George W. 1994. *An Introduction to Gangs.* Bristol, IN: Wyndham Hall Press.

Kornhauser, Ruth Rosner. 1978. *Social Sources of Delinquency: An Appraisal of Analytic Models.* Chicago: University of Chicago Press.

Lasley, James. 1998. *"Designing Out" Gang Homicides and Street Assaults.* Research in Brief. November. Washington, DC: U.S. Department of Justice, National Institute of Justice. NCJ 173398.

Lippitt, Gordon L. 1982. *Organization Renewal: A Holistic Approach to Organization Development,* 2nd ed. New York: Appleton-Century-Crofts.

Maltz, Michael. 1985. "Toward Defining Organized Crime," in *The Politics and Economics of Organized Crime,* ed. Herbert E. Alexander and Gerald E. Caiden. Lexington, MA: D.C. Heath: 21–35.

Maxson, Cheryl, and Malcolm Klein. 1995. "Investigating Gang Structures," *Journal of Gang Research* 3(1): 33–40.

McCorkle, Richard C., and Terance D. Miethe. 1998. "Political and Organizational Response to Gangs: An Examination of a 'Moral Panic' in Nevada," *Justice Quarterly* 15(1): 41–64.

Meyer, John W. 1978. "Strategies for Further Research: Varieties of Environmental Variation," in *Environments and Organizations,* ed. Marshall W. Meyer and Associates. San Francisco: Jossey-Bass: 352–393.

Miethe, Terance D., and Richard C. McCorkle. 1997. "Evaluating Nevada's Anti-Gang Legislation and Gang Prosecution Units," Washington, DC: U.S. Department of Justice, National Institute of Justice. NCJ 171961.

Monti, Daniel J. 1993. "Origins and Problems of Gang Research in the United States," in *Gangs: The Origins and Impact of Contemporary Youth Gangs in the United States,* ed. Scott Cummings and Daniel J. Monti. Albany: State University of New York Press: 3–25.

National Drug Intelligence Center. 1998. *Street Gangs '98: National Street Gang Survey Report—1998.* Johnstown, PA: National Drug Intelligence Center.

Office of Juvenile Justice and Delinquency Prevention. 1999. *1997 National Youth Gang Survey: Summary.* Washington, DC: U.S. Department of Justice, Office of Juvenile Justice and Delinquency Prevention. NCJ 178891.

Parsons, Talcott. 1987. "Suggestions for a Sociological Approach to the Theory of Organizations," in *Classics of Organization Theory,* 2nd ed., ed. Jay M. Shafritz and J. Steven Ott. Chicago: Dorsey Press: 132–146.

Pennell, S., E. Evans, R. Melton, and S. Hinson. 1994. *Down for the Set: Describing and Defining Gangs in San Diego.* San Diego: San Diego Association of Governments, Criminal Justice Research Unit.

Popielarz, Pamela A., and J. Miller McPherson. 1995. "On the Edge or In Between: Niche Position, Niche Overlap, and the Duration of Voluntary Association Memberships," *American Journal of Sociology* 101(3): 698–720.

Regini, Lisa A. 1998. "Combating Gangs: The Need for Innovation," *FBI Law Enforcement Bulletin* 67(2): 25–32.

Sale, R.T. 1971. *The Blackstone Rangers: A Reporter's Account of Time Spent with the Street Gang on Chicago's South Side.* New York: Random House.

Sampson, Rana, and Michael S. Scott. 2000. *Tackling Crime and Other Public-Safety Problems: Case Studies in Problem Solving.* Washington, DC: U.S. Department of Justice, Office of Community Oriented Policing Services. NCJ 181243.

Scott, W. Richard. 1993. *Organizations: Rational, Natural, and Open Systems.* Englewood Cliffs, NJ: Prentice Hall.

Sherman, Lawrence W., Denise Gottfredson, Doris MacKenzie, John Eck, Peter Reuter, and Shawn Bushway. 1998. *Preventing Crime: What Works, What Doesn't, What's Promising, A Report to the United States Congress.* Washington, DC: U.S. Department of Justice, National Institute of Justice. NCJ 165366.

Simmel, Georg. 1902–3. "The Number of Members as Determining the Sociological Form of Groups, I and II," *The American Journal of Sociology* 8:1–46; 138–96.

Spergel, Irving A. 1990. "Youth Gangs: Continuity and Change," in *Crime and Justice: A Review of Research,* ed. Michael Tonry and Norval Morris. Chicago: University of Chicago Press.

———. 1995. *The Youth Gang Problem: A Community Approach.* New York: Oxford University Press.

Spergel, Irving A., with G. David Curry, Ron Chance, Candice Kane, Ruth E. Ross, Alba Alexander, Pamela Rodriguez, Deeda Seed, Edwina Simmons, and Sandra Oh. 1991. *Youth Gangs: Problem and Response.* Chicago: School of Social Service Administration, University of Chicago.

Starbuck, David, James C. Howell, and Donna J. Lindquist (forthcoming). *Hybrids and Other Modern Gangs,* OJJDP Bulletin. Washington, DC: U.S. Department of Justice, Office of Juvenile Justice and Delinquency Prevention.

Starbuck, William H. 1965. "Organizational Growth and Development," in *Handbook of Organizations,* ed. James G. March. Chicago: Rand McNally: 451–533.

Staw, Barry M., and L. L. Cummings, eds. 1990. *The Evolution and Adaptation of Organizations.* Greenwich, CT: JAI Press.

Stinchcombe, Arthur L. 1965. "Social Structure and Organizations," in *Handbook of Organizations,* ed. James G. March. Chicago: Rand McNally: 153–193.

Taylor, Carl S. 1990. *Dangerous Society*. East Lansing, MI: Michigan State University Press.

Thrasher, Frederic M. 1963 [1927]. *The Gang: A Study of 1,313 Gangs in Chicago*. Chicago: University of Chicago Press (originally published in 1927).

Tucker, David J., Jitendra V. Singh, Agnes G. Meinhard, and Robert J. House. 1988. "Ecological and Institutional Sources of Change in Organizational Populations," in *Ecological Models of Organizations,* ed. Glenn R. Carroll. Cambridge, MA: Ballinger: 127–151.

Weber, Max. 1947. *The Theory of Social and Economic Organization,* trans. A. M. Henderson and Talcott Parsons, ed. Talcott Parsons. New York: The Free Press.

Zatz, Marjorie S. 1987. "Chicano Youth Gangs and Crime: The Creation of a Moral Panic," *Contemporary Crises* 11: 129–158. ✦

Chapter 9
Street Gangs

A Cross-National Perspective

Malcolm W. Klein

Street gangs are generally thought to be an American phenomenon, but author Klein offers evidence to the contrary. He describes gang variables and five types of gangs that predominate in the United States, and then demonstrates how the American depictions can be applied to emerging European gangs as well. He notes both similarities and differences between American and European gangs. The definition of a street gang as "any stable, street-oriented youth group whose own identity includes involvement in antisocial activity" appears to be applicable and measurable across nations.

In the fall of the year 2000, an international group of European scholars submitted a proposal for funding to the European Union (Weitekamp, 2000). The purpose was to establish, over a 3-year period, an interactive network of researchers interested in studying street gangs and developing principles for the prevention and control of gang activities. Because it was generally thought up to that time that street gangs were principally an American problem, this chapter will review the history of this new development—known as the Eurogang Program—and place it in the context of this volume. . . . Why should one include a chapter on street gangs outside the United States in such a volume? At least four reasons offer themselves.

1. We have "exported" our American street gang culture abroad. For example, there are Crips in the Netherlands (van Gemert, 2001). As we come to un-derstand foreign variations of our own gang structures, we will learn more about what the sine qua non of street gangs is, and what is peripheral to their necessary nature.

2. The particular forms of European gangs seem similar to those to be found in the United States, although with differences in prevalence and in ethnic makeup. These structural similarities and variations inform us about both European and American youth cultures.

3. The Eurogang Program was initiated by a few Americans on the basis of American gang experiences. We are naturally curious to study our own impact (or lack thereof) in this new setting.

4. The very considerable generic knowledge we have accumulated over the past 70 years in the United States may be quite culture bound. Comparative research elsewhere can illuminate our own knowledge limitations with respect to such well-studied issues as gang location, diffusion, structure, ethnicity, age, gender, cohesiveness, and behavior patterns (including crime).

Gangs Elsewhere

Although this chapter deals principally with the cities of Western Europe, it is clear from a scattered literature that street gangs have been noted in many other locations. Most of this literature, unfortunately, notes but does not describe these gangs: Our empirical knowledge of street gangs in foreign lands is skimpy at best. Here are a number of examples:

- Japan, South Africa, Zambia, Kimshasa, Dakar, the Cameroons, Ceylon (now Sri Lanka), Thailand, Malaysia, Chile, Argentina, India, and Egypt (Clinard & Abbott, 1973)

- Kenya, Tanzania, South Africa, Australia, Mexico, Brazil, Peru, Taiwan, South Korea, Hong Kong, China, and Japan (Spergel, 1995)

- Ghana, Montreal, Australia, Puerto Rico, Jamaica, India, Indonesia, and Thailand (Covey, Menard, & Franzese, 1997). The Ghanaian case is described

Reprinted from: C. Ronald Huff (ed.), *Gangs in America III*, pp. 237–254. Copyright © 2002 by Sage Publications, Inc. Reprinted by permission of Sage Publications, Inc.

in sufficient detail to show resemblance to some American street gangs.

- Canada, Mexico, Japan, South Africa, the Philippines, Hong Kong, China, New Zealand, Australia, and Papua-New Guinea (Klein, 1995). The descriptions cited for the Philippines and Papua-New Guinea (Port Moresby in particular) provide some structural and criminal details that both contrast with and exemplify American counterparts.[1]

- A number of Canadian scholars are now reporting on street gangs in Vancouver, Toronto, Winnipeg, and Montreal. They include Caucasian, Aborigine, Vietnamese, Chinese, and Haitian gangs. What structural information exists to date suggests general similarities to U.S. street gangs, although descriptions range from "youth movements" to "criminal business organizations."

- In New Zealand, a more detailed report by Eggleston (1996) depicts primarily Maori gangs that are clearly crime oriented, male dominated, and involved in intergang rivalries. We are told little about their structures, however.

- In El Salvador, both news reports and visits by American gang experts yield a clear picture of gang culture exported to San Salvador, the capital city, by Salvadoran immigrants to the United States who return or are deported back to that country. *Placets* (graffiti) on the walls advertise *"homies unidos"* (homeboys united).

- In Argentina, DeFleur (1967) many years ago sought counterparts to some highly structured, large, big-city U.S. gangs depicted in American gang treatises of the time. Instead, she found small, leaderless but internally cohesive gangs, quite different in form from what she had anticipated.

In sum, street gangs, or groups subsumed under similar terminology, have been reported in Asia, Africa, Southeast Asia, Latin America, and Canada. Few of the reports, however, have been based on first-hand research. The "gangs" are mostly of unknown size, structure, and behavior patterns. The exceptions, such as those in Canada, Argentina, Papua-New Guinea, and the Philippines, whet the appetite for further study but provide few clues for new directions. Comparative research is badly needed, and the Eurogang Program at last holds promise for an organized approach to the issues at hand.

The Eurogang Program: Definitions and Issues

Although a few American researchers initiated the Eurogang Program, it soon became, by design, a decidedly European venture with Americans as principal consultants. The first step was an informal survey I made of European cities, establishing locations in which street gang activity had emerged during 1980s and 1990s. There followed several meetings of a small steering committee (members from the United States, Canada, Belgium, Holland, Germany, and Sweden) and a series of four workshops between 1997 and 2000 in Germany, Norway, Belgium, and Holland. Other countries represented in one or more of these were Finland, Denmark, England, France, Spain, Italy, Slovenia, Croatia, Greece, and Russia. Street gangs, or "ganglike youth groups" as a few preferred to call them, were found to exist, in some cases in small numbers, in almost all of the European nations. A commonality of interests soon developed among more than 100 participants, most of whom were researchers but some of whom were policymakers in public agencies such as ministries of justice and the police.

Throughout the developmental process, four key issues emerged and drew the most attention, issues whose resolution was required before the agreed-upon goals of cross-national and multimethod research could comfortably be undertaken. The first of these was to achieve a common definition of "street gangs" capable of applying to a variety of such groups as well as distinguishing them from other groups. The latter include motorcycle gangs, prison gangs, terrorist groups, and the very large number of other, less troublesome youth groups that exist in all countries (often school and youth culture based) that are not much of a danger to others.

The second issue, shared less among active gang researchers but more among others becoming interested in the Program's research goals, was the possible creation of a "moral panic" (Cohen, 1972). The concern here was that undertaking research on groups specifically labeled "gangs" could reify the concept, create greater public concern about it, and indeed help to create the phenomenon to a degree greater than originally existed. Some felt it might indeed be a wiser policy to deny or ignore gangs, or at least to develop alternative terminology than the gang terms so common in the United States.

Third, and inextricably tied to the first two, was the issue of setting street gangs into the broader context of youth groups generally. If street gangs are in any sense a unique form of group, we can only know and appreciate their unique qualities through contrast with other youth groups not labeled as gangs. Although this issue has not been a central issue in most American gang research, it has greater meaning in many European countries where there has been a tradition of studying youth groups and youth movements over many decades.

The fourth issue was the most engaging, at least to the American gang scholars. It came to be known as the "Eurogang Paradox."[2] Simply stated, the paradox consists of two elements, the first being the denial by numerous European researchers and policymakers that their jurisdictions have street gangs, because they don't have gangs that are large, highly structured, with strong cultural codes of loyalty and territoriality, and a commitment to violence as seen in American gangs. That is, they don't have "American style" street gangs. The second element of the paradox, of course, is that most American gangs also don't fit this publicly held stereotype of street gangs. Thus the paradox: The denial of gangs in Europe is based on a "typical" American gang that is not at all typical in America.

Very briefly, before moving on to characterizing European gangs as they have been described recently, I will comment on those four issues as they have been addressed in the Eurogang Program. Again, the issues are gang definitions, the concern about moral panic, the context of other youth groups, and the Eurogang Paradox.

Definitions

In a major set of annual surveys of U.S. police agencies designed to assess the prevalence of street gangs, the National Youth Gang Center (NYGC) offered the following approach to defining gangs for its police respondents: "A group of youths or young adults in your jurisdiction that you or other responsible persons in your agency or community are willing to identify or classify as a 'gang.'" The Eurogang participants determined that such a broad definition would be *too* inclusive—almost a "non-definition" as noted by some. But choosing an acceptable alternative proved—as it has for decades in the United States—to be a thorny problem.

The first solution was to accept, for working purposes, a minimal nominal definition that includes the elements of stability over time, street orientation, and a self-identity based on criminal involvement. The definition drafted for these purposes was this: "A street gang (or a problematic youth group corresponding to a street gang elsewhere) is any stable, street-oriented youth group whose own identity includes involvement in antisocial activity" (Weitekamp, 2000).

Note the phrase in parentheses above. For those wishing to avoid gang terminology, the definition can be applied to "problematic youth groups" without explicitly saying, "this is a gang." The second solution was also adopted to meet the concerns of those wishing or needing to avoid gang terminology. This approach, itself having two alternative forms, was to define the issue of whether a group under study is a "gang" or not *operationally*, rather than nominally as above.

The first operational procedure, common to many interview and questionnaire surveys of youth, is to use a set of "funneling" questions. These start with broad questions about one's friends and groups of friends, then narrow slowly to descriptions of groups such as size, activities, reasons for joining, and tendencies to get into trouble. Only at the end is the respondent asked if he or she considers this particular group of friends to be a gang. If the answer is yes, this is generally taken at face value. If the answer is no, the researcher can determine if this is also to be taken at face value or as a denial of "true" gang membership based on the previous answers to the funneling questions. Some of those questions reveal typical gang characteristics.

The second operational procedure is based on the Maxson-Klein typology of gang structures described later in this chapter. The typology describes five gang structures that encompass most gangs found in the United States.[3] It asks youth respondents in two ways to describe their "special group of friends" in line with the five gang types. The first, indirect way is to ask them to describe the group with respect to its size, age range, duration, presence of subgroups, territoriality, and antisocial behavior patterns. These are the dimensions that determine placement of the group in one of the five gang types, or into none of them. The second, more direct way is to present the respondent with very brief scenarios of the five gang types, asking the respondent which of these best describes his special group of friends, or if none of them do.

In sum, the operational definition of a youth's description of his or her group as a street gang can be determined by the funneling questions, or by the indirect or direct approach to the use of the five types of gang structures. The designation of a youth group as nongang or gang is thus achieved by the operations described—that is, by the youth's responses to questions shown in research to distinguish street gangs from other youth groups. These survey approaches can also be applied, with minor modifications, for use in gang observations and ethnographies and for use in surveys of adult experts such as police, school personnel, and community youth agencies. All those procedures are being planned for the developing Eurogang research projects.

Moral Panic

Interestingly, the European colleagues most concerned with creating a moral panic about street gangs tended to be those not yet directly engaged in gang research. Those already so engaged had not found the concern to be very tangible. Nonetheless, the operational definition approach outlined above was designed to make gang research more palatable to those genuinely concerned with the issue. For example, the funneling technique allows one to go all the way through the determination of gang membership by a youth respondent without that youth ever having to admit to gang membership. The phrase adopted—"your special group of friends"—allows avoidance of gang terminology yet permits determination by the researcher of the youth's gang or nongang status.

By the same token, the gang structures approach, both in the questions about size, duration, antisocial activities, and so on, and in the presentation of the five scenarios, uses the word *group*, not gang, in its language. Again, this allows the researcher to determine gang status without directly asking about it. Further, it allows for those youths responding in gang-like fashion to be fitted into one of the five types so that comparisons across sites and with U.S. data can readily be made. Any moral panic resulting from these procedures will not result from the research process, but only from the manner in which the results are presented to the public (if indeed they are made public).

The Youth Group Context

Here, too, the operational approach outlined above serves a secondary purpose, namely the application of gang-relevant survey instruments to a broader array of youth groups. By comparing youth responses from gang and nongang respondents, the distinction between the two types of groups can readily be illuminated. Youth group researchers will undoubtedly wish to ask a far more extensive set of questions in addition, depending on their particular interests. Having the gang comparisons available to them will simply amplify one issue of concern. A fine example can be found in the comparative study in Bremen, Germany, and Denver, Colorado (Huizinga & Schumann, 2001), using common survey instruments applied to large samples of school students in the two cities. A funneling technique for gang determination was employed amid a far broader set of questions about individuals, families, schools, and communities. Excellent contrasts were thus drawn between gang and nongang youth and between both of these cross-nationally.

The Eurogang Paradox

This fourth issue raised during the development of the Eurogang Program has not yet been fully resolved for two reasons. First, the stereotype of American gangs is fairly fixed in many minds and constantly reinforced by naïve, poorly informed representatives of the media and some law enforcement agencies. Second, as the program has expanded its membership, new colleagues continually appear who have not yet been alerted to the nature of the paradox. In my view, following the initiation of the program discussions there have been two principal contributions by the American participants. One is the collaborative process of gang definition statement and measurement. The second, designed to reduce the paradox, is to bring to the European colleagues (admittedly with some repetition and insistence) the most recent data from the 1980s and 1990s on the true nature of U.S. gangs (see, e.g., chaps. 1–7 in Klein, Kerner, Maxson & Weitekamp, 2001). By showing, with both case studies and national surveys, that the stereotypical gang is the exception rather than the rule, and by illustrating the five structural types of the gang typology, the Americans have attempted to demonstrate the variety of gangs in the United States. By doing this, they have allowed European observers to understand that some of their groups, while not fitting the old stereotype, do indeed resemble some of the other, more common U.S. gangs. The resemblance between U.S. and European gangs has been documented (Klein, 1997) and now allows far more useful comparisons of both similarities and differences. It has been a "hard sell," but progress along these lines has been steady.

Characteristics of American Gangs

Though we have established that street gangs probably exist or have existed on every continent, it seems clear that they are most evident in the United States. In attempting to understand street gangs elsewhere, it makes sense to establish their basic elements first in the United States, where seven decades of gang research has taken place. In particular, because American gangs have changed over time and have proliferated in just the past 20 years in particular, it seems sensible to establish the base of knowledge principally on more recent research. The most significant changes have probably taken place with respect to prevalence (there are now thousands of gang-involved jurisdictions), crime patterns (more lethal violence now, due to the availability of modern firearms), and structures (the emergence of several types of non-stereotypical gang forms). In addition to these three characteristics, it seems useful to review several others briefly: location; ethnicity; gender; cultural diffusion; cohesiveness; and two additional crime patterns, versatility and amplification.

Location

In the days of the most "classic" American gang research, from the 1920s to the mid-1970s, gangs known to exist were located principally in large urban centers or their immediate surroundings. These included most notably New York, Philadelphia, Boston, Chicago, Los Angeles, San Francisco, San Antonio, and El Paso. Prior to 1960, there were about 50 communities in these areas with gang problems; street gangs were an urban problem. The number of gang jurisdictions grew slowly but steadily through the mid-1980s, and then exploded to the point that the National Youth Gang Center has reported several *thousand* gang-involved communities, encompassing more than 26,000 gangs and almost 850,000 gang members (NYGC, 2000).

Almost every urban center is now involved, but there are not 3,000 urban centers in the United States; this means that gangs now exist in many large and even many small towns. Recent data from the NYGC (2000) show the following (according to police reports and NYGC's very broad definition):

	Gangs	Members
Large cities:	12,538	482,380
Small cities:	8,413	94,875
Suburban counties:	6,040	176,610
Rural counties:	1,716	26,368

The data are a bit misleading, because NYGC defines as large cities those above 25,000 in population. Nonetheless, it is clear from the above figures that gangs *cannot* be considered just a "big city" problem. For those who think of gangs as an East Coast phenomenon, the NYGC data are equally surprising. Seventy-two percent of reporting jurisdictions in the West indicate active gangs, as opposed to 48% in the Midwest and South and only 29% in the Northeast. The *West Side Story* now has a new meaning.

Clearly, as we look at the street gang situation in Europe or elsewhere, we will need to assess their location in urban *and* non-urban areas. The character of gangs is affected by their location on the landscape.

Ethnicity

In the earlier, classic period, American gangs of many backgrounds were reported: German, Scandinavian, Italian, Polish, Irish, Jewish, and other European immigrant populations fueled the inner-city gangs along with black and Hispanic groups. But with the absorption of most immigrant populations into the multiethnic fabric of our nation, it came to be more and more the still-marginalized minorities—blacks, Hispanics, and to a lesser extent various Asian groups—that have composed most of our modern street gangs. This history makes it clear that it is not a particular nationality, ethnicity, or race that makes up the street gang problem, but rather the disadvantaged, marginalized, and alienated status of youth segments that gravitate to the gang world. Even in the case of Caucasian groups such as the Skinheads, a review of their membership reveals that they are drawn from those who perceive themselves to be socially marginalized.

When we look at the composition of street gangs reported in connection with the Eurogang Program, obviously we should not expect to find a preponderance of blacks or Hispanics, but we should be on the lookout for other marginalized populations there.

Gender

Until recently, the prevalence and behavior of girls in street gangs had received moderate attention at best. A very few autonomous female gangs had been described. More commonly, girls were described either as occasional participants in male gangs or as members of auxiliary groups, as small adjuncts to larger male gangs. It was generally acknowledged that female gang members were fewer in number (ratios of from 1 to 10 to 3 to 10 female to male were noted), younger on average by several years, and less criminally involved than males (although manifesting similarly versatile crime patterns). Female gang members were largely ignored by the police and courts, and stereotypes abounded that the females were sex objects for the males ("toys for boys"), carried concealed weapons for the males, spread rumors to incite rivalries between male gangs, and were generally subservient in a male-dominated street world.

More recently, especially with the advent of feminist criminology, a number of more careful and considered works on female gang members have appeared (see, e.g., Chesney-Lind, Shelden, & Joe, 1996; Fleisher, 1998; Hagedorn & Devitt, 1999; Miller, 2001a; Moore, 1991). Less importance is now given to female subservience

and more to female gang participation, serving specific needs, much as male participation serves such needs. Also, it now appears that the prevalence of female gang members is higher than was estimated earlier (percentages in the 20% to 40% range are more common) and fewer auxiliary groups are reported, with more of the girls to some extent integrated with the boys' groups. Male domination, nonetheless, continues to be the typical pattern. Finally, it is still the case that female gang participation is largely unknown to or downplayed by the police and courts.

The Eurogang Program, unlike the earlier days of American gang research, has been alerted to the issues of female gang members (see Miller, 2001b). Perhaps attention to females early in the development of European gangs will yield more accurate data, although some European scholars, more than Americans, place heavy weight on the issue of "masculinities" (see, e.g., Kersten, 2001).

Cultural Diffusion

In earlier decades, street gangs seemed to appear in major cities as independent phenomena, arising in each case as responses to local patterns of immigration, central city structure, culture clash, and economic disadvantage. None of the earlier gang literature suggested effective ties between gangs in New York and Chicago and Los Angeles and the other known gang locations. Indeed, one noted scholar almost scoffed at the notion of inter-city gang recognition (Campbell, Munce, & Galea, 1982).[4]

Since the mid-1980s, it has become rather commonplace to assign the responsibility for the proliferation of street gangs across the country to one of three processes. The first is a shadow of the earlier thinking: Gangs have emerged in many localities because of similar conditions that are gang-spawning in their nature. These include racism, relative poverty or deprivation, poor local resources, inadequate employment opportunities for youth (and minority youth in particular), and the general marginalization of black, Hispanic, and other minority groups. Many scholars, myself among them, are inclined to this view, noting that the social and political conservatism of the country over the past 20 years has exacerbated these processes.

A second commonly offered explanation

is the advent of crack cocaine and its franchising across the country. Promulgated principally by law enforcement agencies who saw crack cocaine as a new epidemic being fueled by drug kingpins and distributed through the auspices of organized street gang networks, this explanation did receive support from incidents in widely scattered parts of the country. More careful research, however, has downplayed the importance of gang member migration and street gang capacities to market drugs extensively (Decker & Van Winkle, 1996; Hagedorn, 1988; Howell & Gleason, 1999; Klein, 1995; Maxson, 1998).

The third explanation, propounded by myself (Klein, 1995) and a number of police gang experts in the late 1980s, has gained general acceptance over the past decade. It notes the general diffusion of street gang culture—the dress and ornamentation styles, the postures, the argot of gang members—to the general youth population of the country. The press, gang-oriented movies, television news and documentaries, entertainment venues such as MTV, and "gangsta rap" music forms have all served to inculcate original street gang culture into a far broader youth culture. Most young people in America recognize the look, the walk, and the talk of gang members. Many mimic it in part or in whole. Many try it out as a personal style, some to discard it and some to retain it. Play groups, break-dancing groups, taggers, and school peer groups experiment with gang life. For some, it becomes all too real (Hagedorn, 1988; Klein, 1995).

In Europe, a number of new street gangs seem to have taken on the trappings of this gang culture. Needed now is a more careful assessment of the degree to which the exportation of the American style is a cause, or merely the external trappings, of European gang forms.

Cohesiveness

Two characteristics of street gangs, important in themselves, lead to a third. The first of these is group cohesiveness, although we must be careful not to overstate the extent to which gang members are tied to each other. Surprisingly few American scholars have paid much attention to group dynamics within gangs. Notable exceptions have been Yablonsky (1963), Short and Strodtbeck (1965), Jansyn (1966), and Klein

(1971,1995). What has been learned is that group cohesion in gangs is highly variable, both over time and across gangs. Generally, street gangs have only moderate levels of cohesiveness, with the result that this can be reduced sometimes to the point of gang dissolution but also that it can be increased to yield gangs that are more resistant to intervention and more involved in gang-related delinquency and crime. The more cohesive gang usually is the more criminally involved. Paradoxically, data from several projects suggest that the inadvertent effect of direct intervention with street gangs is to *increase* gang cohesiveness and thus gang crime. European policymakers must take very careful note of this process before launching naively into either social welfare *or* suppression programs to deal with their gangs.

Crime Patterns

One finding about street gangs has been consistently reported in research over the past seven decades. For the most part, gangs and gang members do not specialize in particular forms of offending but, rather, display considerable versatility in offending.[5]

Thus it is usually inappropriate to speak of violent gangs or theft gangs or graffiti gangs. They do a little of everything, but alcohol use, minor drug use, petty theft, and vandalism are probably the most common forms of crime. Violent offenses are the exception rather than the rule, a fact consistently overlooked in the media and among political figures. The stereotype of the violent American gang is one important factor underlying the Eurogang Paradox noted earlier.

Crime Amplification

There is, not surprisingly, a selection factor by which more delinquently inclined youth in a neighborhood are more likely to join street gangs than are their less delinquently inclined peers. Perhaps more important, recent longitudinal studies of gangs (Battin, Hill, Abbott, Catalano, & Hawkins, 1998; Huizinga, 1996; Thornberry, Krohn, Lizotte, Smith, & Tobin, 2003) have already confirmed a pattern more informally noted in earlier observational and ethnographic research. Joining a street gang greatly increases one's involvement in criminal activity, and especially in violent activity. Conversely, leaving the gang results in a significant reduction in criminal involvement. It is the combination of group cohesiveness and the crime patterns of gang members that together account for much of this amplification of criminal activity.

It is not just that "birds of a feather flock together." Being with other delinquents is only part of the process; the rest is the triggering of group processes as gang members intermingle and join forces against common enemies (Battin et al., 1998). One sees an amplification of group identity, group pride and status, need for protection, diffusion of responsibility, mutual reinforcement of antisocial moral codes, and similar social psychological processes that both allow and encourage engagement in the very behaviors—criminal behaviors—that give the gang its unique identity. Because normal moderate levels of cohesiveness allow for their own increase, these processes can and do result in serious crime amplification. Because most descriptions of European gangs suggest only moderate levels of cohesiveness and versatile patterns of criminal offending (except among skinhead groups), there is good reason to be worried about crime amplification, much as it has been demonstrated in the United States.

Application to European Gangs

The seven descriptors noted above certainly are not exhaustive. One might add leadership, clique structures, family background, neighborhood characteristics, and so on. Yet the seven listed here provide a sound base from which we might ask about European gangs. There is, however, one additional factor that will help considerably. This is the description of street gang structures.

For this purpose, I turn to the Maxson/Klein (1995) typology of five street gang structures, developed from descriptive data gathered from hundreds of police departments and applied in a preliminary way to European gangs in two publications (Klein, 1997; Klein et al., 2001). As outlined in the pending proposal to the European Union, these five structural types contain descriptors related to subgrouping, size, age range, duration, territoriality, and crime patterns (all are versatile except for the Specialty gangs). Brief scenarios describing the five as seen in the United States are as follows.

Five Street Gang Scenarios

The Traditional Gang

Traditional gangs have generally been in existence for 20 or more years—they keep regenerating themselves. They contain fairly clear subgroups, usually separated by age. O.G.s or Veteranos, Seniors, Juniors, Midgets, and various other names are applied to these different age-based cliques. Sometimes neighborhoods rather than age separate the cliques. More than other gangs, Traditional gangs tend to have a wide age range, sometimes as wide as from 9 or 10 years of age into the 30s. These are usually very large gangs, numbering one hundred or even several hundred members. Almost always, they are territorial in the sense that they identify strongly with their turf, 'hood, or barrio, and claim it as theirs alone.

In sum, this is a large, enduring, territorial gang with a wide range and several internal cliques based on age or area.

The Neotraditional Gang

The Neotraditional gang resembles the Traditional form, but has not been in existence as long—probably no more than 10 years, and often less. It may be medium size—say 50 to 100 members—or also into the hundreds. It probably has developed subgroups or cliques based on age or area, but sometimes may not. The age range is usually smaller than in the classical Traditional gangs. The Neotraditional gang is also very territorial, claiming turf and defending it.

In sum, the Neotraditional gang is a newer territorial gang that looks on its way to becoming Traditional in time. Thus at this point it is subgrouping, but may or may not have achieved territoriality, and size suggests that it is evolving into the Traditional form.

The Compressed Gang

The Compressed gang is small—usually in the size range of up to 50 members—and has not formed subgroups. The age range is probably narrow—10 or fewer years between the younger and older members. The small size, absence of subgroups, and narrow age range may reflect the newness of the group, in existence less than 10 years and maybe for only a few years. Some of these Compressed gangs have become territorial, but many have not.

In sum, Compressed gangs have a relatively short history, short enough that by size, duration, subgrouping, and territoriality it is unclear whether they will grow and solidify into the more traditional forms, or simply remain as less complex groups.

The Collective Gang

The Collective gang looks like the Compressed form, but bigger and with a wider age range—maybe 10 or more years between younger and older members. Size can be under one hundred, but is probably larger. Surprisingly, given these numbers, it has not developed subgroups, and may or may not be a territorial gang. It probably has a 10- to 15-year existence.

In sum, the Collective gang resembles a kind of shapeless mass of adolescent and young adult members that has not developed the distinguishing characteristics of other gangs.

The Specialty Gang

Unlike these other gangs that engage in a wide variety of criminal offenses, crime in this type of group is narrowly focused on a few offenses; the group comes to be characterized by the specialty. The Specialty gang tends to be small—usually 50 or fewer members—without any subgroups in most cases (there are exceptions). It probably has a history of less than 10 years, but has developed a well-defined territory. Its territory may be either residential or based on the opportunities for the particular form of crime in which it specializes. The age range of most Specialty gangs is narrow, but in others is broad.

In sum, the Specialty gang is crime-focused in a narrow way. Its principal purpose is more criminal than social, and its smaller size and form of territoriality may

be a reflection of this focused crime pattern. Typical examples are drug sales gangs and skinhead groups.

Reference to Table 9.1 suggests that modifications may benefit the application of the typology to the European situation. For instance, these relatively new gangs in Europe *at the present time* will seldom reach the size or age-range or duration of the Traditional gangs in the United States. Yet Traditional gangs have been noted in at least three cities—Glasgow, Berlin, and Kazan. The availability of the typology allows a preliminary assessment of the degree to which one can find gangs that are structurally similar in the United States and Europe, thus overcoming the Eurogang Paradox.

Weitekamp's (2001) review of European gang descriptions collected in the book *The Eurogang Paradox* (Klein et al., 2001) reports Traditional gangs in Kazan, Neotraditional and Compressed gangs in Manchester, Specialty Gangs in The Hague and Rotterdam, as well as Compressed gangs in Copenhagen, Frankfurt, and Oslo. Klein (1997) found similar typology counterparts in Paris, Stockholm, Stuttgart, and Brussels. In sum, European nations have street gangs very similar in structure to the street gangs in America. Only future research can reveal variations or prevalence of the types, existence of other types, and the salience of other descriptors.

And what of the seven other gang characteristics listed above; how do they compare in Europe? Here we are severely limited by the few clear depictions currently available in the European gang literature, much of which was written without explicit attention to U.S./European comparisons. I will rely for this analysis on the eight chapters in *The Eurogang Paradox* that describe street gangs in Europe.

Table 9.1
Characteristics of Five Gang Types

Type	Subgroups	Size	Age Range	Duration	Territorial	Crime Versatility
Traditional	Yes	Large (> 100)	Wide (20–30 years)	Long (> 20 years)	Yes	Yes
Neotraditional	Yes	Medium–Large (> 50)	(no pattern)	Short (< 10 years)	Yes	Yes
Compressed	No	Small (< 50)	Narrow (< 10 years)	Short (< 10 years)	(no pattern)	Yes
Collective	No	Medium–Large (> 50)	Medium–Wide (> 10 years)	Medium (10–15 years)	(no pattern)	Yes
Specialty	No	Small (< 50)	Narrow (< 10 years)	Short (< 10 years)	Yes	No

Location

The cities involved in these chapters are Rotterdam, den Haag, Manchester, Oslo, Copenhagen, Frankfurt, Kazan, Paris, and Bremen. Within these cities gang locations are described as inner city in Manchester, Oslo, and Kazan. Suburban locations are suggested in Manchester, Oslo, and Paris. In a number of these European cities, the location in suburban areas is explained by the placement there of housing projects designed for or occupied by immigrant and refugee populations.

Ethnicity

Many European countries, especially following the second World War, have welcomed substantial numbers of immigrants—often as "guest workers" to fill low-paying jobs not acceptable to sufficient numbers of the indigenous population. The second-generation offspring of the guest workers have in some locations gravitated toward street gang structures. In addition, some of these same countries have been receptive to large numbers of refugees from countries experiencing various kinds of nationalism and persecution of minority populations. Younger refugees and second-generation offspring have also fueled some of the gang problems. A review of *The Euro-gang Paradox* reports reveals the following national and ethnic gang compositions:

Holland:	Moroccan, Antillian, and Surinamese
Manchester:	Afro-Caribbean, indigenous white
Oslo:	Vietnamese, Filipino, Pakistani, Somali, Iranian, Moroccan, Turkish, and indigenous white
Copenhagen:	Muslim, indigenous white
Frankfurt:	Turkish, Croatian, Italian, and Russian
Kazan:	Indigenous white, Tatars
Paris:	Algerian
Bremen:	Turkish, indigenous white

Other reports from Stockholm, London, Berlin, Stuttgart, Spain, and Switzerland confirm this highly varied pattern of both indigenous and, especially, nonindigenous gang composition. The contrast to the United States is obviously fairly striking. It should be added that much of the indigenous white gang activity in these European locations, more so than in the United States, is comprised of skinheads and similar racist groups, most of which fit fairly well into the Specialty gang structure.

Gender

With the exception of a mention in the report from Paris, none of the reports in this collection speaks of female gang participation. Whether this reflects a one-sex gang situation or the absence of researchers' attention to the issue cannot be determined. If the former, this is an important departure from the American experience. If the latter, it may be a reflection of a mostly male research enterprise not unlike that found in earlier American studies. The enrollment of female researchers in the Eurogang Program can certainly be encouraged to help open the window on the gender issue there.

Cultural Diffusion

There are no American gangs in Europe, nor have I heard of any American gang members migrating to Europe and influencing gang genesis there. But the reports from Holland, Manchester, and Oslo do suggest that the diffusion of American *gang culture* has had an effect. American gang movies and books (including translations from the English) are specifically cited. And of course much European television fare is imported from the United States, as is gang-oriented popular or rap music. How much we have spread our gang influence is not clear, but it is certain that some level of gang culture diffusion has taken place.

Cohesiveness

The picture on concern for and measurement of gang cohesiveness in Europe is mixed. The reports from Holland, Paris, and Frankfurt make no explicit reference to the topic. The Manchester report suggests low levels, and the Copenhagen and Bremen reports are of medium levels. Some of the Oslo material suggests high gang cohesiveness, and the Kazan report describes a transformation over time from medium to high cohesiveness as those gangs have become more organized and explicitly criminal in focus. None of these reports uses empirical measures of group cohesiveness, to say nothing of common measures. This, then, is a most promising area for future gang research in European settings.

Crime Patterns

The Dutch gangs observed in The Hague and Rotterdam were small Specialty gangs. In Oslo and Paris, both specialized and versatile crime patterns were reported. In all the other sites, versatility was the reported pattern. The parallel to the American experience is quite striking. The patterns of most concern to American officials—drug sales and violence—are in most cases lower in the European cities, and firearm violence there is practically nonexistent. One can only hope this is a difference that will persist.

Crime Amplification

The major effect on levels of criminal activity occasioned by joining street gangs in the United States is mentioned in only three of the European reports, those from Oslo, Kazan, and Bremen. One suspects that this pattern has simply not been a paramount concern for European gang observers, but only future, focused research can clarify this.

Summary

Although European gang research is quite new, and the gangs themselves have had little opportunity to evolve in form, some comparisons to the U.S. situation are already becoming clear. U.S. gangs are far, far more prevalent, and far more involved in serious and lethal violence. Our ethnic gang composition has over time become narrow, whereas that in Europe is highly varied. Still, on both continents street gangs are composed primarily of youth from marginalized segments of their societies. Gender and cohesiveness patterns may be different, but may also only seem so due to a lack of research attention.

But in contrast to these differences, one is struck by the similarities to be found between American and European gang situations (in the absence of, it should be noted, almost any deliberately comparative research). Two sets of attributes, when compared across the two continents, suggest we are viewing one older and one newer variation on a similar theme attributable to common group processes and similar combinations of societal variables that produce marginalization of some youth populations.

First, there are those attributes of gang structure that produce a typology of five gang types roughly applicable in both the United States and Europe. Group placements on subgrouping, size, age range, duration, territoriality, and crime versatility serve to reduce the "Eurogang Paradox" and reveal that current European street gangs can largely be subsumed under the Maxson/Klein typology developed in the United States. To deny street gang existence in Europe, in these circumstances, would be more foolish than useful.

Second, analyses of European gang reports in eight general locations show that, to the extent they are covered, seven gang-relevant descriptions from U.S. research are applicable to European research. One can obtain clarification of European gangs by reference to such variables as location, ethnicity, gender, cultural diffusion, cohesiveness, crime patterns, and crime amplification. These are variables additional to the structural attributes of the typology (except for crime pattern).

There is much room in all this for future research to elucidate the unique natures of European gangs, and the developing Eurogang Program will likely provide such clarification. But the uniqueness will be bounded by the discovered similarities to American street gangs. This means that the American gang knowledge accumulated over the past 70 years provides a major resource for research in Europe, the kind of research not available to the Americans until only very recently. As suggested above, I would urge special attention to group processes and youth marginalization as pivotal concerns for understanding and controlling street gang developments in Europe.

Notes

1. The Port Moresby "Rascals" have been described in Biles (1976), and by Sundeen (1981).

2. A book by that name includes many of the papers produced for the first Eurogang workshop: see Klein et al. (2001).

3. Klein (1997) and Klein et al. (2001) have expanded on the five gang types revealed in the original research by Maxson and Klein (1995). These types have been confirmed in a statewide study in Illinois by Scott (2000) and by the National Youth Gang Center (2000) in a comprehensive national survey of law enforcement agencies.

4. Campbell and her coauthors noted, "youth in one part of the country are relatively ignorant of others' activities until it reaches the

point of mass movement or violence. The net effect is that New York teenagers, already factioned within the city into their own areas, have virtually no knowledge of the situation of gang members in Chicago, Los Angeles, or Philadelphia."

5. This has also been labeled "cafeteria-style" offending ("Smorgasbord offending" has been suggested by a Swedish scholar). The major exception to this versatile pattern is to be found in Specialty gangs described later in this chapter.

References

Battin, S. R., Hill, K. G., Abbott, R. D., Catalano, R. R., & Hawkins, J. D. (1998). The contribution of gang membership to delinquency beyond delinquent friends. *Criminology,* 36(1), 93–115.

Biles, D. (Ed.). (1976). Introduction. In *Crime in Papua New Guinea.* Canberra: Australian Institute of Criminology.

Campbell, A., Munce, S., & Galea, J. (1982). American gangs and British subcultures: A comparison. *International Journal of Offender Therapy and Comparative Criminology,* 26, 76–89.

Chesney-Lind, M., Shelden, R. G., & Joe, K. A. (1996). Girls, delinquency, and gang membership. In C. R. Huff (Ed.), *Gangs in America* (2nd ed., pp. 185–204). Thousand Oaks, CA: Sage.

Clinard, M. B., & Abbott, D. J. (1973). *Crime in developing countries: A comparative perspective.* New York: John Wiley.

Cohen, S. (1972). *Folk devils and moral panics.* London, UK: MacGibbon and Kee.

Covey, H. C., Menard, S., & Franzese, R. J. (1997). *Juvenile gangs* (2nd ed.). Springfield, IL: Charles C Thomas.

Decker, S. H., & Van Winkle, B. (1996). *Life in the gang: Family, friends, and violence.* Cambridge, UK, & New York: Cambridge University Press.

DeFleur, L. (1967). Delinquent gangs in cross-cultural perspective: The case of Cordoba. *Journal of Research in Crime and Delinquency,* 4, 132–141.

Eggleston, E. J. (1996). *Youth perspectives on gangs and crime: An ethnography from New Zealand.* Unpublished manuscript, Massey University, New Zealand.

Fleisher, M. S. (1998). *Dead end kids: Gang girls and the boys they know.* Madison: University of Wisconsin Press.

Hagedorn, J. M. (1988). *People and folks: Gangs, crime and the underclass in a rustbelt city.* Chicago: Lake View.

Hagedorn, J. M., & Devitt, M. L. (1999). Fighting female: The social construction of female gangs. In M. Chesney-Lind & J. Hagedorn (Eds.), *Female gangs in America: Essays on girls, gangs and gender* (pp. 256–276). Chicago: Lake View.

Howell, J. C., & Gleason, D. K. (1999). *Youth gang drug trafficking.* (Juvenile Justice Bulletin, NCJ No. 178282, pp. 1–11). Washington, DC: U.S. Office of Juvenile Justice and Delinquency Prevention.

Huizinga, D. H. (1996). *The influence of delinquent peers, gangs, and co-offending and violence* (Fact Sheet). Washington, DC: U.S. Office of Juvenile Justice and Delinquency Prevention.

Huizinga, D. H., & Schumann, K. F. (2001). Gang membership in Bremen and Denver: Comparative longitudinal data. In M. W. Klein, H.-J. Kerner, C. L. Maxson, & E. G. M. Weitekamp (Eds.), *The Eurogang paradox: Street gangs and youth groups in the U.S. and Europe.* Dordrecht, The Netherlands: Kluwer Academic.

Jansyn, L. (1966). Solidarity and delinquency in a street corner group. *American Sociological Review,* 31, 600–614.

Kersten, J. (2001). Groups of violent young males in Germany. In M. W. Klein, H.-J. Kerner, C. L. Maxson, & E. G. M. Weitekamp (Eds.), *The Eurogang paradox: Street gangs and youth groups in the U.S. and Europe.* Dordrecht, The Netherlands: Kluwer Academic.

Klein, M. W. (1971). *Street gangs and street workers.* Englewood Cliffs, NJ: Prentice Hall.

———. (1995). *The American street gang: Its nature, prevalence, and control.* New York: Oxford University Press.

———. (1997). Gangs in the United States and Europe. *European Journal on Criminal Policy and Research,* 4, 63–80.

Klein, M. W., Kerner, H.-J., Maxson, C. L., & Weitekamp, E. G. M. (Eds.). (2001). *The Eurogang paradox: Street gangs and youth groups in the U.S. and Europe.* Dordrecht, The Netherlands: Kluwer.

Maxson, C. L. (1998). *Gang members on the move* (Juvenile Justice Bulletin, Youth Gang Series, NCJ No. 171153). Washington, DC: U.S. Department of Justice, Office of Juvenile Justice and Delinquency Prevention.

Maxson, C. L., & Klein, M. W. (1995). Investigating gang structures. *Journal of Gang Research,* 3, 33–40.

Miller, J. (2001a). *One of the guys: Girls, gangs and gender.* New York: Oxford University Press.

———. (2001b). Young women's involvement in gangs in the United States: An overview. In M. W. Klein, H.-J. Kerner, C. L. Maxson, & E. G. M. Weitekamp (Eds.), *The Eurogang paradox: Street gangs and youth groups in the U.S. and Europe.* Boston & Dordrecht, The Netherlands: Kluwer Academic.

Moore, J. W. (1991). *Going down to the barrio:*

Homeboys and homegirls in change. Philadelphia: Temple University Press.

National Youth Gang Center. (2000). *1998 National Youth Gang Survey.* Washington, DC: U.S. Department of Justice, Office of Juvenile Justice and Delinquency Prevention.

Scott, G. (2000). *Illinois law enforcement responses to street gangs.* Chicago: Office of the Illinois Attorney General, Gang Crime Prevention Center.

Short, J. F., Jr., & Strodtbeck, F. L. (1965). *Group process and gang delinquency.* Chicago: University of Chicago Press.

Spergel, I. A. (1995). *The youth gang problem: A community approach.* New York: Oxford University Press.

Sundeen, R. A. (1981). Juvenile arrests in Papua New Guinea. In G. F. Jensen (Ed.), *Sociology of delinquency: Current issues.* Beverley Hills, CA: Sage.

Thornberry, T. P., Krohn, M. D., Lizotte, A. J., Smith, C. A., & Tobin, K. (2003). *Gangs and delinquency in developmental perspective.* New York: Cambridge University Press.

van Gemert, F. (2001). Crips in orange: Gangs and groups in the Netherlands. In M. W. Klein, H.-J. Kerner, C. L. Maxson, & E. G. M. Weitekamp (Eds.), *The Eurogang paradox: Street gangs and youth groups in the U.S. and Europe.* Dordrecht, The Netherlands: Kluwer Academic.

Weitekamp, E. G. M. (2000). *Eurogang: A thematic network for comparative, multi-method research on violent youth groups* (The E.U. Eurogang proposal). Tubingen, Germany: Institute of Criminology.

———. (2001). Gangs in Europe: Assessments at the millennium. In M. W. Klein, H.-J. Kerner, C. L. Maxson, & E. G. M. Weitekamp (Eds.), *The Eurogang paradox: Street gangs and youth groups in the U.S. and Europe.* Dordrecht, The Netherlands: Kluwer Academic.

Yablonsky, L. (1963). *The violent gang.* New York: Macmillan. ✦

Chapter 10
Gang Members on the Move

Cheryl L. Maxson

*A*long *with the recognition of the increased proliferation of gangs across the country came various attempts to explain this change. By far the most common of these attempts was to invoke the migration of gang members from major crack cocaine markets, such as Los Angeles, to smaller cities to establish new markets. In this article, Maxson reviews some of the definitional issues and earlier studies of gang migration. She then reports the results of a new national survey of both chronic and emergent gang cities, using police experts as informants on the principal reasons for gang migration. The crack marketing explanation, although applicable in certain situations, generally does little to explain gang proliferation.*

In recent years, local government officials, law enforcement officers, and community organizations have witnessed the emergence and growth of gangs in U.S. cities once thought to be immune to the crime and violence associated with street gangs in large metropolitan areas. Police chiefs, mayors, school officials, community activists, and public health officials have gone so far as to identify this proliferation as an epidemic. Reports of big-city gang members fanning out across the nation seeking new markets for drug distribution have added fuel to concerns about gang proliferation and gang migration.

The increase in gang migration has generated the need for the issue to be assessed

Reprinted from: Cheryl L. Maxson, "Gang Members on the Move." In *Juvenile Justice Bulletin*, October, pp. 1–11. Copyright © 1998 U.S. Department of Justice, Office of Justice Programs, Office of Juvenile Justice and Delinquency Prevention. Reprinted by permission.

based on empirical evidence. As local communities attempt to address gang-related problems in their areas, it is critical that they have a clear understanding of patterns of gang migration and an accurate assessment of local, or indigenous, gang membership.

This Chapter explores how key terms such as *gang, gang proliferation,* and *gang migration* are defined; how and whether gang migration affects gang proliferation; and trends reported in research literature. This Chapter is based in part on work supported by the National Institute of Justice (NIJ) and an article previously published in the *National Institute of Justice Journal* (Maxson, Woods, and Klein, 1996). Findings from a recent University of Southern California (USC) study on street-gang migration are also discussed (Maxson, Woods, and Klein, 1995).

Clarifying the Concepts

Defining the Terms 'Gang,' 'Gang Proliferation,' and 'Gang Migration'

Gang. There has been much debate over the term "gang," but little progress has been made toward widespread acceptance of a uniform definition. Some researchers prefer a broad definition that includes group criminal and noncriminal activities, whereas law enforcement agencies tend to use definitions that expedite the cataloging of groups for purposes of statistical analysis or prosecution. Variations in the forms or structure of gangs make it difficult to put forth one standard definition (Klein and Maxson, 1996). For example, researchers have attempted to draw a distinction between street gangs and drug gangs (Klein, 1995). Drug gangs are perceived as smaller, more cohesive, and more hierarchical than most street gangs and are exclusively focused on conducting drug deals and defending drug territories. Street gangs, on the other hand, engage in a wide array of criminal activity. Drug gangs may be subgroups of street gangs or may develop independently of street gangs. For the purposes of this Chapter and the national surveys on gang migration conducted by USC, gangs were defined as groups of adolescents and/or young adults who see themselves as a group (as do others) and have been involved in enough crime to be of considerable concern to law enforcement and the community (Maxson, Woods, and Klein, 1995). In the USC survey, drug gangs were included in the overall grouping of gangs, but members of motorcycle gangs, prison-based gangs, graffiti taggers, and racial supremacy groups were excluded to narrow the focus to street gangs.

Another challenge in defining the term "gang" is the fluctuating structure of these groups. Over the course of adolescence and young adulthood, individual members move in and out of gangs, continually affecting the gangs' structure (Thornberry et al., 1993). The terms "wannabe," "core," "fringe," "associate," "hardcore," and "O.G." (original gangster) reflect the changing levels of involvement and the fact that the boundaries of gang membership are penetrable. Some researchers argue that the term "member" was created and used by law enforcement, gang researchers, and individuals engaged in gang activity with only a loose consensus of generalized, shared meaning.

Gang Proliferation. The term "gang proliferation" indicates the increase in communities reporting the existence of gangs and gang problems (Knox et al., 1996). While gangs have existed in various forms, degrees, and locations in the United States for many decades, the sheer volume of cities and towns documenting recent gang activity cannot be denied. Some of this increase may be attributed to a heightened awareness of gang issues, redirection of law enforcement attention, widespread training, and national education campaigns. Nevertheless, gangs exist in locations previously unaffected and attract a larger proportion of adolescents than in the past.[1]

Gang Migration. The already difficult task of defining gangs is compounded when the relationship between gang migration and proliferation is addressed. Gang migration—the movement of gang members from one city to another—has been mentioned with increasing frequency in State legislative task force investigations, government-sponsored conferences, and law enforcement accounts at the Federal, State, and local levels (Bonfante, 1995; Hayeslip, 1989; California Council on Criminal Justice, 1989; Genelin and Coplen, 1989; McKinney, 1988; National Drug Intelligence Center, 1994, 1996). For the USC study, migration was broadly defined to include temporary relocations, such as visits to relatives, short

trips to sell drugs or develop other criminal enterprises, and longer stays while escaping crackdowns on gangs or gang activity. More permanent changes, such as residential moves (either individually or with family members) and court placements, were also included. Individuals in the study did not have to participate in gang activity in the destination city to be considered gang migrants. This broad definition of gang migration allowed researchers to investigate the degree of gang-organized and gang-supported expansion of members to other locations, of which little evidence was found. It also allowed researchers to examine variations in gang activity in the destination city and the many reasons for relocating. If the concept of migration was limited to individuals or groups traveling solely for gang-related purposes or at the direction of gang leaders, the patterns of migration would change drastically. Further, collective gang migration is rare, but the migration of individual gang members is not.

Another complication in defining gang migration is the distinction between migrant gang members (migrants) and indigenous gang members, which often fades over time. As migrants settle into new locations, sometimes joining local gangs, their identities may evolve to the point to which their prior gang affiliation no longer exists. This process of assimilation into local gang subcultures has not been addressed in research literature, because law enforcement officers and researchers have only recently begun to discuss gang migration. In future studies, researchers should consider at what point a migrant gang member is no longer perceived as a migrant but as a local gang member in the new location.

The Influence of Gang Migration on Gang Proliferation

The primary focus of this Chapter is to assess whether gang migration has played a major role in gang proliferation. Migrant gang members may stimulate the growth of gangs and gang membership through a variety of processes, such as recruiting locals to establish a branch of the gang in previously unaffected areas. This approach, described as the importation model, involves efforts by gang members to infuse their gang into new cities, primarily to establish new drug markets and other money-making criminal enterprises (Decker and Van Winkle, 1996). This is also referred to as gang franchising (Knox et al., 1996) and gang colonization (Quinn, Tobolowsky, and Downs, 1994). Alternatively, migrants may establish a new gang without structural affiliation to an existing gang. Furthermore, if a sufficient number of individuals from a gang move to a new location, they may replicate a migrant subset of their former gang. No matter what process is used, new local gangs will most likely emerge in response to territorial challenges or perceived protection needs. The city with a single gang is a rare phenomenon (Klein, 1995). Regardless of the pattern of new gang initiation, gang member migration would create an increase in both the numbers of gangs and gang membership.

Another way migrant gangs may stimulate gang proliferation is by introducing new and exciting cultural distinctions from existing gangs. In a city in which gangs exist but are not firmly established, migrant gang members may act as cultural carriers of the folkways, mythologies, and other trappings of more sophisticated urban gangs. They may offer strong distinctions from other gangs and cause a rivalry with existing gangs, such as the rivalry between the Bloods and Crips in southern California and between the People and Folks in the Midwest. Most of the respondents in the 1993 USC phone survey reported that migrants influence local gang rivalries, gang dress codes, and recruiting methods (Maxson, Woods, and Klein, 1995). In addition, the solidification of local gang subcultures may increase the visibility or attractiveness of gangs to local youth. It may also influence the growth of rival gangs.

Conversely, there are a variety of circumstances in which migrant gang members have little or no impact on gang proliferation. If the geographic location allows, migrants may retain their affiliation with their original gangs by commuting to old territories or they may simply discontinue gang activity altogether. In cities with relatively large and established gangs, it is unlikely that migrant gang members would have a noticeable effect on the overall gang environment.

An important related issue is the impact of migrant gang members on local crime patterns.[2] Migrants are generally perceived as contributing to both increased levels of crime and the seriousness of criminal activity (Maxson, Woods, and Klein, 1995). The 1993 USC survey involved telephone interviews with law enforcement in 211 cities that experienced gang migration in 1992. Most of the cities involved in the survey (86 percent) reported that migrant gang members contributed to an increase in local crime rates or patterns primarily in theft (50-percent increase), robbery (35-percent increase), other violent crimes (59-percent increase), and, to a lesser extent, drug sales (24-percent increase). The small increase in drug sale activity can most likely be attributed to competition from established local drug markets. The survey also showed that the type of criminal gang activity was changing to include increased use of firearms and more sophisticated weapons (36-percent increase). Carjackings, fire-bombings, residential robberies, drive-by shootings, and advanced techniques for vehicle theft were also cited on occasion. Changes in the targets of criminal activity and the use of other technological advances were mentioned less frequently.

What Previous Studies Show

The following is a summary of the research literature on the relationship between migration and proliferation. Local law enforcement agencies have become increasingly aware of the usefulness of maintaining systematic information on gangs, yet such data bases hardly meet the scientific standards of reliability and validity. Therefore, the results of the studies described in this section should be viewed as exploratory.

Although a number of national studies dating back to the 1970s have documented an increase in the number of cities and smaller communities reporting street gang activity, the numbers reported by these studies vary (Miller, 1975, 1982; Needle and Stapleton, 1983; Spergel and Curry, 1990; Curry, Ball, and Fox, 1994; Klein, 1995; Curry, 1996). Variations in localities reporting gang activities are attributed to the use of different sampling frames in the national surveys. While the surveys are not compatible, each reports increased gang activity. Miller's 1996 compilation of data from several sources documents gang proliferation during the past three decades and shows that in the 1970s, street gangs existed in the United States in 201 cities and 70 counties (many with cities included in the former count) (Miller, 1996). These figures climbed to 468 and 247, respectively, during the 1980s and to 1,487 and 706 in the 1990s. A nationwide survey conducted by the National Youth Gang Center (NYGC) reported that in 1995 gangs existed in 1,492 cities and 515 counties (OJJDP, 1997). The figures reported by Miller and NYGC are considerably higher than the estimate of 760 jurisdictions reported by Curry and his associates (Curry, Ball, and Decker, 1996) and the projection of 1,200 gang cities derived from the 1992 USC national mail survey (reported in Maxson, Woods, and Klein, 1995). Similarly, the National Drug Intelligence Center (NDIC) reported a much smaller figure of 265 for cities and counties reporting gang activity in 1995 (NDIC, 1996). Of these 265 cities and counties, 182 jurisdictions reported gang "connections" to 234 other cities, but the nature of these relationships was not elaborated on (D. Mehall, NDIC, personal communication, August 20, 1996). With the exception of the Mehall report and that of Maxson, Woods, and Klein (1995), none of the studies addressed the issue of gang migration on a national scale.

With few exceptions, findings on gang migration reported in research literature contrast sharply with the perspectives presented by the media, government agencies, and law enforcement reports. Several researchers have studied gangs in various cities throughout the United States and examined their origin and relationships to gangs in larger cities (primarily Chicago) to examine correlations between gang migration and proliferation on a more regional scale.

Gangs in the Midwestern United States

In 1983, Rosenbaum and Grant identified three Evanston, IL, gangs as "satellites" of major Chicago gangs, but proceeded to emphasize that they "are composed largely of Evanston residents, and in a very real sense, are Evanston gangs" (p. 15). They also found that two indigenous gangs, with no outside connection, contributed disproportionately to levels of violence and were, therefore, "almost totally responsible for increasing fear of crime in the community and forcing current reactions to the problem" (Rosenbaum and Grant, 1983:21). In contrast, the Chicago-connected gangs maintained a lower profile and were more profit oriented in their illegal activities, aspiring "to be more like organized crime" (Rosenbaum and Grant, 1983:21). In other words, the gangs indigenous to Evanston seemed to be more of a threat to the community than the Chicago-based gangs. The conclusion can be drawn that in this particular study, the migration of gangs into Evanston only minimally affected the proliferation of gang activities.

In an extensive study of Milwaukee gangs in 1988, 18 groups were found to use the names and symbols of major Chicago gangs, including identification with such gang confederations as People versus Folk (Hagedorn, 1988). In questioning gang founders on the origins of the gangs, it was determined that only 4 of the 18 were formed directly by gang members who had moved from Chicago to Milwaukee. Further, these members maintained only slight ties to their original Chicago gangs. Despite law enforcement claims to the contrary, no existence of a super-gang (i.e., Chicago) coalition was found in Milwaukee. Founding gang members strongly resented the idea that their gang was in any way tied to the original Chicago gangs (Hagedorn, 1988). In this study, Hagedorn concludes that gang formation in Milwaukee was only minimally affected by the migration of Chicago gangs. If anything, the influence was more cultural than structural, because gangs in smaller cities tend to follow big-city gang traditions and borrow cultural aspects from these gang images.

Further supporting the notion that gang migration only minimally affects proliferation is a 1989 study that determined that gangs in Columbus and Cleveland, OH, originated from streetcorner groups and breakdancing/rapping groups and also from migrating street-gang leaders from Chicago or Los Angeles (Huff, 1989). The study found no evidence that Ohio gangs were directly affiliated with gangs from other cities, particularly Chicago, Detroit, or Los Angeles.

In 1992, researchers examined the role that Chicago gangs played in the emergence of youth gangs in Kenosha, WI (Zevitz and Takata, 1992). Based on interviews with gang members, police analyses, and social service and school records, the study concluded that "the regional gangs in this study were products of local development even though they had a cultural affinity with their metropolitan counterparts. . . . We found no convincing evidence that metropolitan gangs had branched out to the outlying community where our study took place" (Zevitz and Takata, 1992:102). Regular contact between some Chicago and Kenosha gang members reflected kinship or old neighborhood ties rather than the organizational expansion of Chicago gangs.

These findings are echoed in a 1996 study of 99 gang members in St. Louis (Decker and Van Winkle, 1996). A minority (16 percent) of those interviewed suggested that gangs reemerged in St. Louis, MO, through the efforts of gang members from Los Angeles. Several of these migrants had relocated for social reasons, such as visiting relatives. The study also found that St. Louis gangs were more likely to originate as a result of neighborhood conflicts influenced by popular culture rather than from big-city connections.

> The powerful images of Los Angeles gangs, conveyed through movies, clothes, and music, provided a symbolic reference point for these antagonisms. In this way, popular culture provided the symbols and rhetoric of gang affiliation and activities that galvanized neighborhood rivalries. (Decker and Van Winkle, 1996:88)

Another study on gang migration in 1996 surveyed 752 jurisdictions in Illinois (Knox et al., 1996). (Because only 38 percent of the law enforcement agencies responded, these findings should be interpreted cautiously.) The majority of respondents (88 percent) reported that gangs from outside their area had established an influence, that one-fifth or more of their local gang population was attributable to recent arrivals (49 percent), that parental relocation of gang members served to transplant the gang problem to the area (65 percent), and that some of their gang problem was due to gang migration (69 percent). The study concluded that, while the impact of migration varies, "it is still of considerable interest to the law enforcement community" (Knox et al., 1996:78).

Gangs in the Western United States

In a study of drug sales and violence among San Francisco gangs, 550 gang members from 84 different gangs were in-

terviewed (Waldorf, 1993). Of these, only three groups reported relationships with other gangs outside San Francisco. The report concluded that

> . . . most gangs do not have the skills or knowledge to move to other communities and establish new markets for drug sales. While it is true they can and do function on their own turf they are often like fish out of water when they go elsewhere. . . . They are not like organized crime figures (Mafia and Colombian cocaine cartels) who have capital, knowledge and power . . . while it might be romantic to think that the L.A. Bloods and Crips are exceptional, I will remain skeptical that they are more competent than other gangs. (Waldorf, 1993:8)

To the contrary, a 1988 study of inmates in California correctional institutions and law enforcement and correctional officials suggested high levels of mobility among "entrepreneurial" California gang members traveling long distances to establish drug distribution outlets and maintaining close ties to their gangs of origin (Skolnick et al., 1990; Skolnick, 1990). Among all the empirical studies conducted in this area, Skolnick's resonates most closely with the reports from law enforcement previously cited (Bonfante, 1995; Hayeslip, 1989; California Council on Criminal Justice, 1989; Genelin and Coplen, 1989; McKinney, 1988; National Drug Intelligence Center, 1994, 1996).

> Against a backdrop of escalating violence, declining drug prices, and intensified law enforcement, Los Angeles area gang-related drug dealers are seeking new venues to sell the Midas product—crack cocaine. . . . Respondents claim to have either participated in or have knowledge of Blood or Crip crack operations in 22 states and at least 27 cities. In fact, it appears difficult to overstate the penetration of Blood and Crip members into other states. (Skolnick, 1990:8)

But the sheer presence of Crips and Bloods in States other than California is a poor indicator of gang migration. The 1996 NDIC survey identified 180 jurisdictions in 42 States with gangs claiming affiliation with the Bloods and/or Crips. At the same time, the NDIC report cautions against assuming organizational links from gang names.

It is important to note that when a gang

has claimed affiliation with the Bloods or Crips, or a gang has taken the name of a nationally known gang, this does not necessarily indicate that this gang is a part of a group with a national infrastructure. While some gangs have interstate connections and a hierarchical structure, the majority of gangs do not fit this profile. (NDIC, 1996:v)

Gangs in the South Central United States

In a 1994 study of 9 States located in the south central United States, 131 municipal police departments were surveyed; 79 cities completed the mail survey (Quinn, Tobolowsky, and Downs, 1994). Respondents in 44 percent of small cities (populations between 15,000 and 50,000) and 41 percent of large cities (populations greater than 50,000) stated that their largest gang was affiliated with groups in other cities. It is unknown whether the perceived affiliation was based on structural links or on name association. Nearly three-fourths of the 792 gang cities that responded to the 1992 USC mail survey reported that at least some indigenous gangs adopted gang names generally associated with Los Angeles and Chicago (e.g., Bloods, Crips, Vicelords, Gangster Disciples, or Latin Kings). Approximately 60 of these cities had no gang migration.

The National Survey on Gang Migration

In 1992, the University of Southern California conducted a mail survey of law enforcement personnel in approximately 1,100 U.S. cities. The survey was distributed to all cities with a population of more than 100,000 and to more than 900 cities and towns that serve as likely environments for street gangs or gang migration.[3] Law enforcement officials suggested municipalities to include in the survey, and all cities with organizations that investigate gangs were included. To increase the survey pool, the survey asked respondents to list cities to which their local gang members had moved. This sample is best characterized as a purposive sample of gang cities—it is neither representative of all U.S. cities and towns, although all large cities are enumerated fully, nor all gang cities.[4] This survey captured data on the largest number of cities

with gangs identified at the time (and a majority of the cities identified by the NYGC survey in 1995) and is the only systematic enumeration of U.S. cities experiencing gang migration to date. Repeated mailings and telephone follow up resulted in completion of the survey by more than 90 percent of those polled.

To develop descriptions about the nature of gang migration and local responses to it, extensive telephone interviews were conducted with law enforcement officers in 211 cities that reported the arrival of at least 10 migrant gang members in 1991. Interview participants were sampled from a larger pool of 480 cities that cited at least moderate levels of gang migration. Other facets of the study included interviews with community informants and case studies, including personal interviews with migrant gang members.[5]

A primary limitation of this research design is the necessity to rely on law enforcement for depictions of the scope and nature of gang migration. Locally based ethnographic approaches—based on the systematic recording of particular human cultures—would lend a more comprehensive view of the migration situation in individual cities. The USC case studies involved a range of informants whose depictions sometimes contrasted markedly with law enforcement's assessment of the issue. The attempt to extend beyond law enforcement to community respondents produced mixed results, because informants were generally less informed about migration matters in the city as a whole and tended to focus on particular neighborhoods of interest. It would seem that law enforcement is the best available source of information on national patterns of gang migration, but the reader should be wary of the limitations on law enforcement as a source of information on migration. These limitations include the occupational focus of law enforcement on crime (i.e., if migrants are not engaged in a lot of crime, they are less likely to come to the attention of law enforcement), the lack of local data bases with systematically gathered information about migration, and the definitional challenges described earlier in Clarifying the Concepts. Given these limitations, the results from this study should be viewed as exploratory until replicated by further research.

Study Findings

The National Scope of Gang Migration

Approximately 1,000 cities responded to the 1992 mail survey, revealing 710 cities that had experienced gang migration by 1992. The widespread distribution of these cities is reflected in Figure 10.1.[6] Only three States had not experienced gang migration by 1992—New Hampshire, North Dakota, and Vermont. The concentration of migration cities in several regions—most dramatically southern California and the Bay area, the area surrounding Chicago, and southern Florida—may obscure the geographic distribution. Forty-four percent of migration cities are located in the western region of the country, with slightly less prominence in the mid-western (26 percent) and southern (25 percent) portions of the country. Only 5 percent of the migration cities are situated in the northeastern region of the country.

Approximately 80 percent of cities with a population of more than 100,000 have migrant gang members. The overall sample cannot address the proportion of all smaller cities with migration, but the distribution of migration cities by population, shown in Figure 10.1, suggests that this is an issue confronting cities of all sizes. That nearly 100 towns with populations of 10,000 people or less experienced gang migration is striking. This phenomenon is a manifestation of the motivations to relocate and the potential influences of migrant gang members on small-town life and overtaxed law enforcement resources. Moreover, because smaller cities are less likely to have long-standing gang problems, gang migration could be a catalyst for the onset of local gang problems.

The sheer number of cities with migrant gang members and the widespread geographic distribution of these cities across the country is dramatic, but the volume of gang migration presents a far less alarming picture. Survey respondents provided an estimate of the number of migrants that had arrived in their city the year prior to survey completion.[7] Just under half (47 percent) of the 597 cities providing an estimate reported the arrival of no more than 10 mi-

Figure 10.1
Cities Experiencing Gang Member Migration Through 1992

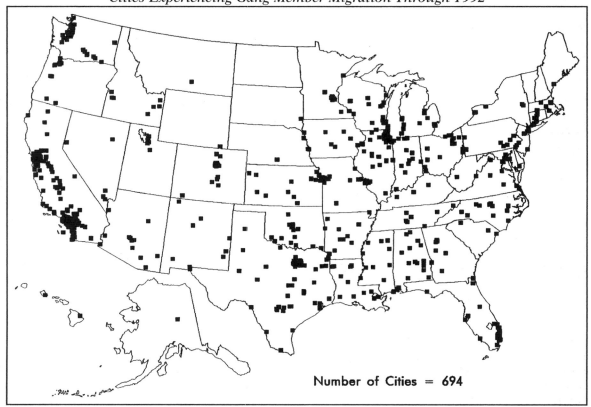

Number of Cities = 694

grants in the prior year. Only 34 cities (6 percent) estimated the arrival of more than 100 migrants during this period. The significance of such numbers would vary by the size of the city, but the large number of cities reporting insubstantial levels of migration suggests that gang migration may not represent a serious problem in many cities.

Survey respondents were asked to provide a demographic profile of migrant gang members. The typical age reported ranged from 13 to 30, and the mean and median age was 18. Female migrants were uncommon; more than 80 percent of the cities noted five or fewer. Compared with the ethnic distribution of gang members nationally, migrant gang members were somewhat more likely to be black. Approximately half of the cities polled in the survey reported that at least 60 percent of migrant gang members were black; predominantly Hispanic distributions emerged in 28 percent of the cities. The predominance of Asian (14 cities or 7 percent) or white (2 cities) migrant gang members was unusual.

Gang Migration and Local Gang Proliferation

The potential for gang migration to have a harmful impact on local gang activity and crime rates may increase substantially if migrant gang members foster the proliferation of local gang problems in their destination cities. This is a pivotal issue, and data of several types are available for elaboration. The characteristics of cities with local gangs can be compared with those of cities with migrant gangs to establish the parameters of the relationship. Of particular interest are the dates of local gang formation and migration onset. Law enforcement perceptions about the causes of local gang problems are also relevant. Lastly, the motivations of gang members to migrate and their patterns of gang activity upon arrival must be considered.

Through the survey of 1,100 cities, it was found that most, but not all, cities that have local gangs also have migrant gang members. Conversely, nearly all cities with gang migration also have local gangs. The 1992 survey identified 792 cities with local gangs; of these cities, 127 (16 percent) reported no experience with gang migration (Table 10.1). Only 45 of the 710 identified migration cities (6 percent) had no indigenous gangs. This simple comparison yields 172 cities (22 percent) in which migration could not have caused the emergence of local gangs, at least through 1992. The large proportion of cities with both local and migrant gang members made it difficult to detect any differences between local gang and migrant gang cities. Distributions across city size categories and geographic region are negligible (data not shown).

Another pertinent point of comparison from the survey is the date of onset of local gangs and the year in which migrant gang members first arrived in cities with local and migrant gang members. (These data are shown in Figure 10.2 with some loss of cases due to the respondents' inability to estimate at least one of the dates.) Only 31 of the cities with local gangs (5 percent) reported the onset of gang migration at least 1 year prior to the emergence of local gangs. Most cities (54 percent) had local gangs prior to gang migration. Adding these 344 cities (i.e., those with local gangs before mi-

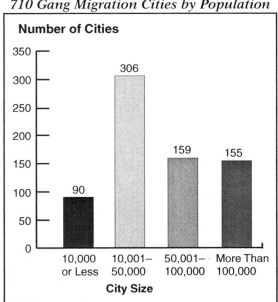

Figure 10.2
710 Gang Migration Cities by Population

Table 10.1
Cities With Local Gangs or Gang Migration

	No Gang Migration	Gang Migration
Cities with no local gangs	182	45
Cities with local gangs	127	665

Source: Maxson, Woods, and Klein (1995).

grants) to the prior figure of 172 cities that have just one or the other gang type yields a total of 516 cities that clearly challenge the notion of migration as the cause of local gang proliferation. While the picture for cities with coincidental onset of the two types of gang members is ambiguous, it seems reasonable to conclude that cities in which migration provides the catalyst for indigenous gang formation are the exception rather than the rule. The telephone interviews confirm this pattern; the majority of informants (81 percent) disagreed with the statement, "Without migration, this city wouldn't have a gang problem."

It can be argued that the concern over gang migration is most pertinent to emerging gang cities. The national gang surveys (Miller, 1996) discussed earlier have shown that the major proliferation of gang cities has occurred since the 1980s.[8] Nearly 70 percent of the 781 gang cities that could provide a date of emergence reported one after 1985. These cities can be characterized as "emergent" rather than "chronic" gang cities (Spergel and Curry, 1990). Emergent gang cities are equally as likely to report

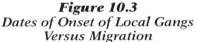

Figure 10.3
Dates of Onset of Local Gangs Versus Migration

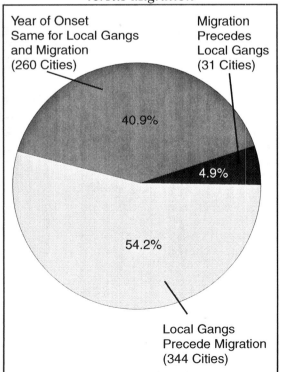

Year of Onset Same for Local Gangs and Migration (260 Cities)

Migration Precedes Local Gangs (31 Cities)

40.9%

4.9%

54.2%

Local Gangs Precede Migration (344 Cities)

gang migration as chronic cities (84 percent of the cities in each group). However, cities with gang onset after 1985 are significantly less likely to report that local gangs preceded gang migration (40 percent versus 88 percent), as might be expected when they are compared with cities with longstanding local gang problems. Emergent cities are more likely to experience the onset of local gangs and migrants in the same year as opposed to chronic cities (53 percent versus 11 percent). The majority of respondents interviewed from emergent gang cities believed that migration was not the cause of local gang problems. This figure was significantly lower for emergent gang cities (73 percent) than for chronic gang cities (93 percent). This shows that the conclusion that migration is not generally the catalyst for gang proliferation holds up, but the exceptions to this general rule can most often be found in emergent gang cities.

Patterns of Gang Migration

Examination of the reasons gang members migrate to other cities and their patterns of gang affiliation in the new city show that migration is not a major catalyst of gang proliferation. Survey interviewers asked participating officers to choose from a list of reasons why most gang members moved into their cities. The most frequently cited reason was that gang members moved with their families (39 percent). When this was combined with the reason of staying with relatives and friends, 57 percent of the survey respondents believed that migrants relocated primarily for social reasons. Drug market expansion was the second most frequently cited motivation (20 percent of cities) for migrating. When this was combined with other criminal opportunities, it created a larger category of illegal attractions, or "pull" motivators, in 32 percent of cities reporting an influx of migrant gangs. "Push" motivators that forced gang members to leave cities, such as law enforcement crackdowns (8 percent), court-ordered relocation, or a desire to escape gangs, were cited in 11 percent of migrant-recipient cities.

Are these patterns of motivation for migrating different in cities with emergent gangs as compared with those cities with chronic local gang problems? The data shown in Table 10.2 provide evidence that they clearly are not. Emergent gang cities have nearly equal proportions of socially

Table 10.2
*Most Frequent Reasons
for Migration Reported by
Chronic and Emergent Gang Cities*

Motivation	Chronic Gang Cities (n=73)	Emergent Gang Cities (n=111)
Social	41 (56%)	63 (57%)
"Pulls"	22 (30%)	37 (33%)
"Pushes"	10 (14%)	11 (10%)

Note: "Pull" motivators (e.g., drug markets) are those that attract gang members to relocate in specific locations. "Push" motivators, such as law enforcement crackdowns, are those that force gang members to leave cities and relocate elsewhere.

motivated gang migration as chronic gang cities. "Pull" motivators (primarily drug market expansion) and "push" motivators are less frequent reasons for gang member relocation than social motivations in both types of city.

There are no differences between the two types of gang cities with regard to patterns of migrant gang activity. Approximately one-third (38 percent) of survey respondents stated that gang migrants established new gangs or recruited for their old gangs; 36 percent reported that gang migrants joined existing local gangs or exclusively retained affiliation with their old gangs. The proportions of each in chronic and emergent gang cities are quite similar (data not shown). Thus, data on motivations for migrating and on migrant patterns in joining gangs provide little support for the view of migrants as primary agents of gang proliferation and no evidence for differential impact on emergent gang cities.

Conclusion

The interpretation of these results should be tempered by an awareness of the limitations of the USC study methodology. The surveys used to collect data relied heavily on law enforcement as a source of information. A logical next step would involve using an array of informants, including courts, schools, and social service providers in addition to community residents and gang members. It should also be noted that the USC data are cross-sectional in nature and cannot adequately describe second- or third-order waves of migration, wherein some individuals may travel from city to city.[9] Another untapped dimension in the USC survey was termed "indirect migration," in which one gang is influenced by another gang that was influenced by a third gang. For example, Pocatello, ID, gangs were heavily influenced by Salt Lake City gangs, which were started by gang members from Los Angeles (R. Olsen, Pocatello Police Department, personal communication, September 24, 1996). Other patterns of sequential mobility were reported on during the USC interviews, but did not occur with sufficient frequency to warrant further analysis.

The findings from the 1992 and 1993 USC surveys provide evidence that gang member migration, although widespread, should not be viewed as the major culprit in the nationwide proliferation of gangs. Local, indigenous gangs usually exist prior to gang migration, and migrants are not generally viewed by local law enforcement as the cause of gang problems. This pattern is less evident in cities in which gangs have emerged more recently, but these municipalities are no more likely to experience gang migration than chronic gang cities. Moreover, the motivations for gang member relocation (i.e., more often socially motivated than driven by crime opportunities) and patterns of gang participation (equally likely to join existing gangs as to retain original affiliation in order to initiate new gangs or branches) do not distinguish migrants in the two types of cities. Proponents of the "outside agitator" hypothesis of gang formation as described by Hagedorn (1988) will find little support in the data available from the USC national study.

On the whole, the USC findings agree with the research literature on gangs cited earlier. Many of the researchers—Rosenbaum and Grant (1983), Hagedorn (1988), Huff (1989), Zevitz and Takata (1992), Decker and Van Winkle (1996), and Waldorf (1993)—found that gang formation was only minimally affected by the diffusion of gang members from other cities. The findings reported by some researchers—Skolnick et al. (1990) and NDIC (1994, 1996)—are less consistent with those reported in the USC study. The Skolnick et al. and NDIC studies focused heavily on drug issues and may have disproportionately represented cities with drug-gang migration or with migrants that moved for drug expansion purposes.[10] Such cities reflect a distinct pattern of gang migration—older gang migrants, traveling longer distances, staying for briefer periods (see Maxson, Woods, and Klein, 1995, for full presentation of these analyses). Research that focuses on drug matters may fail to capture more prevalent trends. Although more often the subject of media coverage, migration for drug distribution purposes is less common than other types of migration. The differential patterns of gang migration, and their effects on local communities, require more research.

In addition, the USC findings are difficult to compare with those reported by Knox et al. (1996). Respondents in the Knox et al. study presented a widespread perception of outside gang influence. This may be the result of exposure to the media and products of the entertainment industry. Klein (1995) and others have suggested that the diffusion of gang culture in the media plays a key role in the proliferation of gang membership. Our nation's youth are hardly dependent on direct contact with gang members for exposure to the more dramatic manifestations of gang culture, which is readily accessible in youth-oriented television programming, popular movies, and the recent spate of "tell-all" books from reputed urban gang leaders. The nature of this influence and its impact on gang participation and expansion have not been investigated systematically but are crucial in understanding fully the dynamics of gang proliferation.

Cities with emerging gang situations should examine the dynamics of their own communities before attributing their gang problems to outside influences. Socioeconomic factors, such as persistent unemployment, residential segregation, and the lack of recreational, educational, and vocational services for youth, are more likely sources of gang formation or expansion than is gang migration.

Notes

1. Few studies attempt to assess the proportion and age of adolescent gang members within a given area. Recent information on self-identified membership from longitudinal projects for representative samples in Denver, CO, and Rochester, NY, (Thornberry and Burch, 1997) is available from the OJJDP-funded Program of Research on the Causes and Correlates of Delinquency. Approximately 5 percent of youth living in "high-risk" neighborhoods in Denver indicated

that they were gang members in any given year (Esbensen, Huizinga, and Weiher, 1993). In Rochester, 30 percent of the sample reported gang membership at some point between the beginning of the seventh grade and the end of high school (Thornberry and Burch, 1997). To address the issue of gang proliferation within Denver or Rochester, new samples would need to be examined to determine whether the proportion of youth joining gangs in these cities has increased since the initial sampling period (nearly 10 years ago).

Prevalence estimates derived from law enforcement identification of gang members have been challenged, as when Reiner (1992) reported that, according to the gang data base maintained for Los Angeles County, 9.5 percent of all men ages 21 to 24 were identified gang members. However, this proportion increased to 47 percent when the analysis was limited to black males ages 21 to 24. This figure has been generally recognized as a vast overstatement of black gang membership.

2. Whether or not migrants provide a catalyst to local gang proliferation, their impact on local crime is of considerable concern to law enforcement.

3. It should be noted that incorporated cities (of all population sizes) were the unit of analysis in this study; unincorporated areas were not included. Whenever cities contracted law enforcement responsibilities to sheriff's departments or State police, such agencies were pursued as respondents. Letters were addressed to the head agency official with a request to pass the survey on to the individual in the department most familiar with the gang situation within the city jurisdiction.

4. A random sample of 60 cities with a population of between 10,000 and 100,000 was surveyed for gang migration or local street-gang presence. Projections from this sample indicate a much larger number of U.S. cities with gang migration than have been identified to date.

5. These data are not presented in this report. Also not included are data from interviews with law enforcement in 15 cities that reported drug-gang migration only. This report refers to street-gang, rather than drug-gang, migration. See earlier discussion under Clarifying the Concepts for the distinction between the two types.

6. A few cities with gang migration were not included in this map because respondents were unable to specify the year of the first arrival of gang members from other cities.

7. A separate estimate of the total number of

migrants was discarded as less reliable than the annual estimate. Even the annual estimate should be considered with caution, as few departments maintained records on gang migration. Some officers had difficulty generalizing to the city as a whole, based upon their own experience, and many migrants presumably do not come to the attention of the police.

8. Klein (1995) provides a highly illustrative series of maps displaying dates of onset of local gang problems using data gathered in the migration study.

9. The interviews with migrant gang members gathered data on multiple moves, but there were too few instances from which to generalize. The author acknowledges Scott Decker for his observation of this limitation of the study design.

10. The Skolnick and NDIC studies employed purposive rather than representative sampling techniques.

Acknowledgements

Support was provided by the National Institute of Justice, grant #91-IJ-CX-K004. Malcolm Klein was co-principal investigator of the study and research assistance was provided by Kristi Woods, Lea Cunningham, and Karen Sternheimer. The author gratefully acknowledges the participation of personnel in hundreds of police departments and community agencies, along with several dozen gang members. Useful comments on an earlier draft were provided by Malcolm Klein, Walter Miller, James Howell, and Scott Decker.

References

Bonfante, J. 1995. Entrepreneurs of crack. *Time,* February 27.

California Council on Criminal Justice. 1989. *State Task Force on Gangs and Drugs: Final Report.* Sacramento, CA: California Council on Criminal Justice.

Curry, G. D. 1996. National youth gang surveys: A review of methods and findings. Unpublished. Tallahassee, FL: National Youth Gang Center, Institute for Intergovernmental Research.

Curry, G. D., Ball, R. A., and Decker, S. H. 1996. Estimating the national scope of gang crime from law enforcement data. In *Gangs in America,* 2d ed., edited by C. R. Huff. Thousand Oaks, CA: Sage Publications.

Curry, G. D., Ball, R. A., and Fox, R. J. 1994. *Gang Crime and Law Enforcement Recordkeeping.* Research in Brief. Washington, DC: U.S.

Department of Justice, Office of Justice Programs, National Institute of Justice.

Decker, S., and Van Winkle, B. 1996. *Life in the Gang.* New York: Cambridge University Press.

Esbensen, F. A., Huizinga, D., and Weiher, A. 1993. Gang and non-gang youth: Differences in explanatory factors. *Journal of Contemporary Criminal Justice* 9:94–116.

Genelin, M., and Coplen, B. 1989. Los Angeles street gangs: Report and recommendations of the countywide Criminal Justice Coordination Committee. Unpublished report of the Interagency Gang Task Force. Los Angeles: Interagency Gang Task Force.

Hagedorn, J. 1988. *People and Folks: Gangs, Crime, and the Underclass in a Rustbelt City.* Chicago: Lakeview Press.

Hayeslip, D. W., Jr. 1989 (March/April). Local-level drug enforcement: New strategies. *NIJ Reports* 213:2–6. Washington, DC: U.S. Department of Justice, Office of Justice Programs, National Institute of Justice.

Huff, C. R. 1989. Youth gangs and public policy. *Crime & Delinquency* 35:524–37.

Klein, M. W. 1995. *The American Street Gang.* New York: Oxford University Press.

Klein, M. W., and Maxson, C. L. 1996. Gang structures, crime patterns, and police responses. Unpublished final report. Los Angeles: Social Science Research Institute, University of Southern California.

Knox, G. W., Houston, J. G., Tromanhauser, E. D., McCurrie, T. F., and Laskey, J. 1996. Addressing and testing the gang migration issue. In *Gangs: A Criminal Justice Approach,* edited by J. M. Miller and J. P. Rush. Cincinnati, OH: Anderson Publishing Company.

Maxson, C. L., Woods, K. J., and Klein, M. W. 1995. Street gang migration in the United States. Unpublished final report. Los Angeles: Social Science Research Institute, University of Southern California.

———. 1996 (February). Street gang migration: How big a threat? *National Institute of Justice Journal* 230:26–31. Washington, DC: U.S. Department of Justice, Office of Justice Programs, National Institute of Justice.

McKinney, K. C. 1988 (September). *Juvenile Gangs: Crime and Drug Trafficking.* Chapter. Washington, DC: U.S. Department of Justice, Office of Justice Programs, Office of Juvenile Justice and Delinquency Prevention.

Miller, W. B. 1975. Violence by youth gangs and youth groups as a crime problem in major American cities. Unpublished. Washington, DC: U.S. Department of Justice, National Institute of Juvenile Justice and Delinquency Prevention.

———. 1982 (Reissued in 1992). *Crime by Youth Gangs and Groups in the United States.* Washington, DC: U.S. Department of Justice, Office of Justice Programs, Office of Juvenile Justice and Delinquency Prevention.

———. 1996. The growth of youth gang problems in the United States: 1970–1995. Unpublished. Tallahassee, FL: National Youth Gang Center, Institute for Intergovernmental Research.

National Drug Intelligence Center. 1994. *Bloods and Crips Gang Survey Report*. Johnstown, PA: National Drug Intelligence Center.

———. 1996. *National Street Gang Survey Report*. Johnstown, PA: National Drug Intelligence Center.

Needle, J. A., and Stapleton, W. V. 1983. *Police Handling of Youth Gangs*. Washington, DC: U.S. Department of Justice, Office of Justice Programs, Office of Juvenile Justice and Delinquency Prevention.

Office of Juvenile Justice and Delinquency Prevention. 1997. *1995 National Youth Gang Survey*. Summary. Washington, DC: U.S. Department of Justice, Office of Justice Programs, Office of Juvenile Justice and Delinquency Prevention.

Quinn, J. F., Tobolowsky, P. M., and Downs, W. T. 1994. The gang problem in large and small cities: An analysis of police perceptions in nine states. *The Gang Journal* 2(2):13–22.

Reiner, I. 1992. *Gangs, Crime, and Violence in Los Angeles*. Los Angeles: Office of the District Attorney of Los Angeles County.

Rosenbaum, D. P., and Grant, J. A. 1983. *Gangs and Youth Problems in Evanston*. Report. Evanston, IL: Northwestern University, Center for Urban Affairs and Policy Research.

Skolnick, J. H. 1990. *Gang Organization and Migration*. Sacramento, CA: Office of the Attorney General of the State of California.

Skolnick, J. H., Correl, T., Navarro, T., and Rabb, R. 1990. The social structure of street drug dealing. *American Journal of Police* 9(1):1–41.

Spergel, I. A., and Curry, G. D. 1990. Strategies and perceived agency effectiveness in dealing with the youth gang problem. In *Gangs in America*, edited by C. R. Huff. Newbury Park, CA: Sage Publications.

Thornberry, T. B., and Burch, J. H. II. 1997 (June). *Gang Members and Delinquent Behavior Chapter*. Washington, DC: U.S. Department of Justice, Office of Justice Programs, Office of Juvenile Justice and Delinquency Prevention.

Thornberry, T. B., Krohn, M. D., Lizotte, A. J., and Chard-Wierschem, D. 1993. The role of juvenile gangs in facilitating delinquent behavior. *Journal of Research in Crime and Delinquency* 30(1):55–87.

Waldorf, D. 1993. When the Crips invaded San Francisco: Gang migration. *The Gang Journal* 1(4).

Zevitz, R. G., and Takata, S. R. 1992. Metropolitan gang influence and the emergence of group delinquency in a regional community. *Journal of Criminal Justice* 20(2):93–106. ✦

Chapter 11
Inside the Fremont Hustlers

Mark S. Fleisher

This chapter is an excerpt from Fleisher's book Dead End Kids, *based on his long-term ethnographic study of a street gang in Kansas City, Missouri. Fleisher captures the fluidity of membership as it mirrors the loose structure of a "collective" gang. In such a loosely structured gang, membership and "tightness" (cohesiveness in other gang literature) are well illustrated in Cara's listing of the subgroups in the Fremont Hustlers. Also pay attention to how different meanings are attached to words; some of these are generic, but some also constitute the special argot of such groups. The "verbal duels" described here remind us that most gang violence is verbal, not physical. The entire selection provides a rich description of the nature of street gang members' interactions and daily life.*

"Membership" in the Fremont Hustlers is a peculiar idea.[1] Wendy, Cara, and Cheri listed 72 males and females on the Fremont Hustler membership roster; however, Fremont kids don't refer to one another as members, nor do they think of themselves as having joined a gang.[2]

"Member," "membership," "join," and "gang" are static notions which fit neither the natural flow of Fremont social life nor the perceptions of Fremont kids. Even the question, Are you a member of the Fremont Hustlers? doesn't match these kids' sense of social logic. The question, Do you hang out on Fremont? makes sense to them but this question didn't bring me closer to understanding the kids' meanings for "joining a

gang" and "gang membership." Fremont kids' perceptions of these issues are more complex than I had imagined.[3]

The social boundary between the Fremont Hustlers—the youth gang—and outsiders is open.[4] Fremont has no formal set of written rules (a charter) specifying what prospective members must do to be admitted and to sustain membership. There are no rules of decorum and, thus, no sanctions for violating those rules. Younger Fremont kids are not required to learn and recite a gang pledge of allegiance or attend lectures given by older members about "proper" behavior. There is no rule preventing drug sellers from being drug users. There is no rule requiring a portion of drug sale profits to be returned to a communal gang bank account or paid as tribute to the leader. There is no leader, no boss, no hierarchy that pulls all 72 kids into coherent organization.[5]

Fremont has no initiation. No one is "beaten in" or "courted in" or ordered to commit violent acts. That behavior, kids said, attracts the cops, and cops are bad for business. Cara said violent initiation is "fucked up and stupid. Who wants ta hang out with niggahs who beat ya ass?" By hanging out and establishing ties with Fremont kids, an outsider is slowly assimilated into the social life at a chill spot.

To these kids, Fremont is defined by the interaction of social histories of families; current and former love relationships; boy-boy, girl-girl, and boy-girl hostilities; envy and bitterness over possessions; current and past crime partnerships; arrests and imprisonment in jails, detention centers, and juvenile treatment facilities; histories of prior gang affiliations; and length of interpersonal affiliation. Kids who have known each other a long time, such as Cara and Wendy, stick together, although there were times when they'd vow never to speak to each other again, but that's typical among adolescents.

Kids' vocabulary helps to describe how they perceive Fremont's social arrangements. Generally speaking, Fremont kids differentiate themselves into one category defined by "time" and another by "tightness." *Tightness* refers to the intensity of a relationship. Kids who hang out together much of the time are said to be tight, and kids who are tight "do shit" (commit crimes, use drugs) together.

Tight also implies to some degree a shared

social history. Most Fremont kids were members of other Kansas City youth gangs before joining the Fremont Hustlers and were together in juvenile detention and treatment facilities; however, being tight doesn't necessarily imply a long-term relationship. Kids can be tight for two weeks or four months and then become bitter enemies. Such volatility is most common among girls.[6] In July 1994, when Wendy and Janet and I met at UMKC, they had been tight for years and said they were inseparable and swore a mutual allegiance forever. Over the next year, Janet and Wendy vied for Steele Bill's attention. Janet won Bill, lost Wendy, and they haven't spoken to each other since then.

Time refers to the hours, days, weeks, and years a kid spends on Fremont. Time spent hanging out on Fremont differentiates kids into four groups. Kids who hang on Fremont most often have established closer ties than kids who don't. Those who don't hang around much are marginal to the gang's principal economic behavior, drug selling.

Kids use expressions for different time categories; I've noted in parentheses the number of days of hang-out time in each category: "here all the time" (six or seven days a week), "here a lot" (three to five days a week), "comes around" (one or two days a week), and "will be here if we need him (or her)" (several days a month). The last group includes kids who didn't appear even once on Fremont between June 1995 and February 1997, but hung out there at some time in the past. These kids are still considered to be Fremont. Fremont Hustlers who have been killed continue as members. The children of Fremont girls are Fremont, too.

A kid who is "here all the time" also is said to be in the "everyday" group. It's common in natural speech for kids to refer to the everyday group as kids "who's in the shit everyday," said Cara. The everyday and here-a-lot groups correspond to the terms *core* and *regular* members, respectively.

There is a segmentary quality to these social groups. Few kids hang out all the time, but dozens of kids are available to the Fremont Hustlers should help be needed. Wendy captured this segmentary quality: "If somebody fucks wid us," she said sternly, "we can get all the help we need."

A subtle difference exists between what it means to "hang out on Fremont" and what it means to be "down with Fremont." To be "down with Fremont" is the expression closest to our use of the term *member*. But being down with Fremont doesn't mean a kid hangs out on Fremont every day.

A number of Fremont kids have been down with other KC gangs. Cara was down with the Southside 39th Street Crips, as well as the 31st Street Eastside Crips, before hooking up with Wendy. Steele Bill has been a 24th Street Crip.

There is a finer distinction as well. I've heard kids ask another kid, "Is he (or she) Fremont or Fremont Fremont?" This is an interesting distinction. Kids, including Cheri, Wendy, Angie, and Roger, who were reared in the Fremont neighborhood and whose family history now links them to the neighborhood are denoted with the label "Fremont Fremont." Afro, by contrast, is a down with Fremont member but is not Fremont Fremont; Wendy said she had "brought him" to Fremont from the east side. Thus, a kid can be Fremont Fremont or Fremont, and either down with or hang out with Fremont. Generally speaking, boys and girls in the everyday and here-a-lot groups are Fremont Fremont and down with Fremont.

Cara, Wendy, Cheri, and I explored how they perceive Fremont social grouping.[7] This was a productive way to learn about social relations from a single-informant, or egocentric, perspective. Simple "social role" labels for gang members as defined by gang researchers, such as "core," "peripheral," "associate," "wannabe," are outsiders' categorizations and simplistic when compared with gang members' perceptions of their own social world.[8] Rather than imposing my labels on each girl's subgrouping, I asked them to give me labels.

Wendy's and Cheri's social groupings are mostly egocentric; that is, each subgrouping is defined with them at the center. The strength of the social ties is denoted with labels such as "my babies," "my real mothafuckas," "kind of cool with, but ain't seen for awhile," "my niggahs," "I'm cool with, but don't fuck with anymore," "people I don't care about," "still all right in my life," "boys I used to talk to" (former lovers), "true bitches" (or "people I hate"). Some labels denote Fremont kids' prior gang affiliation, such as Bloods, Southside (51st Street), Latin Count Brothers, and La Familia. Other labels referred to time spent on Fremont: "hardly come over," "never come over," and "used to come over." Interestingly, Fremont kids who were killed or committed suicide, as well as boys in prison, are still considered to be Fremont members. Imprisoned kids are either labeled "in prison" or are placed in some other group, such as "my mothafuckas." Tyler, a 14-year-old boy killed by Fremont TJ, is always placed in a group with kids who are alive.

Cara's view is much less egocentric than Wendy's and Cheri's, and it has a "fly-on-the-wall" quality. She divides the Fremont Hustlers into these groups: Bloods (friends of Chucky D's from the east side and former Latin Count Brothers); used to visit a lot (girls from the Seven-Miles rap group); grew up on Fremont; in prison; La Familia (members of the gang La Familia, but hang with Fremont anyway); hang together; hang out (these kids are tighter than those in hang together); hardly come around; and Southside.[9] Cara's subgroups, with kids' names and pertinent facts, are listed below.[10]

Bloods: J-Love, JC, and Joe Green.

Used to visit a lot: Kiki, Erica, Felisha, JoJo, Kizzy (all members of the Seven-Miles rap-group; Felisha and Kizzy are sisters). These girls hung out on Fremont in the early days of the Fremont Hustlers. I never met any one of them, although Wendy talked about them, and in the spring of 1997 she started to hang out with several of them, because she was interested in recording rap songs.

Grew up on Fremont: Anthony Contreras, Curly Contreras (these two are brothers; they have three more brothers—Sam, Eddie, and Sal—whom Cara puts in the "hardly come around" group).

In prison: Buck, Dwayne, Snapper, Fremont TJ, Little Man, Rick. Cara put Tyler (RIP) in this category and said it includes kids "who's never coming back." Rick was a crime partner with Anthony and Curly Contreras.

La Familia (also known as KCBs, Kansas City Barrios): Tre, Jacob, JD, John, Chill, Maria, Speedy, Duce. Chill, Maria, and Speedy are cousins. Speedy's sister used to be a member of La Familia.

Hang together (A): Chucky D, Tervis (also called Earl), Steele Bill, Cara, Cheri, Wendy, Joanne, Sequoia. Sequoia is the two-year-old daughter of Joanne and Charles B., Cheri's brother (he was in prison in March 1996 and released in the summer of 1997 but returned a month later on a parole vio-

lation). Joanne has another daughter, Charlene, whose father is Chucky D.

Hang together (B): Johnny Murillo, Steve Holly, Joe Murillo, House of Pain, Cain, Greenbean, Lucky, Wayne, Taz, Zipper. Taz and Zipper were brothers. Taz was 16 when he was killed by Afro in what the police called an accidental shooting. Zipper was 15, a member of La Familia, when a Northeast member shot him in the chest, leaving a scar that looks like a zipper. Zipper is tight with Fremont, despite his affiliation with La Familia. Cheri was once pregnant by a brother of Zipper and Taz; the baby was lost in a spontaneous abortion. One of Taz's brothers told me that Afro intentionally killed Taz, and was released by the police because he is a snitch. Johnny Murillo, Steve Holly, and Joe Murillo are cousins. House of Pain and Cain are brothers.

Hang out (tight): Angie, Chica Bitch, Netta, Donna, Roger, Christina, Melissa, Rosa, Afro. Netta and Donna are sisters (they have a third sister, Teresa). Melissa and Rosa are cousins. Melissa and Lucky are siblings; Christina is their step-sister. Melissa and Lucky's father married Christina's mother. Lucky and Christina had a child born in the spring of 1996. Rosa and Joe Murillo are cousins. Rosa and Afro were lovers and had a baby girl in the fall of 1996. When Rosa was 13 she was shot in the chest by a Northeast member wielding a .38. Afro is a cousin of Cheri and her siblings, Dante and Charles B. Roger and Angie are siblings.

Hardly come around: Dallas, Frosty, Milk, Joey, the Contreras brothers (Sam, Eddie, Sal). Joey is Frosty's little brother. Milk has the dubious distinction of being the only Fremont Hustler to be initiated with a beating.[11] Cara said, "The boys whipped his ass 'cause he's stupid." The Contreras brothers are Fremont's carjackers.

Southside: Bill Bill, Little E, Tony, Scandalous Herb. Bill Bill, Little E, and Tony are brothers; Tony and Bill Bill are twins.

These are perceptions of social groupings and aren't day-to-day operational subgroups within the Fremont Hustlers. Understanding daily social, emotional, and economic dynamics is a complex issue.[12] Recording and analyzing Fremont kids' speech can offer insights.

Two-person relationships and intra- and interclique relations are marked by emotions and behavior, including passivity, standoffishness, friendliness, dependency, anger, aggressiveness, violence, vindictiveness, fearfulness, and withdrawal. These emotions and behavior are captured in the complexity of kids' speech as it's played out in daily social life.

Fremont social life is rich in jokes and laughter, as well as anger, aggression, unresolved disputes, and inter- and intragang incidents of mild to serious violence. Hardly an hour passes without some kid claiming to be pissed off about something or at someone. When one kid gets angry he usually has a lot of companions willing to talk about violence, and some of them are willing to engage in it. Talk about violence is far more common than violent acts.

A number of vocabulary terms connote the quality or affective nature of social ties and, by extension, the likelihood of violence between kids. Three such terms are *niggah*, *dog*, and *mothafucka*. In nearly all instances *niggah* is used without regard to the color of the speaker or the addressee. Sometimes *niggah* is used as a synonym for *homey*, though the terms *home*, *homeboy*, *homegirl*, and *homey* are rarely used in natural conversations.

Rather than denoting racial affiliation, *niggah* is used symbolically for more complex issues. A black, white, or Mexican Fremont boy or girl can call a black, white, or Mexican boy or girl a niggah, as long as the speaker and addressee are "cool," said Wendy.

"Niggah, you ain't shit!" is a common aggressive statement, but it isn't a racial insult to the addressee, who may or may not be black. A common use of *niggah* comes in statements such as, "That niggah over there, he got some."

In natural conversations the term *niggah* is distinguished from *nigger*. *Nigger* is always an insult, but it's a raceless insult used in an already heated conversation. *Nigger* has triggered fights even between black Fremont kids.

The term *dog* has the synonyms *ace deuce* and *number one*. To say "Wha's up, dog?" is a friendly greeting; however, "You're a dog" can, in an already tense situation, trigger a fight.

The term *mothafucka* is used commonly in natural conversations and has a range of connotations as wide as the word *fuck* in colloquial English. In friendly expressions, it is used this way: "You my mothafucka." However, the term *mothafucker*—that is, the

form with the *-er* ending, like *nigger* as opposed to *niggah*—can be an insult and can be directed toward someone during an already tense verbal interaction.

Fremont girls and boys form cliques; however, girls' cliques, more so than boys, act as social units. Wendy and other girls too use the girl's term *my mothafuckas* to denote cliques; boys don't use such terms to label cliques. The term *together* is a synonym for *my mothafuckas*. Cara, Wendy, and Cheri are together, at least most of the time. This means if someone angers Wendy, Cara and Cheri will act with Wendy to support her and oppose her enemy. This works best if the girl who seeks support also controls resources the other girls need. Wendy, for example, had absolute control over her room on Fremont, and Cheri and Cara needed it as a safe spot. Whenever Wendy got pissed off at someone, as she did at Janet for stealing Steele Bill, Cheri and Cara supported Wendy against Janet; however . . . when Wendy's resource disappeared so did her support from Cheri and Cara, and from everyone else on Fremont.

"Sticks and stones can break your bones but words will never hurt you" doesn't apply to Fremont social life. Social life rests on words and how they are uttered and on stylized forms of verbal interaction. Friendly words, angry words, misspoken words, misinterpreted words, filthy words, clean words, all sorts of words are elements in complex social and verbal scenes called verbal duels.

Verbal duels are organized by rules that allow "players" to insult one another, within limits. Verbal duels (structured verbal forms of teasing) publicly verify informal social hierarchies and release tension without violence.

A Fremont insider (a so-called member) may verbally challenge and insult an outsider, as Wendy did a teenage girl walking across Truman by the Quick Trip, but that girl remained silent and didn't exchange insults with Wendy. To do that would have instigated a verbal duel with Wendy's partners in my car, and that might have escalated into a brawl. Fremont Hustlers membership means that only insiders verbally duel (insult, challenge) one another with impunity. Stylized verbal dueling is a privilege of membership.

Cara and Wendy tease Cheri. Cheri teases boys, and because of her reputation as an impulsive and violent girl, boys take it and leave her alone. Girls tease Angie about her hair and aggressiveness; she accepts such teasing as a sign of companionship, rarely ever retaliating with words motivated by angry emotions. In this way, friendships are denoted with teasing.

Fremont kids don't often say things to one another that outsiders would interpret as friendly and affectionate things to say. *Mothafucka, bitch, stank pussy, niggah, dog,* and other terms are signs of companionship if they are spoken correctly between kids whose relationship has already been established and allows for such talk.

Boy-girl, girl-girl, and boy-boy relationships are built on verbal duels. Boys duel by calling each other bitch; girls call each other bitch; boys call girls stank pussy; girls call each other stank pussy; girls accuse each other of sleeping around; and both toss allegations of disloyalty at partners in previous relationships. A girl who wants a boy's attention, or one who is sleeping with a boy, smiles and tolerates his teasing, insults, and accusations.[13]

Boys don't engage in verbal duels as often or as intensely as girls. Boys tease each other momentarily, calling each other bitch or pussy, but verbal dueling, even among boys in the same clique, isn't as elaborate and stylized as it is among girls.

Verbal dueling partnerships exist in pairs, triads, and cliques (four or more) of girls. Wendy, Cara, Cheri, and Angie challenge and insult one another, and emergent among them is an informal pattern of verbal dueling partners. Wendy challenges Cara more often than she does Cheri and Angie. Wendy and Cara tease and challenge Cheri more often than they do Angie. Angie and Wendy tease Cheri more often than they do Cara. Cheri is known for bursts of anger and violent behavior, and girls, as well as boys, tend not to push her.

Verbal duels are stereotyped. When a duel is happening between boys, it's never imbued with the same ferocity as a boy-girl or a girl-girl verbal duel. Nearly always, a boy-boy duel is a brief challenge of a boy's ability or willingness to fight: "You ain't shit," asserts one boy. "Fuck you, niggah. I'll kick your mothafuckin' ass" is a common retort. The "loser" (the second speaker) defers and walks away. The duel ends. A less aggressive boy wouldn't say "You ain't shit" to a more aggressive boy, who might then

punch him. No one ever verbally challenges Chucky D and Afro.

Girl-boy duels happen regularly. Some girls don't duel with boys or other girls and aren't chided or judged to be cowardly for not doing it. Most girls are thrilled to insult boys with terms for male and female genitalia, for excrement, and for challenging a boy's sexual prowess and fighting ability.

Verbal duels are street theater. Verbal duels always occur in public settings, in earshot of others. Verbal duels allow girls to display bravery against boys, adjust social network alliances among themselves, and shift their romantic pairings. During a particularly loud and boisterous performance, kids circle the performers, shouting support for stylistic insults, and laughter reigns. Verbal duels sow the seeds of "domestic" and "dating" violence when such duels run amok. The rules of the verbal duel help to control kids' tendencies to carry aggressive talk too far. When a kid bends verbal dueling rules too far and breaks the unwritten code of conduct, an expected outcome is violence. Controlling their speech helps these kids control their emotions. Once speech rules have been violated, anger pours out of these kids like water gushing from a drainage pipe after a thunderstorm.

Girls always instigate duels with boys. Girl-boy duels are more theatrical than girl-girl duels. Obscenities punctuate the discourse between dueling partners. Boys call girls by the standard list of insulting terms, including *bitch, rotten bitch, stank bitch, pussy, cunt,* and *slut,* among others. Girls retaliate with a vengeance, shouting, "bastard," "prick," "pussy," "bitch," "little dick," and "cocksucker," among others. Girls call one another by the standard list of insults.

Boys and girls toy with the pronunciation of the terms *bitch* and *bastard.* They exaggerate *bitch* until it sounds like "biy-yitch." Girls exaggerate *bastard* until it sounds like "baas-TURD" (emphasis on the second syllable). These stylized pronunciations signal the end of a duel.

Verbal duels can turn violent. *Niggah* signals a challenge by a girl who wants to playfight with a boy. Sometimes, this playful fighting escalates. One Sunday afternoon, I was interviewing Angie at the picnic table next to Wendy's. Other kids were nearby. House of Pain walked over to listen.

"Get outta here, niggah," Angie said to

House of Pain. He looked at her but said nothing. She growled at him a bit more.

He responded, "Fuck you. I'll stand where I want."

She stood up. ""I calling you out, NIGGAH. Wha's up?"

Words were tossed back and forth. House of Pain ended with "You ain't shit, you stank bitch."

That should have ended the duel. He turned and slowly walked away. She kept insulting him and walked after him. House of Pain told her to stop: "Fuck you, bitch. Shut up or I'll kick your ass." That should have been Angie's cue to end it.

She continued to berate him. Wearing a very angry face, he walked up to her, grabbed her by the arm, held her close to him, curled his right hand into a fist, and repeatedly punched her thighs and shoulders. To her cries of pain, an onlooking boy said, "Fuck you, you stank bitch, whatcha do that [push him] for?" Girls paid no attention once the punching ended. They walked away and let Angie rub her wounds by herself.

This scene was awful to watch. I wondered what motivated Angie to persist to the point where words turned to punches. After all, I thought, Angie isn't new to the street, and House of Pain's short fuse is well known. Angie knew that no one would intervene if he beat her.

"Violence doesn't scare me. I'm used to it, it's normal," said Poodle Bitch in a matter-of-fact voice. "I seen shootings and drivebys." Poodle said she had been arrested for assault in a courtroom. She had punched her mother in the face and "knocked that bitch on her fuckin' ass." Roger, Angie's brother, said "It's true," adding, "We used to get into fistfights at home too."

Notes

1. Richard A. Ball and G. David Curry, "The Logic of Definition in Criminology: Purposes and Methods for Defining 'Gangs,'" *Criminology* 33(2) (1995): 225–245, offers an excellent discussion of gang definitions.

2. The vast gang literature is synthesized nicely in Irving Spergel, *The Youth Gang Problem* (New York: Oxford University Press, 1995); and Malcolm Klein, *The American Street Gang: Its Nature, Prevalence and Control* (New York: Oxford University Press, 1995).

3. Gang researchers have systematically sought theories to explain gang formation. Freder-

ick Thrasher's 1927 study, *The Gang* (Chicago: University of Chicago Press), was the first serious research on gangs, and since then gang researchers have created a number of categories of theories linking gangs to poverty, socioeconomic strain, social class (low class, underclass), social disorganization (neighborhood, community), family disorganization, racism, and abnormal personality development.

Despite the search for gang theories or integrated theories of delinquency and gangs, gang researchers haven't looked into the literature on cross-cultural adolescence or on adolescent development. Thus, the focus on gangs has largely been to explain gangs' deviant aspects, with researchers virtually overlooking the universal sociocultural aspects of adolescent social processes. The fact is, most of what we call gang behavior is not especially interesting as a research phenomenon, because it's so commonly a part of adolescent culture. Kids' wishes to hang out with kids like themselves, kids' use of symbolic means (graffiti, clothes, jargon) to sort one group from another, kids' aggressiveness, the impermanence of membership in kids' social groups, kids' rebelliousness against adults, including their families, aren't unique phenomena. Cross-cultural adolescent research has shown that male adolescent aggressiveness is related to increased peer contacts (see Alice Schlegel, "A Cross-Cultural Approach to Adolescence," *Ethos* 23: 1 [1995]:24). Is it really a surprise, then, to find that large groups of American kids (a gang) do more of something (commit crime) than smaller (delinquent) groups?

Bonnie Miller Rubin ("Today's Teens Have Plenty of Picks to Clique," *Chicago Tribune*, National section, Sunday, September 14, 1997, pp. 1, 17) points out that adolescents in large high schools stratify themselves into ranked homogeneous subgroups (skaters, preps, hip-hop, ravers, postgrunge, goths, and stoners); that some kids pretend to be members of a group they really don't belong to (wannabes); that kids shift between groups; that there's conflict between groups; that the school as the adolescent community is fragmented by these subgroups; and the parents are concerned about their kids being in the "wrong" group.

An overemphasis on criminological theories and on adolescent male delinquents seems to have clouded our vision about adolescent delinquent females. Meda Chesney-Lind and Randall G. Shelden's excellent study of girls' delinquency (*Girls, Delinquency and Juvenile Justice* [Pacific Grove, Calif.: Brooks/Cole, 1992]) is narrowly focused on delinquency theory (ecological, strain, differential association, control, labeling) and doesn't cite studies on girls' sociopsychological development or research on nondelinquent-female relationships among themselves and with males. If we don't understand a full range of cross-cultural adolescent female behavior, how are we to pinpoint those behaviors which are unique deviant responses to a range of family and environmental stimuli? In short, we don't understand how much of what we're measuring in female (and male) delinquent and gang behavior is within the range of predictable adolescent behavior in complex urban settings. Why is this such an important issue? Unless we know which adolescent behaviors are natural (and will terminate with adolescence) and which are effects of controllable negative stimuli (family disorganization, for instance), then we won't be able to develop truly effective intervention strategies.

Perhaps the true uniqueness of a "youth gang" is how communities respond to it. Generally speaking, decades of research show that kids in gangs are marginal in school and have been injured by family disorder, among other things. That marginality and injury don't preclude these kids from engaging in universal adolescent sociopsychological processes (homophilous groups, stratification, ranks, aggression); however, so-called gang members act out these processes in an unconventional venue, the street, which alarms adults and engenders a law enforcement (control) response instead of a parental (supportive) response. As an anthropologist observing this scene, it's alarming to watch American adults castigate and alienate their own youth and further injure already victimized adolescents. It isn't youth gangs that should bother America's lawmakers, but rather the dominant culture's response to America's most vulnerable children. America's aggressiveness and punitive reaction to youth gangs as "community evil" marks the abusive nature of our society.

4. Fremont Hustlers fit a common operational definition of gangs as a group involved in illegal activity (Finn-Aage Esbensen and David Huizinga, "Gangs, Drugs, and Delinquency in a Survey of Urban Youth," *Criminology* 31 [1993]:565–569). I prefer the definition in Scott H. Decker and Barrik Van Winkle, *Life in the Gang* (Cambridge: Cambridge University Press, 1996), p. 31; "an age-graded peer group that exhibits some permanence, engages in criminal activity, and has some symbolic representation of membership." The notion of age-grade is important, because we know that gang members in their late teens and early twenties commit most of the violent acts (Spergel, *The Youth Gang Problem*, pp. 33–36). Thus, older gang members in consort with young boys and girls pose a serious problem in the socialization or coercion of young members to be involved in violent acts. How age distribution influences violence in male gangs and in mixed male-female gangs, like the Fremont Hustlers, has not been carefully studied.

5. Malcolm Klein, *Street Gangs and Street Workers* (Englewood Cliffs, N.J.: Prentice Hall, 1971), includes a comprehensive discussion of gang cohesion and leadership. Fremont findings support Klein's and show that external pressures, including poverty, family dysfunction, unemployment, and schools' inadequate responses to difficult kids, have a stronger effect on group cohesion than internal forces, such as a code of conduct and ethos.

6. Few publications focus specifically on females in gangs and female gangs. See, for instance, Lee Bowker and Malcolm Klein, "The Etiology of Female Juvenile Delinquency and Gang Membership: A Test of Psychological and Social Structure Explanations," *Adolescence* 18 (1983):740–751; Joan W. Moore, *Going Down to the Barrio: Homeboys and Homegirls in Change* (Philadelphia: Temple University Press, 1991); Carl Taylor, *Girls, Gangs, Women and Drugs* (East Lansing: Michigan State University Press, 1993), Anne Campbell, *The Girls in the Gang*, 2d ed. (New York: Basil Blackwell, 1991). Also see Ruth Horowitz, *Honor and The American Dream* (New Brunswick, N.J.: Rutgers University Press, 1983).

7. Using the roster elicited on my first day in Fremont, I wrote each of the names of the 72 Fremont Hustlers on its own three-by-five card. I gave the stack of cards to each girl and asked her to sort the cards into as many piles as necessary, as long as each pile had more than one card (see H. Russell Bernard, *Research Methods in Anthropology* [Newbury Park, Calif.: Sage, 1994], pp. 249–252). After each informant had created the piles, I asked why she had grouped those people together.

Pile sorting is useful, but there are a number of difficulties in structured interviews with gang kids in noisy apartments. First, kids want to help each other put cards into piles. I had to tell bystanders to stay quiet. Second, kids see names on cards and start to tell stories about those kids. This is wonderful, but it distracts the informant from the task. Third, kids see names that disturb them. Enemies, former lovers, dead homeys, snitches, and others distract both the informant and the bystanders. If she is upset, either the informant wants to stop the pile sorting or she gets into arguments with bystanders about the names on the cards. Fourth, sorting 72 cards takes time and effort, and then enduring my questions takes even more time and effort. In the end, an hour interview becomes 90–120 minutes, or the kids just abandon the task out of boredom. Fifth, kids have other things going on at the same time. Distractions are endless. Phone calls, buzzing pagers, people knocking at the door, and other kids getting high keep the informant away from the job. Sixth, pile sorting requires good rapport with informants and a fully open channel of communication. I did this pile sorting eight months after arriving on Fremont. Kids are suspicious and without good rapport, they're likely to conceal good data by glossing over kids who are "really in the shit."

In the end, however, pile sorting gave me insights into the internal classification of the Fremont Hustlers through the eyes of three of its longest-standing active members. With these data, I decided who would likely be the best kids to interview next and who could be passed by.

8. Labels such as "core," "peripheral," "associate," "wannabe," or synonyms of these labels, were not used by informants.

9. I elicited these categories in March 1996 and asked Cara to sort the cards as social groups had existed during the gang's 1994–1995 heyday. Social dynamics are continuous; thus, these categories should be viewed as a temporal snapshot. I recorded notes about the kinship relationships within each group, and in some cases between groups, and also noted violent incidents (perpetrator or victim) or other unique characteristics for each kid, as Cara reported them.

10. Fremont girls are in Anne Campbell's (*The Girls in the Gang*) "bad girls" category. "They are not tortured by dreams of upward mobility and have a realistic view of their chances of success in society. They have not done well in school, and when they have money, they spend it. . . . Like the boys in the neighborhood, they enjoy excitement and trouble, which break the monotony of a life in which little attention is given to the future. They like sharp clothes, loud music, alcohol, and soft drugs. They admire toughness and verbal 'smarts.' They may not be going anywhere, but they make the most of where they are" (pp. 7–8).

To be sure, Fremont girls aren't chattle, that is, possessions of gang boys. These girls are staunchly independent, although many have customary adolescent boy-girl relationships. Gang boys are more aggressive than girls and frequently try to control them; in such a case, girls play a passive role. Boy-girl pairings often display violence, as I describe and discuss later. In some cases, a girl will perceive her victimization at the hands of a boy as his affection for her, but I don't think this is unique to gang-affiliated adolescents.

I'm unconvinced that girls, like Cara and Wendy, who have been physically hurt by boys actually believe their own words ("He hit me because he loves me"). If anyone knows about violence, it's these kids, and they know from experience at home that violence isn't love. The public talk equating physical violence and interpersonal affection is a girl's culturally defined rationalization for her inability to escape such a horrible situation. If a gang girl pulls away on her own, her boyfriend will likely beat her more severely. To escape an abusive relationship, a girl needs a new suitor who's stronger and more violent than her current abusive boyfriend. This is how Chucky D and Afro succeed in relationships. No one challenges them, and girls can, in a sense, "hide" behind them. In relationships with them, however, girls pay a price, and that price is obedience and sex.

The more realistic way to escape from these boys is to become pregnant. Once real-life responsibilities face Afro and Chucky D and other Fremont boys, they flee and find new girlfriends. Although pregnant girls don't say it directly, they believe their pregnancy will soften their abusive boyfriends.

11. Anthropologists have reported that social groups with a special purpose, such as a fraternity, commonly have a rite of passage, or initiation, for the prospective members. An initiation rite is the public transformation of social status from, in the case of a gang, a non-gang member to a gang member. Such a rite of passage serves an additional function. It is also a rite of social intensification, which draws group members together and further bonds them on a collective occasion.

It's no surprise to find that a youth gang has a rite of passage. The number of gangs requiring a rite of passage is unknown, although folklore about such rites is plentiful and often apocryphal. Folklore has it that such rituals may include, for instance, being beaten by fellow members or being forced to commit a violent act. Even if such rites of passage occur, it'd be very difficult to know if these are idiosyncratic events or a core feature of gangs as a uniform expression of marginal adolescent culture. By idiosyncratic event, I mean an event that is initiated by a violent boy like Chucky D and his violent companions, who use new members as a means of satisfying their own bloodthirst (see Decker and Van Winkle, *Life in the Gang*, p. 184). In any case, a violent rite of passage certainly isn't unique to inner city gangs. In my college years, fraternities "paddled" initiates, and many still do, although paddling is members' "secret" knowledge.

Gang initiation stories have become so exaggerated that on occasion they reach the news and engender public fear. Over the winter of 1993–94 in central Illinois, local news stations broadcast that gangs were engaged in an egregious violent initiation. It was reported that gang members would drive around at night with the headlights on high beam. When an oncoming car, usually driven by an elderly person, flashed its lights signaling the high beams, the gangsters would turn around and follow the elderly driver to his home and then rob, beat, or kill him. A colleague in the California Youth Authority in Los Angeles told me that such a tale was broadcast on the news there at about the same time it appeared in central Illinois.

While doing Fremont research, Kansas City newscasts reported a violent and bizarre "new" gang initiation. A prospective gangster, the story went, would hide underneath a car in the parking lot of a KC shopping center at night, and when the driver (usually a woman holding bags) stood next to the door to unlock it, the gangster would slash at her ankles with a knife, pull her to the ground and rob her and steal her car. Such an event never occurred in Kansas City. Cara, Wendy, Afro, and Chucky D chuckled when they heard that tale. Chucky D said, "What da fuck d'ya wanna do dat for? Ya getcha clothes dirty and dey ain't no money in it."

12. Social groupings are static representations. To be sure, daily Fremont life isn't static. Pagers helped me to track changing social ties. When a kid gave me his or her pager number, it was a sign of rapport. Old fashioned "low-tech" street ethnography isn't sufficient to keep up with kids who have cars, pagers, and cellular phones, and who shift residences every week or month. "Pager" ethnography helps. I learned to use their pagers and caller identification to my advantage. Kids who know one another's pager numbers, how often kids page one another, whether or not a kid returns a page, how quickly pages are returned, who borrows a pager from whom and then puts his or her own outgoing message on that pager are good data. Boy-girl relationships are traceable with pagers. A girl might carry her boyfriend's pager, and a boy might lend his pager to a girl he wants to sleep with.

Pager numbers are sensitive information. I never had a problem collecting information about drug selling or kids' sex lives, but when I asked for pager numbers and numbers listed on caller identification machines, I often had problems. Even after a long and close association with Cara, she was judicious in giving me caller ID numbers. Their numbers were valuable, and they told me who was contacting whom and how often. Once I had that information, I could ask about the content of the calls and move into the most intimate aspects of kids' social ties.

13. The fundamental gender-linked difference between Fremont girls' and boy' responses to one another is this: girls think about relationships as moral contracts; boys don't. Beyond the street rhetoric of the gang, girls' implicit construction of relationships, especially with boys, includes fairness, reciprocity, and equality. A girl expects that, if she pairs up with a boy and has sex with him, then he will treat her fairly and be responsive to her and their children. In what they perceive to be long-term relationships, girls feel an inherent responsibility toward the boys with whom they are involved, but the boys feels neither reciprocity nor fairness nor equality. This conflict between girls' and boys' underlying conception of the nature of interpersonal relationships is the source of boy-girl physical and emotional abuse. A baby has an important role in the unwitting moral contract between its mother and father, from a girls' perspective. ✦

Chapter 12
The Working Gang

Felix Padilla

In this article, Padilla provides an example of one gang that is organized around the drug trade. The reader should keep in mind that the author is describing only one type of gang structure. Padilla traces the development of this gang into a group organized around making money. He highlights the roles of legislation and the lack of economic opportunities, as well as cultural solidarity. However, in the end the author concludes that the youths' employment in drug sales finds them trapped as highly exploited workers who receive few of the benefits of their labor.

"I'm going to work," Rafael said. "I have to go and make me some bread." The day is April 17, 1989. I had just finished having lunch with Rafael in a local restaurant. Rafael is a member of a Puerto Rican youth gang in Chicago that I have been studying for over two years. He was responding to one of the questions I would ask him as we departed from the restaurant.

"Where can I drive you?" I asked. Of course I knew that he was headed to the usual street location where he had been dealing drugs for several years. After dropping him off, Rafael and a friend boarded a car, which appeared to have been waiting for his arrival. They drove away from the vicinity only to return thirty minutes later carrying a large amount of merchandise he would try selling on this day.

Once back in the neighborhood, he would position himself alongside other dealers to earn a day's pay. Rafael, as well as his co-

workers, were employed by one of the distributors in his gang. Like other workers, they were expected to be at the job for a certain amount of time.

Rafael's work relations with the gang are a clear illustration of the business side of the organization. This is a topic which remains veiled despite a fairly extensive scientific and journalistic literature on youth gangs. In the main, most accounts about gangs and drugs tend to consider "all" teenage drug dealing as an innate activity of the gang. However, this approach overlooks many cases of teenage drug dealing that are not affiliated with or sponsored by the gang.

There are some young men who simply establish drug-dealing networks or crews comprised of several members, but these are not gangs. They lack a formal organization and leadership stratum. Members are not expected to invest time in attending formal meetings. Nor do they pay any form of dues. Members of the network or crew do not consider this group a gang. In other cases, young people who are not affiliated with the gang manage to develop street-level dealing operations on their own. There also are instances of street-level dealing being carried out by gang members working on their own. I will demonstrate below that these three cases are unlikely to materialize where street-level dealing is controlled by a gang, though individuals continue to make attempts to establish these forms of individual undertakings.

The scholarly and journalistic writers do not make a distinction between the times when drug dealing represents a gang activity and a large portion of the earnings go to the organization and the times when drug dealing is an endeavor carried out by nongang members working only for themselves. The discussion that follows will focus primarily on street-level dealers who work for the gang, and who receive a salary for their labor. It also will touch on the experiences of several youngsters who are independent dealers, but who are still part of the gang's occupational structure. They purchase their merchandise from the gang's distributors, utilize the gang-controlled turf for retailing, and are required to pay weekly organizational dues.

The following questions will be considered. What are the reasons for the gang becoming a business organization? What does the gang look like as an entrepreneurial establishment? That is, what are its defining characteristics as a business enterprise? Which cultural elements are used by youngsters for cementing and reinforcing business relations among themselves? What is the gang's occupational structure? How does the gang generate income for itself?

Information for this chapter comes from a two-year study that I have been conducting of a Puerto Rican youth gang in Chicago. I have given the gang the fictitious name of the Diamonds. The neighborhood that serves as the Diamonds' turf is located five miles northwest of the downtown area. For the last twenty years, the neighborhood has been racially and ethnically mixed, comprised of Latino (i.e., Puerto Ricans, Mexican Americans and Cubans) and white residents. Puerto Ricans, who comprise the largest group among Latinos, often refer to this neighborhood as *Suburbia* (pronounced "sooboorbia"). Living there is perceived as a measure of social prosperity and improvement. Census reports confirm this perception. In 1980, almost 40 percent of workers were employed in white-collar occupations. Only 18 percent had incomes below the poverty line and the unemployment rate was 9 percent.

The Diamonds
Become a Business Gang

The history of the Diamonds dates back approximately twenty years, a relatively short period when compared to other Latino youth gangs in Chicago. At first, the Diamonds was a musical group. Members played their music on the street or in local night clubs. In 1970, a member of the musical group was mistaken for a gang member and was killed by a gunshot fired by a youngster from a rival gang. This incident sparked the reorganization of the group into a violent gang. For the next six years the Diamonds provoked fights with other groups. During most of this time, the membership of the Diamonds was quite small. The organization did not divide itself into different sections. Some members used drugs, but in the late 1970s a major change occurred in the thrust of the operations of the gang. It began taking on a businesslike character. No longer were retaliation and violent behavior the mainstays of the organization. Money making through drug dealing came

to represent the gang's chief activity. Several factors account for this change.

Controlled Substance Act

One gang member named Carmelo described one change:

> I remember this older guy from the neighborhood who wanted me to sell for him. He asked several of us to be his dealers. He was offering good money, but I was afraid. I didn't know what he was about. We knew that he was doing something, because all these people used to come to his house all the time. But he never dealt with us before, and then all of sudden he wanted us to work for him. I said no to the guy.

The event that precipitated the development of the gang into a business was the 1971 passage of the Illinois Controlled Substance Act. It carried heavy criminal penalties for adult heroin and cocaine dealers. Well aware that juveniles could always beat the penalties of the newly instituted law, adults who for the most part had controlled drug distribution and dealing up to this point, began enlisting some members from the Diamonds and other gangs to work the streets of particular neighborhoods. Some youngsters like Carmelo refused the job offers. Others agreed. It did not take them or leaders of the gang long to realize that they could profit substantially by controlling neighborhood drug dealing. In other words, these youngsters began to ask the question, why can't we develop our own business?

Gang leaders began thinking about the gang as a wholesaler or investor. It would purchase the merchandise itself and hire its own members, especially the younger ones, to sell at the street level. Because the Diamonds viewed themselves as landlords of several *puntos* or blocks in the neighborhood, the only thing still missing for developing a business operation was the necessary capital with which to purchase large amounts of drugs.

They began pulling their money together. Sometimes two or three of the older members (or leaders) would "go into business." Sometimes the group was larger. At other times, leaders would request that all members make an investment of a certain amount and use this sum for purchasing the drugs with which to open the business.

High Demand for Drugs

The rise of the business side of the gang also was ignited by the increasing demand for drugs, particularly cocaine. The increasing popularity of drug use during the 1970s and the still blossoming international cocaine trade created a situation in which demand outstripped the supply. One distributor recalls the times when, as a street-level dealer, he would sell his merchandise so easily that some customers at times were left without goods. This was the time when the demand was greater than the supply.

Author: How would you compare selling now to years ago?

Carmelo: I was dealing in the streets back in 1974 or so. We did not have the organization that we have now. Now we deal through the gang. So, that was one difference.

Author: What was another difference?

Carmelo: I think it was the amount of reefer and coke, but mainly reefer that were out in the streets. Cocaine was expensive, but reefer, everybody wanted reefer and we were making all kinds of money.

Author: How was that possible?

Carmelo: Like I told you. There was a lot of stuff out there. There were times when I would get my supply in the morning and then go back in the afternoon and get some more. My supplier wanted me out there all the time because the stuff was selling real fast. There were times when I had to turn some of my customers on to somebody else, something I never wanted to do, but if I didn't have the stuff it was better that they cop from other guys. That way they would not want to stop using it. That's what kept us going. Yeah, but, man, that was good, today, well, you seen how that is.

The Nation Coalition

When the business side of gangs grew too large, it had to be better organized. That is when gang nations were built. "My understanding of what the nation means is that we are supposed to respect other groups from the same nation," replied Rafael when I asked him to explain the meaning of the concept. He added that

gangbanging is nothing really hard to do.

In my neighborhood, you have to hang out a lot. Our chief wants us there a lot so nobody else would try to take our neighborhood from us. And we have boundaries, and a little bit of the neighborhood we share with others from the same nation, but of a different affiliation. And we have our territory and if they were to come into our territory, we wouldn't start trouble by getting loud and stuff like that. We all respect each other pretty much, and it's alright.

At a more general level, Rafael was describing the moderate and congenial relations established by rival gangs in Chicago during the early 1980s. Peaceful relations were facilitated by the division of city areas into two gang nations or alliances, People and Folks. Suburbia's various gangs came under the auspices of the latter. No one is really certain of the lineage of the nation alliance, but rumors have it that the alignment was created from formerly rival gangs that were jailed together in 1981. It is also believed that jailed, former leaders of these two parent groups continue to play a significant role in dictating the policies and practices of street gangs in Chicago.

Theoretically, the nation approach was aimed at reducing significantly the degree of intergang violence that had been so common during the 1970s. As indicated by Rafael above, nation gangs were discouraged from invading each other's territories, and agitation and harassment were not to be brought upon coalition members. Indeed, the nation coalition contributed immensely to solidifying the business operation of the gang. "Respect for each other's territories" also came to mean the sharing of the drug consumer market. Each gang was permitted to operate its business from a relatively safe turf or marketplace, selling only to those customers who voluntarily frequented there. No longer was the gang involved in efforts to take over other turfs, hoping to expand its business boundaries beyond its immediate setting. The new nation approach called for the development of a particular gang's business enterprise in its own turf, improving the image and reputation of the business, and making it more attractive to consumers.

Since drug use was so widespread, the most rational business decision was to share the market. It was no longer necessary to fight over turfs. This also freed the neighborhood of gangbanging and provided a fairly safe "shopping area" for prospective customers. A neighborhood that was known for its ongoing gangbanging activities tended to scare off customers.

Members of the Diamonds are committed to mutual understanding and harmony with other gangs but have not abstained entirely from conflict and fighting. In fact, members of the Diamonds believe that the nation alliance has broken down as gangbanging among nation gangs is becoming routine. But the significant point is that when first started, the nation alliance reduced intergang violence substantially and enabled some gangs to establish their organizations as sound business enterprises.

Perceptions of Conventional Work

Youngsters' image of "traditional" jobs was perhaps the leading force that helped to transform the gang into a business venture. These young men began turning to the gang in search of employment opportunities, believing that available conventional work would not be sufficient for delivering the kinds of material goods they wished to secure. One youngster indicated,

> There are some jobs that people can still find, but who wants them? They don't pay. I want a job that can support me. I want a job that I could use my talents—speaking, communicating, selling and a definite goal that I'd be working towards as far as money is concerned.

These young people have a pessimistic appraisal of and outlook toward jobs in the regular economy. They have become increasingly convinced that those "jobs available to them" are essentially meaningless and far from representing the vehicles necessary for overcoming societal barriers to upward mobility. Although these youngsters have been socialized with the conventional cultural belief in achieving material success, they refuse to accept the conventional means to become successful. That is, they do not accept the "American achievement ideology," reflected in middle-class norms, and shown by Horowitz, Kornblum and Williams, and others to be widely supported by ethnic and racial minority parents and teenagers.[1] The ideology stresses that success in school leads to the attainment of managerial and professional jobs, which in turn pave the way for social and economic

advancement. The youngsters' own school experiences and contact with the job market, as well as the futile and frustrating efforts of adults around them to achieve social advancement through menial, dead-end jobs, contradict the American achievement ideology. These young men do not believe in the power of education to serve as the "great equalizer." Nor do they perceive conventional jobs as leading to a successful, meaningful life.

These views reflect the tension between culturally defined goals and the ineffectiveness of socially legitimate means for achieving them that Robert Merton first described and subsequent gang studies confirmed.[2] They point to the absence of avenues and resources necessary for securing rewards which society purports to offer its members.

The decision by members of the Diamonds to sell drugs was informed by their assessment of available opportunities in the regular economy as well as their high level of aspirations. Drug dealing did not arise in deliberate violation of middle-class normative aspirations. The gang represents a "counter organization" geared to achieving things valued by the larger society and countering forces weighing heavily upon their lives. In effect, these youngsters transformed the gang into an income-generating business operation in an unconventional economy in order to "make it" in conventional American society.

Social and Cultural Components of the Ethnic Enterprise

Two questions need to be addressed at this point. First, what are the distinguishing characteristics of the gang that enable it to function as a business organization? Second, what social and cultural devices did the youngsters use for organizing the gang into a reliable money-making enterprise?

The gang has developed its own culture. The gang does this in the same way that the family unit teaches its young the norms, skills, values, beliefs, and traditions of the larger society—and the ways to communicate and reinforce that culture. At the heart of the gang culture is a collective ideology that serves to protect all the members. Collectivism also serves as the major determinant of the gang's efficient development as a business operation. The members' response to their shared conditions and circumstances is collective in the sense that they form a partnership.

For the young people I studied, collectivism translates into an ideology of strength. These young men share a belief that their capacity to earn a living or improve their life can only be realized through a "collective front." In the views of a youngster by the name of Coco, "we are a group, a community, a family—we have to learn to live together. If we separate, we will never have a chance. We need each other even to make sure that we have a spot for selling."

The collectivist nature of the gang can be said to be an extension of the traditional Puerto Rican family. In Puerto Rican immigrant society, as well as in other societies from which many other ethnic and racial groups originated, the family served as the cornerstone of the culture, defining and determining individual and social behavior. Ties between families were cemented by the establishment of *compadrazco* (godparent-godchild) relationships. Relatives by blood and ceremonial ties, as well as friends of the family, were linked together in an intricate network of reciprocal obligations. Individuals who suffered misfortunes were aided by relatives and friends. When they had reestablished themselves, they shared their good fortunes with those who had helped them.

That the gang is rooted in the norms of family life and tradition can be observed from the various descriptions of the gang offered by the youngsters I studied.

Tony: My grandmother took care of me for a long time. I guess this was part of the Puerto Rican tradition at one time. Your grandmother took care of you while your mother and father were away working. Sometimes grandmothers did not believe that their son or daughter were fit to be parents so they took the responsibility of raising their grandchildren. My grandmother is my life. Anybody who messes with my grandmother has to mess with me. The same thing with my aunt.

Author: Which aunt are you referring to?

Tony: This is my mother's sister, which is really weird because they are the same blood but treat me so differently. My aunt is the mother I never had. We are really close. She is the person that I go to when I need someone to tell something to. She always listens to me.

Author: And why does she always listen to you?

Tony: My aunt is this wonderful woman, she's about 35 years old, who is really together. When I'm with her I feel like I can tell her anything that is in my mind. That's what family is all about. This is all in the blood. She cares because she is family. When you have a family, even if it's your aunt or uncle, you know you belong. You will always have someone looking out for you.

Author: In the last interview, you talked a little about the family as it related to the gang. How similar is the gang family to what you're describing now?

Tony: They are very similar. You see a family is like a fist [he pointed to his fist, clenching it and opening it to show that when it's opened it represents five fingers separated from one another]. I know that the five fingers of your hand are supposed to be related; however, what would you prefer having, a hand with five fingers or a closed fist? When the fist is closed the fingers are inseparable; when the fist is opened they stand at a distance from one another. I prefer the closed fist. That's exactly how our gang is—we are very close. To be in our gang you need to have heart. To have heart means that you are truly committed to each other; that you'll do anything for another member because he is part of your family.

In addition to stemming directly from a Puerto Rican family tradition, ethnic solidarity served as another cultural element, used by the youngsters for cementing their business relations. As Puerto Ricans, they expressed feelings of a primordial tie, of blood kinship, said to unify them. This, in turn, provided the basis for trust. As one youngster put it: "The fact that I knew that what I liked was at another person's house— they would talk to me about things like, 'we're going to listen to Salsa music, we're going to have *arroz con gandures* [rice and pot pies]' and some other stuff, I would get more attractive to that than to other things."

Part of the collectivist, communitarian foundation of the gang was also shaped by a base of local consumers or people who are referred by friends. Their willingness to become faithful customers, to continuously purchase available goods, i.e., drugs and stolen merchandise, is viewed by gang members as an indication of membership. These customers become, in the opinion of one youngster, "one of us." The same young man also said: "People from the neighborhood know that they can get smoke, cane, and other things from us. It's risky going to other places. So they protect us. We are safe with them. So we think of them as part of the business."

The significance of collectivism for gang members can be also extracted from their views about the idea of individualism. These youngsters are not in agreement with the view that the successful exercise of individual effort in pursuit of economic and social mobility is applicable to them. To them, individualism means placing oneself at a precarious position. How can they exist or survive without one another? They are fully aware that they do not possess the traditional resources, such as money and high levels of formal education, that are used by members of the middle class to negotiate and advance their individual life chances. They believe that individual effort represents a step toward obliteration. As directly put by one youngster, "By ourselves, we are nobody. We can be had without no problem." Another's remarks were just as straightforward: "This is not a game that you can win by yourself. If you want to win, you do it as a team. If you want to lose, play alone."

Individual success honors those who have achieved it. Failure, and economic failure in particular, stigmatizes those who suffer it. Such failure can only make those who have "failed" the objects of criticism or scorn. It can also be taken to mean that they are inadequate or deficient. The individualization of "success" and "failure" in American society is unacceptable as far as these young men are concerned. For this reason, collectivism is perceived as capable of giving gang members a special sense of purpose and ability—the driving force with which to pursue economic and social success.

Rules of Collectivism

The gang adopted explicit rules aimed at enforcing communitarian behavior and discipline among its members, which was translated into economic activity. Individuals who decided to work on their own were fully aware of the severe penalties associated with such behavior if it led to problems with the "law." For example, members who

are apprehended by the police for selling drugs or stealing on their own may not be entitled to receive the amenities accorded to others who engage in collective action. One youngster, who spent six months in jail, describes the consequences of working alone. "I was left to rot. My people didn't come for me. We were all warned about doing shit by ourselves. I was one who paid for not listening."

Additionally, sullen individual action can lead to severe physical harm, in particular the brutal punishment embellished in one of the most traditional rituals of the gang: the Vs. As explained by one youngster, Vs stand for "violations," which are beatings dispensed to individual members for violating certain rules of the gangs. They are often used in special ceremonies, like initiations or withdrawals of members. During these occasions an individual must walk through a line comprised of other members. The number in the line could range from ten to fifty. The line walk usually lasts three to five minutes and the individual must try to defend himself from the onslaughts of those making up the ranks of the line. If an assault causes the individual to fall, he must return to the beginning of the line and start again. If he gives up, he cannot be excused from the penalty, or accepted as member, or allowed to leave the gang. The most devastating of the Vs are those involving members wishing to quit the gang and those who violate gang rules. One young man described the violations performed during cases when a member leaves the gang:

> There are no rules when they give you a V out. They can use whatever they want on you, they can kick you wherever they want, they pull you on the floor, they can punch you wherever they want, you can't fight back. You just stand there and cover up what you can cover up, and hope that they don't hit one of your weak spots.

I was informed of many instances when individuals who violated certain rules were given severe beatings. The case of Frankie is one example.

> I came out all bruised up and had a broken rib, and that was about it. I just had lumps and bruises all over my face and on my back. It was a lot on my back. But it wasn't as hard really as I thought it would be, so it went pretty fast and I just

hope for the best. I wanted to come out alright [*sic*], alive, at least.

It is to the advantage of individuals to function from the collective perspective of the gang rather than on their own. As gang members, drug dealers are offered a fairly safe marketplace from which to sell their products. The gang's turf, the location in the neighborhood where drug transactions tend to occur, is to be used by members only. In cases when a particular turf has developed a reputation for carrying stocks of reliable and good merchandise, as is true for the turfs of the section of the Diamonds I studied, youngsters can be assured of having an on-going clientele and a profitable business.

Another advantage of a collectivist approach to doing business is found in the symbolic messages this action tends to communicate, particularly to "outsiders." For example, the presence of a group of dealers on a street block or corner, usually taking turns to insure that everyone has an opportunity to make a sale, serves to discourage possible robbery attempts. Customers, users, and others not associated with the gang recognize the danger in trying to burglarize or stick up a group of dealers who are members of a particular gang. In addition, the gang provides individuals with a "reputation," serving as a defense against possible customer snitching. Customers and other individuals would be afraid and hesitant to reveal information about a particular dealer who is viewed as belonging to a particular gang. There is a widespread understanding that to snitch against one is tantamount to revealing information about the entire gang. This is an act youngsters in the streets recognize will provoke retribution and physical violence.

The gang, as representative of a collective unit, carries another advantage. It provides customers with a reputable source from which to purchase drugs and other items. In doing so, it contributes significantly to cementing seller-customer relations. Knowledge about the gang, its territory, its affiliated dealers and overall reputation present customers with the background information necessary for trusting that the merchandise they buy is authentic and good. Customers feel confident that they are not being sold a fraudulent product, or what street-level dealers call "junk."

Finally, the collective approach to selling drugs provides youngsters with protection against police invasion and apprehension. The youngsters I studied worked in groups or crews of at least three members. This work arrangement served as a reliable shield to keep each worker alert and informed of the different predators and threats around them. Otherwise, having to conduct an illicit business from an open and highly visible location, like a street corner, makes arrests a distinct possibility.

Occupational Character

The gang, as a business, is built around a fairly elementary occupational structure. Several leading jobs are found within this structure: drug suppliers/distributors, cocaine and marijuana dealers, and those involving several forms of stealing. This occupational structure, like in other business establishments, is developed in a hierarchical basis, representing a pyramid of power, prestige, authority, and information. One's position on the pyramid is correlated with one's access and possession of these attributes.

At the top level of the gang's occupational hierarchy stands the cocaine and marijuana suppliers or distributors. The number of suppliers/distributors is limited, for the smaller the number the larger the profit. Members of the Diamonds referred to their distributors/suppliers in terms of "leaders," "older guys," or simply "main heads." They thought of the distributors as individuals who had paid their dues by remaining with the gang for a very long period of time. In the process they would have gained knowledge about the drug distribution network and accumulated the necessary money for purchasing bulk quantities of drugs. Distributors hold a virtual monopoly over the purchase and supply of drugs sold by members of the Diamonds.

Author: Who did you purchase your stuff from?

Carlos: I usually bought it from my gang leaders.

Author: So there was a distributor within your gang?

Carlos: Yes, every gang has at least one distributor. There are times when a section may not have one, well these guys then buy from another distributor from the larger gang. My guess is that the older guys took trips to Florida, or meet people half-way. I heard some guys going downtown for the stash. Some of these people were into real estate, restaurants. But it's through some business and the owner of the business was handling the stuff. But this was all done by the older guys, the younger ones never got into this, they couldn't.

Author: I heard you refer to the distributor as the "older guys."

Carlos: Yes, it is the older ones who know what life is all about, who are making money and living a nice life. They are into communicating with one another and making money. But not the youth.

Distributors exercise great influence over street-level dealers through their control over drug sources. A single distributor may have as many as fifteen to twenty youngsters working for him on a regular or periodic basis. The money paid to each youngster, as well as the amount of drugs that he gives on consignment, depends on the type of relationship that is established. If he believes that an individual is not making him money, he will sever the relationship by refusing to supply him. Along with their monopoly over the supplies of cocaine and marijuana, the ability to hire and fire employees gives these distributors a considerable amount of influence over youngsters working at street-level dealing.

The distributor epitomizes success within the gang. He seduces newer members. He is not an illusion or fantasy. Rather, he embodies the dream which the larger society has denied Puerto Rican youngsters. And, in the mind of the youngsters, the distributor represents the one position within the business infrastructure of the gang that they want.

I would see my prez and other heads, you know, two or three cars, and this and that, and they still got jobs, money, you see a bankroll in their pocket, and they be asking you what you want to eat. And this and that, and you be like, "I want to make this money and that money, I want to be like you." And he'll be like, "Ok, well I'll go buy an ounce of reefer, right, cause you ain't got the money to do it." And you know you can't do it.

Since successful drug distribution requires a great deal of secrecy, information about top-level distributors is limited. Contact between the distributor and street-level dealers is restricted to sporadic episodes, most likely involving occasions of drug dispersion and money collection. Distributors are rarely seen on the corners where drugs are presently sold.

Distributors belong to a fairly closed and exclusive club. The few individuals who remain with the gang long enough to achieve this level of job mobility are usually expected to create a new section of the gang in a different area of the neighborhood. They also might be appointed to oversee an existing section that was viewed by the leadership as nonproductive. One young man provides a precise account of the nature of the distributor's job:

In my section, the big guys would never change. They were the distributors, the people everybody wanted to be like but couldn't. They had the control and were not going to give it to anyone. If you got big like them, you had [to] work with another section. They didn't let you compete with them. Why should they? They were going to lose money. But I guess it's not a bad idea to create your section—it's only yours.

In effect, most workers within the Diamonds' job hierarchy occupied the position of street-level cocaine and marijuana dealers—the job directly beneath the distributor/supplier. In most cases dealers sell both drugs, though the preference is toward the cocaine business for its larger profits. Dealing cocaine and marijuana requires possessing available cash in order to purchase the drug from the supplier. Otherwise, youngsters work as sellers for the supplier who "fronts" them a certain amount of drugs—dealers receive a small percentage of the profits. There are other times when the supplier uses gang members to sell cocaine and marijuana by hiring them to make "drops" or "deposits" of specific amounts to individuals outside of the neighborhood. The profits from this job are usually small.

Because of the relatively small profits made by those working for distributors or dealers, the ultimate goal of street-level dealers is to become independent businessmen. That is, they want to amass the necessary amount of dollars to acquire and sell the product without having to share the profits with the distributor. As "independents," the youngsters know very well that the return for their investment and labor will always be higher.

Author: How long did you stay in drug dealing?

Gustavo: I'm still doing it to this day.

Author: What was your biggest profit when you were working for the man?

Gustavo: My biggest profit a week was about $100.00 to $150.00 a week. The profit I was making for the guy was sometimes $1,000 to $2,000.

Author: So you were making very little.

Gustavo: That's right. He was making all the money. There were Saturdays when I would be counting the money that I was going to take him and there were times when on a Saturday he would make $2,000.

Author: Now that you're on your own, how much money do you make?

Gustavo: It varies. If I go and buy $800 worth of cocaine I can make $1,600—a one hundred percent profit. If I package the stuff myself into quarter bags I can make more. Any profit to me is good, as long as it's over $100. But you see, I don't make that kind of money because I don't have the money to buy that quantity.

Author: What has been the most you've ever made?

Gustavo: I bought $400 and took out that plus another $400. And I sold that on a Wednesday, Thursday, and Friday.

Similarly, as independents, dealers determine which drugs to sell, favoring cocaine over others even though the penalties for selling it are more severe. "The money is in cocaine," indicated a youngster as he described the difference between selling cocaine and marijuana. He also stated, "I have spent a lot [of] time working the streets, selling reefers and pills, but I know that I can double whatever I make in these jobs by selling cane."

Dealers from the Diamonds tend to sell both cocaine and marijuana to local consumers, though other buyers come from the "outside." In the majority of the cases, the outside buyers are young, middle-class whites, who have learned through different ways and sources about a particular corner or street block where cocaine can be readily purchased. The thing drug dealers like most about outside buyers is that they tend to become habitual customers, making purchases throughout the course of the week.

Author: You were telling me about some of your customers, and you mentioned how people from the neighborhood are not steady. What do you mean by that?

Carmelo: Friday is the big day. It's payday. That's when most of people come out to make their kill. Actually, the whole weekend is when we sell a lot to people from around here.

Author: And you would not consider that to be steady!

Carmelo: Well, I guess. But, you see my white customers come around all the time. These people have money all the time and don't care about spending it. They come around on a Monday or a Thursday, whenever.

Author: So are you saying that people from the neighborhood make larger purchases that last for the entire week?

Carmelo: Are you kidding? No, they buy a few hits, that's all.

Author: What happens to them during the week?

Carmelo: We work out different things. Sometimes I just give them the stuff and they pay me on Friday. Or, they bring something that they use to trade. For example, I had a guy give me this expensive watch one time. Another left his VCR. So there are different ways that we use.

Marijuana is the most readily sold drug among the youngsters I studied. Not surprisingly, the job of marijuana dealer is the one found most often within the occupational structure of the gang. Marijuana is usually sold to local clients for a very low price. Members of the Diamonds working in marijuana dealing indicated that the common use and popularity of the drug is correlated with customers' perception of it as being relatively mild, pleasurable, and easily manageable. One dealer provided what he believes to be the reasons why users or customers prefer marijuana over other drugs like cocaine.

Because people have the opinion that cocaine is dangerous. And marijuana you just smoke it, it's like smoking a cigarette, you just smoke and get high and that's it. There's not a real big effect on you, you don't get addicted to it. You know, some people do, but they, it's controllable, it's not as bad as cocaine—you get hooked. . . . You know, you get rid of marijuana fast. Marijuana goes better than cocaine.

Youngsters also believe that the legal penalties for dealing marijuana are less severe than those for dealing cocaine. This suggests another explanation for their widespread involvement in marijuana sales. From the dealers' perspective, there is no sign of any significant enforcement apparatus and no cases of severe punishment for possessors of marijuana.

Finally, at the bottom of the gang's occupational hierarchy are those youngsters who make money through stealing. The large number of youngsters involved in acts of stealing are the newer members, called the "Pee Wees" or "Littles." In many cases, stealing represents a "special mission" that Pee Wees are instructed to carry out to demonstrate their loyalty and commitment to the gang. Although these efforts are geared to "proving themselves," they still manage to generate a profit. For other youngsters, stealing becomes a way of life. They work in crews of three or four, and the major item they target is cars. These youngsters become extremely proficient in stealing cars and make a substantial amount of money, though not as much as that generated from drug dealing.

Money-Raising Capacity

Similar to other business organizations, the gang's survival depends on its capacity to develop and maintain a sound financial base. Funds are needed to meet a wide range of organizational needs, such as purchasing weapons, making rent payments, bailing members out of jail, and paying for attorney's fees. The gang's finances are managed primarily through two major sources: one is the organization's own centralized fund, referred to by youngsters as the "box," and the other represents the private funds of the drug supplier/distributor(s) within the gang.

The centralized fund or "box" is established through membership contributions or dues, paid periodically (i.e., weekly, biweekly) to the gang's treasurer. As one youngsters put it: "Without the kitty [box] we would had [*sic*] disappeared a long time ago. We needed all kinds of money to get people out of jail because for a while we were doing some heavy gang-banging. We were paying about $10–15 a week." The sig-

nificance of membership dues in terms of maintaining the gang is also described in detail by another young man:

> Author: How often did you pay dues in your gang?
>
> Hector: We pretty much paid twice a month. We were paying ten dollars per crack. To me that was a lot of money.
>
> Author: What would have happened if you didn't pay?
>
> Hector: But we had to pay—if we didn't the organization would stop. There were times when the president would give us time to raise the money, but we always had to pay. And I guess when you're part of the gang, you care for it. So if you care about the gang, you always find the way to get your hands on some money. It's like if you care for your girlfriend, you always find a way to make her happy. With the gang, you had to find the money to make it happy.

Money for the centralized fund was also secured through other means, for membership dues could only raise a very limited amount. Included in these activities were the stealing and selling of weapons, car parts, and the like. While recalling his early days in the gang as a newcomer, one youngster described his working relationship with senior gang members to whom he was assigned:

> The older guys would always bring me and tell me to go steal or sell this or that. And that this would bring money for me, but most of the money had to be taken to the box for dues. They would tell me that the money would be used for getting me out of jail or any trouble that I might get into later.

A similar account was given by another youngster: "In our gang, we collected dues. Everybody had to pay. Several times I worked together with other guys pulling some jobs, we stole a car and stripped it. The guy in charge took most of the money for the box because we were empty. I guess we didn't mind that much."

The other mode for generating funds for the box is through contributions made periodically by the distributor/supplier. Because the supplier has a vested interest in the maintenance or survival of the gang, there are times when he uses his own funds for resolving certain gang-related matters. The supplier understands quite well that without his monetary donation, the gang might well fall apart. Similarly, he understands that without the gang, he could lose his business. Contributions made by the distributor are geared to protecting his workers, his street-level dealers. If they are apprehended by the police, he puts up the money for getting them out of jail. In the following exchange, Carlos provides a graphic picture of the role of the distributor as a provider toward the well-being of the organization and its members.

Author: How often did the distributor use his money to get members out of jail?

Carlos: Many. We had some times when they pull the money out of their own pockets and one of us would get bailed out. Or sometimes to pay a hospital bill or for someone who got really busted out.

Author: And why did the distributor do this?

Carlos: They would do it really out of their good-will, for the devotion they got for their own gang. And they want everybody in the hood; they figure the more of us who are out there, the better for them.

Author: What were the other reasons the distributor used his money to get people out of jail?

Carlos: One thing you have to understand that is they got their money back. The guy paid him double. It's like an investment because the guy would have to pay him two times what it cost to get him out of jail in the first place.

Author: Did you ever see this happen within your gang?

Carlos: Yes, I saw this happened several times. I even saw it where the big guy borrowed the money and charged double for getting this guy out. He needed money to pay his rent and went and got this money from some other guy and bailed this other one out.

Author: You said earlier that one reason the big guys get others out of trouble situations is to demonstrate to everybody else that they are devoted to the gang and they care for the gang. Elaborate on this.

Carlos: They want to show everybody in the gang that they are devoting everything they have into the gang to make it better. And to take, how can I say it, "look

what I did for you," kind of thing. And they tell everybody, "that's why I'm leader and that's one reason I want all of you to look up to me."

Discussion

In this chapter I have provided a basic sketch of the leading components of the business youth gang. It is clear from the presentation that this kind of enterprise is quite complex. There were many factors contributing to the formation of the gang as a business operation. The examples provided indicate how external forces and conditions combined with internal cultural group dynamics to give rise to systematic and highly organized business relations among gang members.

In addition, although the description presented in the chapter suggests that the gang does indeed provide youngsters with an alternative to unemployment, it is also the case that this form of labor is highly exploitative. The street youth gang of suburbia is far from representing a progressive cultural response to youth labor exploitation. On the contrary, it serves to reproduce that exploitation and oppression.

There are several reasons for this. Contrary to public belief, street-level dealers make little money selling drugs or through stealing. In most cases, these youngsters represent another type of minimum-wage labor. The saturation of the market with mass amounts of drugs as well as the fast rise of so many gangs involved in drug selling have increased availability of drugs and decreased the cost. Youngsters' profit margins are quite small. One youngster explained this turn of events in a very interesting way. "I was planning to make enough to go legit. I wanted to do something with the money I was going to make. I know an older gang member who owns a car wash. I wanted something like that. But as I told you, I worked hard and yet I'm still standing on the corner." Another youngster put it this way:

I guess when we joined the gang, we would see the prez and chief with so much gold and [we'd] think we're going to be the same. But then we have to face the hard facts. There is not much for most of us. But by then, you're too involved, you're a member, people see you and know you now. So you stay—you continue dealing, what else can you do?

In effect, street-level drug dealers are a cheap and permanent labor force used by a few suppliers or distributors within the gang to maintain and enhance their business interests and profits. Although the wages received from selling drugs may be higher than those earned "turning hamburgers at McDonald's," in the case of the street-level dealer upward mobility is highly unlikely. It is to the advantage of the supplier to maintain the subordination and dependency of their street-level dealers. Distributors/suppliers establish the wages of street-level dealers. Suppliers also maintain a large number of youngsters employed, establishing a very real competitive setting and compelling dealers to operate according to the rules established by suppliers.

Additionally, street-level dealing can be regarded as exploitative labor in that the occupation itself is "sporadic, having high peaks and droughts, and is full of uneven demands on [their] time"[3] (Manning and Redlinger, 1983:283). The large majority of the youngsters I studied indicated "working the block" or "standing on the corner" for a good part of their day, for there was not any established time for "making a deal." A transaction could occur at 6:00 A.M. or 12:00 midnight. In addition, competition from other dealers contributed directly to the amount of time youngsters invested working the streets or corners. As one former dealer put it:

> We used to work very long hours. There were other times that we would have to work long past 12 midnight because we got some of these people coming in on Fridays or Saturdays at 2 or 3 in the morning telling us that they just came out of after-hours and they needed it now and they would pay more for it. These were some desperate folks. But you had to deliver otherwise you would lose your clients.

Moreover, the extreme danger of drug dealing adds to the persisting strenuous nature of the occupation. These young people are the ones who do the dirty work of the business, which is often accompanied by physical harm or even death. For youngsters caught doing the gang's dirty work the common consequence is stigmatization by the larger society. Re-entering school is difficult. Obtaining employment in the conventional economy is almost out of the question.

Notes

1. Ruth Horowitz, *Honor and the American Dream* (N.J.: Rutgers University Press, 1983); William Kornblum and Terry Williams, *Growing Up Poor* (Lexington, Mass.: Lexington Books, 1985).

2. Robert K. Merton, *Social Theory and Social Structure* (Glencoe, Ill.: The Free Press, 1957); Richard A. Cloward and Lloyd Ohlin, *Delinquency and Opportunity* (New York: Free Press, 1960); Joan Moore et al., *Homeboys: Gangs, Drugs and Prison in the Barrios of Los Angeles* (Philadelphia: Temple University Press, 1978); Horowitz, *Honor and the American Dream*; Diego Vigil, *Barrio Gangs: Street Life and Identity in Southern California* (Austin: University of Texas Press, 1988).

3. Peter K. Manning and Lawrence J. Redlinger, "Drugs at Work," in *Research in the Sociology of Work*, eds., Ida H. Simpson and Richard L. Simpson (Greenwich, Conn: JAI Press, 1983), p. 283. ✦

Chapter 13
An Overview of the Challenge of Prison Gangs

*Mark S. Fleisher
and Scott H. Decker*

The Modern Gang Reader is concerned principally with street gangs. Prison gangs, terrorist gangs, motorcycle gangs, adult criminal organizations, and drug cartels present significantly different patterns. In some communities, however there have been persistent reports of functional relationships between street gangs and prison gangs. Some membership is shared between them, and sometimes prison gangs seek to dominate street gangs for their own criminal (usually drug-related) goals. Fleisher and Decker bring the character of prison gangs and their control into sharp focus in this chapter, permitting us to speculate more appropriately on how they relate to street gangs as described in the other chapters of this book.

America now imprisons men and women with ease and in very large numbers. At the end of the year 2000, an estimated two million men and women were serving prison terms. The mission of improving the quality of life inside our prisons should be a responsibility shared by correctional administrators and community citizens. Prisons are, after all, public institutions supported by tens of millions of tax dollars and what happens inside of these costly institutions will determine to some degree the success inmates will have after their release. Oddly though, citizens often believe that anyone

Reprinted with the permission of Aspen Publishers from Mark S. Fleisher and Scott H. Decker, "An Overview of the Challenge of Prison Gangs," *Corrections Management Quarterly* (5)1: 1–9. Copyright © 2001.

can offer an intelligent opinion about prison management and inmate programming. In recent years, elected officials have called for tougher punishment in prisons, stripping color televisions, removing weightlifting equipment, and weakening education programs as if doing these rather trivial things will punish inmates further and force them to straighten out their lives and will scare others away from crime. If criminals choose to commit crime, "let them suffer" seems to be the prevailing battle cry of elected officials and citizens alike, who have little formal knowledge of crimogenesis, punishment, and imprisonment.

A parallel argument would let smokers suffer the ravages of cancer because their behavior, above all others, caused their health problem. Similarly, we should allow students who do not choose to study to remain ignorant because their behavior led them to marginal illiteracy. As we sanction cigarette companies for selling a carcinogenic product, as we strive to improve public education, we also should continuously improve prison management and the quality of life inside these costly, tax-supported institutions. We do not advocate coddling inmates but we surely do not advocate allowing millions of imprisoned inmates to live with drug addictions, emotional difficulties, and educational and employment skills so poor that only minimum-wage employment awaits them. These are the disabilities that, to some degree, define the American inmate population, and these same disabilities will damage the quality of life in our communities when these untreated, uneducated, and marginal inmates return home.

Criminologists have argued for decades that persistent criminals often do not have the power to control the destructive forces in their environment, which created their disabilities. Many criminals are, in a real sense, victims of family abuse and neglect, school disciplinary practices that expelled them before they had sufficient education to get a good job, and impoverished neighborhoods well outside the opportunity networks in the dominant community.

Western civilization has used prisons as an experimental site where socially destructive human behavior supposedly is transformed into socially productive behavior. This experiment has yielded consistently poor results. As we begin the next century, we might want to rethink the mission of the prison, shifting the prevailing approach from punishing convicted offenders to using these public institutions as society's last chance to reform men and women who, for whatever reason, have not been able to conform to mainstream community norms.

American history shows prison inmates have, for the most part, been marginal to the dominant economy of the time and were the society's most poorly educated and least well-prepared citizens to hold gainful employment. But now the gap between the social and economic margin and mainstream grows wider and faster than it ever has grown. In the 1950s, a general equivalency diploma (GED) was sufficient to enable employment in America's expanding factory economy, but now the GED affords only minimum-wage employment in the fast-food industry and/or service work in hotels, malls, and restaurants. America's high-tech twenty-first century has decreasing career opportunities for the nearly two million poorly educated American prisoners whose economic future grows more distant from the mainstream economy as the nanoseconds pass. Prisons are our last best chance to help lawbreakers find a lawful, economically stable place in mainstream communities.

That is a lofty mission, indeed, especially with tens of thousands of inmates entering prison annually. To accomplish the difficult job of retraining, educating, and treating inmates, prisons must be well-managed public institutions. Every prison cell house that burns in a disturbance burns millions of tax dollars. Managing prisons is difficult and that task should be delegated exclusively to the correctional experts rather than to elected officials pandering to voters. The highest security prisons hold the most violent and disruptive inmates who are most likely to be as disruptive inside as they were outside. In such places and others of lower security, a social force is operating today that will thwart even our best efforts to create and sustain high-quality prison management. That disruptive social force is prison gangs.

A Brief History of Prison Gangs

Lyman (1989) defines a prison gang as

an organization which operates within the prison system as a self-perpetuating

criminally oriented entity, consisting of a select group of inmates who have established an organized chain of command and are governed by an established code of conduct. The prison gang will usually operate in secrecy and has as its goal to conduct gang activities by controlling their prison environment through intimidation and violence directed toward non-members. (p. 48)

We have only a rudimentary knowledge of prison gangs as social groups operating inside prisons and of the interplay between street gangs and prison gangs. Thus the scope, understanding, and the study of prison gangs are broader and somewhat different from street gangs. One thing we do know: prison gangs are gang researchers' final frontier and prison managers' biggest nightmare.

While we debate prison gang demographics and their distribution in American prisons, we know such groups have been in prisons a long time. The first known American prison gang was the Gypsy Jokers formed in the 1950s in Washington state prisons (Orlando-Morningstar, 1997; Stastny & Tyrnauer, 1983). The first prison gang with nationwide ties was the Mexican Mafia, which emerged in 1957 in the California Department of Corrections.

Camp and Camp (1985) identified approximately 114 gangs with a membership of approximately 13,000 inmates. Of the 49 agencies surveyed, 33 indicated that they had gangs in their system: Pennsylvania reported 15 gangs, Illinois reported 14. Illinois had 5,300 gang members, Pennsylvania had 2,400, and California had 2,050. In Texas, there were nine prison gangs with more than 50 members each, totaling 2,407 (Ralph & Marquart, 1991). Fong (1990) reported eight Texas gangs with 1,174 members. Illinois reported that 34.3 percent of inmates belonged to a prison gang, which was then the highest percent of prison gang-affiliated inmates in the nation (Camp & Camp, 1985).

Lane (1989) reported that the Illinois Department of Corrections (IDOC) estimated the inmate gang population to be nearly 90 percent of the entire population, attributing that number to the importation of gangs from Chicago's streets, which is supported by research (Jacobs, 1974). Rees (1996) shows that Chicago police estimated more than 19,000 gang members in that city and a high percent of IDOC inmates were arrested in Cook County. Other correctional agencies, however, report their gang troubles started inside rather than outside prison walls. Camp and Camp (1985) cite that of the 33 agencies surveyed, 26 reported street counterparts to prison gangs.

Knox and Tromanhauser (1991) suggest there are approximately 100,000 or more prison gang members across the nation. Subsequent to Camp and Camp (1985), the American Correctional Association found that prison gang membership doubled between 1985 and 1992 from 12,624 to 46,190 (Baugh, 1993), with relatively few gang members in minimum security units. Later, Montgomery and Crews (1998) argued that Knox and Tromanhauser overestimated the prison gang population and cited the American Correctional Association's 1993 study that reported some 50,000 prison gang members.

Obtaining data on the number of prison gangs and gang membership has been difficult. Most estimates are now 10 to 20 years old. Fong and Buentello (1991) suggest three major reasons for the lack of prison gang research. First, official documentation on prison gangs is weak. What documentation exists is generally only for departmental use. Second, prison managers are reluctant to allow outside researchers into facilities to conduct prison gang research. Fears over security and concern that research might hamper the welfare of the prison are the oft-cited reasons for excluding prison researchers. Third, prison gang members themselves are secretive and likely would not disclose sensitive information about their prison gang group to outside researchers.

Prison Gangs: Structure and Organization

Prison gangs share organizational similarities. Prison gangs have a structure usually with one person designated as the leader who oversees a council of members who make the group's final decisions. The rank and file form a hierarchy, making these groups look more similar to organized crime than their counterparts on the outside (Decker, Bynum, & Weisel, 1998). The United States Department of Justice (1992) suggests that leaders and hard-core members are some 15–20 percent of a gang's membership and that the majority of members do not have a vested interest in the organization leadership.

Prison gangs, like some street counterparts, have a creed or motto, unique symbols of membership, and a constitution prescribing group behavior. Absolute loyalty to one's gang is required (Marquart & Sorensen, 1997), as is secrecy (Fong & Buentello, 1991). Violent behavior is customary and can be used to move a member upward in the prison hierarchy. Prison gangs focus on the business of crime generally through drug trafficking. Such crime groups have an interest in protecting their membership (Montgomery & Crews, 1998).

Gang members are the essential capital in crime-oriented social groups; likewise, when members want to leave the group, such out-group movement jeopardizes group security, thus the so-called blood in, blood out credo, according to Fong, Vogel, and Buentello (1995). These researchers surveyed 48 former prison gang members who defected and found that the number of gang defectors was proportional to their prison gang's size. A number of reasons were cited for defecting. Most commonly, former members lost interest in gang activities; the next most common reason was refusal to carry out a hit on a non-gang member; and the least common reason for leaving was a disagreement with the direction of the gang's leadership. A small number of former members violated a gang rule and were fearful of a gang violation against them, outgrew a sense of belonging to the gang, turned informant, or refused to commit gang crimes. We do not know, however, how many defectors were killed inside and outside prisons as a percentage of the total number of defectors.

Research suggests there are at least five major prison gangs, each with its own structure and purpose. The Mexican Mafia (*La Eme*) started at the Deuel Vocational Center in Tracy, California, in the 1950s and was California's first prison gang (Hunt, Riegel, Morales & Waldorf, 1993) composed primarily of Chicanos, or Mexican Americans. Entrance into La Eme requires a sponsoring member. Each recruit has to undergo a blood oath to prove his loyalty. The Mexican Mafia does not proscribe killing its members who do not follow instructions. Criminal activities include drug trafficking and conflict with other prison gangs, which is common with the Texas Syndicate, *Mexikanemi,* and the Aryan Brotherhood (AB) (Orlando-Morningstar, 1997).

The Aryan Brotherhood, a white supremacist group, was started in 1967 in California's San Quentin prison by white inmates who wanted to oppose the racial threat of black and Hispanic inmates and/or counter the organization and activities of black and Hispanic gangs (Orlando-Morningstar, 1997). Pelz, Marquart, and Pelz (1991) suggest that the AB held distorted perceptions of blacks and that many Aryans felt that black inmates were taking advantage of white inmates, especially sexually, thus promoting the need to form and/or join the Brotherhood. Joining the AB requires a 6-month probationary period (Marquart & Sorenson, 1997). Initiation, or "making one's bones," requires killing someone. The AB traffics in drugs and has a blood in, blood out rule; natural death is the only nonviolent way out. The Aryan Brotherhood committed eight homicides in 1984, or 32 percent of inmate homicides in the Texas correctional system, and later became known as the "mad dog" of Texas corrections (Pelz, Marquart, & Pelz, 1991).

The Aryan Brotherhood structure within the federal prison system used a three-member council of high-ranking members. Until recently, the federal branch of the Aryan Brotherhood was aligned with the California Aryan Brotherhood, but differences in opinion caused them to split into separate branches. The federal branch no longer cooperates with the Mexican Mafia in such areas as drugs and contract killing within prisons, but as of October 1997, the California branch still continued to associate with the Mexican Mafia. Rees (1996) suggested that the Aryan Brotherhood aligned with other supremacist organizations to strengthen its hold in prisons. The Aryan Brotherhood also has strong chapters on the streets (Valentine, 1995), which allows criminal conduct inside and outside prisons to support each other.

Black Panther George Jackson united black groups such as the Black Liberation Army, Symbionese Liberation Army, and the Weatherman Underground Organization to form one large organization, the Black Guerilla Family, which emerged in San Quentin in 1966. Leaning on a Marxist-Leninist philosophy, the Black Guerilla Family was considered to be one of the more politically

charged revolutionary gangs, which scared prison management and the public (Hunt et al., 1993). Recently, offshoots within the Black Guerilla Family have appeared. California reported the appearance of a related group known as the Black Mafia (Orlando-Morningstar, 1997).

La Nuestra Familia ("our family") was established in the 1960s in California's Soledad prison, although some argue it began in the Deuel Vocational Center (Landre, Miller, & Porter, 1997). The original members were Hispanic inmates from Northern California's agricultural Central Valley who aligned to protect themselves from the Los Angeles–based Mexican Mafia. *La Nuestra Familia* has a formal structure and rules as well as a governing body known as *La Mesa,* or a board of directors. Today, *La Nuestra Familia* still wars against the Mexican Mafia over drug trafficking but the war seems to be easing in California (Orlando-Morningstar, 1997).

The Texas Syndicate emerged in 1958 at Deuel Vocational Institute in California. It appeared at California's Folsom Prison in the early 1970s and at San Quentin in 1976 because other gangs were harassing native Texans. Inmate members are generally Texas Mexican Americans, but now the Texas Syndicate offers membership to Latin Americans and perhaps Guamese as well. The Texas Syndicate opposes other Mexican American gangs, especially those from Los Angeles (Hunt et al., 1993). Dominating the crime agenda is drug trafficking inside and outside prison and selling protection to inmates (Landre et al., 1997).

Like other prison gangs, the Texas Syndicate has a hierarchical structure with a president and vice president and an appointed chairman in each local area, either in a prison or in the community (Orlando-Morningstar, 1997). The chairman watches over that area's vice chairman, captain, lieutenant, sergeant at arms, and soldiers. Lower-ranking members perform the gang's criminal activity. The gang's officials, except for the president and vice president, become soldiers again if they are moved to a different prison, thus avoiding local-level group conflict. Proposals within the gang are voted on, with each member having one vote; the majority decision determines group behavior.

The *Mexikanemi* (known also as the Texas Mexican Mafia) was established in 1984. Its name and symbols cause confusion with the Mexican Mafia. As the largest gang in the Texas prison system, it is emerging in the federal system as well and has been known to kill outside as well as inside prison. The *Mexikanemi* spars with the Mexican Mafia and the Texas Syndicate, although it has been said that the *Mexikanemi* and the Texas Syndicate are aligning themselves against the Mexican Mafia (Orlando-Morningstar, 1997). The *Mexikanemi* has a president, vice president, regional generals, lieutenants, sergeants, and soldiers. The ranking positions are elected by the group based on leadership skills. Members keep their positions unless they are reassigned to a new prison. The *Mexikanemi* has a 12-part constitution. For example, part five says that the sponsoring member is responsible for the person he sponsors; if necessary, a new person may be eliminated by his sponsor (Orlando-Morningstar, 1997).

Hunt et al. (1993) suggest that the *Nortenos* and the *Surenos* are new Chicano gangs in California, along with the New Structure and the Border Brothers. The origins and alliances of these groups are unclear; however, the Border Brothers are comprised of Spanish-speaking Mexican American inmates and tend to remain solitary. Prison officials report that the Border Brothers seem to be gaining membership and control as more Mexican American inmates are convicted and imprisoned.

The Crips and Bloods, traditional Los Angeles street gangs, are gaining strength in the prisons, as well as are the 415s, a group from the San Francisco area (415 is a San Francisco area code). The Federal Bureau of Prisons cites 14 other disruptive groups within the federal system, which have been documented as of 1995, including the Texas Mafia, the Bull Dogs, and the Dirty White Boys (Landre et al., 1997).

Prison Gangs and Violence

Prison gangs dominate the drug business and many researchers argue that prison gangs also are responsible for most prison violence (Ingraham & Wellford, 1987). Motivated by a desire to make money and be at the top of an institution's inmate power structure, prison gangs exploit the inherent weaknesses, resulting from overcrowded, understaffed mega-prisons such as correctional staffers' inability to watch the activi-

ties of say, 3,000–5,000 inmates every moment of each day, month after month.

Where profits are at stake, research on street gangs shows that violence is often the outcome. Inside prisons, the same pattern appears. Camp and Camp (1985) noted that prison gang members were on aggregate 3 percent of the prison population but caused 50 percent or more of the prison violence. In a small confined area with a finite number of drug customers as well as customers of other gang-related services, such as gambling and prostitution (Fleisher, 1989), the stage is set for inter-gang competition (Fong, Vogel, & Buentello, 1992), especially in over-crowded prisons. "Turf wars" occur on the street as well as in prison, where gang members and non-gang members are packed together, leaving few options for retreat to a safe and neutral spot (Gaston, 1996).

Correctional Responses to Prison Gangs

Prison gangs have had adverse effects on prison quality of life. Those adverse effects have motivated correctional responses to crime, disorder, and rule violations. Many correctional agencies have developed policies to control prison gang–affiliated inmates. Carlson outlines the approaches used by major correctional agencies to handle prison gangs [Carlson, 2001].

Since the publication of Clemmer's (1958) classic *The Prison Community*, prison scholars have debated the effect that prison has on the formation of inmate groups and individual behavior. Do inmates form disruptive groups as a result of the actions of prison administrators? Will inmates form disruptive groups as a prison extension of their street behavior (Jacobs, 1977) in spite of the best efforts of prison managers to create a positive environment (Hunt et al., 1993)?

Fong and Buentello (1991) argue that inmates' need for social identity and belonging contribute to the formation of inmate prison groups; however, a need for identity and belonging does not explain the importation of outside gang structures, names, and symbols into a prison where security and continuous oversight are among the institution's principal organizational traits. That inmates form groups based on the need for identity, belonging, personal interests, and race/ethnicity conforms to well-known processes in all human groups, and such behavior inside a prison should not be a surprise. To try to suppress human tendencies to form social groups, as was tried in the early days of the Pennsylvania system, would be pointless as a general management strategy (Knox, 2000). In many respects, however, today's super-maximum security institutions attempt to do just that.

In institutions where prison management controls on inmate crime and violence are weak and where prisons routinely violate inmates' civil rights (Fong et al., 1995; DiIulio, 1987; Ralph and Marquart, 1991), it may be understandable that inmates form tips and cliques to ensure their own physical safety. Given this line of argument, if prisons want fewer inmate tips and cliques and by extension prison gangs, management must step forward proactively and offer inmates a meaningful alternative to prison gangs and gang crime and offer inmates treatment for personal issues such as addiction. Scott's article [Scott, 2001] focuses on altering the prison environment. He argues that prisons, like mainstream communities, must broaden their approach to dealing with prison gangs. Hardening the environment, Scott argues, may fail as a long-term prison control strategy as law enforcement suppression, to the exclusion of social intervention, has failed to quell the street gang problem.

Adjusting prison environments most often happens in court. Jacobs (1977) argues that the courts weakened the authority of correctional officers to control gangs taking control since the earliest cases on inmates' rights; prison administrators are confined within the limits of case law. In [*Corrections Management Quarterly*], Federal Bureau of Prisons' lawyer Daniel Eckhart reviews recent federal legal cases on prison gangs [Eckhart, 2001]. Eckhart's useful article informs correctional administrators who must develop gang control strategies that meet the limits of federal court precedents; such precedents are also useful information to correctional researchers who may evaluate prison control strategies.

Mainline prisons for the most part are expected to house inmates, independent of gang affiliation. Prison suppression and intervention strategies likely will affect gang-affiliated inmates differently from non-gang-affiliated inmates. Why? Shelden (1991) compared 60 gang members (45 black, 15 Hispanic) to 60 non-gang members. There were a number of similarities between the gang and non-gang groups: they shared similar socioeconomic backgrounds, education levels, and marital status; both groups had substance abuse problems. Gang members, however, were more likely to have never been employed, more likely to have a juvenile crime record (30 percent of them had juvenile court records compared with 8 percent of non-gang inmates); 32 percent of the gang members had 15 or more arrests compared with 7 percent of non-members; and gang members also were more likely to have used a weapon than non-members. Krienert and Fleisher show in their article in [*Corrections Management Quarterly*] that new admissions into the Nebraska Department of Corrections who report a prior gang affiliation are significantly different from those who do not report a gang affiliation on many of the same factors Shelden used [Krienert and Fleisher, 2001]. Their research documents the growing nature of this problem.

Shelden's contribution also shows that while imprisoned, gang members were twice as likely to have more than five rule violations, were more likely to violate drug use sanctions, were more likely to fight, and were less likely to be involved in treatment programs. Without in-prison treatment, education, and vocational training, the likelihood that gang-affiliated inmates would be prepared for a lawful lifestyle outside prison is low. The article by Davis and Flannery in [*Corrections Management Quarterly*] deals with special challenges that gang-affiliated inmates pose to therapists [Davis and Flannery, 2001].

How have prison officials responded to prison gangs? Prisons have tried a variety of overt and covert strategies, including the use of inmate informants, the use of segregation units for prison gang members, the isolation of prison gang leaders, the lockdown of entire institutions, the vigorous prosecution of criminal acts committed by prison gang members, the interruption of prison gang members' internal and external communications, and the case-by-case examination of prison gang offenses. There are, however, no published research evaluations testing the efficacy of these suppression strategies on curbing prison gang violence and/or other criminal conduct inside correctional institutions. Below is a brief summary of some of these anti-prison-gang initiatives.

The Texas state legislature passed a bill in September 1985 that made it a "felony for any inmate to possess a weapon" (Ralph & Marquart, 1991, p. 45). The bill also limited the discretionary authority of sentencing judges: inmates convicted of weapons possessions must serve that sentence subsequent to other sentences. Officials believe that laws like this might help to keep inmates, especially those in prison gangs, under control (Ralph & Marquart, 1991).

A popular control procedure is segregation. Inmates are isolated in a cell 23 hours a day, with one hour assigned to recreation and/or other activities. Texas used administrative segregation and put all known prison gang members into segregation in 1985 in the hope of limiting their influence on mainline inmate populations. Violence in the general population has decreased, with nine prison gang–motivated homicides from 1985 to 1990; fewer armed assaults were reported as well. By 1991, segregation housed more than 1,500 gang members (Ralph & Marquart, 1991).

By contrast, Knox (2000) reports that more than half of the 133 prison officials interviewed in a national survey on prison gangs believe a segregation policy is not effective because gang activity still occurs. When an order is issued by a prison gang to commit a violent act, it is carried out, even in a segregation unit. Then, too, segregation is expensive and does not solve the problem of developing better prison management to control prison gangs.

Isolating gang leaders has become a popular control strategy. With a prison gang leader locked down, vertical communication within the gang ideally would weaken and the prison gang group's solidarity eventually would deteriorate. One version of isolating prison gang leaders is to transfer them among institutions or keep them circulating between prisons (United States Department of Justice, 1992). There are no published evaluations of isolation and/or "bus therapy."

Another attempt to reduce gang membership is "jacketing." This involves putting an official note in an inmate's file if he is suspected of being involved with a gang. This note follows him in prison and allows authorities to transfer him to a high-security facility. Many find this process inappropriate because it may involve suspected but unconfirmed gang activity, often reported by a snitch, which leads to incorrectly labeling an inmate as a prison gang member or associate. When so labeled, an inmate can be controlled with threats of segregation and transfer. There are no published evaluations of this approach either.

Correctional agencies now use databases to track prison gang members and gang activities. This allows for effective communication between a correctional agency and a state police agency and improves data accuracy because data can be entered as soon as they are gathered (Gaston, 1996). The New York City Department of Corrections uses a system that allows for digitized photos that document gang members' marks and/or tattoos. Database searches can be done by a tattoo, scar, or other identifying marks. The speed and capacity to update intelligence information make the use of a shared database an effective tool in prison gang management.

Providing alternative programming could become part of prison gang management strategy; however, prison gang members have not embraced such programming. The Hampden County Correctional Center in Ludlow, Massachusetts, developed a graduated program for prison gang members wanting to leave segregation. The program uses movies, discussion sessions, and homework. At the program's end, participants must write a statement certifying they will no longer participate in gang activities. Two years into the program, 190 inmates were enrolled and 17 were returned to segregation for gang activities (Toller & Tsagaris, 1996). Details of the program's evaluation are not available.

Another control strategy is the use of out-of-state transfers, which send key prison gang members out of state in the hope of stopping or slowing a prison gang's activities. If a gang already has been established, it is hoped that such a transfer would disrupt a gang to the point of its demise; however, there are no data showing the effectiveness of this type of control strategy. In fact, transferring a high-ranking prison gang member could be the impetus to transfer his prison gang to yet another institution (United States Department of Justice, 1992).

Correctional agencies have tried to weaken prison gangs by assigning members of different prison gangs to the same work assignment and living quarters in anticipation of limiting the power of one prison over another at a specific place. The Texas Department of Corrections, for instance, assigned prison gang members to two or three high-security lockdown institutions. Illinois tried this approach to no avail because the inmate prison gang population was too large to control effectively within a few locations (United States Department of Justice, 1992). Illinois developed a "gang-free" institution near Springfield, but as yet there are no published evaluations of its effectiveness on reducing gang-related/motivated crime within the Illinois Department of Corrections.

Camp and Camp (1985) surveyed facilities and asked officials which strategies they were most likely to employ against prison gangs. Transfer was cited by 27 of the 33 agencies (such an approach is analogous to schools expelling disruptive students to alternative schools); the use of informers was cited 21 times; prison gang member segregation was cited 20 times; prison gang leader segregation was cited 20 times; facility lockdown was cited 18 times; and vigorous prosecution and interception of prison gang members' communications were cited 16 times.

Knox and Tromanhauser (1991) surveyed prison wardens asking about prison gang control: 70.9 percent advocated bus therapy. Some prison officials tried to quell prison gang disruptions by discussing those disruptions with gang leaders. And another 5.5 percent of the wardens said they ignored prison gangs. These researchers show that fewer than half of the prisons surveyed provided any type of prison gang training; but recently, Knox (2000) shows that correctional officers' training has improved, with a finding that more than two-thirds of the 133 facilities surveyed provided some gang training in 1999.

A Need for More Collaboration

We have little hard data on the demographics of today's prison gangs and the nature and levels of prison gang-related disorder in American prisons. This lack of data is a serious impediment to making progress against a serious and growing problem. The Camp and Camp (1985) inventory of prison gangs describes an earlier era in American corrections. Collaborative research between correctional officials and experienced gang and prison researchers

can yield the data needed to develop effective prison gang intervention and suppression strategies as well as the data needed to test the efficacy of current strategies. Collaboration between correctional agencies and university researchers is a key to creating strong solutions to the difficult, persistent problem posed by prison gangs. Such collaboration should create the programs that will increase the likelihood that prison gang members, leaving institutions after decades of doing time, will remain crime free. Imagine how strange today's job market looks to the inmates who were imprisoned in 1980 or even 1990. To be sure, the challenge of beginning a career, even for a college graduate, is daunting. For a former inmate and a prison gang member, searching to find a lawful path will be difficult and alien.

Efforts to control prison gangs must be matched by thoughtful community initiatives. Such initiatives may include carefully designed community reintegration programs offering specialized education and training to meet the expectations of entry-level high-tech employment. Research shows that prison gangs' criminal influence extends into the community (Fong & Buentello, 1991). The important implication of this observation is that prison gangs will gain a stronger hold in communities if communities do not structure intervention to include more than law enforcement suppression. If that happens, street gangs may become better structured and drug gangs may become more powerful forces in the community. The article by Fleisher and Decker [in *Corrections Management Quarterly*] urges correctional agencies to unite with communities to provide careful, post-imprisonment programming for gang-affiliated inmates [Fleisher and Decker, 2001]. In this way, the response to gangs both on the street and in prison can be comprehensive and integrated.

References

Baugh, D.G. (1993). *Gangs in correctional facilities: A national assessment.* Laurel, MD: American Correctional Association.

Camp, G.M., & Camp, C.G. (1985). *Prison gangs: Their extent, nature, and impact on prisons.* Washington DC: U.S. Government Printing Office.

Carlson, P. (2001). "Prison interventions: Evolving strategies to control security threat groups." *Corrections Management Quarterly,* 5(1), 10–22.

Clemmer, D. (1958). *The prison community.* New York: Holt, Rinehard, and Winston.

Davis, M., & Flannery, D. (2001). "The institutional treatment of gang members." *Corrections Management Quarterly,* 5(1), 37–46.

Decker, S.H., Bynum, T.S., & Weisel, D.L. (1998). Gangs as organized crime groups: A tale of two cities. *Justice Quarterly,* 15, 395–423.

Dilulio, J.J. (1987). *Governing prisons: A comparative study of correctional management.* New York: Free Press.

Eckhart, D. (2001). "Civil Actions Related to Prison Gangs: A Survey of Federal Cases." *Corrections Management Quarterly,* 5(1), 59–64.

Fleisher, M.S. (1989). *Warehousing violence.* Newbury Park, CA: Sage Publications.

Fleisher, M., & Decker, S. (2001). "Going home, staying home: Integrating prison gang members into the community." *Corrections Management Quarterly,* 5(1), 65–77.

Fong, R.S. (1990). The organizational structure of prison gangs: A Texas Case Study. *Federal Probation,* 59, 36–43.

Fong, R.S., & Buentello, S. (1991). The detection of prison gang development: An empirical assessment. *Federal Probation,* 55, 66–69.

Fong, R.S., Vogel, R.E., & Buentello, S. (1992). Prison gang dynamics: A look inside the Texas Department of Corrections. In P.J. Benekos & A.V. Mero (Eds.), *Corrections: Dilemmas and directions,* 57–78. Cincinnati, OH: Anderson Publishing Co.

Gaston, A. (1996). Controlling gangs through teamwork and technology. *Large Jail Network Bulletin,* Annual Issue, 1996, 7–10.

Hunt, G., Riegel, S., Morales, T., & Waldorf, D. (1993). Changes in prison culture: Prison gangs and the case of the "Pepsi generation." *Social Problems,* 40, 398–409.

Ingraham, B.L., & Wellford, C.F. (1987). The totality of conditions test in eighth-amendment litigation. In S.D. Gottfredson & S. McConville (Eds.), *America's correctional crisis: Prison populations and public policy.* New York: Greenwood Press.

Jacobs, J.B. (1974). Street gangs behind bars. *Social Problems,* 21, 395–409.

———. (1977). *Stateville: The penitentiary in mass society.* Chicago: University Chicago Press.

Knox, G.W. (2000). A national assessment of gangs and security threat groups (STGs) in adult correctional institutions: Results of the 1999 Adult Corrections Survey. *Journal of Gang Research,* 7, 1–45.

Knox, G.W., & Tromanhauser, E.D. (1991). Gangs and their control in adult correctional institutions. *The Prison Journal,* 71, 15–22.

Krienert, J., & Fleisher, M. (2001). "Gang membership as a proxy for social deficiencies: A study of Nebraska inmates." *Corrections Management Quarterly,* 5(1), 47–58.

Landre, R., Miller, M., & Porter, D. (1997). *Gangs: A handbook for community awareness.* New York: Facts On File, Inc.

Lane, M.P. (1989, July). Inmate gangs. *Corrections Today,* 51, 98–99.

Lyman, M.D. (1989). *Gangland.* Springfield, IL: Charles C. Thomas.

Marquart, J.W. & Sorensen, J.R. eds., (1997). *Correctional contexts: Contemporary and classical readings.* Los Angeles, CA: Roxbury Pub.

Montgomery, R.H., Jr., & Crews, G. A. (1998). *A history of correctional violence: An examination of reported causes of riots and disturbances.* Lanham, MD: American Correctional Association.

Orlando-Morningstar, D. (1997, October). Prison gangs. *Special Needs Offender Bulletin,* 2, 1–13.

Pelz, M.E., Marquart, J.W., & Pelz, C.T. (1991). Right-wing extremism in the Texas prisons: The rise and fall of the Aryan Brotherhood of Texas. *The Prison Journal,* 71, 23–37.

Ralph, P.H., & Marquart, J.W. (1991). Gang violence in Texas prisons. *The Prison Journal,* 71, 23–37.

Rees, T.A., Jr. (1996, Fall). Joining the gang: A look at youth gang recruitment. *Journal of Gang Research,* 4, 19–25.

Scott, G. (2001). "Broken windows behind bars: Eradicating prison gangs through ecological hardening and symbol cleansing." *Corrections Management Quarterly,* 5(1), 23–36.

Shelden, R.G. (1991). A comparison of gang members and non-gang members in a prison setting. *The Prison Journal,* 71, 50–60.

Stastny, C., & Tyrnauer, G. (1983). *Who rules the joint? The changing political culture of maximum-security prisons in America.* New York: Lexington Books.

Toller, W., & Tsagaris, B. (1996, October). Managing institutional gangs: A practical approach combining security and human services. *Corrections Today,* 58, 100–111.

United States Department of Justice. (1992). *Management strategies in disturbances and with gangs/disruptive groups.* Washington, DC: U.S. Government Printing Office.

Valentine, B. (1995). *Gang intelligence manual.* Boulder, CO: Paladin Press. ✦

Section III

Race, Ethnicity, and Gender in Gangs

Chapter 14
Race and Gender Differences Between Gang and Nongang Youths[1]
Results From a Multi-Site Study

Finn-Aage Esbensen
and L. Thomas Winfree Jr.

Based on survey results from the Gang Resistance Education and Training program (see Chapter 31 for an overview), Esbensen and Winfree report on rates of gang participation among a sample of eighth-grade youths from 14 cities across the United States. As these authors note, the public, policy makers, and even researchers often hold stereotypical views of who the typical gang member is, and often associate gang membership exclusively with young men from minority racial groups, including African Americans, Latinos, and Asians. Findings from the G.R.E.A.T. survey, which sampled youths in geographically and demographically diverse communities, challenge these assumptions; this survey reveals higher than expected gang participation rates both among females and among white youths. Moreover, the disproportionate involvement of gang members in criminal activities is true for female and white gang members, not just minority males. According to the authors, their findings differ considerably from other estimates of gang participation as a result of both their methodological approach and the age of their sample. They

---

conclude by discussing both the strengths and limitations of their approach.

Abstract

Most examinations of youth gangs have been limited to a single city or a single state. In this article we examine gang affiliation in a multi-site survey of 5,935 eighth-grade students in 42 schools located in 11 cities across the United States. We use this diverse sample to examine two related issues: the demographic composition of gangs and the level of delinquent activity of gang members compared with nongang members. Our findings call into question the validity of prevailing notions about the number of girls in gangs and their level of delinquency involvement, and the number of white youths active in gangs and the extent of their illegal activities.

In the past 100 years, volumes of research have been produced describing gangs, gang members, and gang activity. Currently there is heightened concern that although the American violent crime rate is declining, the juvenile violent crime rate is increasing (Fox 1996). Some commentators attribute this increase to the increased role of juvenile gangs in drug trafficking and other illegal activities (Spergel 1995). Combined with the stereotypical image of gang members (e.g., an African-American or Hispanic male), this belief about gang-based drug sales reinforces the myth that the American crime problem is a "minority" problem. On the basis of findings reported in this paper, we are led to question how closely gang affiliation and associated criminal activity are restricted to minority males.

Methodological Issues

Juvenile gangs have often served as the focal point for delinquency research and theoretical development (e.g., Cloward and Ohlin 1960; Cohen 1955; Miller 1958; Short and Strodbeck 1965; Thornberry, Krohn, Lizotte, and Chard-Wierschem 1993). Historically the study of gangs has been descriptive (e.g., Asbury 1927; Campbell 1991; Hagedorn 1988, 1994; Moore 1978; Puffer 1912; Spergel 1966; Thrasher 1927; Vigil 1988); it has relied chiefly on observational methods, thus providing a wealth of information about specific gangs and their members. In spite of some excellent descriptive accounts provided by recent gang researchers (e.g., Campbell 1991; Decker and Van Winkle 1996; Hagedorn 1988, 1994; Harris 1988; MacLeod 1987; Sullivan 1989; Vigil 1988), we have little information about the composition of gangs relative to the adolescent population as a whole. Bursik and Grasmick (1995:154) summarize gang research by stating that the "emphasis has been on the depth of data, rather than the breadth."

More recently, social scientists have turned to two types of quantitative data. First, some gang researchers rely on law enforcement records to describe gang offenses and gang members (e.g., Curry, Ball, and Decker 1996; Curry, Ball, and Fox 1994; Maxson and Klein 1990; Spergel 1990). This body of research parallels the general picture of gang members as disproportionately male and members of ethnic/racial minorities, an image often reinforced by the popular press. Because of enforcement strategies that tend to target individuals with these characteristics, in conjunction with a general reluctance to accept the notion that girls[2] can be gang members, this finding is not surprising.

A second quantitative approach employs survey methods to study gang behavior (e.g., Esbensen and Huizinga 1993; Esbensen, Huizinga, and Weiher 1993; Fagan 1989; Thornberry et al. 1993; Winfree, Backstrom, and Mays 1994). Regardless of study design or research methodology, there is considerable consensus about the high rate of criminal offending among gang members, including crimes against person and property, substance use, and drug distribution and sale.

In spite of this consensus on behavioral traits, the demographic characteristics of gang members remain the subject of considerable disagreement. The primary purpose of the current study is to review the literature and to provide a descriptive account of the differences and similarities between gang and nongang members based on one of the largest general surveys undertaken to assess the American gang problem. We are interested in four questions related to the gender and ethnic composition of gangs:

- What percentage of gang members are female?

- Are girls in the gang as delinquent as boys in the gang?
- What is the ethnic composition of gangs?
- Are members of ethnic minorities in gangs involved disproportionately in delinquent activity?

Gender and Gang Membership

The nature and extent of female delinquency and gang membership is poorly understood. Throughout the history of criminology, female involvement in crime has been a neglected research topic, largely because of the belief that women's level of participation and seriousness of offending are too insignificant to warrant serious attention. For instance, females are not considered in the works of Cohen (1955), Cloward and Ohlin (1960), or most criminological theory and research before 1970. Even in more recent conceptualizations of female delinquency (e.g., Chesney-Lind and Shelden 1992; Triplett and Meyers 1995), female involvement in gangs is largely ignored or presented as an insignificant issue. Chesney-Lind and colleagues (1996:194) refer to girls in the gang as "present but invisible."

Estimates of the prevalence of females in gangs vary greatly, as do descriptions of their involvement in gang activities (e.g., Bjerregaard and Smith 1993; Cohen et al. 1995; Curry et al. 1994; Esbensen and Huizinga 1993; Goldstein and Glick 1994; Huff 1997; Klein and Crawford 1995). Most estimates place the figure in the single digits and perpetuate the stereotype of girls as auxiliary members relegated to gender-specific crimes (i.e., seducing males, concealing weapons, and instigating fights between rival male gangs).

Researchers, however, have begun to question this view of female delinquency. As early as 1967, Klein and Crawford (1995) reported that their caseworkers' "daily contact reports" identified 600 male and 200 female gang members. In other words, 25 percent of the Los Angeles gang members identified by caseworkers in the 1960s were female!

This estimate is consistent with results from recent general surveys. Bjerregaard and Smith (1993) report that 22 percent of girls in their high-risk sample (i.e., from socially disorganized neighborhoods) were gang members. These 60 girls accounted for

31 percent of the self-reported gang members in that survey. Cohen and her colleagues (1995) interviewed approximately 520 youths (age 10 to 18) in their evaluation of 13 drug and gang prevention programs. When program and nonprogram youths were combined, girls accounted for approximately 21 percent of self-proclaimed gang members. Esbensen and Huizinga (1993), during their four years of interviews with high-risk youths in Denver, reported that girls made up 20 to 46 percent of the gang members. When the ages of their longitudinal sample ranged from 11 to 15, 46 percent of the gang members were female. When the sample had reached the age range 13 to 19, girls accounted for only 20 percent of the gang members. These findings tend to support the belief that girls age in and out of gangs earlier than boys.

In contrast to these figures, which are derived primarily from adolescent surveys, other researchers (e.g., Curry, Ball, and Fox 1994; Goldstein and Glick 1994; Huff 1997) report that females account for fewer than 10 percent of the gang members in their studies. For example, a study of 61 large and small police departments yielded a total of 9,092 female gang members, representing less than 4 percent of the total (Curry et al. 1994). Similarly, Goldstein and Glick (1994:9) state that "males continue to outnumber female gang members at a ratio of approximately 20 to 1."

We can identify two main sources of the discrepancy between these two sets of estimates: the research methods utilized to produce the data, and the age of the sample members. Case studies, observational studies, and studies relying on law enforcement data tend to produce lower estimates of female involvement than do general surveys. This difference may well be an artifact of differential recording policies for males and for females. In the operating manual for the Los Angeles Sheriff Department, a youth is classified as a gang member when he or she admits to gang membership. The manual, however, questions the validity of female self-nomination: "These same females will say they are members of the local Crip gang; however, evidence has shown that this is not so" (Operation Safe Streets 1995:40).

The second methodological issue, the age of the sample, may be more significant. The Esbensen and Huizinga (1993) study reported a lower percentage of girl gang members as the sample aged. Additional evidence suggests that girls mature out of gangs at an earlier age than males (e.g., Fishman 1995; Harris 1994; Moore and Hagedorn 1996; Swart 1995). According to Harris (1994), girls are most active in gangs between the ages of 13 and 16. She suggests that "by 17 or 18, interests and activities of individual members are directed toward the larger community rather than toward the gang, and girls begin to leave the active gang milieu" (p. 300). Thus gang samples consisting of older adolescents or gang members in their twenties tend to produce a substantially different picture than studies focusing on youths of middle school and high school age.

Female Delinquency and Gang Membership

Are girls as delinquent as boys, especially in gangs? The prevailing view is that girls account for very little of the violent crime in society; and this also applies to gang crime. Law enforcement data continue to report female delinquency as considerably less prevalent and less violent than male delinquency. In 1995, for example, girls under age 18 accounted for only 14.6 percent of juvenile arrests for violent crimes and 26 percent of juvenile arrests for property crimes (U.S. Department of Justice 1996:217).

With respect to female gang activity, the Denver Youth Survey reveals that girl gang members account for only a small percentage of all active offenders but commit more violent crimes than do nongang boys (Huizinga 1997). The stereotype of the girl as sex object and limited participant in the gang's delinquent activity apparently requires reexamination. For example, in Rosenbaum's (1991) study of 70 female gang members who were wards of the California Youth Authority, none of the females mentioned sex as playing a role in her gang involvement. Several of the girls in Huff's (1997) study, however, reported that they were forced to engage in sexual activity with male gang members. In a clarification of these opposing findings, Miller (1997) states that the girl's status in the gang determines whether she will be subject to forced sex with the gang boys. Thus it may be that this stereotype of gang girls as sex objects is more an artifact of the data-collection technique and of the age of the youths sampled than of the actual distribution of the behavior in the targeted population. Furthermore, the traditional focus on girls' sexual activity may have distracted attention from their "other" delinquent pursuits.

Anecdotal observations in the mass media suggest that females have become more violent and more crime-oriented in recent years. Evidence supporting such increases, however, is largely missing (see the critique of the media construction of girl gangs by Chesney-Lind, Shelden, and Joe [1996]). In an attempt to address this issue of a "new violent female offender," Huizinga and Esbensen (1991) compared self-reported data from the 1978 National Youth Survey with 1989 data from the Denver Youth Survey; they found no evidence of an increase in violent offending by females. Moreover, in his comprehensive review of the literature, Spergel (1995:58) concludes that "there is no clear evidence that female gang members are increasingly involved in serious gang violence." Chesney-Lind and her colleagues (1996:189) note similarly that the "rise in girls' arrests more or less parallels increases in arrests of male youth."

Race, Ethnicity, and Gang Membership

In spite of questions about the generalizability and reliability of ethnographic gang studies, such studies have proved to be a rich source of information about the ethnic and racial composition of gangs (e.g., Campbell 1991; Hagedorn 1988; Moore 1978, 1991; Vigil 1988). This depth of coverage, however, may have engendered one of gang research's greatest racial myths: One consequence of these studies is an assumption that gang members are youths from ethnic or racial minority backgrounds (e.g., Fagan 1989; Spergel 1990). Police-based studies often support these conclusions. In the national survey conducted by Curry and colleagues (1994), approximately 90 percent of gang members are African-American or Hispanic. Spergel (1995:59) concluded his review by stating that the "dominant proportions of blacks and Hispanics identified as gang members based on police reporting seem hardly to have changed, although the numbers have increased in the past twenty years."

As with gang research in general, much of what is known about ethnicity and gangs is derived from case studies of specific gangs or cities. Yet even the more general surveys of youths do not include diverse enough samples to adequately address the race/ethnicity composition of gangs. The Denver and Rochester longitudinal studies (e.g., Bjerregaard and Smith 1993; Esbensen and Huizinga 1993; Thornberry et al. 1993) were concentrated in high-risk neighborhoods; such neighborhoods, by definition, include disproportionate numbers of racial and ethnic minorities. In the Denver Youth Survey, for instance, African-American or Hispanic youths accounted for almost 80 percent of the entire sample and approximately 90 percent of gang members (Esbensen and Huizinga 1993). Such samples hardly permit examination of gang membership by ethnicity.

The emergence of the underclass concept (Wilson 1987) as an explanation for the apparent increase in gangs (Hagedorn 1988; Vigil 1988) has focused attention on ethnic and racial minority gang membership. This perspective can be seen as an outgrowth of social disorganization theory (Shaw and McKay 1942), historically the dominant social structural explanation for gang activity. Covey, Menard, and Franzese summarize the effect of ethnicity on gang membership:

> Racial differences in the frequency of gang formation such as the relative scarcity of non-Hispanic, white, ethnic gangs (Campbell 1984) may be explainable in terms of the smaller proportion of the non-Hispanic European American population that live in neighborhoods characterized by high rates of poverty, welfare dependency, single-parent households, and other symptoms that characterize social disorganization. (1997:240)

The early gang studies by Thrasher (1927), Puffer (1912), and Asbury (1927) were a rich source of information about white urban gangs. These gangs were described according to nationality, not race or ethnicity; not until the 1950s did commentators identify gang members by race or ethnicity (Spergel 1995:8). This apparent change in gang composition is tied closely to the social disorganization of urban areas and the research focus on urban youths. As researchers expand their efforts to include a more representative sample of the general population, the problem is likely to be redefined. The 1995 National Youth Gang Survey, a survey of law enforcement agencies, illustrates how expanding the sample can affect the apparent parameters of the problem. That survey, which included nonurban law enforcement agencies, found gangs to be present in communities with fewer than 10,000 inhabitants (National Youth Gang Center 1997). With this wider coverage, it seems inevitable that the description of the demographic (especially racial) composition of gang members will change.

Gang Membership, Ethnicity, and Rates of Offending

In addition to the ethnic composition of gangs, another important issue is the extent of involvement in delinquent activity within the gang. Are minority gang youths more delinquent than white gang members? Among the researchers who have examined differential rates of adolescents' offending by race/ethnicity (e.g., Curry and Spergel 1992; Elliott and Ageton 1980; Huizinga and Elliott 1987; Lyons, Henggeller, and Hall 1992; Sellers, Winfree, and Griffiths 1993; Winfree, Mays, and Vigil-Backstrom 1994), relatively few have explored whether differences in offending exist within the gang. Two studies that compared Hispanic with Caucasian gang members produced mixed results. Lyons, Henggeller, and Hall (1992) found slightly lower rates of self-reported offending among Hispanic youths; Winfree and his colleagues (1994) found no difference between the two groups. In their comparison of African-American with Hispanic gang members in Chicago, Curry and Spergel (1992) found higher offending rates among African-American males.

Most investigations of gang offending have been restricted to ethnically or racially homogeneous gangs. Therefore, the issue of ethnic differences in offending has rarely been explored. Many ethnographic and case studies of gang members, as discussed above, tend to have limited generalizability. Similarly, some of the general surveys reported recently have been restricted to "high-risk" areas and thus limit the ability to examine ethnic differences in offending.

In the current multi-site study, considerable population and geographic diversity allows for closer examination of the gender and ethnic composition of gangs. We use this diverse sample from 11 cities to examine the demographic characteristics of gang members in relation to nongang members and to investigate behavioral differences and similarities between males and females

and four ethnic groups (whites, African-Americans, Hispanics, and Asians).

Research Design

This investigation of demographic and behavioral differences between gang and nongang youths is part of a larger evaluation of the Gang Resistance Education and Training (G.R.E.A.T.) program, a school-based gang prevention program. Therefore, evaluation objectives dictated site selection and sampling procedures. Because the G.R.E.A.T. program is administered to seventh-grade students, we surveyed eighth-grade students to allow for a one-year follow-up while at the same time guaranteeing that none of the sample members was currently enrolled in the program. We conducted this multi-site, multi-state cross-sectional survey in spring 1995. Site selection was limited to cities in which the G.R.E.A.T. program had been delivered during the 1993–1994 school year, when the targeted students were in grade 7.[3]

Site Selection

We used records provided by the Bureau of Alcohol, Tobacco, and Firearms, the federal agency supervising the G.R.E.A.T. program, to identify prospective sites that met two criteria. First, only agencies with two or more officers trained before January 1994 to teach G.R.E.A.T. were considered eligible.[4]

Second, to increase the geographic and demographic diversity of the sample, we excluded some potential cities from consideration.[5] We made exploratory contacts with more than 30 different law enforcement agencies to determine whether adequate numbers of students were participating in the classroom-based program.

Fifteen of these sites met this preliminary requirement. Reasons for exclusion at this stage varied: Some cities had not yet implemented the program; not all of the sites had processed enough students through the program in the previous year to allow for the retrospective data collection planned; and in some situations, the police had instructed all seventh-grade students, making it impossible to construct a comparison group of students who had not received G.R.E.A.T. Subsequently we submitted formal proposals requesting participation to the public school districts at these 15 sites.

We reached agreements with 11 of the sites. Three districts declined participation; at the fourth site, it was determined on closer scrutiny that all of the seventh-grade students in the district had participated in the program during the previous year. The 11 cross-sectional sites selected were Las Cruces, NM; Omaha, NE; Phoenix, AZ; Philadelphia, PA; Kansas City, MO; Milwaukee, WI; Orlando, FL; Will County, IL; Providence, RI; Pocatello, ID; and Torrance, CA. These sites provide a diverse sample. One or more can be described by the following characteristics: large urban area, small city, racially and ethnically homogeneous, racially and ethnically heterogeneous, East Coast, West Coast, Midwest, inner-city, working-class, and middle-class.

At the selected sites, schools that had offered G.R.E.A.T. during the past two years were selected and questionnaires were administered in groups to all eighth-grade students in attendance on the specified day.[6] Attendance rates varied from a low of 75 percent at one Kansas City middle school to a high of 93 percent at several schools in Will County and Pocatello.

We obtained a final sample of 5,935 eighth-grade students representing 315 classrooms in 42 different schools. Passive consent procedures (i.e., a procedure requiring parents to respond only if they do not want their child to participate in a research project) were approved everywhere but at the Torrance site. The number of parental refusals at each school ranged from zero to 2 percent (at one school). Thus participation rates (the percentage of students in attendance on the day of administration who actually completed questionnaires) varied between 98 and 100 percent at the passive consent sites. Participation rates in Torrance, where active consent procedures were required, ranged from 53 percent to 75 percent of all eighth-grade students in each of the four schools.[7]

This public school-based sample has the standard limitations associated with school-based surveys: exclusion of private-school students, exclusion of truant, sick, and/or tardy students, and the possible under-representation of "high-risk" youths. With this warning in mind, the current sample is composed of all eighth-grade students in attendance on the days when questionnaires were administered in these 11 jurisdictions. The sample includes primarily 13- to 15-year-old students attending public schools in a cross-section of communities in the continental United States. This sample is not random, and generalizations cannot be made to the adolescent population as a whole.

Students from these 11 jurisdictions, however, represent the following types of communities: large urban areas in which most of the students belong to a racial or ethnic minority (Philadelphia, Phoenix, Milwaukee, and Kansas City); medium-sized cities (population ranging between 100,000 and 500,000) with considerable racial and/or ethnic heterogeneity (Providence and Orlando); medium-sized cities with a majority of white students but a substantial minority enrollment (Omaha and Torrance); a small city (fewer than 100,000 inhabitants) with an ethnically diverse student population (Las Cruces); a small, racially homogeneous (white) city (Pocatello); and a rural area in which more than 80 percent of the student population is white (Will County). This diversity in locations and sample characteristics permits exploration of the distribution of gang affiliation and delinquent activity in an age group generally excluded from "gang research."

Measures

The questionnaires given to students consisted of demographic, attitudinal, and behavioral measures. In this paper we examine only demographic variables (gender, age, race/ethnicity, and family composition) and behavioral traits (self-reported delinquency and gang membership). Self-reported delinquency and gang affiliation were asked of respondents toward the end of the questionnaire. This reporting technique has been used widely during the past 40 years and provides a good measure of actual behavior rather than a reactive measure of police response to behavior (e.g., Hindelang, Hirschi, and Weis 1981; Huizinga 1991; Huizinga and Elliott 1987). Respondents were asked whether they had ever engaged in any of 17 distinct delinquent acts, whether they had ever used any of five different types of drugs, and whether they had ever been in a gang. Students indicating that they had engaged in these behaviors then were asked to report how many times during the past 12 months they had committed each offense. Students indicating that they had belonged to a gang were asked to answer additional gang-related questions.

We created four different measures of self-reported delinquency for the analyses reported here: property offenses, crimes against persons, drug use, and illegal drug sales (see appendix). To correct for the skewness of self-reported data, we truncated individual items at 12. Upon creation of each composite score, we truncated the score again at 12.[8]

Gang membership was determined through self-identification. As with most social phenomena, issues of definition arise.[9] By relying on self-definition, we adhere to law enforcement officers' primary criteria for identifying "official" gang members. In the current research, two filter questions introduce the gang-specific section of the questionnaire: "Have you ever been a gang member?" and "Are you now in a gang?" Given the current sample, in which almost all the respondents are under age 15, even an affirmative response to the first question followed by a negative response to the second may indicate a recent gang affiliation.

In an attempt to limit our sample of gang members to "delinquent gangs," we employed a restrictive definition of gang status: We classified as gang members only those youths who reported ever having been in a gang and who reported that their gangs engaged in at least one type of delinquent behavior (fighting other gangs, stealing cars, stealing in general, or robbing people). This strategy resulted in identification of 623 gang members, representing 10.6 percent of the sample.

Results

In this paper we focus on gender and ethnicity. To put results in perspective, however, we first provide a demographic description of the whole sample. Approximately half of the sample is female (52 percent). Most of the respondents live in intact homes (62 percent); that is, they indicated that both a mother and a father (including stepparents) were present in the home. The sample is ethnically diverse: Whites account for 40 percent of the respondents, African-Americans 27 percent, Hispanics 19 percent, Asians 6 percent, and other groups 8 percent. As would be expected with an eighth-grade sample, most of the respondents are between 13 and 15

years old; 60 percent are 14 years old. According to data provided by the school districts included in this study, the sample characteristics are similar—indeed, virtually identical—to the districts' student profiles. In Las Cruces middle schools, for example, 36 percent of the students are Caucasian, 61 percent are Hispanic, and 4 percent are classified as "other." Our Las Cruces sample is 34 percent Caucasian, 57 percent Hispanic, and 9 percent "other." In Milwaukee, our sample contains 27 percent white and 56 percent African-American students, compared with 25 percent and 61 percent respectively in the district.

At the beginning of this paper we posed two questions about the gender and ethnic composition of gangs. Table 14.1 reveals that (1) there are more girls in gangs than is commonly assumed and (2) that whites account for a larger portion of gang members than official reports suggest. In agreement with much of the emerging gang research but contrary to prevailing stereotypes about the male-dominated nature of gangs, fully 38 percent of the gang members in this eighth-grade sample are females. This figure still indicates that females are underrepresented among gang members, but to a far lesser extent than is commonly assumed when older samples are studied.

Also, contrary to popular perception, 25 percent of the gang members are white. Although minority youths account for most gang members, white youths are not as absent as "official" estimates suggest. As discussed previously, much of the previous gang literature relied on case studies of gangs or surveys limited to predominantly minority samples. This sample reveals that white youths are less likely to be involved in gangs than are African-American and Hispanic youths, but not to the extent suggested by past research. In fact, if we include some of the "other" category, which includes white youths who identified themselves as American, Italian, German, Portuguese, and the like, the ethnic difference in gang membership is reduced even further.

In keeping with earlier assessments of the demographic characteristics of gangs, this sample reveals that younger youths are underrepresented in gangs and that gang members are more likely than nongang members to live with a single parent. Even in this limited age sample, the youths age 13 and under account for only 17 percent of

Table 14.1
Demographic Characteristics of Gang and Nongang Youths

	Nongang			Gang			Total Sample	
	N	Row%	Col%	N	Row%	Col%	N	Col%
Sex*								
Male	2,412	86	46	380	14	62	2,792	48
Female	2,793	92	54	237	8	38	3,030	52
	5,205	89		617	11			
Race*								
White	2,187	94	42	150	6	25	2,337	41
African-American	1,339	88	26	188	12	31	1,527	27
Hispanic	924	86	18	153	14	25	1,077	19
Asian	317	92	6	28	8	5	345	6
Other	389	81	8	94	20	15	483	8
	5,156	89		613	11			
Family Structure*								
Single-parent	1,559	86	30	249	14	40	1,808	31
Intact	3,301	92	64	292	8	47	3,593	62
Other	336	81	7	78	19	13	414	7
	5,196	89		619	11			
Age*								
13 and under	1,585	94	31	101	6	17	1,686	29
14	3,119	90	60	367	11	61	3,486	60
15 and over	468	77	9	138	23	23	606	11
	5,172	89		606	11			

*$p < .001$

gang members but represent 31 percent of the nongang sample. At the other extreme, 23 percent of gang members but only 9 percent of nongang members are 15 or older. A minority of all youths live in single-parent homes, but gang members report living in single-parent homes more frequently (40 percent) than do nongang youths (30 percent). These demographic characteristics suggest possible qualitative differences between gang and nongang youths' living situations.

Table 14.2 reports the mean annual rates of offending for male and female gang and nongang members. The appendix lists the individual items constituting each subset of delinquent activity. In agreement with past research, girls report lower rates of offending than do boys, with one exception: The male-female difference in drug use among gang members is not statistically significant at the .001 level. The ratio of male to female offending within the two groups (gang and nongang) is in the general range of 1.5:1; the actual range is from 1.15:1 for drug use among gang members to 2.53:1 for drug sales among nongang youths. More interesting perhaps, is the ratio of gang girls' self-reported offending relative to nongang boys' delinquency rates: For each comparison, the gang girls are considerably more delinquent than the nongang boys. For crimes against persons, the gang girls commit 2.34 offenses to every one for the nongang boys. Evidence for a link between gang membership and drug dealing (with a ratio of 5.24:1) is found in the comparison of gang girls' involvement in drug sales with that of nongang boys.

Table 14.3 presents results from an analysis comparing annual offending rates by ethnicity while controlling for gang affiliation. Among nongang members, we found no differences for rates of property offending. For crimes against person, drug sales, and drug use, the Asian youths reported the lowest levels of activity. The African American youths reported the highest levels of crimes against person, while the white, Hispanic, and "other" youths indicated the highest levels of drug use. These figures suggest the possibility of a slight degree of offense specialization by ethnicity.

A different picture emerges among the gang youths. We found relatively few statistically significant differences between the

Table 14.2
Self-Reported Delinquency (SRD) by Gender, Controlling for Gang Membership[a]

	Nongang		Gang		Ratio of Female Gang to Male Nongang
	Male	Female	Male	Female	
Property[b,c]	.79	.47	3.15	1.99	2.5 :1
Person[b,c]	.80	.50	2.76	1.87	2.34:1
Drug Sale[b,c]	.38	.15	3.27	1.99	5.24:1
Drug Use[b]	1.08	.93	4.03	3.49	3.23:1
N =	2,412	2,793	380	239	

[a] The SRD scores reflect the average number of offenses for respondents in each of these categories. To control for extreme scores, all items were truncated at 12. All composite scores were also truncated at 12.
[b] Differences between male and female nongang members were statistically significant at $p < .001$. Separate-variance t-tests were used.
[c] Differences between male and female gang members were statistically significant at $p < .001$. Separate-variance t-tests were used.

self-reported delinquent acts across the ethnic subgroups. African American gang members reported lower levels of drug use than the other groups; the Asian gang members indicated less involvement in drug trafficking than white and "other" adolescents. Overall, however, the similarities between the different groups are quite remarkable, especially in light of the ethnic differences found among nongang youths.

Table 14.3 makes clear that the gang members are significantly more delinquent than their nongang peers. Within each ethnic group, the gang youths report three to 36 times more delinquency than the nongang youths. The smallest ratio of gang to non-

Table 14.3
Self-Reported Delinquency (SRD) by Ethnicity, Controlling for Gang Membership[a]

	White	African-American	Hispanic	Asian	Other
Nongang					
Property	.67	.55	.61	.57	.68
Person[b,c,d,e,g,h,i]	.59	.86	.53	.35	.70
Drug sale[c,e,g,i]	.24	.29	.26	.03	.36
Drug use[b,c,d,e,f,g,i]	1.15	.74	1.10	.48	1.22
N =	2,187	1,339	924	317	389
Gang					
Property[h]	3.07	2.47	2.21	3.04	3.49
Person[i]	2.45	2.53	2.22	1.70	2.77
Drug sale[c,i]	2.99	2.62	2.57	1.10	3.79
Drug use[b,d,f]	4.51	2.65	4.32	3.64	4.47
N =	150	188	153	28	94
Ratio of Gang to Nongang Offending, by Ethnicity					
Property	4.58:1	4.49:1	3.62:1	5.33:1	5.13:1
Person	3.64:1	2.94:1	4.19:1	4.86:1	3.96:1
Drug sale	12.46:1	9.03:1	9.88:1	36.67:1	10.53:1
Drug use	3.92:1	3.58:1	3.93:1	7.58:1	3.66:1

[a]The SRD scores reflect the average number of offenses for respondents in each of these categories. To control for extreme scores, all items were truncated at 12. All composite scores were also truncated at 12.

The following comparisons were statistically significant at the .01 level using separate-variance t-tests.

[b]White/African American
[c]White/Asian
[d]African-American/Hispanic
[e]African-American/Asian
[f]African American/Other
[g]Hispanic/Asian
[h]Hispanic/Other
[i]Asian/Other

gang activity is crimes against persons among the African-American youths. The greatest difference (36.67:1) is found between Asian gang members and nongang members with regard to drug sales.

Summary

We posed four research questions at the beginning of this paper, and attempted to address each one. First, what percentage of gang members are female? With our finding that 38 percent of gang members in our sample are female, this study contributes to the growing body of research reporting greater rates of female participation in gangs than was previously acknowledged (e.g., Bjerregaard and Smith 1993; Cohen et al. 1995; Esbensen and Huizinga 1993; Thornberry et al. 1993). Is this involvement of females in gangs a new phenomenon, or have females been systematically excluded from gang research? Although we will probably never know the answer, we contend that much of the discrepancy in estimates of female gang participation is attributable to two related methodological issues: the data-collection method and the age of the sample.

Field research, as Campbell (1991) suggests, has tended to be conducted by male researchers on male subjects; thus it has failed to identify female participants except through the eyes of male gang members. This has posed problems not only in identifying gang girls but also in describing girls' role in gangs. Older adolescents and young adults frequently serve as objects of field studies. Hagedorn (1988), for example, studied the "top dogs" in the formation of Milwaukee gangs. Campbell (1991) reports on case studies of three gang "girls," one of whom did not join the gang until her late twenties. Vigil's (1988) gang boys were 16 to 23 years old. These older samples fail to identify gang girls captured in general surveys of younger samples because the girls "mature out" of gangs earlier than boys (e.g., Harris 1994; Moore and Hagedorn 1996). Decker and Van Winkle (1996) include a much wider age range in their St. Louis study of gang members (from 13 to 29), with a mean of 16.9. Their snowball approach, however, produced only seven female gang members, compared with 92 males. Also, these gang girls "were often recruited in groups of two or through their boyfriends" (Decker and Van Winkle 1996:57). Field studies, through a combination of relying on older respondents and reliance on snowball sampling techniques, have systematically excluded girls from field studies.

The current study introduces its own limitations. The eighth-grade sample may exclude some high-risk students—that is, truants and expelled students—whose absence biases the estimates of gang membership provided in our analyses. In addition, in view of some evidence that girls exit gangs at an earlier age than boys, this young sample may over-represent the actual distribution of girls in gangs. Our purpose here is not to claim that one method or one estimate is better than the other, but to clarify the great disparity in estimates of female participation in gangs. In this spirit, we encourage future researchers to include not only multiple methods but also diverse age groups, and to consider the possibility that gangs are not the exclusive domain of young males.

Our second research question concerned the relative delinquency levels of girls and boys in the gang. Our findings do not support the notion that gang girls are mere sex objects with no involvement in the violent acts that the gang boys commit. The gang girls commit the same variety of offenses as the boys, but at a slightly lower frequency. Further, the gang girls are two to five times more delinquent than the nongang boys. These findings are consistent with recent longitudinal analyses from the Denver Youth Survey (Huizinga 1997) and Miller's (1997) fieldwork in Columbus, Ohio. It is time for a conscientious inclusion of females in the study of gangs not only for academic reasons, but also for identifying and designing gang prevention programs that include girls in the target population.

Analyses assessing the ethnic composition of gangs confirmed the stereotype that gang members are disproportionately members of ethnic and racial minorities. Although our findings are consistent with prior research, white involvement in gangs in this sample is greater (25 percent of gang members) than has generally been reported. One problem is that much of the research conducted during the past 30 years simply has been unable to address the race/ethnicity issue. Field studies are often unsuccessful in identifying white gang members or, by design, are limited to studying specific racial or ethnic groups. Decker and Van Winkle's (1996) St. Louis study, in which they found only four white gang members, is representative of field studies that fail to "recruit" white gang members. The authors state: "The racial composition of our sample merits some comment. We are aware of white gangs in the city of St. Louis that have been in existence for several years. However, we were not able to gain access to members of these gangs through our street contacts" (Decker and Van Winkle 1996:57). They add that the same limitation applied to their identification of Asian gang youths in the city.

Exclusion of white youths from gang research is not limited to field research. Surveys also tend to over sample minority populations (e.g., Esbensen and Huizinga 1993; Fagan 1989; Thornberry et al. 1993). In their study of gang affiliation in "high-risk" Denver neighborhoods, for example, Esbensen and Huizinga (1993) had a sample containing 90 percent minority youths, a disproportionate representation. This kind of sample bias does not permit a realistic assessment of the racial composition of gangs. Our research identifies a need for more surveys of the general adolescent population to clarify the extent of gang activity among different racial and ethnic groups.

The fourth research question raised the issue of differential involvement in delinquent activity by ethnicity. Although we found ethnic differences in rates of offending among nongang members, gang membership seems to be an equal opportunity promoter of delinquent behavior. All gang members, regardless of ethnicity, reported considerably higher levels of delinquency than their nongang ethnic counterparts.

By answering these four questions, we believe we have accomplished one final, critical goal: We have identified several unintentional biases inherent in most of the current gang research strategies. These biases have the potential to overestimate the male and minority composition of gangs while concurrently underestimating or ignoring female and white involvement. Other methods, however, may lead to overestimation of females' involvement in gangs and illegal activity. We believe that to contextualize the American gang problem as completely as possible, we must incorporate results from these methodologies and diverse samples. We hope that our analyses of data from this sample of eighth-grade students attending 42 public schools in 11 very different settings has contributed to an understanding of American youth gangs at the end of the twentieth century.

Appendix: Self-Reported Delinquency Scales and Items

Property Offenses: Stole or tried to steal something worth less than $50; stole or tried to steal something worth more than $50; went into or tried to go into a building to steal something; stole or tried to steal a motor vehicle.

Person Offenses: Hit someone with the idea of hurting them; attacked someone with a weapon; used a weapon or force to get money or things from people; shot at someone because you were told to by someone else.

Drug Sales: Sold marijuana; sold other illegal drugs such as heroin, cocaine, crack, or LSD.

Drug Use: Used tobacco products; used alcohol; used marijuana; paint, glue, or other things you inhale to get high; used other illegal drugs.

Notes

1. An earlier version of this paper was presented at the 1995 annual meetings of the Academy of Criminal Justice Sciences, Las Vegas. This research is supported under Award 94-IJ-CX-0058 from the National Institute of Justice, Office of Justice Programs, U.S. Department of Justice. Points of view in this document are those of the authors and do not necessarily represent the official position of the U.S. Department of Justice. We would like to thank our colleagues Fran Bernat, Libby Deschenes, Wayne Osgood, Chris Sellers, Ron Taylor, and Ron Vogel for their contributions to this research enterprise. We also acknowledge the excellent work of our research assistants, who were responsible for much of the data collection. Larry Mays and the anonymous reviewers provided valuable comments.

2. Throughout this paper we consciously use the term girls rather than young women in support of young women's movement to reclaim their power as girls, absent the negative connotations of the past. In her recent address to the Academy of Criminal Justice Sciences, Christine Alder (1997) introduced us to this new perspective.

3. In another paper, Esbensen and Osgood (1997) examined program effects, and included preexisting differences between the G.R.E.A.T. program students and the comparison group. They found no systematic demographic differences between the two groups.

4. Officers interested in becoming certified G.R.E.A.T. instructors apply for training through the G.R.E.A.T. office at the Bureau of Alcohol, Tobacco, and Firearms headquarters. Currently there is a waiting list, but in the early years officers were trained within a few months of their initial inquiry. Our selection of sites was influenced by the number of officers who had been trained at each site. This site selection was not dictated either by the funding agency or by others involved in the G.R.E.A.T. program.

5. Because the program originated in Phoenix, cities in Arizona and New Mexico were overrepresented in the early stages of the G.R.E.A.T. program. Thus cities such as Albuquerque, Tucson, Scottsdale, and other smaller southwestern cities were excluded from the eligible pool of potential sites. At most sites it was possible to identify schools in which the G.R.E.A.T. program had been administered to some but not all of the students as seventh-grade pupils. In Will County and Milwaukee, however, it was necessary to select entire schools as the treatment and control groups because G.R.E.A.T. instruction had been delivered to or withheld from all seventh-grade pupils in those schools.

6. We wish to acknowledge the following research assistants for their contribution to the data-collection process: Karen Arboit and Lesley Harris from California State University at Long Beach; Danette Sandoval Monnet and Dana Lynskey from New Mexico State University; Lesley Brandt, Jennifer West, and Annette Miller from the University of Nebraska at Omaha; and Leanne Jacobsen from Temple University.

7. Five weeks of intensive efforts to obtain active parental consent in Torrance produced an overall return rate of 90 percent (72 percent consents and 18 percent refusals). In spite of repeated mailings, telephone calls, and incentives, 10 percent of the parents failed to return the consent form. Ninety percent of students with parental permission completed the questionnaires. (For a discussion of active parental consent procedures and their effect on response rates, see Esbensen et al. 1996.)

8. The skewness of self-report frequency data presents analytic problems. Various approaches can be used in attempts to remedy this problem, including transforming the data with the natural log, truncating at the 90th percentile (Nagin and Smith 1990), or truncating the high-frequency responses according to some conceptual reasoning. We chose to truncate items at 12 on the premise that monthly commission of most of these acts constitutes high-frequency offending. Thus we can examine these high-frequency offenders without sacrificing the detail of open-ended self-report techniques.

9. For further discussion of this definitional issue, see Decker and Kempf-Leonard (1991), Maxson and Klein (1990), or Winfree et al. (1992). We agree with Klein (1995) that the illegal activities of gangs are a matter of research and policy interest. For this reason we restrict our definition of gangs to include only youths who reported that their gangs are involved in illegal activities.

References

Alder, C. 1997. "Passionate and Willful Young Women: Confronting Practices." Presented at the annual meetings of the Academy of Criminal Justice Sciences, Louisville.

Asbury, H. 1927. *The Gangs of New York.* New York: Capricorn.

Bjerregaard, B. and C. Smith. 1993. "Gender Differences in Gang Participation, Delinquency, and Substance Use." *Journal of Quantitative Criminology* 4:329–55.

Bursik, R. J., Jr. and H. G. Grasmick. 1995. "The Collection of Data for Gang Research." Pp. 154–57 in *The Modern Gang Reader,* edited by M. W. Klein, C. L. Maxson, and J. Miller. Los Angeles: Roxbury.

Campbell, A. 1984. *The Girls in the Gang.* Cambridge, MA: Basil Blackwell.

———. 1991. *The Girls in the Gang,* 2nd ed. Cambridge, MA: Basil Blackwell.

Chesney-Lind, M. and R. G. Shelden. 1992. *Girls: Delinquency and Juvenile Justice.* Pacific Grove, CA: Brooks/Cole.

Chesney-Lind, M., R. G. Shelden, and K. A. Joe. 1996. "Girls, Delinquency, and Gang Membership." Pp. 185–204 in *Gangs in America,* 2nd ed., edited by C. R. Huff. Thousand Oaks, CA: Sage.

Cloward, R. and L. E. Ohlin. 1960. *Delinquency and Opportunity.* New York: Free Press.

Cohen, A. 1955. *Delinquent Boys: The Culture of the Gang.* Glencoe, IL: Free Press.

Cohen, M. I., K. Williams, A. M. Bekelman, and S. Crosse. 1995. "Evaluation of the National Youth Gang Drug Prevention Program." Pp. 266–75 in *The Modern Gang Reader,* edited by M. W. Klein, C. L. Maxson, and J. Miller. Los Angeles, CA: Roxbury.

Covey, H. C., S. Menard, and R. Franzese. 1997. *Juvenile Gangs,* 2nd ed. Springfield, IL: Thomas.

Curry, G. D., R. A. Ball, and S. H. Decker. 1996. *Estimating the National Scope of Gang Crime from Law Enforcement Data.* Washington, DC: U.S. Department of Justice.

Curry, G. D., R. A. Ball, and R. J. Fox. 1994. *Gang Crime and Law Enforcement Record Keeping.* Washington, DC: U.S. Department of Justice.

Curry, G. D. and I. A. Spergel. 1992. "Gang Involvement and Delinquency among Hispanic and African-American Adolescent Males." *Journal of Research in Crime and Delinquency* 29:273–91.

Decker, S. H. and K. Kempf-Leonard. 1991. "Constructing Gangs: The Social Definition of Youth Activities." *Criminal Justice Police Review* 5:271–91.

Decker, S. H. and B. Van Winkle. 1996. *Life in the Gang: Family, Friends, and Violence.* New York: Cambridge University Press.

Elliott, D. S. and S. S. Ageton. 1980. "Reconciling Race and Class Differences in Estimates of Delinquency." *American Sociological Review* 45:95–110.

Esbensen, F.-A., E. P. Deschenes, R. E. Vogel, J. West, K. Arboit, and L. Harris. 1996. "Active Parental Consent in School-Based Research: An Examination of Ethical and Methodological Issues." *Evaluation Review* 20:737-753.

Esbensen, F.-A. and D. Huizinga. 1993. "Gangs, Drugs, and Delinquency in a Survey of Urban Youth." *Criminology* 31:565–589.

Esbensen, F.-A., D. Huizinga, and A. W. Weiher. 1993. "Gang and Non-gang Youth: Differences in Explanatory Variables." *Journal of Contemporary Criminal Justice* 9:94–116.

Esbensen, F.-A. and D. W. Osgood. 1997. *National Evaluation of G.R.E.A.T.* Washington, DC: U.S. Department of Justice.

Fagan, J. 1989. "The Social Organization of Drug Use and Drug Dealing among Urban Gangs." *Criminology* 27:633–69.

Fishman, L. T. 1995. "The Vice Queens: An Ethnographic Study of Black Female Gang Behavior." Pp. 83–92 in *The Modern Gang Reader,* edited by M. W. Klein, C. L. Maxson, and J. Miller. Los Angeles: Roxbury.

Fox, J. A. 1996. *Trends in Juvenile Violence: A Report to the United States Attorney General on Current and Future Rates of Juvenile Offending.* Washington, DC: U.S. Department of Justice.

Goldstein, A. P. and B. Glick. 1994. *The Prosocial Gang: Implementing Aggression Replacement Training.* Thousand Oaks, CA: Sage.

Hagedorn, J. M. 1988. *People and Folks: Gangs, Crime, and the Underclass in a Rustbelt City.* Chicago: Lakeview.

———. 1994. "Homeboys, Dope Fiends, Legits, and New Jacks." *Criminology* 32:197–219.

Harris, M. C. 1988. *Cholas: Latino Girls and Gangs.* New York: AMS.

———. 1994. "Cholas, Mexican-American Girls, and Gangs." *Sex Roles* 30:289–301.

Hindelang, M. J., T. Hirschi, and J. G. Weis. 1981. *Measuring Delinquency.* Beverly Hills: Sage.

Huff, C. R. 1997. "The Criminal Behavior of Gang Members in Ohio, Colorado, and Florida." Presented at the annual meetings of the Western Society of Criminology, Honolulu.

Huizinga, D. 1991. "Assessing Violent Behavior with Self-Reports." Pp. 47–66 in *Neuropsychology of Aggression,* edited by J. Milner. Boston: Kluwer.

———. 1997. "Gangs and the Volume of Crime." Presented at the annual meetings of the Western Society of Criminology, Honolulu.

Huizinga, D. and D. S. Elliott. 1987. "Juvenile Offenders: Prevalence, Offender Incidence, and Arrest Rates by Race." *Crime and Delinquency* 33:206–23.

Huizinga, D. and F.-A. Esbensen. 1991. "Are There Changes in Female Delinquency and Are There Changes in Underlying Explanatory Factors?" Presented at the annual meetings of the American Society of Criminology, San Francisco.

Klein, M. W. 1995. *The American Street Gang: Its Nature, Prevalence, and Control.* New York: Oxford University Press.

Klein, M. W. and L. Y. Crawford. 1995. "Groups, Gangs, and Cohesiveness." Pp. 160–67 in *The Modern Gang Reader,* edited by M. W. Klein, C. L. Maxson, and J. Miller. Los Angeles: Roxbury.

Lyons, J.-M., S. Henggeller, and J. A. Hall. 1992. "The Family Relations, Peer Associations, and Criminal Activities of Caucasians and Hispanic-American Gang Members." *Journal of Child Psychology* 20:439–49.

MacLeod, J. 1987. *Ain't No Makin' It: Leveled Aspirations in a Low-Income Neighborhood.* Boulder: Westview.

Maxson, C. L. and M. W. Klein. 1990. "Street Gang Violence: Twice as Great or Half as Great?" Pp. 71–100 in *Gangs in America,* edited by C. R. Huff. Newbury Park, CA: Sage.

Miller, J. 1997. "Gender and Victimization Risk among Young Women in Gangs." Presented at the National Research and Evaluation Conference, Washington, DC.

Miller, W. B. 1958. "Lower Class Culture as a Generating Milieu for Gang Delinquency." *Journal of Social Issues* 14:5–19.

Moore, J. W. 1978. *Homeboys: Gangs, Drugs, and Prison in the Barrios of Los Angeles.* Philadelphia: Temple University Press.

———. 1991. *Going Down to the Barrio: Homeboys and Homegirls in Change.* Philadelphia: Temple University Press.

Moore, J. W. and J. M. Hagedorn. 1996. "What Happens to Girls in the Gang?" Pp. 205–19 in *Gangs in America,* 2nd ed., edited by C. R. Huff. Thousand Oaks, CA: Sage.

Nagin, D. S. and D. A. Smith. 1990. "Participation in and Frequency of Delinquent Behavior: A Test for Structural Differences." *Quantitative Criminology* 6:335–365.

National Youth Gang Center. 1997. *1995 National Gang Survey.* Tallahassee: National Youth Gang Center.

Operation Safe Streets (OSS) Street Gang Detail. 1995. "L.A. Style: A Street Gang Manual of the Los Angeles County Sheriff's Department." Pp. 34–45 in *The Modern Gang Reader,* edited by M. W. Klein, C. L. Maxson, and J. Miller. Los Angeles: Roxbury.

Puffer, J. A. 1912. *The Boy and His Gang.* Boston: Houghton Mifflin.

Rosenbaum, J. L. 1991. "The Female Gang Member: A Look at the California Problem." Unpublished manuscript, California State University at Fullerton.

Sellers, C. S., L. T. Winfree Jr., and C. T. Griffiths. 1993. "Legal Attitudes, Permissive Norm Qualities, and Substance Use: A Comparison of American Indian and Non-Indian Youth." *Journal of Drug Issues* 23:493–513.

Shaw, C. R. and H. D. McKay. 1942. *Juvenile Delinquency and Urban Areas.* Chicago: University of Chicago Press.

Short, J. F. and F. L. Strodtbeck. 1965. *Group Process and Gang Delinquency.* Chicago: University of Chicago Press.

Spergel, I. A. 1966. *Street Gang Work: Theory and Practice.* Reading, MA: Addison-Wesley.

———. 1990. "Youth Gangs: Continuity and Change." Pp. 171–275 in *Crime and Justice: An Annual Review of Research,* edited by N. Morris and M. Tonry. Chicago: University of Chicago Press.

———. 1995. *The Youth Gang Problem.* New York: Oxford University Press.

Sullivan, M. L. 1989. *Getting Paid: Youth Crime and Work in the Inner City.* Ithaca: Cornell University Press.

Swart, W. J. 1995. "Female Gang Delinquency: A Search for 'Acceptably Deviant Behavior'." Pp. 78–92 in *The Modern Gang Reader,* edited by M. W. Klein, C. L. Maxson, and J. Miller. Los Angeles: Roxbury.

Thornberry, T. P., M. D. Krohn, A. J. Lizotte, and D. Chard-Wierschem. 1993. "The Role of Juvenile Gangs in Facilitating Delinquent Behavior." *Journal of Research in Crime and Delinquency* 30:55–87.

Thrasher, F. M. 1927. *The Gang: A Study of One Thousand Three Hundred Thirteen Gangs in Chicago.* Chicago: University of Chicago Press.

Triplett, R. and L. Meyers. 1995. "Evaluating Contextual Patterns of Delinquency: Gender-Based Differences." *Justice Quarterly* 12:59–84.

U.S. Department of Justice. 1996. *Crime in the United States, 1995.* Washington, DC: U.S. Department of Justice.

Vigil, J. D. 1988. *Barrio Gangs: Street Life and Identity in Southern California.* Austin: University of Texas Press.

Wilson, W. J. 1987. *The Truly Disadvantaged: The Inner City, the Underclass, and Public Policy.* Chicago: University of Chicago Press.

Winfree, L. T., T. V. Backstrom, and G. L. Mays. 1994. "Social Learning Theory, Self-Reported Delinquency, and Youth Gangs: A New Twist on a General Theory of Crime and Delinquency." *Youth and Society* 26:147–77.

Winfree, L. T., G. L. Mays, and T. Vigil-Backstrom. 1994. "Youth Gangs and Incarcerated Delinquents: Exploring the Ties between Gang Membership, Delinquency, and Social Learning Theory." *Justice Quarterly* 11:229–56. ✦

Chapter 15
Chinese Gangs and Extortion

Ko-Lin Chin

Ethnic variations in gang formation result from differences in social and economic opportunities, community structures, and cultural values. In this article, Chin describes the involvement of Chinese youth gangs in the extortion of community businesses. According to the author, Chinese gangs are closely tied to the social and economic organization of their communities. Because the communities in which they evolve tend to be prosperous, and because they draw on Chinese subcultural norms, these gangs are able to take advantage of both legitimate and illegitimate opportunities for money and power that are not available to gang members of other ethnic groups.

Before 1965, with the exception of group conflicts among the tongs[1] in the late nineteenth and early twentieth centuries (Dillon, 1962; Gong & Grant, 1930), crime rates within the Chinese communities in North America were very low (Beach, 1932; Mac-Gill, 1938). Chinese immigrants were generally law-abiding, hardworking, and peaceful. Official statistics show that the most common offenses were victimless crimes such as prostitution, opium smoking, drunkenness, and disorderly conduct (Tracy, 1980). Offenders were primarily adults who indulged in these culturally sanctioned recreational activities as a respite from work. Among Chinese adolescents, delinquency was also uncommon (Sung, 1977).

In considering the tranquility of Chinese communities in the past, however, it is important to note that before 1965 there were

Reprinted from: C. Ronald Huff (ed.), *Gangs in America*, pp. 129–145. Copyright © 1990 by Sage Publications, Inc. Reprinted by permission.

few Chinese teenagers in the United States, a result of the Chinese Exclusion Act passed in 1882 and the National Origins Act of 1924 (Fessler, 1983; Sung, 1979). The Immigration and Naturalization Act of 1965 was a turning point in the history of Chinese immigration because it not only made China a "preferred" nation but also established priorities for admission based largely on family relationships; those already living in the United States could initiate the immigration process for their families overseas (Kwong, 1987; Takagi & Platt, 1978).

Since 1965, the increasing number of Chinese immigrating to the United States has affected the stability of the Chinese communities in unprecedented ways. Traditional groups such as the family and district associations were ill prepared to cope with the influx. Because there were few social service agencies to help the newcomers, they were left mostly on their own to resolve housing, employment, education, and health problems (R. Chin, 1977; Huang & Pilisuk, 1977).

This breakdown in support, coupled with the growth of the Chinese population in isolated and fragmented communities, brought a corresponding increase in criminal activities among the Chinese (Bresler, 1981; Posner, 1988; President's Commission on Organized Crime, 1984; Robertson, 1977). Chinese gangs sprang up in San Francisco (Emch, 1973; Loo, 1976), Los Angeles (Los Angeles County Sheriffs Department, 1984), Boston (Roache, 1988), Toronto (Allen & Thomas, 1987), Vancouver (Robinson & Joe, 1980), and New York City (Chang, 1972; K. Chin, 1986). Although the number of active Chinese gang members is relatively small (there are no more than 2,000 Chinese gang members in the whole country), their involvement in some of the nation's worst gang-related violence (e.g., Daly, 1983) and heroin trafficking (U.S. Senate, 1986) has drawn the attention of law enforcement authorities. Recently, local and federal authorities have predicted that Chinese criminal organizations will emerge as the number one organized crime problem in the 1990s, when they become a dominant force in heroin trafficking, alien smuggling, money laundering, and other racketeering activities (U.S. Department of Justice, 1985, 1988, 1989; U.S. Department of State, 1988).

Although Chinese gangs have been active in the United States for more than 20 years, most of our knowledge about them has come from police and journalists. Other than a few scholarly studies carried out 10 or 15 years ago (Loo, 1976; Miller, 1975; Robinson & Joe, 1980), there has been no recent research on Chinese gangs. Thus it is imperative to improve our understanding of a social problem that law enforcement authorities have suggested is of paramount importance.

This chapter describes the individual and group characteristics of New York City's Chinese gangs and compares them with street gangs of other ethnic groups. Additionally, the social processes and functions of extortion—the type of illegal activity routinely and systematically committed by the Chinese gangs—also are considered.

This study was based on four types of data: ethnographic interviews, field notes, official reports and documents, and newspapers and magazines. People who were familiar with Chinese gangs or who had been victimized by gang members were interviewed, including members of the tongs and street gangs, social service providers, officials of civic associations, reporters, police officers, prosecutors, federal law enforcement officials, and victims.

To supplement interview data, I spent some time in the field. Most of my observations were made in gambling dens or bars where gang members hang out. I also reviewed and analyzed official reports and documents, and examined indictment materials and sentencing memoranda related to Chinese gangs. Finally, hundreds of English- and Chinese-language newspaper and magazine articles on Chinese gangs were collected and categorized by type of criminal organization, geographical area, and type of crime.

Demographic Characteristics

Sex

Like other ethnic gangs, Chinese gangs are composed predominantly of males. Although young females do hang around with members or live in the gangs' apartments, they are not initiated into the gangs. Except for carrying guns for their boyfriends, the girls are not involved in either property or violent crime.

Age

According to a police report, members' ages range from 13 to 37 (New York City Police Department, 1983). The mean age for the 192 registered gang members is 22.7. Most members are in their late teens or early 20s. Because the report included active, inactive, suspected, and imprisoned members, the sample may overrepresent seasoned members. Those who are new members may not yet be known to the police.

Country of Origin

In the 1960s and 1970s, most gang members were young immigrants from Hong Kong. A few were American- or Taiwan-born. Of the 25 Ghost Shadows indicted in 1985, for example, 24 were born in Hong Kong. Since the late 1970s, some Chinese gangs have recruited many Vietnam-born Chinese (President's Commission on Organized Crime, 1984). In the 1980s, many young immigrants from China were being recruited. Recently, some Korean youths also were inducted into the newly established Chinese gangs. So far, Chinese gangs have not recruited anyone who is of non-Asian origin. Most gang members, with the exception of a Taiwanese gang, speak the Cantonese dialect.

Structural Characteristics

Size

Each gang has on average about 20 to 50 hard-core members, a few inactive members, and some peripheral members. When conflicts among gangs are intense, they may seek reinforcements from other cities. Law enforcement authorities estimate a total of 200 to 400 active Chinese gang members in New York City, belonging to about nine gangs.

Organization

The structures of the gangs vary. The Ghost Shadows, for example, have four or five leaders at the top, the so-called *tai lou* (big brothers). Most other gangs have either one or two leaders. Under the leaders are a few "lieutenants," or associate leaders, in command of the street soldiers. At the bottom of the hierarchy are the street soldiers, who guard the streets and commit most of the extortion, robbery, and street violence. They are known as the *ma jai* (little horses).

Leaders maintain direct contact with certain tong elders and receive payment from them or from the gambling houses in the community. The leaders are the only liaisons between the tongs and the gangs. Leaders rarely are involved in street violence, although they give the orders. Whenever a leader wants somebody harassed or assaulted, he instructs the street leaders or members to carry out the assignment. The leader may provide the hit man with guns and pay him as a reward after he fulfills the "contract." Usually, the leader monitors the action from a nearby restaurant or gang apartment.

Although the associate leaders do not have much power in the administration of the gang, they control the ordinary members. Therefore, it is not surprising that street soldiers are more loyal to their immediate bosses than to the top leaders. Street leaders usually recruit the ordinary members. Although street leaders sometimes are involved in carrying out assignments, their usual role is that of "steerer"—they bring the street soldiers to their target and identify it for them. Street leaders do not initiate plans to attack specific people.

Among ordinary members, a few tough ones are known as "shooters"; they carry out most of the gang's assaults. The primary function of the soldiers is to watch the streets, guard the gambling places, and collect protection fees.

Most gangs have their own apartments, which are occupied mainly by street soldiers and are used as headquarters and for ammunition storage. The leaders do not live in them, although they drop by occasionally.

Except for the Ghost Shadows and the Flying Dragons, the gangs do not have splinter groups in other cities. The Ghost Shadows have chapters in Boston, Chicago, Baltimore, Houston, and Toronto, and police in New York City believe that the groups are nationally—or even internationally—linked.

Recruitment and Membership

Some youths join the gangs voluntarily, while others are coerced. Before the mid-1970s, most youths were volunteers. Members treated one another as brothers, and it appeared that there was much camaraderie among them. From the mid-1970s through the early 1980s, however, many youths joined the gangs out of fear. Gangs have employed both subtle and crude methods to recruit new members. Gang members may

treat a potential member to a good meal, show him their expensive cars, and provide him with the companionship of teenage girls. Impressionable adolescents may decide to join the gang to enjoy the putative benefits of membership. If potential recruits are unimpressed by what the gang offers, gang members send street soldiers to beat them up, a crude way of convincing them that their lives are more secure if they are gang members than if they are alone.

Usually, gang members recruit youths who are vulnerable—those who are not doing well in school or who have already dropped out. Young newcomers who have little or no command of English, poor academic records, and few job prospects are the most likely to find gang life attractive and exciting. Gang youths also approach adolescents who hang around video arcades, basketball courts, bars, and street corners, and those who talk and act arrogantly. Recruitment activities are carried out by both seasoned members and those who have been in the gang for only a short time.

Once a youth decides to join the gang, he goes through an initiation ceremony that is a simplified version of the Chinese secret societies' recruiting rituals. The youth takes his oaths, burns yellow paper, and drinks wine mixed with blood in front of the gang leaders and the altar of General Kwan, a heroic figure of the secret societies. The oaths taken by new recruits are, in essence, similar to the 36 oaths of the secret societies (see Bresler, 1981; K. Chin, 1990).

Dynamic Characteristics

Conformity to peer pressure is a strong characteristic of Chinese gang members. For instance, after six Ghost Shadows abducted and raped a White woman, two of the offenders initially opposed killing the victim. When the other four argued that she had to be killed, however, the two immediately consented. Nevertheless, group cohesion appears to be weak. Intragang conflicts erupt frequently, and members sometimes transfer from one gang to another. Within a Chinese gang there are usually two or more cliques, each consisting of a leader, one or more associate leaders, and several soldiers. These cliques usually distrust and dislike one another, and the tensions among them are exacerbated easily whenever illegal gains are not distributed properly. A review of the history of Chinese gangs in New York City indicates that leaders constantly are plotting to have one another killed (K. Chin, 1990). A Chinese gang leader is more likely to be killed by his associates than by a rival.

Some intragang conflicts are instigated by tong elders who are associated with a particular clique. These mentors prefer to have a divided rather than a united gang; therefore, they intervene to ensure that no particular clique gains enough power to challenge the supremacy of the tong.

Attachment to the gang is not absolute. To date, no gang member has been attacked by his peers simply because he decided to leave the gang. If a member joins a rival gang, however, he can provoke retaliation from his former associates. On the other hand, if the leaders of the two groups involved can reach agreement about the transfer of members, changing membership and allegiance can be arranged satisfactorily.

Comparison of Chinese Gangs With Other Ethnic Gangs

How different are Chinese gangs from other ethnic gangs? Some researchers report that Chinese gangs are similar to other ethnic gangs in several ways. For instance, Robinson and Joe (1980) found that the characteristics of the Chinese gangs in Vancouver were identical to those of American gangs. The gangs Robinson and Joe studied, however, were atypical in the sense that they were not related to community organizations as Chinese immigrant gangs in San Francisco and New York City are. They resembled American street-corner gangs or athletic clubs, and were similar to the American-born Chinese gangs that were active in the early 1960s, a period when Chinese gangs were not yet institutionalized by community associations.

Like Robinson and Joe, Takagi and Platt (1978) suggest that Chinese gangs—like other ethnic gangs—are involved only in petty crimes. In their view, the tongs and other adult associations, rather than the gangs, are responsible for the organized racketeering activities and violence within the Chinese communities. Takagi and Platt's findings are not supported by other data. Violence in Chinatown is, in most instances, instigated by Chinese gangs (K. Chin, 1990).

In contrast to scholars of gang delinquency, law enforcement authorities argue that Chinese gangs are unlike other ethnic street gangs. A former captain of the New York City Police Department suggests that Chinese gangs should not even be considered as "youth" gangs because of the way they are controlled and the age of the leaders:

> [Chinese gangs] are well-controlled and held accountable to the various associations in the Chinatown area. They are the soldiers of Oriental organized crime, with strong ties to cities throughout the United States. The associations have international ties in banking, real estate, and import/export businesses and are suspected of being involved in narcotics and alien smuggling. Members of the street gangs range in age from the mid-teens to early twenties. The street leaders are in their early twenties and thirties, with the highest leader being a mature middle-age or senior adult generally in charge of one of the associations. (New York City Police Department, 1983, p. 3)

The data collected for this study revealed that Chinese gangs have the following unique characteristics that set them apart from other ethnic gangs. First, they are closely associated with and are controlled by powerful community organization. Second, gang leaders invest their money in legitimate businesses and spend a large amount of time doing business. Third, Chinese gangs form national or international networks. Fourth, the gangs are influenced to a great extent by Chinese secret societies and the norms and values of the Triad[2] subculture. Fifth, gang members normally do not go through various stages in which they graduate from delinquent behavior to serious crime. New members often are assigned to carry out the most serious assaults. Sixth, Chinese gangs control large amounts of money, and making money is their main motive. Finally, Chinese gangs systematically victimize the businesses in their communities in ways no ordinary street gangs possibly could. In sum, their strong affiliation with powerful adult organizations, their high level of mobility, and their businesslike methods of wiping out rivals suggest that they more closely resemble adult criminal organizations than typical youth gangs that are concerned mainly with dress codes, turf, and involvement in nonutilitarian, negativistic activities (Cohen, 1955).

According to data collected for this study,

Chinese gangs resemble Cloward and Oh-lin's (1960) "criminal gangs." Chinese gangs develop in ethnic communities in which adult criminal groups exist and in which the adult criminals serve as mentors and role models for the gang members. They not only provide the youths with jobs but also offer them an opportunity structure in ille-gitimate activities. The youths can start working as street soldiers and then go on to become lieutenants, gang leaders, and (eventually) core members of the tong. Thus, a street youth can work his way up to become a respected, wealthy community leader through the structure of illegal activi-ties provided by adult organizations, if he can survive his years as a gang member.

Nevertheless, gangs such as the Ghost Shadows and the Flying Dragons do not strictly follow the subculture pattern in Cloward and Ohlin's classification. Their long history of street violence shows that, besides securing income, the gangs fought constantly with rival gangs to establish their power to shake down the community. This use of violence to win status is consistent with Cloward and Ohlin's definition of "con-flict gangs." It is hard to imagine, in any case, how criminal gangs could protect their illegal sources of income without violently subduing rival gangs to prevent them from encroaching on their territory. Although gang involvement in street violence is not condoned by the adult organizations and is not in the best interests of the gangs them-selves, apparently the gangs believe that they must instill fear in rival groups as well as in the community as a whole.

What is the evidence for Cloward and Ohlin's third delinquent subculture, the retreatist? In a study of gangs in three cities, Fagan (1989) found drug use widespread among Black, Hispanic, and White gangs, regardless of the city. Moore's (1978) Los Angeles gangs and Hagedorn's (1988) Mil-waukee gangs were involved heavily in drug use and dealing. Drug use among Chinese gang members, however, is rare. Moreover, although gang leaders are involved in drug trafficking, they themselves are not drug users. Tong members do not tolerate drug use in the gangs, and the gangs themselves are reluctant to recruit anyone who uses drugs. If a member begins using drugs, he is expelled from the gang.

Thus Chinese gangs have the characteris-tics of two of the subcultures described by Cloward and Ohlin: the criminal and the conflict subcultures. Because gang leaders are concerned primarily with the lucrative heroin trade and investment in legitimate businesses and are closely associated with certain tong leaders, they adhere more to norms and values of the criminal subculture as depicted by Cloward and Ohlin. Young members are concerned mostly with their macho image and therefore are more prone to commit violent acts and predatory crimes. These young members seem to be most congruent with Cloward and Ohlin's conflict gangs. Consequently, instead of la-beling Chinese gangs as either criminal or conflict gangs, it is perhaps more important to consider the ages and ranks of the gang members and their criminal propensities.

Unlike Chinese gangs that are closely as-sociated with the well-established adult groups, gangs formed by young Chinese im-migrants from Vietnam and Taiwan have no adult group to emulate. As a result, these gangs are not as well organized as the Chi-natown gangs. Without the stable income from protection and extortion operations that Chinatown gangs enjoy, and without a lucrative commercial district to claim as a territory, Vietnamese and Taiwanese gangs are forced to become involved primarily in extortion, robbery, and burglary. These gangs resemble Cloward and Ohlin's con-flict gangs because they are prone to exces-sive use of violence, they lack supervision by adult criminal elements, and they are out-side the illegitimate opportunity structure.

Protection and Extortion

The booming economy and the gambling industry in the Chinese community have provided Chinese gangs with ample crimi-nal opportunities. Of the businesses in the community, gambling clubs are the most in need of the gangs' protection. In order to op-erate smoothly, the clubs must rely on gang members to protect them and their custom-ers from the police, intruders, and the gangs themselves. To perform these jobs, a few members are dispersed in the street where the gambling club is located. Three or four members guard the entrance, while some stay inside. Members carry beepers to com-municate with one another. Street leaders in the gang's nearby apartments oversee the entire operation. Nightclubs and massage parlors owned by Chinese and catering to

Chinese patrons also require protection. These businesses need gang members to protect them from members of other gangs.

Gangs supplement their primary activity of guarding gambling dens and adjacent streets with another criminal activity: systematic extortion of Chinese businesses. Police estimate that at least 80 percent to 90 percent of Chinese businesses have to pay one or more gangs regularly or occasionally. Only those merchants who are close to the hierarchy of the tongs are said to be able to avoid paying the gangs.

Techniques of Extortion

According to police officers, prosecutors, and victims interviewed, the gangs primarily use two forms of extortion. One explicit technique is for gang members to demand money. Usually, gang members approach a new business during its opening ceremony and ask for *li shi* (lucky money). After the owner pays, they show up again later and identify themselves as gang members, explain how the racket works, and indicate that it is better to pay than to refuse. Occasionally, gang members tell the owners that they need money for food, or to help their "brothers" who have been arrested. There are also times when gang members will ask businessmen to "invest" in their business or give them a "loan."

In the second extortion technique, the demand for money is implicit. For example, the gang members will try to sell festival-related goods such as firecrackers or plants to business establishments for an inflated price. Sometimes, gang members may simply tell store owners that protection from the gang is provided to their businesses.

Gangs employ several common practices. First, a group of youths may enter a restaurant during the lunch or dinner hour, and each of them occupies a table. They tell the manager that they are waiting for friends. They sit for hours, and they act in rowdy fashion to intimidate customers. They may fight with each other, smash the dishes, or insist on remaining in the restaurant after closing hours. An experienced manager knows what the disruptive youths want.

Second, young men may go into a restaurant and order the finest dishes on the menu. When they leave, they write "Shadows" or "Dragons" on the back of the bill and do not pay. Third, some gang members may dine in a restaurant but refuse to pay the bill. While they argue with the manager about it, two or three fellow members walk in and pretend to be customers. They appear to be sympathetic to the manager and chastise the youths who refuse to pay. When the "show" is over, a gang member calls up the manager, demands protection money, and tells the manager that if similar incidents happen in the future, his gang will protect the restaurant. This technique is known as *hei bai lian* (black and white faces), meaning that while members play the role of the "bad guys," leaders will act as the "good guys" who ask money from the frightened victim.

The fourth method is called *tai jiau tsi* (carrying a sedan chair). Gang members will try to flatter a potential victim by calling him "Big Brother" and acting as though they are his loyal followers. If the businessman is unaware of the gang's tactic and associates himself with the gang, he may find out that it is too late for him to get rid of the label "Big Brother." As a "Big Brother," the victim has no other real benefits except to provide financial support to the gang.

The fifth approach is known as *wo di* (literally, undercover). A gang member infiltrates a business by seeking a job there. During his tenure he collects information about the owner, where he lives, when the business will accumulate the maximum amount of cash, and other matters. The gang member provides the information to his associates to draw up an extortion or robbery plan.

Most of the time, the owners negotiate about the amount of payment, but they do not bicker about whether they are going to pay. When the gang gets a victim paying, a schedule is arranged: several hundred dollars monthly for large stores; less than a hundred dollars per week for modest businesses. The gang usually has designated collectors and keeps records of its income from extortion.

If a retail business refuses to pay, then the gang may vandalize, burglarize, rob, or set fire to the shop. The owner then usually relents and cooperates. In some instances gangs have beaten, shot at, or killed business and retail store owners. For those who do pay, the amount demanded by crime groups escalates rapidly, or another gang will show up soon with the same demand. When businesses are no longer able to meet the gangs' demands, they close down, move to another area, or report the crime to the police. Usually, most business owners try to satisfy the gangs by paying them the first few times. Only when they find out that they have to pay more than one gang or that their payments increase rapidly will they turn to law enforcement for help.

Types of Extortion

Extortion in Chinese communities may be classified into four types. The primary objective of the first and most prevalent type of extortion is monetary gain. The offenders and victim may not know each other prior to the incident, and the extortionate act may be perpetrated without the knowledge of the tong associated with the gang. Regardless of how the victim reacts to the offender's demand, he or she is unlikely to be assaulted physically by the offender in this type of extortion.

The second type is symbolic extortion, which is used as a display of power to indicate control over a territory. Monetary gain is not the major goal; gang members usually demand only free food or other small items such as cigarettes. They also may ask for heavy discounts from restaurant owners. This type of extortion occurs almost on a daily basis, and the victims are usually small store owners or peddlers who do businesses within a tightly controlled gang territory.

The third type is extortion for revenge. Offenders extort victims because of something the victims did to the gang previously, or the gang is hired by a victim's adversary to extort the victim as a form of revenge. Because monetary gain is not the motivating factor, victims are likely to be robbed, beaten up, or killed even if they do not resist the perpetrators. Extortion is used simply as a cover for vengeance.

The fourth type is instrumental extortion, which is used to intimidate the victim into backing down in certain business or personal conflicts. In this type of extortion, the victims are also vulnerable to assault and harassment. The extortionate act is, more than anything else, a message sent to the victim by his rival through the gang members. Gang members also may rob or extort money from the victims for their own sakes. Conflicts pertaining to business territories and business or gambling debts usually result in instrumental extortion activity.

Extortion and Territory

Through extortion, the gangs assert their firm control over certain territories in New York City's Chinese communities. When two or more gangs claim control of a specific area, or when the area is occupied by a weaker gang, store owners within that territory have to pay more than one gang. Currently, Canal Street and East Broadway, the rapidly expanding streets of Chinatown, have no single powerful gang that can claim exclusive sovereignty. Consequently, some of the store owners in those areas have to pay as many as five gangs simultaneously.

The same is true for the Chinese communities in Queens and Brooklyn. Although the White Tigers, The Green Dragons, and a Taiwanese gang are the three most active gangs in these newly established communities, more powerful gangs from Manhattan's Chinatown occasionally invade the area to commit extortion. When two or more gangs are active in a particular area and attempt to extort from the same victim simultaneously, street violence erupts as a result of the power struggle.

Before 1980, most extortionate activities were confined to Manhattan's Chinatown. Only occasionally would gang members venture outside Chinatown to extort money. Beginning in 1980, however, the gangs rapidly spread their extortionate activities to other parts of Manhattan, Queens, Brooklyn, Long Island, New Jersey, and Connecticut. Unlike extortionate activities within Manhattan's Chinatown, which are mostly spontaneous and cost the victims fairly small amounts of money, out-of-state extortion is well planned, and gang members tend to demand rather large amounts.

Since 1984, businessmen in Queens and Brooklyn have been extorted frequently. Unlike in Manhattan's Chinatown, gangs in these areas have no gambling establishments from which to collect protection money. As a result, the only likely source of funds is extortion or robbery of stores in the community. The lack of knowledge about the gangs by local precincts has also contributed to the rapid increase in extortion. In addition, business owners in Queens and Brooklyn are not protected by tongs or other traditional organizations as are business owners in Manhattan's Chinatown.

Conclusion

In order to understand Asian crime groups, the research and law enforcement communities need to broaden their perspectives. Concepts that are adequate for explaining Italian, Black, and Hispanic crime groups may not be adequate for examining criminal organizations of Asian origin. Because Asian people have diverse cultural heritages, we also need to identify the unique features of each Asian ethnic group.

We can isolate three unique characteristics that cause Chinese gangs to persist. First, unlike Black and Hispanic gangs (Hagedorn, 1988; Moore, 1978), Chinese gangs are not based on youth fads or illicit drug use. Instead, they are closely related to their communities' social and economic life. This relationship enables Chinese gangs to become deeply enmeshed in the legitimate and illegitimate enterprises in their communities. Opportunities for money, power, and prestige through various ventures are bestowed on Chinese gang members. No such distinctive opportunity exists for other minority gangs.

Second, unlike other ethnic gangs—which operate primarily in deteriorated, poor neighborhoods—Chinese gangs flourish in rapidly developing and economically robust Chinese communities that are tied closely to Chinese societies in Southeast Asia. Chinese gangs thus can become engaged in economically rewarding domestic and international ventures. Other ethnic gangs are hampered by both the lack of lucrative criminal opportunities in their own neighborhoods and the absence of contacts outside those neighborhoods.

Third, Chinese gang members are embedded in the legendary Triad subculture, a subculture established and maintained by members of the Chinese secret societies. By emulating Triad initiation rites and internalizing Triad norms and values, they can claim a certain legitimacy within their communities. This legitimacy enables them to instill a level of fear that no other ethnic gangs can match, because the community does not view them merely as street thugs.

Nevertheless, the nature, values, and norms of Chinese gangs could change in the future. Chinese gangs with no ties to the tongs or Triad subculture are emerging in newly established Chinese communities. We are now observing the rise of Vietnamese-Chinese and Fujianese gangs (Badey, 1988; Meskill, 1989). Both groups are not only unfamiliar with Triad norms and values, but their criminal patterns—such as street mugging and household robbery—are markedly different from those of the traditional Triad-inspired gangs.

Author's Note

I am grateful to Colleen Cosgrove for her comments. This chapter is excerpted from *Chinese Subculture and Criminality: Non-Traditional Crime Groups in America* (Contributions in Criminology and Penology, No. 29, Greenwood Press, an imprint of Greenwood Publishing Group, Inc., Westport, CT, 1990). Copyright © 1990 by Ko-Lin Chin. Reprinted with permission of the publisher.

Notes

1. *Tong* means "hall" or "gathering place." Tongs were first established in the United States during the mid-nineteenth century by the first wave of Chinese gold field and railroad workers as self-help groups. Bloody conflicts among the tongs are known as "tong wars." The most powerful tongs in New York City are the Chih Kung, the On Leong, and the Hip Sing. Since the 1960s, in order to improve their image, the tongs have been renamed as associations. The heads of these associations are normally influential and well-respected community leaders.

2. *Triad* means a "triangle of heaven, earth, and man." Triad societies are secret societies formed by patriotic Chinese three centuries ago to fight against the oppressive and corrupt Ch'ing dynasty. When the Ch'ing government collapsed and the Republic of China was established in 1912, some of the societies began to be involved in criminal activities.

References

Allen, G., & Thomas, L. (1987). Orphans of war. *Toronto Globe and Mail*, 1(12), 34–57.

Badey, J. R. (1988). *Dragons and tigers*. Loomis, CA: Palmer Enterprises.

Beach, W. G. (1932). *Oriental crime in California*. Stanford, CA: Stanford University Press.

Bresler, F. (1981). *The Chinese Mafia*. New York: Stein & Day.

Chang, H. (1972). Die today, die tomorrow: The rise and fall of Chinatown gangs. *Bridge Magazine*, 2, 10–15.

Chin, K. (1986). *Chinese triad societies, tongs, organized crime, and street gangs in Asia and the United States*. Unpublished doctoral dissertation, University of Pennsylvania.

————. (1990). *Chinese subculture and criminality: Non-traditional crime groups in America.* Westport, CT: Greenwood.

Chin, R. (1977). New York Chinatown today: Community in crisis. *Amerasia Journal,* 1(1), 1–32.

Cloward, R. A., & Ohlin, L. E. (1960). *Delinquency and opportunity: A theory of delinquent gangs.* New York: Free Press.

Cohen, A. K. (1955). *Delinquent boys: The culture of the gang.* Glencoe, IL: Free Press.

Daly, M. (1983, February). The war for Chinatown. *New York Magazine,* 31–38.

Dillon, R. H. (1962). *The hatchet men.* New York: Coward-McCann.

Emch, T. (1973, September 9). The Chinatown murders. *San Francisco Sunday Examiner and Chronicle.*

Fagan, J. (1989). The social organization of drug use and drug dealing among urban gangs. *Criminology,* 27(4), 633–669.

Fessler, L. W. (Ed.). (1983). *Chinese in America: Stereotyped past, changing present.* New York: Vantage.

Gong, Y. E., & Grant, B. (1930). *Tong war!* New York: N. L. Brown.

Hagedorn, J. M. (1988). *People and folks: Gangs, crime, and the underclass in a rustbelt city.* Chicago: Lake View.

Huang, K., & Pilisuk, M. (1977). At the threshold of the Golden Gate: Special problems of a neglected minority. *American Journal of Orthopsychiatry,* 47, 701–713.

Kwong, P. (1987). *The new Chinatown.* New York: Hill & Wang.

Loo, C. K. (1976). *The emergence of San Francisco Chinese juvenile gangs from the 1950s to the present.* Unpublished master's thesis, San Jose State University.

Los Angeles County Sheriff's Department (1984). *Asian criminal activities survey.* Los Angeles: Author.

MacGill, H. G. (1938). The Oriental delinquent in the Vancouver juvenile court. *Sociology and Social Research,* 12, 428–438.

Meskill, P. (1989, February 5). In the eye of the storm. *New York Daily News Magazine,* pp. 10–16.

Miller, W. B. (1975). *Violence by youth gangs and youth groups as a crime problem in major American cities.* Report to the National Institute for Juvenile Justice and Delinquency Prevention.

Moore, J. W. (1978). *Homeboys: Gangs, drugs, and prison in the barrios of Los Angeles.* Philadelphia: Temple University Press.

New York City Police Department, Fifth Precinct (1983). *Gang intelligence information.* New York: Author.

Posner, G. (1988). *Warlords of crime.* New York: McGraw-Hill.

President's Commission on Organized Crime (1984). *Organized crime of Asian origin: Record of hearing III—October 23–25, 1984, New York, New York.* Washington, DC: U.S. Government Printing Office.

Roache, F. M. (1988, January). Organized crime in Boston's Chinatown. *Police Chief,* pp. 48–51.

Robertson, F. (1977). *Triangle of death.* London: Routledge & Kegan Paul.

Robinson, N., & Joe, D. (1980). Gangs in Chinatown. *McGill Journal of Education,* 15, 149–162.

Sung, B. L. (1977). *Gangs in New York's Chinatown* (Monograph No. 6). New York: City College of New York, Department of Asian Studies.

————. (1979). *Transplanted Chinese children.* New York: City College of New York, Department of Asian Studies.

Takagi, P., & Platt, T. (1978). Behind the gilded ghetto. *Crime and Social Justice,* 9, 2–25.

Tracy, C. A. (1980, Winter). Race, crime and social policy. *Crime and Social Justice,* pp. 11–25.

U.S. Department of Justice (1985). *Oriental organized crime: A report of a research project conducted by the Organized Crime Section* (Federal Bureau of Investigation, Criminal Investigative Division). Washington, DC: U.S. Government Printing Office.

————. (1988). *Report on Asian organized crime.* (Criminal Division). Washington, DC: U.S. Government Printing Office.

————. (1989). *The INS enforcement approach to Chinese crime groups* (Immigration and Naturalization Service, Investigative Division). Washington, DC: U.S. Government Printing Office.

U.S. Department of State. (1988). *Hong Kong 1997: Its impact on Chinese organized crime in the United States* (Foreign Service Institute). Washington, DC: U.S. Government Printing Office.

U.S. Senate (1986). *Emerging criminal groups* (Hearings before the Permanent Subcommittee on Investigations of the Committee on Governmental Affairs). Washington, DC: U.S. Government Printing Office. ✦

Chapter 16
Patterns of Ethnic Violence in a Frankfurt Street Gang[1]

Hermann Tertilt

In Chapter 9, Malcolm Klein suggested that many European gangs resemble those in the United States. This chapter describes one such group, composed of Turkish immigrant youth in Germany. Author Tertilt's emphasis is on interethnic violence, Turks against Germans. In addition, the description gives one a sense of the perspectives of these marginalized youth, who are even less accepted in their host country than are many of the minority groups that form the bulk of U.S. gangs. Note his final comment about "segregation, degradation and humiliation" as the roots of the violence among the Turkish Power Boys gang.

I have my own rights my own rules
I have my own fights my own fools
I know my friends and my enemies
I know who I am and how to be

If you punch me I'll punch you
*   back*
Punching you I'll swing my flag
I'm a warrior against the time
My weapon is my lyric and my
*   power is my rhyme*

Reprinted from: Malcolm W. Klein, Hans-Jürgen Kerner, Cheryl L. Maxson, and Elmar G. E. Weitekamp (eds.), *The Eurogang Paradox: Street Gangs and Youth Groups in the U.S. and Europe*, pp. 181–193. Copyright © 2001 by Kluwer Academic Publishers. Reprinted with kind permission from Springer Science and Business Media.

There are some, they don't
*   understand me*
They think I'm running for money
But I won't cry when I am sad
And I won't run when I'm afraid

I'm not the black man
I'm not the white man
I'm just the type between them
I'm a Turkish man in a foreign land

Introduction

This rap was originally written in English by a sixteen-year-old Turkish boy, Hayrettin, who lives in Frankfurt. He was a member of the Turkish Power Boys, a street gang formed at the beginning of the 1990s. His group became known more for violent attacks than for raps or lyrics. The best example of such violence was a series of muggings in the autumn of 1990. In more than 40 cases, the police at this time accused the members of the gang of brutally beating up German youths and of stealing their jackets.

Since the end of the 1980s, gangs such as the Turkish Power Boys have appeared in almost all the big German cities. They are characterized by brutality and street crimes. What is new about this gang phenomenon in the German Republic is that the gang recruits sons of immigrant families and proclaim to the world their ethnic identity. At the beginning of 1990, only five such groups existed in Frankfurt. During that year, this number increased to 25. The police estimated that by the end of that year some 500 youths had organized themselves into violent cliques in the city. Some of these gangs used the names of their parents' home countries and identified themselves in nationalist terms (Croatia boys, Italy boys, Russ boys, Turkish Power Boys). Other gangs reflected local Frankfurt districts in their names (Ring Boys, Ginnheimer Posse, Süd Boys, Ahorn Boys, Sinai Boys). Yet others formed their gang names without reference to any territorial origin (Le Mur, La Mina, Los Desperados, Los Lobos, Bomber Boys or Club 77). In all these gangs male youths of the second immigrant generation are represented, occasionally in a multi-ethnic composition. The majority of members were Turkish youths, with Germans playing, according to the police, "an absolutely unimportant role." It is clear from the contemporary context that the Turkish Power Boys did not originate as an isolated phenomenon but were part of a whole immigrant subculture dominated by Turkish youths.

The German public reacted to the phenomenon of gang violence with shock, incomprehension and disdain. Police controls were strengthened within the city, and the deportation of "criminal foreigners" became not only the subject of political debate but also a reality.

I examined the Turkish Power Boys and their acts of violence over a course of a two-year field study and have presented my conclusions in an ethnography. From early 1991 until the break-up of the gang in autumn 1992 (and after that, in further contact with single youths until 1994), I made very detailed observations of this gang, took part in their daily lives and interviewed them personally or as a group. I spent almost every afternoon with the boys, met them in bars, ate and drank with them, played table football and billiards with them, went where they went, attended their parties, visited their families, their court trials, etc. My interest in the Turkish Power Boys had nothing to do with criminology in the sense of solving their crimes: my goal was to interpret the phenomenon of violence from the subjective perspectives of the youths. I tried to understand how ethnically motivated violence correlates with the social circumstances of the second immigrant generation in Germany.

The first part of this article portrays briefly the two-year history of the gang. It sets the background for an understanding of the second part, in which I deal extensively with the stealing of jackets as an example of ethnically motivated violence. The third part interprets these violent acts. I see in these acts the attempt of immigrant youths to free themselves from the low levels of self-esteem that have been forced upon them by German society.

The Turkish Power Boys Gang

In the summer of 1990, four schoolboys from a Frankfurt secondary modern school founded the Turkish Power Boys gang. In the course of time, about 50 boys aged between 13 and 18 years joined this gang. The group came into being through a loose network of Turkish friendships, to which a few members of other immigrant groups also belonged—but never Germans! The most striking aspect of the gang's composition was the very different education backgrounds of the members. One-third of the members attended intermediate school, a third attended secondary modern school, and the rest went to grammar and vocational schools. The last third also included two boys who went to a "special school." The deciding basis for the strength of the relationships among the members was the common experience of growing up as immigrant children in an urban neighborhood, and not, as is usual for other peer groups, educational standards. Their parents occupied the lowest paid trades as unqualified workers (such as refuse disposal, cleaning crew, factory).

The boys did not see their future in Germany as permanent. Through brotherhood with the gang, the youths could face up to, often aggressively, their status as "illegitimate children"[2] in society. Some of the Turkish Power Boys were strongly delinquent, some only occasionally, and yet others not all. All of them, however, identified with the violence and crimes carried out by other gang members. The spectrum of delinquencies ranged from petty crime such as shoplifting, truancy, and rowdy behavior to drug abuse and grievous bodily harm, as well as car theft, kiosk robberies, muggings, and other offenses connected with the acquisition of money. However, crime only represented a small portion of the gang's activities. Friendship and solidarity, respect and recognition, masculinity and courage, girls, music, football and billiards were significant to the everyday life of the group, as well as unbearable boredom. During the initial phases of the group's development, there was no apparent hierarchical structure. They collectively practiced jacket theft [and saw it] as important. Bomber jackets with prestigious designer names were much sought after objects. These were held as status symbols by the youths, and were stolen more for personal reputation than for financial gain. Even months after their "infamous" deeds, the boys raved to me about them:

Ismail: In half a year we made more hits than other gangs made in one whole year. We did that within one month—took so many jackets, too money, beat up guys. . . .

Why did you do this?

Ismail: Just for fun. It used to be "in." Everybody did it.

Veli: It shows power, man.

And from whom do you take the jackets?

Muzaffer: Above all from Germans.

What types of jackets? A certain kind?

Ismail: Bomber jackets, Chevignons, leathers, we don't care. . . .

Veli: The main thing is the jacket.

Muzaffer: But it has to be a good jacket!

In their crimes, the boys followed the overall rule: "Only from Germans! We have always ripped it off the Germans." Opportunities for stealing jackets were offered in public parks or on fairgrounds, though jackets were also stolen in the Frankfurt underground or on streets where the gang had their hangouts, looking for trouble with Germans.

At the end of the first phase of its existence, the gang was shaken by a wave of arrests. Consequently, the gang reorganized by establishing a leadership of four members resulting in the replacement of its initial egalitarian structure by a type of oligarchy. At the same time, the gang's meeting point moved away from the streets to a public youth club.

This second phase of the gang's existence, from spring to autumn 1991, was marked by the leadership's decision to stop the thefts. Instead, the gang started to exchange blows (usually on an "athletic" level) with rival gangs. When "their" youth club closed down that autumn, the gang's meeting point went again somewhere else. They established their hangout at the local community center where they also were no longer under social workers' care. At that stage the gang showed obvious signs of dissolution; the leaders distanced themselves from the others and some members started to consume hard drugs, such as heroin. The drug abuse split the gang into two parties: one that smoked or snorted heroin regularly, the other that rejected drugs.

The ones who became addicted had to face a series of severe personal and social changes. The drug consumption had to be kept secret from family and, in part, even from friends due to a feeling of disgrace. When the parents found out about their child's addiction, out of shame and dishonor the boys often fled their homes. Some would spend days away from home, sleep at their friends' houses or in cheap hotels in the city center. Others had to repeat one class because of regular truancy; again others were suspended from school completely. The drug-taking boys more increasingly had to face the daily burden of addicts, finding themselves in a vicious circle: the need for the drug and the difficulty of financing it. Consequently, the problem of heroin purchase led to drug-related crimes and theft became a part of everyday life again. The consumption of heroin and the drug-related crimes resulted in police investigations, further arrests and court trials. Within the gang, conflicts also arose between the heroin consumers and those who kept their distance from drugs. The addicted among the friends had offended the sense of solidarity by becoming disloyal and unreliable; their appointments and promises did not count anymore. In autumn 1992, the final dissolution of the Turkish Power Boys took place.

My short summary of the gang history shows the independence of violence and the structure of the group. Violence had at first a ritualistic character, but then the behavior very much shifted in connection with the structural transformation of the gang on the whole. With the increase of drug abuse the attacks on Germans served primarily the acquisition of money than—as originally—a humiliation in public.

Making *Tokat*

Initially the Turkish Power Boys had become known for their attacks on German youths; their names even reached beyond the city limits. By using the example of jacket *tokat*, as the boys called the thefts, I would like to discuss the direction which ethnic violence took in practice and the rules that it followed.[3] The expression *tokat* is borrowed from the Turkish and means "slap in the face." In their jargon, however, the boys changed its meaning into "theft of jackets" which they obviously used as a slander against Germans. "Making *tokat*" referred not only to the stealing of jackets but also of other items such as Walkmans, hats, neck chains, wallets, or even bikes.

The leaders of the gang explained to me how they usually proceeded in a *tokat:* generally as a group, or at least in pairs, but never alone. Also characteristic of a *tokat* was its spontaneity. "With me it was like this," illustrated Yildirim. "When I took a jacket I didn't leave the house thinking, 'Okay, today I'm gonna take a jacket.' It was more like; I walk around and somebody walks by and I look at him—that's it, we're gonna take his jacket." The victims of these thefts were nearly always German boys who "could afford expensive jackets." "Especially when it's a German and he's got a little bit shorter hair, like skinheads, then he's worse off than us and so we take his jacket away," emphasized Veli. In the Turkish Power Boys' perception, the roles of victim and perpetrator were clearly assigned according to national origin. Only "Germans" could be victims, only "foreigners" could be perpetrators.

> Hayrettin: The people who make jacket *tokat*, that's always foreigners. And I mean which one of us looks like a German? Nobody! I've been wearing my bomber jacket for six or seven years. And nobody's ever said: "Hey, how come you've gotta bomber jacket. . . !" Probably because I'm a Turk and nobody gets on my nerves 'cause I'm Turkish.

The provoking of a potential victim always preceded the *tokat*. Veli describes a typical scene:

> Veli: It depends on our mood, you know. If we want to take a jacket then we always act cool and walk on normally, you know. And then when we see a good jacket, a really good one, then we'll go up to you and talk to you. And I say, "Hey, don't I know you from somewhere?" I've done that before. "Aren't you so and so?" and stuff. And then: "Take your jacket off, you asshole!" If he doesn't do it, then we beat him up a bit. And then he has to take it off. That's how it goes.

If the victims were intimidated by such provocations, and reacted with anxiety, they would be forced by further threats to hand over their jackets. "Then you say, 'Take off your jacket!' And if he doesn't do it you punch him, and then he takes it off anyway. So it would be cleverer for him if he took his jacket off straight away before he gets punched." To enforce the intimidation, the boys also used weapons, such as knives or pistols, or they simply grouped around and administered fear by simply outnumbering their victims.

Whoever tried defending himself and refused to take off his jacket straight away had to count on a beating up. "We even like it when somebody tries to defend himself," emphasized Muzaffer and justified this by saying, "When we take the jacket and the guy doesn't defend himself, then we don't have fun. It's more fun when you get a punch yourself. Then you get aggressive quicker and punch back."

Without doubt, the boys' accounts were not at all exaggerated; they tell of petty theft true to reality from the perpetrator's point of view. In the court trials, the witnesses' statements and confessions gave similar impressions of these violations. I would like to quote from one of the recorded jacket thefts reported in a ruling against one of the gang members:

> On the evening of the 15th of August 1990, the accused Dogan, in accompaniment of further members of the Turkish Power Boys (one of [whom], Biçakçi, was tried separately), demanded the surrendering of jackets from witnesses Krüger, Weiß, and Kopp at about 20.15 during the journey from Flestplatz to City Centre on the tram line 18. Biçakçi knocked witness Weiß's baseball cap off his head and asked the witnesses Krüger and Kopp whether their baseball jackets were authentic. As he pulled the witness Krüger's jacket from behind to look at the label, the witness stood up, upon which Biçakçi hit him twice flat-handedly on the right cheek. Then Biçakçi pulled the right sleeve of the witness's jacket while two accomplices standing behind the witness pulled the witness's arm up behind his back. All participants tore the jacket from the witness's body and left the tram at the next stop.[4]

The victims, according to the boys, normally reacted defensively and tried to calm them down in order to avoid a conflict. "Most of them are shit-scared," described Arif as the usual pattern of reaction. The German youths tried to prevent a clash by saying, "Hey, knock it off, hey stop it, quit it." The boys were very well aware of the humiliation they imposed on their victims. Their motives for the *tokat* seemed trivial. "We only do it to have fun," reasoned Veli. "We go out, see the guy with the jacket, take the jacket, and are happy, you know." The act of taking the jacket must have been especially satisfying. "That was the greatest. Everybody did it," Safir described the situation, "because those rich Germans, they had the Chevignon-jackets."

I asked the boys whether they could justify their actions. On the one hand their motto was: "I don't give a shit if a German gets his jacket stolen or not." On the other hand, however, some of the boys had a guilty conscience and showed sympathy towards their victims.

> Muzzafer: Like I took a jacket and at night—I swear to God—sometime I couldn't sleep, you know, 'cause I took the jacket. I always said to myself, "Hey, how would it be if somebody came up to you and wanted your jacket, you know? How would you feel?" Sometimes I thought about that in the early morning. I couldn't sleep on the nights when I ripped someone off.

To identify with the victim was obviously one of the largest psychological hindrances to being violent. However, Hayrettin and Ismail did not agree with Musaffer's account. They tried to provide a moral justification for the *tokat* and created from their point of view the social context in which they seemed to justify their violence:

> Hayrettin: I never have a guilty conscience. I mean, that's life, *c'est la vie*. Every guy in Frankfurt knows that if he buys a Chevignon-jacket it might get stolen. You shouldn't buy a jacket if you don't have the right friends. That's life: You've gotta look at it like that. Some are born as Turks in a dangerous neighborhood, in a bad area. Someone else is born a German. That's why! Look. I have my friends. I make jacket *tokat*. And people are scared of me. That's life. One guy is born a black and is called a "nigger," but he beats up whites. And the whites are scared of him. But they say "fucking nigger" anyway.

> Ismail: And they say "fucking Turk" to us. Okay, they're right—we are bad. But there are other guys too who are really nice. And they say "fucking Turk" to them too 'cause other Turks do bad things. When they say "fucking Turk" then they mean every Turk, you know. But there are Turks who are okay. They don't do bad stuff, they go to work, go to school, have their own friends. And they say "fucking Turk," "wog," "get out of Germany," "we don't want to have you here!" That's how the whole crap started, you know.

> Hayrettin: I wouldn't say that. I say the Germans started it. Say, ten years ago the Germans started it. "Turks take away our jobs, our houses. . . " Not because of the beating-up, making *tokat*—that didn't exist back then. This is how they started: "fucking Turks." They made that up. And then the Turks answered: "You say fucking Turks to us so then we start fucking you: take your jacket off!" That's how it started. Now of course the Turks are worse because they exaggerated it all. I have to admit it even though I'm a Turk. But when someone says "fucking Turk" to me then I really feel like going and beating him up.

What is remarkable about this discussion is the concept of social reality behind *tokat* which Hayrettin and Ismail evoke. It is based on the construction of two classes whose respective affiliation is determined by birth. Both classes struggle against each other. Xenophobia on the one hand and ethnic violence on the other characterize the two fronts. Ethnic violence appears to be a legitimate way of self-maintenance in this scenario; it is one way of dealing with conflicts by answering to humiliation with humiliating aggressiveness. The evocation of two antagonistic classes is indicative of the social situation in which the boys are part of an ethnic minority. In the same way, this construction also neutralizes the scruples of being violent and helps the boys to ignore the victim's point of view.

Discussion

At the beginning of my field study, long before I gained a comprehensive impression of the extent of the delinquency and whilst trying to get close contact to the gang, I was frequently confronted with violence myself. My first contact with the Turkish Power Boys took place in January 1991 in a youth club where the boys used to meet. At this first occasion I was threatened and attacked without having delivered any appropriate motive. I could not explain to myself why I had become a target to their verbal and physical attacks. The boys' violent provocation remained a mystery to me and I could only put it down to pure bloodthirstiness. Naturally, I had tried to explain it to myself by thinking that the boys wanted to test the water with me to determine what my reaction as an outsider would be. However, these rationalizations were anything but satisfactory given the great number of attacks.

Only the method of participant observation and dialogue with the boys allowed me more and more to gain an understanding of their violence. The process of establishing such a dialogue was difficult due to distrust and hostility. Later, in a conversation with one of my attackers, it became clear to me why I had been violated. He justified it by pointing out that Germans were treated in Turkey "like kings," whereas the Turks were treated "like niggers" in Germany. It was made apparent that his aggression was not addressed to my own behavior, but to my status as a German, a representative of the ethnic majority.

Before I was able to consider the relationship of dominance and subordination between the German majority and the Turkish minority, I followed up one other approach. The correlation of foreign behavioral patterns with "cultural values" might be a prejudice of my profession: cultural anthropology. I myself tended to apply this type of interpretation. While I was gaining more and more security within the gang, I got to know the masculine bearings of the boys; the challenging, boastful *machismo* with which they carried out conflicts. I was sure I could find a connection between their virile *habitus* determined by their Turkish background and the group's violence. The strongly developed consciousness of *machismo* on the Turkish part and the weak one on the part of German youths seemed to me to cry out for disaster. This cultural (mis)interpretation prevented me from discovering the other side of the already sovereign and seemingly superior gang members. Not until one year later, when we were sitting over our fourth beer, did I learn how the status "foreigner" damaged their self-esteem. It seemed to me that the boys had incorporated the degrading picture of themselves with which they were confronted in German society. However, the boys could not admit to this, neither in the gang's daily life nor in front of my microphone. On the contrary, they told anecdotes about their violence with an attitude of detachment. To them brutality was a matter of course and hardly questioned in respect of the victim.

The court and police records make evident the considerable brutality with which the boys committed their crimes. The following case is an excerpt from a police record and documents the progress of a conflict:

> Around 18.40 the accused, Koca, situated himself in the path of witness Neumann, who was riding along Burgstraße on his mountain bike. As the witness got off his bike the accomplices of the accused circled the witness. One of the unknown assailants [not all perpetrators were identified—H.T.] pressed a knife against the victim's thigh and another held a pistol in his hand. The accused, Koca, took the victim's Walkman, gold chain with pendant, as well as a ring. Then the accused, Karadeniz, hit the witness Neumann in the face, pulled him off his mountain bike and grabbed the bike. The unknown assailant with the pistol grabbed the victim by the T-shirt. The accused Çevik kicked the victim karate-style once in the nose and once in the back. He also "head-butted" the victim, breaking his nose.[5]

In many instances it was characteristic that the progress of punishable acts did not follow the pattern of challenge and reaction, i.e., this was not a defense of one's honor. Violence was rather targeted at the humiliation of the victim. The victim was brutally "head-butted" after he had been robbed. If the attack had purely been instrumental in getting their "loot" it would have been enough to leave the boy alone.

The gang members repeatedly used the "crooked" glance from the Germans as a motive for an act of violence. From this glance they automatically inferred a contemptuous image of themselves. Striking out meant a legitimated striking back at the Germans. At least, some of their accounts indicated this. With phrases like "I'm gonna give it to him now" or "got no respect for the Germans," "don't talk, just punch him in the face, just punch" they projected their own humiliation onto their victims. The Germans were faced forcefully with the same degradation with which the boys associated their own low self-esteem. Thus the stare of Germans remains significant as a banal trigger for violence. "Then they all look at us as if we are the biggest thieves," Muzaffer claims as he describes the start of a violent conflict between Germans and gang members. He continues by saying, "So I went up to him and said, 'What are you staring at? Something up, or what?' "

I consider the violence resulting from such situations as an attempt by the Turkish

Power Boys to become liberated from a damaged self-image. The idea of revenge is expressed here—a type of equalized injustice—namely the experience of injustice is rewarded with injustice. My interpretation of this violence phenomenon is based on a notion of normal migrant youths that in their violence, react to an abnormal cultural situation. So the German manner of dealing with foreigners by segregation, degradation and humiliation is one of the main factors to consider when explaining the violence of the Turkish Power Boys and other migrant gangs.

Notes

1. This article first appeared in the *International Journal on Minority and Group Rights* (1997) 4: 341–352. Kluwer Law International. Translated by Léonie G. Avery.

2. In German cities like Frankfurt, nearly half of the juvenile population has a German passport. Thus most of the members of the Turkish Power Boys were born and brought up in Germany but still hold the status of a "foreigner" which is passed on from generation to generation. This systematic form of discrimination and the withholding of rights (such as the right to vote) are based on a social consensus that still clings to the picture of an ethnically homogeneous German *volksgemeinschaft*.

3. I only witnessed the crimes committed by the gang on exceptional occasions. I gained a great portion of my information through the boys' accounts, newspapers articles, and the court trials that I visited. The boys also allowed me to study their various criminal records. A systematic insight into the complete court trial files was not possible for confidentiality reasons.

4. All information that could lead to a positive identification of any person has been changed.

5. All information that could lead to a positive identification of any person has been changed.

References

Hermann, L. (1991). Straßenraub in Frankfurt am Main—Gewöhnung an ein versbrechen? ["Street robbery in Frankfurt—Getting used to a crime"] In: Hessische Polizeinundschau, Heft 3/1991, S.9.

Tertilt, H. (1995). Turkish Power Boys. Ethnographic einer Jugendbande [An Ethnography of a Street Gang]. Frankfurt: Shurkamp. ✦

Chapter 17
Female Gangs

A Focus on Research

Joan Moore and John Hagedorn

There may be no component of the street-gang scene that has been first more ignored, and then more stereotyped than the place of females in street-gang membership. The police and courts consistently underestimate the prevalence of gang girls. The media just as consistently portray gang girls either as "toys for boys" or as aberrations of acceptable female roles. With increasing research on girl gang members and greater appreciation of gendered perspectives, criminologists are coming to a better understanding of female gang membership. Moore and Hagedorn present a comprehensive and updated statement on the issues involved and offer suggestions for the direction of future research on female gangs and gang members.

Much of the research on gangs has ignored females or trivialized female gangs.[1] Influential early studies of gangs, which for years shaped the research agenda, concentrated almost exclusively on males. The implicit message of these studies was that female gangs were unimportant. Even within the past decade an expert commented: "The notion seems to be that female gangs and their members are 'pale imitations' of male gangs" (Spergel, 1995, p. 90).

Given the lack of research, much of what has been written about female gangs and then reproduced in textbooks has been based on the reports of journalists and social workers and on the statements of male gang members. With the exception of a very few early studies, gang researchers did not

Reprinted from: Joan Moore and John Hagedorn, "Female Gangs: A Focus on Research," *OJJDP Juvenile Justice Bulletin*. Washington, DC: U.S. Department of Justice, National Institute of Justice, March 2001, NCJ 186159.

begin to take female gangs seriously until the 1980s, when Campbell's (1984a) book on New York gangs appeared. Even now, there continue to be methodological problems with many reports on female gangs. This bulletin summarizes both past and current research on female gangs and draws attention to programmatic and research needs. It considers the underlying reasons for female gang membership, assesses the delinquency and criminal activity of female gang members, examines how ethnicity and gender norms may influence female gang behavior, and discusses the long-term consequences of gang membership for females. It concludes with some proposals for future research.

Early Reports:
A History of Stereotypes

Gangs are studied because they are of social concern. That concern stems from typically "masculine" acts of vandalism, violence, and other serious threats. It was often assumed that females did not take part in such behavior, so early researchers were not interested in the delinquency of female gang members.[2] Researchers and journalists saw gangs as a quintessentially male phenomenon. Thus, most early reports focused on whether female gangs were "real" gangs or merely satellites of male groups. One review concluded that in these early studies, "girls were defined solely in terms of their . . . relations to male gang members" (Campbell, 1990, p. 166).

"Sex objects or tomboys"—these are the images that, until recently, dominated the literature on female gang members. Individual females were portrayed in terms of their sexual activity, with an occasional mention of their functions as weapon carriers for male gang members (e.g., Spergel, 1964). Even when describing female gang members as tomboys, researchers emphasized that the females' motivations were focused on males. Miller (1973, p. 34), for instance, explained that "the behavior of the [girls] . . . appeared to be predicated on the assumption that the way to get boys to like you was to be like them rather than [sexually] accessible to them." Campbell (1984a) points out that "sex object" and "tomboy" are both variants of the "bad girl" role. Good girls are modest and feminine; bad girls are not.

These studies were conducted before

women entered the labor market in such large numbers as they do today. It was an era when most people viewed homemaking as the only acceptable goal for women. The studies reflected the widespread notion that for males, gang membership might involve delinquency, but it does not violate gender-role norms. However, gang membership for females was more shocking because it involved real deviance and seriously violated gender-role norms.

The accuracy of early descriptions of female gang members as sex objects and tomboys is difficult to judge because there are not enough reliable data in these reports. Most historical information about female gangs comes from journalists (e.g., Asbury, 1927; Rice, 1963), who were likely to emphasize the sensational, and from social workers (e.g., Hanson, 1964; Welfare Council of New York City, 1950), who were likely to emphasize members' personal problems. Both sources fed the "bad girl" stereotype.

However, in retrospect, the early skepticism about whether female gangs were "real gangs" seems odd. It seems to have been based on a very narrow view of what a gang really is. Gangs—male and female alike—differ greatly from one another. Those differences affect the behavior of young members and their chances of maturing into conventional, law-abiding adults. A female gang may be autonomous or allied with a male gang, or female gang members may be part of a fully gender-integrated gang (Miller, 1975). Unfortunately, there is not enough information to determine how each kind of gang structure affects the members' behavior (Miller and Brunson, 2000). Existing information does indicate, however, that joining a gang—regardless of the gang's structure—is a significant act for an adolescent female, often with important consequences later in life.

Number of Female Gang Members

Both male and female gangs proliferated in the 1980s and 1990s. Although the percentage of gang members who were female is difficult to ascertain, all sources agree the numbers were significant.

Nationwide surveys of law enforcement agencies provide the most widely used data, although they have limitations. The first such survey, conducted in the mid-1970s, estimated that 10 percent of all gang members were female (Miller, 1975). Some 20 years later, in 1992, another nationwide survey found that only 3.7 percent of all gang members were female (Spergel, 1995). A criminologist associated with the latter survey commented that this low proportion may have resulted because 32 percent of the surveyed jurisdictions did not, "as a matter of policy," identify females as gang members (Curry and Decker, 1998, p. 98). Two other nationwide surveys of law enforcement agencies, conducted in 1996 and 1998, estimated that 11 percent and 8 percent, respectively, of all gang members were female (Moore and Terrett, 1998; National Youth Gang Center, 2000).

Other sources provide figures that are much higher than most law enforcement estimates. In surveys of youth in a wide range of cities, for example, the proportion of self-identified gang members who were female ranged from 8 to 38 percent, and the proportion of females surveyed who claimed gang membership ranged from 9 to 22 percent (Bjerregaard and Smith, 1993; Cohen et al., 1994; Esbensen and Huizinga, 1993; Esbensen and Deschenes, 1998; Esbensen and Osgood, 1997; Fagan, 1990). Such surveys provide a valuable supplement to police sources, despite some limitations (which are discussed [below]). The high number of female gang members recorded in self-report studies may reflect the younger ages of survey respondents compared with the ages of youth on police rosters: females tend to drop out of gang life at earlier ages than males, often because of pregnancy (cf. Moore, 1991). Finally, field research, although its reports are usually limited to one time and place, can offer additional insights. For example, in San Antonio, TX, field research has identified groups of girls who consistently hang out with male gangs. Even though they rarely define themselves as gangs, they may be seen as "gangs" by outsiders (Valdez and Cepeda, 1998). In some cities, females constitute up to one-third of the members in some gang cliques but are completely absent in others (Moore, 1991).

Surprisingly, female gangs are somewhat more likely to be found in small cities and rural areas than in large cities. Their ethnicity varies from one region to another, with African American gangs predominant in the Midwest and Northeast and Latina gangs predominant in the Southwest (National Youth Gang Center, 2000).

Being in a Gang: The Background

Joining a gang is a significant, potentially life-altering, event. The reasons for any single juvenile's joining a gang are complex and personal. Though most females join gangs for friendship and self-affirmation (Campbell, 1984a, 1987; Moore, 1991), recent research has begun to shed some light on economic and family pressures motivating many young women to join gangs.

Economic and Ethnic Forces

Throughout the 20th century, poverty and economic marginality were associated with the emergence of youth gangs, but in the 1980s and early 1990s, the loss of hundreds of thousands of factory jobs made conditions even worse in America's inner cities.[3] Hagedorn's (1988) study of gang formation in Milwaukee, WI, a city then suffering economic decline, shows that although the parents of most gang members usually held good jobs, these jobs had disappeared by the time their children were grown. It is not surprising that gangs proliferated rapidly during this period, not only in Milwaukee but throughout the Nation.[4] (See Hagedorn, 1988, 1998; Moore, 1991; Padilla, 1992; Taylor, 1990, 1993.) An informal economy flourished. Although much of the work associated with this economy was legal, a substantial portion involved drug dealing and other illicit activities, and gang members joined in. (See [below] for a more extensive discussion of the drug-dealing activities of female gang members.) In Chicago, IL, for example, economically successful gangs—female and male—became significant community institutions, sometimes offering resources and protection to neighbors (Venkatesh, 1996, 1998).

Female gang members have been affected not only by these economic shifts but by recent changes in the welfare system. Welfare has been an important economic resource for many of them. In Los Angeles, CA, for example, Mexican American gang members active in the 1950s and 1970s became pregnant, on average, at age 18. They tended to rely on welfare, combined with work and help from their families, to survive (Moore and Long, 1987). Similar patterns were found in Milwaukee in the 1990s (Hage-

dorn, 1998). However, welfare reforms introduced in the mid-1990s have reduced or eliminated welfare payments. Because female gang members often face significant barriers to legitimate employment, it is unclear what they will do to replace welfare support.

Ethnic marginality often lies behind economic marginality. In the 1920s, most gang members were children of European immigrants (Thrasher, 1927). By the 1980s, most were African American and Latino. In recent years, large-scale immigration from Spanish-speaking countries and from Asia has changed the ethnic composition of the United States. Increasingly, gangs tend to be Latino and Asian (National Youth Gang Center, 2000). Because ethnicity is closely related to gender roles (as discussed [below]), this nationwide shift in ethnicity has important implications for female gangs.

Family Pressure

There is one aspect of female gang life that does not seem to be changing—the gang as a refuge for young women who have been victimized at home. The available research consistently shows that high proportions of female gang members have experienced sexual abuse at home. In Los Angeles, for example, 29 percent of a large representative sample of Mexican American female gang members had been sexually abused at home, and their homes were more likely than those of male gang members to include drug users and persons arrested for crimes (Moore, 1991, 1994). Another study found that almost two-thirds of female gang members interviewed in Hawaii had been sexually abused at home. Many had run away and had joined gangs to obtain protection from abusive families (Joe and Chesney-Lind, 1995; Chesney-Lind, Shelden, and Joe, 1996).[5] A recent report sums up young women's reasons for joining a gang: "[T]he vast majority noted family problems as contributing factors," citing drug addiction and abuse as the most common problems (Miller, 2001).

Joining a gang can be an assertion of independence not only from family, but also from cultural and class constraints. In joining a gang, young Puerto Rican women in New York felt that they would be able to express themselves as assimilated Americans, spending money freely and standing up for themselves. "[They] construct . . . an image of the gang that counterpoints the suffocating futures they face" (Campbell, 1990, p. 173). In Los Angeles, Mexican American gangs were described as "a substitute institution . . . [providing] meaning and identity" (Quicker, 1983, p. 28) or "their own system in which they [could] belong," in the absence of "clear or satisfactory access to adult status" (Harris, 1988, p. 166). In San Francisco, CA, a large, multiethnic study of female gang members describes them as "resisting normative forms of femininity" but also as "devising alternative forms of femininity" (Joe-Laidler and Hunt, 2001).

Sex: Stereotyping and Victimization

"Sex object" was one of the early stereotypes of female gang members, and the interest in the sex lives of female gang members still persists. Early reports about the easy sexual availability of female gang members came almost exclusively from male gang members (e.g., Short and Strodtbeck, 1965). Even some recent reports present similar male perceptions as fact, with no attempt at verification (Sanchez-Jankowski, 1991). However, male gang members may be indulging their own fantasies. In a recent study, male gang members told researchers that group sex was an initiation ritual for female gang members, but female gang members dismissed the idea as ludicrous (Decker and Van Winkle, 1996).

In Los Angeles, a large random sample of male and female Mexican American gang members was asked about the role of women in the gang (Moore, 1991). Half of the male members claimed that female members were "possessions." This response not only referred to the females' sexual exploitation but also reflected the males' general need to be in charge. The other half of the male members felt that female members were respected and treated like family. (About two-thirds of the female members vehemently denied that they were treated like possessions.)

In San Antonio, where there are many Mexican American gangs but few female gangs or gang members, most females who associate with male gang members are respected. But "hoodrats"—females involved in "frequent partying, drug using, participation in illegal activities and multiple sexual encounters"—are not deemed worthy of respect (Valdez and Cepeda, 1998, pp. 6–7).

Although male gang members may exaggerate their sexual domination over female members, there are reports from females that they have been sexually exploited by males within the gang. In San Francisco, females from an immigrant Salvadoran gang reportedly often were sexually victimized by male gang members, although this rarely happened in a nearby Mexican American gang (Brotherton, 1996). Sexual abuse and exploitation by male gang members were also reported by some subsets of female gang members in Columbus, OH (Miller, 1998); Milwaukee (Hagedorn, 1998); Phoenix, AZ (Portillos, 1999); Chicago (Venkatesh, 1998); and Los Angeles (Moore, 1991).[6] Some of these reports may have been from females who were only marginal to the gang. In Milwaukee, for example, females controlled admission to their gang (a female auxiliary to the male gang), but female "wannabes" seeking to become members thought that males controlled admission. The male members tricked some female wannabes into group sex by telling them it was an initiation ritual. It was not, and females who participated in the group sex did not become members of the gang (Hagedorn and Devitt, 1999). A similar situation existed in Phoenix (Portillos, 1999). Evidence of sexual exploitation of female gang members at home and within their gangs is one reason for considering female gang membership a serious social concern.

Delinquency and Criminality of Female Gang Members

Whether female gangs are seen as a serious problem depends in large part on the level of their delinquent and criminal activities and the types of offenses they commit. Unfortunately, getting definitive information about these topics is difficult. It means working through many detailed studies, often conducted in several cities that differ in important ways. The findings of these studies are not easily generalized, but some conclusions can be drawn. This section reviews three major sources of information, draws some general conclusions about female gang members' delinquency and criminality, and then focuses on female gang members' involvement in drug dealing.

Sources of Information About Female Gang Offending

There are three major sources of information about female gang members' criminality and delinquency: law enforcement agency reports, surveys of at-risk youth, and field studies. These sources supplement each other and offer a basis for drawing some conclusions about female gang members' offending.

Law Enforcement Agency Reports. Law enforcement reports on arrests of female gang members have been compiled for several large cities. They offer the only information available about female gang members' actual involvement with the justice system. However, because police have traditionally underarrested females, these reports may well understate the involvement of female gang members in crime (see Chesney-Lind, Shelden, and Joe, 1996; Taylor, 1993).[7] Only one nationwide survey of law enforcement agencies (conducted in 1992) asked about the criminality of female gang members (Curry, Ball, and Fox, 1994) and, as noted previously, that survey probably underestimated the problem because, "as a matter of policy," many jurisdictions did not count females as gang members (Curry and Decker, 1998). An additional problem with law enforcement agency reports as a source of information is that jurisdictions often differ in how they identify an offense as "gang related."[8]

Surveys of At-Risk Youth. Surveys of at-risk adolescents (who are usually contacted at a school or social service agency) provide a different perspective. Among other questions, these surveys typically ask about respondents' gang involvement and about whether and how often they have committed certain offenses. These surveys are the only source of information about how the delinquency of gang youth differs from that of nongang youth. However, youth answering a questionnaire may be tempted either to conceal or to exaggerate delinquency. Since most surveys are anonymous, such self-reports are difficult to verify. However, a study of middle school males in Chicago found that a little more than half (51.5 percent) of those who self-reported both delinquency and gang involvement had also been identified by the police as delinquent (Curry, 2000). Almost all of the youth whom police identified as gang members also self-reported gang membership (Curry, 2000).

This study's finding of a disparity between self-reported and police-reported delinquency rates may indicate that respondents exaggerated their delinquency, escaped police detection, or dropped out of the gang before the police were able to identify them.

Field Studies. Field studies have a venerable tradition in gang research and continue to be a major source of insight about gang life. Many of these studies, however, do not raise the issue of criminality, and most are confined to one time and one place, making it difficult to generalize from their findings. More important, since gang females are usually difficult to reach, researchers often report on very small and/or seriously unrepresentative samples of female gang members. Although field research offers a level of understanding of individual motivation and gang social structure not available through other sources, findings from such studies must be approached critically.

Levels of Offending

Many, but not all, female gang members are involved in some kind of delinquency or criminality. Youth surveys consistently show that delinquency rates of female gang members are lower than those of male gang members but higher than those of nongang females and even nongang males (Esbensen and Huizinga, 1993; Bjerregaard and Smith, 1993; Fagan, 1990). In Rochester, NY, for example, 66 percent of female gang members and 82 percent of male gang members reported involvement in at least one serious delinquent act, compared with only 7 percent of nongang females and 11 percent of nongang males (Bjerregaard and Smith, 1993). By contrast, a survey of youth in three cities—Chicago, Los Angeles, and San Diego—classified 40 percent of female gang members and 15 percent of male gang members as, at most, "petty delinquents." The three-city study also found that although 33 percent of the female gang members and 43 percent of the males reported using hard drugs, almost one-third of the females and 25 percent of the males said they were not using drugs or alcohol at all (Fagan, 1990).

Types of Offenses

In general, female gang members commit fewer violent crimes than male gang members and are more inclined to property crimes and status offenses.[9] These gender patterns were found in a nationwide 1992 survey of law enforcement agencies and also in analyses of data on arrests from Honolulu, HI, and Chicago (Curry, Ball, and Fox, 1994; Chesney-Lind, Shelden, and Joe, 1996; Block et al., 1996). In Chicago, the disparity was very large. Not only were male gang members more likely than female gang members to commit serious crimes, but there were a great many more male gang members than females (and police may also have been more likely to arrest males). Between 1965 and 1994, the number of arrests of male gang members was much greater than that for females: "[t]he ratio of males to females was 15.6:1 for nonlethal violence [and] 39:1 for drug offenses," and only 1.1 percent of offenders in gang-related homicides were female (Block et al., 1996, p. 10).

Some might conclude from these data that female gang members are not violent enough to be of concern. However, an 11-city survey of eighth graders undertaken in the mid-1990s found that more than 90 percent of both male and female gang members reported having engaged in one or more violent acts in the previous 12 months (Esbensen and Osgood, 1997). The researchers found that 78 percent of female gang members reported being involved in gang fights, 65 percent reported carrying a weapon for protection, and 39 percent reported attacking someone with a weapon (Deschenes and Esbensen, 1999). These and similar findings prompted the authors of this study to recommend that gang prevention and intervention efforts be directed specifically at females.

Drug Dealing

Drug offenses are among the most common offenses committed by female gang members. In Los Angeles County, an analysis of lifetime arrest records of female gang members revealed that drug offenses were the most frequent cause for arrest (California Department of Justice, 1997). Special tabulations from Chicago show that between 1993 and 1996, either drug offenses or violent offenses were the most common cause for arrest of female gang members.[10]

Law enforcement records document but do not explain these high rates of drug arrests for female gang members. Several field studies, however, provide some related insights into female gang members' participation in drug dealing, perhaps the most

important criminal activity of the 1990s. In the early 1980s, Moore and Mata (1981) interviewed 85 heroin-addicted Mexican American female gang members about their experiences in dealing heroin in Los Angeles. Female dealers, who were often addicts themselves, frequently obtained their stock of heroin from their own suppliers and occasionally from relatives. A few females began to deal drugs when their dealing husbands went to prison. Most female dealers were working for someone else, although there were a few powerful female career dealers.[11] The drug-dealing patterns of these women may be used—with caution—to illustrate drug-dealing patterns of other Mexican American gang members prior to the cocaine/crack epidemic that began in the mid-1980s in most cities. By extrapolating from the Moore and Mata findings, it can be estimated that 20 percent of all Mexican American female gang members in this period may have dealt heroin at some time during their careers.

A 1990s study (Moore and Hagedorn, 1996) of African American and Latina female gang members in Milwaukee documents a very different situation. Many more females were dealing drugs, although they were less likely to do so than were males. About one-half of the female gang members and three-quarters of the male gang members had sold cocaine at some time in their lives. The proportion was higher for Latina females (72 percent) and Latino males (81 percent) than for African American females (31 percent) and males (69 percent). In at least one African American gang neighborhood, two drug houses were run independently by females whose male relatives were in a gang.

These findings indicate that, by the 1990s, drug dealing was much more common among female gang members in Milwaukee than it had been among female gang members in Los Angeles a decade earlier. A 1990s study in San Francisco found that drug dealing in an African American gang was important enough to cause a rift between male and female gang members. Female members became so dissatisfied with the income they were receiving from male dealers that they withdrew from the gang and went into business for themselves (Lauderback, Hansen, and Waldorf, 1992). A later report on this female gang contrasted its complete control over drug dealing with the less extensive or nonexistent drug-dealing activities of females in two other gangs: a nearby Mexican American gang, whose female members were permitted to deal as independent individuals, and an immigrant Salvadoran gang, whose female members were subservient to the male members and were not allowed to deal drugs (Brotherton, 1996). Female gang members (mostly African American) in Columbus, OH, also reported being explicitly debarred from selling drugs (Miller, 1998).

Taylor (1993) presents the most extensive examination to date of drug dealing by female gang members. He followed up his study of Detroit's dangerous "corporate gangs"—that is, gangs organized for "financial gain by criminal action" (1993, p. 19)—with a companion book on female gangs. Taylor traces the female presence in Detroit's gangs back to the 1950s, but it was not until the 1970s, with the growing presence of hard drugs and the emergence of more criminally oriented ("commercial") gangs, that females began to play a more active role. By the 1980s, corporate gangs dominated Detroit's street economy, and by the 1990s, females were involved in both autonomous (all-female) and gender-integrated selling crews. Taylor's study leaves little doubt that the position of females in the drug dealing business has changed, contemporaneous with the devastating collapse of job opportunities in Detroit's inner city and the parallel collapse of neighborhood social structures.[12] Taylor's historical perspective provides a context for other studies discussed in this bulletin. As drug dealing became more common among gang members, autonomous female dealers occasionally emerged. There is also a great deal of local variation, as shown by the contrasting roles of Latinas in Los Angeles (Moore and Mata, 1981), Milwaukee (Moore and Hagedorn, 1996), and San Francisco (Brotherton, 1996).

Ethnicity and Gender Roles in the Gang

Most female gangs are either African American or Latina, although there are small but increasing numbers of Asian and white female gangs. Autonomy and male dominance, which are ongoing issues for all female gangs, tend to vary with ethnicity. For example, gender expectations in each ethnic group might suggest that African American and white female gang members would be more autonomous and Latinas more subordinate to males. They usually are, but not always. In other words, there is no universal ethnic continuum. Indeed, some factors related to female autonomy and male dominance affect gang members regardless of ethnicity. Male unemployment and the incarceration of the many males who are convicted of illegal economic activities remove males from both Latino and African American households. As a result, women must rely on their own resources to support themselves and their children.

African American and Latina Gangs

One of the first researchers to investigate African American female gangs was Laura Fishman, who was on a team studying an African American female gang in Chicago in the early 1960s. Later, in a reanalysis of her field notes, Fishman argued that although the women in this gang were likely to play subordinate roles, they also showed elements of autonomy, committing "male crimes" and invading rival gang territory (Fishman, 1988, 1998). Autonomy was the keynote in a study of African American female gang members in Philadelphia, PA, in the 1970s. Most of the gangs were gender integrated and seemed to reflect gender equality: "The female is an intrinsic part of the gang's group identity who participates in gang activities . . . rather than just ancillary activities" (Brown, 1977, p. 226). Taylor, studying Detroit gangs (1993), concurs. Former female gang members reported that even though police ignored them, they were just as involved in gang warfare, drinking, and sex as the male members of their gangs. Taylor also found females in all types of gangs—from rowdy neighborhood groups to corporate, drug-dealing enterprises.

Further evidence of autonomy among African American female gangs was found in a substantial field study comparing African American and Latina (mostly Puerto Rican) gangs in Milwaukee in the 1990s. African American females were more likely than Latinas to feel that they, not the male gang members, controlled their gangs. By the time they had reached their late twenties, most of the African American and Latina females had ceased to participate in their gangs. African Americans were more likely than Latinas to be employed, less likely to be on welfare, more likely to have moved away from their old gang neighborhoods, and less likely to use cocaine (Hagedorn and Devitt, 1999; Hagedorn, Torres, and Giglio, 1998). The comparison showed that "[f]or Latinas, . . . gang membership tended to have a significant influence on their later lives, but for African American[s] . . . the gang tended to be an episode" (Moore and Hagedorn, 1996, p. 210).

Latina gangs (Mexican Americans in the Southwest and Puerto Ricans in New York) have been studied more than African American female gangs. Latina gangs have been continuously present in Los Angeles since the 1930s. Interviews with a large, representative sample of Latina females and Latino males from Los Angeles gangs active in the 1950s and 1970s revealed considerable change. The earlier female gangs were more autonomous and, although they fought rival female gangs, they did not fight side-by-side with males. The more recent female gang members did. They were also more likely to use hard drugs (see Long, 1990) and to feel that the gang played an important part in their lives.[13] In both periods, female gang members were more likely than male gang members to come from troubled families and were far more likely to have run away from home. Another study of Mexican American gangs in Los Angeles reported that even though the female gangs were auxiliaries to male gangs, they often acted independently and their cliques held firmly to an egalitarian norm (Quicker, 1983). Indications of assertiveness were also found in a study of Mexican American female gang members in Phoenix (Moore, Vigil, and Levy, 1995). However, another study in Phoenix reported a persistent and pervasive double standard among Mexican American gang members—particularly when it came to sexuality (Portillos, 1999).

New York's Puerto Rican female gangs were first analyzed in lengthy biographies of former members (Campbell, 1984a).[14] Within their gangs, females took on different roles—"loose" girls versus "good" girls or "mother figures" versus "tomboys"—but all were dominated by males. Campbell (1984b) analyzed 64 fights involving Puerto Rican female gang members and found that most were generated by domestic conflicts and challenges to honor rather than by gang issues. Opponents of females in these fights were just as likely to be male as female.

Campbell argued that female gang members are deeply conservative regarding gender roles. She was also one of the first researchers to discuss the importance of motherhood to female gang members and to note their desire to maintain a reputation within the gang as good mothers (Campbell, 1987).

The number of gangs declined sharply in New York in the 1980s and early 1990s. However, when Puerto Ricans began going to prison in large numbers, new gangs emerged in prison and on the streets. These new gangs included the Latin Kings (Curtis and Hamid, 1997). Preliminary research on the Latin Queens (the female counterpart to the Latin Kings) corroborates Campbell's observation that male domination in Puerto Rican gangs tends to socially isolate females (Hamid, 1996). However, in the mid-1990s, when increasing numbers of Latin Kings were imprisoned, the females' roles changed dramatically. The Latin Queens who remained in the neighborhood became leaders, maintaining communication between incarcerated Kings and gang members still on the streets. The street branches of the Latin Kings became distinct from the prison branches. As females became more important, these street branches became more likely to emphasize community problem solving and to discourage violence (see also Venkatesh, 1998). By the late 1990s, the prison and street branches were in conflict (Curtis, John Jay College, personal communication, 1998). The high rates of imprisonment that have accompanied the Nation's war on drugs may have generated similar changes in gangs elsewhere, but these changes have not yet been documented. This is an important area for research.

In Milwaukee, slight differences in perceptions of autonomy were found between Mexican American and Puerto Rican members of the major Latina gangs. (Large samples from eight gangs, including almost all members of the largest gang, were interviewed in the mid-1990s.) Whereas Mexican Americans saw their gang as a separate, female clique of the male gang, Puerto Rican females saw themselves as part of the male gang. Hagedorn and Devitt (1999) concluded that the difference might be explained by the fact that Puerto Rican females were more likely to have boyfriends or relatives among the male gang's leadership, which was predominantly Puerto Rican.

The number of immigrants is increasing in Latino communities, and immigrant gangs are forming in a number of cities. A study in San Francisco compared Mexican American, immigrant Salvadoran, and African American female gangs and, as discussed [above], found distinctly different patterns of sexual exploitation by male members and drug dealing activity among females from one gang to another. However, both Latina gangs—but not the African American gang—were fighting gangs and were highly territorial (Brotherton, 1996). This study supports the argument that communitywide ethnic patterns of gender relations—in particular, relative degrees of subordination—are directly reflected in gangs.

Other Ethnic Groups

White female gangs have rarely been studied except for a brief report on an Irish gang that was active in Boston, MA, in the early 1970s (Miller, 1973).[15] Members of the female gang were arrested for truancy, theft, drinking, and vandalism. According to the report, these females, known as "Molls," wanted to be accepted by their affiliated male gang and "gloried in" their dependency on the male gang (Miller, 1973, p. 35).

A student of New York City's Chinese gangs remarked that "[w]omen are an essential part of Chinese gangs, although they are not allowed to be members" and noted that these women were a major source of gang conflict (Chin, 1996, p. 173). Unfortunately, the author did not elaborate on this point. These Chinese gangs appear to be criminal organizations rather than traditional youth street gangs. A Los Angeles newspaper reported that there were six female Vietnamese gangs involved in violence in the Orange County area (Klein, 1995), but as with immigrant Latino gangs, there have been few studies on male Asian immigrant gangs in the mainland United States and none on their female counterparts.

Long-Term Consequences

Although joining a gang is only an adolescent episode for some females, for others it is a turning point and a gateway to a life offering very little chance for a socially acceptable career. Researchers are divided in their assessment of gang membership for females, some arguing that it is "liberating"

and some that it causes "social injury" (see Curry, 1998).

Some authors studying Mexican American gangs in Los Angeles imply that once a female leaves a gang, the gang's influence on her life ends (Quicker, 1983; Harris, 1988), but others disagree (Moore and Hagedorn, 1996; Moore, 1991). In the 1990s, most African American female gang members in Milwaukee regarded their gang involvement as an adolescent episode, but for Puerto Ricans in Milwaukee, as for Mexican Americans in Los Angeles, gang membership had long-term consequences. In Los Angeles, Mexican Americans who joined a gang were likely to be from families that were already stigmatized by conventional community residents. Joining a gang and wearing its conspicuous clothes further labeled them as unacceptable to the wider community. Many had joined the gang to escape abusive families, but gang membership actually constricted their futures. Membership virtually ruled out marrying nongang mates. Most female gang members married male gang members whose careers often involved repeated imprisonments. (By contrast, only one-fifth of the male gang members married females from the gang.) When they were young, these Mexican Americans, like Puerto Ricans in New York City, glamorized the gang, but on mature reflection, most felt that joining a gang had been a mistake (Moore, 1991).

Regardless of the cultural context, there is one constant in the later life of most female gang members: most have children. Most male gang members also have children, but the consequences are greater for females. When male gang members in Los Angeles were asked about major turning points in their teens and twenties, they usually talked about the gang, drugs, or arrests. By contrast, females referred to motherhood and marriage. Although most males abandoned responsibility for their children, most females reared their own children (Moore, 1991). In Milwaukee, as gang involvement in the drug business became riskier, women with children were more likely to opt for safer, if less lucrative, means of support (Hagedorn, 1998).

Taking Female Gangs Seriously: Areas for Future Research

The historic lack of research on female gangs suggests that almost every aspect of female gang members' lives requires further research and analysis. In listing research needs, therefore, this bulletin must be highly selective. The following proposed areas of research draw specifically on the analyses in this bulletin:

- **Female gang formation.** As discussed previously, several studies have shown that gang formation (for both males and females) is related to deteriorating inner-city economic conditions. However, no research has been conducted in the many cities where economic conditions improved during the 1990s to determine whether there has been a commensurate decline in gang formation or in the persistence of gang membership into adulthood. General economic conditions influence male and female gangs alike, but a related issue applies specifically to women: how welfare reform and the elimination of Aid to Families With Dependent Children affect female gang formation and gang persistence.

- **Reasons for joining gangs.** As most studies show, friendship, solidarity, self-affirmation, and a sense of new possibilities were found to motivate young inner-city females to join and remain in gangs. Several studies found that the female gang may be a refuge from physical and sexual abuse at home. Although sexual victimization is difficult to study, an understanding of it is relevant to programs designed to keep adolescent females out of gangs and programs designed to intervene with or provide safe havens for female gang members once they are in gangs. Additional research that provides a better understanding of why females join gangs may help communities develop prevention programs to deter female gang membership.

- **Ethnicity.** Because it bears so heavily on gender roles, ethnicity is important in understanding how female gangs function and is also relevant to program design. More research is needed on this topic, particularly with regard to Latina and Asian immigrant gangs, white gangs, and multiethnic gangs.

- **Gender roles in gangs.** Additional research is needed on the roles of females in drug gangs. Field research is

also needed on female gang members' involvement in other economic activities—legal and illegal—and their participation in violence. This research should focus on the gender structure of gangs (i.e., whether females form an autonomous gang, a female auxiliary of a male gang, or part of a gender-integrated gang).

- **Delinquency and criminality.** More substantial data on female gang members' delinquency and criminality are needed. Two possibilities for developing such data are described below:

  — **Continue national surveys of local law enforcement agencies.** Despite acknowledged problems of police underreporting and of varying local definitions of what constitutes a gang or a gang-related offense, surveys of law enforcement agencies provide a valuable look at changes over time.

  — **Use existing law enforcement data sets.** Drawing on local reports, two State agencies have compiled valuable data on female gang members' offense patterns: the Illinois Criminal Justice Information Authority analyzed the annual offense patterns of male and female gang members in Chicago and the California Department of Justice analyzed the lifetime arrest records of female gang members in Los Angeles. These data sets could be used as models for other States with endemic gang problems.

- **Later-life consequences of female gang membership.** Studies using systematic samples of former female gang members could identify factors associated with their success or failure in later life. Such studies would be useful for understanding the long-term consequences of female gang membership. In particular, research is needed on the incarceration experiences of female gang members and the role of female gangs in jails and prisons. More information is also needed about drug use and access to drug rehabilitation among female gang members. It is also important to know whether certain families have developed a tradition of gang membership and whether female gang members are more likely than male gang members to transmit that tradition to their children. There is no research to date on the children of female gang members.

Conclusion

Many aspects of female gang functioning and the lives of female gang members remain a mystery because relatively few researchers have considered female gangs worthy of study. In addition, researchers face serious obstacles to the study of female gangs and, because of these obstacles, they often settle for unrepresentative samples. Gangs are highly suspicious of researchers and cooperate with them only under unusual circumstances. Female gang members, in particular, have been averse to talking about sexual abuse, whether it occurred at home or within the gang. Some field researchers have been able to work effectively with gangs to obtain representative samples and trustworthy data. Other researchers avoid resistance and what they perceive to be the danger involved in direct field studies. These researchers contact gang members through community agencies, probation and parole offices, and incarceration facilities, but each of these strategies entails unknowable biases in sampling and in response sets (see Hagedorn, 1990).

Unfortunately, female gangs have received little programmatic attention. The Family and Youth Services Bureau of the U.S. Department of Health and Human Services had a program that explicitly addressed female gang members, but the program lasted only 3 years. The 1990s brought recognition within the Federal Government that female and male offenders have different programmatic needs. For example, the 1992 reauthorization of the Juvenile Justice and Delinquency Prevention Act of 1974 specifically mandated more programmatic focus on female delinquent offenders. Several national programs have made efforts to reach females. Notable among these are programs created by the Boys & Girls Clubs of America that are directed at reducing or eliminating gangs and the Office of Juvenile Justice and Delinquency Prevention's (OJJDP's) Comprehensive Communitywide Approach to Gang Prevention, Intervention, and Suppression,

which is directed at gang-involved youth and their communities. OJJDP's program includes efforts addressed to females who are or who have been gang members. Across the five sites in this demonstration program, females represent 20 percent of the targeted youth. These programs offer a foundation to build on, but much more work needs to be done to address the needs of females involved with gangs.

Notes

1. In general, this [article] views a gang as an unsupervised group of youth that defines itself as a gang and develops its own norms and criteria for membership. Gang members are more responsive to peer socialization than to conventional agents of socialization, and the gang may become quasi-institutionalized (i.e., it may develop the capacity for self-perpetuation). This definition excludes hate groups, motorcycle gangs, and other exclusively adult gangs. The focus of this [article] is on female gangs. This term refers to gangs containing only female members: some of these gangs are autonomous and some are affiliated with male gangs. The term also refers to gangs that are controlled and dominated by females but that may include male members. The term "female gang members" refers both to individuals who are members of female gangs and to those who are members of gender-integrated gangs.

2. Although most early reports emphasized female gang members' departure from conventional gender-role norms, a recent report from Chesney-Lind, Shelden, and Joe (1996) observed that the media produced a counterintuitive (and dubious) stereotype of female gang members as violent and out of control.

3. The long-term effects of economic restructuring are summed up in the title of W.J. Wilson's 1996 book *When Work Disappears*. Industrial jobs were replaced by part-time or temporary work, with salaries that were often insufficient to support families. Under such conditions, the transition from adolescence to self-supporting adulthood became even more difficult for poorly educated young people than before.

4. One study of city characteristics found that the decline in manufacturing employment was strongly correlated with a rise in urban crime rates and the number of gangs (Jackson, 1995).

5. This study offers a rare analysis of Asian female gangs. Most of the 13 female gang members in the study were either Hawaiian,

Samoan, or Filipina. The authors indicated that ethnicity was a major organizing principle of the gangs (Joe and Chesney-Lind, 1995).

6. All of these studies involved African American, Mexican American, and Puerto Rican females.

7. A female gang member in Detroit, MI, commented that "the boys would get all the blame" for whatever the girls did (Taylor, 1993, p. 33).

8. Many jurisdictions count an offense as "gang related" if it is committed by a gang member. A few jurisdictions, like Chicago . . . , require a gang-related motive.

9. Status offenses include underage drinking, truancy, curfew violations, incorrigibility, and running away. These offenses would not be defined as offenses if committed by adults.

10. Neither the Los Angeles nor the Chicago source includes data on male gang arrestees. However, Block and colleagues (1996) found that in Chicago, between 1965 and 1994, drug offenses accounted for approximately 30 percent of arrests of both male and female gang members.

11. In these Mexican American gangs, heroin dealing was not an activity of the gang as a whole. Instead, individuals or pairs would go into business, and many hired fellow gang members.

12. Some researchers feel that Taylor's portrayal of the changing role of female gang members in Detroit is offensive, arguing that it revives a stereotype of the "liberated female crook" dating from the mid-1970s (Chesney-Lind, Shelden, and Joe, 1996). At that time, Adler (1975) contended that female criminality showed a new pattern of masculine-style violence and attributed this pattern to the egalitarian ideology of the women's movement. However, later analysis showed that the premise underlying the idea (i.e., that violent offenses had increased among females) was erroneous (Steffensmeier, 1980). Unfortunately, the anecdotal nature of Taylor's report makes it difficult to resolve this issue.

13. Another study of Mexican American gangs in Los Angeles also acknowledged the female gang's deviant behavior, its drug culture, and its violence, arguing that females emulated the males (Harris, 1988). See also Hunt, Joe-Laidler, and MacKenzie (2000) for the importance of drinking (alcohol) in the daily lives of female gang members.

14. A social worker's memoir of a year spent with a 12-member Puerto Rican female gang appeared earlier. Hanson (1964) reported both fighting and histories of early molestation, neglect, and abuse from family members and male gang members alike.

15. Other ethnic groups include white, Asian, and multiethnic gangs; all have been increasing. Surveys of law enforcement agencies in 1996 and 1998 showed more whites in gangs than before—14 and 12 percent (Moore and Terrett, 1998; National Youth Gang Center, 2000)—and a survey of eighth graders in 11 cities showed that 25 percent of all gang members were white (Esbensen and Osgood, 1997). The 1996 survey also reported that almost half of all gangs were multiethnic (Moore and Terrett, 1998), and the 1998 survey reported that 6 percent were Asian.

References

Adler, F. 1975. *Sisters in Crime.* New York, NY: McGraw-Hill.

Asbury, H. 1927. *The Gangs of New York.* New York, NY: Blue Ribbon.

Bjerregaard, B., and Smith, C. 1993. Gender differences in gang participation, delinquency, and substance abuse. *Journal of Quantitative Criminology* 9:329–355.

Block, C.R., Christakos, A., Jacob, A., and Przybylski, R. 1996. *Street Gangs and Crime: Patterns and Trends in Chicago.* Research Bulletin. Chicago, IL: Illinois Criminal Justice Information Authority.

Brotherton, D. 1996. "Smartness," "Toughness," and "Autonomy:" Drug use in the context of gang female delinquency. *Journal of Drug Issues* 26:261–277.

Brown, W.K. 1977. Black female gangs in Philadelphia. *International Journal of Offender Therapy and Comparative Criminology* 21:221–228.

California Department of Justice. 1997. *Female Gang Members—Arrest Records Reviewed.* Sacramento, CA: Office of the Attorney General.

Campbell, A. 1984a. *The Girls in the Gang.* Oxford, England: Basil Blackwell.

———. 1984b. Girls' talk: The social representation of aggression by female gang members. *Criminal Justice and Behavior* 11:139–156.

———. 1987. Self definition by rejection. *Social Problems* 34:451–466.

———. 1990. Female participation in gangs. In *Gangs in America,* edited by C.R. Huff. Newbury Park, CA: Sage Publications.

Chesney-Lind, M., Shelden, R., and Joe, K. 1996. Girls, delinquency, and gang membership. In *Gangs in America,* 2d ed., edited by C.R. Huff. Newbury Park, CA: Sage Publications.

Chin, K. 1996. Gang violence in Chinatown. In *Gangs in America,* 2d ed., edited by C.R. Huff. Newbury Park, CA: Sage Publications.

Cohen, M.I., Williams, K., Bekelman, A.M., and Crosse, S. 1994. *Evaluation of the National*

Youth Gang Drug Prevention Program. Report to the Administration on Children, Youth and Families, U.S. Department of Health and Human Services. Washington, DC: U.S. Government Printing Office.

Curry, G.D. 1998. Responding to female gang involvement. In *Female Gangs in America,* edited by J. Hagedorn and M. Chesney-Lind. Chicago, IL: Lakeview Press.

———. 2000. Research note: Self-reported gang involvement and officially recorded delinquency. *Criminology* 38:100–118.

Curry, G.D., Ball, R.A., and Fox, R.J. 1994. *Gang Crime and Law Enforcement Recordkeeping.* Research in Brief. Washington, DC: U.S. Department of Justice, Office of Justice Programs, National Institute of Justice.

Curry, D., and Decker, S. 1998. *Confronting Gangs.* Los Angeles, CA: Roxbury.

Curtis, R., and Hamid, A. 1997. State sponsored violence in New York City and indigenous attempts to contain it: The mediating role of the third crown (sgt. at arms) of the Latin Kings. Unpublished paper. New York, NY: John Jay College.

Decker, S., and Van Winkle, B. 1996. *Life in the Gang.* New York: Cambridge University Press.

Deschenes, E.P., and Esbensen, F. 1999. Violence in gangs: Gender differences in perceptions and behavior. *Journal of Quantitative Criminology* 15:63–96.

Esbensen, F., and Deschenes, E.P. 1998. A multisite examination of youth gang membership: Does gender matter? *Criminology* 36:799–827.

Esbensen, F., and Huizinga, D. 1993. Gangs, drugs and delinquency in a survey of urban youth. *Criminology* 31:565–589.

Esbensen, F., and Osgood, D.W. 1997. *National Evaluation of G.R.E.A.T.* Research in Brief. Washington, DC: U.S. Department of Justice, Office of Justice Programs, National Institute of Justice.

Fagan, J. 1990. Social processes of delinquency and drug use among urban gangs. In *Gangs in America,* edited by C.R. Huff. Newbury Park, CA: Sage Publications.

Fishman, L. 1988. The Vice Queens: An ethnographic study of black female gang behavior. Paper presented at the American Society of Criminology Meetings, Chicago, IL.

———. 1998. Black female gang behavior: An historical and ethnographic perspective. In *Female Gangs in America,* edited by M. Chesney-Lind and J. Hagedorn. Chicago, IL: Lakeview Press.

Hagedorn, J. 1988. *People and Folks.* Chicago, IL: Lakeview Press.

———. 1990. Back in the field again. In *Gangs in America,* edited by C.R. Huff. Newbury Park, CA: Sage Publications.

———. 1998. *People and Folks.* 2d ed. Chicago, IL: Lakeview Press.

Hagedorn, J., and Devitt, M. 1999. Fighting females: The social construction of the female gang. In *Female Gangs in America,* edited by M. Chesney-Lind and J. Hagedorn. Chicago, IL: Lakeview Press.

Hagedorn, J., Torres, J., and Giglio, G. 1998. Cocaine, kicks and strain: Patterns of substance abuse in Milwaukee gangs. *Contemporary Drug Problems* 15:133–145.

Hamid, A. 1996. Resurgence of drugs/gangs/violence in New York City. Unpublished manuscript. New York, NY: John Jay College.

Hanson, K. 1964. *Rebels in the Streets.* Englewood Cliffs, NJ: Prentice-Hall.

Harris, M. 1988. *Cholas: Latino Girls and Gangs.* New York, NY: AMS Press.

Hunt, G., Joe-Laidler, K., and MacKenzie, K. 2000. "Chillin', being dogged and getting buzzed": Alcohol in the lives of female gang members. *Drugs: Education, Prevention, and Policy* 7(4):331–354.

Jackson, P. 1995. Crime, youth gangs, and urban transition: The social dislocations of post-industrial economic development. *Justice Quarterly* 8:379–387.

Joe, K., and Chesney-Lind, M. 1995. "Just Every Mother's Angel": An analysis of gender and ethnic variations in youth gang membership. *Gender & Society* 9:408–431.

Joe-Laidler, K., and Hunt, G. 2001. Accomplishing femininity among the girls in the gang. *British Journal of Criminology.*

Klein, M. 1995. *The American Street Gang.* New York, NY: Oxford University Press.

Lauderback, D., Hansen, J., and Waldorf, D. 1992. "Sisters Are Doin' It for Themselves": A black female gang in San Francisco. *The Gang Journal* 1:57–72.

Long, J. 1990. Drug use patterns in two Los Angeles barrio gangs. In *Drugs in Hispanic Communities,* edited by R. Glick and J. Moore. New Brunswick, NJ: Rutgers University Press.

Miller, J. 1998. Gender and victimization risk among young women in youth gangs. *Journal of Research in Crime and Delinquency* 35:429–453.

———. 2001. *One of the Guys? Girls, Gangs and Gender.* New York, NY: Oxford University Press.

Miller, J., and Brunson, R. 2000. Gender dynamics in youth gangs: A comparison of males' and females' accounts. *Justice Quarterly* 17(3):419–448.

Miller, W. 1973. The Molls. *Society* 11:32–33.

———. 1975. *Violence by Youth Gangs and Youth Groups as a Problem in Major American Cities.* Washington, DC: U.S. Department of Justice, Law Enforcement Assistance Administration, National Institute for Juvenile Justice and Delinquency Prevention.

Moore, J.W. 1991. *Going Down to the Barrio.* Philadelphia, PA: Temple University Press.

———. 1994. The chola life course: Chicana heroin users and the barrio gang. *International Journal of the Addictions* 29:1115–1126.

Moore, J.W., and Hagedorn, J. 1996. What happens to girls in the gang? In *Gangs in America*, 2d ed., edited by C.R. Huff. Thousand Oaks, CA: Sage Publications.

Moore, J.W., and Long, J. 1987. *Final Report: Youth Culture vs. Individual Factors in Adult Drug Use*. Los Angeles, CA: Community Systems Research, Inc.

Moore, J.W., and Mata, A. 1981. *Women and Heroin in Chicano Communities*. Final Report for the National Institute on Drug Abuse. Los Angeles, CA: Chicano Pinto Research Project.

Moore, J.W., Vigil, J.D., and Levy, J. 1995. Huisas of the street. *Latino Studies Journal* 6:27–48.

Moore, J., and Terrett, C. 1998. *Highlights of the 1996 National Youth Gang Survey*. Tallahassee, FL: National Youth Gang Center.

National Youth Gang Center. 2000. *1998 National Youth Gang Survey*. Washington, DC: U.S. Department of Justice, Office of Justice Programs, Office of Juvenile Justice and Delinquency Prevention.

Padilla, F. 1992. *The Gang as an American Enterprise*. New Brunswick, NJ: Rutgers University Press.

Portillos, E.L. 1999. Women, men and gangs: The social construction of gender in the barrio. In *Female Gangs in America*, edited by M. Chesney-Lind and J. Hagedorn. Chicago, IL: Lakeview Press.

Quicker, J. 1983. *Homegirls: Characterizing Chicana Gangs*. San Pedro, CA: International Universities Press.

Rice, R. 1963. A reporter at large: The Persian Queens. *New Yorker* 39(October 19):153–187.

Sanchez-Jankowski, M. 1991. *Islands in the Street*. Berkeley, CA: University of California Press.

Short, J., and Strodtbeck, F. 1965. *Group Processes and Gang Delinquency*. Chicago, IL: University of Chicago Press.

Spergel, I. 1964. *Racketville, Slumtown, Haulburg*. Chicago, IL: University of Chicago Press.

———. 1995. *The Youth Gang Problem*. New York, NY: Oxford University Press.

Steffensmeier, D. 1980. Sex differences in patterns of adult crime: 1965–1977: A review and assessment. *Social Forces* 58:1080–1108.

Taylor, C. 1990. *Dangerous Society*. East Lansing, MI: Michigan State University Press.

———. 1993. *Girls, Gangs, Women and Drugs*. East Lansing, MI: Michigan State University Press.

Thrasher, F. 1927. *The Gang*. Chicago, IL: University of Chicago Press.

Valdez, A., and Cepeda, A. 1998. Homegirls, chicks, and kicking it: Females associated with Mexican American male gangs. Unpublished paper. San Antonio, TX: University of Texas at San Antonio.

Venkatesh, S.A. 1996. The gang in the community. In *Gangs in America*, 2d ed., edited by C.R. Huff. Thousand Oaks, CA: Sage Publications.

———. 1998. Gender and outlaw capitalism: A historical account of the Black Sisters United "girl gang." *Signs* 23:683–709.

Welfare Council of New York City. 1950. *Working With Teenage Groups: A Report on the Central Harlem Project*. New York, NY: Welfare Council of New York City.

Wilson, W.J. 1996. *When Work Disappears*. Chicago, IL: University of Chicago Press. ✦

Chapter 18
The Impact of Sex Composition on Gangs and Gang Member Delinquency

Dana Peterson, Jody Miller, and Finn-Aage Esbensen

The slowly increasing literature on female gang membership has paid scant attention to how various mixes of male and female memberships affect gang delinquency. This chapter presents two unusual thrusts. First, it deliberately sets out to test opposing theories. Second, it considers how different ratios of males to females in gangs might shape the perspectives and behavior of the gangs. The findings are in some ways quite surprising, even beyond the demonstration that sex composition makes a difference. The reader should note that the data came from eighth graders, the majority of whom are under 15 years of age. Similar research on older gang members, where female membership declines rapidly, might not yield such clear results.

The organizational structure of American youth gangs is a topic of considerable interest to researchers and policymakers. Although gangs are often discussed as though they were a monolithic phenomenon, researchers have paid increasing attention to variations across gangs, using a variety of frameworks to classify gangs according to

their organization, duration, and activities. For instance, Spergel and Curry (1993) distinguish among gangs in chronic and emergent cities; Fagan (1989) distinguishes among gangs with differing patterns of drug use, selling, and other criminal activities; and Taylor (1990) distinguishes among scavenger, territorial, and corporate gangs. In perhaps the most comprehensive study to date, Klein and Maxson (1996) distinguish between five types of gangs—traditional, neotraditional, compressed, collective, and specialty gangs—according to a series of dimensions: size, age range, duration, subgroupings, territoriality, and crime patterns.

Despite this attention to organizational structure, few studies have considered the impact of sex composition on gangs and their members, and only recently have researchers moved beyond Miller's (1975) now decades-old typification of female gang involvement as occurring within auxiliary, mixed, or independent groups. However, there are reasons to consider the issue an important one, not just for female gang members, but also for males. Scholars in the sociology of organizations have long recognized sex composition as a key feature shaping interactional dynamics within groups (see, e.g., Blalock, 1967; Blau, 1977; Gutek, 1985; Kanter, 1977a, 1977b). Moreover, several recent qualitative studies of female gang involvement suggest that the sex composition of gangs, as well as other organizational factors, have an impact on girls' experiences and activities within these groups (Joe-Laidler and Hunt, 1997; Miller, 2001; Nurge, 1998). Another recent study also points to the importance of sex composition for understanding some facets of male gang involvement (Miller and Brunson, 2000).

Utilizing a quantitative approach, this paper adds to the small body of literature on the topic. Drawing from a sample of male and female gang youths from 11 cities, we examine whether sex composition within gangs has an impact on gang members' characterizations of their gangs' organization and activities, as well as their individual participation in delinquency. By focusing specifically on sex as a structural feature of gangs, our goal is to contribute to a more complex picture of its impact on gangs and their male and female members.

Sex Composition and Its Impact Within Groups

A central research question in organizational sociology is the impact of demographic composition on the normative features of groups as well as majority and minority group members' experiences and behaviors. Earlier theoretical approaches were *generic*, in that they suggest that *any* group in the numeric minority will face similar experiences based on their proportion within a given group (see Blau, 1977; Kanter, 1977a, 1977b). More recently, minority group members' social position is also recognized as an important consideration. These *institutional* approaches suggest that members of numeric minorities will have different experiences within groups, "depending upon the social significance of particular demographic characteristics in society at large and in the particular organization" (Konrad et al., 1992:115; see also Gutek, 1985). Thus, theorists adopting an institutional approach argue that females in majority male groups will have different experiences than males in majority female groups, largely because of asymmetrical social definitions of masculinity and femininity and their links with sexual inequality.

Several competing theoretical approaches have been brought to bear on the impact of sex ratios within groups, each of which has received some empirical support. Blau's (1977) examination of the quantitative properties of social structure is a purely generic theory of the impact of group proportion on intergroup interaction. He suggests that the amount of intergroup association between two groups, and thus the nature of majority-minority group interactions, can be predicted based on the statistical probabilities associated with group proportion. Specifically, Blau (1977:250) states that "the rate of intergroup associations between two groups is higher for the smaller of the two." That is, when females are a smaller proportion of the total group, for purely numeric reasons, they will have more interactions with male group members, although male members will have few interactions with females. When females are a larger proportion of the total group, they will have fewer opportunities to interact with male members and will have more

interactions with other females. In these more heterogeneous groups—where males are not a clear majority—male group members will have increased interactions with females and intergroup interactions overall will be increased. Further, Blau (1977:80–81) suggests that intergroup contact improves minority/majority relations:

> When group differences are conspicuous and intergroup relations are rare, group pressures [on dominant group members] are likely to arise that further discourage the deviant practice of associating with members of the outgroup.... [I]ncreases in heterogeneity, by making intergroup relations less rare, weaken ingroup pressures that inhibit sociable interaction with members of outgroups and thus lessen discrimination against outgroups.

Consequently, Blau's theory would suggest that heterogeneous groups should be those with the most cooperative between-gender relations (see also South et al., 1983).

One of Blau's predictions is that males in primarily male groups will have fewer interactions with female members than males in groups with more females. Likewise, in her seminal work on sex ratios and organizations, Kanter (1977a:966; see also Kanter, 1977b) distinguishes between skewed groups, in which "there is a large preponderance of one type over another" such that individuals in the numerically smaller type are tokens, versus tilted or balanced groups, in which the numeric minority has a larger and sizeable representation within the group. She suggests that when groups "begin to move toward less extreme distributions . . . dominants are just a majority and tokens a minority. Minority members are potentially allies, can form coalitions, and can affect the culture of the group" (Kanter, 1977a:966). Kanter extends Blau's theory through an examination of the effects—in addition to ratio of contacts—of token membership in skewed groups. She argues that the most extreme effects of minority membership will be experienced among tokens, and she reports that female tokens in primarily male groups are subject to three perceptual phenomena: "visibility (tokens capture a disproportionate awareness share), polarization (differences between tokens and dominants are exaggerated), and assimilation (tokens' attributes are distorted to fit preexisting generalizations about their social type)" (Kanter, 1977a:965). Thus, she argues that female tokens in primarily male groups will be more marginalized and less accepted within the group than women in either tilted or balanced groups.

Kanter's theory has received some empirical support when the minority group under examination is female (see, e.g., Spangler et al., 1978; Yoder et al., 1983), whereas studies of males as token minorities fail to support Kanter's hypotheses (see, e.g., Fairhurst and Snavely, 1983b; Heikes, 1991). Much of the research testing Kanter's approach offers credence to the *institutional* rather than the *generic* character of the impact of demographic composition: It is not necessarily pure numbers that affect the experiences of group members, but rather a combination of the number of males and females and other factors, such as the status of group members, gender stereotyping, and the activities and goals of the group (see, e.g., Fairhurst and Snavely, 1983a, 1983b; Gutek, 1985; Konrad et al., 1992; Williams, 1992; Yoder, 1991). Particularly in groups that are male-dominated and associated with stereotypically masculine traits, females may have an especially difficult time integrating in the group (Gutek, 1985).

An alternative set of hypotheses emerges from Blalock's (1967) majority group power theory. Researchers who have applied Blalock's theory to sex and gender suggest a backlash effect. That is, when women's numbers increase within a group setting, their presence is experienced as a greater threat than when they remain a token minority. Consequently, majority group members (in this case, males) are more likely to take action against members of the minority group (females) in what Kanter calls tilted or balanced groups. Thus, while Kanter argues that women in tilted or balanced groups are less marginalized because they are better able to shape the culture of the group, and Blau would suggest increased and improved relations between women and men in such groups, Blalock's theory instead would suggest greater social and behavioral distance between males and females as they approach more equal numbers in groups.

Majority group power theory is predicated on the assumption of competition between majority (male) and minority (female) group members, such that an encroaching number of minority members will be perceived as a threat to the higher status group. This threat will be dealt with by increased negative action and control in an effort to maintain the dominant group's position. By contrast, the theory would also predict that when females remain tokens in primarily male groups, they must rely on males for access to the group's resources, and thus, do not pose a competitive threat. Majority group power theory has been particularly well supported in the literature on race (e.g., Baker et al., 1989; Chiricos et al., 1997; Covington and Taylor, 1991; Wordes and Bynum, 1995), but has also received some empirical support with regard to gender (see South et al., 1982).

The theories reviewed thus far have been tested in settings such as organizations, work groups, and ecological communities. They provide consistent evidence, despite conflicting findings, that "purely numeric factors can and do exert fundamental influences on patterns of social interaction" (South et al., 1982:598). Whether these factors operate in the ways predicted by Blau (1977), Kanter (1977a, 1977b), Blalock (1967), or others is a focal point of debate. Some scholars suggest the issue should be examined in the specific context of the particular groups in question, particularly given evidence against the utility of a generic approach (Konrad et al., 1992; South et al., 1983). Although this body of research demonstrates the importance of groups' sex composition as a line of inquiry, how sex composition affects gang members' activities, and whether it is associated with other organizational features of gangs, is an issue that has received little empirical examination. In the next section, we further document the utility of such an approach.

Sex, Gender, and Gang Involvement

Research consistently indicates that both males and females are involved in gangs in fairly large numbers (see Bjerregaard and Smith, 1993; Esbensen and Deschenes, 1998). Estimates suggest that males account for approximately 54% to 80% of gang members, and females 20% to 46% (Esbensen and Huizinga, 1993; Esbensen and Winfree, 1998; Winfree et al., 1992). There is also evidence of variation in sex composition across gangs. Although standard approaches for categorizing (presumably or implicitly) male gangs continue to focus on a broad range of issues exclusive of sex (see, for example, Jankowski, 1991; Klein and Maxson, 1996; Spergel and Curry, 1993; Taylor, 1990), studies of female gang types focus specifically on sex organization, most often drawing from Walter Miller's (1975) tripartite classification: (1) mixed-sex gangs with both female and male members, (2) female gangs that are affiliated with male gangs, which he refers to as "auxiliary" gangs, and (3) independent female gangs (but see Hagedorn and Devitt, 1999; Nurge, 1998).

There are several case studies of these various gang types (see Fleisher, 1998; Lauderback et al., 1992; Quicker, 1983), but less evidence of their prevalence. Curry's (1997) study of female gang members in three cities found that only 6.4% of girls described being in autonomous female gangs, while 57.3% described their gangs as mixed-sex, and another 36.4% said they were in female gangs affiliated with male gangs. Miller (2001) and Nurge (1998) report that the majority of girls in their studies were in groups that were mixed-sex rather than "auxiliary" or female-only, but with varying sex compositions. For example, of the 42 members of mixed-sex gangs in Miller's (2001) sample, 74% were in groups that were majority-male, with just under a third (31%) in gangs in which 80% or more of the members were males. Likewise, Miller and Brunson (2000) note that 61% of the male gang members they interviewed reported being in mixed-sex rather than male-only gangs, with two-thirds of those in mixed-sex gangs reporting that their groups were 80% or more male.

Given the import of sex composition in shaping group dynamics, the variation reported within gangs would appear to be a significant issue. Kanter (1977a) notes that often conclusions drawn about differences between males and females, and attributed to "gender roles" or cultural differences between women and men, are in fact more appropriately attributable to situational or structural factors such as the sex composition of groups. Indeed, the fact that sex composition has been shown to influence group members' experiences could help explain the sometimes disparate findings scholars report about young women in gangs (see Curry, 1998, for an overview).

Several debates and incongruous findings exist within the literature on female gang involvement. Curry (1998), for example, notes the tension between perspectives that focus on gangs as "liberating" for their female members, as evidenced by solidarity and support among female members (see, e.g., Campbell, 1990; Lauderback et al., 1992; Taylor, 1993), and those perspectives that focus on the "social injury" young women experience in and as a consequence of their participation in gangs, resulting in part from sexual inequality and exploitation within these groups (see, for example, Fleisher, 1998; Miller, 1998; Moore, 1991).

In addition, several scholars report greater variation in young women's participation in delinquent activities than young men's. Although it is evident that young women in gangs have higher rates of delinquency than their nongang peers, both male and female (Bjerregaard and Smith, 1993; Esbensen and Winfree, 1998; Thornberry et al., 1993), several studies have noted "a bimodal distribution [for girls], with nearly as many multiple index offenders as petty delinquents" (Fagan, 1990:201; see also Miller, 2001). Moreover, there is debate concerning whether participation in delinquency, particularly of a violent nature, is a normative feature of gang involvement for females. Although scholars have long argued that delinquency is a predominant normative feature of youth gangs (see Decker, 1996; Klein, 1995), some scholars have argued that this is not the case for young women (see Campbell, 1993; Joe and Chesney-Lind, 1995). For example, Joe and Chesney-Lind (1995:224, 228) report that "for boys, fighting—even looking for fights—is a major activity within the gang. . . . For girls, violence (gang and otherwise) is not celebrated and normative. . . ." Other scholars suggest that female gang members' lesser involvement in serious gang crime is not a function of differences in the norms adopted by males and females, but instead results from "the structural exclusion of women from male delinquent activities" (Bowker et al., 1980:516). That is, male gang members block young women's participation in central activities within the gang.

As Curry (1998:109) suggests, some of these disparate findings may result from different perspectives, whereas from the dialectical perspective he proposes "there is really no theoretical problem in the same social activity being simultaneously rewarding and destructive." It may also be that the discrepancies found in various studies of female gang involvement result in part from variations in the sex composition of those gangs under investigation—a feature that most research on female gang involvement has overlooked. Miller's (2001) qualitative study provides some preliminary evidence of the importance of sex composition within gangs by examining how the sex composition of girls' gangs shapes their experiences and perceptions. She reports that girls in primarily female gangs (whether independent or affiliated with male gangs), as well as girls in mixed-sex gangs with a substantial proportion of female members, are more likely to emphasize the social and relational aspects of their gangs, particularly their friendships with other girls. As noted, this is in keeping with a number of studies that highlight these features of young women's gang involvement (Campbell, 1990; Joe and Chesney-Lind, 1995; Lauderback, et al., 1992).

On the other hand, Miller (2001) reports that girls in gangs which Kanter (1977a) would classify as skewed or tilted in favor of males were more likely to emphasize the delinquent aspects of gang life and to describe themselves as "one of the guys." Likewise, Miller and Brunson's (2000) study of male gang members suggests that young men in "balanced" groups highlighted the social aspects of their interactions with female gang members, but differentiate males' and females' participation in delinquent activities. Young men in "skewed" gangs, with a vast majority of male members, embraced the few young women in their gangs as "one of the guys," and described these girls as essentially equal partners in many of their delinquent endeavors.

These findings, as noted earlier, suggest that taking sex composition into account could help explain some of the incongruent findings with regard to sex that arise in studies of gangs. Our goal in the present study is to address these issues. Specifically, we pose two general research questions, as follows:

1. Are there differences in gang characteristics, activities, and members' experiences depending on the sex composition of the gang? Stated differently, can gangs of differing sex compositions be distinguished by their organizational characteristics, activi-

ties, and their members' participation in delinquency?

2. Do descriptions of gang activities and individual delinquency differ for males and females in varying gang types? For example, do females in one gang type differ from females in other gang types (i.e., within-sex, across-gang type comparisons), and do males and females within gang types differ from each other (i.e., between-sex, within-gang type comparisons)?

The first of these questions will allow us to explore how the sex composition of the gang is related to the gang's characteristics and the activities—both prosocial and delinquent—in which the gang is involved. The second question will provide insight into how the sex composition of the gang operates for both male and female members of these gangs. Comparing both within and across sex will help to disentangle whether effects, if any, are associated with sex differences or the sex composition of the gang. Given the significance of delinquency as both a key normative feature and activity of gang members, our examination of delinquency also provides the opportunity to test the relative import of the theoretical perspectives reviewed above.

For example, Kanter's work would lead us to predict that due to their marginalization, female members of majority male gangs will have lower rates of delinquency than their male counterparts in these gangs. By contrast, Kanter and Blau's theories both would predict that females' delinquency in mixed-sex (what we will call "sex-balanced" in our study) gangs will more closely match that of the males in their gangs than in other groups. Moreover, assuming (as Kanter suggests) that a larger proportion of female members affects the culture of the group, if delinquency is of less normative significance for females than males, we would also expect lower rates of delinquency among males in sex-balanced than in majority-male or all-male gangs, and the lowest rates of delinquency in majority-female and all-female gangs. Blalock's majority group power theory would suggest opposite predictions: Not only will girls in sex-balanced groups be less delinquent than their female counterparts in primarily male gangs, but there will be greater differences between male and female delinquency in sex-balanced groups, resulting from Blalock's prediction of greater social and behavioral distance between males and females as they approach more equal numbers in groups. . . .

Research Design, Site Selection, and Measures

[Data for this study come from the Gang Resistance Education and Training (G.R.E.A.T.) program evaluation. See Chapter 14 in this volume for a description of site selection, sample limitations, and additional measurement techniques—Eds.]

[We] categorized gang youth according to their reports of the sex composition of their gangs. In an open-ended question, respondents were asked to record the number of males and number of females in their gangs. Although a substantial number of gang members failed to provide complete data on the number of males and females in their gangs, we did receive enough valid responses to enable us to make our intended comparisons. Of the 623 gang members in the full sample, 369 (59%) provided sufficient information. Analyses were conducted to compare those who gave insufficient information—and who were thus excluded from the present study—to those who provided the necessary information. No statistically significant differences between the two groups were found for the demographic or behavioral variables under examination in this study.

If the respondents indicated a positive number of one sex and no members of the other sex, they were classified as being in "all-male" or "all-female" gangs. Gang members were classified as being members of "majority-male" or "majority-female" gangs if the majority sex comprised at least two-thirds of the gang. Those who reported that neither sex exceeded two-thirds of the gang membership were classified as being in "sex-balanced" gangs.[1] We also examined youths' self-defined place in their gang. Five concentric circles were drawn on a chalkboard, with the center circle labeled "1" and representing the center of the gang, and the outer circle labeled "5," representing the periphery of the gang. Respondents were asked to circle the number that best described their place in their gang. Those circling 1 or 2 were considered "core" gang members and those circling 3, 4, or 5 were considered "noncore."

Youths were then asked to describe their gangs in terms of structural and organizational characteristics and behaviors. In response to the question, "Do the following describe your gang?" gang members were asked to circle as many answers as applied, including such possibilities as "There are initiation rites" and "The gang has established leaders." In terms of their gangs' activities, particularly the group's involvement in delinquency, gang members responded to the question, "Does your gang do the following things?" by circling as many answers (for example, "Get in fights with other gangs" and "Steal things") as applied. With respect to delinquency comparisons among males and females in gangs of differing sex compositions, we examined annual frequency[2] (i.e., "how many times in the past 12 months have you . . .") of self-reported participation in a range of delinquent acts, including property crimes, crimes against persons, and drug sales.

Results

Consistent with the findings of Curry (1997), Miller (2001), and Nurge (1998), our sample of 369 gang members includes youths in gangs with varied sex compositions. Approximately 45% of male gang members described their gangs as having a majority of male members; 38% said their gangs were sex-balanced; 16% were in all-male gangs; and just under 1% (2 cases) reported being in gangs that were majority-female. Young women were more likely than young men to describe belonging to sex-balanced, rather than majority-male, gangs. Fully 64% of girls described their gangs as sex-balanced, followed by 30% in majority-male gangs, and 13% in majority-female (eight cases) or all-female (ten cases) gangs. In keeping with reports that gangs are primarily masculine enterprises, the least prevalent gang types in our study were female-only and majority-female gangs. Nonetheless, gangs with both male and female membership were by far the most common. Of the total sample of 369 gang members, only 10% percent reported membership in male-only gangs. Our goal here is to explore whether and how sex composition is related to other gang characteristics and activities and gang member behaviors.

Table 18.1 reports demographic characteristics of male and female gang members, as well as their self-defined place in their gangs. The dispersion of ages among males was consistent across gang types—under one-fifth were 13 or younger, the majority were age 14, and approximately 25% were 15 or older. This pattern was similar for girls in sex-balanced gangs, but not for girls in majority-male or all-/majority-female gangs. In majority-male gangs, approximately one-quarter were 13 or younger, and fully 44% of girls in majority- or all-female gangs were 13 or younger. Half of the girls in all-/majority-female gangs were age 14, along with 70% of girls in majority-male gangs. These differences among females were statistically significant, as were the differences between males in all-male gangs and females in primarily female gangs. Evidence from longitudinal research suggests that girls' gang involvement tends to be of a shorter duration than boys', with girls' peak gang involvement around eighth and ninth grades (Thornberry, 1999). Our data suggests this is most likely to be the case in primarily female and primarily male gangs.

There was no significant variation by race among gangs of different sex compositions.[3] African-American males were the largest proportion of boys in all-male gangs, but they were much more likely to be in gangs with female membership, as was the case for all males, regardless of race. Likewise, several studies indicate that African-American girls are more likely to be in independent female gangs than other girls (Lauderback et al., 1992; Taylor, 1993). Although four of the ten girls in our sample reporting membership in all-female gangs were African-American, this represents only 11% of the African-American female gang members.[4]

With regard to self-defined place in the gang, the membership appears to be fairly evenly split between those claiming core and noncore positions within their gangs. However, fewer females in majority-male gangs reported holding central positions in their gangs than girls in other gang types. In addition, the proportion of females in majority-male gangs who were core members was lower compared with males in those gangs, and a greater proportion of females than males in sex-balanced gangs reported holding core positions. The former of these findings appears to offer support for Kanter's (1977a, 1977b) and Blau's (1977) predictions of greater marginalization for minorities in unbalanced groups compared with groups with relatively equal numbers. However, because male participation in majority-female groups is rare, we are unable to ascertain whether this is a generic phenomenon or if it applies primarily to minorities who are not just in the numeric minority, but also hold less power within American society at large (e.g., females; see Gutek, 1985; Konrad et al., 1992).[5]

Table 18.1
Gang Member Characteristics by Sex and Gang Type[a]

	All Male	All/Majority Female	Majority Male		Sex Balanced	
	M n=37	F n=18	M n=105	F n=31	M n=87	F n=86
Age:[b,c]						
13 and under	14%	44%	16%	23%	11%	17%
14	60%	50%	58%	70%	62%	59%
15 and over	26%	6%	26%	7%	27%	25%
Race:						
White	22%	33%	29%	29%	29%	23%
African-American	44%	33%	29%	26%	35%	26%
Hispanic	11%	17%	26%	23%	19%	24%
Other	22%	17%	16%	23%	18%	27%
Place in Gang:						
Core	50%	64%	52%	39%	44%	57%
Non-Core	50%	36%	48%	61%	56%	43%

[a]For all analyses, both within-sex, across gang type and between-sex, within-gang type comparisons were conducted. Only statistically significant results from these comparisons are reported in the table.
[b]Chi-square test, p < .05, comparison between females.
[c]Chi-square test, p < .05, comparison of males in all-male gangs to females in all/majority female gangs.

Gang Characteristics and Activities

Table 18.2 reports youths' descriptions of key characteristics of their gangs. Here, we examine whether boys and girls across gang types, as well as boys and girls in the same gang types, characterized their gangs differently. We did not find differences between males and females within the same gang types with regard to their descriptions of gang characteristics. However, there were some differences within-sex, across-gang types. Specifically, males in all-male gangs reported the lowest levels of gang organization and males in sex-balanced gangs the highest. Statistically significant differences were reported by boys for the following organizational characteristics of their gangs: specific rules, regular meetings, and the adoption of symbols or colors. Nonetheless, with the exception of having regular meetings, the majority of males and females in all gang types reported these characteristics.

The results for girls were less straightforward. Girls in all- or majority-female gangs were less likely to report regular meetings or specific rules than were girls in the other gang types, but otherwise girls' descriptions of gang characteristics were consistent across gang types. The only finding of statistically significant differences for girls was for the gangs' regular meetings. No significant differences were found between girls and boys in the same gang types. Given the extent that these features of gang organization vary across cities (Klein and Maxson, 1996), the overall lack of striking differences may be a result of our multicity sampling. Moreover, whether these characteristics are actual measures of gang organization,

or are more aptly a reflection of gang characteristics as they are influenced by the cultural diffusion of gangs, remains an open question (see Klein, 1995; Miller, 2001). Nonetheless, our findings do suggest that on the whole the sex composition of youths' gangs does not appear to be significantly related to other organizational characteristics of these girls' groups, although three of five significant differences for characteristics of boys' gangs suggest some relationship.

In terms of gang activities, however, the differences are somewhat more dramatic for females. Table 18.3 reports the results of gang members' descriptions of the activities of their gangs, including both prosocial and delinquent behaviors. Although these differences are not statistically significant, boys in all-male gangs, and particularly girls in all- or majority-female gangs, were the most likely to report that their gangs were involved in prosocial activities, as measured by helping out in the community. Moreover, girls in all- or majority-female gangs described their groups as substantially and, in some cases, significantly less involved in delinquency than their female counterparts in sex-balanced and majority-male gangs. A much smaller proportion of girls in majority-/all-female gangs reported the gang's involvement in all measures of delinquency, and they were significantly less likely to report that the gang fought with other gangs, stole cars, sold marijuana, or sold illegal drugs other than marijuana.

Likewise, boys in sex-balanced and majority-male gangs reported comparable rates of delinquency for their gangs, whereas boys in all-male gangs reported lower rates of gang delinquency. However,

Table 18.2
Gang Characteristics by Sex and Gang Type[a]

| | All Male | All/Majority Female | Majority Male | | Sex Balanced | |
| | M | F | M | F | M | F |
	n=37	n=18	n=105	n=31	n=87	n=86
Initiation Rites	65%	78%	74%	76%	77%	78%
Established Leaders	79%	83%	76%	79%	83%	89%
Regular Meetings[b,c]	33%	39%	58%	52%	66%	67%
Specific Rules[b]	60%	67%	71%	87%	84%	87%
Symbols or Colors[b]	78%	83%	90%	100%	94%	88%

[a]For all analyses, both within-sex, across-gang type and between-sex, within-gang type comparisons were conducted. Only statistically significant results from these comparisons are reported in the table.
[b]Chi-square test, p < .05, comparison between males.
[c]Chi-square test, p < .05, comparison between females.

Table 18.3
Gang Activities by Sex and Gang Type[a]

	All Male	All/Majority Female	Majority Male		Sex Balanced	
	M n=37	F n=18	M n=105	F n=31	M n=87	F n=86
Help in Community	38%	41%	30%	15%	25%	26%
Fight Other Gangs[b]	87%	78%	93%	94%	90%	95%
Steal Things	60%	71%	78%	90%	70%	77%
Rob Others	51%	41%	61%	73%	68%	62%
Steal Cars[b]	60%	47%	73%	87%	73%	69%
Sell Marijuana[b,c]	69%	69%	80%	97%	85%	84%
Sell Other Drugs[b]	49%	24%	64%	72%	64%	67%
Damage or Destroy Property	66%	77%	82%	90%	81%	79%

[a]For all analyses, both within-sex, across gang type and between-sex, within gang type comparisons were conducted. Only statistically significant results from these comparisons are reported in the table.
[b]Chi-square test, p < .05, comparison between females.
[c]Chi-square test, p < .05, comparison of males to females in majority-male gangs.

none of the differences among males' descriptions of their gangs' activities was statistically significant. Males and females within gang types were fairly similar in their descriptions of gang activities, with one exception. Females in majority-male gangs were significantly more likely than males in those gangs to report that their gangs sold marijuana (97% compared to 80%). Overall, based on member reports, it appears that majority-/all-female gangs were the least delinquent groups, followed by all-male gangs, whereas sex-balanced and majority-male gangs were more delinquent and were quite similar with regard to the gangs' involvement in delinquent activities.

If gang members' reports of their gangs' activities are a reflection of the goals and norms of these groups, these differences between single-sex and majority-female gangs versus sex-balanced and majority-male gangs are noteworthy. In keeping with the findings of other scholars (Campbell, 1993; Joe and Chesney-Lind, 1995), our findings suggest that delinquency, particularly of a serious nature, is a less normative feature of primarily female gangs than other gangs. To interpret this as a function of differences between male and female values, however, is problematic, given the comparably low rates of reported delinquency among all-male gangs. Instead, sex composition appears to be the salient issue: Gangs with both male and female membership (with the exception of primarily female gangs) are those most likely to be oriented toward delinquent activities.

Gang Member Delinquency

Finally, we turn to gang members' reports of their participation in delinquency. Comparing groups with both male and female membership based on their sex composition (e.g., sex-balanced versus majority-male gangs), recall that Kanter's and Blau's theories would lead us to predict the greatest differences in rates of delinquency would occur when comparing males and females in majority-male gangs. Both theorists suggest females' marginalization in majority-male groups will result in exclusion from the primary status-enhancing activities of the group (e.g., delinquency; see Decker, 1996; Klein, 1995). Moreover, if delinquency is less normative for females than males, Kanter and Blau would also predict that both males and females in sex-balanced gangs would have lower rates of delinquency than males in majority-male gangs, given females' increased influence on the groups' norms and activities. In contrast, Blalock's majority group power theory predicts the opposite: The greatest difference in rates of delinquency will be found in sex-balanced, rather than majority-male groups. As females' numbers increase within the group, male members are more likely to exclude them from the gangs' primary activities to reduce the threat of territorial encroachment on normatively "masculine" endeavors. Blalock's theory would also predict that female members of majority-male gangs must rely on males for access to group rewards and acceptance and, thus, pose less of a threat to male group

Table 18.4

Male to Female t-Test Comparisons of Delinquency Frequency within Gang Types

	All Male	All/Majority Female	Majority Male		Sex Balanced	
	M n=37	F n=18	M n=105	F n=31	M n=87	F n=86
Damage Property	4.32 (4.48)	3.33 (4.72)	5.76 (4.62)	4.67 (4.74)	5.51* (5.01)	3.54 (4.42)
Illegally Spray Paint	4.03* (4.93)	1.00 (2.50)	5.51* (5.41)	3.80 (4.69)	4.52* (5.07)	2.68 (4.19)
Steal Less Than $50	3.66 (4.54)	3.00 (4.75)	5.71 (5.02)	4.93 (4.83)	4.28 (5.03)	3.77 (4.47)
Steal More Than $50	1.56* (2.51)	.12 (.49)	3.67 (4.34)	2.27 (3.89)	3.56* (4.81)	1.50 (2.94)
Go into Building to Steal Something	2.19 (4.13)	1.44 (3.76)	3.59 (4.84)	2.93 (4.39)	2.37 (3.99)	2.17 (3.91)
Steal Motor Vehicle	1.51* (3.37)	.17 (.38)	2.05 (3.51)	1.71 (3.23)	3.37* (4.62)	1.17 (2.61)
Sell Marijuana	2.21 (3.91)	2.24 (4.24)	5.47* (5.48)	3.86 (4.99)	3.97* (5.04)	2.83 (4.36)
Sell Other Drugs	1.50* (3.68)	.29 (1.21)	3.03 (4.96)	3.10 (5.15)	2.90* (4.80)	1.50 (3.61)
Carry Hidden Weapon	5.29* (4.94)	2.44 (4.16)	6.98 (5.13)	6.63 (4.95)	6.92* (5.29)	3.48 (4.59)
Rob Someone	.97* (2.04)	.00 (.00)	2.33 (4.17)	1.87 (4.06)	1.84* (3.76)	.86 (2.66)
Hit Someone with Idea to Hurt Him/Her	4.82 (4.59)	5.44 (4.69)	6.25 (4.82)	5.86 (4.67)	5.70* (5.13)	5.00 (4.61)
Participate in Gang Fights	3.97 (4.08)	2.50 (4.31)	5.63 (4.69)	4.93 (4.91)	5.46* (4.89)	4.35 (4.25)
Attack Someone with a Weapon	2.24* (3.34)	.17 (.71)	3.09 (4.29)	3.03 (4.57)	2.61* (4.30)	1.58 (3.00)
Shoot at Someone	.62* (1.38)	.00 (.00)	1.57 (3.43)	1.47 (3.25)	1.85* (3.82)	.78 (2.33)

*p < .05, comparison of males to females within gang types.

members. Consequently, they are less likely to be systematically blocked from the gangs' activities than are girls in sex-balanced groups.

Tables 18.4 and 18.5 report gang members' self-reported frequency of participation in a variety of delinquent acts by sex and gang type. In line with the predictions of Blalock (1967), *t*-tests comparing males and females within gang types (Table 18.4) reveal significant differences between males and females in sex-balanced gangs on nearly every measure, but few differences between males and females in majority-male gangs. Among youths in sex-balanced gangs, fe-

male members were significantly less involved than male members in 12 of the 14 measures of delinquency. Only for two property offenses—stealing less than $50 and going into a building to steal something—were females' rates comparable to those of young men. They were significantly less involved in serious property offending (stealing more than $50, stealing cars), drug sales, carrying hidden weapons, as well as all violent offenses recorded.

In contrast, there were only two significant differences between males and females in majority-male gangs: Female members were significantly less involved in illegal

Table 18.5

t-Test Comparisons of Property and Person Delinquency Frequencies by Sex and Gang Type[a]

	All Male	All/Majority Female	Majority Male		Sex Balanced	
	M n=37	F n=18	M n=105	F n=31	M n=87	F n=86
Property Offense Index[b,c,f]	2.16 (2.40)	1.16 (1.97)	3.77 (3.58)	2.98 (3.24)	3.52 (3.69)	2.14 (2.72)
Person Offense Index[b,c,d,e,f]	2.15 (2.17)	1.36 (1.17)	3.30 (3.26)	3.03 (3.42)	3.16 (3.39)	2.10 (2.40)

[a]For all analyses, both within-sex, across-gang type and between-sex, within-gang type comparisons were conducted. Only statistically significant results from these comparisons are reported in the table.
[b]p< .05, comparison between males in all-male and majority-male gangs.
[c]p< .05, comparison between males in all-male and sex-balanced gangs.
[d]p< .05, comparison between females in all/majority female gangs and majority-male gangs.
[e]p< .05, comparison of males in all-male gangs to females in all/majority-female gangs.
[f]p< .05, comparison of males to females in sex-balanced gangs.

spray painting and selling marijuana. However, their frequencies of involvement in the other 12 illegal activities—including violent offenses—were not significantly lower than were the frequencies of involvement of their male counterparts in majority-male gangs. The final between-sex comparison reveals that girls in majority-/all-female gangs were less frequently involved in delinquency than males in all-male gangs, with significant differences reported for 8 of the 14 offenses measured, particularly more serious offenses (stealing more than $50, stealing cars, selling drugs other than marijuana, carrying hidden weapons, committing robberies, attacking others and shooting at someone).

In order to facilitate within-sex comparisons across gang types, we examined two indices of delinquent behavior: property offenses (stealing less than $50, stealing more than $50, going into a building to steal something, and stealing motor vehicles) and person offenses (hitting someone with the idea of hurting him/her, attacking someone with a weapon, robbing someone, and shooting at someone). As Table 18.5 reveals, males in all-male gangs were significantly less involved in property offenses and offenses against persons than were males in either majority-male or sex-balanced gangs. No significant differences emerged between males in majority-male and sex-balanced gangs, as would be expected if increased female membership shifted the norms and activities of gangs towards more prosocial activities. Females in majority- or all-female gangs had lower frequencies of delinquency than their counterparts in sex-balanced and majority-male gangs, and they were significantly less involved in person offending than females in majority-male gangs.

Again, as predicted by Blalock's majority group power theory, between-sex differences were found for those youths in sex-balanced gangs. Males in this gang type reported greater rates than did females of both property and person offending. Females in primarily female gangs also differed significantly from males in all-male gangs in rates of offending against persons.

Overall, girls in all- and majority-female gangs had the lowest rates of delinquency, followed by girls in sex-balanced gangs, boys in all-male gangs, girls in majority-male gangs, boys in sex-balanced gangs, and finally, boys in gangs with a majority of male members. Thus, membership in a gang with a minority of female members and a majority of males was correlated with higher rates of delinquency for both males and females. In fact, it is notable that girls in majority-male gangs were more delinquent than boys in all-male gangs.

Discussion

Prior to discussing the relevance of our findings, we would like to acknowledge three methodological limitations of our work: the cross-sectional research design, the relative young age of our gang members, and missing data for a number of respondents on the sex composition measure. First, at the suggestion of one reviewer, analyses were conducted to compare current and former gang members on delinquency. As expected, these analyses did reveal several significant differences; however, there was no differential attrition across gang types, so these differences should not affect the overall pattern of our results, except in underestimation of these behaviors. Second, even though our sample is young and sex composition of groups may have different effects at different ages, we can have confidence in our results based on the fact that qualitative studies with older samples have found similar patterns regarding the impact of sex structure on males' and females' experiences within the gang (see Miller, 1998; Miller and Brunson, 2000). Finally, no statistically significant differences were found on any of the key variables between gang members who provided the required information about their gangs' sex composition and gang members who failed to provide this information. Thus, we have no reason to believe that the findings reported here cannot generalize to our entire gang member sample.

With these limitations in mind, the goal of this study was to explore the relationship of gang sex composition to both gang characteristics and activities and individual gang members' delinquent behavior. We examined within-sex differences across gang types in order to investigate whether males and females within gangs of one particular sex composition provided similar or different descriptions from their same-sex peers in other gang types. In addition, we examined whether males and females within gangs of the same sex composition characterized their gangs and activities in the same or differing ways. These analyses allowed us to examine (1) whether gangs of differing sex compositions can be distinguished by their characteristics and activities, as well as by the delinquency of their members; and (2) whether differences in gang members' descriptions appear to result from sex differences or from the sex structure of their gangs.

As highlighted above, literature from the field of organizational sociology strongly suggests the latter (i.e., the impact of sex structure) more so than the former (normative sex differences, for instance, resulting from "gender role" differences). Our findings are consistent with this literature. With regard to descriptions of gang characteristics and activities, for example, youths in all-male and all-/majority-female gangs reported fewer of the organizational features typically associated with youth gangs (e.g., leadership, meetings, the adoption of symbols or colors), although these differences were not marked. Likewise, youths in all-male and all-/majority-female gangs reported their gangs' greater participation in prosocial activities and lesser participation in delinquency than youths in other gang types.[6] We also found significant differences in individual delinquency across gang type and (in the case of sex-balanced gangs) across sex.

In testing the demographic composition theories proffered by organizational sociology, our findings support the significant influence of sex composition on male and female group members' behavior. Specifically, we find much stronger support for Blalock's (1967) majority-group power theory than the theories of Kanter (1977a, 1977b) or Blau (1977). Both of the latter theories would lead us to predict the greatest sex differences among youths in majority-male gangs, resulting from the marginalization of female tokens. They would also predict that a larger proportion of female members may influence the normative features of the group, such that (assuming delinquency is a "masculine" norm) males in sex-balanced gangs would have considerably lower rates of delinquency than would males in majority-male gangs.

In contrast, Blalock's (1967) minority-group threat hypothesis suggests that as the proportion of the lower status group (i.e., females) increases, the higher status group (i.e., males) increases negative action and control in an effort to maintain a dominant position. Thus, it would be in sex-balanced gangs—those with a sizeable proportion of female members—that the greater sex differences would emerge with regard to participation in delinquency. Our findings are in line with this prediction. Males and females in majority-male gangs did not report significantly different rates of offending, while males and females in sex-balanced gangs did. Thus, it may be that males in sex-balanced gangs, in which the percentage of females is nearly equal that of males, feel a gendered status threat and respond by narrowing girls' opportunities for involvement in "masculine" activities such as delinquency[7] (see also Bowker et al., 1980; Miller, 2001). By contrast, males in majority-male gangs feel little status threat from the small number of females in their gangs, and thus, these females are granted greater freedom (see also Miller and Brunson, 2000).

Our findings are also somewhat consistent with prior research indicating that groups consisting of both males and females are more prone to delinquency than other group types (Giordano, 1978; Warr, 1996). In our study, youths in majority-male and sex-balanced gangs described both their gangs and themselves as involved in the greatest amounts of delinquent behavior. This was true for both males and females in these gang types, despite the differences reported for individual delinquency by girls and boys in sex-balanced gangs. Giordano (1978) and Warr (1996) have suggested that females learn their delinquent behavior from males in these groups, as their results show that females in groups with both male and female membership exhibit far greater delinquency than do those in exclusively female groups.

Such an interpretation would follow the argument that girls are less oriented toward delinquency than boys, as a result of gender or cultural differences between males and females. Increased rates of female delinquency, thus, result from girls learning and adapting to the masculine behavioral norms of the group. In fact, Kanter (1977a) explicitly makes this suggestion when she analyzes tokens' responses to their marginalized position. She suggests that female tokens typically adopt two strategies: overachievement according to the "masculine" standards of the group; and attempting to become "socially invisible"—to "minimize their sexual attributes so as to blend unnoticeably into the predominant male culture" (Kanter, 1977a:974; see also Konrad et al., 1992). Although this could be an explanation for the high rates of delinquency reported by females in majority-male gangs, we did not find evidence to suggest that these girls' opportunities for participation in delinquency were blocked in the first place, as evidenced by our data's support of Blalock's (1967) majority-group power theory. Miller and Brunson's (2000) work likewise suggests that males in majority-male gangs accept female members as "one of the guys" and describe girls' participation in many of the gang's delinquent activities, whereas males in mixed-sex gangs note stronger differences in male and female gang members' delinquent activities. Thus, it does not appear that tokenism has a marginalizing effect on girls in majority-male gangs.[8]

Moreover, in contrast to perspectives that assume cultural differences between males and females at the outset, our research also indicates that males in all-male gangs are far less delinquent than males are in other gang types, and even less delinquent than girls in majority-male gangs. This calls into some question Giordano's (1978) and Warr's (1996) gendered social learning approach. In fact, at first glance, this finding seemed puzzling, even to us. Some sex-composition theories would lead us to believe that all-male groups would tend to be the most aggressive and competitive in their orientation. Gutek (1985), for example, argues that sex-role spillover in male-dominated groups results in the adoption of stereotypical masculine traits that come to define the group.

Our findings offer challenge to this perspective, as well as to those of Giordano and Warr. We appear to be witnessing a phenomenon associated with the gendered organization of groups, not simply the interplay of differences between males and females. If gang delinquency is both a normative feature of gangs and a decidedly "masculine" one, it is enacted most strongly by males in gangs with female membership, as witnessed by their significantly higher rates of delinquency than their counterparts in all-male gangs. These findings attest to the fluidity of masculinity and femininity—they are *situationally* defined and enacted, rather

than resulting from deeply entrenched gender differences (see Connell, 1987, 1995; West and Fenstermaker, 1995). In the case of gangs, it appears that the participation of females in these groups results in increased levels of male delinquency, regardless of the activities of female members themselves.[9]

Finally, we suggested at the outset that a number of discrepant reports regarding female gang involvement might be accounted for by considering the import of gangs' sex compositions, particularly as these may impact the norms and activities of these groups. As we have just discussed, the examination of sex composition can help address the question of whether delinquency is a normative feature of girls' gang activities, as well as differences in reported rates of girls' participation in delinquency. Another series of debates concerns whether gangs offer their female members the solidarity, support, and "sisterhood" of other girls (see, e.g., Campbell, 1990; Joe and Chesney-Lind, 1995; Lauderback et al., 1992; Taylor, 1993), versus reports that some female gang members tend to be male-identified and critical rather than supportive of other girls (see Miller, 2001). Again, our findings suggest that attention to gangs' sex structures may help account for these differences.[10] Studies of girls in mixed-sex and especially all- or majority-female gangs would most likely sustain the former explanation, and studies of girls in majority-male gangs the latter.

In sum, our findings support organizational sociologists' assertion that some differences often attributed to gender or cultural differences between males and females are more appropriately attributable to group structure. They also are consistent with the observations of qualitative studies (Joe-Laidler and Hunt, 1997; Miller, 2001; Miller and Brunson, 2000; Nurge, 1998) that the sex composition of gangs, independent of sex, plays an important part in shaping the norms and activities of gangs and their members. Just as other gang research indicates the importance of considering such factors as geographic location, organizational structure and age (see Esbensen et al., 1999; Klein and Maxson, 1996), our findings highlight the significance of the gang's sex structure. Attention to this issue is an important line of inquiry for future research on gang and group delinquency.

Notes

1. Because only two young men reported membership in majority-female gangs, they were not included in the analyses that follow. Females in majority-female and all-female gangs were combined for the analysis ($N = 18$).

2. The skewness of self-report frequency data presents analysis problems. Various approaches can be used in attempts to remedy this problem, including transforming the data using the natural log, truncating at the 90th percentile (Nagin and Smith, 1990), or truncating the high-frequency responses according to some conceptual reasoning. We chose to truncate items at 12. Our premise is that commission by eighth graders of most of these acts on a monthly basis constitutes high-frequency offending. In support of this, frequency data indicated that few respondents committed more than 12 of each offense during the designated time period. We are thus able to examine these high-frequency offenders without sacrificing the detail of open-ended self-report techniques.

3. The "other" category includes a small number of Asian and American Indian youths, but is primarily composed of youths who describe themselves as biracial, multi-racial, or members of "white" ethnic groups (e.g., Italian, Irish).

4. Other research suggests that Hispanic girls are more likely to be found in "auxiliary" branches of male gangs (Curry, 1997; Lauderback et al., 1992; Quicker, 1983). Given the nature of our measure of sex composition, this is not an issue we are able to address.

5. Of the two young men in our study reporting membership in majority-female gangs, one described himself as a core member, the other as noncore.

6. Our restricted definition of gang membership may have excluded some groups that were more prosocial in nature. It is telling that even among these delinquent gangs, all-male and primarily female gangs appear to be more prosocial and less delinquent than do other gang types.

7. Nonetheless, there is also evidence that some young women choose to exclude themselves from delinquent activities they find dangerous or morally troubling—exclusionary practices by young men are but one factor in a larger set of gendered processes (see Miller, 1998, 2001; Miller and Decker, 2001).

8. An operating factor that may be involved is that males dictate who is allowed to join the gang (see Miller and Brunson, 2000), so that only those females who demonstrate "male" qualities such as "toughness" succeed in gaining access to male-dominated gangs. Control of entrée may also serve to lessen the status threat girls pose—a situation that would be different in the workplace, where male coworkers have little input into the hiring practices of the organization.

9. Another possibility that may be considered is that the interaction of boys and girls may somehow stimulate delinquency; for example, as one reviewer suggested, it may be that boys in mixed-sex gangs feel the need to "show off" more so than boys in all-male gangs, and this may account for some of the differences in delinquency involvement.

10. Likewise, although we did not examine victimization in this study, some preliminary evidence suggests that girls' social injury within gangs (see Curry, 1998) may also be shaped by the sex composition of these groups (see Joe-Laidler and Hunt, 1997; Miller and Brunson, 2000).

References

Baker, Robert L., Birgitte R. Mednick, and Linn Carothers. 1989. Association of age, gender, and ethnicity with victimization in and out of school. Youth and Society 20:320–341.

Bjerregaard, Beth and Carolyn Smith. 1993. Gender differences in gang participation, delinquency, and substance use. Journal of Quantitative Criminology 4:329–355.

Blalock, Hubert M. 1967. Toward a Theory of Minority-Group Relations. New York: John Wiley & Sons, Inc.

Blau, Peter M. 1977. Inequality and Heterogeneity: A Primitive Theory of Social Structure. New York: The Free Press.

Bowker, Lee H., Helen Shimota Gross, and Malcolm W. Klein. 1980. Female participation in delinquent gang activities. Adolescence 15:509–519.

Campbell, Anne. 1990. On the invisibility of the female delinquent peer group. Women & Criminal Justice 2:41–62.

———. 1993. Men, Women, and Aggression. New York: Basic Books.

Chiricos, Ted, Michael Hogan, and Marc Gertz. 1997. Racial composition of neighborhood and fear of crime. Criminology 35:107–132.

Connell, Robert W. 1987. Gender and Power. Stanford: Stanford University Press.

———. 1995. Masculinities. Berkeley: University of California Press.

Covington, Jeanette and Ralph B. Taylor. 1991. Fear of crime in urban residential neighborhoods: Implications of between- and within-neighborhood sources for current models. Sociological Quarterly 32:231–249.

Curry, G. David. 1997. Selected statistics on female gang involvement. Paper presented at the Fifth Joint National Conference on Gangs, Schools, and Communities, Orlando, Florida.

———. 1998. Female Gang Involvement. Journal of Research in Crime and Delinquency 35:100–118.

Decker, Scott H. 1996. Collective and normative features of gang violence. Justice Quarterly 3:243–264.

Esbensen, Finn-Aage and Elizabeth Piper Deschenes. 1998. A multi-site examination of youth gang membership: Does gender matter? Criminology 36:799–827.

Esbensen, Finn-Aage, Elizabeth Piper Deschenes, and L. Thomas Winfree, Jr. 1999. Differences between gang girls and gang boys: Results from a multi-site survey. Youth and Society 31:27–53.

Esbensen, Finn-Aage and David Huizinga. 1993. Gangs, drugs and delinquency in a survey of urban youth. Criminology 31:565–590.

Esbensen, Finn-Aage and L. Thomas Winfree, Jr. 1998. Race and gender differences between gang and non-gang youths: Results from a multi-site survey. Justice Quarterly 15:505–526.

Fagan, Jeffrey. 1989. The social organization of drug use and drug dealing among urban gangs. Criminology 27:633–667.

———. 1990. Social processes of delinquency and drug use among urban gangs. In C. Ronald Huff (ed.), Gangs in America. Newbury Park, CA: Sage.

Fairhurst, Gail Theus and B. Kay Snavely. 1983a. Majority and token minority group relationships: Power acquisition and communication. Academy of Management Review 8:292–300.

———. 1983b. A test of the social isolation of male tokens. Academy of Management Journal 26:353–361.

Fleisher, Mark S. 1998. Dead End Kids: Gang Girls and the Boys They Know. Madison: Wisconsin University Press.

Giordano, Peggy. 1978. Research note: Girls, guys, and gangs: The changing social context of female delinquency. Journal of Criminal Law and Criminology 69:126–132.

Gutek, Barbara A. 1985. Sex and the Workplace. San Francisco: Jossey-Bass.

Hagedorn, John M. and Mary Devitt. 1999. Fighting female: The social construction of female gangs. In Meda Chesney-Lind and John Hagedorn (eds.), Female Gangs in America: Essays on Girls, Gangs and Gender. Chicago: Lakeview Press.

Heikes, Joel E. 1991. When men are the minority: The case of men in nursing. Sociological Quarterly 32:89–401.

Jankowski, Martin Sánchez. 1991. Islands in the Streets: Gangs and American Urban Society. Berkeley: University of California Press.

Joe, Karen A. and Meda Chesney-Lind. 1995 'Just

every mother's angel': An analysis of gender and ethnic variations in youth gang membership. Gender & Society 9:408–430.

Joe-Laidler, Karen A. and Geoffrey Hunt. 1997. Violence and social organization in female gangs. Social Justice 24:148–169.

Kanter, Rosabeth Moss. 1977a. Some effects of proportions on group life: Skewed sex ratios and responses to token women. American Journal of Sociology 82:965–990.

———. 1977b. Men and Women of the Corporation. New York: Basic Books.

Klein, Malcolm W. 1995. The American Street Gang. New York: Oxford University Press.

Klein, Malcolm W. and Cheryl L. Maxson. 1996. Gang structures, crime patterns, and police responses. Final Report to the National Institute of Justice.

Konrad, Alison M., Susan Winter, and Barbara A. Gutek. 1992. Diversity in work group sex composition: Implications for majority and minority members. Research in the Sociology of Organizations 10:115–140.

Lauderback, David, Joy Hansen, and Dan Waldorf. 1992. 'Sisters are doin' it for themselves': A Black female gang in San Francisco. The Gang Journal 1:57–70.

Miller, Jody. 1998. Gender and victimization risk among young women in gangs. Journal of Research in Crime and Delinquency 35:429–453.

———. 2001. One of the Guys: Girls, Gangs and Gender. New York: Oxford University Press.

Miller, Jody and Rod K. Brunson. 2000. Gender dynamics in youth gangs: A comparison of males' and females' accounts. Justice Quarterly 17:419–448.

Miller, Jody and Scott H. Decker. 2001. Young women and gang violence: An examination of gender, street offending and violent victimization in gangs. Justice Quarterly 18:115–140.

Miller, Walter. 1975. Violence by Youth Gangs and Youth Groups as a Crime Problem in Major American Cities. Washington, DC: Government Printing Office.

Moore, Joan. 1991. Going Down to the Barrio: Homeboys and Homegirls in Change. Philadelphia: Temple University Press.

Nagin, Daniel S. and Douglas A. Smith. 1990. Participation in and frequency of delinquent behavior: A test for structural differences. Journal of Quantitative Criminology 6:335–365.

Nurge, Dana. 1998. Female gangs and cliques in Boston: What's the difference? Paper presented at the Annual Meeting of the American Society of Criminology, Washington D.C.

Quicker, John C. 1983. Homegirls: Characterizing Chicana Gangs. San Pedro, CA: International University Press.

South, Scott J., Charles M. Bonjean, William T. Markham and Judy Corder. 1982. Social structure and intergroup interaction: Men and women of the federal bureaucracy. American Sociological Review 47:587–599.

———. 1983. Female labor force participation and the organizational experiences of male workers. The Sociological Quarterly 24:367–380.

Spangler, Eve, Marsha A. Gordon, and Ronald M. Pipkin. 1978. Token women: An empirical test of Kanter's hypothesis. American Journal of Sociology 84:160–170.

Spergel, Irving A. and G. David Curry. 1993. The National Youth Gang Survey: A research and developmental process. In Arnold P. Goldstein and C. Ronald Huff (eds.), The Gang Intervention Handbook. Champaign, IL: Research Press.

Taylor, Carl S. 1990. Gang imperialism. In C. Ronald Huff (ed.), Gangs in America. Newbury Park: Sage Publications.

———. 1993. Girls, Gangs, Women and Drugs. East Lansing: Michigan State University Press.

Thornberry, Terence P. 1999. Personal correspondence, April 2.

Thornberry, Terence P., Marvin D. Krohn, Alan J. Lizotte and Deborah Chard-Wierschem. 1993. The role of juvenile gangs in facilitating delinquent behavior. Journal of Research in Crime and Delinquency 30:75–85.

Warr, Mark. 1996. Organization and instigation in delinquent groups. Criminology 34:11–37.

West, Candace and Sarah Fenstermaker. 1995. Doing difference. Gender & Society 9:8–37.

Williams, Christine L. 1992. The glass escalator: Hidden advantages for men in the 'female' professions. Social Problems 39:253–267.

Winfree, L. Thomas, Jr., Kathy Fuller, Teresa Vigil, and G. Larry Mays. 1992. The definition and measurement of 'gang status': Policy implications for juvenile justice. Juvenile and Family Court Journal 43:29–37.

Wordes, Madeline and Timothy S. Bynum. 1995. Policing juveniles: Is there a bias against youths of color? In Kimberly Kempf-Leonard, Carl E. Pope, and William H. Feyerherm (eds.), Minorities in Juvenile Justice. Thousand Oaks, CA: Sage Publications, Inc.

Yoder, Janice D. 1991. Rethinking tokenism: Looking beyond the numbers. Gender & Society 5:178–192.

Yoder, Janice D., Jerome Adams, and Howard T. Prince. 1983. The price of a token. Journal of Political and Military Sociology 11:325–337. ✦

Section IV

Gangs, Violence, and Drugs

Chapter 19
Membership in Youth Gangs and Involvement in Serious and Violent Offending

Terence P. Thornberry

Drawing from his own and several additional longitudinal studies, Thornberry reviews the current state of knowledge concerning the significant relationship between youth gang membership and participation in serious and violent crime. He highlights three important findings: First, gang members are not only disproportionately involved in offending, but they are also responsible for the majority of those serious and violent acts committed by adolescents. Second, gang membership has a facilitation effect on delinquency. That is, youths have higher rates of serious and violent offending while they are active gang members than they do prior to or after they are gang-involved. Finally, gang youths' associations with delinquent peers cannot fully account for this relationship between gang membership and offending. Instead, there is something unique about gang membership itself that increases youths' participation in serious and violent crime. As Thornberry concludes, these findings indicate the importance of focusing on gang youths as targets for prevention and intervention in order to reduce crime.

Reprinted from: R. Loeber and D. P. Farrington (eds.), *Serious and Violent Juvenile Offenders*, pp. 147–166. Copyright © 1998 by Sage Publications, Inc. Reprinted by permission.

The Contribution of Gang Members to the Volume of Delinquency

Prior studies have demonstrated that gang members are significantly more involved in delinquency, especially serious delinquency, than are nonmembers. Despite the uniformity of this finding, we have surprisingly few estimates of the proportion of all delinquent or criminal acts for which gang members are responsible. That is, although we know that gang members have higher rates of offending than do nonmembers, we do not know how much of the total amount of crime is attributable to them. This is an important issue: If gang members are responsible for a very large proportion of all offenses, effective gang intervention may be a necessary ingredient in efforts to reduce the overall amount of crime in society.

The most straightforward way of addressing this analytic issue is to compare the proportion of gang members in the population with their proportionate share of the number of crimes reported. For example, if gang members represent 10 percent of the population we would expect them to be responsible for approximately 10 percent of the crimes committed, if there were *no relationship* between gang membership and criminal involvement. To the extent that their proportionate share of crimes exceeds 10 percent, one can conclude that they are disproportionately contributing to the volume of crime in society. Results from four studies are presented in Table 19.1.

Fagan (1990) analyzed a general adolescent sample by combining a cluster sample of high school students and a "snowball" sample of dropouts in San Diego, Los Angeles, and Chicago. He found the prevalence of gang membership to be 23 percent during the year prior to the interview. Although only 23 percent of the population, gang members account for 67 percent of felony assaults, 66 percent of minor assaults, and 66 percent of robberies during that same time period. Fagan reported similar percentages for various forms of theft, ranging from 56 percent of minor thefts to 72 percent of felony thefts. Gang members are also disproportionately involved in weapons offenses, illegal services, drug use, and drug sales.

Thornberry (1996) examined cumulative measures of gang membership and self-reported delinquency in the Rochester Youth Development Study. Thirty percent of the Rochester sample reported being a member of a street gang prior to the end of high school. Although slightly less than one-third of the population, gang members accounted for two-thirds of the acts of general delinquency that were self-reported over a 4-year period, covering the junior high school and high school years. These gang members were also responsible for 86 percent of the serious acts of delinquency, 68 percent of the violent acts of delinquency, and 70 percent of the drug sales that were reported. Gang members, as compared to their share in the population, also had much higher rates of moderate and minor delinquency, property offenses, public disorder offenses, and alcohol and drug use.

Battin, Hill, Hawkins, Catalano, and Abbott (1996) report very similar patterns of results for gang members in the Seattle Social Development Project. Although gang members comprised only 15 percent of the total sample, they accounted for 85 percent of the robberies that were committed between Grades 7 and 12. They also accounted for at least 50 percent of all the other forms of delinquency measured in that project. These percentages ranged from 51 percent for minor assault to 62 percent for drug selling.

Using data from the Denver Youth Survey, Huizinga (1997) reported very similar results. Between 1988 and 1992, 14 percent of the Denver sample were gang members. They [were] responsible for 79 percent of the acts of serious violence, 71 percent of serious property offenses, and 87 percent of drug sales, however. They [were] also disproportionately involved in public disorder offenses, alcohol use, and marijuana use.[1]

Table 19.1
Percentage of Delinquent Acts Committed by Gang Members, Results From Four Projects

Three-City Gang Study, Fagan (1990)	%	Denver Youth Survey, Huizinga (1997)	%
Prevalence of gang membership (1 year)	23	**Cumulative prevalence of gang membership (Waves 1–5)**	14
Percentage of offenses		**Cumulative percentage of delinquent acts**	
Felony assault	67	Serious violence	79
Minor assault	66	Serious property	71
Robbery	66	Public disorder	44
Felony theft	72	Alcohol use	42
Minor theft	56	Marijuana use	53
Extortion	60	Drug sales	87
Property damage	61		
Weapons	53		
Illegal services	70		
Alcohol use	59		
Drug use	55		
Drug sales	71		
Rochester Youth Development Study, Thornberry (1996)	%	Seattle Social Development Project, Battin, Hill, Hawkins, Catalano, and Abbott (1996)	%
Cumulative prevalence of gang membership (Waves 1–9)	30	**Cumulative prevalence of gang membership (Grades 7–12)**	15
Cumulative percentage of delinquent acts		**Cumulative percentage of delinquent acts**	
General delinquency	65	Minor assault	51
Serious	86	Robbery	85
Moderate	67	Felony theft	54
Minor	59	Minor theft	53
Violent	68	Damaged property	59
Property	68	Drug selling	62
Street	64	General delinquency	58
Public disorder	60		
Alcohol use	63		
Drug use	61		
Drug sales	70		

The results of these studies confirm the finding of the many earlier studies that gang members have higher rates of involvement in delinquency than do non-gang members. They go beyond those results, however, to indicate that gang members, although representing a minority of the overall population, are responsible for the majority of the delinquent acts. These two findings are not duplicative. The first observation, that gang members are significantly more likely to be involved in delinquency than are non-gang members, can hold even if the second observation does not. That is, gang members could be responsible for only slightly more delinquent acts than their proportionate share in the population and still be significantly different from non-gang members. The results in these studies suggest, however, that this is not the case. Not only are gang members significantly different from non-gang members, they also account for the lion's share of all delinquent acts that are reported. Also, the proportionate contribution of gang members to delinquency is most pronounced for the more serious forms of delinquency. That is, gang members account for a very large proportion of felony offenses, serious offenses, violent offenses, and drug sales. Their contribution to more minor forms of delinquency, although still large, is somewhat muted.

The Facilitation Effect of Gang Membership on Delinquency

The previous section has shown that gang members have higher rates of delinquency than non-gang members and also that gang members account for a disproportionate share of the crime problem relative to their share of the population. Those analyses, however, do not identify the processes by which this relationship is brought about.

Thornberry et al. (1993) have identified three models that could account for this relationship. The first is a social selection model. It suggests that gangs recruit or attract individuals who are already involved in delinquency and violence. If this is the case, then prior to periods of active gang membership, gang members should be more heavily involved in delinquency and violence than are non-gang members. The second model is a facilitation model. In this model, the norms and group processes of the gang are thought to facilitate involve-ment in delinquency and violence. If this model is accurate, then gang members would not be particularly different from nonmembers prior to or after their periods of active gang membership; during that period, however, they would be much more extensively involved in delinquency and violence. The third model is a mixed model. It suggests that both selection and facilitation effects are at work.

In their empirical analysis, limited to the male respondents in the Rochester Youth Development Study, Thornberry et al. (1993) report strong support for the facilitation model and virtually no support for the selection model:

> Perhaps the strongest support for the social facilitation model is found in the analysis of the type of behavior most often associated with gangs—crimes against the person. . . . Gang members have higher rates of person offenses only when they are active gang members. Of particular interest is the drop-off in the rate of person crimes once boys leave the gang. The means for crimes against the person for boys when they are active members of the gang are, by and large, at least twice as high as when they are not. Clearly, being in the gang is generative of violent behavior among these boys. (pp. 80–81)

A gang facilitation effect was also observed for general delinquency, drug sales, and to a somewhat lesser extent drug use. It was not, however, observed for property offenses.

Since the publication of these findings, several studies have replicated the facilitation effect that gang membership has on delinquency. Esbensen and Huizinga (1993) report that "prevalence rates for each type of [delinquent] behavior are highest during the gang member's year of actual gang membership" (p. 577). They also report some elevation in the prevalence of delinquency in the year prior to joining a gang. Thus, the results from the Denver Youth Survey offer support for a mixed model, combining both selection and facilitation models.

Hill, Howell, Hawkins, and Battin (1996) examined this issue in the Seattle Social Development Project. For violent delinquency their results are quite similar to those reported by Thornberry et al. (1993). Mean levels of violence are particularly elevated during the years of active gang membership. Violent delinquency is only slightly elevated in the year prior to joining a gang and reduces quite substantially in the years following active gang membership. With the exception of drug sales, similar findings are observed for other types of delinquency. During periods of active gang membership, involvement in drug sales is quite high (Hill et al., 1996). Unlike other forms of delinquency, however, involvement in drug sales remains high after the individual leaves the gang. This finding has also been observed in more recent analyses of the Rochester Youth Development Study data (Bjerregaard & Lizotte, 1995; Lizotte, Howard, Krohn, & Thornberry, 1997).

The most recent investigation of this issue has been conducted in the Montreal longitudinal study by Tremblay (personal communication, November 1996). The Montreal study is based on 1,034 boys who attended kindergarten in 1984 in one of 53 low socioeconomic status schools in Montreal. The screening criteria "created a homogeneous low socioeconomic status, white, French-speaking sample" (Tremblay, Pihl, Vitaro, & Dobkin, 1994, p. 733). In replicating the study by Thornberry et al. (1993), Tremblay used self-reported data on gang membership and on delinquency and drug use for the 3-year period when the respondents were 14, 15, and 16 years of age.

The results for violent offenses are consistent with the facilitation model. Violent offending is higher during the year(s) of gang membership than either prior to or following active membership. Prior to joining the gang, gang members have somewhat higher rates of violent offending than do nonmembers, but the predominant change in behavior patterns occurs during periods of active gang membership. A similar pattern is observed for general delinquency and property crimes. As reported by Hill et al. (1996) and Bjerregaard and Lizotte (1995), drug selling exhibits a somewhat different pattern. Involvement in drug sales increases during periods of gang membership, and it remains high after the youth leaves the gang.

The findings by Tremblay are important for several reasons. Prior studies of the facilitation effect were conducted in American cities and based on samples of gang members that were predominantly African American or Hispanic. Tremblay shows very similar effects in a large Canadian city with an exclusively white, French-speaking sample. The similarity of results suggests that gang processes may be quite similar in diverse settings.

Controlling for Risk Factors

Gang members have higher rates of delinquency, especially violent delinquency, when they are active gang members, and it appears that gang membership facilitates this increase. It is possible, however, that gang members have elevated rates of violence, not because of a gang facilitation effect but because of the accumulation of risk in their backgrounds. . . . [G]ang members have substantial deficits in many social and psychological domains. As a result, it may not be gang membership that brings about the observed increase in violence; the increase may instead be caused by risk factors that are related both to gang membership and to violent behavior. Indeed, Le Blanc and Lanctot (in press) claim that Thornberry et al.'s (1993) conclusion that there is a gang facilitation effect is premature: "We tend to favor the enhancement causal model. The delinquent with lower self- and social control joins a gang, and the group activates its offending. . . . To thoroughly verify the nature of the causal role of the gang longitudinal data sets should be reanalyzed controlling for self- and social control characteristics of individuals" (p. 13).

To begin examining this possibility, we further examine data from the Rochester Youth Development Study.[2] Involvement in violent delinquency is grouped into the same three annual periods analyzed in Thornberry et al. (1993) and then regressed on a dummy variable indicating whether the subject was a gang member during that year and a variety of prior risk factors (Table 19.2). The inclusion of the dummy variable allows us to assess the facilitative effect of active gang membership on violent behavior net of the impact of antecedent variables. The antecedent variables are drawn from different domains and are among the strongest risk factors for gang membership . . . and for violence. . . . The specific risk factors that are included are family poverty level, parental supervision, commitment to school, experiencing negative life events, prior involvement in violence, and associating with delinquent peers. The risk factors are measured at the wave prior to the year of gang membership.[3] The analysis is limited to males because of the relatively small number of female gang members at later waves.

The results in Table 19.2 suggest that the relationship between gang membership and concurrent involvement in violent delinquency is not spurious. Even when family poverty level, parental supervision, commitment to school, experiencing negative life events, prior involvement in violence, and associating with delinquent peers are held constant, gang membership exerts a strong impact on the incidence of violent behavior at all 3 years.[4] In the equation for Year 1, for example, the standardized coefficient for gang membership is .26, approximately the same magnitude of coefficients observed for prior violence (.18) and for association with delinquent peers (.32), generally two of the strongest predictors of delinquent behavior (see Thornberry & Krohn, 1997). Indeed, across the years, gang membership has the largest impact on violent behavior.

Summary

Several recent longitudinal studies provide rather consistent support for the facilitation effect described by Thornberry et al. (1993). Rates of delinquency, especially violent delinquency and drug sales, are particularly high during periods of active gang membership. There is evidence of some selection effect in that gang members have somewhat higher rates of involvement in delinquency prior to joining the gang, but this effect is less consistent and less powerful than the facilitation effect. Also, there tends to be a general drop-off in delinquency following the period of gang membership, with the notable exception of drug sales. In that case, the gangs appear both to facilitate entry into drug-selling markets and to facilitate continuation of involvement in those markets even after the individual leaves the gang. Finally, the impact of gang membership on concurrent involvement in violent delinquency was examined when major risk factors are held constant. Based on results from the Rochester Youth Development Study, the gang exerts a strong facilitative effect on violent behavior even when prior involvement in violence and several important risk factors are controlled. The pattern of results reported here, using a complementary methodology, is concordant with the portrait of gang behavior that is typically presented in the ethnographic literature (e.g., Hagedorn, 1988; Klein, 1995).

Gangs and Delinquent Peer Groups

One of the most consistent correlates of delinquency is association with delinquent peers (Thornberry & Krohn, 1997). Because youth gangs obviously constitute one form of a delinquent peer group, it is not clear whether the effects of gang membership described in this chapter are a function of gang membership or simply a function of association with delinquent peers.

Several gang researchers suggest that delinquent peer groups and gangs are qualitatively different. For example, Joan Moore (1991) has concluded that "gangs are no longer just at the rowdy end of the continuum of local adolescent groups—they are now really outside the continuum" (p. 132). Klein (1995) makes a similar point: "Street gangs are something special, something qualitatively different from other groups and from other categories of law breakers" (p. 197). Although these and other gang researchers view gangs as qualitatively different, there is virtually no quantitative research investigating this hypothesis. Because of that, several recent longitudinal studies have begun to investigate this issue.

Table 19.2
Predicting the Incidence of
Self-Reported Violence, Rochester
Youth Development Study, Males Only
(standardized OLS regression coefficients)

Risk Factor	Self-Reported Violence (logged)		
	Year 1[a]	Year 2[b]	Year 3[c]
Gang membership	.26***	.34***	.32***
Family poverty level	.04	−.06	.00
Parental supervision	−.10**	−.06	.01
Commitment to school	−.01	−.04	.02
Negative life events	.13***	.15***	.20***
Prior violence	.18***	.08*	.13**
Delinquent peers	.32***	.13**	.16***
R^2	.46	.31	.28
N	512	487	430

[a]Year 1 violence combines data from Waves 2 and 3; risk factors are from Wave 2.
[b]Year 2 violence combines data from Waves 4 and 5; risk factors are from Wave 3.
[c]Year 3 violence combines data from Waves 6 and 7; risk factors are from Wave 5.
*p < .05.   **p < .01.   ***p < .001.

In the Rochester Youth Development Study, we classified the male respondents into five groups at each interview wave.[5] One group consists of active gang members at that wave. Respondents who were not gang members were divided into quartiles based on their score on a scale measuring their association with delinquent peers, also at that wave. The most important comparison concerns the non-gang members in the highest quartile (those with the greatest number of delinquent peers) and the gang members. If Moore and Klein are correct, gang members will have substantially higher rates of delinquency than will the non-gang members who associate with highly delinquent peer groups. If, on the other hand, gangs are simply another variant of highly delinquent peer groups, these two groups should not differ in terms of their delinquency.

Table 19.3 presents results for the logged incidence of violent delinquency. At all eight waves, gang members report committing violent offenses at significantly higher rates than do the nonmembers who associate with highly delinquent peer groups. For example, at Wave 2 the mean number of violent offenses for the gang members is 1.44 as compared to a mean of .87 for the nonmembers who associate with highly delinquent peers. There are even larger differences at the later waves: At Wave 9 the mean for the nonmembers who associate with highly delinquent peer groups is .27, whereas the mean for the gang members is 1.05. All of the differences between the nonmembers in the highly delinquent peer

group and the gang members are statistically significant.[6]

Battin, Hill, Hawkins, et al. (1996) examined this issue with Seattle data. They created three groups: (a) those youth who were ever gang members from the 7th through the 12th grades, (b) those youth who were members of non-gang law-violating youth groups, and (c) those who were neither. To establish the second group, they selected those youth who were never in a gang but for whom the majority of their three best friends had been arrested or who had done things to get them into trouble with the police. They then calculated the mean incidence of delinquency that each group reported committing between the 7th and 12th grades.

The results are quite similar to those in the Rochester study. Gang members reported substantially higher levels of involvement in all the offense types that were examined: minor assault, robbery, felony theft, minor theft, property damage, drug selling, and general delinquency. For minor assault, for example, the mean number of offenses reported by the gang members is 45.9 as compared to 14.1 for members of the law-violating youth groups. The mean number of robberies reported by gang members is 2.0, but it is only 0.2 for members of the nongang law-violating youth groups.

Finally, Huizinga (1996) examined this topic using data from the Denver Youth Survey, in which "youth aged 14–19 in 1991 were classified into four groups—those who had low, medium, and high involvement with delinquent friends, and those who were gang members" (p. 1). For both males

Table 19.3
Mean Logged Incidence of Self-Reported Violent Delinquency by Gang Membership and by Level of Delinquent Peer Groups, Rochester Youth Development Study, Males Only

| Interview Wave | Non-Gang Members | | | | Gang Members |
	Low Delinquent Peers	Moderately Low Delinquent Peers	Moderately High Delinquent Peers	High Delinquent Peers	
2	.11	.17	.38	.87	1.44*
3	.05	.13	.24	.58	1.73*
4	.05	.08	.25	.64	1.44*
5	.04	.09	.22	.50	1.29*
6	.04	.05	.15	.51	1.26*
7	.03	.09	.17	.38	1.11*
8	.01	.11	.22	.32	1.57*
9	.02	.03	.15	.27	1.05*

*$p < .05$ (one-tailed test) between the last two groups; non-gang members with high delinquent peers versus gang members.

and females, he observed higher levels of serious assaults and total assaults for the gang members as compared to the nonmembers who had highly delinquent peers. For example, among the males, 72 percent of the gang members reported involvement in serious assault, whereas only 20 percent of the nonmembers with highly delinquent peers did so. For the females, 72 percent of the gang members reported involvement in serious assault, and only 13 percent of the nonmembers with highly delinquent peers did so.

Battin, Hill, Hawkins, et al. (1996) tested this hypothesis from a causal modeling perspective. They used measures of association with delinquent peers and of gang membership to predict various forms of delinquent activity. Even when association with delinquent peers is included in the equation, the effect of gang membership is sizable and significant. This model was tested for a variety of outcomes—violence, theft, drug use, and drug selling, and for both self-reported and court-reported data—with similar results.

In line with the predictions by Klein and Moore, these three recent longitudinal studies find that gang membership appears to be qualitatively different from associating with delinquent peers in terms of its impact on delinquent behavior. Even when compared to nonmembers who associate with highly delinquent peer groups, gang members have substantially higher rates of delinquency. . . .

Discussion

The findings reported here, especially in the context of recent trend data, provide cause for great concern. Gang members are clearly major contributors to the level of serious and violent crime in American society—especially while they are active gang members. Moreover, Klein (1995), Curry et al. (1996a, 1996b), and the National Youth Gang Center (1997) report a massive expansion of gangs in recent years. As recently as the mid-1980s, gangs were found in relatively few, and generally very large, cities. By the mid-1990s, however, gangs have spread to virtually all large and middle-sized cities and to many smaller cities and towns. Given the facilitation effect that gangs appear to have on violent and serious delinquency, it is little wonder that the overall rate of these crimes for youth has increased so sharply during the past 10 years.

These findings highlight the importance of focusing on youth gangs as important targets for prevention and treatment programs. If gang members are indeed responsible for the majority of serious and violent delinquent acts, as suggested by all studies that have examined this topic, then it is unlikely that we will be successful in reducing the overall rate of serious delinquency unless we can bring gangs under control. That will not be an easy task, however.

Recent surveys to identify prevention programs that effectively reduce delinquency uniformly report that we have few, if any, truly effective gang prevention and suppression programs. In his masterful review of the scene, Klein (1995) has concluded that "the simple fact is that much of our local response and most of our state and federal responses to gang problems are way off base—conceptually misguided, poorly implemented, halfheartedly pursued" (p. 19). The conclusions reached by Spergel (1995), Howell (1995, 1998), and others are hardly more encouraging. Effectively intervening in street gangs has proven remarkably difficult.

It seems, therefore, that one of the highest priorities that we can have in our effort to reduce the level of serious and violent delinquency in American society is to develop effective intervention programs for street gangs. This is, and will be, a most difficult challenge (see Howell, 1998). It will not be done overnight and will require a carefully thought-out, long-term commitment to a "strategy of search" (see Thornberry, 1976). That is, potentially effective programs will have to be faithfully implemented and very carefully evaluated in a slow, iterative process that might eventually lead to the identification of effective programs. It is unlikely that any other approach will succeed. Yet the data reviewed in this chapter suggest the centrality of gangs to the production of serious and violent delinquency, and therefore the centrality of gang prevention to the reduction of serious and violent delinquency.

Author's Note

This study was prepared under Grant 86-JN-CX-0007 (S-3) from the Office of Juvenile Justice and Delinquency Prevention, Office of Justice Programs, U.S. Department of Justice; Grant 5 R01 DA05512-02 from the National Institute on Drug Abuse; and Grant SES-8912274 from the National Science Foundation. I would like to thank Kim

Tobin-Carambia for her assistance in developing this chapter. I would also like to thank Darnell F. Hawkins, James C. Howell, Malcolm W. Klein, Alan J. Lizotte, Walter B. Miller, and Carolyn A. Smith for helpful comments on earlier drafts.

Notes

1. Because cumulative measures were used in the Rochester, Seattle, and Denver analyses, some of the offenses for which the gang members are responsible were committed either prior to or subsequent to periods of active gang membership. Because of the temporal patterning of membership and offending, however (see following section), it is likely that many of these offenses were committed while the gang members were actively involved in the gang.

2. I would like to thank David Farrington also for suggesting this line of analysis.

3. There is some overlap between risk factors and gang membership in the analysis for Year 1 because, with the exception of prior violence, the risk factors are measured at Wave 2 and gang membership combines data from Waves 2 and 3. This was unavoidable as not all risk factors were measured at Wave 1.

4. Equations also were estimated excluding association with delinquent peers because of the conceptual and empirical overlap between delinquent peers and gang membership. There were no substantive changes in the results when this was done.

5. These data are based only on males because of the relatively low base rate of female gang membership at later waves.

6. We also restricted the nonmembers to those in the top decile on the delinquent peer measure and to the top n respondents, where n is equal to the number of gang members at the particular wave. Differences between gang members and nonmembers are still large and statistically significant.

References

Battin, S., K. G. Hill, J. D. Hawkins, R. F. Catalano and R. Abbott. 1996. "Testing Gang Membership and Association With Antisocial Peers as Independent Predictors of Antisocial Behavior: Gang Members Compared to Non-gang Members of Law-violating Youth Groups." Paper presented at the annual meeting of the American Society of Criminology, Chicago.

Bjerregaard, B., and A. J. Lizotte. 1995. "Gun Ownership and Gang Membership." *Journal of Criminal Law and Criminology* 86:37–58.

Curry, G. D., R. A. Ball and S. H. Decker. 1996a.

"Estimating the National Scope of Gang Crime From Law Enforcement Data." *Research in Brief*. Washington, D.C.: National Institute of Justice.

Curry, G. D., R. A. Ball and S. H. Decker. 1996b. "Estimating the National Scope of Gang Crime From Law Enforcement Data." Pp. 266–275 in *Gangs in America*, 2nd Edition, edited by C. R. Huff. Thousand Oaks, CA: Sage Publications.

Esbensen, F. and D. Huizinga. 1993. "Gangs, Drugs, and Delinquency in a Survey of Urban Youth." *Criminology* 31:565–589.

Fagan, J. 1990. "Social Processes of Delinquency and Drug Use Among Urban Gangs." Pp. 183–219 in *Gangs in America*, edited by C. Ronald Huff. Newbury Park, CA: Sage Publications.

Hagedorn, John M. 1988. *People and Folks: Gangs, Crime and The Underclass in a Rustbelt City*. Chicago: Lake View Press.

Hill, K. G., J. C. Howell, J. D. Hawkins and S. R. Battin. 1996. "Risk Factors in Childhood for Adolescent Gang Membership: Results from the Seattle Social Development Project." Manuscript under review.

Howell, J. C., ed. 1995. *Guide for Implementing the Comprehensive Strategy for Serious, Violent and Chronic Juvenile Offenders*. Washington, D.C.: U.S. Department of Justice, Office of Juvenile Justice and Delinquency Prevention.

Howell, J. C. 1998. "Promising Programs for Youth Gang Violence Prevention and Intervention." Pp. 284–312 in *Serious and Violent Juvenile Offenders: Risk Factors and Successful Interventions*, edited by R. Loeber and D. Farrington. Thousand Oaks, CA: Sage Publications.

Huizinga, D. H. 1996. *The Influence of Delinquent Peers, Gangs and Co-offending on Violence*. Fact sheet prepared for the U.S. Department of Justice, Office of Juvenile Justice and Delinquency Prevention.

———. 1997. "Gangs and the Volume of Crime." Paper presented at the annual meeting of the Western Society of Criminology, Honolulu, HI.

Klein, M. W. 1995. *The American Street Gang: Its Nature, Prevalence and Control*. New York: Oxford University Press.

Le Blanc, M. and N. Lanctot. In press. "Social and Psychological Characteristics of Gang Members According to the Gang Structure and Its Subcultural and Ethnic Makeup." *Journal of Gang Research*.

Lizotte, A. J., G. J. Howard, M. D. Krohn and T. P. Thornberry. 1997. "Patterns of Carrying Firearms Among Juveniles." *Valparaiso University Law Review* 31:375–393.

Moore, J. 1991. *Going Down to the Barrio: Homeboys and Homegirls in Change*. Philadelphia: Temple University Press.

National Youth Gang Center. 1997. *The 1995 National Youth Gang Survey*. Washington, D.C.:

U.S. Department of Justice, Office of Juvenile Justice and Delinquency Prevention.

Spergel, I. A. 1995. *The Youth Gang Problem: A Community Approach.* New York: Oxford University Press.

Thornberry, T. P. 1976. "The Once and Future Promise of the Rehabilitative Idea." *Journal of Criminal Law and Criminology* 67:117–122.

———. 1996. *The Contribution of Gang Members to the Volume of Delinquency.* Fact sheet prepared for the U.S. Department of Justice, Office of Juvenile Justice and Delinquency Prevention.

Thornberry, T. P. and M. D. Krohn. 1997. "Peers, Drug Use and Delinquency." Pp. 218–233 in *Handbook of Antisocial Behavior,* edited by D. Stoff, J. Breiling and J. D. Maser. New York: John Wiley.

Thornberry, T. P., M. D. Krohn, A. J. Lizotte and D. Chard-Wierschem. 1993. "The Role of Juvenile Gangs in Facilitating Delinquent Behavior." *Journal of Research in Crime and Delinquency* 30:75–85.

Tremblay, R. E. 1996. Personal communication, November.

Tremblay, R. E., R. O. Pihl, F. Vitaro and P. L. Dobkin. 1994. "Predicting Early Onset of Male Antisocial Behavior From Preschool Behavior." *Archives of General Psychiatry* 51:732–739. ✦

Chapter 20
Gang Involvement and Delinquency in a Middle School Population

G. David Curry, Scott H. Decker, and Arlen Egley Jr.

Sources of street-gang data are numerous: youth surveys and interviews, police records, street observations and ethnography, correctional records, school and family reports, and the media. None yield identical findings, yet each has advantages for selected purposes. We need to be able to assess the value of each data source. In this study, the authors look at two critical issues, level of gang involvement and level of delinquency involvement. They do this by comparing youth self-reports and independently recorded data from court records, which principally reflect arrests. The data reveal the expected concordance between levels of gang and delinquency involvement, a pattern revealed in both sources of data.

The relationship between self-reported gang membership and self-reported delinquency has been widely reported by researchers and repeatedly substantiated by empirical research (Spergel, 1990). This body of research has consistently found a positive correlation between self-reported gang membership and self-reported delinquency (Battin, Hill, Abbott, Catalano, & Hawkins, 1998; Esbensen & Huizinga, 1993; Esbensen & Winfree, 1998; Fagan, 1990;

Reprinted from: G. David Curry, Scott H. Decker, and Arlen Egley Jr. "Gang Involvement and Delinquency in a Middle School Population." *Justice Quarterly* 19(2): 275–292. Copyright © 2002 by Academy of Criminal Justice Sciences. Reprinted with permission of the Academy of Criminal Justice Sciences.

Howell, 1994; Huff, 1996; Thornberry, Thornberry, Krohn, Lizotte, & Chard-Wierschem, 1993). Similarly, the relationship between self-reported delinquency and officially recorded delinquency (Elliott, Huizinga, & Morse 1987; Farrington, 1989; Hartstone & Hansen, 1984; Hawkins et al., 1998) has been systematically explored. The relationship between gang membership and officially recorded delinquency has not been studied as thoroughly, however.

In the past decade, a considerable body of new evidence has been produced in support of this relationship. Using samples of high school students and dropouts from Chicago, Los Angeles, and San Diego, Fagan (1989, 1990) found that youths who identified themselves as gang members had higher levels of self-reported delinquent behavior than did their nongang counterparts. From the longitudinal Denver Youth Survey, Esbensen and Huizinga (1993) concluded that gang members self-report two to three times as much delinquency as do nongang members. In a comparable longitudinal study for a representative sample of Rochester, New York, youths, Thornberry et al. (1993) reported that gang-involved youths were significantly more likely to report involvement in violence and other forms of delinquency. By following youths over time, the Rochester researchers revealed that gang membership is a transitional process, with delinquent activity increasing during periods of self-reported gang membership and declining afterward. In another analysis of the Rochester data, Bjerregaard and Lizotte (1995) found that self-reported gang members were twice as likely to report carrying firearms and three times as likely to report selling drugs.

Using longitudinal data on a sample of Seattle youths, Battin et al. (1998) discovered that gang members reported significantly more acts of violence and general delinquency than did nongang members. The researchers determined that differences in self-reported delinquency were also reflected in juvenile court reports of delinquency. In addition, they controlled for differences in having delinquent friends to reveal that gang membership is associated with delinquency above and beyond the propensity to have delinquent friends (see also, Thornberry, 1998).

Despite this research, several important questions remain about the relationship between gang membership and delinquency. The first has to do with levels of membership. It is clear that operationalizing gang membership as a simple dichotomy (i.e., member, nonmember) has many virtues from a measurement standpoint. However, this parsimony may miss important substantive variation in *levels* of membership, especially with younger adolescents, whose membership may be more transitory and reflect patterns of age-graded friendships. For middle school adolescents (ages 12–14), their involvement in gangs may reflect their diverse constellation of friends, some of whom may be gang members and some of whom may not (Decker & Van Winkle, 1996; Hagedorn, 1998). Thus, it is possible to be *involved* in gang activities as a consequence of one's friendships with gang members but not claim membership.

Although previous studies uncovered a relationship between self-reported gang membership and delinquency, research has yet to examine whether the same relationship holds for those who are involved with gang members without claiming membership themselves. We hypothesize that, given gang members' higher levels of involvement in crime, associating with gang members has a stronger effect on self-reported involvement in crime than associating with delinquent nongang peers would have. The longitudinal work of Battin et al. (1998) and Thornberry et al. (1993) provide the basis for our speculation in this regard. This is one of the key issues this article examines. As dependent variables, we used both self-reported and official measures of delinquency. It is a well-established principle in measurement theory that the strongest indication of external validity occurs when two measures of the same trait from different measurement systems are related (Campbell & Fiske, 1959). Measuring the level of delinquency by both self-reports and official records provides such a test and follows Battin et al.'s (1998) practice. In this article, we use referral to juvenile court as the measure of official involvement in delinquency.

Gang Problems in St. Louis

The most recent gang problem in St. Louis emerged in the late 1980s and the early 1990s. As with many U.S. cities, St. Louis had been the scene of reported gang problems during other periods dating back

more than a century. In the 19th century, gangs of German and Irish youths fought in neighborhoods just north of what was then downtown. In his study of gangs in early 20th-century Chicago, Thrasher (1927) referred to gangs existing at that time in St. Louis. In the years following World War II, the city experienced the first appearance of African American gangs, with gangs battling for the same neighborhoods as their Euro-American predecessors and distinguishing their rivalries with the same colors of blue and red. Still, when W. Miller (1975) studied St. Louis in the 1970s, he concluded that the city did not have a gang crime problem. By the late 1980s, St. Louis was identified by a national study (Spergel & Curry, 1993) as having an "emerging" gang problem. By 1991, St. Louis made its first contribution to a national tabulation of gang statistics. In that year, the St. Louis Police Department reported 33 gangs and 8 gang homicides. During the mid-1990s, gang-related homicides had grown to be a significant portion of all homicides in St. Louis (Rosenfeld, Bray, & Egley, 1999). By this time, Decker and Van Winkle (1996) had undertaken their field study of 99 active gang members that would reveal gangs in St. Louis to be disorganized yet extremely violent.

The Structure of Gangs and Patterns of Gang Involvement

Theoretical patterns of gang involvement are closely related to theories about gang structure. Hypothetical models of gang structure range from highly structured, hierarchical organizations to loosely structured manifestations of collective behavior. At one end of this continuum are the observations of Sánchez-Jankowski (1991), who portrayed gangs as hierarchical organizations with clearly established leaders and rational goals and actions. Taylor (1990) described some of the gangs he found in Detroit similarly and labeled them "corporate" gangs. Padilla (1992) examined the transformation of a Chicago youth gang into a more rationally organized and efficient drug-selling enterprise.

These highly structured gangs are in contrast to the gangs observed by other researchers. For Thrasher (1927, p. 202), the gang was, above all, a primary group based on informality and face-to-face association. The conflict gangs observed by Spergel

(1964) were neither "permanent" nor "stable." The gangs that Short and Strodtbeck (1965, p. 196) studied were "very fluid," and in the view of the members interviewed by Suttles (1968, p. 176), the gang was a "happy coincidence" and "spontaneous cohesion." More recently, Hagedorn (1998) depicted Milwaukee gangs as dynamic, age-graded subgroups in which the informal patterns of association varied over time. Participation in and the level of organization of St. Louis gangs were portrayed by Decker (1996) as increasing and decreasing in conjunction with patterns of violence. Decker referred to gangs as forms of collective behavior, rather than complex organizations. In a study of organizational structure in four gangs identified by the police as potential organized crime groups in Chicago and San Diego, Decker, Bynum and Weisel (1998) found that only one of the gangs displayed any kind of sustained organizational structure, and that gang fell short of what could be called "organized crime."

Different theoretical processes of how youths become gang members are associated with the highly organized and the loosely organized perspectives of gang organization. Rationally organized gangs with well-defined structures suggest rational processes for admitting or recruiting members. As Sánchez-Jankowski (1991) reported, becoming a member of a well-organized gang required two explicit decisions. The individual decided to become a member, and the gang decided to permit membership. Gang members joined gangs primarily for material gain but also for recreation and commitment to community. On the other side of the process, gangs recruited members as needed to strengthen existing resources or to gain organizational control of new resources. In this model, the line between a member and a nonmember was distinct.

Under the theoretical model of loosely organized gangs, the nature of membership is quite different. From Spergel's (1964), research in New York, "Identification as a member of a gang . . . was not a stable, permanent, once-and-for-all social fact (p. 66). . . . One youngster might, for a relatively short period of time, 'hang around' a group and be recognized almost immediately as a member of that group. Another individual would be present a great deal of the time with the group and be regarded clearly as a non-member or as a member of another group" (pp. 66–67). Vigil (1988), for Los Angeles barrio gangs, and Decker and Van Winkle (1996, p. 67), for emerging St. Louis gangs, portrayed the process of joining a gang as gradual, sometimes taking years. According to Decker and Van Winkle (p. 68), "On average, members of our sample heard about their gang while they were 12, started hanging out with gang members at 13, and joined before their 14th birthday. This suggests a gradual process of affiliation rather than one of active recruitment." From her ethnographic study of female gang members in Columbus, Ohio, and St. Louis, J. Miller (2001) reached a similar conclusion of gradual gang involvement for girls.

The model of loosely organized gangs with gradual processes of affiliation is conducive to the identification of different levels of gang membership. Thrasher (1927) spoke of the inner circle, the rank and file, and fringe members. Vigil (1988) classified members as regular, peripheral, and temporary. Hagedorn (1998, p. 90) noted a division between "main groups" and "wanna be's" in Milwaukee gangs, but added, "A 'wanna be' this week may be in the 'main group' next week."

How youths come to be involved in gangs has important implications for variation in gang behavior. When gangs are highly organized and membership is well defined, it would be expected that one would find members and nonmembers. When gangs are loosely structured manifestations of collective behavior, one should find, in addition to members and nonmembers, a population of youths who are neither completely members nor nonmembers, but something in between. In this study of St. Louis, where gangs have been observed to be loosely organized, it should be possible to identify youths with differential levels of gang involvement somewhere short of gang membership. In an earlier analysis, Decker and Curry (2000) found that distinguishing between levels of gang involvement was important in understanding youths' gang-related perceptions and experiences. In this article, we explore the relationship between different levels of gang involvement and delinquency.

Research Design

The design is one that has been frequently used in studies of delinquency

(Curry & Spergel, 1992; Esbensen & Huiz-inga, 1993; Esbensen & Winfree, 1998; Fagan, 1990). A population of students attending middle school classes was surveyed within a classroom setting and asked about their involvement in a variety of behaviors. In cooperation with the St. Louis Public Schools, three middle schools were selected on the basis of their proximity or distance from concentrations of gang homicides. Two of these three schools were in poor neighborhoods with considerable gang activity. The third was in a predominantly middle-class neighborhood with little or no gang activity, and the majority of students in this school did not reside in the surrounding community. Two additional schools that were included in the study were the St. Louis Public Schools "Tri-A" Academies. These two academies are reserved for students with disciplinary or legal problems. By combining these three types of schools (from poor neighborhoods with gang problems, from a middle-class neighborhood with few gang problems, and from the Tri-A Academies), we believe that the respondents reflect the general character of students in this urban district.

The survey was administered in the spring semester of the 1995–96 school year. The response rate among students attending school was high, as is inevitably the case, when students and teachers are offered an alternative to regular class activities. Participating schools were paid $20 per completed survey for the purchase of educational supplies. Passive parental consent was used. Only 17 parents requested that their children not participate in the survey. In one classroom, all students collectively refused to participate; the research assistants reported that students (who may have been gang members) announced that decision for their classmates. The greatest detriment to participation was school attendance. Although we had access to school records and were able to code each instrument with students' identification numbers, school officials could not tell us whether students were absent or had changed schools. In other school studies in which absentees could be clearly identified (Curry & Spergel, 1992), absentees were more likely to have school disciplinary and delinquency records than were attending students.

Measurement

Gang membership was measured by the student's answers to the questions, "Do you belong to a gang?" and "Have you been a member of a gang in the past?" We treated affirmative answers to either question as evidence of ever having been a member of a gang, following the practice of Esbensen and Winfree (1998) for identifying gang membership in samples in which most respondents are younger than age 15. In this study, no additional criteria were imposed on the self-reporting of gang membership. This follows the recommendation of Esbensen, Winfree, He, and Taylor (2001, p. 124), who found self-nomination to be a "particularly robust measure of gang membership capable of distinguishing gang from non-gang youth." In their study, along a continuum of an increasingly restrictive definition of gang membership, the greatest difference in gang behaviors and attitudes was observed between youths who had never been gang members and youths who self-reported only current or prior gang involvement. In another study, Esbensen and Huizinga (1993) required that respondents also answer one of two items about their group's illegal activity. Since our main concern was to examine the relationship between the level of gang membership and delinquency, we did not impose any requirement for illegal activity on our operational definition of gang membership. This measurement strategy avoided the potential tautology of establishing the relationship between membership and delinquency in our operational definition (Ball & Curry, 1995; Short, 1998).

Gang involvement was measured by four of eight criteria used by Curry and Spergel (1992) to measure gang involvement other than self-reported membership in a gang. Curry and Spergel found that self-reported measures of gang-related behavior, independent of membership, were significantly related to levels of delinquency. The specific four measures we used are shown in Table 20.1. Self-reported delinquency was measured by answers to a number of items asking if youths had committed a particular delinquent act. Most of these items were taken from other instruments used to study self-reported delinquency. Officially recorded delinquency was measured by linking students' files to referrals to the St. Louis City Family Court for either a status

Table 20.1
*Gang Involvement Behavior Items
for Nongang Members (n = 453)*

	n	%
Have gang members as friends	168	37.1%
Worn gang colors	137	30.2%
Hang out with gang members	107	23.6%
Flashed gang signs	90	19.9%

Note: Unanswered items treated as not reported.

offense or a delinquency offense.[1] All court referrals for delinquency were captured for each student who completed a survey.

Findings

Prevalence of Gang Membership

All the students at two of the middle schools and one of the academies were African American. At the third middle school, the majority of students in the sample (62.1%) were white. Of the 533 respondents to the survey, 80 (15.0%) reported being either currently or formerly a gang member. The prevalence of gang membership is somewhat higher than the 10.6% reported in the multisite, 11-city survey of youths conducted by Esbensen and colleagues (see Esbensen & Winfree, 1998). This difference is most likely the result of the use of a more restrictive definition in the latter study. Elsewhere, using a similar classification procedure as the present survey, Esbensen et al. (2001) reported that 16.8% of the sample responded as ever having been a gang member.

There were differences associated with gender and race. With regard to gender, 18.1% of the boys and 11.5% of the girls reported ever being a gang member (a statistically significant difference at the .05 level). These observed prevalence levels of gang membership are slightly higher than the 13.6% for boys and 7.8% for girls reported by Esbensen and Winfree (1998) and are, in part, likely to be the result of the difference in classification procedures and the extent of gang problems in the study sites. With regard to race, overall, only five white students (8.2%) identified themselves as ever having been gang members. The expected values for white students were too small to compute a chi-square comparing the prevalence of gang membership for whites and African Americans. The overall percentage of African American respondents who reported ever having been gang members was 15.9%, but at the predominantly white school, 28.6% of the African Americans did so (a statistically significant difference at the .05 level).[2]

Prevalence of Gang Involvement

Treating any one of the gang-related behaviors in Table 20.1 as being gang involved, it is possible to examine the proportion of youths who reported never being a gang member who reported some level of gang involvement (see Table 20.2). Of the 453 respondents who reported never having been a gang member, 260 (57.4%) reported at least one kind of gang involvement. With regard to gender, 59.1% of the boys and 55.6% of the girls who were never gang members reported some level of gang involvement. This difference is not statistically significant and suggests that knowledge of and involvement in gang behavior is quite high, even for nonmembers. With regard to race, 60.1% of the African American youths and 37.5% of

Table 20.2
Students' Characteristics and Gang Involvement

Characteristics	Total		Gang Member		Gang Involved	
	Reported	%	Reported	%[a]	Reported	%[a]
African American	471	88.4	75	15.9[b]	238	50.5*
White	61	11.4	5	8.2	21	34.4
Hispanic[c]	1	0.2	0	0.0	1	100.0
Male[b]	281	52.7	51	18.1*	136	48.4[b]
Female	252	47.3	29	11.5	124	49.2

[a]Level of statistical signifance of chi-square test.
[b]Not statistically significant at .05.
[c]Category not included in statistical computations.
*p < .05

the white youths who were not gang members reported some level of gang involvement (a statistically significant difference at the .01 level). The one Latino in the survey reported that he had friends who were gang members. The finding that the majority of nonmembers reported some level of gang involvement underscores the pervasive effect of gangs among middle school students in these neighborhoods. It suggests that the influence of gangs on nongang members may be greater than previous studies have estimated.

Gang Involvement and Self-Reported Delinquency

Separating respondents into gang members, nongang members, and nonmembers who have some level of gang involvement gave us an opportunity to expand what we know about the status of being involved with yet not a member of a gang. Given the empirically established relationship between gang membership and delinquency, any status that is defined by the social space between gang member and nonmember should be differentially associated with delinquency. In Table 20.3, nonmembers with gang involvement are labeled "gang involved."

The respondents were asked about their participation in a range of delinquent behaviors, including serious, minor, and drug offenses. Table 20.3 shows the relationships between level of gang involvement and self-reported delinquency. For each of the 12 self-reported delinquent offenses, the differences (as measured by gamma) across the three levels of gang involvement are statistically significant at the .001 level. For all 12 self-reported delinquency items, the prevalence rate for gang-involved youths is both greater than that of youths who were not gang involved and lower than that of those who self-reported gang membership.[3]

For all but one of the measures, the paired comparisons between nonmembers with no gang involvement and nonmembers with gang involvement is statistically significant at the .05 level (at least). The exception is stealing something worth more than $50, for which 3.6% of nonmembers not gang involved and 8.1% of the gang-involved nonmembers stand significantly apart from the 30% reported by gang members. A smaller number of the self-reported delinquency items differentiate between gang-involved nonmembers and gang members. Most notable, the prevalence rate for using violence against another person among gang-involved youths (55.8%) is more than double that of youths who reported no gang

Table 20.3
Gang Status and Self-Reported Delinquency and Victimization

Delinquency or Victimization	Noninvolved (n = 193)		Gang Involved (n = 260)		Gang Member (n = 80)	
	Reported	%[a]	Reported	%[a]	Reported	%
Thrown objects at cars or people	29	15.0***	93	35.8**	44	55.0
Damaged or destroyed property	18	9.3***	68	26.2[b]	29	36.3
Ran away from home	11	5.7**	36	13.8[b]	15	18.8
Stole something less than $50	19	9.8*	48	18.5[b]	21	26.3
Stole something more than $50	7	3.6[b]	21	8.1***	24	30.0
Bought, held, or sold stolen goods	10	5.2***	39	15.0***	27	33.8
Used violence against someone	49	25.4***	145	55.8[b]	52	65.0
Own or possess a gun	4	2.1***	27	10.4***	30	37.5
Carried a gun	6	3.1*	21	8.1***	25	31.3
Used beer or wine	30	15.5*	61	23.5***	42	52.5
Used hard liquor	8	4.1*	26	10.0***	32	40.0
Used marijuana	13	6.7***	45	17.3***	42	52.5
Threatened with a gun	15	7.8[b]	35	13.5***	26	32.5
Shot at with a gun	8	4.1***	39	15.0*	22	27.5
Injured by gunshot	3	1.6[b]	11	4.2**	10	12.5

Note: Gamma across all three groups is statistically significant at .001 level for all items.
[a]Level of statistical significance of chi-square test results between adjacent two groups.
[b]Not statistically significant at .05.
* p < .05, ** p < .01, *** p < .001.

involvement (25.4%) and approaches that of self-reported gang members (65.0%).

Gang Involvement and Victimization

The relationship between offending and victimization has been well established in research on delinquency (Lauritsen, Sampson, & Laub, 1991) and has received support in the gang literature (Decker & Van Winkle, 1996; Moore, 1991). Decker (1996) reported that more than a dozen of his 99 respondents had been killed within five years of the conclusion of his study. These results show that gang members have violent victimization rates that exceed those of nonmembers. Victimization was measured by self-reports of being threatened with a gun, shot at, or injured by gunshot. Table 20.3 illustrates that gang membership is as strongly associated with victimization as offending. But at least in one case, having been shot at, gang-involved nonmembers are more than three times as likely to report affirmatively than nonmembers with no gang involvement. Those who reported ever having been a gang member were more than four times more likely than nongang members with no gang involvement to have been victimized in each of the listed events. For example, 12.5% of the gang members reported having been injured by gunshot, over four times that of non-gang-involved non-members (1.6%) and almost three times the rate reported by gang-involved nonmembers (4.2%).

Taken together, these findings are congruous with the contagion of violence purported to be associated with gang activity (Decker, 1996). Initial acts of gang-related violence arouse and expand the willingness of others to engage in retaliatory violence. Within this spatial concentration, gang members may often assume the role of victim, perpetrator, or witness to violence. From the method of measurement used in this survey, it is impossible to conclude with certainty that gang members in this sample were necessarily involved in gang-related violence. However, it is noteworthy that the association among gang membership, delinquency, and victimization was observed and categorically supported among a sample of young adolescent gang members.

Gang Involvement and Officially Recorded Delinquency

While recent research has continued to support the link between gang member-ship and self-reported offending, the link between gang membership and officially recorded delinquency is not as frequently documented. From a survey of young adolescents in Chicago, Curry (2000) found that among those who self-reported both gang involvement and delinquency, over half were arrested for at least one delinquent act in the subsequent five years, and over half of those who were so arrested were apprehended for involvement in a gang-motivated offense. Thus, these findings suggest that there is a considerable overlap between youth-based surveys and official records regarding adolescents' gang membership and delinquency.

From an analysis of the data of referrals to the St. Louis Family Court, it was possible to examine the relationship between self-reported gang membership and referrals to the court. All court referrals between September 1993 and December 31, 2000, were checked for matches with the respondents to the survey on child's name, date of birth, and address listed in the school records. Respondents with either status-offense referrals or delinquency referrals between 1993 and 2000 were identified. Although the survey data were essentially cross-sectional, it was possible to add some degree of chronological structure to the analysis by classifying each referral as being before or after the administration of the survey.

Table 20.4 compares the court referral records for respondents who identified themselves as gang members, nonmembers with some gang involvement, and nonmembers with no gang involvement. As should be expected, rates of referral prior to the survey (when the respondents were younger) were appreciably lower than in the five years following the survey. The status-offense referral rates for each of the three gang-involvement groups before the survey was administered were not significantly different. In fact, the nonmembers who reported gang involvement in the survey had a slightly lower rate of referrals for status offenses prior to the survey. The referral rates for delinquency before the survey varied in the ordinal direction found for self-reported delinquency, increasing from nonmembers with no gang involvement to nonmembers with gang involvement to self-reported members. The difference across the three categories was statistically significant at the

Table 20.4
Gang Status and Officially Recorded Delinquency

Officially Recorded Delinquency	Noninvolved (n = 193)		Gang Involved (n = 260)		Gang Member (n = 80)	
	Reported	%[a]	Reported	%[a]	Reported	%
Referred for status offense prior to survey	9	4.7[b]	10	3.8[b]	5	6.3
Referred for status offense post survey	30	15.5***	74	28.5[b]	29	36.3
Referred for delinquency prior to survey	11	5.7[b]	23	8.8[b]	12	15.0
Referred for delinquency post survey	48	24.9**	96	36.9[b]	39	48.8
Mean times referred for delinquency post survey	0.58*		1.12***		2.03	

Note: Gamma across all three groups is statistically significant at .001 level for all items except for status offense referral.
[a]Level of statistical significance of chi-square test results between adjacent two groups.
[b]Not statistically significant at .05
* p < .05, ** p < .01, *** p < .001

.05 level, but the differences between consecutive pairs of categories were not statistically significant.

Table 20.4 reveals that the same rank-order relationship holds between the three levels of gang involvement and officially recorded delinquency. Nonmembers with gang involvement were more likely to have been referred for status offenses than were nonmembers with no gang involvement. Nonmembers with gang involvement were more likely to have been referred for delinquency after the survey than were nonmembers with no gang involvement. Just over one-third of the gang-involved youths (36.9%) were referred to the juvenile court for a delinquent offense, below the prevalence rate for gang members (48.8%), yet significantly greater than that of youths who were not gang involved (24.9%). The differences between noninvolved youth and both gang-involved groups within each type of referral after the survey are statistically significant. On the whole, these results provide strong evidence of an intermediary status between gang membership and nonmembership, whereby even a minimal amount of involvement in gang-related behaviors clearly separates these youths from their uninvolved peers in terms of self-reported and officially recorded delinquency.

The proportions referred in the five years following the survey were significantly different at the .001 level. The proportion of non-gang youths referred was four times that referred prior to the survey, as was the proportion of gang-involved nonmember youths. While the increase in the proportion of gang members who were referred after the survey was only three times the proportion of members referred prior to the survey, the amplification of the greater initial proportion resulted in a much larger gap between the nongang and gang-involved youths. This difference in officially recorded delinquent offending underscores the importance of self-reported gang membership as a predictor of delinquency (Esbensen et al., 2001; Esbensen & Winfree, 1998).

These results unequivocally demonstrate that increased involvement in gang-related behaviors for adolescents significantly enhances the risk of delinquency and victimization. This finding highlights both the significance of gang involvement for offending and the role of engaging in gang behavior, short of full-fledged membership, in enhancing offending. The increased levels of offending associated with engaging in gang behaviors are quite dramatic, underscoring the need to address both gang-involved and marginally gang-involved youths.

Conclusion

This article has demonstrated that the relationship between self-reported gang membership and delinquency found in other cities holds for St. Louis.[4] Since the survey was conducted in middle schools, it is safe to conclude that the relationship between gang membership and delinquency emerges in early adolescence. Whereas most previous surveys have shown the relationship between self-reported gang involvement and self-reported delinquency, this study also found a statistically significant relationship between self-reported gang membership and referral to the juvenile court for delinquency.

In addition to identifying a distinction between gang members and nonmembers with respect to delinquency, the survey identified an interstitial status between full-fledged gang membership and nonmembership. Nonmember gang involvement was measured using a set of criteria developed by Curry and Spergel (1992) in studying Chicago youths. The St. Louis Police Department Gang Unit uses the designation "gang associate" to identify suspects who are known to have some association with gangs but are not known to be members. We think that this designation may be useful in research. It is comparable to labels used in other research, such as "peripheral members," "marginal members," and "wanna be's." The significance of this gang-associate status is demonstrated by its strong relationship to delinquency. For a range of measures of self-reported and officially recorded delinquency, the prevalence of offending for this group was shown to be between that of gang members and nonmembers who were not involved in gang behavior. The delinquent involvement of this group of associate members lies along a scale between full-fledged members and nonmembers.

A longitudinal survey design is required to discover if identified gang associates are in a transitional phase that would, in some cases, lead to full gang membership or if their association with gangs would fade. Still, one may draw conclusions about the social structure and dynamics of gang involvement. While the study found that self-perceived gang membership is an important predictor of delinquency, it demonstrated that marginal gang involvement is associated with a level of risk of delinquency and violence that is greater than that experienced by nonmembers.

Implications for Research and Policy

This study joins others (Esbensen & Winfree, 1998) in showing that the relationship between gang membership and delinquency emerges in early adolescence. The findings also indicate that engaging in gang behaviors is strongly and consistently associated with involvement in a variety of forms of delinquency and victimization. Thus, associating with gang members ("hanging out") and engaging in gang behaviors (adopting gang

mannerisms) both have important consequences for delinquency, even for nongang members. It is not necessary for an individual to self-report gang membership to experience the delinquency-enhancing effects of gang membership. This finding supports the need for early prevention and intervention programs with youths and families, especially in neighborhoods with high levels of gang membership or in families with older siblings who belong to gangs. This finding also underscores the need for gang intervention programs that deal with actively involved gang members, as well as individuals who are peripheral to the gang. Minimizing the influences of gang members on peripheral members or nonmembers should pay dividends for both delinquency prevention and intervention efforts. We also believe that this finding should be particularly relevant for programming directed at young girls who may not (yet) be active gang members, but who may associate with such individuals either through familial or associational ties.

The image of the gang that is supported by these findings is one of a loosely structured organization. As was noted in prior studies in St. Louis (Decker, 1996; Decker & Van Winkle, 1996), gang activity can be best viewed as a form of collective behavior, with many youths perceiving themselves, at least at some point in time, as gang members. However, other youths who do not consider themselves ever to have been gang members continue to associate with gangs and gang members and are differentially involved in the overall patterns of gang-related crime and delinquency. This finding may also be true for individuals who once were gang members and have cut their formal ties with the gang, but still maintain friendships with gang members and occasionally engage in gang behavior with them.

Suppression approaches that treat gangs as organized crime groups have been shown to be inappropriate responses to most gangs (Decker et al., 1998). The more loosely structured nature of gang organization calls for more comprehensive responses that require a range of coordinated prevention, intervention, and suppression activities. This finding seems particularly appropriate for adolescents of the age range in our study. The emphasis in gang programming over the past decade has been on suppression (Decker & Curry, 2000; Spergel & Curry,

1993). Such approaches have gang members as their focus and hence may miss a significant number of gang-involved youths who may not be identified as gang members or may not identify themselves as such, particularly those who are younger adolescents. Suppression efforts appear to be operating at maximum capacity, that is, there appears to be little excess capacity in law enforcement efforts to address gangs. The findings about suppression highlight the need for programs that focus on the broad range of differentially involved gang youths and their range of different problems and needs.

Notes

1. These data were provided through the cooperation of the St. Louis Family Court.
2. The source of this difference remains unknown to us, but it may be that some African American students perceive themselves differently at an integrated school or feel the need to affiliate with a gang (for protection) in such a setting.
3. From a longitudinal study of Seattle youths, Battin et al. (1998) concluded that the effect of gang membership on self-reported delinquency remained statistically significant even when having delinquent friends was controlled. To examine the possibility that our measure of gang involvement may simply be a proxy for delinquent friends, we controlled for four variables related to information about friends' delinquency. These variables were positively related to self-reported and officially recorded delinquency as well as gang-involvement status. In a series of logistic regression analyses (17), we regressed each of the last eight self-reported delinquency measures, the three victimization measures, and the two post-survey measures of family court referrals on gang involvement (as a three-value categorical variable) and the report of delinquent friends. For only one of the self-reported delinquency measures, stealing something worth less than $50, was the coefficient for delinquent friends statistically significant when gang involvement was not. In the others, either gang involvement alone was a statistically significant predictor of the outcome variable or both gang involvement and having delinquent friends were statistically significant predictors. Therefore, gang involvement had an independent effect on delinquency beyond that attributed to delinquent friends. The table of results is available from the authors.
4. It should be noted that this was not a ran-

dom sample, so it is not feasible to generalize to other populations.

References

Ball, R. A., & Curry, G. D. (1995). The logic of definition in criminology: Purposes and methods for defining "gangs." *Criminology, 33,* 225–245.

Battin, S. R., Hill, K. G., Abbott, R. D., Catalano, R. P., & Hawkins, J. D. (1998). The contribution of gang membership to delinquency beyond delinquent friends. *Criminology, 36,* 93–115.

Bjerregaard, B., & Lizotte, A. J. (1995). Gun ownership and gang membership. *Journal of Criminal Law and Criminology, 86,* 37–58.

Campbell, D., & Fiske, D. (1959). Convergent and discriminant validation by the multi-trait-multi-method matrix. *Psychological Bulletin, 56,* 81–105.

Curry, G. D. (2000). Self-reported gang involvement and officially recorded delinquency. *Criminology, 38,* 100–118.

Curry, G. D., & Spergel, I. A. (1992). Gang involvement and delinquency among Hispanic and African-American adolescent males. *Journal of Research on Crime and Delinquency, 29,* 273–291.

Decker, S. H. (1996). Collective and normative features of gang violence. *Justice Quarterly, 13,* 243–264.

Decker, S. H., Bynum, T., & Weisel, D. (1998). A tale of two cities: Gangs as organized crime groups. *Justice Quarterly, 15,* 395–425.

Decker, S. H., & Curry, G. D. (2000). Addressing key features of gang membership: Measuring the involvement of young members. *Journal of Criminal Justice, 28,* 473–482.

Decker, S. H., & Van Winkle, B. (1996). *Life in the gang: Family, friends, and violence.* New York: Cambridge University Press.

Elliott, D. S., Huizinga, D., & Morse, B. (1987). Self-reported violent offending: A descriptive analysis of juvenile violent offenders and their offending careers. *Journal of Interpersonal Violence, 1,* 472–514.

Esbensen, F.-A., & Huizinga, D. (1993). Gangs, drugs, and delinquency in a survey of urban youth. *Criminology, 31,* 565–587.

Esbensen, F.-A., & Winfree, L. T. (1998). Race and gender differences between gang and nongang youths: Results from a multisite survey. *Justice Quarterly, 15,* 505–523.

Esbensen, F.-A., Winfree, L. T., He, N., & Taylor, T. J. (2001). Youth gangs and definitional issues: When is a gang a gang, and why does it matter? *Crime and Delinquency, 47,* 105–130.

Fagan, J. (1989). The social organization of drug use and drug dealing among urban gangs. *Criminology, 27,* 633–669.

———. (1990). Social processes of delinquency and drug use among urban gangs. In C. R.

Huff (Ed.), *Gangs in America* (pp. 183–219). Thousand Oaks, CA: Sage.

Farrington, D. P. (1989). Early predictors of adolescent aggression and adult violence. *Violence and Victims, 4,* 79–100.

Hagedorn, J. M. (1998). *People and folks: Gangs, crime, and the underclass in a rustbelt city* (2nd ed.). Chicago: Lakeview Press.

Hartstone, E., & Hansen, K. V. (1984). The violent juvenile offender: An empirical portrait. In R. A. Mathias, P. De Muro, & R. S. Allinson (Eds.), *Violent juvenile offenders* (pp. 83–112). San Francisco: National Council on Crime and Delinquency.

Hawkins, J. D., Herrenkohl, T., Farrington, D. P., Brewer, D., Catalano, R. F., & Karachi, T. W. (1998). A review of predictors of youth violence. In R. Loeber & D. P. Farrington (Eds.), *Serious and violent juvenile offenders: Risk factors and successful interventions* (pp. 106–146). Thousand Oaks, CA: Sage.

Howell, J. (1994). *Gangs fact sheet.* Washington, DC: U.S. Department of Justice, Office of Juvenile Justice and Delinquency Prevention.

Huff, C. R. (1996). The criminal behavior of gang members and nongang at-risk youth. In C. R. Huff (Ed.), in *Gangs in America* (2nd ed., pp. 75–102). Thousand Oaks, CA: Sage.

Lauritsen, J. L., Sampson, R. J., & Laub, J. H. (1991). The link between offending and victimization among adolescents. *Criminology, 29,* 265–292.

Miller, J. (2001). *One of the guys: Girls, gangs, and gender.* New York: Oxford University Press.

Miller, W. B. (1975). *Violence by youth gangs and youth groups as a crime problem in major American cities.* Washington, DC: U.S. Government Printing Office.

Moore, J. (1991). *Going down to the barrio: Homeboys and homegirls in change.* Philadelphia: Temple University Press.

Padilla, F. M. (1992). *The gang as an American enterprise.* New Brunswick, NJ: Rutgers University Press.

Rosenfeld, R., Bray, T. M., & Egley, Jr., A. (1999). Facilitating violence: A comparison of gang-motivated, gang-affiliated, and nongang youth homicides. *Journal of Quantitative Criminology, 15,* 495–516.

Sánchez-Jankowski, M. S. (1991). *Islands in the street: Gangs and American urban society.* Berkeley: University of California Press.

Short, J. F. (1998). The level of explanation problem revisited: The American Society of Criminology 1997 presidential address. *Criminology, 36,* 3–36.

Short, J. F., & Strodtbeck, F. L. (1965). *Group process and gang delinquency.* Chicago: University of Chicago Press.

Spergel, I. A. (1964). *Racketville, slumtown, haulburg.* Chicago: University of Chicago Press.

———. (1990). Youth gangs: Continuity and change. In M. Tonry & N. Morris (Eds.), *Crime and justice: A review of research,* Vol. 12 (pp. 171–275). Chicago: University of Chicago Press.

Spergel, I. A., & Curry, G. D. (1993). The National Youth Gang Survey: Research and development process. In A. Goldstein & C. R. Huff (Eds.), *Gang intervention handbook* (pp. 359–400). Champaign-Urbana, IL: Research Press.

Suttles, G. (1968). *The social order of the slum.* Chicago: University of Chicago Press.

Taylor, C. S. (1990). *Dangerous society.* East Lansing: Michigan State University Press.

Thornberry, T. (1998). Membership in youth gangs and involvement in serious and violent offending. In R. Loeber & D. P. Farrington (Eds.), *Serious and violent juvenile offenders: Risk factors and successful interventions* (pp. 147–166). Thousand Oaks, CA: Sage.

Thornberry, T., Krohn, M. D., Lizotte, A. J., & Chard-Wierschem, D. (1993). The role of juvenile gangs in facilitating delinquent behavior. *Journal of Research in Crime and Delinquency, 30,* 55–87.

Thrasher, F. (1927). *The gang: A study of 1,313 gangs in Chicago.* Chicago: University of Chicago Press.

Vigil, J. D. (1988). *Barrio gangs: Street life and identity in southern California.* Austin: University of Texas Press. ✦

Chapter 21
Situations of Violence in the Lives of Girl Gang Members

Geoffrey Hunt
and Karen Joe-Laidler

We don't normally associate violence with fe-males, but Hunt and Joe-Laidler provide a close-up view of its antecedents and patterns among female gang members with three dif-ferent ethnic backgrounds in the San Fran-cisco Bay Region. These women are both perpetrators and victims. They come from in-dependent gangs and male-auxiliary gangs. The variety of experience is as notable as its severity. However, we warn the reader about generalizing from these findings to other fe-male gang members, because in this study the women are unusually old for gang girls, most of whom desist from gang activity several years earlier. Hunt and Joe-Laidler paint a picture for unusual women who have ex-tended their gang careers.

Women and violence has become a topic of increasing concern. Women's involve-ment in perpetrating violence, especially girl gang members, also has raised national concern. The participation of young women in gangs and gang violence has caused pub-lic consternation as they are perceived to be violating traditional notions of femininity. In spite of this increased concern and bur-geoning literature, significant gaps still exist

Reprinted from: *Health Care for Women International* 22:363–384. Copyright © 2001 from *Health Care for Women International* by Geoffrey Hunt and Karen Joe-Laidler. Reproduced by permission of Taylor & Francis, Inc., http://www.taylorandfrancis.com.

in our understanding of the role of young women in gangs, the nature and extent of fe-male gang members' victimization, and the extent of their involvement in perpetrating violence. The purpose of this paper is to ex-amine the role of violence in the lives of fe-male gang members.

The analysis draws from the qualitative and quantitative data of an ongoing com-parative study on ethnic youth gangs in the San Francisco Bay Area. The analysis is or-ganized around the situations of violence these young women face from early child-hood within the family setting to their cur-rent status within the gang and on the streets.

Over the last decade, public concern has risen over the problems of women as vic-tims and offenders of violence. Justice and health agencies have initiated research and programs to address the issues associated with women and violence. The National Crime Victimization Survey found that 30.4 per 1,000 women had been victims of crimes of violence in 1998 (Bureau of Justice Statis-tics [BJS], 2000a). Research on female vio-lence over the last 20 years has shown that the "most common assailant is a man known to the woman, often her male inti-mate" (Crowell & Burgess, 1996, p. 29). An estimated 30% of all female murder victims are killed by intimate partners, a finding consistent since 1976 (BJS, 2000b). Inti-mate male-on-female victimization also pre-dominates for both sexual and physical assault for African Americans, Hispanics, Whites, and urban and rural populations (BJS, 1999; Chesney-Lind, 1997; Crowell & Burgess, 1996). Women between the ages of 12 to 18 experience the highest rates of vic-timization, a characteristic that is true for homicides, sexual assaults, and intimate partner violence (Crowell & Burgess, 1996; Reiss & Roth, 1993). The rates of victimiza-tion for crimes of violence among female ju-veniles differs as well. For 1998, the rate of violent victimization among 12- to 15-year-old females is 62.3 per 100,000; the rate among 16- to 19-year-old females is 72.6 per 100,000; and the rate among 20- to 24-year-old females is 59.0 per 100,000. These rates are significantly higher compared with adult females (the rate among 25- to 34-year-olds is 35.2 per 100,000). Among the highest risk of violent victimization (16- to 19-year-olds), the major forms of violent vic-timization include, in rank order, simple assault, attempted violence, and aggravated assault (BJS, 2000a). This group also had the highest rate of rape victimization in that year—10.0 per 100,000.

Although fewer studies have been conducted on violence against minority women, certain differences are discernible. African American women are more likely to report physical violence in intimate relationships than White (non-Hispanic) women (Asbury, 1987; Cazenave & Straus, 1990; Crowell & Burgess, 1996; Durant, Cadenhead, Pendergrast, & Slavens, 1994; Sorenson, 1996; Straus & Gelles, 1986). Results from studies on Hispanic women and violence are inconclusive, with some of them reporting Hispanic women being at a higher risk of violence than non-Hispanics, while others report the risk to be lower or at the same level (Sorenson, 1996; Sorenson & Telles, 1991; Straus & Smith, 1990). Little or no survey data exist on violence against Asian American women (Ho, 1990). According to the National Violence Against Women Survey, however, Asian Pacific Americans reported significantly lower rates of personal violence than other ethnic groups. This finding is not necessarily linked to lower rates of violence in this group (Tjaden & Thoennes, 2000). Instead, researchers suggest that Asian Pacific Americans are highly resistant to reporting because of their strict adherence to traditional values, which emphasize personal sacrifice for family harmony and discourage disclosure of conflict and abuse in the family (Abraham, 2000; Crowell & Burgess, 1996; Lum, 1998).

Women's involvement in perpetrating violence also has raised national concern. According to self-reported victimization, females account for an estimated 14% of violent offenders, or an annual average of 2.1 million violent female offenders (BJS, 1999). Three out of four of violent victimizations committed by females were for simple assault (BJS, 1999). Slightly more than one-third of offenders were described by victims of violence as being Black, and 1 in 10 were described as being of another ethnic minority group. Based on victims' self reports, approximately 28% of violent female offenders are under the age of 21. This proportion is similar to that of male juvenile offenders (26% of all violent male offenders). According to arrests data, females accounted for 22% of all arrests in 1998, 17% of violent offenses (including murder, rape, robbery, and aggravated assault), and 29% of property crimes. Juvenile females accounted for 22% of all female arrests. The arrest rates for violent offenses were higher for female juveniles at 126 per 100,000 compared with 91 per 100,000 for female adults (BJS, 1999).

These statistics highlight the extent to which young minority women are at risk for violence, both as victims and as perpetrators. One arena in which minority women appear particularly at risk is in gangs. Recently the increasing concern over their participation in gangs (Chesney-Lind, Shelden, & Joe, 1996) has focused primarily on assumptions of an increase in young minority women's membership in gangs and participation in violence. Although exact participation rates of female involvement in gangs, crime, and violence remain unknown, even less information is available about the nature and extent of female gang members' victimization.

Female gang participation has generated much public concern and media attention, in part because they are becoming more visible, and also because they are presumed to be rebelling against traditional notions of femininity. The popular image of female gang members portrays these "bad girls" as even more problematic than their male counterparts because they challenge traditional gender roles. Official estimates of the number of youth involved in gangs have increased dramatically over the past decade. Currently, more than 90% of the nation's largest cities report youth gang problems, an increase from about half in 1983, and police estimates now put the number of gangs at 4,881 and the number of gang members at approximately 249,324 (Chesney-Lind, Shelden, & Joe, 1996; Curry, Ball, & Fox, 1994). Recent studies have noted that girl gang membership is also increasing (Esbensen, Huizinga, & Weiher, 1993; Fagan, 1990a; Winfree et al., 1992). Female membership in gangs is estimated to be between 10% to 30% of all gang members (Campbell, 1984; Chesney-Lind, 1993; Curry, Ball, & Fox, 1994; Esbensen & Huizinga, 1993; Fagan, 1990b; Klein, 1995; Moore, 1991), figures much higher than those supplied by official data.

Despite a shift in interest from what Inciardi, Horowitz, and Pottieger (1993) have called the "garden variety" delinquent to that of the serious delinquent (Horowitz,

1990), researchers traditionally have neglected or downplayed the roles that females play in street gangs as well as the social processes and consequences of their involvement in gangs.[1] Male gang researchers traditionally characterized female members as maladjusted tomboys or sexual deviants who, in either case, were no more than mere appendages to male members of the gang (Joe & Chesney-Lind, 1995). This traditional view stands in stark contrast to recent public discussions about female gang members, which indicate that female gang members are no longer simply the "molls" of male gang members, but also are establishing their own ground and taking on an active independent role in crime and violence (Chesney-Lind, 1993). In spite of these more recent efforts to study the girls in the gang and dispel popular characterizations of them as "gun packing wild women," questions remain about the violence with which these young women are confronted. To what extent do these young women experience violence in their lives? Does the violence that they experience take place solely on the streets, or do they experience violence within their home lives? Are these women solely victims of this violence, or do they on occasions instigate violence? If so, then what are the reasons for this violence and to whom are they violent?

In answering these questions, this article challenges recent portrayals of the demonic character of female gang members by examining the violence-prone situations in which these young women operate.

Research Methods

The data for this analysis are drawn from a long-term, comparative ethnographic study of ethnic gangs in the San Francisco Bay Area that began in 1991 and continues to the present. From 1991 to 1993, we conducted face-to-face interviews with more than 600 self-identified male and female gang members. (See Waldorf, 1993, and Joe, 1993.) The 65 female gang members interviewed were from 7 different groups and were located using the snowball sampling approach (Biernacki & Waldorf, 1981). This sampling strategy relied on respondents referring members of their group or other groups to be interviewed. The same technique was used in our second study, which extended our comparative research to Southeast Asian gangs in the same locale. In this effort, we interviewed 91 male and 19 female Southeast Asian gang members from 1993 through 1994. At present, we are engaged in a third study that revisits and explores other contemporary gang issues among males and females in the San Francisco Bay Area. We have 57 completed female interviews from the current study and have included these cases for this analysis. From the three studies, then, we will be drawing on a total sample size of 141 interviews with female gang members.

For years sociologists have been debating the definition of gangs, and the debate continues with little resolution. For the purposes of our research we have adopted Klein's (1971) definition, which as Miller (1996) has noted, is one of the most influential and longstanding. Klein argues that the term "street gang" refers to any group of youths who "a) are generally perceived as a distinct aggregation by others in their neighborhood, b) recognize themselves as a denotable group, [and] c) have been involved in a sufficient number of [illegal] incidents to call forth a consistent negative response from neighborhood residents and/or enforcement agencies" (Klein, 1971, p. 13). In addition to using this definition, we allowed our respondents to tell us if they were gang members or not. We did this early on in the interviews by asking if they were part of a clique or group and if they were, did they have a name for the group. In this way we attempted to supplement the gang definition by allowing the individual to identify himself or herself as a gang member. Finally, given the experience of many of our interviewers, they were able to detect, early on in an interview, if the respondent had little knowledge of gang life and was primarily a "wannabe" gang member.

The in-depth interview involved a two-step process in which the interviewee first answered a series of questions from a quantitative schedule. The second step entailed a tape-recorded session, and members reflected on questions from a semistructured guide about their gang experiences. This combined approach of qualitative and social survey methodology provided an opportunity to focus on the groups' histories, organization, and activities, and the gang members' demographics, alcohol and drug use, history and involvement with the group, and prior contact with the criminal justice system. We also asked the young women about power relations and gender expectations within the group, with the various males in their lives and with their families. The interviews were conducted in a variety of settings ranging from the respondent's or peer's residence to parks, church youth centers, and coffee shops. Interviews lasted from 90 minutes to 3 hours. We provided respondents with a $65 honorarium in recognition of their participation and time.

Sample

The 141 young women in this study are members of one of 44 different gangs. Table 21.1 offers an overview of their personal characteristics. The 17 African American women belonged to 1 of 6 groups. Unlike any of the other ethnic groups, 4 of the African American female gangs organize themselves as "independent" groups without any ties to a male group. The members of the "independent" groups have been lifelong friends, growing up in the same neighborhood. The other two gangs are part of larger "mixed-gender" groups that include female and male members. The African American women in the sample are older than the females of other ethnic gangs, ranging between the ages of 14 and 27, with a median age of 23 years.

Table 21.1
Personal Characteristics of Girls in the Gang

	African American (n = 17)	Latina (n = 98)	Asian American (n = 26)	Total (n = 141)
Age (median)	23	18	18	18
Place of birth				
United States	100%	61%	27%	60%
Mexico/Latin America	0%	39%	0%	27%
Vietnam	0%	0%	73%	13%
Domestic unit prior to 16 yrs of age				
Mother & father (incl. stepparent)	53%	34%	61%	41%
One parent	35%	52%	23%	45%
Other	12%	14%	8%	13%
Unknown	0%	0%	8%	1%
Education completed				
9th grade or less	24%	42%	23%	36%
10th grade	24%	16%	23%	18%
11th grade	35%	21%	35%	26%
12th grade+	17%	20%	11%	18%
Unknown	0%	0%	8%	1%
Employed full/part time	0%	30%	15%	23%
If employed, type of work				
Skilled	0%	21%	50%	24%
Service industry	0%	55%	25%	52%
Unskilled/semiskilled	0%	24%	25%	24%
Primary source of income				
Job	0%	25%	15%	20%
Family/friends	6%	40%	73%	42%
Public assistance	35%	16%	0%	15%
Hustles	41%	4%	12%	10%
Combination	18%	15%	0%	13%
Marital status				
Single	71%	78%	92%	80%
Living together/married	23%	21%	8%	19%
Separated	6%	1%	0%	1%
% with or expecting children	82%	43%	8%	41%

Note: Percentages may not total 100% because of rounding.

The African American women come from highly marginalized backgrounds. Although slightly more than half of them report that they have lived principally with their mother and father until their midteen years, one of the parents, usually the father who was unemployed or in unskilled labor work, often left home for months at a time because of alcohol and drugs. More than one-third of them have lived only with their mother and have had very limited or no contact at all with their fathers. Their mothers tend to be either working in the service sector or unemployed. The girls rely principally on hustling (drug sales and shoplifting) and public assistance to support themselves and their children.

Among the other ethnic groups, the majority of the young women belong to "auxiliary" groups attached to male gangs. All of the Latina and 17 of the Asian Pacific American girls belong to one of these groups that consider themselves "separate but equal" to their male counterparts. These young women range in age from 14 to 32, with a median of 18 years of age. The Latinas come from more diverse communities and backgrounds compared with the African American girls. Nearly 40% of the Latinas were born in Mexico or Latin America and immigrated with at least one parent. Almost 30% of the girls have lived with their mother and father. Nearly half of the girls indicate that they have lived principally with their mothers, and several of them state that their fathers had either left the family or returned to their native land. When fathers were present, they were skilled, semiskilled, or unskilled laborers. Most mothers worked in the service sector or in unskilled positions. Among the 98 Latinas, approximately one-third report that at least one of their parents has had problems with alcohol or drugs.

The Asian American females were similar in age to the Latinas, with a median of 18 years of age and ranging in age between 15 to 21. The majority of Asian American girls are Chinese, Chinese Vietnamese, and Vietnamese who have immigrated from Vietnam. The girls come from different neighborhoods, primarily working-class houses and flats. More than 60% of them live with both parents. The respondents' fathers work in small businesses and semiskilled jobs, and their mothers are employed in small businesses or in semiskilled or service industry jobs. Most of the girls are still attending school and rely on their family and friends for money. Only one is living with her partner and expecting a baby.

Domains of Violence

Three domains of violence exist in the lives of girl gang members: the street, the family, and relationships with boyfriends.

Violence on the Streets

This section examines the situations of violence these young women encounter on the streets. The range of situations varies depending upon the organization of the girl's gang. Although the "independent" and "separate-but-together" gangs report some similar situations of violence, the latter group of gangs describe many other serious incidents. These other violence-prone situations are related, in large part, to their associations and activities with their male counterparts.[2]

Females in Independent Gangs. On the street, the women in the independent gangs confront two main situations of potential and real violence. These situations are associated with selling drugs and competition with females in other gangs.

These young women describe themselves as being autonomous from males and pride themselves on being able to care for themselves and their children, despite having had to drop out of school. They have devised a number of income-generating strategies, including "boosting" (selling stolen goods) and drug dealing. Because they are on their own, they take precautions on the streets because they recognized that they are potential targets for "drug fiends and robbers." Security for these girls is found in numbers. In addition to relying on their homegirls for protection, they adopted a variety of other precautionary strategies. According to these young women, one way to avoid potential violence is to steer clear of certain areas at particular times of the day. The girls live by the rule of avoiding the streets late at night, when males dominate the streets. Other rules for reducing their vulnerability involve locations for dealing, such as not selling through car windows, and preferences for selling indoors, like in crackhouses. Also, every one of the girls discussed the importance of carrying weapons to deal with potential danger, and admitted to carrying a knife or gun.

As with most gangs, these young women find themselves in conflict with females from other gangs over two main issues: men and turf. For example, according to the women in one gang, conflict with their major rival began in a dispute over men.

(I) How did these rivalries start?

(R) . . . About our men.

(I) Meanin'?

(R) Somebody in that group will want our men.

(I) And that's what you guys fight about?

(R) Yes.

(I) Do you ever fight about any other things besides your guys?

(R) No.

These young women believe that men in the mixed gender gangs encourage their own homegirls to take an aggressive stance against the females in independent gangs, thereby instigating the rivalries. Others believe that rivalries start not because of men but over turf and its association with drug sales. In either case, the women recognize the dangers of their rivals and their men. They are aware of the realities of constantly being a potential victim as well as a potential assailant. As women operating in independent groups, they rely on each other for protection, and as a precautionary measure they try to avoid going into their rivals' territory.

Females in Separate-but-Together Gangs. Compared with the young women in the independent gangs, females in other gangs face more situations of potential and real violence. Five situations are identified.

The first situation of violence involves initiations into the gang. Founding members of a group rarely participate in any initiation ceremonies. However, once the group is established, later initiates typically experience the ceremony and rituals of "jumping in." This "rite of passage" involves either "passing the line," or fighting with a gang member one-on-one. In fighting one-on-one, the potential gang member is matched with a girl of comparable build and strength, or in some cases the novitiate herself chooses her combatant as long as she does not "choose a wimp." Because the girls are connected with male gangs, potential gang members might be required

to fight a homeboy, but this occurs less frequently. In one case this male-on-female violence led to serious injuries and the practice was stopped: "One of the guys hit a girl in the back really bad. So they decided guys will hit guys and girls will hit girls." This type of initiation does not happen in independent female gangs. Instead of requiring new members to fight to prove their eligibility, the young women in independent gangs insist on potential members proving themselves by stealing from local department stores.

A second situation of violence involves conflict with male members of other gangs. According to the respondents, gangs have clear rules about females staying away from particular settings of violence, like fights between males or drive-by shootings. A few girls, however, report having had to jump in to help in unfair male-on-male fighting situations, such as when one of their homeboys was attacked by three or more rivals. As intended, their intervention broke up the fight, as the rival males refuse to hit the women. Nevertheless, these young women are in a highly vulnerable position given their association with their male counterparts.

Unlike the independent gangs, the women in the separate-but-together gangs, because of their affiliation with male groups, face another situation of potential violence involving rivalries with other similarly structured gangs. Although the separate-but-together homegirls know that their own involvement in violent situations among males might stop a fight, at the same time they became targets for violence generally associated with males (for example, drive-by shootings).

A third situation, similar to that experienced by the young women in the independent gangs, occurs when women in separate-but-together gangs find themselves in situations of conflict with homegirls from other gangs. However, in contrast to the African Americans much of this potential and real violence is instigated by the girls' own homeboys:

(I) Do the boys expect the girls to act a certain way?

(R) Sometimes. Like sometimes when you are all hanging together and the guys say, "Hey, go jump that girl," right, for no reason. You don't want to.

(I) If you guys don't do it, then what happens? Do they let it go?

(R) Well sometimes they'll hit you, but just playing.

According to some respondents, one reason for this instigation is that their homeboys like to see girls fighting. However, the girls in both types of groups do not like to be provoked into fighting with rival homegirls by any males (whether they were the rivals' boyfriends or their own homeboys). Some girls see male provocation as senseless and domineering.

A fourth situation involves internal conflict between female members of a gang. In contrast with the women in the independent gangs, women in the separate-but-together groups admit that they got into fights among themselves, usually because of gossiping, "talking shit," drinking and getting drunk, or conflicts over men. In relation to gossiping, or "talking shit" (making derogatory comments about a homegirl's reputation), other researchers of gang life (Dietrich, 1998; Moore, 1991) note that notions of respect and honor are vitally important characteristics for a homegirl's life, and many of the Latinas describe the elements of a "good reputation":

> [It means] that you are not a ho, that you don't fuck all the homeboys. Even though sometimes you don't do it, everybody talks. So a good reputation is that you take care of your shit. And you respect your elders, and you don't go around the home boys, getting loaded and going to bed with them.

Once a homegirl becomes identified as a "ho," it is difficult for her to regain her good reputation: "I don't want that name. 'Cause the name sticks with you. I don't care if you stop being a slut off the street, it sticks with you. So it's very important to keep a ladylike profile." Within this context of honor, respect, and a fear of achieving a bad reputation, the homegirls often referred to others "talking shit." When "talking shit" occurs, homegirls confront each other, demand a recantation or an explanation, and if it is not forthcoming, then violence can and does occur.

Internal fighting also takes place in the context of "partying" and drinking. Alcohol is a major theme in street life and "hanging out,"[3] especially among the Latinas and the African Americans. For the auxiliary gangs, drinking occurs in both public and private settings, and in many of the accounts of conflict between the homegirls, drinking and getting drunk plays an important contributory role.

Another issue that leads to conflict between homegirls within the same gang are disputes over males. Whereas descriptions of homeboy-instigated violence and fighting over men between homegirls were completely absent in the interviews with the women in the independent gangs, for the Latinas and Asian Americans this type of violence accounts for the majority of conflicts between homegirls. Other cases of homegirl conflict are occasioned by rivalry and jealousy between girls over individual homeboys. Fortunately, internal fights are confined to "regular" fistfighting, and do not involve weapons.

The fifth situation of violence for women in separate-but-together gangs involves conflict between homegirls and homeboys in the same gang. Because the males and females hold a collective identity, the young women indicate that they feel protected not only by the knowledge that their homegirls back them up, but also that their homeboys are there to defend them or avenge males who disrespect or assault them. This protection is known as "being down." It reinforces the traditional gender roles as well as the masculine character of the streets. Moreover, few homegirls describe their homeboys as being oppressively controlling over their lives or physically abusive to them, although some talk about the homeboys being verbally abusive, "talking mean," or occasionally "just playing." Sometimes they use other male members (especially the girls' brothers, if they are members) to keep aggressive male members in check. For example, protection by their homeboys also occurs when homegirls wish to defend themselves from unwelcomed advances from other homeboys. For example, a Latina described a situation where she called on her homeboys to beat up another homeboy because he had been sexually aggressive toward her:

> I remember this guy . . . that motherfucker cornered me and grabbed my ass and then tried to kiss me. I was like, "Get your motherfucking ass away from me." And he was like, he goes, "Hey you are cute though. You need to be with me." And blah, blah, and like it was every day

right after school. . . . Alba and I walked together . . . we went to the house and some of the guys [homeboys] were there. And I said, "Hey you guys I want you to kick this guy's ass." And they are like, "What did he do?" I am like, "This fucking guy tried to kiss me and grab my ass." They are like, "Okay." So they kicked his ass the next day. They kicked his ass good too.

Although the girls take some comfort in this solidarity, they are paradoxically victims of their male protectors, a situation absent among females in the independent gangs. Such a situation is most strikingly conveyed in this young woman's recounting of being raped by a fellow homeboy:

He gave me a lot of respect, you know. I used to go to his house drink up, smoke. And he used to really take care of me and I put a lot of trust on him. And once I smoked a leyo with him and I thought he was going to be cool with me. . . . I was by myself. He brought me to his house. I mean, we were at his house and then he brought me into his brother's room. He locked me in and took off my clothes. And I couldn't talk, you know. And I was telling him, "Let me go. Let me go. Don't do this to me. I'm your homegirl." . . . And I was going, "Let me go. Let me go." And he was slapping me. . . . They took me to San Francisco General Hospital and . . . they told me I was okay. And if I wanted to press charges on him 'cause I had really big bumps on my head and my face. . . . I thought I was going to feel embarrassed, everybody looking at me saying, "She got raped." I told nobody, but everybody knew. And they were looking at him bad. They were going to break his window. And then he called me up and he cried. He used to write me letters and he used to tell me that he loved me. And that he just wanted to have me in his arms and everything. And I said, "You shouldn't do that in the first place 'cause I was your homegirl and everything."

These girls' experiences suggest a complex relationship with their male counterparts in which the girls simultaneously are protected from potentially aggressive situations, but also are open to sexual victimization by their protectors.

Violence in the Family

Girl gang members' relationships with their parents and other family members are varied and complex, with some reporting strong family ties, others describing violent confrontations or sexual and physical abuse, and others expressing extreme hatred (Moore & Hagedorn, 1996).[4] Two significant relationships can be identified from the homegirls' discussions of family: relations with their mothers and relations with fathers and stepfathers.

Mothers. The most significant relationship for the majority of the young women is with their mothers. Most describe generally positive ties with their mothers, seeing their mothers in traditional terms as well as accommodating to changes in the mother's role and position in the family. However, even within these more positive accounts, the young women make references to the disruptive features in their family. One 15-year-old respondent, who reports having a good relationship with her mother, casually remarks that she currently is living with her sister. When asked why, she replied " 'Cause my mom got locked up. . . . 'Cause of drugs. Shooting up."

Disruptions to their relationships surface in ways in which the girls feel they have little control. A few respondents find their relationship changing with their mothers when the latter becomes involved with men:

Me and my mom, always had a good relationship, but for like a year, I moved away from her and we stopped talking 'cause she got with this other guy and, you know, I just didn't like it. . . . I felt that this guy was like, just using her, and I didn't, I couldn't stand it 'cause it was my mom, you know, and I've always been pretty much with my mother, I've always had a good relationship.

In contrast to these more positive accounts, many homegirls describe conflictual relationships with their mothers. More than half of the sample blame their mothers for the problems in the home. Of these, more than one-half attribute problems to their mothers' drinking or drug use. Even so, some of the girls accept their mothers' problems and assume the parental role over the mother as well as over younger siblings.

Two respondents' criticisms of their mothers stem from their mothers' failure to protect them from their stepfathers' sexual molestation and assaults. The respondents report that their trust in their mothers has been undermined and that a "lot of hatred" now exists in the home, making living together an impossibility. However, in almost all the cases, even when the women report hostile and negative relations with their mothers some level of interaction still occurs, and only in a few cases is interaction completely broken.

In spite of these respondents' negative feelings toward their mothers, they nevertheless maintain ties with their mothers, partly out of familial loyalty and love, but also for instrumental reasons. It is their mothers who they turn to in times of need. Although a few respondents express strong feelings of animosity toward their mothers for past behaviors, they rely on them for help in looking after their children, shelter, and even protection. This seemingly contradictory behavior is strikingly highlighted in one case, where the respondent, although having described her mother in the early part of the interview in lurid terms, for example, "a fuckin' bitch" and "a fuckin' drunk," later on proudly describes how, having got in a fight with an older woman, she telephones her mother to come and defend her, and how her mother, having "hunted down" the older woman, "kicks her ass":

> I went and called my mom. I said the bitch wants to fuck with me. I said, "Mom, drop off my son and come and look at my face 'cause she got two hits on me," and I said, "Mom, get over here. I just fought this bitch and she's as old as you." . . . She came and said, "Where's this bitch at?" I was like, "Oh man, my mom's from New York, you know, and my mom all hunting that bitch down," and I didn't get to see her kick her ass, but, you know, everybody was like, "Damn it, look at Maria's mom." They thought I was going to go snitch and call the cops. I said, "Nah, I'm calling someone better. I'm calling my mom."

The intricacy of these relations and intensity of feelings expressed by these young women toward their mothers also can be seen from those cases where the respondents recounted situations where they had physically defended their mothers. The defense of, and sense of loyalty to, their mothers also came through in their home lives, as the young women often witnessed conflict between their parents or between their mothers and mothers' boyfriend or spouse. Nearly half of the women reported such incidents of violence in the home and most of the time they sided with their mothers.

Fathers and Stepfathers. Just as their relationships with their mothers were varied, so also are their relationships with their fathers, although not as extensive or complex. However, in comparing their relationships with their mothers with those of their fathers, one significant difference emerges. Female gang members have less to say about their fathers. Fewer than one-fourth provide information about these relationships. In some cases, they mention their fathers only in passing; in others, their fathers seem to be nonexistent. This feature is not surprising when we consider the small proportion of respondents, approximately a third, who have lived with their fathers for most of the time until their sixteenth birthday. Although some respondents describe growing up as "just normal" and having good relationships with their fathers, many in the course of the interview recount situations of tension and disruption within the family.

Alcohol and drug consumption and alcohol-related violence play a much more significant role in the accounts of their relationships with their fathers as opposed to their mothers—a characteristic also evident in the discussions of their stepfathers. Accounts of the latter are in general more negative than those pertaining to their fathers. Like the accounts of their fathers, the majority of the stepfathers are described either in passing or in harsh terms such as, "He disgusts me," and "I hate him a lot." Sometimes tension has resulted in violence, especially between the respondents' mothers and fathers/stepfathers or between their mothers and their boyfriends. The matter-of-fact way in which these incidences of family violence are described suggests that they were often regular occurrences within the family.

As many writers have noted (Campbell, 1991; Joe & Chesney-Lind, 1995; Moore, 1991), violence between parents, between siblings, and between parents and children are commonplace in homegirls' stories of their families, and homegirls are often witness to, and the victims of, multiple incidents of abuse in their homes, whether from their fathers/stepfathers, mothers, or siblings.

Violence directed at the respondent is the most common reason provided by respondents for negative feelings toward their fathers or stepfathers. The most extreme form of violence described by the young women is rape or sexual molestation. In the three cases where this had occurred, stepfathers account for two of the perpetrators, and the best friend of the father for the third. In the case of the father's best friend, the young woman describes how she hates her father not only because she blames him for his best friend raping her, but also because of his violence toward her—he often points a gun at her head. She also notes in her account that these events are the reasons why she herself is violent today:

> I would get like hate for my dad, 'cause he didn't take care, he left me alone when he was supposed to take care of me and his best friend raped me when I was 7. . . . That's why I got so violent, you know, where I could just kill somebody . . . 'cause that anger that was inside of me. . . . I feel a lot of that frustration, you know, those people hurt me, man, they hurt me when they do that to me, and that's why I guess I got to a point where I said nothing's gonna hurt me no more, nobody's gonna see me shed a tear for nothing that they did to me. I remember when my dad used to put a gun to my head, it took all fear away from me from dying. . . . Everything was always stripped from me. I didn't have nothing no more. . . . Something in me was already taken away as a little girl.

Other young women remember violent events with their mothers' boyfriends. In the following example, the young woman describes her attempts to protect her mother, who she notes was beaten on a regular basis:

> He would always beat up on my mom, and I was the one that would call the police because my sister would get scared and go and run and put herself in a corner. They were usually at night. We are trying to go to sleep and we always wake up to my mom screaming. I would wake up and my sister would be all scared and I would be like, "It is okay. I will call the police." Every single time I would try and help my mom. Try to beat him with something. I would always grab some shit and . . . throw it at him or something and try to get him off her. That motherfucker was strong.

Despite the ups and downs in the young women's relationships with their mothers, they nevertheless maintain emotional and instrumental ties. In many cases, relationships are reciprocal in the sense that at times mothers provide the nurturing and protective role for their daughters, and at other times the daughters assume the motherly role of caregiver and protector. This intimacy and reciprocal care-giving is largely absent in the young women's relationships with their fathers, where interaction is best characterized as distant, periodic, and strained. In essence, their relationship is nonrelational. Only a few of the female gang members describe feelings of affection and warmth toward their fathers.

Family disruption is a major reason for running away, with the homegirls citing problems with their mothers or stepfathers or parental drug use. More than half of the sample has run away from home at least once, some for only a day, whereas others left home for up to 2 years, some as many as 20 times. Yet leaving the family for however long is not always because the respondents wish to escape family conflict. Other reasons for running away include a desire to be independent, the attraction of life outside the family, and, in one case, simply the desire to attend a rave.

Violence With Boyfriends

In spite of the dangers that exists for the homegirls on the street, conflict with boyfriends at home is the most significant arena for violence. The girls quickly learn that the men in their lives have a number of general assumptions about women. Our respondents uniformly agree that the men in their lives had certain conventional expectations of them. For example, Natalie, a 24-year-old African American girl in an independent group, succinctly summarizes this common view: "He just want me to act *like a woman* [her emphasis]." The girls are very clear on what the men define as "acting like a woman." One key defining feature was for the women to be domestic. Many of the young women complain that they are constantly cleaning and cooking when they hang out with their boyfriends at somebody's house, when they are partying, or attending barbecues and picnics at the park. The girls' reaction to these expectations vary, with some accepting this "feminine duty" and others completely rejecting it by confronting the men.

In addition to the requirement of fulfilling domestic chores, boyfriends also demand that the women bring in their share of the household income. If the woman does not comply, then violence could occur. For example, as Tanya, a 23-year-old African American girl makes clear:

> He wants me to do everything for him. He wants me to cook his dinner, wash his clothes and shit, and he slaps me around when I don't do it . . . because I didn't have his dinner ready when he came from outside selling his dope. And I didn't have his tennis shoes—wasn't white enough one time—so he beat me up. He is mean to me at times. He wants to control me. I go out to make money for my kids and he wants my money so he can invest it in his dope and get more dope. I am like, "What if somebody take it off him, where is my money?" It is gone. He wants me to be just down for him and do whatever he wants. He wants me to sell dope for him. But I don't. I sell it for myself to make money for my kids.

Others in similar situations, indicate that although they would attempt to fulfill the domestic requirements, they are nevertheless unwilling to be "duped" into giving their income, usually from drug dealing or shoplifting, to them.

According to the women, boyfriends, and to an extent homeboys, hold other traditional expectations of them. In particular, they were expected to act within the confines of "appropriate womanly behavior." The lists of "don'ts" included "not to flirt with men, not to sleep with men other than your boyfriend, not to take drugs or too much alcohol, and not to be foulmouthed," especially in the presence of "others." Controls over the women increase when a homeboy assumes the role of a boyfriend. Activities that the young women previously had been involved in now became curtailed. For example, boyfriends often disapprove of the homegirls hanging out on the streets:

> My boyfriend is alright, but he is a pain in the ass. He don't want me to be hanging out. He thinks he can own me. He won't let me do nothing. He won't let me go out with my friends and hang out. When I leave without permission, when I come back he just gets mad and slaps me.

As Dietrich has noted, boyfriends expected their girlfriends to be " 'regular jainas' who stayed home and waited for their men to return" (1998, p. 146). The homegirls recognize that lovers constantly preach and regulate their behavior in large part to protect their own image and status; that is, they did not want to be associated in any meaningful way with "bad girls," who are simply for fun. But they do not want reputable girls to make them out as fools. It is his image that is to be protected as "master," rather than as "fool."

They also recognize the power associated with their boyfriends' expectations. The consequences of completely defying or resisting these expectations can be severe, involving violence. Although many of the women describe their ideal man as a "gentleman" who treats them well and respects them, "I want a guy who like has a car, has money, has good looks, nice, and is not going to talk shit to me and not going to threaten me," many of the women described how they were constantly in and out of abusive relationships. For example, the respondent who described above her ideal man went on to say, when asked to compare the qualities of her ideal man with the homeboys she had dated:

> (I) Are those the kind of boys that you have been dating?

> (R) No. The guys that I usually date don't have cars, they don't have money, and if they do it is drug money. They want to fight with me, they want to talk shit to me, they want to threaten me. They are cute; that's about all they are good for.

Overall, the women dislike, and in some cases reject, aggressive attempts to make them conform to more traditional notions of feminity, including sexual chastity, staying at home, cooking, and looking after children.

Conclusion

What then can we conclude from this material? First and most obviously, girl gang members experience an extensive amount of violence in their lives whether on the streets, in their family lives, or in their relationships with their boyfriends and lovers. Second, they experience the violence not solely as victims, but on some occasions they act as the instigators of the violence. Although many of the accounts given by these young women describe situations where they had violence done to them, they also describe occasions where they have been violent toward others. In the context of the family, respondents often describe their violent behavior as defending family members or family honor. Third, on some occasions they are neither victims nor instigators but witnesses. In discussing their home lives, our respondents describe having witnessed violence between their mothers and fathers, stepfathers, or mothers' boyfriends. Finally, when we consider the impact of social organization and violence in the gang we find that the women in auxiliary gangs are more subject to "violence-prone situations" than those in the independent gang. Although all the respondents recount a variety of violent situations that had to be confronted on a daily basis, the risk of being harmed appears to have been present in many more settings for the young women in the auxiliary groups than for those in the independent groups. Whereas the former confront potential violence both inside and outside the gang, the women in the independent gangs have to deal only with potential violence outside the gang. Their own homegirls provide a refuge for them and are reliable and dependable. For the others, violence is perpetrated not only by men but also by their own homegirls. Whereas the women in the independent gangs feel safe among their fictive family of "sisters," the auxiliary gang girls describe a number of situations where they have to protect themselves and their reputations from other "sisters."

The main focus of this article has been to examine the different situations of violence female gang members encounter both on the streets and in their private lives with lovers and family. We have tried to contextualize their involvement in these situations of violence sometimes as offenders (or more precisely as defenders of their honor and reputations and personal safety), but also as victims living in a tension-filled, sometimes hostile, environment. It is not that they seek out violent encounters, but rather, they must seek out a place at home, on the street, and in a marginalized community, and in doing so they may have to resort to violence to protect themselves. Importantly, however, we must underscore that in seeking out a place at home and on the streets, violence, although present, does not consume these young women's everyday lives. Much of their everyday lives entail getting together to talk and shop, to hang out, and to care for their children. Their reasons for joining the group, after all, are related to their desire to

have and create a sense of family (Joe & Chesney-Lind, 1995).

Notes

1. Exceptions to this include the work of Bowker and Klein, 1983; Brotherton, 1996; Brown, 1977; Campbell, 1984 and 1991; Chesney-Lind and Hagedorn, 1999; Fishman, 1988; Harris, 1988; Hunt, MacKenzie, and Joe-Laidler, 2000; Joe-Laidler and Hunt, 1997; Miller, 2001; Moore, 1991; Ostner, 1986; Quicker, 1983.

2. For a more detailed discussion of the relationship of gang organization and violence see Joe-Laidler and Hunt, 1997.

3. For a fuller discussion of the role of alcohol in the lives of female gang members see Hunt, Joe-Laidler, and MacKenzie, 2000.

4. For a fuller discussion of girl gang members' relationships with family members see Hunt, MacKenzie, and Joe-Laidler, 2000.

References

Abraham, M. (2000). *Speaking the unspeakable: Marital violence among South Asian immigrants in the United States.* New Brunswick: Rutgers.

Asbury, J. (1987). African-American women in violent relationships: An exploration of cultural differences. In R. L. Hampton (Ed.), *Violence in the Black family: Correlates and consequences* (pp. 89–105). Lexington, MA: Lexington Books.

Biernacki, P., & Waldorf, D. (1981). Snowball sampling: Problems and techniques of chain referral sampling. *Sociological Methods and Research,* 10(2), 141–163.

Bowker, L. H., & Klein, M. W. (1983). The etiology of female juvenile delinquency and gang membership: A test of psychological and social structural explanations. *Adolescence,* 18(72), 739–751.

Brotherton, D. C. (1996). "Smartness," "toughness," and "autonomy": Drug use in the context of gang female delinquency. *Journal of Drug Issues,* 26, 261–277.

Brown, W. K. (1977). Black female gangs in Philadelphia. *International Journal of Offender Therapy and Comparative Criminology,* 21(3), 221–228.

Bureau of Justice Statistics (BJS). (1999). *Women Offenders: Special Report.* Washington, DC: U.S. Department of Justice.

———. (2000a). *Criminal Victimization in the U.S. 1998, Statistical Tables. National Crime Victimization Survey.* Washington, DC: U.S. Department of Justice.

———. (2000b). *Intimate Partner Violence: Special Report.* Washington, DC: U.S. Department of Justice.

Campbell, A. (1984). *The girls in the gang.* New Brunswick: Rutgers University Press.

———. (1991). *The girls in the gang* (2nd ed.). Cambridge, MA: Basil Blackwell.

Cazenave, N. A., & Straus, M. A. (1990). Race, class, network embeddedness, and family violence: A search for potent support systems. In M. A. Straus & R. J. Gelles (Eds.), *Physical violence in American families: Risk factors and adaptions to violence in 8,145 families* (pp. 321–339). New Brunswick: Transaction.

Chesney-Lind, M. (1993). Girls, gangs and violence: Anatomy of a backlash. *Humanity and Society,* 17(3), 321–344.

———. (1997). *The female offender: Girls, women, and crime.* Thousand Oaks, CA: Sage.

Chesney-Lind, M., & Hagedorn, J. M. (Eds.). (1999). *Female gangs in America.* Chicago: Lake View Press.

Chesney-Lind, M., Shelden, R. G., & Joe, K. A. (1996). Girls, delinquency, and gang membership. In C. R. Huff (Ed.), *Gangs in America* (2nd ed., pp. 185–204). Thousand Oaks, CA: Sage.

Crowell, N. A., & Burgess, A. W. (Eds.). (1996). *Understanding violence against women.* Washington, DC: National Academy Press.

Curry, G. D., Ball, R. A., & Fox, R. J. (1994). *Gang crime and law enforcement recordkeeping.* Washington, DC: National Institute of Justice.

Dietrich, L. C. (1998). *Chicana adolescents: Bitches, 'hos, and schoolgirls.* Westport, CT: Praeger.

Durant, R. H., Cadenhead, C., Pendergrast, R. A., & Slavens, G. (1994). Factors associated with the use of violence among urban black adolescents. *American Journal of Public Health,* 84(4), 612–617.

Esbensen, F., & Huizinga, D. (1993). Gangs, drugs, and delinquency in a survey of urban youth. *Criminology,* 31(4), 565–589.

Esbensen, F., Huizinga, D., & Weiher, A. W. (1993). Gang and non-gang youth: Differences in explanatory factors. *Journal of Contemporary Criminal Justice,* 9, 94–116.

Fagan, J. (1990a). Intoxication and aggression. In M. Tonry & J. Q. Wilson (Eds.), *Drugs and crime* (pp. 241–320). Chicago: University of Chicago Press.

———. (1990b). Social processes of delinquency and drug use among urban gangs. In C. R. Huff (Ed.), *Gangs in America* (pp. 183–219). Newbury Park, CA: Sage.

Fishman, L. (1988). *The vice queens: An ethnographic study of female gang behavior.* Paper presented at the American Society of Criminology, University of Vermont, Burlington.

Harris, M. (1988). *Cholas: Latino girls and gangs.* New York: AMS.

Ho, C. K. (1990). An analysis of domestic violence in Asian American communities: A multicultural approach to counseling. *Women and Therapy,* 9, 129–150.

Horowitz, R. (1990). Sociological perspectives on gangs: Conflicting definitions and concepts. In C. R. Huff (Ed.), *Gangs in America* (pp. 37–54). Newbury Park, CA: Sage.

Hunt, G., MacKenzie, K., & Joe-Laidler, K. (2000). I'm calling my mom: The meaning of family and kinship among homegirls. *Justice Quarterly,* 17(1), 1–31.

Hunt, G., Joe-Laidler, K., & MacKenzie, K. (2000). "Chillin', being dogged and getting buzzed": Alcohol in the lives of female gang members. *Drugs: Education, Prevention and Policy,* 7(4), 331–353.

Inciardi, J. A., Horowitz, R., & Pottieger, A. E. (1993). *Street kids, street drugs, street crime: An examination of drug use and serious delinquency in America.* Belmont: Wadsworth.

Joe, K. (1993). Getting into the gang: Methodological issues in studying ethnic gangs. In M. D. L. Rosa & J. L. R. Adrados (Eds.), *Drug abuse among minority youth: Advances in research and methodology* (pp. 234–257). Rockville, MD: U.S. Department of Health and Human Services, National Institute on Drug Abuse.

Joe, K., & Chesney-Lind, M. (1995). Just every mother's angel: An analysis of gender and ethnic variations in youth gang membership. *Gender and Society,* 9(4), 408–431.

Joe-Laidler, K. A., & Hunt, G. (1997). Violence and social organization in female gangs. *Social Justice,* 24(4), 148–169.

Klein, M. W. (1971). *Street gangs and street workers.* Englewood Cliffs, NJ: Prentice Hall.

———. (1995). *The American street gang: Its nature, prevalence, and control.* New York, NY: Oxford University Press.

Lum, J. (1998). Family violence. In L. C. Lee & N. W. S. Lane (Eds.), *Handbook of Asian American psychology* (pp. 505–525). Thousand Oaks: Sage.

Miller, J. A. (1996). *Female gang involvement in a Midwestern city: Correlates, nature and meanings.* Unpublished doctoral dissertation, University of Southern California, Los Angeles.

———. (2001). *One of the guys: Girls, gangs, and gender.* New York: Oxford University Press.

Moore, J. W. (1991). *Going down to the barrio: Homeboys and homegirls in change.* Philadelphia: Temple University Press.

Moore, J. W., & Hagedorn, J. M. (1996). What happens to girls in the gang? In C. R. Huff (Ed.), *Gangs in America* (2nd ed., pp. 205–218). Thousand Oaks, CA: Sage.

Ostner, I. (1986). Die Entdeckung der Madchen. Neue Perspektiven fur die. *Kolner-Zeitschrift-fur Soziologie-und-Sozialpsychologie,* 38, 352–371.

Quicker, J. C. (1983). *Homegirls: Characterizing*

Chicana gangs. Los Angeles: International University Press.

Reiss, A. J., & Roth, J. A. (Eds.). (1993). *Understanding and preventing violence.* Washington, DC: National Academy Press.

Sorenson, S. B. (1996). Violence against women: Examining ethnic differences and commonalities. *Evaluation Review, 20,* 123–145.

Sorenson, S. B., & Telles, C. A. (1991). Self-reports of spousal violence in a Mexican-American and non-Hispanic white population. *Violence and Victims, 6*(1), 3–15.

Straus, M. A., & Gelles, R. J. (1986). Societal change and change in family violence from 1975 to 1985 as revealed by two national surveys. *Journal of Marriage and the Family, 48,* 465–479.

Straus, M. A., & Smith, C. (1990). Violence in Hispanic families in the United States: Incidence rates and structural interpretations. In M. A. Straus & R. J. Gelles (Eds.), *Physical violence in American families: Risk factors and adaptations to violence in 8,145 families* (pp. 341–367). New Brunswick: Transaction.

Tjaden, P., & Thoennes, N. (2000). *Extent, nature and consequences of intimate partner violence.* Washington, DC: National Institute of Justice.

Waldorf, D. (1993). *Final Report of the Crack Sales, Gangs and Violence Study.* (NIDA Report). San Francisco: Institute for Scientific Analysis.

Winfree, L. T., Fuller, K., Vigil, T., & Mays, G. L. (1992). The definition and measurement of "gang status": Policy implications for juvenile justice. *Juvenile Family Court Journal, 43*(1), 29–37. ✦

Chapter 22
Defining Gang Homicide:
An Updated Look at Member and Motive Approaches[1]

Cheryl L. Maxson
and Malcolm W. Klein

Law enforcement agencies adopt different definitional policies for tabulating and reporting "gang-related" crime. A major distinction is whether gang features are fundamental to the motive of the incident or whether gang members participate regardless of the motive. Maxson and Klein apply the two definitional approaches to Los Angeles homicide data and find that the difference between the resulting case groups is less than one might expect. Although departments using the motive definition will report far fewer numbers of gang-related crimes, the overall character of the two types of gang cases is quite similar. However, depictions of drug aspects of gang homicide appear to be influenced by definitional approach.

Attempts to develop generalizations across cities about the prevalence of gang violence need to take these definitional stances into account. However, characterizations about the nature of gang violence are less vulnerable to definitional variations. The implications of different definitional styles may be more or less important depending upon the purposes for which these data are utilized.

In our chapter for the first edition of *Gangs in America* (Maxson and Klein, 1990), we

Reprinted from: C. Ronald Huff (ed.), *Gangs in America*, 2nd ed., pp. 3–20. Copyright © 1990 by Sage Publications, Inc. Reprinted by permission.

presented Los Angeles homicide data from the years 1978 through 1982 to investigate the implications of two approaches to defining gang crime—the member versus motive definitions. In the current edition, we utilize homicide incidents from 1988 and 1989 to update our previous findings and to examine whether or not drug aspects introduce differences in the definitional analyses.

The recent proliferation of U.S. cities with street gang activity increases the importance of investigating the relationships between gangs, violence and drug distribution. A recent study by the authors estimates about 1,100 gang-involved cities and towns (Klein, 1995)—cities of all shapes and sizes. Curry, Ball, and Decker (1995) report a national estimate of 735 jurisdictions with a population of at least 25,000 with gang crime problems. Our law enforcement respondents share a deep concern about the violence and drug activity reportedly associated with gangs in cities both large and small.[2] Furthermore, the implications of different law enforcement approaches to definitions of street gangs, gang membership and gang-related crime extend to the vast array of cities; police officials are grappling with developing methods of counting, reporting and understanding their gang problems.

But it is to Los Angeles, one of the "traditional" gang areas, often referred to as the gang "capital" of the United States, that we turned to address our research questions. The grim figure of 779 gang homicides occurring in the county of Los Angeles in 1994 provides corroboration for this appellation (McBride, Los Angeles Sheriff's Department, personal communication, August 21, 1995). We will, as before, refer to two definitional approaches, gang-member versus gang-motive homicides. The first are defined as having a gang member on either the assailant or victim side; the second are defined in terms of group-loyalty vs. individual interest as the principal reason for the act. The primary research questions can be stated quite simply: Updating the implications of using member versus motive definitions of gang homicides,

- How many homicides appear to result from gang motives? Has the proportion of gang-motivated cases changed from 1978–82 levels?

- What incident and participant characteristics distinguish member-defined gang cases from motive-defined gang cases? Are there different distinguishing characteristics when each group of cases is compared with nongang cases? Are there different patterns in each of these comparisons involving 1988–89 homicides from those found in 1978–82 homicides?

- How successful are these characteristics in classifying member-defined gang versus nongang cases and motive-defined gang versus nongang homicides? Are the classification rates similar to those found in earlier years?

Combining the drug and definition issues,

- What aspects of drug involvement distinguish member-defined gang cases from motive-defined gang cases, and each from their nongang counterparts?

- Is the classification of gang (member and motive) versus nongang cases improved by the consideration of aspects of drug involvement?

Following a brief discussion of the definitional issue and an overview of the study methods, we present the current Los Angeles data to address each of the research questions. We conclude with the implications of these findings for knowledge about gang violence in Los Angeles and elsewhere.

Definitional Approaches to 'Gang-Related' Crime

Law enforcement procedures for defining gang-related crime take on increased significance in the current context of the proliferation of cities with street gang problems. Despite the resurgence of ethnographic gang studies, these are limited in both the number of gangs and the cities investigated. Law enforcement is currently the best source available for comparisons of gang prevalence and violence. The definitional approaches adopted by these newer gang cities will have a distinct impact on perceptions of the scope and nature of gang violence in this country. There is a lack of consensus among law enforcement (Curry, Ball, and Fox, 1994; Curry et al., 1995; Spergel, 1988) and, for that matter, among researchers (Curry, 1991; Ehrensaft and Spergel, 1991), regarding the optimal definitional approach. There is even disagree-

ment as to the presumed value of adopting common definitions (Decker and Kempf-Leonard, 1991; Horowitz, 1990). Ball and Curry (1995) recently lodged the following criticism against their academic coworkers: "Unfortunately . . . few if any gang researchers and theorists have been sufficiently conscious of their own definitional stances, with the result that their definitions have carried too many latent connotations, treated correlates or consequences as properties or causes, or contributed to similar errors of logic" (p. 239). Yet, a recent symposium of street gang experts from state and local law enforcement agencies across the country issued a call for standardized definitions and provided a model based upon the consensus reached at this meeting (National Drug Intelligence Center [NDIC], 1995).

Among law enforcement agencies, there are two basic approaches to defining gang-related violence. Officials in Los Angeles and many other cities have adopted a rather broad definitional policy, designating an incident as gang-related if either the suspect or victim is a gang member. This is the approach recommended by the NDIC gathering described above. Officials in Chicago and other cities apply the more stringent criterion of a direct link to gang function. In Chicago, there must be positive evidence that gang activity or gang membership was the motive for the encounter (Block, 1991). Examples of such motives are retaliation, territoriality, recruitment, and "representing" (graffiti, wearing gang colors, shouting gang slogans, etc.) (Bobrowski, 1988). We refer to these two approaches as "gang-member" and "gang-motive" definitions. (See Maxson and Klein, 1990, for a detailed description of these definitional approaches.) A recent national survey of prosecutors in 192 jurisdictions that have addressed gangs found that equal numbers in large jurisdictions adopted each approach (Institute for Law and Justice, 1994). More small jurisdictions (59 percent) use the narrower definition, that is, a crime committed by a gang member for the benefit of a gang.

For the current study, we posed questions regarding the implications of the two definitional approaches. The first is a prevalence question: What proportion of the homicides designated as gang-involved by the member definition would also satisfy the motive requirement? This analysis has both operational and statistical significance. Gang homicides are often assigned to investigators with special gang expertise, which may produce more positive investigative outcomes (Maxson, Klein, and Gordon, 1990). The number of gang homicides reported would certainly differ. In 1994, law enforcement gang experts in the city of Los Angeles tallied 370 gang homicides, or a whopping 44 percent of all homicides occurring in the city in that year (Los Angeles Police Department, personal communication, August 23, 1995). On the other hand, the Chicago Police Department reported a 1994 figure of 293 gang homicides, a more moderate 32 percent of all homicides for that year (D. Hilbring, Chicago Police Department, personal communication, August 23, 1995).[3]

The second research question addresses the impact of the two definitional approaches on descriptions of the *nature* of gang homicide, particularly in comparison with nongang incidents. If the characteristics of the two types of gang cases are similar and the differences between gang and nongang incidents remain stable, then elements of gang violence can be compared from city to city, despite different operational approaches to defining gang-related crime. Legitimate, cross-city comparisons provide a foundation for building generalized knowledge about gangs.

That, in essence, was the conclusion we drew from the earlier analyses of two data sets made up of gang and nongang homicides that occurred in the city of Los Angeles and in county areas patrolled by the Los Angeles Sheriff's Department (LASD) (Maxson and Klein, 1990). The Los Angeles Police Department (LAPD) homicides were drawn from three station areas over the years 1979–1981; the LASD data spanned the years 1978–1982 and included all 19 station areas. The two data sets were analyzed separately, but the conclusions held for both jurisdictions: Applying the criterion of the presence of a gang motive reduced the number of gang homicides by about half, but for the most part, the qualitative differences between gang and nongang cases were constant, regardless of the definitional criteria used.

We noted some variation between the two jurisdictions, but these differences were minor in contrast with the overall stability of gang versus nongang distinctions. We confirmed the conclusions emerging from the bivariate analyses with discriminant analysis techniques, noting once again some differences, but an overall pattern of consistency between the two definitional approaches.

We wondered whether these conclusions would hold up in more recent homicides and furthermore whether drug aspects of homicides might introduce some differences in the definitional analyses that we were not able to examine in the earlier project. Thus, we were able to combine our interests in both the drug and definitional aspects of gang violence with analyses of current gang and nongang homicides while updating our prior findings.

Method

Our current study includes homicides from five station areas in South Central Los Angeles, selected due to high levels of gang and drug activity. Three of the five stations were within the jurisdiction of the LAPD and two were county areas handled by the LASD. The data from the two departments are combined for all analyses reported in this chapter.

Gang and nongang homicides occurring in the five station areas during 1988 and 1989 were sampled using a random stratified approach to yield equal numbers of each type for collection. Officer-involved shootings and the few cases handled by specialized units other than the homicide division were deleted from the population. Lists of "gang-involved" cases were supplied by each jurisdiction's specialized gang unit. Both departments employ broad definitions of gang involvement including membership of participants on either side, behavioral indications during the incident, and other gang indicators that may emerge during the course of the investigation. In a previous study, we found the application of these criteria to homicide cases to be relatively stable over time in both jurisdictions (Klein, Gordon, and Maxson, 1986; Maxson, Gordon, and Klein, 1985). The sampling procedures resulted in 201 gang and 201 nongang homicides, reflecting about two-thirds of the gang homicides and slightly less of the nongang homicides. Despite the inclusion of two station areas from the LASD jurisdiction, it should be noted that about three-fourths of these cases are from LAPD.

A team of data collectors extracted information from extensive homicide investigation files. On occasion, files could not be located, and in a few instances, access was denied by the detective in possession of the case material; these cases were replaced by randomly selected cases from the remaining population. Coded items included descriptors of the incident (e.g., setting, automobile involvement, weapons, related case charges, additional injuries, and gang motives), participants (e.g., numbers on each side, relationship, demographics of designated victims and suspects, and stated gang affiliations), and an extensive list of drug indicators (use and sales paraphernalia, drugs found in investigation, autopsy results, drug use or sales by participants, aspects of the location, and drug motives). Intercoder reliability was assessed by duplicate coding of 10 percent of the sample. Overall, reliabilities were quite high (over .90), but it should be noted that the data collection was closely supervised, with lots of involvement by senior staff in coding decisions.

Findings

Assessing the Implications of Different Definitional Approaches

We begin with the basic question of how many of the homicides labeled as gang-involved by Los Angeles gang units, utilizing the broad member definition, would retain their gang status under the more stringent motive criterion. Then moving beyond the issue of case numbers, we use the incident and participant characteristics to explore the differences between the two types of gang cases and the respective gang-nongang comparisons. Finally, discriminant analytic techniques permit an assessment of the overall impact of these variables on distinguishing gang from nongang homicides. We examine whether the motive approach produces a "purified" set of gang cases, more clearly distinct from nongang cases, with a wholly different character from homicides categorized using the member criterion.

Of the 201 homicides labeled by the gang units as gang-member involved, 120 (60 percent) also had statements of gang motives present in the case file investigation materials. Similar motive statements also appeared in 8 (4 percent) of the 201 nongang homicides.[4] Both figures are slightly higher than those found in the 1978–82 homicides.

In the earlier study, 52 percent of the member-defined gang homicides and 2 percent of the nongang homicides included statements of gang motives. This difference over time may reflect changes in the nature of gang activity, increased sensitivity of law enforcement investigators to gang issues, differences in the sampling strategies employed in the two studies, or some combination of these factors.

Clearly, a narrow definition such as Chicago's would reduce the reported Los Angeles rate significantly. The revised 1994 figure for the city of Los Angeles would be in the neighborhood of 222 gang-related homicides, as compared with the 370 incidents reported using the member definition.[5] Both figures are high and represent substantial human and social costs, but one could reasonably question whether 222 homicides would have provoked the intense law enforcement and press reactions to gang activity that we have observed over the last several years in Los Angeles. Moreover, the new figure for Los Angeles is considerably lower than Chicago's total of 293. When the issue is *prevalence*, that is, the volume of gang activity, clearly comparisons between cities with different definitional styles would be quite inappropriate.

Putting aside the issue of comparative incident counts, we now turn to the question of, "So what?" If reducing the pool of gang incidents to the presumably more "pure," motivated cases does not substantially alter the descriptions of gang violence, then comparisons regarding the *nature* of gang activity between cities with different definitional policies may be quite legitimate.

We approached this issue by utilizing a series of variables describing the incidents and participants and comparing gang with nongang cases. This required construction of a new data set made up of the 128 identified gang-motive cases and a comparable group of 128 nongang cases, sampled randomly from a reconstituted population of the remaining homicides. This reconstitution was a complex procedure, but allowed those member-defined gang cases *not* meeting the motive criteria to fall within the nongang motive group. For the comparison member-defined data set, we sampled 128 gang and 128 nongang cases from the original 402 cases.[6] Table 22.1 shows the bivariate comparisons of gang-nongang differences in case characteristics, employing first the member definition and then the motive definition.

The construction of Table 22.1 permits several types of comparisons. Characteristics of the two types of gang cases are displayed in the first and fourth columns.[7] There is a striking similarity between the two sets of percentages and means. Motive-defined gang cases are slightly more likely to occur on the street and are slightly less likely to involve participants with a clear prior relationship than member-defined incidents. These differences are minimal and not substantially significant. In fact, comparing the incident and participant characteristics of the two types of gang cases suggests that we are not dealing with two distinct types at all. Descriptions of the nature of gang homicide categorized by either definitional approach are for all intents and purposes identical.

Does the similarity between the two types of gang cases extend to comparisons between the two groups of nongang homicides? Employing the motive definition results in the transfer of some member-defined gang cases[8] into the nongang population and may alter the aggregated character of the nongang comparison pool.

A cursory review of the second and fifth columns of Table 22.1 suggests that the two groups of nongang cases show more differences than the two sets of gang cases. Presence of automobiles, associated charges, and other (than the homicide) victim injuries are higher in nongang cases using the gang-motive approach than in nongang incidents under the member approach. This pattern suggests increased gang aspects of nongang cases when the gang-motive standard is applied. The direction of the slight differences in the participant characteristics (more participants, proportionally more males, more blacks, of younger ages) is consistent with this interpretation. Does this slight change in the nature of nongang homicides affect descriptions of the differences between gang and nongang incidents? The relevant comparisons are displayed by the two vertical halves of Table 22.1, with particular reference to the significance tests reported in the third and sixth columns.

The overall consistency between the two vertical halves of Table 22.1 is quite remarkable. With only a few exceptions, the same variables significantly differentiate gang from nongang homicides, and there are no reversals of direction. Consistent with the 1978–1982 incidents, the presence of associated charges seems to differentiate gang cases under one definitional approach but

Table 22.1
Characteristics of Gang and Nongang Homicides Using Member and Motive Definitions

	Member-Defined			Motive-Defined		
	Gang (n = 128)[b]	Nongang (n = 128)[b]	p[a]	Gang (n = 128)[b]	Nongang (n = 128)[b]	p[a]
Late afternoon-to-evening occurrence	49%	32%	**	52%	34%	**
Automobile present	80%	44%	***	83%	54%	***
Street location	58%	35%	***	65%	32%	***
Fear/threat of retaliation	37%	20%	**	40%	19%	***
Associated charge: violent	41%	16%	***	38%	30%	NS
Associated charge: robbery	6%	6%	NS	2%	13%	***
Gun(s) present	95%	74%	***	98%	76%	***
Other victim injuries present	38%	12%	***	38%	20%	**
Clear prior relationship	24%	48%	***	18%	47%	***
Mean number victim participants	4.13	1.79	**	4.47	1.95	**
Mean number suspect participants	2.70	1.71	***	2.83	1.95	***
Proportion male victims	.88	.73	***	.92	.78	***
Proportion male suspects	.96	.85	**	.98	.89	***
Proportion black suspects	.86	.88	NS	.84	.82	NS
Mean age victims	24.2	33.1	***	22.7	31.8	***
Mean age suspects	20.5	29.6	***	19.7	26.5	***

Notes: NS = not significant.
[a]Significance levels were determined by chi-squares or *t*-tests (*$p < .05$; **$p < .01$; ***$p < .001$).
[b]Numbers of cases included in each analysis vary according to missing values.

not the other, as exemplified by the lower proportion of nongang member-defined cases with additional violent offenses.

It appears that the motive approach is associated with a lower likelihood of gang designation when robbery is a feature of the case. This is hardly surprising and very consistent with conceptual distinctions between the member and motive definitions. Personal gain, rather than gang benefit, is more often viewed as the offender's primary motive. Perhaps more surprising is the marked similarity between the two definitional approaches in most of the incident and participant descriptors.

A more mixed picture emerges when we turn to more sophisticated, multivariate techniques in order to examine these distinctions further. Discriminant analysis organizes all the variables in such a way as to maximize their capacity to discriminate gang from nongang cases. The standardized coefficients reported in Table 22.2 show the relative contribution of each variable toward distinguishing gang from nongang incidents. The drug variables were not included in this analysis, and associated violent charges were dropped due to high correlations with other variables. The rank ordering of the size of the coefficients is provided in parentheses to facilitate the comparison between the two data sets. Eta squared (eta^2) is a measure of the ability of the discriminant function to explain the variance between gang and nongang cases.

In both data sets, mean age of suspects emerges as by far the strongest discriminator between gang and nongang incidents. The value of eta squared and the classification results are similar, although slightly higher in the motive-defined analysis. The overall pattern is one of shared variables, but in a departure from the bivariate results, three variables did not achieve sufficient discriminatory power to enter the motive-defined function. Two of these variables, mean age of victims and automobile presence, ranked quite high in the member-defined function. Consistent with the bivariate analysis, robbery as an associated case offense figured prominently in the motive function, but was the lowest-ranked variable in the member function. The rank-order correlation (rho) between the two columns of figures is a quite low .19. Further examination of the variable rankings in the discriminant analyses performed previously

Table 22.2
Gang Versus Nongang Discriminant Analysis Results: Member- and Motive-Defined Comparisons

	Member-Defined[a]	Motive-Defined[a]
Mean age, suspects	−.555 (1)	−.603 (1)
Number suspect participants	.243 (2)	.239 (6)
Mean age, victims	−.224 (3)	N.S.
Automobile present	.219 (4)	N.S.
Clear prior relationship	−.207 (5)	.266 (3)
Other victim injuries present	.190 (6)	.192 (9)
Proportion male suspects	.184 (7)	.253 (4)
Proportion black suspects	.170 (8)	.239 (7)
Late afternoon-to-evening occurrence	.166 (9)	.154 (11)
Fear/threat of retaliation present	.162 (10)	.243 (5)
Number victim participants	.150 (11)	.217 (8)
Gun(s) present	.139 (12)	.179 (10)
Proportion male victims	.139 (13)	N.S.
Associated charge: robbery	−.117 (14)	−.444 (2)
Street location	N.S.	.129 (12)
Variance explained (eta^2)	.429	.461
Classification success (%)		
Gang	85.5	91.3
Nongang	71.4	75.0
Overall	80.6	83.4

Notes: NS = not significant.

[a]Weights are standardized canonical discriminant function coefficients. Negative valence indicates inverse relationship with gang. Relative rankings are noted in parentheses. Member-defined analysis includes 113 gang cases and 98 nongang cases (45 cases dropped for missing values on at least one variable). Motive-defined analysis includes 115 gang cases and 108 nongang cases (33 cases dropped for missing values).

on the older LAPD and LASD homicide data sets shows equally low correlations.

Overall, data presented in Tables 22.1 and 22.2 do not suggest that drastic changes in the depiction of gang homicides or in the characterization of the differences between gang and nongang incidents occur when different operational approaches to gang crime definitions are applied by law enforcement. Descriptions of the *nongang* comparison group may be more vulnerable to definitional variations, but on the whole, we find a large measure of stability in the gang/nongang comparisons, at least at the bivariate level.

Multivariate analyses are less supportive of a stance that definitional policies make little difference in depictions of the character of gang violence. Despite similarities between the results of discriminant analyses of the two data sets, there are marked differences in the contributions that a few variables make to the discriminant functions. The import of robbery as an associated charge for the motive-derived function makes sense. It is possible that victim age and automobile presence failed to enter the motive function as a consequence of special features of robbery incidents, but there were too few such cases to examine this speculation. Expanding the analysis to include drug aspects of the incident may prove useful.

Combining the Drug and Definition Issues

The presence of robbery as an associated case offense affects whether or not a homicide would be handled as a gang crime in departments, depending upon their different definitional policies. Drug involvement may well have a similar impact. Drug information was collected on quite specific items, most of which did not produce sufficiently high frequencies to support analyses of gang-nongang differences. This fact in itself throws some doubt on the purportedly close relationship between gangs, drugs, and violence. Alternatively, we computed variables that represent more general aspects of drug involvement and reflect the gang-drug issues in South Central Los Angeles. Most drug (excluding alcohol) mentions were coded to indicate the type of drug involved. From these, we computed a variable for any *mention of cocaine* in the case. The *presence of any type of sales* or *distributional aspect* of the case could derive from the nature of the incident location, sales involvement by participants on either side, or motives related to drug distribution. Finally

mentions of any drug-related motive for the homicide includes conflicts over drug use, although these are far less frequent than motives stemming from drug distribution (for example, conflicts over drug territory and dealer rip-offs). In Table 22.3, we present the data on the three drug dimensions in gang and nongang incidents reflecting the two definitional approaches.

If drug sales are *not* intrinsically related to gang affairs, then one would expect the three drug dimensions to be less apparent in gang-motivated cases than in member-defined gang cases.[9] In comparing the first and fourth columns in Table 22.3, it appears that employing the gang-motive definition reduces the proportion of gang cases with cocaine involvement, drug sales aspects, or drug motives (see Note 8). Two of these, cocaine involvement and the presence of drug motives, appear with similar frequency in nongang cases, regardless of whether they are "nongang" by virtue of no gang members or no gang motive (see columns two and five in Table 22.3). But the third, the proportion of nongang cases with an aspect of drug sales, is higher when the gang-motive criterion is employed.

Drug aspects of the incidents do distinguish gang from nongang cases, but these vary by definitional approach. For this analysis, we tested for gang versus nongang differences by comparing columns one and two (member approach) and then, columns four and five (motive approach) in Table 22.3. The statistical tests for the significance of these respective differences are reported in the third and sixth column. Drug sales involvement separates gang-member cases from nongang incidents, but not from gang-motivated cases. Neither cocaine presence nor drug motives distinguishes gang-member cases from their nongang

Table 22.3
Drug Characteristics of Gang and Nongang Homicides Using Member and Motive Definitions

	Member-Defined			Motive-Defined		
	Gang (n = 128)[b]	Nongang (n = 128)[b]	p[a]	Gang (n = 128)[b]	Nongang (n = 128)[b]	p[a]
Cocaine involved	37%	47%	NS	29%	48%	**
Drug sales aspect	41%	28%	*	34%	37%	NS
Drug motive mentioned	20%	27%	NS	12%	28%	***

Notes: NS = not significant.
[a]Significance levels were determined by chi-squares or t-tests (*p < .05; **p < .01; ***p < .001).
[b]Numbers of cases included in each analysis varies according to missing values.

counterparts. On the other hand, both of these features differentiate motive-defined gang cases from nongang cases. These findings would be surprising to those who argue a close gang-drug-violence connection. Drug motives and cocaine involvement are *less* common in gang-motivated than in nongang homicides.

These bivariate results of the drug variables revealed interesting gang-nongang distinctions that varied between the two definitional styles. The "purification" of gang features resulting from the application of the motive approach reveals that drug aspects are important in distinguishing gang from nongang cases—cocaine and drug motives are more often featured in nongang cases.

Once again, we turned to discriminant analysis strategies to examine the relative impact of the drug variables. Unfortunately, the three drug dimensions have high intercorrelations that permitted the inclusion of only one drug variable in the multivariate analysis. A separate set of discriminant analyses was performed with the same set of incident and participant variables, plus mention of a drug motive.

As shown in Table 22.4, the drug motive variable entered both member and motive functions and ranked quite high (second) in the motive-defined data set. From the bivariate results, low ranking of drug motive in the member-defined function was not surprising. But the summary statistics (eta squared and classification) were affected only minimally by the inclusion of drug motive, nor did it appear to influence the relative contributions of the other variables. The rank-order correlations between the two member-defined functions (i.e., with and without the drug motive variable) and between the two motive-defined functions both exceeded .95. Clearly, our quest to explain the differential contribution of variables to gang-nongang distinctions has not been aided by the inclusion of drug motive.

Conclusion

Overall, these analyses of 1988 and 1989 incidents confirm our prior conclusions about the implications of different law enforcement policies regarding the designation of gang homicides. Adopting the narrower, motive criterion substantially reduces the number of gang homicides re-

Table 22.4

Gang Versus Nongang Discriminant Analysis Results: Member- and Motive-Defined Comparisons (Drug Motive Included)

	Member-Defined[a]	Motive-Defined[a]
Mean age, suspects	−.532 (1)	−.582 (1)
Mean age, victims	−.241 (2)	N.S.
Number suspect participants	.235 (3)	.259 (8)
Automobile present	.212 (4)	N.S.
Clear prior relationship	−.200 (5)	−.309 (5)
Proportion male suspects	.198 (6)	.310 (4)
Other victim injuries present	.188 (7)	.176 (10)
Proportion black suspects	.184 (8)	.277 (7)
Fear/threat of retaliation present	.169 (9)	.278 (6)
Late afternoon-to-evening occurrence	.162 (10)	.141 (12)
Gun(s) present	.158 (11)	.195 (9)
Drug motive mentioned	***−.158 (12)***	***−.397 (2)***
Number victim participants	.146 (13)	.175 (11)
Proportion male victims	.129 (14)	N.S.
Associated charge: robbery	N.S.	−.372 (3)
Street location	N.S.	N.S.
Variance explained (eta²)	.432	.495
Classification success (%)		
Gang	86.8	91.3
Nongang	74.5	75.9
Overall	81.3	83.9

Notes: NS = not significant.
[a]Weights are standardized canonical discriminant function coefficients. Negative valence indicates inverse relationship with gang. Relative rankings are noted in parentheses. Member-defined analysis includes 113 gang cases and 98 nongang cases (45 cases dropped for missing values on at least one variable). Motive-defined analysis includes 115 gang cases and 108 nongang cases (33 cases dropped for missing values).

ported by jurisdictions confronting violent gang activity. Comparisons of rates between jurisdictions embracing different definitional approaches are clearly *not* valid unless motive information is available to restructure a member-defined population of incidents (or conversely, if member information is available on non-motive but gang member–involved cases).

Cross-city comparisons of bivariate descriptions of gang, as compared with nongang, homicide characteristics *are* appropriate, but within certain limitations. On the one hand, the use of firearms, participant demographics, and the number of and relationship between participants are among the many examples of case characteristics that appear to be unaffected by definitional styles. On the other hand, comparisons of drug involvement and additional violent offenses should be approached with extreme caution.

Other general statements can be derived from the data on drug aspects of homicide. The finding that drug motives and cocaine mentions appear more commonly in non-gang cases but sales involvement is more frequent in gang incidents is interesting because most of the specific drug motives mentioned concerned sales rather than use. This suggests that although participants in gang homicides are more likely to have roles in the sales or distribution of drugs, this sales involvement may be less likely to figure as a "cause" of the homicide than in nongang cases. These findings do not support a strong connection between gang drug sales and violence. If anything, the sales-violence connection seems stronger in nongang cases. In any case, the term "drug-related" is just as ambiguous as is the term "gang-related." The "involved" versus "motivated" distinctions could be applied to an analysis of drug homicides just as we have used the member versus motive categories to investigate gang homicides.

Applying motive versus more general gang involvement criteria certainly results in different prevalence rates. Drug aspects emerge less frequently in cases designated as "gang" under the motive criterion. Given the ubiquitous association between gangs, drugs, and violence in the popular media, one wonders whether the connection would be made less readily if motive became the primary consideration for police (or media) reports of violence. Different definitional approaches to labeling gang and drug aspects of homicides could result in varying social constructions about the nature of gang and drug violence connections.

Since the use of discriminant analytic techniques is relatively limited in law enforcement circles, it remains for researchers to be somewhat troubled by the multivariate results. Frankly, we are stymied as to how to interpret the intricacies of the performance of certain variables and must fall back on the customary positions of caution and the call for more research of this type. In particular, it would be helpful if data from other cities could be investigated with similar analytic techniques.

Finally, there is the issue of which approach is better, more valid, or more useful.

For local law enforcement, it is probably *most* important to apply definitional policies consistently, regardless of the type of definition used. Both approaches are vulnerable to the availability of information. Motives can be quite difficult to determine, even with the resources usually devoted to homicide investigation; motive information often is not available for other types of offenses. Reliable gang rosters are quite costly to develop and maintain, require a strong commitment to intelligence gathering, and place emphasis on systematic application of criteria for gang membership.

For research purposes, the broader member approach provides the data to examine incident-based characteristics of all homicides involving gang members. Data are also available on the subset of incidents closely tied to gang function or operations. Thus, there is more information accessible to researchers with the member definition. Finally, both definitional approaches present opportunities for valid comparisons between cities, a prerequisite for developing a comprehensive understanding of the nature of gang violence.

Notes

1. This research was supported by the Harry Frank Guggenheim Foundation and the Southern California Injury Prevention center (under the auspices of the Public Health Service Centers for Disease Control grant # R49/CCR903622). We are grateful to officials in the Los Angeles Police Department and the Los Angeles Sheriff's Department for their cooperation. Many thanks also to the team of USC students who helped collect these data, under the supervision of the ever-vigilant Lea C. Cunningham. Points of view expressed herein are solely those of the authors.

2. Space limitations do not permit an extended discussion here of street gang involvement in drug distribution. Perceptions of a tight or highly organized connection between gangs and drugs have been supported by some research (Mieczkowski, 1986; Padilla, 1992; Sanchez-Jankowski, 1991; Skolnick, 1990; Taylor, 1990), but also severely challenged by many recent studies (Block and Block, 1994; Decker and Van Winkle, 1994; Esbensen and Huizinga, 1993; Fagan, 1989; Hagedorn, 1994; Klein and Maxson, 1994; Maxson, 1995; Moore, 1990; Waldorf and Lauderback, 1993). Interested readers should refer to the recent reviews of this literature by Klein (1995) and Decker (1995).

3. The 1994 figure of 293 gang homicides in Chicago represents a marked increase over the 1993 figure of 129. Follow-up inquiries with the Chicago Police Department's Crime Analysis Unit confirmed the 1994 count. This unit has the official responsibility for designating gang homicides. Officials report that the command structure implemented a new definition in 1994 and encouraged the practice of inferring gang motive in ambiguous cases. The current Chicago definition of gang-related homicides is, "The offender must be a gang member and any of the following apply: 1) the offender is engaged in any activity which furthers the gang enterprise; or 2) the by-product of the offender's gang activity results in a death."

Crime Analysis Unit personnel report their perception that there has been a genuine increase in both turf and drug-motivated incidents, but also acknowledge that the application of the new definition would produce higher gang homicide numbers than in prior years. This exemplifies the importance of examining shifts and definitional stances; Chicago perhaps should be removed from the group of cities that are thought to employ the "Chicago definition."

4. A brief review of the summary descriptions of these cases suggested two patterns. In most cases, there was speculation about various motives without confirmatory reports by witnesses or participants. In a few cases, the drug issues dominated the gang issues. Both patterns are also present in the gang incidents with gang motives, however, so it is not clear why these eight cases were not designated as "gang" by the units.

5. It should be noted that Los Angeles city figures, rather than county, are more appropriate for comparison with Chicago.

6. Data collectors recorded all statements of gang affiliation in the investigation files. It is interesting to note that 11 percent of the member-defined gang cases had no affiliation statements while 22 percent of the member-defined nongang cases had gang members possibly involved in the incident. Apparently, even the more inclusive definitional approach based upon gang status of the participants does not result in designating all cases with gang aspects as "gang crimes." The motive-defined nongang cases had only a slightly higher percentage (29 percent) of incidents with gang members involved.

7. Because the same cases can appear in both the member and motive categories, statistical tests would be inappropriate.

8. That is, those with gang members involved but without gang motives expressed as the cause of the incident.

9. Using a database maintained by the LAPD homicide unit, Meehan and O'Carroll (1992) found a much lower rate of narcotics involvement in gang-motivated homicides. "Gang motive" was entered by detectives in 345 of the 2,162 homicides occurring between January 1, 1986, and August 31, 1988. Only 18 of the 345 homicides also were coded positively by detectives as "narcotics involved." Meehan and O'Carroll examined investigation files on a subset (adolescent victims who died in South Central Los Angeles in a 20-month period) of the homicides in the LAPD database and report similar results. Although the number of gang-motive homicides we identified would be reduced by limitation to only those cases with clear *confirmation* of the gang motive (available in about 60 percent of the 128 homicides with gang motives mentioned in our data set), this would still not account for the much lower figure reported by Meehan and O'Carroll.

References

Ball, R. A., & Curry, G. D. (1995). The logic of definition in criminology: Purposes and methods for defining "gangs." *Criminology*, 33(2), 225–245.

Block, C. R. (1991). *Early warning system for street gang violence crisis areas*. Chicago: Illinois Criminal Justice Information Authority.

Block, C. R., & Block, R. (1994). Street gang crime in Chicago. *Research in Brief*. Washington, D.C.: National Institute of Justice, Office of Justice Programs, U.S. Department of Justice.

Bobrowski, L. J. (1988). Collecting, organizing and reporting street gang crime. Chicago: Chicago Police Department, Special Functions Group.

Curry, G. D. (1991, November). Measuring street gang–related homicide. Paper presentation, American Society of Criminology annual meetings.

Curry, G. D., Ball, R. A., & Decker, S. H. (1995). An update on gang crime and law enforcement recordkeeping. St. Louis: University of Missouri, Department of Criminology and Criminal Justice.

Curry, G. D., Ball, R. A., & Fox, Robert J. (1994). Gang crime and law enforcement recordkeeping. *Research in Brief*. Washington, D.C.: National Institute of Justice, Office of Justice Programs, U.S. Department of Justice.

Decker, S. (1995). Gangs, gang members and drug sales. St. Louis: University of Missouri, Department of Criminology and Criminal Justice.

Decker, S., & Kempf-Leonard, K. (1991). Constructing gangs: The social construction of youth activities. *Criminal Justice Policy Review*, 4, 271–291.

Decker, S., & Van Winkle, B. (1994). Slinging dope: The role of gangs and gang members in drug sales. *Justice Quarterly*, 583–604.

Ehrensaft, K., & Spergel, I. (1991). *Police technical assistance manual. Youth Gang Suppression and Intervention Program.* Chicago: University of Chicago, School of Social Service Administration.

Esbensen, F. A., & Huizinga, D. (1993). Gangs, drugs, and delinquency in a survey of urban youth. *Criminology*, 31, 565–586.

Fagan, J. (1989). The social organization of drug use and drug dealing among urban gangs. *Criminology*, 27, 633–667.

Hagedorn, J. M. (1994). Homeboys, dope fiends, legits and new jacks. *Criminology*, 32, 197–219.

Hilbring, D. (1995). Commander, Gang Crime Section, Chicago Police Department. Personal communication, August 23, 1995.

Horowitz, R. (1990). Sociological perspectives on gangs. In C. R. Huff (Ed.), *Gangs in America*. Newbury Park, CA: Sage Publications.

Institute for Law and Justice (1994). Gang prosecution in the United States. Final report prepared for the National Institute of Justice. Alexandria, VA: Institute for Law and Justice.

Klein, M. W. (1995). *The American street gang*. New York: Oxford University Press.

Klein, M. W., Gordon, M. A., & Maxson, C. L. (1986). The impact of police investigations on police-reported rates of gang and nongang homicides. *Criminology*, 24, 489–512.

Klein, M. W., & Maxson, C. L. (1994). Gangs and cocaine trafficking. In D. MacKenzie & C. Uchida (Eds.), *Drugs and the criminal justice system: Evaluating public policy initiatives*. Newbury Park, CA: Sage Publications.

Los Angeles Police Department (1995). Gang Information Section and Press Relations. Personal communication, August 23, 1995.

Maxson, C. L. (1995). Street gangs and drug sales in two suburban cities. *Research in Brief*. Washington, D.C.: National Institute of Justice, Office of Justice Programs, U.S. Department of Justice.

Maxson, C. L., Gordon, M. A., & Klein, M. W. (1985). Differences between gang and nongang homicides. *Criminology*, 23(2), 209–222.

Maxson, C. L., & Klein, M. W. (1990). Street gang violence: Twice as great, or half as great? In C. R. Huff (Ed.), *Gangs in America*. Newbury Park, CA: Sage Publications.

Maxson, C. L., Klein, M. W., & Gordon, M. A. (1990). Street gang violence as a generalizable pattern. Los Angeles: University of Southern California, Social Science Research Institute.

McBride, W. (1995). Sergeant, Operation Safe Streets, Los Angeles Sheriff's Department. Personal communication, August 21, 1995.

Meehan, P. J., & O'Carroll, P. (1992). Gangs, drugs, and homicide in Los Angeles. *American Journal of Diseases of Children*, 146, 683–687.

Mieczkowski, T. (1986). Geeking up and throwing down: Heroin street life in Detroit. *Criminology*, 24, 645–666.

Moore, J. (1990). Gangs, drugs, and violence. In M. De La Rosa, E. Y. Lambert, & B. Gropper (Eds.), *Drugs and violence: Causes, correlates and consequences*. Washington, D.C.: NIDA Research Monograph Series.

National Drug Intelligence Center (NDIC) (1995). NDIC Street Gang Symposium: Selected findings. Jonestown, PA: NDIC.

Padilla, F. (1992). *The gang as an American enterprise*. New Brunswick, NJ: Rutgers University Press.

Sanchez-Jankowski, M. (1991). *Islands in the street*. Berkeley, CA: University of California Press.

Skolnick, J. H. (1990). The social structure of street drug dealing. *American Journal of Police*, 9, 1–41.

Spergel, I. A. (1988). *Report of the Law Enforcement Youth Gang Symposium*. Chicago: University of Chicago, School of Social Service Administration.

Taylor, C. S. (1990). *Dangerous society*. East Lansing, MI: Michigan State University Press.

Waldorf, D., & Lauderback, D. (1993). Gang drug sales in San Francisco: Organized or freelance? Alameda, CA: Institute for Scientific Analysis. ✦

Chapter 23
Gang Homicide in LA, 1981–2001

George Tita and Allan Abrahamse

Los Angeles has long been called the street gang capital of America—deservedly so. Not far behind comes Chicago and its immediate environs. Not surprisingly, Los Angeles and Chicago have also been the principal centers of various gang control practices and policies of prevention, intervention, and suppression. The data presented in this chapter make it clear that gang violence, homicide in particular, is qualitatively different from other forms of homicide, exhibiting some different patterns. There is, as other gang researchers have noted, something different and special about street-gang homicide. While data such as those provided here have long been accessible to authorities in Los Angeles, it is notable that such data have largely not been used to develop gang-control programs. Rather, these programs, from prevention to suppression, have been driven by philosophical and political ideologies unrelated to the accumulated knowledge about the nature of street-gang activity. The authors provide some data-based directions that future gang-control planning might take.

During the last 40 years, as Figure 23.1 shows, California experienced three "epochs" of increasing homicide rates: a prolonged 15-year climb between 1965 and 1980, a five-year period from 1989 through 1993, and a period that began about 1999 and appears to be continuing today.

This paper examines the period following the first epoch and characterizes the overall

patterns in terms of the demographic composition of victims and the motivating circumstances of the incident. In particular, we consider how the most recent, seemingly ongoing epoch compares in terms of demography and circumstances (especially factors relating to gangs) with the 1989–1993 period of increase. Similarities between the two time periods suggest that the current upward trend might be relatively short-lived. With overall rates of violence at or below historic lows at the beginning of the most recent increase, one can only hope that short-lived or not, it will not result in the intense violence experienced in the early 1990s.

Broadly stated, our goal is to quantify how changes in the pattern and level of homicide in Los Angeles County compare with similar changes in the remainder of the state. Being the most populated area of the state, some say that Los Angeles County "drives" California's homicide rate and that gang homicide is largely responsible for changes in the local Los Angeles rate. We show that there is some support for this point of view; furthermore, that changes in levels and patterns of homicide in Los Angeles could serve as an early indicator of change for the rest of the state.

Next, we move beyond the aggregate state and county-level data to portray violence within one particularly violent area of the city of Los Angeles. As part of an on-going study of the impact of racial/ethnic succession on local homicide rates, we have collected data directly from police files for a study on the changing nature of homicide in the Southeast Area of the Los Angeles Police Department (LAPD). This area, which includes the community of Watts, often ranks as either the first or second most violent place among the 18 LAPD Areas. In addition to examining changes in the patterns of the demographic composition of victims and perpetrators of homicide, the data also include a more refined treatment of the motivating circumstances of the event. Unlike the annual Cal-DOJ Homicide File, these data permit one to bifurcate the universe of "gang homicide" into "gang motivated" homicides and simply "gang member" homicides. The former is strictly predicated on the activities of the collective group (a drive-by against one's enemy; settling a score within the gang; a dispute over respect or turf). The latter include those activities

Reprinted from: George Tita and Allan Abrahamse, "Gang Homicide in LA, 1981–2001," March 2004, in *At the Local Level: Perspectives on Violence Prevention*, Number 3, pp. 1–20. Published by the California Attorney General's Office. Reprinted by permission.

Figure 23.1
Homicide Rate in California, 1961–2002

undertaken by members of gangs, but not for the promotion of the gang's reputation or power, and include robberies, arguments, and domestic/familial homicides where either the victim or the offender is a known gang member.

Finally, this research concludes with a set of recommendations for how policy makers can best address homicide throughout the state. Recognizing that many types of homicides have fallen, and that the majority of citizens are now facing much lower risk of violent victimization than at any time in the last 20 years, we first remind policy makers to "do no harm." That is, we should determine why most types of homicides have demonstrated dramatic decreases over time and be sure that any new policy does not disturb the existing programs/efforts aimed at reducing such types of homicide as intimate partner/domestic. Unfortunately, while rates have dropped, homicide still remains as the leading cause of death for young minority males, especially African Americans, living in impoverished urban settings. Too, much of this violence appears to be centered on gang activity within Los Angeles County/City. In closing, we caution against the development and implementation of any policy aimed at reducing violence without first looking more closely at the appropriate types of data. The usefulness of a "problem solving approach" is well documented and we adhere to the principles that "more information is better than less information" when formulating policy strategies.

On the Risk of Becoming a Homicide Victim in California, 1981–2001

This section provides a broad summary of the nature of homicide in California over the two decades between 1981 and 2001. All statistics are calculated using the entire 21-year data series, a viewpoint that obscures some important trends that have occurred over this period of time, but allows us to focus on some broad facts about homicide that have remained essentially the same. (We will turn to examining some of these trends in the next section.) The broad facts about homicide that we want to highlight are these: that the risk of becoming a homicide victim depends strongly on gender, age, ethnicity, and where you live, and depending on these demographic facts, different types of homicides pose different risks.

As Figure 23.2 shows, the risk of becoming a homicide victim depends strongly on gender and age. However, the relationship between homicide risk and age and gender is complicated. While both sexes face a maximum risk during early adulthood, except for the youngest victims males always face a higher risk than females. The risk is appallingly high for neonates, relatively low for elementary school kids; it rises rapidly during the teen-age years, falls steadily during most of early adulthood and middle age, then begins to rise again among the elderly. What's going on here?

The answer is: there are different kinds of

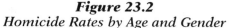

Figure 23.2
Homicide Rates by Age and Gender

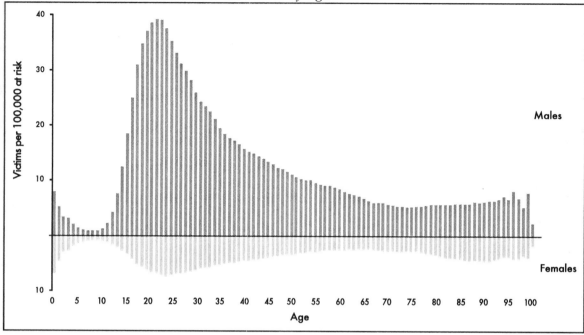

homicides, and these different kinds of homicides pose different risks for men and women, the young, the middle aged and the old. We have identified nine distinct types of homicides, listed in Table 23.1, that differ strongly in the age and gender characteristics of victims. In all but two of these types, most victims are males. The two exceptions are homicides that occur in the course of rape, and spousal or intimate partner homicides. Homicides in which the victim was related to or acquainted with the offender and no gun was involved account for a very large fraction of homicides of children. Homicides that occurred in the course of some

other crime but in which no gun was involved (e.g., strong-arm robbery, burglary) account for many of the homicides of older victims. Fights, arguments, gang killings and other gun-related homicides largely involve males, mostly young ones, and these types of homicides will be considered in more detail below.

Figure 23.3 shows the risk of becoming a gang-homicide victim by age and gender. Males between the ages of 15 and 35 face the bulk of the risk, with a sharp rise for teenagers, a rapid fall after age 20.

The reader will probably not be surprised to note that homicide victimization rates dif-

Table 23.1
Nine Homicide Types

Description	Number	Pct male	Average age of victim	Frequent mode for:
Rape	717	3	35	Women
Killed by relative without gun	2250	57	22	Infants
Spouse, intimate partner	3243	32	41	Women
Fight, argument, etc., without gun	4732	79	34	Older adults
Other crime (e.g., robbery) without gun	5457	70	42	Adults over age 65
Killed by acquaintance without gun	6115	74	32	Children
Other crime (e.g., robbery) with gun	9884	90	33	Males
Gang killing	10138	95	22	Males age 10–17
Fight, argument, etc., with gun	19379	85	30	Men, all other ages
All homicides	61915	80	31	

Figure 23.3
Age and Gender of Gang Victims Are Overwhelmingly Young Males

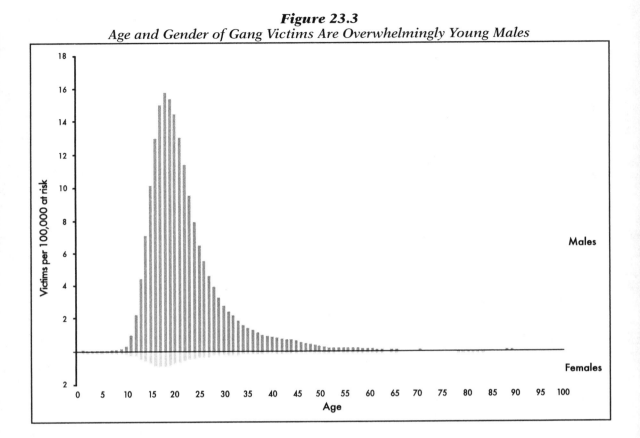

fer sharply by race/ethnicity. As Table 23.2 shows, the victimization rate among African Americans is higher than that among persons of Hispanic origin, and that rate, in turn, is higher than the rate for everyone else. This contrast holds for almost all types of homicides. These facts have important consequences for an ethnically diverse state like California, especially in Los Angeles County.

The homicide victimization is sharply higher in Los Angeles than in the rest of the state. As Table 23.3 shows, this contrast holds across all homicide types, but it is particularly pronounced for gang homicides. The overall victimization rate in Los Angeles County is a little over twice that in the rest of the state, the gang victimization rate is almost seven times higher.

Table 23.2
Homicides per 100,000 by Homicide Type, Race/Ethnicity and Gender

	African American		Hispanic		Everyone Else	
	Males	Females	Males	Females	Males	Females
Rape	0.0	0.8	0.0	0.1	0.0	0.2
Argument, relative, no gun	1.5	1.0	0.5	0.3	0.3	0.2
Spouse, intimate partner	1.5	1.4	0.2	0.6	0.3	0.6
Argument, stranger, no gun	3.2	1.2	2.0	0.2	0.6	0.2
Felony, no gun	3.7	1.5	1.3	0.3	0.9	0.5
Argument, acquaintance, no gun	5.4	1.9	1.9	0.4	0.8	0.4
Robbery, burglary, etc., with gun	14.1	1.4	3.6	0.3	1.3	0.2
Gang killing	14.7	1.0	6.5	0.3	0.3	0.0
Argument, stranger, with gun	23.1	3.8	8.2	1.0	2.1	0.6
All homicides	67.3	14.1	24.1	3.5	6.7	3.1

Table 23.3
Victimization Rates in Los Angeles County Contrasted with Rest of the State

	Los Angeles	Rest of California
Rape	0.2	0.1
Argument, relative, no gun	0.4	0.3
Spouse, intimate partner	0.6	0.5
Argument, stranger, no gun	1.0	0.6
Felony, no gun	1.2	0.7
Argument, acquaintance, no gun	1.2	0.9
Robbery, burglary, etc., with gun	2.7	1.1
Gang killing	4.0	0.6
Argument, stranger, with gun	4.6	2.5
All homicides	15.9	7.3

Homicide Trends, 1981–2001

The statistics we have presented were obtained from data aggregated over the previous two decades. As promised, we now turn to an examination of trends that can be seen during this period.

As Figure 23.4 shows, after a decade of relatively high homicide rates in California, from 1993 until 1999 rates declined every year. In 1998, they fell to a level that had not been seen since the late 1960s. In 2000, we experienced the first increase in six years, followed by a sharper increase in 2001.

The trend in gang-related homicides has a similar shape, but the contrasts are much sharper. Figure 23.5 shows that changes in the homicide rate for gang killings of males are more pronounced than are changes in the overall rate. Between 1999 and 2001, the overall rate rose by about 7%; gang killings among males age 18–24 almost doubled.

Gang-related homicides have always represented a larger fraction of all homicides in Los Angeles than outside Los Angeles, and this contrast has grown over the last two decades, and especially in the last few years. Figure 23.6 illustrates this fact. In 1981, gang killings represented about 10% of all Los Angeles homicides, compared to about 4% in the rest of the state. In 2001, almost half of all homicides in Los Angeles were gang-related, compared to about 14% elsewhere.

It is probable that law enforcement is lately more inclined to identify certain classes of homicides as gang-related than in earlier years, and possible that Los Angeles law enforcement agencies are more likely to do so than agencies in other parts of the state. However, it seems unlikely that such reporting differences could explain the entire contrast seen here.

The recent rise in gang killings is much steeper in Los Angeles than in the rest of the state. Furthermore, there are more gang killings in Los Angeles than would be expected on the basis of demography alone.

Figure 23.4
Homicide Victims per 100,000 Population, 1981–2001

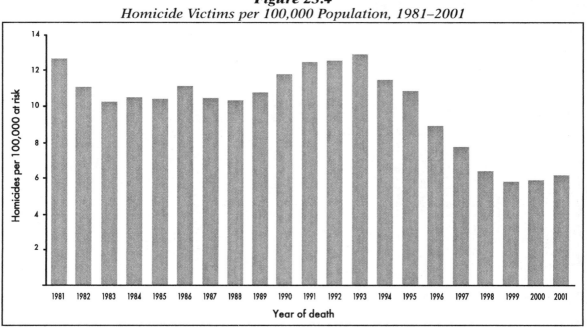

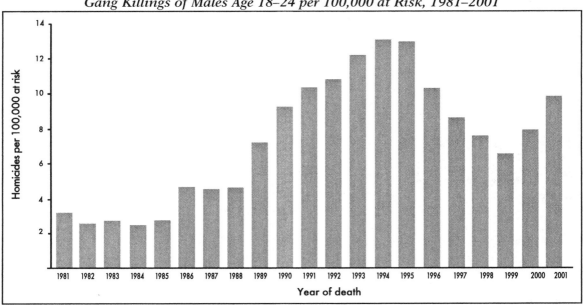

Figure 23.5
Gang Killings of Males Age 18–24 per 100,000 at Risk, 1981–2001

Assuming similar demographic composition of victims, Figure 23.7 compares the actual number of gang homicides with the number that would have occurred in these two places if the homicides were directly proportional to the population size, controlling for age and race. As the chart shows, there are far more gang killings in Los Angeles County, as compared to the rest of the state, than can be accounted for by differences in the composition of the population.

California experienced a dramatic in-

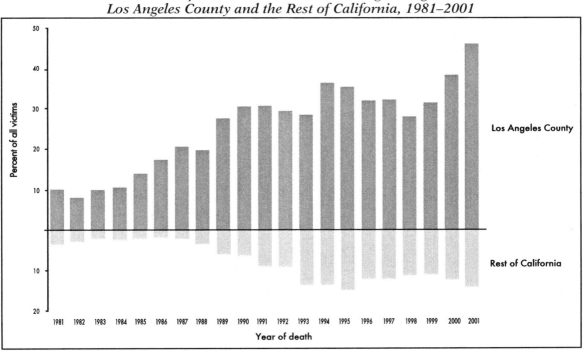

Figure 23.6
*Percent of All Homicides That Are Gang Killings in
Los Angeles County and the Rest of California, 1981–2001*

Figure 23.7
*Number of Gang Killings in Los Angeles County and in the Rest of California
Contrasted with the Expected Number on the Basis of Demography, 1981–2001*[1]

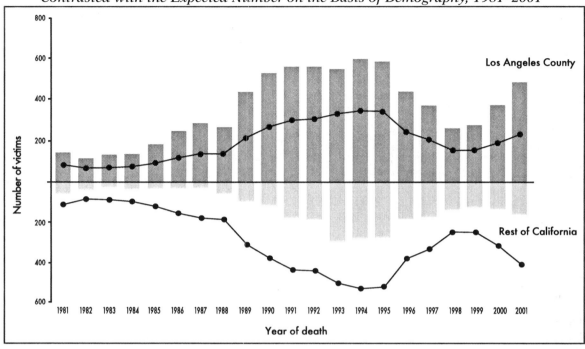

Figure 23.8
Gang Killings of Hispanic Males Age 10–24

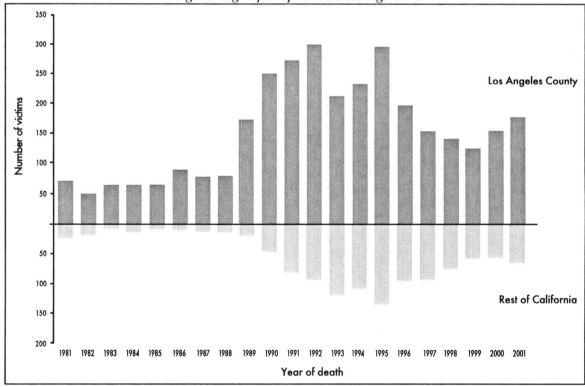

Table 23.4
Gang Homicides of Hispanic Males
in Los Angeles County, 1988–1992

	10–17	18–24	Both groups
1988	25	54	79
1989	71	101	172
1990	99	152	251
1991	104	169	273
1992	120	179	299

crease in gang killings of young Hispanic males in the late 1980s. Figure 23.8 plots the number of such killings for the 20-year period in Los Angeles and outside Los Angeles; Table 23.4 shows the actual numbers for the five-year period in Los Angeles, for younger and older members of this age class.

For the younger group, the number of such killings nearly tripled between 1988 and 1989. The number of such deaths declined after 1992 but has never returned to the levels prior to 1989. The sharp rise in Hispanic gang killings in 1988 in Los Angeles County was followed, about a year later, with a somewhat less pronounced rise outside of Los Angeles.

Cook and Laub have named these sorts of lasting structural changes as "hang overs" of the youth homicide epidemic that peaked nationally in 1993. For Hispanics involved in gang homicide, 1995 was the peak year. Though not as pronounced, we are again experiencing an increase in Hispanic victimization.

The patterns for African American victims of gang violence are somewhat similar to those of Hispanics, though the increase for African Americans began several years prior to the Hispanic increase and peaked one year earlier, in 1994. Figure 23.9 shows the number of such homicides of African American males age 10–24.

What is most troubling is that after a dramatic decrease of more than 50% from the peak in 1994 to the bottom of the trough in 1998, the 2001 rate for Los Angeles County is once again at 1994 levels. While the rate of decline was similar among African American and Hispanic victims of gang violence, the most recent rate of growth for African American victimization far exceeds the rate of growth for Hispanic victims.

To examine the issue in more depth, we use a detailed longitudinal data set of homi-

Figure 23.9
Gang Killings of African American Males Age 10–24

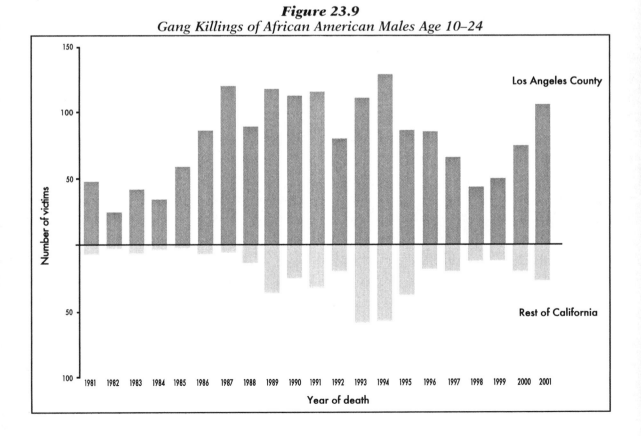

cides in the Southeast Policing Area of Los Angeles. The data include all homicides recorded between 1980 and 2000 and includes information taken from two sources: the actual LAPD homicide case file, and a summary database maintained by LAPD's Robbery Homicide Division named "HitMan." The summary data provided detailed information on the offender(s) and victim, but tended to include less specific information about the motivation behind the killing.

Southeast is a historically black area that includes the neighborhoods of Athens Park, Avalon Gardens, and Watts. It also contains some of the largest concentrations of public housing west of the Mississippi River, including Nickerson Gardens and Jordan Downs. Southeast Los Angeles has experienced both economic and social problems over the last two decades including high levels of poverty, dense public housing, and—through the processes of "de-industrialization"—a shrinking job base. This area is also known for its open-air drug markets, urban street gangs and high levels of violence. According to 1990 census figures, Southeast represents almost four percent (3.75%) of the city's total population. However, from 1980–2000, this area accounted

for more than eleven percent (11.8%) of all homicides, illustrating a concentration of violence in this area of the city.

The Southeast neighborhoods are also experiencing substantial racial and ethnic succession. Until recently, the population of Southeast was almost exclusively black. However, beginning in the 1980s and continuing today, the black population is migrating out of Southeast and is being replaced by Latinos from Mexico, Honduras and El Salvador. In 1980, nearly 80% of the population described itself as Black, with Hispanics comprising only 16%. The 1990 Census reports that African-Americans maintain a slim majority in Southeast comprising 56% of the population while the percent of population that is Hispanic has increased to 40%.

While the demographic composition of the neighborhood has changed dramatically, the composition of its homicide victims has not. African Americans always represent the majority of homicide victims in the neighborhood (see Figure 23.10). For most of the period, the number of homicide victims in both groups has risen and fallen in tandem and the Latino rate has consistently been approximately 2.5–3 times lower

Figure 23.10
Homicides in Southeast Los Angeles

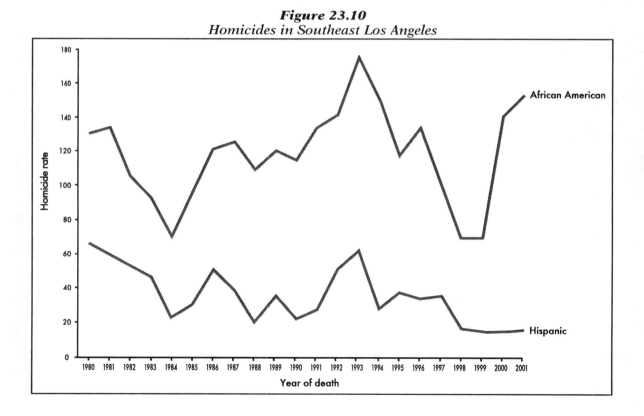

Table 23.5
*Number of Homicides
in Southeast, by Type*

Homicide type	Count	Percent
Gang	578	29
Drug	138	7
Domestic violence	144	7
Robbery	383	19
Fights and arguments	454	23
Other	299	15
Total	1996	100

than the Black rate. However, what is striking in this graph is the divergence of patterns beginning in 2000/2001 (and anecdotally continuing for 2002). The growth of homicide in Southeast and other communities of the city of Los Angeles that still contain a sizable population of African Americans is exclusively the result of Black-on-Black violence, mostly concentrated within gang disputes.

Table 23.5 provides the distribution of homicides by motive over the study period. Homicide involving gang members is the single largest category among the data, representing 29% of all homicides, followed closely by the escalation of arguments (includes both stranger and non-stranger victim-offender relationships) at nearly 23% of all events.

As defined above, the gang category captures any homicide involving a gang member as either victim or offender. Looking closer, we found that of the 578 events known to involve a gang member, 308 centered on inter-gang disputes, 43 involved intra-gang disputes, 28 of the homicides had no information in the case file regarding the motive, and an additional 39 cases spread among all other motive classifications. The summary information contained within "HitMan" did not elaborate beyond "gang" for motive and includes the remaining 160 cases.[2] Consistent with other research on this issue, these gangs do not appear to be killing each other over drug issues, at least not in ways apparent within the homicide case files.[3]

Other Kinds of Homicides Show a Different Pattern

It is important to point out that some other kinds of homicides have *not* been in-

creasing recently, and in fact, have been falling steadily for the last 20 years. Furthermore, the distribution of these homicides between Los Angeles County and the rest of the state is strictly proportional to the population of these two regions.

Figure 23.11 shows the number of victims killed in the course of rape, in Los Angeles County and in the rest of the state, for the 21-year period under study. As in Figure 23.7, the bars represent actual counts, the lines represent estimated counts under the assumption that these killings would have been found in either of the two regions strictly on the basis of population, controlling for ethnicity and age.

As the figure demonstrates, there has been a sharp decline in the number of rape-related homicides, a decline that began around 1987, and shows no sign of reversal. Furthermore, while during the first half of the two-decade period displayed here, Los Angeles County appeared to experience somewhat more of its share of these homicides in proportion to its ethnic and age distribution, that contrast disappeared around 1991.

Homicides called "arguments with a stranger, gun involved," a characterization that probably applies to most gang killings, rose in the late 1980s, and fell after that. While the drop has stalled in the last few years, these homicides have not begun to climb as rapidly as gang homicides. It is possible that many homicides classified as this type some years ago would now be classified as gang homicide.

Figure 23.12 describes "non-gun felony homicides," that is, homicides that occurred during the commission of a crime, but one in which a gun was not used. This is a homicide type that frequently results in the death of an older individual. Such homicides have been steadily declining for the last 20 years, and for the last 10 years, at least, are no more prevalent in Los Angeles County than in the rest of the state, after controlling for ethnicity and the age distribution of the population.

Conclusions and Policy Recommendations

The foregoing brief overview of homicide in California during the period 1981 through 2001 suggests the following:

Figure 23.11
Homicides Involving Rape

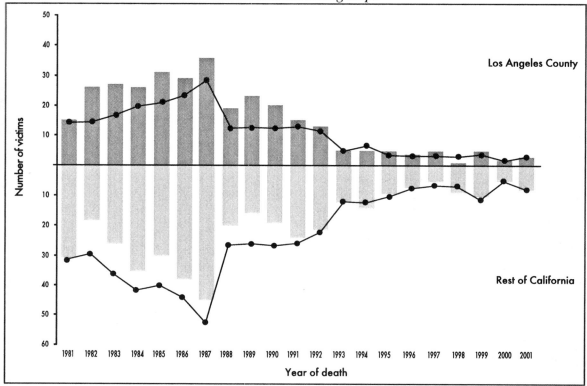

Figure 23.12
Non-Gun Felony Homicides

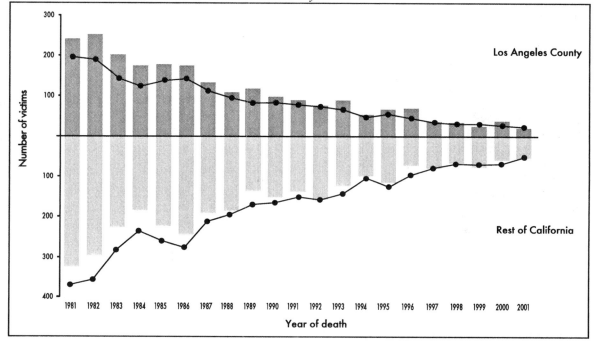

1. A sharp decline in homicides that began about 1993 appears to have reversed itself beginning in 2000, and homicide rates are now increasing. This increase shares certain similarities with the historically high rates experienced in the early 1990s in that minority youth are once again overrepresented among the population of participants. Both periods are also characterized by growth in gang homicide.

2. There are also important differences between the two upswings in violence. Much, if not most, of the current increase can be attributed to gang killings. In 1999 there were a total of 1,977 homicides in the state of California. In 2001, there were 2,178, an increase of 201 homicides. Over the same time period, the number of gang homicides in Los Angeles County rose from 277 in 1999 to 486 in 2001, an increase of 209 incidents. Given that our analysis has demonstrated that all other types of homicides continue to decrease or at least stay level over this period, clearly, gang homicide in Los Angeles County is solely responsible for the statewide increase. During the early 1990s all types of homicides were increasing.

3. The youth homicide epidemic that peaked in 1993 resulted in historically high levels for African-American youth (a group with a long history of high homicide rates). It also appears that whatever was driving the increase during that period "spread" into the Latino community. After years of relatively stable levels of violent victimization, young Latino males also experienced historically high rates of homicide victimization. During the current resurgence in violence, rates for both groups are rising, but African-American rates are rising much faster. This point is underscored below (see Point 5).

4. Los Angeles County appears to experience more gang killings than the rest of the state, even after controlling for ethnic, racial and age differences. For other kinds of homicide, Los Angeles' experience is similar to the rest of the state. This suggests that what truly sets Los Angeles apart from the remainder of California is not a general propensity for violent behavior, but rather the existence of a specific milieu that has fostered the development of a violent gang culture unlike any other gang culture in the state.

5. In the beginning, an increase in gang killings may affect only a small area (e.g., Southeast Los Angeles) and may involve only one demographic class (e.g., very young African-American males). But such violence may soon spread to other areas and groups. This has not been the case with respect to the current upswing in violence in Los Angeles. While the number of Latino gangs has always exceeded the number of Black gangs in the city, and Latino gangs have demonstrated an equal propensity for violent behavior (at least during the early 1990s), the current increase in homicide is limited to lethal attacks among warring Black gangs. However, it should be noted that Latino gang violence lagged Black gang violence by 2–3 years in the late 1980s/early 1990s as well.

6. If an increase in gang killings is seen in Los Angeles, an increase may be seen very soon elsewhere in other parts of the state. There is, however, probably no reason to assume that problems *always* begin in Los Angeles. In trying to understand patterns of gang violence, one is often frustrated by the seemingly "random" nature of the changing levels of violence among gangs. Gangs in other cities are likely to react to "random" events within their own city, not to what is going on in Los Angeles.

These observations lead us to the following policy recommendations:

1. First of all, "do no harm." Significant decreases in some kinds of homicide have been seen in the last 20 years, and are continuing, and despite the recent rise in gang killings, the rate of such killings is much lower than it was a decade ago. We need to learn what has worked, and why, then reinforce these processes, and do nothing to disrupt them.

2. Tailor specific interventions to specific problems, in specific places. The immediate problem appears to have begun with African-American gangs in Los

Angeles County. We need to deal with that problem, locally, and then guard against the problem spreading to other areas. We also must learn what is currently insulating Latino gangs from following the lead of the Black gangs and also participating in gang violence. In areas of the City of Los Angeles where racial/ethnic succession is resulting in Latinos now comprising the majority in what have traditionally been African-American neighborhoods, gangs comprised of Latino members often share the same geographic space with gangs comprised of African-American members. Yet these groups are displaying very different patterns and levels of violence. Contrary to many sociological theories, there is also very little inter-ethnic/inter-racial lethal violence.

3. Since the data suggest that problems that begin in one place may spread to another, the State should implement a homicide surveillance system, similar to systems used by the public health community, to provide an early warning of a rise in homicide within particular communities. The system needs to work fast enough to provide a warning within a few months of the beginning of the problem. It also needs to be fine-tuned with respect to geography and demography. It does not need to wait until a homicide is "solved," nor does it have to be highly concerned with details or even perfect accuracy. A system that could capture and publish a modest amount of information (age, race, sex, circumstance, census tract) about almost every suspected homicide victim (two or three thousand a year) within a month of the event would provide a important tool for detecting and reacting to upswings in violence in the State.

We conclude with the following general observation. There is no such thing as "*A Homicide Problem.*" There are many homicide problems. Even labeling something as a "gang" homicide masks important aspects that need to be understood before enacting policy; for example, whether the homicide was motivated by gang rivalry, or the protection of drug markets, or was merely an argument that involved young males who happened to be gang members. This makes it difficult, at best, to offer more concrete policy recommendations for addressing the current upswing in violence. However, given that so much of the violence involves gangs, one might consider a "pulling levers" strategy first developed by Boston's Operation Ceasefire (also known as the Boston Gun Project.) This nationally renowned intervention, implemented to address Boston's youth gun violence problem during the mid-1990s, exploited the social structure of gangs by making it known that if a gang continued to commit acts of gun violence, then any member of that gang would receive increased attention from the criminal justice system by stepping up such activities as probation/parole searches and the enforcement of non-felony warrants. At the same time, the community and social service providers stood ready to offer their services and guidance to those youth ready to eschew a violent lifestyle. The results were remarkable, with youth gun homicide rates falling to nearly zero for an extended period of time.

This "pulling levers" approach has been demonstrated to work within several areas of California, including the city of Stockton and the Boyle Heights neighborhood of Los Angeles. Each of these efforts has relied on the "problem solving" approach where the design of the intervention is driven by data analysis. Both targeted an activity (gun violence) rather than an affiliation (gang membership.) What makes this approach especially appealing in Los Angeles is that the message trumpeted by the intervention is not one of "a war on gangs"—a message the community has grown weary of. Instead, the message of the project is both simple and clear—to reduce gun violence in a community where the great majority of these acts happen to be committed by gang members. It is much easier for a community to support an effort aimed at reducing the killing of its youth than it is to support an effort that declares war on its youth.

Notes:

1. The height of the bars in this figure represents actual counts. The plot points connected by lines represent estimates of the number of homicides that would have been seen if the number of homicides was directly proportional to the population, controlling for age and race. For example, in 2001 there were nine African American ho-

Chapter 24
Street Gang Crime in Chicago

Carolyn Rebecca Block
and Richard Block

In this report prepared for the U.S. Department of Justice, the Blocks draw from extensive data on gang crime in Chicago. The definition of gang crime is limited to actions specifically linked to gang function. The complexity of the relationship between crime and gang involvement is revealed in the ebb and flow of gang homicide over a 25-year period, in the differential patterns of lethal and nonlethal violence, and in the variations in level and type of crime among the 40 major street gangs active in this city. The Blocks have pioneered the use of computer mapping to enhance intervention efforts. By identifying concentrations of gang crime in certain neighborhoods, "hotspots" can be pinpointed to focus law enforcement and prevention resources.

Street gang activity—legal and illegal, violent and nonviolent, lethal and non-lethal—occurs disproportionately among neighborhoods and population groups. Types of incidents tend to cluster and increase in bursts in specific neighborhoods and among specific gangs.

Neighborhoods often differ sharply in the predominant type of street gang–motivated incidents they experience. For example, one city neighborhood may be unaffected by street gang activity, while another close by may be a marketplace for a street gang's

Issues and Findings

Discussed in the Brief

A study supported by the National Institute of Justice of street gang–motivated violence in one major U.S. city—Chicago. Analysis of police homicide records over 26 years and gang-motivated incident records over 3 years revealed the street gang affiliation of every offender and the location of each offense, which gives a detailed picture of gang activity and the relationships of individual, gang, and neighborhood characteristics.

Key Issues

Gangs—and gang-related violence and drug trafficking—are growing problems across the country. Street gangs and the crimes in which they engage cannot be viewed as monolithic: One neighborhood may be unaffected, while nearby, another is the marketplace for a gang's drug operation or the center of lethal turf battles. Bursts of gang-related violence appear among specific gangs and suddenly stop.

Key Findings

For a 3-year period, 1987–1990, the study results included the following:
- Gang-related, high-crime neighborhoods can be classified into three types: turf hot spots, where gangs fight over territory control; drug hot spots, where gang-motivated drug offenses concentrate; and turf and drug hot spots, where gang-motivated crimes relate to both.
- Gang involvement in violence and homicide is more often turf-related than drug-related. Only 8 of 288 gang-motivated homicides were related to drugs.
- The city's four largest street gangs were identified with most of the street gang crime. Representing 51 percent of all street gang members, they accounted for 69 percent of recorded criminal incidents.
- The rate of street gang–motivated crime in the 2 most dangerous areas was 76 times that of the 2 safest.
- A gun was the lethal weapon used in almost all gang-motivated homicides. Use of high-caliber, automatic, or semiautomatic weapons dramatically increased.

These and other findings of the research have policy implications for formulating intervention strategies:
- Programs to reduce nonlethal street gang violence must be targeted to the specific street gang problems in each neighborhood.
- Effective intervention strategies must be built on continuously updated information.

Target Audience

Law enforcement officials, community leaders, policymakers, and researchers.

drug operation, and yet a third may be plagued by frequent and lethal turf battles.

In addition, the chief criminal activities of one street gang often differ from those of another. For example, one outbreak of lethal street gang violence may be characterized by escalating retribution and revenge, while another may be associated with expansion of a drug business into new territory. Consequently, street gangs and the crimes in which they engage cannot be viewed as monolithic in nature.

This Research in Brief describes these and other patterns of street gang–related violence in a major U.S. city—Chicago. All available information, including Chicago police records of illegal street gang–motivated activity—from vandalism to drug offenses to violent offenses (both lethal and nonlethal)—was examined across time, neighborhood, and street gang affiliation. Individual, gang-level, and neighborhood-level characteristics were also analyzed to determine the relationships among these three factors. The results of the analysis give one of the most complete pictures of street gang crime available today.

Study Methodology

Researchers examined Chicago gang homicide data over a 26-year period, from 1965 through 1990, and detailed information on other gang-related crime from 1987 to 1990. Two methods of analysis were used to determine the extent to which neighborhoods differed in the type and concentration of street gang activity and to examine the neighborhood characteristics that were associated with high levels of lethal and nonlethal street gang activity.[1] The information analyzed was primarily from Chicago Police Department (CPD) records, which were organized into three sets of data on Chicago homicides, street gang–motivated offenses, and street gang territories. Neighborhood characteristics and population data for rate calculation were obtained from the U.S. Bureau of the Census. This information was gathered by tract and aggregated into the 77 Chicago community areas (Exhibit 24.1).[2]

Researchers geocoded the address of each homicide and street gang–motivated incident. Boundaries of the community areas were mapped, geocoded offenses were aggregated by community area, and offenses were analyzed in relation to population and other community characteristics. Finally, the densest concentrations (hot spot areas) of individual addresses of street gang–related incidents were identified regardless of arbitrary boundaries and related to gang turfs, gang activity, and community characteristics.

Data on Homicides

One of the largest and most detailed data sets on violence ever collected in the United States, the Chicago homicide data set contains information on every homicide in police records from 1965 to 1990.[3] More than 200 variables were collected for the 19,323 homicides in this data set. The crime analysis unit of the Chicago Police Department has maintained a summary—Murder Analysis Report (MAR)—of each homicide over the 26-year period. On the basis of these reports, 1,311 homicides were classified as street gang–motivated.

Data on Street Gang–Motivated Offenses

This data set included information on 17,085 criminal offenses that occurred from 1987 to 1990 that were classified by the police as street gang–related. These offenses were categorized as follows:

- 288 homicides.
- 8,828 nonlethal violent offenses (aggravated and simple assault and battery).
- 5,888 drug offenses (violations related to possession or sale of hard or soft drugs).
- 2,081 other offenses (includes more than 100 specific crimes ranging from liquor law violations to intimidation, mob action, vandalism, robbery, and weapons law violations).[4]

Data on Street Gang Territory Boundaries

This data set included the location of street gang territory boundaries in early 1991. These boundaries were based on maps drawn by street gang officers in Chicago's 26 districts, who identified the territories of 45 street gangs—both major and minor—and noted areas that were in dispute between one or more street gangs.[5]

Defining Gang Affiliation

These three data sets included several possible aspects of street gang affiliation for each incident—for example, the street gang affiliation of the offender or offenders, the

Exhibit 24.1
Non-Lethal and Lethal Street Gang Motivated Crimes: 1987–1990

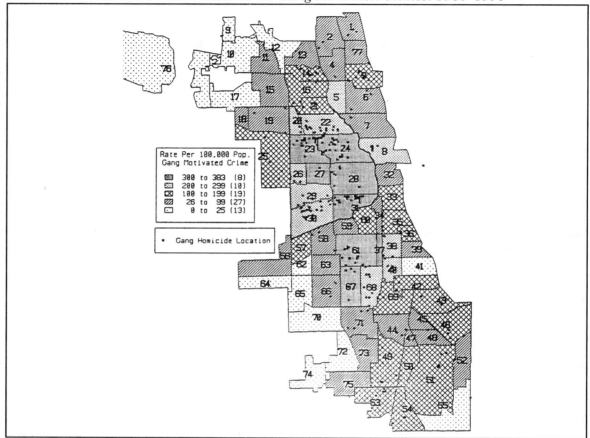

Source: Chicago Police Department.

affiliation of the victim or victims (if any), and the location of the incident within the boundaries of a gang's turf. In this study researchers classified street gang–motivated criminal incidents according to the affiliation of the offender(s).

Street Gangs in the City

More than 40 major street gangs are active in the city of Chicago.[6] Researchers in this study concentrated on the four largest and most criminally active street gangs, each of which was responsible for at least 1,000 police-recorded criminal incidents from 1987 to 1990:

- Black Gangster Disciples Nation (BGDN). Descended from the Woodlawn Disciples, BGDN is strongest on Chicago's South Side. The gang is known for its turf wars with the Blackstone Rangers in the late 1960s

and early 1970s and the Black Disciples in 1991.[7]

- Latin Disciples. A racially and ethnically mixed street gang allied with BGDN, the Latin Disciples operate mainly in the integrated Northwest Side neighborhoods of Humboldt Park and Logan Square.[8]

- Latin Kings. The oldest (over 25 years) and largest Latino street gang in Chicago, the Latin Kings operate throughout the city in Latino and racially and ethnically mixed neighborhoods. The gang is particularly active in the growing Mexican neighborhoods on the Southwest Side.

- Vice Lords. One of the oldest street gangs in Chicago, the Vice Lords date from the 1950s. The gang operates throughout the city, but is strongest in the very poor West Side neighborhoods that have never recovered from the destruction that followed the death of Dr. Martin Luther King in 1968.[9]

Members of BGDN and the Vice Lords are almost all black men, while the Latin Disciples and Latin Kings are predominantly Latino men. Rough police department estimates indicate that the 19,000 members of these four gangs constitute about half of all Chicago street gang members.

In the mid-1980s BGDN and the Latin Disciples formed the Folk Alliance. Soon after the Latin Kings and Vice Lords formed the People alliance. Both "super alliances" of street gangs appeared following an increase of street gang–related homicide.

The contrasting size and longevity of Chicago black and Latino street gangs is in part a reflection of the city's population dynamics. In general, the black population of Chicago has declined[10] and some black neighborhoods have been abandoned, while the Latino population has grown and the population of Latino neighborhoods has climbed. For example, over the past 25 years, the population of East Garfield Park (area 27) has fallen by 60 percent and many commercial and residential buildings have been lost, while the population of South Lawndale (area 30) has expanded by 31 percent and changed from a Czech to a Mexican neighborhood (now called Little Village).

With the growth of the Latino population and the expansion of Latino neighborhoods, many small street gangs have emerged. Given their limited territories, these small neighborhood street gangs battle each other frequently and often have to defend their turf against the more established Latino street gangs.

Criminal Activities of Street Gangs

From 1987 to 1990, the four largest street gangs were also the most criminally active. They accounted for 69 percent of all street gang–motivated crimes and 56 percent of all street gang–motivated homicides in which the street gang affiliation of the offender was known. Of the 17,085 street gang–motivated offenses recorded during this period, BGDN was responsible for 4,843 offenses; the Vice Lords for 3,116; the Latin Kings for 2,868; and the Latin Disciples for 1,011.

However, taken as a whole, street gangs other than the top four were responsible for more police-recorded offenses (5,207

Definition of a Street Gang

The Chicago Police Department defines "street gang" as an association of individuals who exhibit the following characteristics in varying degrees:

- A gang name and recognizable symbols.
- A geographic territory.
- A regular meeting pattern.
- An organized, continuous course of criminality.

An incident is defined as street gang–related if the evidence indicates that the action grew out of a street gang function. Gang membership is not enough to determine gang-relatedness. To determine if an incident is street gang–related, police investigators analyze each case for application of the following criteria:

- Representing—Offenses growing out of a signification of gang identity or alliance (such as hand signs, language, and clothing).
- Recruitment—Offenses relating to recruiting members for a street gang, which include intimidating a victim or witness.
- Extortion—Efforts to compel membership or to exact tribute for the gang.
- Turf violation—Offenses committed to disrespect another gang's territory.
- Prestige—Offenses committed either to glorify the street gang or to gain rank within the gang.
- Personal conflict—Conflicts involving leadership or punitive action within the rank and file of a gang.
- Vice—Activities generally involving the street-level distribution of narcotics by street gang members.
- Retaliation—Acts of revenge for offenses against the gang by rival gang members.[11]

---

from 1987 to 1990) than any one of the top four. Many of these smaller street gangs were relatively new, predominantly Latino, and fighting among themselves over limited turfs.

Drug Offenses

The four major street gangs varied sharply in the degree to which drug crimes dominated their illegal activity (Exhibit 24.2). For example, of the 2,868 incidents committed by the Latin Kings from 1987 through 1990, only 19 percent were drug offenses, compared to 56 percent of the 3,116 incidents attributed to the Vice Lords. More incidents of cocaine possession (the most common drug offense) were attributed to the Vice Lords or to the Black Gangster Disciples Nation than to all other street gangs

Exhibit 24.2
Street Gang Incidents: 1987–1990 Four Largest and Other Gangs

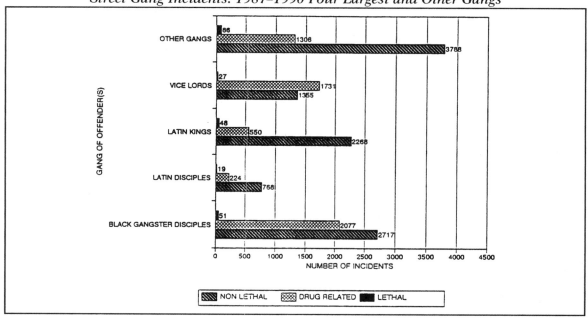

combined. The Vice Lords were also active in heroin possession offenses, with twice as many incidents attributed to them than to all other street gangs combined.

The reintroduction of heroin to Chicago by the Vice Lords and Black Gangster Disciples Nation was particularly disturbing to police and community workers. From 1987 to 1990, the number of incidents of possession of white heroin rapidly escalated from 11 to 165, while possession of brown heroin declined from 77 to 64, probably reflecting the reentry of Asian heroin into the Chicago market. Meanwhile, the number of incidents of hard drug possession involving the Latin Kings, Latin Disciples, and other street gangs remained low.

Only 8 of the 288 street gang–motivated homicides between 1987 and 1990 were drug related.[12] Five of these, all of which occurred in 1989 or 1990, were related to the business of drugs. As researchers in Los Angeles also found, the connection between street gangs, drugs, and homicide was weak and could not explain the rapid increase in homicide in the late 1980s.[13]

Competition, Violence, and Other Confrontations Over Turf

Most of the nonlethal, nondrug offenses attributed to street gangs were violent confrontations (assault and battery) or damage to property (graffiti); see Exhibit 24.3. Other Index crimes such as robbery and burglary were relatively rare, and only six sexual assaults were determined to be street gang–motivated from 1987 to 1990.[14]

Violent incidents involving the Vice Lords or BGDN were evenly divided between simple battery and assault (no weapon) and aggravated battery and assault. Offenses attributed to the Latin Disciples, Latin Kings, or smaller street gangs (which were also mostly Latino) were more likely to be aggravated than simple assault or battery.

The Vice Lords' West Side turf (see Exhibit 24.4) was remarkably free of graffiti. The gang was so much in command that they did not need many physical markers to identify their turf. In contrast, the constricted turfs of the smaller street gangs were well marked with graffiti and other identifiers. Driving south on Pulaski Road from Vice Lords' turf in North Lawndale (area 29) toward Two Sixers', Deuces', and Latin Vikings' territories in South Lawndale (area 30), researchers observed a remarkable transformation in neighborhoods. In North Lawndale stood many abandoned factories and apartments and empty lots, but not much graffiti. In thriving South Lawndale (Little Village), buildings were covered with multiple layers of insignia. Competing for scarce territory, the street

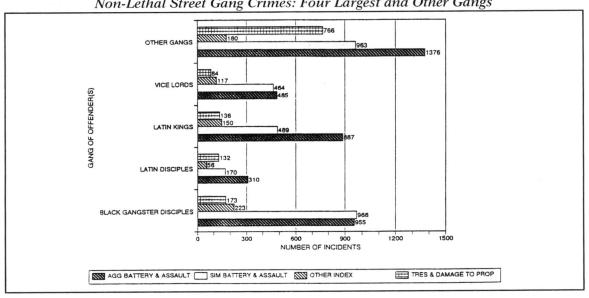

Exhibit 24.3
Non-Lethal Street Gang Crimes: Four Largest and Other Gangs

gangs in Little Village had to identify and violently defend their domains.

Both the amount of graffiti and number of violent turf defense incidents appear related to competition. West Side gangs knew which neighborhoods were under the Vice Lords' control and infrequently challenged that control. In contrast, battles between rival street gangs were a regular occurrence in the expanding Mexican neighborhoods on the Southwest Side. Thus, symbolic "face maintenance," graffiti contests, and violent territorial defense actions were relatively frequent in street gangs more threatened by competition.

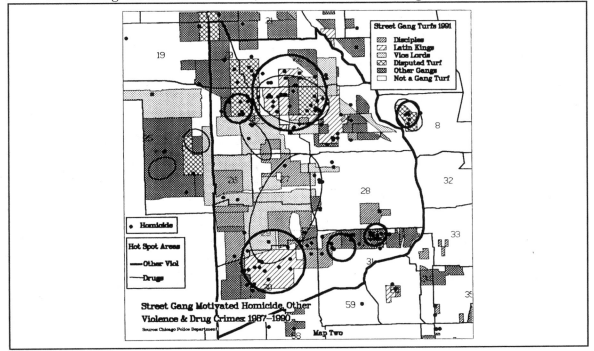

Exhibit 24.4
Street Gang–Motivated Homicide, Other Violence, and Drug Crimes: 1987–1990

Trends in Homicides

In contrast to domestic or acquaintance killings, street gang homicides occurred in bursts (Exhibit 24.5).[15] Years with only a few homicides were punctuated by years with many. In 1965 only 11 street gang–motivated homicides occurred (2.8 percent of all homicides); but in 1970, 70 occurred (8.7 percent of the total). The risk of being murdered in a street gang confrontation was more than five times higher in 1970 than in 1965. This early surge in homicide reflected BGDN wars on Chicago's South Side.

By 1975 the number of street gang–motivated homicides was again as low as the mid-1960s, even though 1974 and 1975 were record years for other types of homicide. This brief respite was followed by eruptions of lethal street gang violence in 1979 and again in 1981, when there were 65 and 83 deaths, respectively. However, the formation in the mid-1980s of the two gang super alliances, People and Folk, may have brought relative stability in street gang–motivated violence for a few years. Only 50 street gang–motivated homicides were recorded in 1987, and the total number of Chicago homicides reached the lowest point in 20 years.

Unfortunately, the rivalries that developed both between and within alliances in the mid-1980s generated even more violence later in the decade when street gang–motivated homicide increased sharply to 101 in 1990 (then an all-time high) and surpassed that to 121 in 1991 and 133 in 1992. Although the overall level of homicide also increased rapidly in those years, street gang–motivated homicide increased faster. It accounted for 12 percent of all homicides in 1990 and was responsible for 33 percent of the total increase from 1987 through 1990.

If street gang–motivated homicide is directly related to other street gang–motivated incidents and if the proportion of incidents with a lethal outcome does not change, then the pattern over time of lethal incidents should parallel the pattern of nonlethal incidents. Although the data show some similarity in the short-term pattern of street gang–motivated lethal versus nonlethal incidents, the overall trend is very different (see Exhibit 24.6).[16]

- In 1987, 1 street gang–motivated homicide occurred for every 44 street gang–motivated personal violence offenses known to the police.

- In 1990 there was 1 death for every 20 police-recorded crimes of personal violence.

Indeed, the number of street gang–motivated deaths in a typical month increased sharply over the 3-year period, even though the number of nonlethal violent incidents

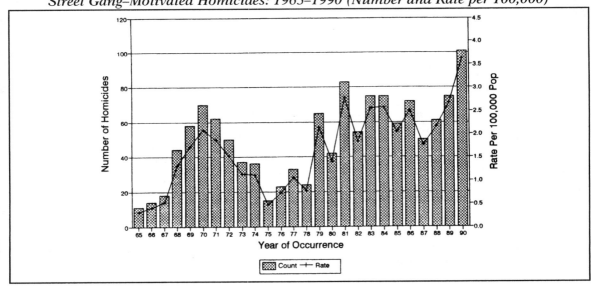

Exhibit 24.5
Street Gang–Motivated Homicides: 1965–1990 (Number and Rate per 100,000)

Exhibit 24.6
ı Street Gang–Motivated Violence: Lethal and Nonlethal (3-Month Moving Averages)

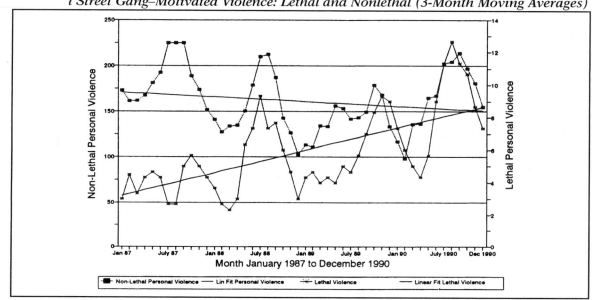

declined slightly. These divergent trends in lethal and nonlethal violence indicate that the proportion of incidents with a lethal outcome has increased.

The Role of Guns

One explanation for the increasing lethality of street gang–motivated violent incidents could be an increase in gang use of guns. From 1987 to 1990, the proportion of nonlethal street gang–motivated violent offenses that were committed with a gun increased slightly from 27.3 percent to 31.5 percent. In contrast, a gun was the lethal weapon in almost all street gang–motivated homicides—96 percent in 1987 and 94 percent in 1990.

Furthermore, the proportion of murder weapons that were automatics or semiautomatics increased from 22 percent to 31 percent over the 3 years (from 11 to 31 deaths from 1987 to 1990). In addition, deaths by large-caliber guns (38 or greater) increased from 13 in 1987 to 39 in 1990.

Overall the number of street gang–motivated homicides increased from 51 in 1987 to 101 in 1990. The number killed with an automatic or semiautomatic (any caliber) or with a nonautomatic gun of 38 caliber or greater increased from 24 to 70 from 1987 to 1990. Virtually the entire increase in the number of street gang–motivated homi-

cides seems attributable to an increase in the use of high-caliber, automatic, or semi-automatic weapons.

Street Gang Activity by Community Area

Every community area in Chicago had at least one street gang–motivated offense between 1987 and 1990. However, the two most dangerous communities, East Garfield Park (area 27) and Humboldt Park (area 23), had a mean annual rate of street gang–motivated crimes (381.5) that was 76 times the mean annual rate (5.0) in the two least dangerous neighborhoods, Mt. Greenwood (area 74) and Edison Park (area 9); see Exhibit 24.1. The community areas with the highest levels of street gang–motivated crime were on the West Side (areas 23, 24, 27, 28, and 31); in the south central neighborhoods of New City (area 61) and Fuller Park (area 37); and in West Englewood (area 67), the scene of a burst of street gang violence in 1990 and 1991.

Homicides

Street gang–motivated homicides were also concentrated in two corridors on the Northwest and Southwest Sides. Of Chicago's 77 community areas, 17 had no street gang–motivated homicide from 1965 to

1990. Many had only one. None of the 13 community areas with the lowest rates of street gang–motivated crime had a street gang–motivated homicide between 1987 and 1990. At the other extreme, the Lower West Side (area 31) averaged more than 6 street gang–motivated homicides per 100,000 people per year over that same time period.

The risk of becoming a homicide victim or offender was far higher for young Latino men than for other Latinos or for non-Latino whites, and equal to that for young black men. The risk of homicide for other Latinos was not exceptionally high,[17] but the risk of homicide for non-Latino blacks was higher than for non-Latino whites, regardless of age or gender, and higher than for all Latinos except young men.

These individual differences were reflected in community differences as well.

Community Differences

Black neighborhoods with high rates of street gang homicide also had high rates of other forms of homicide. But this was not necessarily true in other communities. For example, the mostly mixed and Latino neighborhoods on the Northwest and Southwest Sides had many street gang–motivated killings, but relatively few killings for other reasons.[18] As a result, the rate of street gang–motivated homicide and the rate of other forms of homicide from 1987 though 1990 were only weakly correlated (.287) across community areas.

Compared to the relationship over time (Exhibit 24.6), the relationship between lethal and nonlethal violence across geographic areas appeared to be higher, but the strength of the relationship depended on the type of violence. Five of the six community areas with the highest rates of street gang–motivated nonlethal personal violence (assault and battery) also ranked among the six with the highest rates of street gang–motivated homicide. In contrast, only one of the six community areas that had the highest rate of street gang–motivated drug crime in the years 1987 to 1990 also ranked among the top six in street gang–motivated homicide rates. Only one community area, Humboldt Park (area 23), ranked among the top six in all three rates—street gang–motivated lethal violence, nonlethal personal violence, and drug offenses. Overall the correlation across the 77 community areas be-

tween rates of street gang–motivated drug crime and homicide was moderate (.401), while the correlation was much stronger (.728) between street gang–motivated homicide and rates of street gang–motivated assault and battery.

Hot Spot Areas of Street Gang Activity

Fifty-one percent of the city's street gang–motivated homicides and 35 percent of nonlethal street gang–motivated offenses occurred in 10 community areas on the West Side. Three kinds of neighborhood situations can be seen in this West Side map (Exhibit 24.4).[19]

- Neighborhoods with a turf hot spot area (heavy concentration of nonlethal personal violent activity to defend turf).
- Neighborhoods with a drug hot spot area (heavy concentration of street gang–motivated drug offenses).
- Neighborhoods plagued by both a turf and drug hot spot area.

Residents in these neighborhoods tend to view street gang activity very differently. For example, a resident living in a drug hot spot area is likely to consider the neighborhood street gang problem to be primarily a drug problem. A resident living in a turf hot spot area may consider the neighborhood street gang problem to revolve around violent defense of turf. And a resident of a community in which a drug and a turf hot spot area intersect experiences the worst of both.

In specific neighborhood areas, the link between incidents of street gang–motivated nonlethal and lethal personal violence was far stronger than that between drug crimes and lethal violence. For example, street gang–motivated homicides tended to occur within or close to the boundaries of turf hot spot areas, and only rarely in drug hot spot areas except when a drug hot spot area intersected a turf hot spot area.[20] Of the 169 street gang–motivated homicides in the 10 community areas shown in Exhibit 24.4, 94 occurred in hot spot areas, as follows: 37 in neighborhoods where a drug hot spot area and a turf hot spot area intersected (28 in Humboldt Park, 4 in Little Village, and 5 in Cabrini Green), 48 in turf hot spot areas only, and 9 in drug hot spot areas only. The turf hot spot area in Little Village (in the southwest corner) experienced more than 7 homicides per square mile, while the Pilsen hot spot area (southeast corner) experienced 48, and the turf hot spot area around Humboldt Park, which intersected with a drug hot spot area, was the site of 16 homicides per square mile over the 3-year period.

Highlights of Major Findings

This study painted a more complete picture of the reality of street gang crime than is usually the case in studies of gangs. By analyzing police records of lethal and nonlethal street gang–motivated crimes, examining temporal and spatial patterns of those crimes, and describing the criminal activities of Chicago's four largest street gangs, researchers sought to uncover typical patterns of street gang life.

The patterns of street gang activity can be summarized as follows:

- Chicago's largest street gangs can be identified with most of the city's street gang crime. These four street gangs (representing about 10 percent of all street gangs and 51 percent of the estimated number of all street gang members) accounted for 69 percent of police-recorded street gang–motivated criminal incidents and 55 percent of all street gang–motivated homicides from 1987 to 1990.

- Street gangs varied in the types of activities in which they were engaged. Some specialized in incidents of expressive violence while others focused on instrumental violence (see "Expressive Versus Instrumental Violence"). For example, the Vice Lords and BGDN were much more involved in acts of instrumental violence (such as possession or sale of drugs), while the Latin Disciples, Latin Kings, and smaller gangs specialized in acts of expressive violence (such as turf defense). Most of the criminal activity in smaller street gangs centered on representation turf defense. The most lethal street gang hot spot areas are along disputed boundaries between small street gangs.

- Types of street gang crime clustered in specific neighborhoods. Street gangs specializing in instrumental violence were strongest in disrupted and declining neighborhoods. Street gangs specializing in expressive violence were strongest and most violent in relatively prosperous neighborhoods with expanding populations.

- The rate of street gang–motivated crime in the 2 most dangerous Chicago communities was 76 times that of the 2 safest. However, every community area in Chicago had at least one street gang–motivated criminal incident between 1987 and 1990.

- Most of the lethal gang-related crimes occurred in neighborhoods where street gang activity centered on turf battles, not in neighborhoods where street gang activity focused on drug offenses. Of 288 street gang–motivated homicides from 1987 to 1990, only 8 also involved drug use or a drug-related motive.

- A gun was the lethal weapon in almost all Chicago street gang–motivated homicides from 1987 to 1990. Incidents involving a high-caliber, automatic, or semiautomatic weapon accounted for most of the increase in homicides over this period.

- Many community areas with high levels of lethal and nonlethal street gang–motivated personal violence and homicide had relatively low levels of other forms of homicide. Although hot spot areas of street gang–motivated drug offenses were usually low in street gang homicide, some were high in other kinds of homicide.

Policy Implications

As this report shows, street gang violence has been a continuing problem in Chicago since the late 1960s. The years 1990, 1991, and 1992 broke records for street gang violence, and the number of incidents continued to grow in 1993.

Intervention programs whose aim is to reduce nonlethal street gang violence will probably also reduce lethal violence. To be effective, however, these intervention programs must be built on a foundation of current information about the types of street gangs and street gang activity in each specific neighborhood.

As shown by this research, street gang–motivated crime is not random. In Chicago it occurred in specific neighborhoods and was concentrated in limited time periods.

Expressive Versus Instrumental Violence

A growing body of literature indicates that violence is not one type of event but many.[21] Almost all acts of lethal violence begin as another type of confrontation—for example, as an argument between spouses, a fight or brawl between acquaintances, a robbery, an act of sexual violence, or a street gang confrontation—that escalates to death. To understand lethal violence, the reasons why some—and only some—of these violent events become lethal must first be understood. The answer differs for those fatal and nonfatal "sibling" offenses such as assault homicide and assault compared to robbery homicide and robbery, which occupy different points on the expressive-versus-instrumental continuum.

In general, the dynamics of a violent situation are governed by the degree to which *expressive* versus *instrumental* motives predominate as the assailant's primary and immediate goal. In an expressive violent confrontation, the primary goal is violence or injury itself, and other motives are secondary. In contrast, the primary purpose of an act of instrumental violence is not to hurt, injure, or kill, but to acquire money or property. In addition, situational factors—such as possession of a weapon—that might affect the likelihood of a fatal outcome operate differently in expressive and instrumental confrontations.

Street gang–motivated violence often contains many expressive aspects—such as impulsive and emotional defense of one's identity as a gang member, defense and glorification of the reputation of the gang and gang members, and expansion of the membership and territory of the gang. Though some of these turf activities may involve acquisition, the primary motive is expressive. On the other hand, other types of street gang violence, such as formation and maintenance of a lucrative drug business and other entrepreneurial activities, are fundamentally instrumental. In this study researchers found that some gangs specialized in expressive violence, while others specialized in instrumental violence.

Some street gangs spent much of their time defending or expanding their turf while others were actively involved in the business of illegal drugs. Programs to reduce street gang–motivated violence must recognize these differences. For example, a program to reduce gang involvement in drugs in a community in which gang members are most concerned with defense of turf has little chance of success.

Furthermore, because the predominant type of street gang activity in a neighborhood may change from year to year or month to month, and because the level of street gang–motivated violence tends to occur in spurts, effective intervention strategies must be built on continuously updated information.

Another focus of control over gang violence should be on weapons. The death weapon in almost all gang-motivated homicides in Chicago was a gun, and much of the increase in gang-motivated homicides from 1987 to 1990 was an increase in killings with large-caliber, automatic, or semiautomatic weapons. Therefore, reducing the availability of these most dangerous weapons may also reduce the risk of death in street gang–plagued communities.

Street gang membership, street gang–related violence, and other illegal street gang activity must be understood in light of both long-term or chronic social patterns, and current or acute conditions. Street gang patterns and trends reflect not only chronic problems, such as racial and class discrimination and adjustment of immigrants, but also acute, often rapidly changing problems stemming from the existing economic situation, weapon availability, drug markets, and the spatial arrangement of street gang territories across a city.

Obviously, the chronic problem of street gang violence cannot be solved with a quick fix; the ultimate solution rests on a coordinated criminal justice response, changes in educational opportunities, racial and ethnic attitudes, and job structure. On the other hand, while waiting for these long-term strategies to take effect, lives can be saved and serious injury prevented by targeting the causes of short-term or acute escalations in violence levels.[22]

Notes

1. Two types of spatial analysis were used: correlational community area analysis and identification of hot spot areas of dense street gang activity concentrations. Hot spot areas were identified using the hot spot ellipse capability of the STAC (Spatial and Temporal Analysis of Crime) package, which was developed by the Illinois Criminal Justice Information Authority. STAC used an iterative search that identified the densest clusters of events on the map, calculated a standard deviational ellipse fitting each cluster, and mapped the events and the ellipses. STAC delineated, regardless of artificial boundaries, the areas of the map that contained the densest clusters of events. It was thus a database-driven, objective tool for identifying nonarbitrary summary areas from the actual scatter of events on the map.

r further information about STAC, see C. R. Block, "Hot Spots and Isocrimes in Law Enforcement Decisionmaking," paper presented at the Conference on Police and Community Responses to Drugs: Frontline Strategies in the Drug War, University of Illinois at Chicago, December 1990.

2. Community areas are aggregations of census tracts, usually including several neighborhoods but sometimes only one, identified by an official name and number. Since the Chicago School sociologists first identified them in the 1930s, a plethora of data has been collected and analyzed by community area. For more detail, see Exhibit 24.1 and Chicago Factbook Consortium, *Local Community Fact Book: Chicago Metropolitan Area* (Chicago: University of Illinois Department of Sociology, 1980).

3. Data from 1965 through 1981 are currently available in the National Archive of Criminal Justice Data of the Inter-University Consortium for Political and Social Research, and a completely updated data set from 1965 through 1990 is being prepared for the archive. The ultimate source of all information for all years was the Murder Analysis Report (MAR), a two-page summary of each homicide maintained since 1965 by the Crime Analysis Unit of the Chicago Police Department. Since its inception in 1965, MAR has consistently flagged cases in which there was positive evidence that the homicide was motivated by street gang activity.

4. Although a single incident may have involved multiple offenders or multiple victims, data were analyzed at the incident level. If more than one offense occurred in an incident, the incident was classified according to the most serious violation. All data are from 1987 to 1990, except for homicides; the homicide data include murders that occurred from 1965 to 1990.

5. It is quite possible that the territories defined by police officers differ from the territories that would be defined by street gang members, agency workers, community members, or even by police officers assigned to another division such as narcotics. Also, because street gangs disappear, merge, or change names over time, it would have been preferable to have a turf map that was contemporaneous with the street gang incident data. However, the turfs are probably a fairly accurate representation of the later part of the study period.

6. Chicago Police Department, Gang Crime Section, "Street Gangs" (internal report), 1992.

7. In the 1960s and 1970s, the Woodlawn Disciples battled the Blackstone Rangers (later called the Black P Stone Nation and then changed to El Rukins), which resulted in an upsurge in homicides. In 1991, renamed BGDN, the gang fought the normally allied Black Disciples gang for control of Englewood.

8. Much of the discussion on gang structure, history, and current activities depends upon two police department sources: L. J. Bobrowski, "Collecting, Organizing, and Reporting Street Gang Crime," paper presented at the annual meeting of the American Society of Criminology, Chicago, 1988; and Chicago Police Department, "Street Gangs," 1992.

9. R. J. Sampson and W. J. Wilson, "Toward a Theory of Race, Crime, and Urban Inequality," paper presented at the annual meeting of the American Society of Criminology, San Francisco, 1991.

10. C. R. Block, "Lethal Violence in the Chicago Latino Community," in *Homicide: The Victim-Offender Connection*, ed. A. V. Wilson (Cincinnati, OH: Anderson Pub. Co., 1993), 267–342.

11. For further information, see Bobrowski, "Collecting, Organizing and Reporting Street Gang Crime," and Chicago Police Department, "Street Gangs," 1992.

12. A homicide was defined as drug-related if drugs were a motivation for the crime or if the victim or offender was under the influence of drugs during the incident. Drug-motivated homicides included those involving the business or sale of drugs, those that resulted from a crime committed to get drugs or money for drugs, those that resulted from an argument or confrontation about drugs, and "other" (such as an infant starving to death because both parents were high). This definition follows that of P. J. Goldstein, "The Drugs/Violence Nexus: A Tripartite Conceptual Framework," *Journal of Drug Issues* 14 (1985): 493–506. Note that drug-related information was not available for nonlethal incidents.

13. M. W. Klein, C. L. Maxson, and L. C. Cunningham, " 'Crack,' Street Gangs, and Violence," *Criminology* 29(4) (1991): 701–717.

14. Non-Index offenses, such as intimidation, mob action, and weapons and liquor law violations, are not shown in Exhibit 24.3.

15. Yearly totals in Exhibit 24.5, which refer to the year of occurrence of the homicide (year of the incident) may differ from police totals, which refer to the year in which the police "booked" the offense.

16. The data here are 3-month moving averages.

17. C. R. Block, "Lethal Violence in the Chicago Latino Community," 1993.

18. R. Block and C. R. Block, "Homicide Syndromes and Vulnerability: Violence in Chicago's Community Areas Over 25 Years," in *Studies on Crime and Crime Prevention,* v. 1. (Oslo/Stockholm: Scandinavian University Press, 1992), 61–87.
19. Because of space considerations, the actual locations of the drug or nonlethal violent incidents that formed the basis for these hot spot areas are not depicted in Exhibit 24.4. The location of street gang–motivated homicides, which were not included in the calculation of the hot spot area ellipses shown on the map, are depicted by black dots.
20. Note that only nonlethal offenses, not homicides, were included in the calculation of hot spot areas depicted in Exhibit 24.4.
21. For more information on this issue, see R. Block and C. R. Block, "Homicide Syndromes and Vulnerability," 1992.
22. The authors acknowledge also the assistance of the Chicago Police Department in preparing this study, especially Commander Robert Dart of the Gang Crime Section, Commander James Maurer of Area Four Violent Crimes, Gang Crimes Specialist Lawrence J. Bobrowski of the Bureau of Operational Services, and Detective Al Kettman (retired) of the Crime Analysis Unit. Findings and conclusions of the research reported here are those of the authors and do not necessarily reflect the official position or policies of the U.S. Department of Justice.

References

Block, Carolyn Rebecca. "Hot Spots and Iso-crimes in Law Enforcement Decisionmaking." Paper presented at the Conference on Police and Community Responses to Drugs: Frontline Strategies in the Drug War. University of Illinois at Chicago, December 1990.

———. "Lethal Violence in the Chicago Latino Community." In *Homicide: The Victim-Offender Connection,* ed. Anna V. Wilson. Cincinnati, OH: Anderson Pub. Co., 1993, pp. 267–342.

Block, Richard, and Carolyn Rebecca Block. "Homicide Syndromes and Vulnerability: Violence in Chicago's Community Areas Over 25 Years." *Studies on Crime and Crime Prevention,* v. 1. Oslo/ Stockholm: Scandinavian University Press, 1992, pp. 61–87.

Bobrowski, Lawrence J. "Collecting, Organizing, and Reporting Street Gang Crime." Paper presented at the annual meeting of the American Society of Criminology, Chicago, 1988.

Chicago Factbook Consortium. *Local Community Fact Book: Chicago Metropolitan Area, 1980.* Chicago: University of Illinois Department of Sociology, 1980.

Chicago Police Department, Gang Crime Section. "Street Gangs." Internal report, 1992.

Goldstein, Paul J. "The Drugs/Violence Nexus: A Tripartite Conceptual Framework." *Journal of Drug Issues* 14 (1985): 493–506.

Klein, Malcolm W., Cheryl L. Maxson, and Lea C. Cunningham. " 'Crack,' Street Gangs, and Violence." *Criminology* 29(4) (1991): 701–717.

Sampson, Robert J., and William Julius Wilson. "Toward a Theory of Race, Crime, and Urban Inequality." Paper presented at the annual meeting of the American Society of Criminology, San Francisco, 1991. ✦

Chapter 25
'Getting High and Getting By'

Dimensions of Drug Selling Behaviors Among American Mexican Gang Members in South Texas

Avelardo Valdez
and Stephen J. Sifaneck

The relationship of street gangs to drug sales remains a source of contention. Most gang researchers find the relationship to be episodic and overstated in public debate, while law enforcement officials generally refer to a close and direct engagement of gangs in drug distribution. Valdez and Sifaneck contribute to clarifying the issues by showing how different types of gangs become involved in varying forms of drug use, selling, and dealing. Such differentiations help to break down simple, stereotypic notions about the gang/drug connections.

Research on gangs and drug dealing has generally found it difficult to discern the role that gangs and gang members play in drug markets, and the relationship between gang members' drug use and drug selling behaviors (Howell and Gleason 1999). Studies have reportedly found that most gangs' major illegal activity is associated with the marketing of drugs, especially in low-income urban minority communities (Moore 1978; Covey, Menard, and Franzese

1992; Chin 1995; Spergel 1995). The degree, however, to which gangs are involved is found to vary from one community to another, often times among gangs within the same neighborhood (Hagedorn 1988; Padilla 1992a; Morales 2001). Most studies, however, have found that even though drug selling is common among individual gang members, it is not a primary focus of the street gang itself (Klein 1995). Rather, drug sales develop almost as an unintended consequence of drug use by gang members as it does among other drug users. This article addresses the various roles of gang members in drug sales, the structure and function of the gangs, and the relationship to other actors in the drug market, especially adult prison gangs. The purpose here is to address an important gap in our knowledge of the gang's participation in drug market in relationship to other actors.

Mexican American Illegal Drug Market

In South Texas, the geographic context of this article, marijuana and heroin account for more than half of the total seizures of these drugs in the United States (ONDCP 2002). The Office of National Drug Control Policy (ONDCP) pursuant to the Anti-Drug Abuse Act of 1988 designated the Southwest Border, which encompasses the entire 2,000 mile border one to two counties deep, as a High Intensity Drug Traffic Area (HIDTA). These are areas that are identified as having the most critical drug trafficking problems that adversely impact the United States. Within the Southwest, South Texas is identified as a primary staging area for large-scale, bi-national, narcotic trafficking operations and a common source of marijuana, cocaine, and heroin.

The business of illegal drugs in South Texas is similar in its structure to those in other regions of the United States (Johnson et al. 1990; Adler 1993). Considering the proximity of Mexico (a few hours' drive from several large southwestern U.S. cities) trafficking operations are, however, somewhat different from distribution operations in other regions of the U.S. Drug dealing operations typically involve a bi-national hierarchic structure comprising of Mexican Americans and Mexicans. Mexican Americans living near the U.S./Mexico border and involved in drug distribution have more direct access to primary illegal drug sources than others who must go through multiple layers of middle-men, which decreases profits and increases risks. Cultivating a drug connection in Mexico may also be easier for a Mexican American who may be more acceptable to a Mexican dealer since they share a common ethnic background. This type of access for persons in the Southwest makes it unnecessary for them to develop an organizational hierarchy to traffic in drugs as opposed to those residing in cities and towns located in other areas of the U.S. These factors result in highly decentralized drug markets in the Southwest characterized by multiple small-time drug entrepreneurs with ties to Mexican distributors along with larger international cartels.

One other factor that has begun to characterize the drug market in Mexican American communities in the Southwest is the presence of Chicano prison gangs. There are few studies that describe the role of prison gangs in drug sales and their relationship to juvenile and adult gangs outside the prison either in Mexican American communities or others. Jacobs' (1974) study is one of the few to address the prison/street nexus. In that study, however, he describes how inmate culture is actually imported from the outside by street gangs into the prison. What seems to be occurring in U.S. Mexican communities is actually the opposite: adult prison gangs are influencing the community's illegal activities from inside the prison. The participation of "pintos" (a term used in the barrio by Mexican Americans to describe ex-convicts) in the drug market was initially described in Moore's *Homeboys* (1978). At that time in Los Angeles (and we speculate throughout the Southwest), prison gangs were selling drugs on "a relatively small-scale" and did "see their business as a lifetime commitment to a deviant role" (Moore 1978:149). Their role in the drug market in states like California and Texas seems to have substantially increased over the last two decades based on reports from law enforcement in these two states (although there is little information on these groups in the academic literature). In the Texas prison system, gang membership grew substantially during the 1990s (Cornyn 1999). As members of these prison gangs were released (paroled) from penal institutions, they began to organize themselves into a criminal network engaged in drug dealing and other illegal activities. This same pattern has been reported in California and other states with large concentrations of incarcerated Mexican Americans.

Juvenile Gangs, Drug Distribution, Dealing, Selling, and Organization

The term *youth gang* is used in this study to refer to groups of adolescents[1] who engage in collective acts of delinquency and violence, and are perceived by others and themselves as a distinct group. Moreover, the group has a structured hierarchy with rituals, symbols (colors, signs, etc.) and is associated with a territory. Research in the past twenty years has yielded a large amount of data on youth gangs and their role in the distribution of drugs (Fagan 1996; Hagedorn 1994a, 1994b; Klein 1995; Padilla 1992b; Taylor 1990; Venkatesh 1997; Waldorf 1993; Hagedorn, Torres, and Giglio 1998). Dolan and Finney (1984), Moore (1978) and Spergel (1995) have all suggested that youths involved in gang activities are more likely to be involved in the drug trade than other adolescents. During the crack epidemic of the late 1980s and early 1990s, the distribution of this drug was often linked to juvenile drug gangs or "crews" in large U.S. cities like New York and Chicago (Mieczkowski 1986; Padilla 1992a; Sullivan 1989; Williams 1989). Taylor (1990) and others have suggested that the growth of gang membership is due to resources made available through the gang's connection to drug markets. Declining economic conditions in many minority urban communities increased juvenile involvement in illegal drug markets (Hagedorn 1988). In the case of New York City, drug suppliers often used juveniles to retail their wares and avoid the risk of harsh sentences adults faced under the Rockefeller drug laws (Williams 1989).

Many researchers such as Skolnick et al. (1990) have argued that drug dealing by gangs is carried out by highly structured organized crime units. As well, Jankowski (1991:131–32) proposed that gangs were cohesive and structured organizations which all had a relationship with organized crime. Applying contingency theory from the literature on organizations, Hagedorn et al. (1998) explores the relationship between gangs and drug selling among minorities in Milwaukee. His findings show that a gang whose drug sales were limited to people within the neighborhood, i.e. their low-income neighbors, are likely to be less organized as a drug gang than those gangs who sell to people outside the neighborhood, especially to middle-class and affluent Whites.

Most contemporary literature reports youth gangs to be rarely involved in large-scale drug distribution activities as an organized gang function (Decker and Van Winkle 1996; Klein 1995). As described by Howell and Gleason (1999:2), "Distribution implies organizational management and control, as opposed to individual involvement in selling drugs directly to individual buyers." Waldorf and Lauderback's (1993) study found Latino and African-American street gangs in San Francisco to be loosely organized with individuals engaged in freelance, rather than organized, drug distribution entities. Skolnick et al. (1990) did find that African-American gangs are more likely to be "instrumental" and vertically organized than "cultural" Latino gangs. In his description, the instrumental gangs are more dedicated to the organized sale of drugs and the cultural gangs are closer to the classic notion of neighborhood corner groups. Mieczkowski (1986) has argued, as well, that crack in Detroit was distributed by small entrepreneurs rather than a large organization.

Drug Use, Drug Selling Behaviors, Drug Dealing, and Distribution

Research over three decades has established the intersection between different types of illegal drug use and drug selling (Hunt 1990; Hunt, Lipton, and Spunt 1984; Preble and Casey 1969). Users who serve as intermediaries for other users in drug transactions seem to be a consistent phenomenon. This has been observed with some consistency across the different types of illegal drug markets (marijuana, crack, cocaine, heroin) in varied geographic contexts for over 30 years (Andrade, Sifaneck and Neaigus 1999; Furst et al. 1997). For insistence, Sifaneck (1996) has observed a relationship between chronic marijuana users in New York City who played various roles in the distribution, some essentially becoming "subsistence dealers" of the drug in order to pay for their own use.

There have been few noninstitutionalized, or community-based studies of Mexican American drug use and selling/dealing especially among gang members (Bullington 1977; Moore 1978; Sanders 1994). In Moore's (1978:85) study of East Los Angeles' drug market, she states "drug dealers did employ members of their own barrios in a hierarchy that included non-addicted dealers, addicted dealers (who in turn would supply addict-pushers who sold heroin for use rather than profit), and finally the consumer addict." Individual gang members who dealt drugs operated in the same manner. A consistent finding in these few published studies is that users often paid for their drugs, as Preble and Casey (1969) found among New Yorkers, "by taking care of business," that is, with involvement in drug sales.

In this study we identify and describe the different types of drug use, selling behaviors, and dealing found among members of 26 active gangs in a large metropolitan area in South Texas. We explore the different dimensions of relationships that are involved in constructing a typology of Mexican American gang membership, and the distribution and use of drugs in the Mexican American illegal drug market. Finally, we discuss the implications of current public policies pertaining to gang formation and drug distribution.

Method

This research evolved from a study of Mexican American gangs in South Texas, whose focus was to identify and distinguish the relationship between gang violence and drug use among male gangs. The study used multiple methods, including ethnographic field observations, focus groups, and life history/intensive interviews with 160 male gang members sampled in a large Southwestern city (see Yin et al. 1996). The study was delimited to two areas of the city's Mexican American population, encompassing centers of commerce and residency for this group. These areas also have the highest concentration of delinquent behavior and Mexican American gang activity as well as underclass characteristics (Kasarda 1993). This delimitation was based on secondary data such as the U.S. Census, criminal justice data, public housing statistics, and previous published governmental reports and studies.

After identifying two study areas, two indigenous field workers began the social mapping of these communities, using systematic field observations and recording extensive field notes. Using Wiebel's (1993) indigenous outreach model, fieldworkers were selected based on their knowledge and familiarity with the targeted community and their ability to provide entrée to groups of Mexican American juvenile gang members. The social mapping stage of the study lasted approximately six months, although field work was a continuous process lasting a total of four years. Social mapping assisted us in the identification of gangs and where the target groups congregate, such as public parks, public housing spaces, playgrounds, recreational centers, downtown areas, neighborhood businesses and specific neighborhoods. In conducting this initial fieldwork, field workers were able to establish "an ethnographic presence" (Sifaneck and Neaigus 2001) and maintain a high visibility within the targeted community to help legitimize the project in the community. After this was accomplished, the field workers began to make contacts with the gang members, gain their trust, and obtain access to their social networks. The primary goals of the field workers were to establish rapport with the gang members, maintain nonjudgmental attitudes, and to promote candid and accurate reporting by respondents during data collection and the interview process.

After gaining access, rapport, and trust, field workers began to collect observational data based on gang hangouts mentioned previously. Results of this fieldwork were recorded in daily field notes that were shared and discussed with the research team. All efforts were made not to use information from school officials or police agencies in order to avoid associating the project with these authorities. Attention was focused on the primacy of developing and maintaining networks and a research presence in these communities and among the gangs in these areas.

The fieldwork resulted in identifying all 26 active juvenile gangs and their respective rosters in this area whose cumulative membership totaled 404 persons. The validity and accuracy of gang rosters were checked using at least three of four collateral sources: "gatekeepers," gang member contacts, key respondents, and field workers' observations. Gatekeepers control access to information, other individuals and places (Hammersley and Atkinson 1995, LeCompte and Schensul 1999). Fieldworkers were able to acquire information for initially classifying membership (leader, core, peripherals), gang type, and to delineate the gang's territory (neighborhood). Using this information, we designed a stratified sample that generated the 160 gang members interviewed for this study. A monetary incentive of $50 was provided to the gang member for participating in the interview. In order to protect the identities of the study participants, actual names of the gangs and gang members were known only to the field workers and the project administrator. Any reference to individual members or organizations was based on pseudonyms or identification number assigned by the administrator. As well, fictitious names were given to all geographic and other physical locations.

For the purpose of this paper emphasis will be on drug selling and drug use pattern information elicited from respondents at various times during the life history/intensive interview. Scenario questions provided the respondents' gangs' two major illegal activities (Page 1990). This scenario included specifics on the activity such as the individual in charge, the subject's participation and the distribution of profits. Additionally, a closed-ended question elicited data on the gangs' frequency of dealing during the last year. Individual level data was also collected by asking respondents their frequency of drug selling during the last year as well as the characteristics of their customers. The field note and life history/intensive interview data were combined into an electronic qualitative database. The data was then analyzed and contextualized for themes and commonalities. After the analysis of the data, we developed a typology based on distinct themes.

Dimensions of Drug Selling Behaviors and Drug Dealing Among Gang Members

Based on the analysis of our qualitative data gathered during field observations and life history interviews, two dimensions have emerged (see Figure 25.1) that shape and influence behavior associated with drug use and dealing among gang members. These are dimensions, not absolute points, and there is room for overlap between categories (Bailey 1994).

Figure 25.1
A Typology of Drug Dealers and
User/Sellers in Street and Drug Gangs

	Street Gang	Drug Gang
User/Seller	Homeboy	Slanger
Dealer	Hustler	Baller

The first dimension focuses on to what extent the gang as an organization is a drug dealing criminal enterprise. At one extreme are gangs who are not involved as a gang in drug dealing activity. These street gangs are traditional, territory-based gangs located in diverse neighborhoods ranging from public housing projects to single-family residential neighborhoods. Nineteen of the 26 gangs in this study were identified as street gangs. They encompass the various types of youth gangs described in the literature, but exclude criminal gangs which overlap with our drug gang category (Morales 2001). Street gangs generally are not hierarchical, although they adhere to some gang rituals such as identification with distinct colors, hand signs, and gang "placas" or symbols. They are involved in "cafeteria-style" crimes including auto theft, burglary, robbery, vandalism, criminal mischief, and petty crime. These crimes tend to be more individual and less organized. The gang member demonstrates more individual agency in his own activities and behavior. Violent behavior tends to be more random and personal rather than purposeful. The gang does offer protection from rival gangs or others in the community who threaten them. This protection is extended to those members who are involved in drug selling and dealing activities.

At the other end of this dimension are those gangs that are organized, criminal, drug dealing enterprises. These drug gangs, that comprised 7 out of the 26 gangs, usually function as a hierarchy with a clearly defined leadership that shares in the profits generated among all gang members involved in the business. Klein (1995:130) suggests these gangs exist in communities where there are "an adequate market of users, a sufficiently uncontrolled neighborhood, and connections with at least mid-level distributors." They may consist of several independent cliques that function under the protective umbrella of a gang. These gangs are distinct from other gangs in that they are not concerned with territorial issues or "turf violations," and do not engage in random acts of violence such as drive-by shootings. Violence among these gangs tends to be more systemic, i.e. related to drug distribution (Goldstein 1985). For instance, little importance is placed on identifying their territory with gang tags, even when other gangs tag their neighborhoods. Members are discouraged from engaging in more expressive acts of violence such as drive-by shootings, random assaults, and personal fights. According to several members, these types of violent acts draw unnecessary attention from the police, which could lead to exposure of covert drug dealing operations. Not all members of these gangs are involved in dealing drugs, some may be involved in other criminal enterprises such as auto theft and fencing stolen goods. Others, especially the younger members, may simply be involved in the gang "socially" without engaging in any criminal activity except occasional fights with rival gang members.

The second dimension identified by our analysis is based on an individual gang member's role in selling and dealing drugs within the gang. The one extreme of this dimension is the user/seller who is primarily buying drugs for personal consumption, and selling a portion of the drugs to offset the costs associated with his drug use. This behavior tends to occur among users who are in the early stages of drug using careers or who have established a relatively controlled regular (daily or weekly) drug use pattern. A user/seller is typically a young gang member who smokes marijuana on a daily basis with friends and acquaintances in the context of socializing. Marijuana purchased by these types of members is usually a quarter ounce that sells for $20 to $30 in a typical barrio neighborhood. An average daily user may purchase a quarter ounce every 3 to 4 days. This does not necessarily mean that the person is smoking the entire quarter ounce himself, since marijuana is a drug that is generally shared with other users. Any profits generated by such a transaction are usually in the form of the drug involved. This pattern of marijuana use and purchasing behavior is common among most gang members in this community.

The other extreme of this dimension includes the dealers, gang members who deal drugs (marijuana, cocaine, and heroin) for their own profit. These persons are connected with criminal networks that provide easy or reliable access to the drug market. They are either dealing as an individual, or with a group of other gang members, or with individuals outside the gang. Profits generated by dealers vary from a highly lucrative business that may afford a newer model car, jewelry, stereo, and other accruements of wealth in the barrio, to barely enough money to sustain or distinguish the person from other nondealing "homeboys." Drug use among these members varies from not using any drugs at all to those that have become heavy users of cocaine and heroin. The crossclassification of the subjects by the two dimensions result in a two-fold typology (see Figure 25.1).

Homeboys: Drug User/Sellers in Nondealing Gangs

Homeboys are gang members who belong to a street gang whose criminal behavior tends to be more individual, less organized, and less gang directed. Violent behavior tends to be more random and personal as opposed to more purposeful such as physically injuring someone because of an unpaid debt. Except for gang turf disputes, most violence is centered on interpersonal fights and random situational acts of violence often associated with male bravado. Most of these user/sellers usually buy just what they are going to use to get "high" and sell small remaining quantities to reduce the costs associated with their own consumption. Drug selling behaviors exhibited by these homeboys are essentially independent and separate from any formal link to a collective gang activity. These members usually "score" small amounts for themselves, friends and other associates. They may act as a middleman for members who may not have access to a connection. But, the primary feature of this user is that his drug selling is motivated more by the desire for pharmacological effects of a drug than desire to make a profit. One heroin sniffer stated, "Yeah, I am selling drugs, but only so I can get my own stuff. The gang don't have shit to do with this."

The Circle is a gang whose members exemplify this individualized selling/buying activity.[2] Members of the Circle are like many of the other gang members in this study: they smoked marijuana on a daily basis and stayed high most of the day. Most gang members in the Circle, like other members in this category, tend to sell small amounts of marijuana. They would usually sell marijuana to other gang members, friends and acquaintances in the neighborhood. The quantity they sold was usually $10 bags. They would also occasionally sell cocaine in a similar fashion in $10 and $20 units.

A gang member commenting on selling and dealing in his gang said, "None of them deal, they mostly just buy it and smoke it or sniff it or whatever." Even though the gang is not a drug dealing gang, in most cases, there is usually a "veterano" who is the source for the user/seller gang members. Veterano literally translates to veteran in English, and in Chicano street jargon is reserved for an older experienced criminal drug user. The primary source for the Circle was "Fat Boy," an older gang member who was marginally affiliated with the gang. He was linked through relatives to one of the prison gangs in the area who had connections to higher level dealers. Fat Boy operated with full knowledge of the gang leadership that consisted of a leader and two seconds. The leadership themselves had [interest in neither] dealing nor the profits generated by Fat Boy. The Circle was territorial, and involved in activities associated with protecting their turf, while drug dealing was not a primary interest.

The majority of the gang members buying from Fat Boy were relatively young, averaging from 15 to 18 years old, and had few dependable drug connections. As some of Fat Boy's customers got a little wiser they started to develop their own connections outside the gang. For instance, Julio was sent to an alternative school after being expelled from his high school. At the alternative school he met someone who introduced him to a cocaine connection. Julio eventually began to use this connection rather than Fat Boy.

Another nondealing gang is the Invaders. This gang is located in a low-income, residential area characterized by modest and older single-family homes. The neighborhood is accessible by car only through a couple of major streets, making it difficult for rival gang members or anyone else to enter the area unobtrusively. The gang consists of approximately twenty members ranging in age from 14 to 18. Their primary illegal activity is "gang banging." This includes protecting the gang's turf from rival gangs, drive-by shootings, fights and assaults. The Invaders also have a reputation as a party gang known for heavy use of marijuana, cocaine, and alcohol. The members seem to fall in the user/seller category with the majority involved in small-time drug selling, primarily marijuana sales.

Up in the Sky (UIS) is a gang that in the initial months of the research project had been classified as a "tagging crew." This is a group of individuals whose major activity focuses on spray-painting walls, alleyways, street signs, and buildings in a highly individualistic style described as "graffiti art." The general public, and school and police authorities often confuse tagging crew art for gang graffiti. In fact, tagging crew art is much more elaborate than gang graffiti, which is primarily used to mark off territory. These tagging crews are often in competition with each other for the most elaborate tags and the best location. Prestige is bestowed on those that display their art in the highest places (i.e., tops of buildings, freeway crossings).

Members of tagging crews vary according to the roles played in the organization's tagging functions such as "bombers" and "crew members." Bombers are members who actually create the works identified as graffiti art, while the crew provide support as assistants or lookouts. There are also members who are the "partyers." They are attracted to the gang because of the group's social activities, which include the frequent use of marijuana and alcohol, and the occasional use of cocaine. The leader of the UIS was a charismatic 19-year-old whose father was a police officer. In an interview, the leader stated, "In the beginning we didn't let in anyone into the gang that wasn't a tagger. But, as we started to get shit from other gangs we let them in." These nontaggers were attracted to the gang because of the party aspect of the group, but did have to meet gang obligations like fighting rivals.

The members of this gang were primarily homeboys. A few of the gang members, including the leader, had a connection with an older acquaintance from whom he bought ½ to 1 ounce of marijuana at a time. He would resell the drug to the other members at a slightly higher cost than he purchased it to cover the cost of the marijuana he used. Other members of this crew were involved in a similar practice. According to the leader, "No one was making any money off the stuff." However, as tension mounted between UIS members and other rivals they began to organize themselves more as a gang. As the crew began to diversify, the group's activities expanded to more profit-oriented drug dealing by certain homeboys. The crew's identity as a gang was solidified when they successfully defended themselves in a gang fight with one of the most notorious gangs in the area.

Hustlers: Drug Dealers in Nondealing Gangs

Gang members identified as hustlers deal drugs for profit within a street gang that is not characterized as a drug dealing organization. However, it does provide protection to hustlers within the territory controlled by the gang. Protection is extended to those persons because they are members of the organization rather than because of their drug selling activities. Profits generated by these hustlers are their own and are not used to support the collective activities of the street gang.

The Chicano Dudes are one of the largest and most violent street gangs on the city's West Side. There were approximately 59 members in the gang at the time of the study. Its territory is one of the largest public housing projects in the Mexican American community. The neighborhoods they dominate are filled with the gang's tags on building walls, commercial billboards, and traffic signs.

The leader of the Chicano Dudes is Mark Sanchez who took over the gang after the previous leader was sent to prison for attempted murder. Most of the gang's drug selling is controlled by Mark as an individual, not as leader of the gang. The dealers do not, and are not expected to share profits with the gang. The gang serves a lucrative drug market within a geographic territory they control, although Mark, "his boys," and the other hustlers sell outside this territory. It is the public housing territory, however, that the gang protects through intimidation and violence. Members are expected to support and defend the gang's collective interests, often through violence, and may be required to participate in a drive-by shooting, an assault, or a gang fight. Violating this expectation could have serious repercussions, as one field worker's notes recount:

> Last night Jesse, an ex-Chicano Dude who turned Vida [an adult prison gang] got an order to jump on a Chicano Dude who broke a car window of a sister who is still a Chicano Dude, with him. He did his job, and roughed up Tony, the one who broke the window. The Chicano Dude who went along, Robert, did not do anything but observe the situation. This all happened around 9:00 p.m. till 11:00 p.m. Mark, the head of Chicano Dudes, sent a group of seven boys to find Jesse, and beat him. They also found Robert, and beat him for watching.

Mark Sanchez maintained the loyalty of a close-knit group of gang members who were primarily older gang members (OGs). Some of these members were involved in his drug dealing and others were not. They were used by Mark as his "backup" (protection) to deal with clients who were giving him trouble or not paying their drug debts. This selective group was given special treatment by Mark such as being provided a lawyer and bond if arrested. If members were incarcerated, he was also known to provide protection while "locked up."

As Mark's drug dealing operation expanded, he began to sell drugs to other gangs on the West Side of San Antonio. When asked if this conflicted with his obligations as leader of the Chicano Dudes, one community researcher stated, "No, the dealing was seen as separate from the gang's business such as protecting its turf. But, Mark would use gang members to back up his business." Toward the end of the study Mark's dealing operations were even expanding outside the gang community into other criminal social networks that put him in conflict with one of the adult prison gangs.

There were other members of the gang selling and dealing drugs that were not part of Mark's clique and operated independently. One of these was a young charismatic gang member named Sparks who was the leader of a set within the Dudes comprised of the gang's pee wees. "I really love these little guys, and try to take care of them," he commented to us in an interview conducted by one of the authors of this paper. "I try and make sure they don't get into too much trouble, especially staying away from the 'brown' [heroin]." Over the years of the study, as the Dudes evolved into primarily a drug dealing gang under the tyrannical control of Mark, Sparks stayed loyal to the principles of the gang. However, Sparks was dealing marijuana, cocaine and heroin to other gang members and people outside the gang. With profits from these deals he was able to purchase marijuana for his own use (which he smoked on daily basis) and support himself economically.

"Biggie" was another member of the Chicano Dudes who was dealing independently. He was the leader of set or clique within the gang located in a different section of the "courts" (public housing projects) they controlled. According to our fieldworkers, he sold ounces of cocaine and heroin. What made Biggie different from the other hustlers is that [he] used his leadership of a major sub-set of the Chicano Dudes as front for his drug business. "He would even give out gang v's [violations] for late payments and members who were getting addicted to heroin." According to several sources, other gang members loyal to Biggie fatally beat one of Biggie's crew for a violation. Biggie was given the leeway in these matters by Mark, as long as he remained loyal to him.

One of the distinctions of the Chicano Dudes was its independence from Vida Loca, an adult prison gang that operated in the same area as his gang. Over the years the prison gang had attempted to control the Chicano Dudes, particularly its drug trade. Mark Sanchez was one of the few gang leaders to stand up to them. He did this through his own violent behavior and the loyalty of several OGs who were not intimidated by these adults. Only recently did this independence begin to weaken when a rival gang associated with Vida Loca seriously injured Sanchez in an aborted attempt on his life. His vulnerability to the prison gang and personal accumulation of wealth started to affect the loyalty of many of his members to the gang and his leadership. Over the course of this study, this gang became to transform itself more into a dealing gang as its dealing activities became its primary activity.

Slangers: Drug User/Sellers in Drug-Dealing Gangs

Gang members in this category are characterized as user/sellers in gangs that are organized as drug dealing enterprises. Slangers are members who either chose not to participate in the higher levels of the gang's organized drug dealing activities or who are excluded from those circles for various reasons. However, the slangers continue to use and sell drugs at an individual level mostly to help off-set costs associated with their drug use and to support themselves economically. In the vernacular of the gangs, these members are dealing to "get high and get by." The slangers stand in contrast to the hardcore dealer members in the drug gang who are heavily involved in the gang's higher level organized drug distribution activities.

Varrio La Paloma (VLP) is a gang that is located in San Miguel Public Housing Project, one of the oldest courts on the Westside. The gang's activities have recently expanded to a working-class suburban subdivision outside the barrio after public housing authorities displaced many project families to this location. There are approximately 100 hard-core and 80 marginal members in this gang. Organizationally, this dealing gang has several sets or subgroups of members. Each of the sets has a head that is under the command of a leader. VLP is an older established gang and one of the few gangs whose former members were parents and other relatives who have in the past participated in this same gang.

The distribution of drugs by the VLP was controlled by the leader of the gang and his closest gang associates, primarily older hard core members, including two of his brothers. There were several cliques of members who were responsible for different tasks or functions associated with the gang's drug business. VLP leadership had connections to wholesale drug distributors who were associated with independent adult criminals with ties to Mexico. The actual drug distribution in the barrios was conducted by slangers. The slangers were "fronted" drugs by the gang's leadership for retail sale. Fronting is a form of credit or consignment in the drug culture given to sellers who agree to pay for the drugs within an agreed upon time. Amount of profits accrued by the slangers depends on their mode of distribution. One report from the field stated,

> How much money a slanger made depended on how you cut it, or whether you resold it in smaller qualities. If one of the guy's in the crew got an eight ball [3½ grams] of cocaine from Leo for $100, he might mix it with a gram of cut for about a $50 profit if he sold the whole amount. Or, he could make more profits if he bagged it up in smaller quantities and sold it that way like 10s and 20s bags [dollars].

Selling in smaller units entails higher risks because of the higher volume of customers needed to get rid of the "batch."

Interestingly, the VLP's status as a drug dealing gang is a relatively recent phenomena and is in response to the emergence of the prison gangs in the community during the last 10 years. They became involved in a serious conflict with the adult prison gang, which was attempting to enforce its diez porciento (10%) take from VLP's total sales. At that time, drug dealing was conducted on an individual basis by gang members. In order to protect their share of the drug market, the gang's dealers began to organize their drug business around the gang. This allowed them to use the gang's organization to protect themselves from the prison gang attempting to control the drug market in their community.

This conflict culminated when two adult prison gang members were murdered by a VLP member when he refused to cooperate with him. One of our fieldworkers described the time he met the VLP member soon after the shoot-out incident:

> Georgie walked with the help of two crutches as he approached the car. Vida put out a contract on him because he refused to pay the 10% commission on his drug sales. Georgie had started out selling dime bags of heroin. Shortly thereafter, he was selling three to four ounces of heroin and coke a week. That's when Vida started asking for their 10%. He said, "They sent two hit men. The men shot first hitting me in the thigh and the knee. I was shooting on the way down and killed them both. I gave the gun to Ray-Ray, who stashed it before the police got there." Georgie was upset because none of the VLP got down for him.

Eventually, after serious threats of retaliation from both sides, the VLP and the prison gang reached a compromise. The VLP would be allowed to sell cocaine and marijuana, but the heroin trade would be the exclusive right of the prison gang even within the San Miguel Courts.

As previously mentioned, slangers are those members on the lower end of the gang's dealing hierarchy. Slangers may include many of the younger members who were excluded from more serious drug dealing operations because of the legal risks and violence associated with these activities. This protective attitude was even stronger if the younger member was a sibling of the older veteranos drug dealers. One of these types told us, "There was no way my carnalito [younger brother] was going to get involved." However, these members continued to engage in user/seller behavior to economically supplement their recreational drug use. What distinguishes these slangers from other user/sellers is the high-level protection and reputation of the drug gang. In fact, outsiders often treated them as full-fledged "ballers" (described in the following section) because of their drug dealing gang affiliation.

Another category of slangers in the VLP were gang members who voluntarily decided not to participate in the gang dealing activities, although to continue user/seller behavior. These often included VLP members on probation and parole. In these types of cases, the person fears that an arrest for drug dealing could result in a long prison term. This threat is often a deterrent to becoming involved in the gang's organized drug dealing. In other cases, the veterano may be experiencing a process of maturing out of the gang life style. In these situations the member is often emotionally attached to a woman whose child he may have fathered. He may have also found a job that offered a good salary and some stability. At this point in his life, the veterano may be considering dropping out of the gang scene. However, he may still be using drugs, especially marijuana, and since he has solid connections to drug dealers, he will continue to sell to a few trusted customers to compensate for his own drug use. As one of these slangers put it, "I am selling enough to cover my own huesos [bones]."

Ballers: Drug Dealers—Drug-Dealing Gangs

As discussed, drug gangs are those organized as a criminal enterprise with profits distributed either to the gang as an entity or equally among the gang members active in the organization. Ballers are the individuals within these gangs who control the drug distribution business. One gang member commented, "These are the batos [guys] making all the feria [money], jewelry, and fancy cars. They have the big connections." The ballers usually sit atop the gang's hierarchy and comprise a leadership structure that provides protection to members against rival gangs and predatory adult criminals. Among these gang members, heroin use was generally discouraged, although as the gangs began to deal heroin, many ballers began shabanging[3] (noninjection) and/or picando (injecting), and some subsequently became addicted. One of the distinctions of ballers from seller-dealers, slangers and homeboys is their generally lower visibility and the higher volume of drugs they deal. "You don't see these guys on the street selling drugs like those others," an older gangster (OG) member mentioned to us in an interview. Furthermore, they avoid ostentatious aggressive behavior that attracts law enforcement like drive-by shootings. Violence among ballers is also more purposeful and revolved around business transactions as discussed in Goldstein's drug-nexus typology (1985).

The Nine-Ball Crew (NBC) is a dealing gang located in La Luna Courts, another large city housing project. This gang was distinct from other youth gangs in its direct ties to Vida Loca. This prison gang controlled the heroin trade in this community by imposing the 10 percent rule that it enforced through violence and intimidation. The gang leader's stepfather was one of the heads of the prison gang. Over the last few years, they have recruited several gangs, and subsequently their members, to distribute heroin for them. Although the relationship between a youth gang and the adult prison gang is initially based on drug distribution, the youth gang often becomes a subsidiary of the prison gang. The control of Vida Loca over the NBCs is their most successful example of this process. During the course of the study, a Nine-Baller shot the leader of the Chicano Dudes for refusing to pay the adult prison gang a percentage of his profit. The hit was an attempt by the adult prison gang to solidify their control of the drug trade in this area.

The Nine-Ball Crew is highly organized,

with a leader and two second-heads or lieu-tenants, a hard-core membership of 20 members and approximately 30 others. The leader of this gang is Juan, a baller, who tightly rules the gang. He is 23 years old and has been described as "cold-blooded and vicious." His control of the gang is solidified by the support of his five brothers, who are active in the gang. The NBC drug market is primarily in the La Luna Courts and nearby vicinity, where there is little competition from other sellers and dealers. The selling of drugs is coordinated by one of Juan's brothers and another member identified as an original gangster (OG). The gang's hardcore membership, under the direct supervision of the two heads, is responsible for the distribution and sale of the drugs. Ballers, such as Juan and his OGs, are the primary sources of drugs for other slangers, hustlers, homeboys, and other drug sellers in the community. When one of the NBC members was asked about Juan, he said

> Yeah, he's the main guy that controls the drugs. He says who is going to sell and who ain't going to sell. If you're selling without permission and don't bring money to him you're going to get in trouble, get a v.

Another well recognized baller was Pio Gomez, who operated out of a public-housing complex on the near West Side. What distinguished him from some of the other ballers was that he was not a member of one of the drug gangs. He was actually a childhood friend of a leader of the Chicano Dudes. This widely acknowledged relationship among gangs members and the community allowed him to run his drug business as if he was a high-ranking member of a drug gang. This provided him the "street muscle" to deal with those who tried to interfere in his business or refused to pay their debts to him and his crew. Through independent adult dealers and other dealing gangs, including Mark from the Chicano Dudes, he would acquire kilos of cocaine and ounces of heroin. Pio broke these larger quantities into ounces, half ounces, quarter ounces and eight-balls (3½ grams) that he fronted to his crew. His crew, which consisted of gang members and other young men, distributed the drugs to slangers in the courts and the surrounding neighborhoods. Over the course of the study, Pio generated a great deal of money, spending it in a very

conspicuous manner. One gang member stated, "Everyone considered Pio a baller. He bought a brand new silver Eclipse. He had gold chains, expensive watches that stood out like a sore thumb. But, he never got busted. Some of his crew did, but not him."

During the period of this study there were gang members who moved from one category of the typology to another. El Gato, the leader of the Deep West, transformed himself from a slanger to baller, and finally was recruited as a "soldier" by Vida Loca. El Gato used his gang members as runners in an area on the western outskirts of the Mexican American community. At the height of his dealing career, he was distributing large amounts of cocaine and heroin. When El Gato was finally arrested, it was for possession with intent to distribute 6 ounces of cocaine and 4 ounces of heroin, an amount he would sell through his crew 2 or 3 times a week. Most of these drugs were fronted to other gang members or other independent drug sellers. To make sure that his gang members stayed loyal and in his services, he was known for giving away $10 to $20 bags of heroin to them. As [a] result, many of his hard-core slangers became addicted and were less useful to his operation, especially in collection efforts. As El Gato started to lose key members to heroin addiction and increased police pressure, he started to create alliances with the prison gang that eventually recruited him as a full-fledged member.

Although many of the dealing gangs, and subsequently the ballers, were generating large amounts of money, others were not. One informant told us, "the VLP as a gang wasn't selling nothing compared to a couple of guys [a set] associated with the Chicano Dudes." He went on to explain how the VLP were really small-time in the larger drug market in the community, although the VLP did manage to control through violence a corner of that market in the courts. "These guys were not driving around in new cars, and flashing money around. These guys were small time, many couldn't even pay their utility bills." However, even those ballers and hustlers like Mark Sanchez that were perceived as "making money" were not wealthy enough to invest in legitimate businesses like more successful criminals such as those in larger illegitimate enterprises.

Discussion and Conclusion

We have attempted to develop a framework for describing and understanding the relationships among drug use, gang membership, and drug distribution and gang membership in the context of a Mexican American community in South Texas. We constructed this framework along two dimensions: (1) the gang's organizational structure defined by involvement in drug dealing; and (2) the individual gang member's role in using, selling and dealing drugs. The analysis of the two dimensions resulted in a fourfold typology. The typology encompasses a wide range of connections and intersections between gangs, their individual members, and the selling of illegal drugs within the wider distribution system.

Malcolm Klein (1995:132) asserts that a clear distinction exists between street and drug gangs (Howell and Gleason 1999). He posits that few gangs are involved as an organization in drug distribution in entrepreneurial marketing of drugs because of key structural limitations. For example, drug dealing requires a hierarchical and cohesive organization, dependable leadership, a business focus, and avoidance of opportunistic "cafeteria-style" crimes. Our findings generally corroborate Klein's theory as applied to the Mexican Americans in South Texas. However, our data suggests that Klein underestimates the extent to which street gangs and gang members are fluid in their drug dealing roles and are susceptible to existing, adult based drug distribution systems.

Findings from this study suggest that gang members' involvement in selling and dealing is influenced by the presence of adult criminals in key members' social network. Many of the gang members are related by family ties to adult criminals who are prison gang members active in drug distribution. Moore (1994) similarly described the importance of the "cholo" family in sustaining a wide array of delinquent and criminal behavior among Mexican Americans in Los Angeles (Vigil 1988 and Moore 1994). This "intergenerational closure" provides a social cohesiveness to the street gang that sharply contrasts to that in Chicago that has been related to positive social outcomes (Sampson, Morenoff, and Earls 1999). Nonetheless, the capacity of adult criminal family relationships to influence and intervene in the lives of young males provides a marker for distinguishing the Mexican American gangs in this study.

The inclusion of the second dimension pertaining to drug user/seller and dealer roles in the construction of our typology provides a more comprehensive understanding of gangs and the drug distribution system. The appreciation of the subtle yet complex roles played by individual gang members in this system has been overlooked by some gang researchers. An exception has been the work of Spergel (1995) who recognized a fluidity and similarity in the roles of members in street and drug gangs. Our typology contributes to this recognition by explicating the multiplicity of roles that individual gang members play in the drug distribution system that is not necessarily dictated by gang structure, i.e. street vs. drug gang.

The role of gang members in this system is often obscured because of the fact that most gang members are more frequent users and sellers of drugs compared to other non-gang youth. But as Spergel (1995) concludes, this does not mean that the majority of gang members are dealers as we have defined them by our typology nor that the gangs they belong to are necessarily criminal drug organizations. What emerges from our data is that some gangs have nothing to do with the dealing of drugs. This was clearly illustrated by the "tagging crew" who spent their time, energy and money on elaborate, although illegal, displays of public art, and not the selling of illegal drugs.

Another important finding of this study is that drug selling and dealing is not only related to extended family networks but also to the larger social context of the gang. Thus, the gang can offer to drug sellers and dealers protection in exchange for their commitment and obligation to the gang. As a result, the role of the gang in the distribution of drugs in the community is difficult to discern and is obscured to most outsiders. For instance, protection may often be misperceived by police as evidence that a gang is a drug dealing enterprise when in reality members may be operating independently from the gang. Often law enforcement personnel indiscriminately extend this flawed perception to all Mexican American youth living in these neighborhoods. This misconception may lead to continual harassment, shakedowns and detainment of many innocent youth.

A serious consequence of this perception is very often drug law enforcement that indiscriminately arrests and prosecutes offenders without distinguishing the differences that constitute our four distinct types. Even those "homeboys" arrested for minor violations of drug laws, such as possession of small amounts of marijuana, get caught up in a criminal justice system that often treat them like "ballers," leading to serious lifelong consequences. Our typology suggests that a more variegated law enforcement and balanced social intervention policy is needed to address the complexity of the situation.

The analysis presented here suggests the need for police, judges and district attorneys to understand the relationship between the use of illegal drugs by poor youth and the diverse operative roles these youth may play in the distribution of these drugs. Police need to be trained in recognizing the differences in the "homeboy" user/seller who is affiliated with a street gang from "slangers" and "ballers" who are the persons really dealing drugs. Judges also need more discretion in the sentencing of those who violate drug laws. Mandatory sentencing minimums need to be balanced with social work and treatment options for "homeboys," and in certain cases "hustlers" and "slangers." These changes in policy would shift the emphasis away from a wholesale punishment approach, usually in the form of incarceration, to a refined rehabilitation approach involving creative applications of drug treatment, job training, and probationary social work.

In closing, the methodological limitations of our study need to be acknowledged. Common with other ethnographic and qualitative studies, the generalizability of the results is limited to other communities. Ethnographic studies of drug dealing often arrive at seemingly contradictory findings in relatively similar communities (Hagedorn 1988; Taylor 1990). South Texas, with its proximity to Mexican trafficking operations, may present so special a context that replication of our gang drug dealing typology without essential modifications would be problematic. However, confidence in the generalizability of our typology is increased in that we were able to find and distinguish street and drug gangs and membership behavior in South Texas as has been widely done elsewhere. This is complemented by the inclusion in our analysis of the mechanism of intergenerational closure to help explain the variation we discovered. A deeper and more extended program of qualitative research needs to be initiated in cities in diverse regions and with gang members of other ethnicities in order to further evaluate the significance of the findings from this single study.

Notes

1. In the literature there are very different definitions of what constitutes an adolescent gang (Klein 1971; Miller 1975; Moore 1978; Yablonsky 1962), often based on the researcher's relationship to the gang and source of information. The definition used in study is based on our experiences in working with gangs in San Antonio.

2. All the names of gangs and gang members are aliases. Some of the descriptive characteristics have been altered to prevent identification of the actual participants, gangs, and neighborhoods.

3. *Shabanging* is a term used by these youth to describe intranasal use of heroin, typically via a plastic nasal spray bottle. The heroin is diluted with water and sprayed into the nasal cavity with the plastic device.

References

Adler, Patricia A. 1993. *Wheeling and Dealing: An Ethnography of an Upper-Level Drug Dealing and Smuggling Community*. New York: Columbia University Press.

Andrade, Xavier, Stephen J. Sifaneck, and Alan Neaigus. 1999. "Dope Sniffers in New York City: An Ethnography of Heroin Markets and Patterns of Use." *Journal of Drug Issues* 29:271–98.

Bailey, Kenneth B. 1994. *Typologies and Taxonomies: An Introduction to Classification Techniques*. Thousand Oaks, CA: Sage.

Bullington, Bruce. 1977. *Heroin Use in the Barrio*. Lexington, MA: Lexington Books.

Chin, Ko-Lin. 1995. "Chinese Gangs and Extortion." Pp. 46–52 in *The Modern Gang Reader*, edited by M. W. Klein, C. L. Maxson, and J. Miller. Los Angeles, CA: Roxbury.

Cornyn, John. 1999. "Gangs in Texas: 1999." Austin, TX: Office of the Attorney General, State of Texas. Retrieved August 15, 2003 from http://www.oag.state.tx.us/AG_Publications/pdfs71999gangs.pdf.

Covey, Herbert C., Scott Menard, and Robert J. Franzese. 1992. *Juvenile Gangs*. Springfield, IL: Charles C. Thomas.

Decker, Scott and Barrik Van Winkle. 1996.

"Slinging Dope: The Role of Gangs and Gang Members in Drug Sales." *Justice Quarterly* 11:583–604.

Dolan, Edward F. and Shan Finney. 1984. *Youth Gangs.* New York: Julian Messner.

Fagan, Jeffery. 1996. "Gangs, Drugs, and Neighborhood Change." Pp. 39–74 in *Gangs in America,* edited by C. R. Huff. Newbury Park, CA: Sage.

Furst, Terry R., Richard S. Curtis, Bruce D. Johnson, and Douglas S. Goldsmith. 1997. "The Rise of the Street Middleman/Woman in a Declining Drug Market." *Addiction Research* 5:1–26.

Goldstein, Paul J. 1985. "The Drugs/Violence Nexus: A Tripartite Conceptual Framework." *Journal of Drug Issues* 15:493–506.

Hagedorn, John. 1988. *People and Folks: Gangs, Crime and the Underclass in a Rust Belt City.* Chicago: Lake View Press.

———. 1994a. "Neighborhoods, Markets, and Gang Drug Organization." *Journal of Research in Crime and Delinquency* 31:264–94.

———. 1994b. "Homeboys, Dope Fiends, Legits, and New Jacks." *Criminology* 32:197–219.

Hagedorn, John, Jose Torres, and Greg Giglio. 1998. "Cocaine, Kicks, and Strain: Patterns of Substance Use in Milwaukee Gangs." *Contemporary Drug Problems* 25:113–45.

Hammersley, Martyn and Paul Atkinson. 1995. *Ethnography, Principles in Practice.* London: Routledge.

Howell, James C. and Debra K. Gleason. 1999. *Youth Gang Drug Trafficking.* Washington, DC: US Department of Justice, Office of Justice Programs, Office of Juvenile Justice and Delinquency Prevention.

Hunt, Dana E. 1990. "Drugs and Consensual Crimes: Drug Dealing and Prostitution." Pp. 159–202 in *Crime and Justice: An Annual Review of Research, vol. 13: Drugs and Crime,* edited by J.Q.W.A.M. Tonry. Chicago: University of Chicago Press.

Hunt, Dana E., Douglas S. Lipton, and Barry Spunt. 1984. "Patterns of Criminal Activity Among Methadone Clients and Current Narcotics Users Not in Treatment." *Journal of Drug Issues* 14:687–702.

Jacobs, James B. 1974. "Street Gangs Behind Bars." *Social Problems* 21:395–409.

Jankowski, Martin Sanchez. 1991. *Islands in the Street: Gangs and American Urban Society.* Berkeley: University of California Press.

Johnson, Bruce D., Terry Williams, Kojo A. Dei, and Harry Sanabria. 1990. "Drug Abuse in the Inner City: Impact on Hard-Drug Users and the Community." Pp. 9–30 in *Drugs and Crime,* vol. 13, edited by M. Tonry, N. Morris, and N.I.O. Justice. Chicago: The University of Chicago Press.

Kasarda, John D. 1993. *Urban Underclass Database: An Overview and Machine-Readable File Documentation.* New York: Social Science Research Council.

Klein, Malcolm. 1971. *Street Gangs and Street Workers.* Englewood Cliffs, NJ: Prentice Hall.

———. 1995. *The American Street Gang.* New York: Oxford Press.

LeCompte, Margaret D. and Jean J. Schensul. 1999. *Designing & Conducting Ethnographic Research, Ethnographer's Toolkit, Vol. 1.* Walnut Creek, CA: Altamira Press.

Mieczkowski, Thomas. 1986. "Geeking Up and Throwing Down: Heroin Street Life in Detroit." *Criminology* 24:645–65.

Miller, Walter B. 1975. *Violence by Youth Gangs and Youth Groups As a Crime Problem in Major American Cities.* Washington, DC: Department of Justice.

Moore, Joan. 1978. *Homeboys: Gangs, Drugs, and Prison in the Barrios of Los Angeles.* Philadelphia: Temple University Press.

———. 1994. "The Chola Life Course: Chicana Heroin Users and the Barrio Gang." *The International Journal of the Addictions* 29:1115–26.

Morales, Armando T. 2001. "Urban and Suburban Gangs: The Psychosocial Crisis Spreads." Pp. 397–433 in *Social Work: A Profession of Many Faces,* 9th ed., edited by A. T. Morales and B. W. Sheafor. Boston, MA: Allyn & Bacon.

Office of National Drug Control Policy, High Intensity Drug Trafficking Areas. 2002. "Southwest Border HIDTA South Texas Partnership." Retrieved August 15, 2003 from http://www.whitehousedrugpolicy.gov/hidta/frames_stex.html.

Padilla, Felix M. 1992a. *The Gang As an American Enterprise.* New Brunswick, NJ: Rutgers University Press.

———. 1992b. *Becoming a Gang Member: The Gang As an American Enterprise.* New Brunswick, NJ: Rutgers University Press.

Page, Bryan. 1990. "Shooting Scenarios and Risk of HIV-1 Infection." *The American Behavioral Scientist* 33:478.

Preble, Edward and John J. Casey. 1969. "Taking Care of Business—The Heroin User's Life on the Street." *The International Journal of the Addictions* 4:1–24.

Sampson, Robert J., Jeffery D. Morenoff, and Felton Earls. 1999. "Beyond Social Capital: Spatial Dynamic of Collective Efficacy for Children." *American Sociological Review* 64:633–60.

Sanders, William B. 1994. *Gangbangs and Drive-by.* New York: Aldine de Gruyter.

Sifaneck, Stephen J. 1996. "Regulating Cannabis: An Ethnographic Analysis of the Sale and Use of Cannabis in New York City and Rotterdam." Unpublished Ph.D. Dissertation. City University of New York (CUNY), New York.

Sifaneck, Stephen J. and Alan Neaigus. 2001. "The Ethnographic Accessing, Sampling and

Screening of Hidden Populations: Heroin Sniffers in New York City." *Addiction Research and Theory* 9:519–43.

Skolnick, Jerome H., Theodore Correll, Elizabeth Navarro, and Roger Rabb. 1990. "The Social Structure of Street Drug Dealings." *American Journal of Police* 9:1–41.

Spergel, Irving A. 1995. *The Youth Gang Problem: A Community Approach.* New York: Oxford University Press.

Sullivan, Mercer L. 1989. *Getting Paid: Youth Crime and Work in the Inner City.* Ithaca, NY: Cornell University Press.

Taylor, Carl. 1990. *Dangerous Society.* East Lansing: Michigan State University Press.

Venkatesh, Sudhir A. 1997. "The Social Organization of a Street Gang Activity in an Urban Ghetto." *American Journal of Sociology* 103:82–111.

Vigil, Diego. 1988. *Barrio Gangs.* Austin: University of Texas Press.

Waldorf, Dan. 1993. *When the Crips Invaded San Francisco: Gang Migration-Homeboy Study.* Alameda, CA: Institute for Scientific Analysis.

Waldorf, Dan and David Lauderback. 1993. *Gang Drug Sales in San Francisco: Organized or Freelance?* Alameda, CA: Institute for Scientific Analysis.

Wiebel, Wayne. 1993. *The Indigenous Leader Outreach Model: Intervention Manual.* Rockville, MD: National Institute on Drug Abuse.

Williams, Terry. 1989. *The Cocaine Kids: The Inside Story of a Teenage Drug Ring.* Redding, MA: Addison-Wesley.

Yablonsky, Lewis. 1962. *The Violent Gang.* New York: McMillan.

Yin, Zenong, Avelardo Valdez, Alberto G. Mata Jr., and Charles Kaplan. 1996. "Developing a Field-Intensive Methodology for Generating a Randomized Sample for Gang Research." *Free Inquiry—Special Issue: Gang, Drugs and Violence* 24:195–204. ✦

Section V

Programs and Policies

Chapter 26
Public Policy Responses to Gangs:
Evaluating the Outcomes

Noelle E. Fearn,
Scott H. Decker,
and G. David Curry

Street gangs in the United States come in many forms. In this chapter, the authors describe a plethora of federal and local governmental efforts initiated in the last decade to respond to gangs. These responses take the form of suppression, social intervention, organizational change, community mobilization, and the provision of social opportunities. How well does the response match the problem? Do the responses focus attention on the immediate or deep-rooted causes of gang activity? Do the responses take into account gang process and dynamics, the functions that gangs serve for disadvantaged youngsters? Sound policies rest on a thorough understanding of the phenomenon they attempt to address. Consider these initiatives in light of the depictions of gangs and gang activity provided in the prior sections of this volume. Is there a good fit between knowledge and response?

Introduction

Designing public policy to respond to gangs is difficult. Based on police respondents, the National Youth Gang Center estimated that in 1996, 51 percent of jurisdictions reported having a gang. These jurisdictions included 816,000 gang members in 30,500 youth gangs across the United States (National Youth Gang Center 1999). Moore and Cook (1999) summarized data from the 1998 National Youth Gang Survey and reported 28,700 gangs with 780,000 gang members nationwide. Others (Maxson and Klein 1994) document large movement of gang members across American cities. The current cycle of gang activity is different than in previous eras as it is spread across more cities, is more violent, and is more deeply entrenched than was the case earlier (Klein 1995). Contemporary gangs have greater access to automobiles and high-powered firearms than did their predecessors. The growth of the underclass has also contributed to the growth of gangs (Jackson 1991; Vigil 1988; Klein 1995). Gangs also appear to be spreading beyond the boundaries of cities and gaining a foothold in suburban and rural communities (Klein 1995). These circumstances make responding to gangs a difficult task.

It is a truism that we cannot respond effectively to gangs unless we understand them. Public perceptions of gangs are shaped more by media images, such as the evening news or movies, than by a solid understanding of what gangs are. Most understanding of gangs comes from the criminal justice system and is the by-product of reporting on only the most criminal or delinquent members of gangs. This is important given that our conceptions of gangs are critical to determining the way we respond to them. Decker and Leonard (1991) found that members of an anti-gang task force based their knowledge of gangs on the media, a source considered the least reliable. The popular perception sees gangs as well-organized groups of men committed to a profit-making enterprise and organized around a common set of goals. However, there is little or no evidence to support these views. These facts provide a backdrop for our attempts to compare the policy responses to gangs to the magnitude and nature of the gang problem.

Despite a veritable explosion of gang research in the past decade, there has been little effort to catalogue the responses to gang problems in a systematic fashion (but see Howell 1997 and 1998). These responses have been implemented by a variety of levels of government, and address the problem in different ways. While some interventions have been supported by the federal government, others have their locus in local governments. Some of these responses have emphasized prevention, while others have concentrated on intervention after the commission of an offense. We present this review by using the Spergel and Curry (1993) typology of responses to gang problems.

Responding to Gang-Related Crime and Delinquency

No response to gang-related crime and delinquency can hope to be effective unless it focuses attention on both the immediate causes of gangs, as well as background factors. Such efforts must be undertaken with the understanding that institutions in the community must be addressed at the same time that individual behavior is addressed by programs. The immediate causes of gangs include the threats that other gangs generate to personal safety, the values that reinforce violence, and the limited availability of legitimate activities where gang members live. Background factors that cause the growth of gangs include the concentration of poverty, unemployment, and the decline of the family in American cities. And no matter what level is chosen for intervention, solutions will not be easy.

Spergel and Curry (1993) surveyed law enforcement agencies in over 250 cities for the Office of Juvenile Justice and Delinquency Prevention (OJJDP) and identified five basic gang intervention strategies. The general categories of gang intervention include efforts oriented around suppression, social intervention, organizational change, community mobilization, and social opportunities provision. Interestingly, the survey reported that the response that was employed most often, suppression, was viewed as the least successful intervention strategy. Conversely, the social opportunities provision was viewed as the most successful strategy, though it was employed least often by the cities. The contrast between the perceptions of what was a successful strategy

and what was used in these jurisdictions is quite notable.

Suppression strategies include law enforcement and criminal justice interventions such as arrest, imprisonment, and surveillance. Forty-four percent of the responding agencies reported that suppression was their primary strategy in responding to gangs. By itself, suppression will not affect the growth of gangs or the crimes committed by gang members. To be effective, suppression strategies need to be part of a larger group of responses to the crimes of gang members. Klein (1995) has argued that suppression efforts should not be implemented in ways that increase the status of gang members. Gang suppression may also exacerbate the racial disproportionality of arrest. It is likely that prison gangs will grow as a result of suppression efforts.

Social intervention approaches focus on short-term, more immediate interventions, particularly in response to acts of violence or personal crises. Thirty-two percent of the law enforcement agencies surveyed said that they used social intervention strategies such as crisis intervention, treatment for youths and their families, and social service referrals. Because gang members and their families often find themselves in personal crises, such as arrests, injuries, or threats to their personal well-being, the use of crisis intervention and the provision of social services to gang members and their families is an important response. Gang members frequently are victims of violence or witnesses to friends' victimization. The use of crisis intervention services in such instances is promising. Crisis responses should be available at emergency rooms and should be mobilized by law enforcement, health care, or community groups, and attempt to integrate families. Interventions targeted at families are important because of their focus on root causes and long-term change. In addition, most gang members have siblings or cousins whose well-being may be adversely affected by the gang member. This magnifies the potential impact of family interventions.

Organizational change requires the creation of a broad consensus about gang problems within cities. Forming a task force is typical of such a response. These task forces typically target the proximate causes of gangs and by themselves cannot solve gang problems. Organizational change was selected by 11 percent of the respondents. In general, organizational change and other efforts aimed at creating, modifying, and expanding policies, practices, and legislation regarding gangs can lead to an awareness of the gang problems in the community and mobilize efforts to address them, or produce a new set of relations among agencies and groups who respond to such problems. Putting together task forces and focus groups in order to address the needs of particular communities with local gang problems is an example of this type of response to gangs. Organizational change will only be successful if it has the support of the community and groups in those neighborhoods where gangs operate, optimally including local politicians and the private sector.

The fundamental causes of gangs are addressed by community mobilization strategies. This strategy coordinates and targets services so that the needs of gang members may be met more effectively. This strategy was selected by only 9 percent of cities as their modal response to gangs. Community mobilization focuses on cooperation across agencies and is designed to produce better coordination of existing services and resident groups. City services are seldom offered or merged in ways that are effective in meeting the needs of gang members who often have little contact with social institutions. Effective community mobilization must include both immediate social institutions such as the family, but also schools, community agencies and groups, churches, public health agencies, and the criminal and juvenile justice systems.

Social opportunities attempt to expand job prospects and educational resources. Similar to community mobilization, this type of response confronts the fundamental causes of gang formation and gang membership. The smallest number of cities, 5 percent, reported that their primary response was to provide social opportunities to gang members. These gang intervention efforts incorporate job creation, training, and residential placements designed to reshape values, peer commitments, and institutional participation by gang members and those at risk for membership. The underlying value of such an approach is to expand social capital and create new values among gang members by integrating them into legitimate social institutions.

Contemporary Responses to Gangs

In the 1980s and 1990s, the United States came to depend increasingly on suppression as the major response to gang crime problems. Often the dependence on suppression leads to the exclusion of nonjustice agencies as well as other, more effective, responses to gang problems. As we noted above, the strategy of suppression was the most common response to gang problems reported by respondents to the 1988 OJJDP national survey. Despite this, most respondents regarded it as the least effective response and there is broad recognition that no single response can be effective in responding to gangs (Spergel and Curry 1993). Only a balanced approach that combines suppression and other interventions, especially social opportunities, can provide a successful intervention. Below, we review a number of major policy initiatives directed at gangs in the 1990s, frame these initiatives within the Spergel-Curry intervention typology, and assess their long-term prospects for success. Public policy responses to gang activity and gang membership can come from three government levels: federal, state, and local. The next section of this chapter presents the current response to gang problems by these distinct government levels. The responses may take on the identity of legislative and/or programmatic initiatives in order to provide prevention, intervention, and/or suppression of gang problems.

Gang Legislation

By 1993, 14 of the 50 states had enacted statutes specifically directed at criminal gang activity. A review conducted by the Institute for Law and Justice (1993) groups gang legislation into two major categories: (1) legislation that provides criminal sanctions for the justice system against offenders in gang-related crimes and (2) legislation that provides civil remedies for the victims of gang crime. Criminal sanction legislation most often enhances sentences for those found guilty of committing a gang-related crime or makes provisions for segregating incarcerated gang members. Civil remedy approaches have most often attempted to empower citizens to file civil suits against gang members collectively or individually. A major impediment to the effectiveness of gang legislation is court rulings that several specific legislative acts violate the First Amendment rights of gang members (e.g., United States Supreme Court ruling, June 10, 1999; *Chicago v. Moralez* No. 97–1121).

Gang legislation constitutes a unique kind of organizational development and change in response to gang-related crime. Many law enforcement agencies engage in efforts to initiate or modify legislation related to gangs or the gang problem or try to influence legislation pertaining to gangs. Perhaps the best known gang legislation and one that has served as a model for other jurisdictions is California's 1988 STEP (Street Terrorism Enforcement and Prevention) Act (California Penal Code Section 186). STEP provides a definition of a criminal street gang and enhanced penalties for individuals convicted under such statutes. In addition to the STEP Act, local ordinances in many California cities allow the police to obtain a civil injunction against named gang members that prohibit those gang members from congregating in public, carrying beepers, drinking in public, and other behaviors. In their review of gang legislation in California over a ten-year period, Jackson and Rudman (1993) argue that most gang legislation represented a form of moral panic that was overwhelmingly devoted to gang suppression and influenced by law enforcement. Thus, the legislation failed to include any of the provisions found in the more effective strategies aimed at the fundamental causes of gangs and gang membership.

Maxson and Allen (1997) provides the only evaluation of the impact of a civil injunction in California. Maxson reviews the process and outcome of the implementation of this civil process in Inglewood, CA. She notes that the gang members who were served with these injunctions (in the form of temporary restraining orders) seemed confused and unaware of what was happening when they were civilly served with the injunction on the street and during their court appearance. In addition, she noted that the grant funding was depleted before the injunction could be fully implemented and found no evidence that violent crime decreased in the target area following the issuance of the injunction.

Federal Policy and Gangs

DHHS's Youth Gang Drug Prevention Program

In 1988, the Youth Gang Drug Prevention Program was established in the Administration on Children, Youth, and Families (ACYF), part of the U.S. Department of Health and Human Services (DHHS). Applications for the first round of funding focused on single-purpose demonstration projects and innovative support programs for at-risk youths and their families. Sixteen consortium projects were funded for three years. In design, these programs constituted a federally initiated, coordinated, and monitored commitment to community organization strategic responses to gang crime problems. This commitment was on a scale that was historically without precedent. Nine more consortium projects were funded in 1992 with a total of $5.9 million, each for a period of five years for up to $750,000 per year. The consortium projects received the bulk of Youth Gang Drug Prevention Program funding. However, the ACYF program included a number of projects employing social intervention strategies. Over the five years of the program, projects provided peer counseling, family education, youth empowerment, mentoring, crisis intervention, community restitution, and recreation. Priority funding areas for the delivery of services also targeted intergenerational gang families, adolescent females, and new immigrant and refugee youth gangs.

The explicit goals of the Youth Gang Drug Prevention Program mandated by Congress in its creation included facilitating federal, state, and local cooperation and coordination of the agencies responding to gang and drug crime problems. Funding solicitations required applicant programs to incorporate a local evaluation plan, and an independent national level evaluation was funded for the 52 projects initially funded in 1989. The national evaluation (Cohen et al. 1995) concluded that while local programs were generally effective in reducing delinquency and drug use among youth participants, *the programs were not successful at preventing or reducing gang involvement*. In 1995, the gang component of the program came to an end.

OJJDP's Comprehensive Response to America's Gang Problem

The first national assessments of the U.S. gang problem and the establishment in 1988 of the National Youth Gang Suppression and Intervention Program by the Office of Juvenile Justice and Delinquency Prevention (OJJDP) were important parts of the federal response to gangs. The program set three goals: (1) identify and assess promising approaches and strategies for dealing with the youth gang problem, (2) develop prototypes or models from the information thereby gained, and (3) produce technical assistance manuals for those who would implement the models (Spergel and Curry 1993). The project included 12 prototypes or models for gang program development and 12 technical assistance manuals corresponding to each prototype. The major outcome of the project was OJJDP's resolution that community-wide responses were required for dealing with local level gang problems (Bryant 1989).

The Spergel Model. The Spergel model has become the driving force in the OJJDP response to gangs. It has a flexible format that is useful for responding to gang problems at the community level. It focuses on the formation of partnerships between local private and public agencies (including law enforcement) to provide educational, emotional, and treatment services for youth at risk of or already involved in gangs. Separate required components of the Spergel model focus on community mobilization and employment programs, with one agency acting as the lead or mobilizing agency. In addition, law enforcement plays a central role in this process. Key agencies that must be involved include the police, grassroots neighborhood organizations, and some form of employment or job training program. The guidelines for community mobilization are intended to facilitate interagency cooperation and minimize interagency conflict. Under funding from OJJDP, five demonstration sites received funding to implement and test the Spergel model in a variety of urban settings with coordinated technical assistance and a systematic evaluation led by Spergel. In addition, in the Chicago community of Little Village, Spergel (1994; Spergel and Grossman 1994) has

been working with a network of police, outreach youth workers, probation officers, court service workers, and former gang members to reduce violence between two warring coalitions of Latino street gangs. Preliminary evaluation results of this project indicate a reduction in gang-related homicides, increased community organization and mobilization, and the channeling of gang-involved youths into educational programs and jobs (Spergel 1999).

Safe Futures. As the first few years of the 1990s brought record increases in levels of juvenile violence, OJJDP became convinced that the problems of serious, violent, and chronic offending and gang-related crime were related. The Comprehensive Strategy (another OJJDP program) focuses on strengthening the families, strengthening the juvenile justice system, providing opportunities for youth, mobilizing communities, and breaking the cycle of violence. This strategy is separated into two components: one for at-risk youth and one for delinquent youth. The difference between the Comprehensive Strategy and the Spergel model is the separate program objectives for at-risk versus delinquent youth. Social opportunities and prevention techniques are saved for at-risk youth while graduated sanctions, prosecution, and other suppression techniques are used on the delinquent youth. The Spergel model does not make the same separation. The Spergel model argues for a combination of all prevention and intervention strategies along with the formation of local partnerships. It was decided that a major effort needed to be undertaken to test the utility of both the Comprehensive Strategy and the Spergel model in specifically targeted geographic settings. The policy result was the Safe Futures Program. With funding from OJJDP, Safe Futures Programs have been established in four urban sites (Boston, Seattle, Contra Costa County, CA, and St. Louis), one rural site (Imperial Valley, CA), and one Indian Reservation (Fort Belknap, MT). Funding for Safe Futures projects is larger ($1.4 million per year) and extended over a longer period of time (a five-year commitment) than funding for previous comparable efforts. All sites were initially funded in the fall of 1996.

The Safe Futures programs incorporate specific suppression, opportunities provision, and neighborhood focused services. As such, they are consistent with the Spergel model, and likely to provide a full test of the effectiveness of this model, which integrates suppression with community mobilization. One key characteristic of Safe Futures is very close monitoring by OJJDP and a series of consultants hired through technical assistance contracts. Often it is difficult to determine the impact of a program. Programs look and operate substantially different from the initial plan. The technical assistance and close oversight is designed to overcome these difficulties. A local evaluation is mandated for each site, and all sites are participating in a national evaluation. It is too early in the funding cycle to know the effect of the interventions. However, one thing is clear: Mounting large-scale interventions designed to change the delivery of services to youths is very difficult. A few sites have struggled with local issues to implement the Spergel model. For example, in St. Louis, the Safe Futures site has had difficulty integrating law enforcement—a key component of the model—into service delivery and client identification.

Community-Oriented Policing Services

Anti-Gang Initiative. Community-oriented policing represents an even broader federal effort to respond to crime in a way that integrates law enforcement into a cooperative, community problem-solving framework. This strategy is aimed at establishing a partnership between law enforcement and people in the community. It focuses on getting officers more involved in their communities with the hopes that better and more familiar relationships between the police and the community will facilitate lower crime rates and strengthened community relationships. In 1996, the Community Oriented Policing Services (COPS) office in the Justice Department launched a 15-city Anti-Gang Initiative (AGI). Instead of being selected through a competitive application process, the 15 cities were selected for their consistency in providing gang-related crime statistics to the Justice Department surveys described above. Funding was mandated to be spent on community policing efforts, to improve data collection, to integrate law enforcement agencies into community-wide responses to gangs, and to provide a safer setting in which less suppressive response programs can be given a chance to develop. In total, $11 million was made available to the cities, in $1 million or $500,000 alloca-

tions depending on city size. The sites included Austin, Boston, Chicago, Dallas, Detroit, Indianapolis, Jersey City, Kansas City, Los Angeles, Miami, Oakland, Orange County, Phoenix, Salt Lake City, and St. Louis.

The Anti-Gang Initiative set three specific goals: (1) develop strategies to reduce gang-related problems, (2) develop strategies to reduce gang-related drug trafficking problems, and (3) reduce the fear instilled by gang-related activities. Each jurisdiction was required to develop a formal written characterization of their local gang problem to include the number of gangs, members, age ranges, reasons for joining a gang, source and location of recruitment, location of activities, reasons for migration, and incidents of gang-related crime. These characterizations called for considerable detail that in most cities was simply not available through traditional law enforcement data gathering. Local researchers were included in the process of developing the view of gangs in some cities.

Eight specific strategies were identified. Three of the departments (Detroit, Jersey City, and St. Louis) chose to use special curfew enforcement strategies to target juveniles out after curfew hours. Six jurisdictions (Boston, Indianapolis, Miami, Oakland, Phoenix, and St. Louis) emphasized the need to coordinate their funded activities with ongoing efforts to combat drugs and gangs that were already in place. In Boston, this meant that the AGI effort was specifically linked to the Safe Futures funding received from OJJDP, and in Phoenix a tie was developed between the G.R.E.A.T. program (Gang Resistance Education and Training, a school-based gang prevention program targeted at junior high students) and AGI efforts.

The most popular strategy was Organizational Development and Change. Spergel and Curry (1993) have identified this as a core response strategy of law enforcement to gang problems. Eleven of the 15 departments used some form of this strategy. Typically, this approach attempts to enhance existing interventions by changing an overall organization or strategic response by bringing new partners to the table. This often meant that police departments sought out the assistance of other law enforcement partners, but also turned to the schools or social service agencies for help. Six cities saw information sharing as a key strategy to be funded by AGI monies. Often this meant the use of enhanced technology to provide presentations, transfer data, or conduct analyses. For example, many cities took the opportunity to use Geographic Information System technology to map gang, drug, and youth crime activities.

Eight of the jurisdictions chose to track gang members through the use of an enhanced or expanded database. In this way, they sought to better understand the number and nature of membership, and use that information for developing additional strategies and tactics of suppression. Nine of the jurisdictions specifically included schools as a partner in their COPS-funded Anti-Gang Initiative. Often this meant enhancing G.R.E.A.T. or PAL (Police Athletic League) activities, but in some cases new partnerships were developed. Finally, eight of the jurisdictions mounted a community organization strategy, seeking to engage citizens and neighborhoods in crime prevention and control. Typically this meant that presentations and meetings were held.

Each jurisdiction was required to set aside 5 percent of total funds for the purposes of conducting an evaluation. These evaluations were largely focused on process issues, given the small amount of money available and limited time frame. Unfortunately, to date there has been no effort to make those evaluations available in a form that could shed light on the feasibility, impact, or future of such interventions. What is clear from those sites with completed evaluations is that those areas of intervention that the police controlled themselves (i.e., suppression) generally worked according to plan. However, partnership ventures were considerably more difficult to accomplish. Given the Spergel model's insistence on linking suppression and opportunities provision, the likely impact of these efforts is temporary or quite small.

Youth Firearms Violence Initiative. Another COPS response to increased levels of firearm violence among youth was the Youth Firearms Violence Initiative (YFVI). This federal initiative targeted groups at high risk for the use of firearms in the commission of crimes, and youth gangs were one criterion for the design of interventions. Ten cities were selected to each receive $1 million for a one-year period to reduce violent firearms crime by youth. Departments were to develop innovative programs that enhanced proactive crime control efforts and prevention programs targeted at young persons. Specifically, the COPS office wanted evidence that the number of violent firearm crimes committed by youth declined. Additionally, the agency expected that the number of firearms-related gang offenses and the number of firearms-related drug offenses would decline. Each participating department was required to develop new initiatives in three areas: (1) innovative strategies or tactics, (2) community policing orientation, and (3) new information systems. The 10 cities included Birmingham, AL, Bridgeport, CT, Milwaukee, WI, Richmond, VA, Seattle, WA, Baltimore, MD, Cleveland, OH, Inglewood, CA, Salinas, CA, and San Antonio, TX. Local evaluations and a national evaluation were completed examining the efforts of each site.

There was considerable variation across the participating sites regarding the strategies and tactics employed to achieve these objectives. Not surprisingly, most strategies emphasized enforcement, although some combined enforcement with prevention. The tactics included such things as focusing on specific targets (gangs), neighborhoods, firearms crimes, and the use of dedicated units to address these issues specifically. Inglewood employed among the most innovative strategies. Inglewood is a medium-sized city in the Los Angeles area with predominantly African-American and Hispanic residents. Inglewood chose to target a single neighborhood of relatively small size. A full-time prosecutor and probation officer worked with the police department. The prosecutor worked to develop the civil injunction that was discussed above and is becoming a popular tactic in California. The probation officer was responsible for seizing hundreds of firearms from youth on probation, employing his powers to search the residences of his probationers. The officers' efforts serve as an example of the kind of innovative work that can be forged between different agencies of the criminal justice system. Unfortunately, these partnerships—seen as critical to the success of the prevention and suppression of crime—vanished when grant funding ended. This raises the important issue of sustainability, that is, the extent to which innovations and partnerships will continue once the federal money runs out.

The national evaluation demonstrated that these interventions, in most cities, were accompanied by reductions in gun offenses. A specific geographic area similar to the program area was chosen for comparison purposes and gun offenses were tracked by week. The tracking of gun offenses occurred during the two-year period prior to YFVI efforts and the one-year period after the program. In each of the five impact evaluation sites (Bridgeport, Seattle, Baltimore, Inglewood, Salinas), the decline in gun offenses per week was greater for the program area than for the comparison area. While this is not conclusive proof that YFVI was solely responsible for the observed declines, it is consistent with that hypothesis. In almost every case, YFVI was strictly a suppression program; only rarely did it effectively integrate the activities of social service or prevention activities. However, in those cities where such activities were integrated (especially Milwaukee and Seattle), those activities and relationships remained in place well after the conclusion of the program.

State and Local Policy Examples

The Illinois Gang Crime Prevention Center

In 1995, the governor of Illinois established the Governor's Commission on Gangs and appointed the Illinois attorney general to serve as the chairman. The Commission was to be responsible for generating practical solutions to the growing street gang problem in Illinois. Following nine months of research focused on examining the gang problem in Illinois as well as community mobilization, future legislation, public awareness and parental education, law enforcement, and safety in schools, the Commission recommended a comprehensive strategy to integrate suppression, prevention, and intervention strategies and the creation of an organization to focus on reducing gang activity statewide (Governor's Commission on Gangs 1996). The Gang Crime Prevention Center (GCPC) was designed and created to serve this function. The Center began operating on July 1, 1997. The GCPC was separated into four units: community mobilization, program development, research and information services, and operations. These units work together to develop, implement, and evaluate organization- and neighborhood-based programs.

The GCPC has utilized a seven-step program development process to create, fund, and implement five gang prevention pilot programs in Illinois: (1) collaboration and problem definition, (2) site assessment and target population, (3) approach and mission, (4) strategy and resource development, (5) implementation and operation, (6) monitoring and evaluation, and (7) modification and evolution. The five pilot programs, implemented in 1998, include two court-based (Early Intervention Probation and Evening Reporting Center) and three school-based (Student Covenant for the Future, Mentoring/Tutoring, and Right Track Truancy Reduction) programs. Each of these programs is concerned with preventing gang membership and intervention and suppression for active gang members (Leverentz 1999).

The Early Intervention Probation program focuses on youth already involved, to some extent, with gangs, delinquent activities, and the juvenile justice system. The Evening Reporting Center (ERC) also utilizes intervention and suppression techniques for youth previously exposed to the juvenile justice system. The ERC is modeled after the Eight Percent Solution in Orange County, California. This program, similar to the one in California, focuses on youth most likely to become the chronic, serious offenders of tomorrow. The programs identify and intervene with youth who are headed towards a criminal career. Objectives include both individual skill building and family-oriented services (Schumacher and Kurz 2000). As is the case with the two court-based programs, the three school-based programs are located in specific geographic locations throughout the state of Illinois. Lovejoy Elementary School is the home of the Mentoring/Tutoring program, Kelly High School houses the Student Covenant for the Future, and Springfield was chosen as the site of the Right Track Truancy Reduction program. These five sites were chosen by the Gang Crime Prevention Center because of the specific target population and objectives for each of the programs. The two court-based programs target youth already exposed to gangs and gang activities and utilize intervention and suppression strategies. The school-based programs, specifically the Mentoring/Tutoring Program, target younger recipients and opt for prevention as a goal. However, both the Student Covenant and Truancy programs include intervention and suppression strategies along with prevention measures. Without exception, all of these programs involve some kind of partnership between community agencies, schools, and/or law enforcement agencies. Some of the participants involved with the programs include the Attorney General's Office, the public school districts, the Illinois Retired Teachers' Association, probation and parole departments, the mental health department, the Department of Human Services, the Department of Children and Family Services, Social Service Programs, and law enforcement agencies.

The Gang Crime Prevention Center is currently being evaluated with regards to the implementation, process, and impact of its pilot programs and its role in developing, implementing, overseeing, evaluating, and replicating social programs. Preliminary implementation results indicate that with the exception of the Evening Reporting Center, the programs have broader foci than just gangs. Also, some of the programs (Mentoring/Tutoring, Student Covenant, and Right Track Truancy) do not emphasize gangs as a central program component. Participants in at least one of the programs, the Mentoring/Tutoring program, dissuade any discussion of gangs and gang membership. These participants focus on academic tutoring and emotional/social mentoring. This is so the youth will do better in school and thus stay there (in school) and (hopefully) away from gangs.

These programs provide social, emotional, behavioral, or academic benefits for the participants but do not seem to be targeting at-risk or gang-involved youth for the purposes expressed in the Governor's Commission on Gangs report (Governor's Commission on Gangs 1996). The direction of these programs has changed from the original plans (implementation changes) as well as during the life of the program (process changes). The sustainability and replicability of these pilot programs are problematic issues as the programs do not focus as much on gang prevention and intervention as originally intended. However, these programs represent an important state-level response in a state with serious gang problems.

The Boston Gun Suppression Project

Perhaps no single intervention in the 1990s has received as much public attention as the Boston Gun Suppression Project (Kennedy, Piehl, and Braga 1996; Boston Police Department and Partners 1997). Also known as Ceasefire, this project has been replicated in a number of cities across the country, including Minneapolis, where it has been carefully evaluated (Kennedy and Braga 1998). At its heart, Ceasefire employs the SARA (Scanning, Analysis, Response, and Assessment) problem-solving model to assess youth violence. The SARA model requires that local jurisdictions gather data to determine the nature of local problems, analyze those data, and, based on the results of those analyses, design a response to solve problems. The final step of the SARA model requires that the response be carefully assessed and recalibrated. The apparent success of this intervention largely rests on two features: (1) careful background work conducted to understand the nature of youth firearms markets and (2) partnerships among the participating groups. Kennedy and his colleagues determined that the youth firearm market was different from that of adults, was comprised of a relatively small group of serious offenders, was largely based on fear of attack by rival youth who often were gang members, and that the primary means of acquiring guns by young people was theft. These findings led Kennedy and his colleagues to conclude that traditional methods of intervention, such as intelligence gathering and arrest, by themselves may not be successful.

The Boston Gun Project involves a large interagency working group that consists of representatives from the local police department, the Bureau of Alcohol, Tobacco, and Firearms (ATF), the U.S. Attorney, the local prosecutor, the departments of probation and parole, city youth outreach workers, the school district, and Kennedy's research team. The working group met regularly to review research and operational findings, and it is from these meetings that a response plan was developed. Two complementary strategies were developed, one that attempted to disrupt the illegal firearms market on the supply side, and the other targeted at the demand side. On the supply side, ATF worked with local police, prosecutors, and the U.S. Attorney to step up gun tracing and prosecution efforts. It is the demand side where the most interesting interventions were developed, however. Probation and parole officers engaged in night visits to their clients to enforce routine conditions of sentence such as curfews and room searches that heretofore had not been regularly enforced. This was coupled with a series of dramatic meetings with local gang members attended by key law enforcement officials to announce and demonstrate the effects of a zero-tolerance policy for the use of guns by youth in a number of Boston neighborhoods.

The initial evaluations of the Boston Gun Project have demonstrated that the program was quite successful. Youth gun crime, particularly homicide, recorded dramatic declines in Boston, even greater declines than throughout the rest of the nation. Kennedy, Piehl, and Braga (1996) conducted both a process and outcome evaluation that demonstrated key components of the project. Kennedy and Braga (1998) replicated the Ceasefire project in Minneapolis with similar results. What are the key features of this effort to reduce gang firearm violence that appear to have made it successful? First, the intervention is based on data that come from local law enforcement and are presented in a way that leads naturally to policy interventions. Second, the use of data to guide the project did not end once the intervention began. Rather, the researchers continued to collect data and use it to refine the intervention on an on-going basis. Third, the intervention combined the efforts of a variety of committed groups and individuals. As Spergel and Curry remind us, no program based on a single form of intervention is likely to achieve success. By combining suppression at a number of levels (federal, state, and local) with social opportunities provision and broader based enforcement (probation and parole), Boston appears to have found ways to get a handle on its gang problem. These findings suggest that a mixture of Spergel-Curry strategies, especially combining suppression with social opportunities and perhaps crisis intervention, may be the most promising approach in responding to gangs.

A Different Public Policy Response for Female Gang Members?

Until the 1980s and 1990s, the majority of gang research focused on young men (Joe-Laidler and Hunt 1997; Curry 1998). Females were often overlooked, ignored, and/or marginalized in the literature regarding gang involvement and strategies for

reducing gang activities and gang membership. Over the last 15 years, however, there has been an increase in research concerned with females and their roles within (and alongside) gangs (Curry 1998). While this "female-focused" body of gang research has continued to grow, there has been little change in the traditional response to gangs (i.e., suppression). This illuminates a critical gap since ideally policy responses should be theoretically grounded (Curry 1999). In other words, responses to gangs and gang membership should be implemented based on research that indicates its potential to affect decisions to join and maintain a relationship to a gang.

Most female gang research has been of a qualitative nature, utilizing in-depth interviews and ethnographic accounts (see for example, Fleisher 1998; Hunt, Mackenzie, and Joe-Laidler 2000; Joe-Laidler and Hunt 1997; Miller 2001). Much of the response to female gang involvement has come in the form of increased awareness and recognition of its existence. More and more research is being conducted on females and gangs and is seen by some as a response in itself. According to one gang researcher, "research on a subject increases in conjunction with increased public and policy concern and, perhaps just as important, funding resources" (Curry 1999:134). Thus, although research by itself might not be exactly what we think of as a response or a solution to the problem of female gang involvement, it is a beginning. While the female gang research continues to expand, public policy responses aimed at female gang involvement have been almost nonexistent.

Public policy responses to female gang members (aside from research) have taken on a social service and/or law enforcement focus. An NIJ law enforcement survey was conducted in 1992 and many of the law enforcement agencies provided either no information regarding female gang involvement or reported that they had no female gang members (Curry 1999). This contradicts the presence of females in gangs and female gangs described in other kinds of research (ethnographic and self-report studies; see Fleisher 1998; Hunt, Mackenzie, and Joe-Laidler 2000; Joe-Laidler and Hunt 1997; Miller 2001). The small number of reported female gang members (as compared to male members) and the lack of official statistics collected on female gang members and their activities has indeed contributed to the neglect of these individuals when policy decisions are being made. While the law enforcement response to females in gangs has been limited basically to increased reporting and suppression techniques, varied social services responses emerged (and have already begun to decline) in the early nineties (Curry 1999).

The majority of these social service programs were funded by Congress in 1989 under the administration of the Department of Health and Human Services Family Youth Services Bureau (FYSB). In 1990, the FYSB solicited programs for the prevention and intervention of female gang involvement. Overall 13 programs focused on preventing and intervening in female gang involvement were created and implemented in different sites by 1992. The services provided by these new programs varied and included: building self-esteem, providing social activities and recreation, individual and group counseling, education and employment support, mentoring, and conflict resolution skills. A couple of problems emerged with the focus and process of these programs. First, some of the programs received female participants from the juvenile court and many of these girls did not identify themselves as gang members. In addition, at least one of the programs would not allow current gang members and many of the participants in several of the programs were former gang members (Curry 1999). Thus, programs that were supposed to prevent female gang membership and activities were not actually recruiting, receiving, and accepting the proper target population. Out of all of these social service programs three were evaluated: Boston, Seattle and Pueblo, CO (Curry 1999). The evaluation results indicated that, "while the programs may have had some effect on reducing delinquency and drug-use, actual reductions in gang activity associated with program efforts could not be identified" (Curry 1999:149).

As a result of these evaluation findings, and a reemerging emphasis on law enforcement strategies, the FYSB programs gradually diminished. By 1995 all gang-focused program features had disappeared and by 1998 much of FYSB's program funding was withdrawn. As discussed in Curry (1999) this group of programs was the only federally funded attempt to prevent and intervene in female gang involvement. The disappearance of these programs is similar to (yet much more short-lived than) the continuous cycle of research, law enforcement, and social service responses to (male) gang involvement in which programs are initiated but fail to be accurately implemented, include the correct population, or provide viable services and opportunities for youth.

Conclusion

The last decade produced an unprecedented increase in gangs, gun assaults, and youth homicide. These increases have spurred federal and local governments to action. In the search for appropriate responses to these problems, suppression has been the strategy most often adopted. This makes sense for a variety of political and pragmatic reasons; after all, the police are a visible and generally popular resource in the effort to combat crime. However, such responses are not likely to be successful on their own. When suppression occurs in a vacuum, when it is not accompanied by other, more supportive, actions, the chances of making lasting changes in gang crime are diminished.

A number of federal initiatives that emphasize suppression or social opportunities provision have been undertaken in the last decade. The COPS Office's Anti-Gang Initiative is a good example of programs that were based almost exclusively on suppression. This is counterbalanced by the effort of DHHS in its Youth Gang Drug Prevention program. This heavily funded federal effort focused exclusively on opportunities provision. While the evaluation data do not enable a definitive conclusion about the effectiveness of these interventions, it is clear that they have not made substantial inroads into the gang problem in the communities where they were funded because of their failure to implement a balanced response. If there is a single message in this chapter, it is that law enforcement and social opportunities provision must work hand-in-hand if successful interventions are to be implemented.

The success of any initiative, as demonstrated by the Boston Gun Project, hinges largely on its ability to integrate a number of approaches. Gangs are not monolithic, as the recent work of Klein and Maxson (1995) has demonstrated. Klein and Maxson produced a typology of gang structures, based on the size of the gang, its age, involvement in crime, and other salient characteristics. Their typology reinforces the diversity of gangs, and consequently the need for a variety of responses. The key to a successful response to gangs is the recognition that gangs vary by type, within and between cities, and that successful responses must be built on a solid knowledge base. Klein is often critical of the police because they characterize gangs and gang members as overly organized, more seriously criminal, and more dedicated to the gang than is actually the case. He argues that this conception of gangs and gang members dominates the public and criminal justice understanding of this phenomenon, thereby distorting the fact that most gang members are loosely committed to their gang, that they are involved in a wide range of mostly minor criminal and delinquent acts, and that gangs are not effective vehicles for social organization. Without multiple sources of information and a coordinated response that involves suppression, community mobilization, and social opportunities provision, little progress will be made in responding to such gangs.

References

Boston Police Department and Partners. 1997. *The Boston Strategy to Prevent Youth Violence.* Boston Police Department.

Bryant, D. 1989. *Community-Wide Responses Crucial for Dealing with Youth Gangs.* Washington, D.C.: Juvenile Justice Bulletin, Office of Juvenile Justice and Delinquency Prevention, U.S. Department of Justice.

Cohen, M., K. Williams, A. Beckman, and S. Crosse. 1995. "Evaluation of the National Youth Gang Drug Prevention Program," in M. Klein, C. Maxson, and J. Miller (Eds.) *The Modern Gang Reader.* Los Angeles: Roxbury, 266–275.

Curry, G. D. 1998. "Female Gang Involvement." *Journal of Research in Crime and Delinquency* 35:100–118.

———. 1999. "Responding to Female Gang Involvement," in M. Chesney-Lind and J. M. Hagedorn (Eds.) *Female Gangs in America: Essays on Girls, Gangs, and Gender.* Chicago: Lake View Press, 133–153.

Decker, S. H., and K. L. Leonard. 1991. "Constructing Gangs: The Social Construction of Youth Activities." *Criminal Justice Policy Review* 4:271–291.

Fleisher, M. S. 1998. *Dead End Kids: Gang Girls and the Boys They Know.* Madison; London: University of Wisconsin Press.

Governor's Commission on Gangs. 1996. *Mobilizing Illinois: Report and Recommendations to the Governor.* Chicago: Office of the Attorney General of Illinois

Howell, J. C. 1997. "Youth Gangs." Office of Juvenile Justice and Delinquency Prevention. Washington, D.C.: U.S. Department of Justice.

———. 1998. "Youth Gangs: An Overview." Office of Juvenile Justice and Delinquency Prevention. Washington, D.C.: U.S. Department of Justice.

Hunt, G., K. MacKenzie, and K. Joe-Laidler. 2000. " 'I'm Calling My Mom': The Meaning of Family and Kinship Among Homegirls." *Justice Quarterly* 17:802–831.

Institute for Law and Justice. 1993. *Gang Prosecution Legislative Review.* Report prepared for the National Institute of Justice. Washington, D.C.: U.S. Department of Justice.

Jackson, P. I. 1991. "Crime, Youth Gangs, and Urban Transition: The Social Dislocations of Postindustrial Development." *Justice Quarterly* 8:379–398.

Jackson, P. J., with C. Rudman. 1993. "Moral Panic and the Response to Gangs in California," in S. Cummins and D. Monti (Eds.) *The Origins and Impact of Contemporary Youth Gangs in the United States.* Albany: SUNY Press, 257–275.

Joe-Laidler, K., and G. Hunt. 1997. "Violence and Social Organization in Female Gangs." *Social Justice* 24:148–169.

Kennedy, D., and A. Braga. 1998. "Homicide in Minneapolis." *Homicide Studies* 2:263–290.

Kennedy, D., A. Piehl, and A. Braga. 1996. "Youth Violence in Boston: Gun Markets, Serious Youth Offenders, and a Use-Reduction Strategy." *Law and Contemporary Problems* 59:147–196.

Klein, M. 1995. *The American Street Gang.* New York: Oxford.

Klein, M., and C. Maxson. 1995. "Investigating Gang Structures." *Journal of Gang Research* 3:33–40.

Leverentz, Andrea. 1999. "Pilot Programs: An Interim Report." Research and Information Services Unit, Illinois Gang Crime Prevention Center.

Maxson, C. L. and T. Allen 1997. An Evaluation of the City of Inglewood's Youth Firearms Violence Initiative. University of Southern California, Los Angeles.

Maxson, C., and M. Klein. 1994. "The Scope of Street Gang Migration in the U.S." Presentation. Gangs Working Group. Washington, D.C.: National Institute of Justice.

Miller, J. 2001. *One of the Guys.* New York: Oxford University Press.

Moore, J. P., and I. L. Cook. 1999. "Highlights of the 1998 National Youth Gang Survey." *OJJDP Fact Sheet.* Washington, D.C.: Office of Juvenile Justice and Delinquency Prevention.

National Youth Gang Center. 1999. *1997 National Youth Gang Survey.* Washington, D.C.: U.S. Department of Justice, Office of Juvenile Justice and Delinquency Prevention.

Schumacher, M. A., and G. A. Kurz. 2000. *The 8% Solution: Preventing Serious, Repeat Juvenile Crime.* Thousand Oaks, CA: Sage Publications, Inc.

Spergel, I. 1994. *Gang Suppression and Intervention: Problem and Response.* Washington, D.C.: Office of Juvenile Justice and Delinquency Prevention.

———. 1999. *Evaluation of the Little Village Gang Violence Reduction Project.* Chicago: Illinois Criminal Justice Information Authority.

Spergel, I., and G. D. Curry. 1993. "The National Youth Gang Survey: A Research and Development Process," in A. P. Goldstein and C. R. Huff (Eds.) *Gang Intervention Handbook.* Champaign, IL: Research Press, pp. 359–400.

Spergel, I., and S. Grossman. 1994. *Gang Violence and Crime Theory: Gang Violence Reduction Project.* Presentation at the American Society of Criminology Annual Meetings. Miami, FL.

Vigil, J. D. 1988. *Barrio Gangs.* Austin: University of Texas Press. ✦

Chapter 27
G-Dog and the Homeboys

Celeste Fremon

Given the vast array of gang intervention approaches and the sometimes hopeless sense that nothing works, we include this inspirational story of one individual's efforts to make a difference. In the following article, Fremon describes the one-man gang reform program found in Father Gregory Boyle of East Los Angeles. He offers schooling, job programs and counseling to the gang members in his community, as well as a caring, supportive relationship with these youths. While he touches the lives of so many of the gang members around him, it remains inevitable that the efforts of one person can do little to diminish the escalation of gang activity and violence.

At exactly 7 p.m. on an uncommonly warm night in early March, 1990, some 300 mourners, most of them members of the Latino gang the East L.A. Dukes, descend upon Dolores Mission Church at the corner of 3rd and Gless streets in Boyle Heights. They arrive by the carload and cram themselves into the scarred wooden pews that fill the sanctuary. As they file into the small stucco building, they cast edgy glances toward the street, as if expecting trouble. They are here for the funeral of Hector Vasquez, a.k.a. Flaco, 17, killed by a single shot to the head two nights before in a drive-by incident that took place at the nearby Aliso Village housing project.

The attire worn this night conforms to the unwritten gang code of dress. Girl gang members wear their hair long at the bottom

Reprinted from: Celeste Fremon, "G-Dog and the Homeboys," *Los Angeles Times*, August 11, 1991. Copyright © 1991 by the *Los Angeles Times*. Reprinted by permission.

and teased high at the crown, their lipstick blood-red. The boys sport perfectly pressed white Penney's T-shirts, dark Pendleton shirts and cotton work pants called Dickies, worn four sizes too big and belted, a contemporary interpretation of the old pachuco style. About 20 boys and girls wear sweat shirts emblazoned with iron-on Old English lettering that reads: "IN LOVING MEMORY OF OUR HOMIE FLACO R.I.P."

Outside the church, the police are very much in evidence. A couple of black-and-whites sit, just around the corner, motors running. Two beige unmarked cars, the kind favored by the LAPD's special gang unit, and one plain white Housing Police sedan continuously circle the block.

At first, the mood in the church is tense, expectant. But when taped synthesizer music throbs from loudspeakers, the sound seems to open an emotional spigot. The shoulders of the mourners start to shake with grief.

Behind the altar, a bearded man in glasses and priest's vestments sits quietly, watching the crying gangsters. When the music ends, Father Gregory Boyle rises and, taking a microphone, steps down to a point smack in front of the first row of mourners. From a distance, with his receding hair line and beard going to gray, he looks well past middle age. Up close, he is clearly much younger, not yet even 40.

Boyle takes a breath. "I knew Flaco for a long time," he says, his gaze traveling from face to face in the pews. "He used to work here at the church. I knew him as a very loving, great-hearted and kind man." Boyle pauses. "And now we shouldn't ask who killed Flaco, but rather *what* killed him. Flaco died of a disease that is killing La Raza, a disease called gang-banging." The crowd shifts nervously.

"So how do we honor Flaco's memory?" Boyle asks. "We will honor him best by doing what he would want us to do." Another pause. "He would want us to stop killing each other."

All at once, there is a commotion in the sixth row. A hard-eyed kid of 18 with the street name Magoo stands bolt upright and makes his way to the center aisle. Slowly, deliberately, he walks down the aisle, until he stands in front of Boyle, staring the priest straight in the eye. Then he turns and walks out a side door.

The air in the church is as brittle as glass

when Boyle begins speaking again: "If we *knew* Flaco and *loved* Flaco, then we would stop killing each other."

Four more gangsters stand and walk out. Boyle's face reddens and then turns pale, as the mourners wait to see what he will do. Finally his jaw sets. "I loved Flaco," he says, his eyes starting to tear. "And I swear on Flaco's dead body that he would want us to stop killing each other."

The words explode in crisp, stunning bursts like so many rounds of live ammunition. Two more gang members get up and leave—but these boys walk with their heads down, their gaits rapid and scuttling. The rest of the mourners sit stock still, transfixed by the ferocity of Boyle's gaze. "We honor his memory," he says quietly, "if we can do this."

Father Gregory Boyle is the pastor of Dolores Mission Church, which serves a parish that is unique in several ways. First, it is the poorest in the Catholic Archdiocese of Los Angeles—it is dominated by a pair of housing projects: Pico Gardens and Aliso Village. Second, within the parish boundaries, which enclose about two square miles of Boyle Heights east of the Los Angeles River, seven Latino gangs and one African-American gang claim neighborhoods. This means that in an area smaller than the UCLA campus there are eight separate armies of adolescents, each equipped with small- and large-caliber weapons, each of which may be at war with one or more of the others at any given moment.

The Clarence Street Locos is the largest of the gangs, with close to 100 members; Rascals is the smallest, with 30 or so. The rest—Al Capone, the East L.A. Dukes, Cuatro Flats, The Mob Crew (TMC, for short), Primera Flats and the East Coast Crips (the single black gang in this predominantly Latino area)—hover in size from 50 to 80 teenage boys and young men. However large the membership, the " 'hood," or territory, that each gang claims is minuscule—no more than a block or two square. A member of one gang cannot safely walk the half-block from his mother's apartment to the corner store if that store is in enemy territory—much less walk the five or 10 blocks (across as many 'hoods) to reach his assigned junior high or high school.

According to statistics compiled by the Hollenbeck Division of the LAPD, gang-related crimes in East Los Angeles were up a sobering 20 percent from 1989 to 1990 and are rising again, up 11 percent over the same period last year. It is hardly surprising, therefore, that in his five years as parish priest Greg Boyle has buried 17 kids who were shot to death by rival gang members, and two who were shot to death by sheriff's deputies.[1] He himself has been in the line of fire seven times.

This is the tragic heart of the barrio, a bleak and scary part of Los Angeles that much of the rest of the city would like to block from its consciousness. Here junkies and baseheads pump gas for handouts at self-service filling stations, and bullet craters in the stucco walls of houses and stores serve as mnemonic devices, reminders of where this kid was killed, that one wounded. Yet surface impressions are not the whole of the matter in this parish: Beyond the most insistent images of gang violence, poverty and despair, a more redemptive vision comes into focus, a vision that comes clearest around Father Boyle.

Boyle lives simply. He wears the same burgundy zip-front sweat shirt every cold day, and the same rotating selection of five shirts when the days are sunny. His sleeping quarters are half a mile from the church, in a 1913-vintage two-story clapboard dwelling that he shares with six other Jesuits.

His days are long. They start at 7 a.m., often with a trip to Juvenile Court to testify in a gang member's behalf. They end close to midnight when Boyle takes one last bicycle ride around the projects to make sure that no trouble is brewing. In between, along with two assistants at Dolores Mission, he performs the conventional range of pastoral duties: saying Mass, hearing confessions, officiating at weddings and funerals or simply working in his monastic-cell of an office, dealing with parish business.

Whenever the door to Boyle's office opens, gang members swoop in like baby chicks for a feeding. They come to him to have their hair cut, to ask for a job through his Jobs for a Future program, to sign up to feed the homeless (to comply with court-ordered community service), to ask for admission to Dolores Mission Alternative, the school that he started as a sort of Last Chance U. for gang members. But mostly they come to hang out, to talk, to tease and be teased, to laugh. Around Boyle, the gangsters' defensive "screw you" expressions drop away. Twelve-year-old wanna-bes and

20-year-old tough-eyed *veteranos* jockey to be the favored child and sit next to Boyle in his car on his daily errands. They aren't afraid to cry in his presence. They find any excuse to touch him. The gangsters have even christened Boyle with his own placa, his street name: G-Dog. But most simply call him G.

"G. is always there when you need him," says one precariously reformed gangster. "I don't have a dad. So I think of him like my father. Even when I was in jail, he always had time to talk to me. Even when nobody else was there for me. And, you know, when I wanted to stop gang-banging, sometimes I would have so much anger that I wanted to do something, kill somebody. But I would talk to Father Greg and he would help me so I didn't explode inside. He's the one we can all look up to."

The term "dysfunctional family," one of the fashionable buzz phrases of the 90s, acquires a special meaning in the Dolores Mission parish. Not long ago, on a whim, Boyle sat down at his computer and made a list of all the gang kids who immediately came to mind. Next to each name he wrote a coded description of the youth's family situation: "AB" for father absent; "A" for alcoholic father; "AA" for alcoholic and abusive; "ABU" for just plain abusive, "S" for stepfather, "I" for intact original family.

"I didn't stack the deck or anything," he explains. "I just wrote down 67 names sort of stream-of-consciousness. I found that most fathers were absent. The second biggest categories were alcoholic and alcoholic/abusive." Out of 67 kids, only three had intact families with fathers who were not alcoholic or abusive.

Pick three, any three, of the gang members that hover around Boyle's door and delve into their family dynamics and the stories will disturb your sleep. There is Bandito[2], whose father died two years ago of a heroin overdose. There is Smiley[2], whose father is continually drunk and abusive. There is Gato[2], whose basehead mother sold his only warm jacket to buy another hit. Or Gustavo Martinez, Javier Villa and Guadalupe Lopez—Grumpy, Termite and Scoobie, respectively.

Grumpy's father was gone long before he was born. His mother beat him with the plug-end of the television cord, with the garden hose, a spiked belt—anything she could find. The beatings were so severe that she

was jailed several times for child abuse. Some abusive parents are by turns affectionate and rejecting. Not this mother. In all the years of Grumpy's upbringing, he never received a birthday gift or a Christmas gift or even a card.

"Imagine," says Boyle, "not one piece of concrete evidence of caring from a parent throughout a whole childhood."

In Termite's case, the blows were not to the body. His mother always professed great love for him. His father never hit him. What his father did was tell him he was worthless, despicable and generally a bad seed. Even now, when Boyle drops Termite at home, a call will sometimes come minutes later. It will be Termite pleading to sleep in Boyle's office for the night. "My dad locked me out," he will say.

"I know he cares about me," says Termite, as if the words are a spell capable of making it so. But when pushed on the subject he averts his eyes. "I guess mostly he just acts like I'm not there."

Sometimes it is not the parents but life in the barrio that provides the abuse. Scoobie's last memory of his alcoholic father was when he was 3; his dad knocked his mother off her feet, cuffed Scoobie to the floor and snarled: "What're you lookin' at?" Scoobie's mother gathered her kids and fled. However, the hotel in which she found shelter was so crime-ridden that, before he was 5, Scoobie witnessed three lurid murders, virtually on his doorstep. Add to that the problems of a young single mother with no resources and no child care and the picture becomes still bleaker.

Scoobie's mother padlocked her pre-school-age children in a darkened hotel room while she went to work for the day. "She was trying to keep us safe," says Scoobie. When he is asked if his childhood had any happy times, he thinks for a moment: "I remember this one day when my mom took us all to the park and let us run around. It was so great, you know. For once we weren't stuffed up in that little room. And we felt, I don't know, just—free!"

So what does a barrio kid do when family and society have failed him? When he turns 14 or 15, he joins a gang, a surrogate family, where he finds loyalty, self-definition, discipline, even love of a sort. "We all want to be attached to something," says Diego Vigil, an anthropology professor at USC who has studied gangs. "We want to connect and commit. If we can't find anywhere else to connect and commit, we'll connect and commit to the streets. The gang takes over the parenting, the schooling and the policing."

On a Sunday afternoon in January, 1991, Father Boyle takes Scoobie and Grumpy shopping for clothes. Both of them are large kids, bulky and muscular, each with a proclivity for fast, funny patter delivered half in English, half in Spanish. They are members of the Mob Crew and the Clarence Street Locos, respectively—traditionally friendly gangs whose neighborhoods are close to the church. Scoobie is 19 and Grumpy is 20, both *veteranos*, both too old to attend Dolores Mission Alternative. They are desperate to find employment. Their shopping destination is Sears. The idea is to get them non-gangster attire to wear to job interviews.

In the men's department, Boyle pulls out pants and shirts for them to try on. He is careful to choose light colors. Grumpy and Scoobie keep edging back in the direction of the gangster look: dark colors and a baggy fit.

"Hey G., these pants are too tight," wails Scoobie. In reality, the pants fit perfectly.

"They're fine," Boyle counters, and Scoobie relents.

"Look," Boyle says to Scoobie and Grumpy as he hands the cashier a Sears credit card, "I'm spending a lot of bank on this today, and the deal is you have to be dressed and in my office every morning at 9 a.m., ready to look for work." The two nod obediently and assure Boyle that they will indeed comply.

Both Scoobie and Grumpy are staying in Casa Miguel Pro, the temporary residence that Dolores Mission maintains for homeless women and children. "I'm trying an experiment in letting them stay there," Boyle explains. "A lot of folks aren't exactly thrilled that I'm doing this. But right now neither of them has anywhere else they can go."

After the shopping trip, Scoobie irons his new tan pants and shirt striped in shades of blue. Next he takes a bath. Finally he puts on the freshly pressed clothes and looks in a communal mirror.

"That ain't me . . ." he says softly to the mirror. He stands back a little and looks again. "I look like a regular person," he says, his expression so happy it borders on giddi-ness. "Not like the police say, not like another *gang member.*"

When Greg Boyle first came to Dolores Mission in early July, 1986, at age 32 the youngest pastor in the L.A. Archdiocese, he hardly seemed likely to become "the gang priest." Raised in comfortable Windsor Square on the outskirts of Hancock Park, one of eight children of a third-generation dairyman, he attended Loyola High School, the Jesuit-run boys' school on Venice Boulevard, from 1968 to 1972. It was a wildly inspiring four years for an idealistic Catholic kid. His teachers led peace marches protesting the Vietnam War, and activist Jesuits were making news all over the country as liberation theology—which marries social justice to spiritual renewal—came to full flower.

Boyle spent the next 13 years in religious training, culminating in his 1984 ordination in Los Angeles. He was posted to Bolivia, the poorest country in the Western Hemisphere, where he became the parish priest in a small village. The experience radicalized the young, middle-class priest from Southern California. "Bolivia turned me absolutely inside out," says Boyle. "After Bolivia my life was forever changed." He realized he wanted to work with the poor. And few places were poorer than Dolores Mission.

Boyle's first year in the parish was tense and difficult. The priest before him had been a venerable *Mexicano*, and the community was slow to warm up to an Anglo, especially one so young. Since so few parishioners came to him, he decided to go to them. Every afternoon without fail, Boyle walked for hours through the neighborhood, particularly through the housing projects where most of his parishioners lived. He talked to people, listened to their complaints, played with their children. Over time he noticed that the majority of the complaints centered upon one issue: gangs.

Boyle made an effort to get to know the gangsters. He began by learning their names. At first, they brutally rejected the *gavacho* who spoke only passable Spanish. But he kept going back to them. "And you know," he says, "at some point it becomes sort of flattering that the priest knows who you are." Then he started going to Juvenile Hall to visit when kids got locked up, bringing messages from their homeboys. Or he'd rush to the hospital if they got shot.

He noticed that the kids who got into the

most trouble were the kids who were not in school, and the reasons they were not in school were invariably gang-related. Either they had gotten kicked out of school because they had been fighting with enemy gang members, or the school itself was in enemy territory and deemed unsafe by the kids.

So in September, 1988, Father Boyle and one of his associates at Dolores Mission, Father Tom Smolich, opened a junior high and high school for gang members only. Dolores Mission Alternative was started on the third floor of Dolores Mission Elementary, the church's grammar school. Through home study and specially designed classes, the school aimed to get the kids back on an educational track, or at the least to help them pass the high-school equivalency exam.

Boyle also started hiring gang members to work around the church at $5 an hour. "And before I knew it there was no turning back," he laughs. "I felt like I sort of related to the gang members. They were fun and warm and eternally interesting. So gradually," he says, "it became a ministry within a ministry."

The rest of the parish, however, didn't find the gangsters quite so "warm" and "interesting." They saw only hair-netted homeboys doing heaven-knows-what in the same building with uniformed parochial-school children. Worse yet, these same "criminal types" were hanging out at the church as if it was their personal clubhouse. In the fall of 1989, Boyle's most virulent critics circulated a petition asking then-Archbishop Roger M. Mahony to remove him from the parish altogether.

Things came to a head one October night. Boyle had called a meeting to clear the air. The school basement was packed with Boyle supporters and *contras* when a swarm of gang members unexpectedly walked in, underlining the tension in the room. One by one, the homies got up and talked: "We're human beings, and we need help. And Father Greg is helping us."

Slowly the tension began to lift. Parish parents rose to speak: "Father Greg is right," they said. "These gang members are not the enemy. They are our children. And if we don't help them no one will."

That was the turning point. The parish stopped fighting Boyle's programs and began adopting them as their own. In short order, the Comité Pro Paz en el Barrio, the

Committee for Peace in the Barrio, was formed to address the gang situation. Parish mothers who had never before attended so much as a PTA meeting suddenly became activists in the gangsters' behalf, organizing a peace march, holding a gang conference.

"What is going on at Pico-Aliso is very different than anything else I've seen elsewhere in the city," says Yolanda Chavez, for the last two years Mayor Tom Bradley's official liaison to the L.A. Latino community. "A lot of people are well-meaning, but they don't help people organize themselves. They do things for them. Father Greg's goal is always to help the people help themselves. He has become a focal point for their strength, empowering the community to provide the gang members with alternatives."

Scoobie has been job-hunting for three weeks straight, but now he is sitting in Boyle's office and he looks terrible. His lips and jaw are bruised and swollen. His hands are cut up, and an incisor on the lower left side of his jaw is broken. He has just returned from the dentist. Boyle will pay the dental bills, which may be close to a thousand dollars.

It happened two nights ago, says Scoobie, when he was stopped by two uniformed police officers. He was doing nothing in particular—just hanging out with the homies when the officers ordered him up against a car with his hands over his head. "Then they pushed me down on my knees," he says. Scoobie responded with a four-letter suggestion. At that point, according to Scoobie, one of the cops hit him in the mouth with a billy club. Then, he says, the cops made him lie down spread-eagled and stepped on his hands. Finally the police let him go without an arrest.

One of the activist parish mothers, Pam McDuffie, took Scoobie to the Hollenbeck Police Station to report the incident. The case is currently under investigation by Internal Affairs, but Boyle believes Scoobie's story implicitly. "This is one of many, many cases of the police beating the kids down," he says.

A few days after Scoobie's trip to the dentist, there is new trouble. Boyle arrives at his office in the morning to find a message on his answering machine. "Hey G.," says a young voice, "tell Grumpy I don't have the money for the gun but I'll have the money soon." Boyle stares at the machine boggle-eyed. It is nearly inconceivable that some-one would leave such a message with him.

Boyle goes upstairs to Grumpy's room, and in a kind of false wall in the closet he finds a gun-cleaning kit and a metal strong-box. The box is heavy and the lid is stuck. Boyle carts it down to his office and shuts the door before prying the lid open. Inside, he finds $178 in cash, a neat list of investors and a box of 9-millimeter Beretta shells.

Boyle shuts the box, puts it in a desk drawer and waits for Grumpy's inevitable appearance. The confrontation goes as follows:

"Do you have a gun?"

"No, G."

"Are you collecting money for a gun?"

"No, G."

Boyle opens the drawer to reveal the strong box. "You've really let me down," he says quietly.

Grumpy's face turns to stone. "When do you want me to leave?" he asks. Then eyes averted and brimming, he turns and walks out.

Two hours later Grumpy is back. "G., I know I let you down! I let you down, *gacho*! I let you down big time!"

Boyle cannot bring himself to make Grumpy leave. "I know tough love is some-times required," he philosophizes later. "I just don't know how tough the love should be."

A solution to the gang problem has been eluding Los Angeles Police Department for decades, and from law enforcement's point of view, the "love" should be very tough in-deed. The ongoing police anti-gang program is dubbed Operation Hammer. "Hammer is a strategy in which we keep the pressure on," says Captain Nick Salicos, recently of the Hollenbeck Division. "On a Friday or a Saturday night, we go out with 30 or 40 offi-cers to known gang locations and arrest gang members for anything we can. Drinking beer in public. Anything." If the crime can be shown to be gang related, and the arrestee is a known gang member, the sentence can be "enhanced"—made longer.

"The police try to make life as miserable as possible for gang members," Boyle says, "which is really redundant since gang mem-bers' lives are already miserable enough, thank you very much. And they hate me, I guess, because, No. 1, I refuse to snitch on gang members. No. 2, they can't understand how I could care about these kids. And I can't understand why they insist on criminalizing every kid in this community."

A visit to Hollenbeck Police Station re-veals that Boyle is correct; the police don't like him much. Mention the priest's name to most Hollenbeck officers and there is invari-ably much rolling of eyes, followed by re-marks that range from the suggestion that Boyle is "well-meaning but dangerously naive" to veiled charges that he is an acces-sory to gang crimes to intimations that he is under the influence of Communists.

A ride-along in a black-and-white pro-vides an instructive perspective. The streets seem meaner from inside a patrol car. The stares the police gather are hostile, threat-ening. "Although our job is to try to prevent gang crime," explains Detective Jack Fors-man of the LAPD's special gang unit, CRASH (Community Resources Against Street Hoodlums), "more often than not we can do little more than pick up the pieces once a crime has been committed."

"What I don't get," adds another officer who requested anonymity, "is why Father Boyle refuses to preach against using guns and being in gangs."

The remark infuriates Boyle. "Aside from the fact that it just isn't true," he bristles, "it has no respect for the complexity of the issue. It's Nancy Reagan writ large: 'Just Say No' to gangs. I would say getting kids out of gangs is the whole point of my work here. But what is ultimately persuasive is a job and self-esteem and education and having the kid feel that he or she can put together in his or her imagination a future that is via-ble. Now I can sit there and say, 'Get out of the gang!' but I don't know what value that would have. If any of this is going to be suc-cessful, you have to accept folks where they are. What they always get is: 'Where you are is a horrible place and you'd better change.' Well, look how successful that's been."

Boyle sighs wearily. "Part of the prob-lem," he says, "is that when you're poor in the city of Los Angeles, you're hard-pressed to imagine a future for yourself. And if you can't imagine a future, then you're not going to care a lot about the present. And then anything can happen."

Although his approach is controversial, Boyle is by no means the only person work-ing with gangs who decries the Just Say No approach as simplistic. "We have tried that," says Chavez from Mayor Bradley's office, "and it hasn't worked. Force hasn't worked.

Police harassment hasn't worked. Jail and Juvenile Hall hasn't worked. Without options, gangs will thrive."

Mary Ridgeway and John Tuchek are the two officers in the L.A. County Probation Department's East L.A. Gang Unit who deal with arrested juveniles from Pico Gardens or Aliso Village. "There is the illusion," says Tuchek, "that we are rehabilitating these kids. And I'm here to tell you that the truth is we aren't even trying to rehabilitate them. We used to. But that doesn't happen down here any more. That's why what Father Greg is doing is so important. He's their only resource."

Ridgeway puts it another way. "At best, we can only deal with a fraction of the kids for a very short period of time, while he's there for all of them, all of the time. Father Greg and I are, in many ways, coming from a different point of view philosophically," she continues. "There are kids that I think should be locked up who he is reluctant to give up on—like a kid we both know who, fortunately, now is in Soledad. He was trouble every minute he was out on the streets."

"But, see," she smiles, "Father Greg loves everybody. In all my years in probation I've met maybe two people who have his courage. He's the kind of person we all wish we could be."

In the month after Boyle finds Grumpy's gun fund, the Pico-Aliso gangs begin to turn up the heat. By early March, Boyle is depressed. "Things have been awful around here," he says one Monday morning. It seems that Looney, an East Coast Crip, was killed on Thursday as a payback for Clown, a Primera Flats kid who was shot by a Crip in September, 1990.

"That's how the game works," says Boyle grimly. The night after Looney was killed, two Latinos, one a transient and the other a basehead, were killed. No one is sure if these killings were gang-related or not. Moreover, the Crips and Al Capone, gangs that have traditionally gotten along, have had two fights in less than 48 hours.

The bad news didn't stop there. At about 8 p.m. on Saturday night, a kid from the Clarence Street Locos was headed down Gless Street to buy a beer when a Cuatro Flats kid approached him. Words were exchanged. Immediately each boy marched off to find his homies. In seconds, members of both gangs appeared from around corners, like magic rabbits, and began mad-dogging and dissing each other—glaring and shouting insults. A kid named Diablo from Cuatro hit Solo from Clarence, and someone yelled, "It's on!" War had been declared.

Suddenly, 80 gang members were blocking the intersection of 4th and Gless. Fists were flying, heads were bashed, ghetto blasters were swinging. All the while voices screamed, "It's on. It's on!"

It was then that Boyle showed up, almost by chance. He had just dropped a kid off at home when he saw traffic backed up, he pulled over and raced to investigate. Then the situation became surreal. Into a tangle of brawling gangsters ran Boyle, grabbing arms and shrieking every four-letter word he could think of. At his screamed orders, the Clarence group backed up. Cuatro stopped swinging and halted its advance. On the edge of the action, kids on bikes still circled, shotguns bulging underneath their Pendletons.

Finally, Boyle was able to herd the Clarence kids across 4th and down Gless; the Cuatro force moved off, dispersing into the neighborhood.

Afterward, Boyle was walking alongside Mando, who, with his identical twin, has a lot of juice with the Clarence Street Locos. "You *yelled* at us, G.," said Mando, shaking his head in genuine shock. "You used the *F word!*"

"In the moment," says Boyle later, "I'll do any damn thing that works."

It's raining. Four homies—Termite, Grumpy, Green and Critter—are hanging out in Boyle's office as he opens mail and does paper work.

Critter, a slim, handsome kid with long, fringed eyelashes and a heartbreaker's smile, rubs Boyle's ever-expanding forehead with the palm of his hand as Boyle unsuccessfully bats him away. "I'm rubbing your bumper for luck, G.!" says Critter, moving in for another rub.

"Hey, G.," interrupts Grumpy, "How come you're in such a good mood?" Turning to Green: "Have you ever noticed that whenever G. is in a good mood it rains?" Grumpy pauses, possessed of a new thought. "Hey, you think maybe G. is actually Mother Nature in disguise? That means the drought is his fault, right? You think the drought is your fault, G.?"

Boyle looks up at Grumpy. "Here's a letter here from a couple who want to adopt a child," he says, deadpan. "What do you think, Grumps? You think it's right for you?"

"Only if the *madre* is proper," sniffs Grumpy. Meanwhile, the imagined scene of an unsuspecting young couple being introduced to their new "child"—a 6-foot, 200-pound tattooed homie named Grumpy—throws the rest of the room into spasms of hilarity.

Grumpy is discouraged about his job prospects. He has been answering want ads for weeks to no avail, he says. "You go in there and you fill out an application. Then they say they'll call you but you can tell they're looking at your tattoos and they're not gonna, you know? It's like, when you leave, you see your application flying out the window made into a paper airplane."

Nonetheless, Grumpy has heard that applications are being taken at the post office on 1st Street. "C'mon, let's go," he says to Green.

"Nah," says Green, "they won't hire us."

"C'mon homes," Grumpy persists. "Let's just try it. Let's go." He attempts to drag Green.

"C'mon homes." But Green remains immovable. Finally, Grumpy sits back down with a sigh. No one goes to the post office this day.

After the homies vacate his office, Boyle stares dolefully at his checkbook. "Right now, I have a hundred dollars in the bank. And I have to pay the kids working for me on Friday." He looks up. "But, you know, it's weird. Somehow the money always shows up. It usually happens on Thursday, my day off. There'll be no money in the bank on Wednesday and then I'll come in on Friday and there'll be a couple of checks on my desk. Checks coming from nowhere when they had to come—that's happened at least 50 times since I first came here." Boyle pauses. "It's not like I think it comes from God. My spirituality doesn't really take that form. But I do feel that if the work is meant to be done, somehow there'll be a way."

"Now all I have to do is find $150,000 to give kids jobs this summer," he continues. "Invariably, the violence in the neighborhood decreases in direct proportion to how many kids are working at any given time."

With the Jobs for a Future program, Boyle usually has three or four construction and maintenance crews working on church projects. In addition, he is on the phone daily to local businesses asking them to hire homies. "We will pay their salaries," he tells the potential employers. "All you have to do is give them a place to work." Boyle adds: "Of course, it would be great if the employers would pay the salaries. But unfortunately, that rarely happens."

"The myth about gang members and jobs," says Boyle, "is how're you gonna keep 'em down on the farm when they're making money hand over fist selling drugs—the implication being that they will never want to accept an honest job. Well, I have kids stop me on the street every single day of the week asking for jobs. And a lot of times these are kids I know are slanging, which is the street term for selling crack cocaine. I always say, 'If I get you a job, it means no more slanging.' And I've never once said that to a kid who didn't jump at the chance to do an honest day's work instead of selling drugs."

Four days later it is Saint Patrick's Day, a generally uneventful Sunday until Grumpy approaches Boyle, his clothes and hands covered in paint. "Oh, I've been doing some painting at Rascal's house," he says, in answer to Boyle's questioning look. Then he screws his face into a grimace. "You know, G.," he says. "I'm not going to look for a job anymore."

Boyle's expression darkens. "Why?" he asks.

"I'm just not going to," replies Grumpy. "No more job hunting."

Boyle looks truly distressed by this news. "What are you talking about . . . ?" Boyle begins.

"Nope. I'm not looking for a job any more," is all Grumpy will say.

Boyle throws up his hands. "What the hell am I supposed to do? Support you for the rest of your life?"

Finally, Grumpy's face breaks into a gigantic grin. "I'm not going to look for a job any more BECAUSE I FOUND A JOB, G.," he shouts. "I'm a painter! I'm painting stereo speakers!"

The rest of the day, Boyle cannot restrain himself. He tells Grumpy how proud he is, over and over. Grumpy tries to stay cool but his happiness is obvious and irrepressible.

Termite is one of the regulars in and around Boyle's office. He is 16, has the huge, dark eyes of a yearling deer and a smile that unfolds fast, wide and bright. His hair is cut Marine short, shaved by Boyle with the No. 4 attachment of the church's clippers. On his upper lip there sprouts a pale hint of brown velvet. When he is happy, Termite's face is transformed into that of a deliciously mischievous child. In repose, his expression suggests someone waiting patiently for a punishment. At all times, his shoulders slump more than is natural.

Termite is a Clarence Street Loco, jumped into the gang less than a year ago. So far, his gang-banging has been confined to compulsive tagging: Walk in any direction from Dolores Mission and you soon see the spray-painted message "CSL *soy* Termite." Termite is not a kid drawn to violence. "I don't mind if you want to go head up," he says. "But it would be better if nobody had guns."

Since last summer, Termite has been pestering Boyle for a job. Finally, the priest has talked a local self-storage company into hiring two homies, courtesy of Dolores Mission. Termite and Stranger, a kid from The Mob Crew, get the call.

The timing is fortuitous. Termite's father has just gone to visit family in Mexico, and with the weight of his dad's anger briefly lifted, Termite is a new person. Instead of partying with the homies till all hours, he asks Boyle to drive him home before dark every night. He has all but stopped tagging and has started showing up at the alternative school every day.

The day before Termite and Stranger are to start work, Boyle drives them to meet their new boss, the manager of the storage company, a matter-of-fact woman named Yolanda. The boys listen quietly while she explains their duties—gofering and general cleanup. Afterward Boyle takes the two kids to McDonald's to celebrate.

"We won't let you down, G." says Termite.

One week later, events have derailed Termite's promise. On the first Sunday in April, at about 5 p.m., Boyle is driving across 1st Street, from East L.A. Dukes territory in Aliso Village toward the church. He sees a group of five Clarence kids, Grumpy and Termite among them, running in Pecan Park near the baseball diamond. It is not a playful run. Termite has a long stick under his jacket, as if he's packing a shotgun. On instinct, Boyle turns to look behind him and sees a group of East L.A. Dukes near home plate, also running. The Dukes are sworn enemies of the Clarence Street Locos.

Boyle swerves his car to a halt on the wrong side of the street, rolls down his window and yells to the Clarence kids to get the blankety-blank out of there. Amazingly they do. As he raises his hand to open his door, there is a terrifying BOOM-BOOM-BOOM-BOOM-BOOM. Just behind Boyle's head, the car's rear window on the driver's side shatters. When the shooting stops, Boyle gets out to confront the Dukes. They disappear fast as lightning.

Later, he drives back into Dukes territory. This time he finds them. "Did you want to f––kin' kill me?" he yells, hoping to shock them into a new state of consciousness. "I prayed you would hit me so then maybe it would end. I'd be willing to die to end this." The Dukes stare at him, then at the missing car window and the bullet holes in his car, one in the door frame no more than an inch from where Boyle's head had been. They murmur frantic, ineffectual apologies.

Then one boy looks up just in time to see two gangsters on the hill above them— East Coast Crips. An instant later the noise comes again: BOOM-BOOM-BOOM-BOOM-BOOM-BOOM. Everyone dives behind Boyle's car as the sky rains bullets. Miraculously, no one is hit. Instead a bullet has punctured the car's right rear tire, just missing the gas tank, and come to rest inside the trunk.

The next day, Boyle wakes up with no obvious ill effects from the near misses except for a piercing headache. The pain is localized just behind his ear, where neck meets skull. In other words, about where the door-frame bullet would have hit if it had taken only a slightly different course.

As usual, violence spawns more violence. On Monday morning, when Boyle arrives at the church, he gets a call from Yolanda, the manager of the storage facility where Termite and Stranger are working. She is going to have to fire Termite, she says. It seems that on Friday he not only crashed the facility's motorized cart, but, when he was supposed to remove graffiti from a wall, he replaced it with new inscriptions: "CSL *soy* Termite."

It does not strike Boyle as entirely coincidental that Termite's father returned from Mexico a few hours before Termite began this orgy of acting out. Nor does it help matters that the mood of the Clarence homies in general is restless. Two Clarence Street homeboys have been killed by Dukes since January, 1990, and Clarence has not yet retaliated. After yesterday's shooting, they will probably begin to feel intolerably pressed. And most of the pressure will fall on the little heads, the younger gang members like Termite who have yet to prove themselves.

Boyle takes Termite to lunch to break the bad news about the job. First he gives him a stern lecture about responsibility and consequences. Then he turns Good Cop and assures Termite that losing the job is not the end of the world. "You know I'll never give up on you," Boyle says. *Te quiero mucho,* he says finally. *"Como si fueras mi hijo"* ("I love you as if you were my son"). At this, Termite starts to cry. Once started he cries for a long while.

At the end of the day, Termite's actions are swinging farther out of control; he gets into a fight with one of his own homies. When Boyle sees him again, he is covered in blood. "It's nothin'," he mumbles.

Then at about 2 the next afternoon, Father Smolich sees Termite deep in Dukes territory with a can of spray paint; he is crossing out Dukes graffiti and replacing it with his own. It is a dangerously provocative act, considering the events of the last two days. Smolich demands that Termite hand over the spray can. Termite dances rebelliously away.

Two hours later, Termite is back in Clarence territory, on the pay phone at the corner of Third and Pecan streets talking with his girlfriend, Joanna. He sees Li'l Diablo[2], another "new bootie" from Clarence, walking north toward 1st Street and Pecan Park, and sensing that something is up, he follows. All at once, Termite sees what is up: Li'l Diablo has a gun, and there is a group of Dukes gathered in the park. Termite watches as Li'l Diablo raises the gun, a .22, and fires one shot into the air. The Dukes scatter, running for the projects across 1st Street. Li'l Diablo drops his weapon and runs in the other direction.

At first Termite follows him. But then, on an impulse he cannot later adequately explain, Termite turns back and picks up the gun. Then he points it in the direction of the by-now faraway Dukes and empties it. Most of the bullets fall harmlessly to the pavement. However, one bullet strays into an apartment on Via Las Vegas, where a 6-year-old girl named Jackie is watching television with her mother. Jackie kicks up her small foot just in time for it to meet the bullet. Blood spurts, and her mother begins to scream.

Holding the empty gun, Termite stands on the sidewalk still as a statue for a long moment. Finally he runs.

In short order, the neighborhood is alive with rumor, and word of what has happened quickly reaches Boyle. It is hours before he finds Termite, milling nervously with some other homies a block from the church. Wordlessly, Termite climbs into Boyle's car.

"I know what happened," Boyle tells him. "Did you do it?"

There is a silence. "Yeah," Termite says without meeting Boyle's gaze.

Boyle informs him that he has hit a little girl. Termite is horrified. "A lot of people say," Boyle tells him, "that in order to be a man you have to shoot a gun. But I'm telling you that isn't true. The truth is, in order to be a man you need to take responsibility for your actions. That means you need to turn yourself in."

Termite starts to protest. Then he is quiet for a long while. "Let's go, G." he says finally.

Inside Hollenbeck Police Station, two CRASH officers order Termite to spread his legs. As the officers briskly frisk him, he stands with his lips pursed, trying not to cry.

Everyone who meets Greg Boyle seems to go through the same two-step process. Step one is as follows: "Hey, this guy is really some kind of a saint!" And then step two: "There's got to be a dark side."

Yet when you get to know Boyle well, you find no ominous recesses of the psyche or murky hidden agendas. There are small things: a healthy-size ego, or the way he at times seems more quarrelsome with the police than might be necessary. But nothing you'd call dark. What you do find, however, is a man in the grip of a paradox.

The other priests at Dolores Mission, however fond they are of the gang members, admit that they keep an emotional distance between themselves and a situation that can be overwhelming and tragic on a daily basis. For Boyle, there seems to be no distance. He cares for the gang members as if they were literally his own children. Certainly it is Boyle's offer of unconditional love that is the source of his magic. Pure love heals. But what happens if you give your heart to 10 dozen kids, many of whom will die violently and young, the rest of whom are dying slow deaths of the spirit?

"Burn-out is the cost, I think," Boyle says. "Because I'm so invested in each kid, tragedies and potential tragedies kind of get into my gut in a way they probably don't get into other folks'." He laughs nervously. "A lot of it is the classic ministerial occupational hazard of co-dependency, where you get too invested. Only it's kind of writ larger here, I think. And it's also parental. It's like, 'Oh my God, my kid hasn't come home yet and it's midnight' times a hundred."

The analogy of Boyle as parent can lead to still riskier territory. If you ask most parents what they would die for, they reply, "My children." Boyle grows uncharacteristically quiet when the question is posed to him. "I would die for these kids," he says finally. "I don't know how that would play itself out. But I don't think there would be any question. It's not a choice, you know," he says. "It just is."

This is not the first time Boyle has considered the possibility. The day the Dukes' gunfire hit his car and came within an inch of killing him, he realized that a line had been crossed. It was not that they had tried to kill him; it was that they had known he was in the line of fire and they had shot anyway.

Two weeks later he had another close call. Late at night, Boyle was walking one of the younger kids home when the boy whispered, "Look out." Boyle turned to see gangsters, guns at the ready, creeping along the bushes that fringe the Santa Ana Freeway on the east edge of Aliso Village. They were headed toward a group of TMC homies. But this time, seeing Boyle, no one shot.

"It was very similar to the day that the Dukes shot," Boyle says. "But that time I arrived a split second too late and the action had already been put in motion. This time I think I arrived just early enough to stop it."

"As I walked home that night I felt so weird. I kept saying to myself, 'I really think this is where my life will end. I'm going to die in this barrio.' "

He pauses, his eyes searching some interior distance. "But you know, what should I do differently? Would I not have intervened that day between Clarence and East L.A.? Just kept driving instead? I don't think that would be possible."

"So what should I do differently?"

The question hangs in the air like smoke after a fire.

Even Dukes were impressed by the fact that Termite had turned himself in. "That's *firme*! That's *firme*!" they said. But Termite's father assessed his actions differently. We could have gotten you to Mexico, he told

Termite, his voice scathing. "Can't you do anything right?"

At Termite's court hearing, his fortunes take an unexpected turn. His public defender—a fast-talking, upwardly mobile fellow named Brady Sullivan—not only undermines a witness's testimony but also gets Termite's confession thrown out on a *Miranda* violation. Termite is set free.

As far as Boyle is concerned, this is good news and bad news. The good news is that a sensitive kid with no prior record will not get two to five in a California Youth Authority lockup. "Termite is a wonderful, wonderful kid," Boyle says. "And he shot a little girl. A lot of people can't hold those two thoughts together. But, the task of a true human being is do precisely that."

The bad news is that Termite will not go on a badly needed, if enforced, vacation. Instead, he will be back in the neighborhood and back in the gang life.

At first, Termite is euphoric at being free. But soon, reality sets in; the Dolores Mission neighborhood is no longer a safe place for him. His mother talks about sending him to live with an aunt in San Bernardino or his grandmother in Mexico, but Termite doesn't want to go. He says he wants to be near his girlfriend Joanna, a sunny-natured girl of 14. His mother relents on the condition that Termite stay away from the church and the projects.

For two weeks straight, Termite spends his days cooped up in a darkened house with his dad, who works at night. Predictably, it isn't long before the situation blows itself to smithereens. Termite is back hanging out, staying at friends' houses, tagging everything he can find, particularly in East L.A. Dukes territory.

Word is soon on the street that Termite is a marked man. His mother has answered the phone at home and heard the death threats. "It's hard to know what to do," Boyle worries out loud. "I don't want him to feel boxed in. When that happens a kid is likely to feel that the only thing to do is to go out in a blaze of glory, or take somebody else out in a blaze of glory."

When it is mentioned to Termite that he is all but asking to be killed, he cocks his head quizzically. "Sometimes I just don't care. Sometimes I feel like I want to die," he says, then looks away, "and I don't know why."

A week later, the inevitable has happened: Termite has been shot. He was hanging out with homies from both Clarence and TMC near the corner store at Gless and 4th. A truck whizzed by and dozens of bullets were fired. Only one connected. It grazed the left side of Termite's head above his ear and blew a crater an inch-and-a-half deep and six inches in diameter in the stucco wall behind him. There was lots of blood, but no serious damage.

No one knows for sure who the shooters were—or who the intended target was. But Termite believes he knows. "I didn't tell anybody," he says, "but I was thinking while I was lying there on the ground, 'This bullet was meant for me.'"

Like the volume of a boom box turned up notch by notch, the violence around Dolores Mission grows in frequency and intensity as the days move from spring to summer and on toward fall. Grumpy gets a bullet in the stomach. Two Jobs for a Future construction workers are shot on two different nights. Thumper, from Cuatro Flats, who was out walking with his girlfriend, has his hair parted down the middle by a bullet that skimmed neatly across the top of his skull. Sniper, from TMC, is shot twice in the shoulder and once below the heart. All his wounds are through-and-throughs—the .38-caliber bullets passed straight through his body and out again. An hour and a half after he is rushed to White Memorial Hospital emergency room, Sniper is back on the street, a jacket over his bandages. "He has no insurance so they wouldn't give him any pain killers," says Boyle, "not even some Tylenol."

And yet there are bright spots. Grumpy recovers and is still employed. Green finds a job making conga drums. Scoobie makes it onto one of Boyle's construction crews, and his foreman gives him rave reviews. The morning after Critter receives his diploma from Roosevelt High School (with some help from Mission Alternative) on the stage of the Shrine Auditorium, he starts a new job at a downtown law firm. "I think maybe after a while they're going to let me do some computer work," says Critter happily. "I told 'em I got an A-plus in my last computer class."

And then there is Termite. After he was shot, he asked if he could move into Casa Miguel Pro with Grumpy. "Casa Pro is supposed to be for mothers and children," explains Boyle. "If I let Termite in it would just open the flood gates. Grumpy genuinely has

nowhere else he can go, but if I gave a room to every kid who has an intolerable family situation I could fill up Casa Pro plus the Hilton."

In the end Boyle found a compromise. He told Termite he could sleep on the floor of his office. For a time, things seemed to settle down.

Then, a few weeks later, the shooting starts again. Boyle is at Aliso Village talking to a group of TMC homies when unidentified gangsters open fire with automatics and "gauges"—shotguns. The shooting goes on for nearly two minutes. But, as is often the case, the gangsters are bad shots and no one is seriously hurt.

The next day, Termite is picked up by the police. He had been wandering in Dukes territory, carrying a loaded .38. He pleads guilty to a carrying a concealed weapon and is given a minimum sentence—approximately six months—in a county probation department youth camp.

It is 9:55 p.m. and Boyle has finished his bicycle rounds through the projects; things are quiet and he grows contemplative. "You know," he says, "people are always asking me what I consider to be my victories. But I can never think of things that way. With these kids, all you can do is take one a day at a time. A lot of days it's two steps forward and four steps back. On other days it's like the line in Tennessee Williams' play, 'A Streetcar Named Desire': 'Sometimes there's God so quickly.' Then it's joy upon joy, grace upon grace."

Grace or none, it is clear that Boyle loves this place and the job. "You go where the life is," he says. "And the life for me is here in this parish—especially with these kids. The happiness they bring me is beyond anything I can express in words. In the truest and most absolute sense, this work is a vocation." He laughs softly. "And for good or ill I can do no other."

There is an irony here. In July, 1992, Greg Boyle will in fact "do other." A Jesuit is normally assigned to a particular post for six years, no more. The goal is detachment—it should be the work, not the person, on which redemption depends.

Next summer marks the end of Boyle's assignment as pastor of Dolores Mission. He is then expected to spend the next 12 months in prayer, study and renewal before he takes his final vows. (Jesuits wait until a man hits his middle years before final vows are offered.)

"After that," says Boyle, "I'll probably be able to come back here in some capacity, maybe as director of the school." But not even this is a sure thing.

When asked what effect his departure will have on the homeboys, Boyle is quick to be reassuring. "It'll be fine. The structures are in place now—the school, the Comité Pro Paz, the Jobs for a Future program. I am by no means irreplaceable at Dolores Mission."

Maybe, and maybe not. A look into the faces of the gang members who love Boyle as they love no one else in the world makes you wonder. One thing is sure: For good or ill, by this time next year, Father Gregory Boyle will be gone.[3]

Notes

1. Editors' note: The article was written in 1991. By the end of 1994, Father Boyle had buried his 39th gang member in this parish.

2. The name of this gang member—and others so marked—has been changed.

3. Editors' note: And in 1994, Father Boyle returned to continue his work with his "homies," finding jobs and burial sites. ✦

Chapter 28
New Approaches to the Strategic Prevention of Gang and Group-Involved Violence

Anthony A. Braga,
David M. Kennedy,
and George E. Tita

A *widely heralded approach to the reduction of gang violence was initiated with the Boston Gun Project in the 1990s, and has been repeated in diverse forms in other areas of the country. Because it is based principally upon deterrence theory (a favorite of conservative scholars) but also involves community-level participation (a favorite of liberal scholars), the approach has received support from both sides of the political spectrum. The authors describe the general approach and its application in a number of different settings. The strategy appears to be conceptually appropriate, and preliminary findings are said to be encouraging. We note, however, that the evaluations tend to be* post hoc *(after the fact), and not experimentally designed. We are reminded that promise is not fulfillment, and that planned evaluations are required before we jump on any gang-control bandwagon.*

A number of jurisdictions have been experimenting with new problem-solving frameworks to prevent gang and group-involved violence. These new strategic approaches have shown promising results in the reduction of violence. Pioneered in Boston, these new initiatives have followed a core set of activities to reduce violence. These activities have included the "pulling levers" focused deterrence strategy, designed to prevent violence by and among chronic offenders and groups of chronic offenders; the convening of an interagency working group representing a wide range of criminal justice and social service capabilities; and jurisdiction-specific assessments of violence dynamics, perpetrator and victim characteristics, and related issues such as drug market characteristics and patterns of weapons use and acquisition. All of these initiatives have been facilitated by a close, more or less real-time, partnership between researchers and practitioners. In many jurisdictions, an initial interest in "juvenile violence" or "gun violence" has shifted, as the problem assessments have proceeded, to a focus on understanding and controlling violence, regardless of age or weapon type, associated with chronic offenders and groups of chronic offenders. This chapter traces the development of these new problem-solving frameworks, discusses the commonalities and divergences across jurisdictions that have experimented with these approaches, and synthesizes the key elements of the new strategic prevention frameworks.

The Development of the New Strategic Prevention Frameworks: The Boston Gun Project

The Boston Gun Project was a problem-solving enterprise expressly aimed at taking on a serious, large-scale crime problem—homicide victimization among young people in Boston. Like many large cities in the United States, Boston experienced a large, sudden increase in youth homicide between the late 1980s and early 1990s. Boston youth homicide (ages 24 and under) increased 230%—from 22 victims in 1987 to 73 victims in 1990 (Braga, Kennedy, Waring, & Piehl, 2001). Youth homicide remained high well after the 1990 peak; Boston averaged 44 youth homicides per year between 1991 and 1995 (Braga et al., 2001). The Boston Gun

Project proceeded by (a) assembling an interagency working group of largely line-level criminal justice and other practitioners; (b) applying quantitative and qualitative research techniques to create an assessment of the nature of, and dynamics driving, youth violence in Boston; (c) developing an intervention designed to have a substantial, near-term impact on youth homicide; (d) implementing and adapting the intervention; and (e) evaluating the intervention's impact (Kennedy, Piehl, & Braga, 1996). The Project began in early 1995 and implemented what is now known as the Operation Ceasefire intervention, which began in the late spring of 1996.

The trajectory of the Project and of Ceasefire is by now well known and extensively documented (Kennedy et al., 1996; Kennedy, Braga, & Piehl, 1997; Kennedy, 1997; Kennedy, 1998; Kennedy, 2001; Braga et al., 2001). Briefly, the working group of law enforcement personnel, youth workers, and researchers diagnosed the youth violence problem in Boston as one of patterned, largely vendetta-like ("beef") hostility among a small population of chronically criminal offenders, and particularly among those involved in some 60 loose, informal, mostly neighborhood-based groups (these groups were called "gangs" in Boston, but were not Chicago- or LA-style gangs). As this diagnosis developed, the focus of the Project shifted from its initial framework of "juvenile violence" and "gun violence" to "gang violence." The Operation Ceasefire "pulling-levers" strategy was designed to deter violence by reaching out directly to gangs, saying explicitly that violence would no longer be tolerated, and backing up that message by "pulling every lever" legally available when violence occurred (Kennedy, 1997, 1998). Simultaneously, youth workers, probation and parole officers, and later churches and other community groups offered gang members services and other kinds of help. The Ceasefire Working Group delivered this message in formal meetings with gang members; through individual police and probation contacts with gang members; through meetings with inmates of secure juvenile facilities in the city; and through gang outreach workers. The deterrence message was not a deal with gang members to stop violence. Rather, it was a promise to gang members that violent behavior would evoke an immediate and intense response. If gangs committed other crimes but refrained from violence, the normal workings of police, prosecutors, and the rest of the criminal justice system would deal with these matters. But if gang members hurt people, the Working Group focused its enforcement actions on them.

A central hypothesis within the Working Group was the idea that a meaningful period of substantially reduced youth violence might serve as a "firebreak" and result in a relatively long-lasting reduction in future youth violence (Kennedy et al., 1996). The idea was that youth violence in Boston had become a self-sustaining cycle among a relatively small number of youth, with objectively high levels of risk leading to nominally self-protective behavior such as gun acquisition and use, gang formation, tough "street" behavior, and the like: behavior that then became an additional input into the cycle of violence (Kennedy et al., 1996). If this cycle could be interrupted, a new equilibrium at a lower level of risk and violence might be established, perhaps without the need for continued high levels of either deterrent or facilitative intervention. The larger hope was that a successful intervention to reduce gang violence in the short term would have a disproportionate, sustainable impact in the long term.

A large reduction in the yearly number of Boston youth homicides followed immediately after Operation Ceasefire was implemented in mid-1996. As discussed earlier, Boston averaged 44 youth homicides per year between 1991 and 1995. In 1996, with Ceasefire in place for roughly half the year, the number of Boston youth homicides decreased to 26 and then further decreased to 15 youth homicides in 1997, a level below that characteristic of Boston in the pre-epidemic period. The low level of youth homicides has continued through 1998 (18) and 1999 (15; Braga & Kennedy, 2001). A formal evaluation of Operation Ceasefire revealed that the intervention was associated with a 63% decrease in the monthly number of Boston youth homicides, a 32% decrease in the monthly number of shots-fired calls, a 25% decrease in the monthly number of gun assaults, and, in one high-risk police district given special attention in the evaluation, a 44% decrease in the monthly number of youth gun assault incidents (Braga et al., 2001). The evaluation also suggested that Boston's significant youth homicide reduction associated with Operation Ceasefire was distinct when compared with youth homicide trends in most major U.S. and New England cities (Braga et al., 2001).

Experiences in Other Jurisdictions

At first blush, the effectiveness of the Operation Ceasefire intervention in preventing violence may seem unique to Boston. Operation Ceasefire was constructed largely from the assets and capacities available in Boston at the time and deliberately tailored to the city's particular violence problem. Operational capacities of criminal justice agencies in other cities will be different, and youth violence problems in other cities will have important distinguishing characteristics. However, the basic working group problem-solving process and the pulling-levers approach to deterring chronic offenders are transferable to violence problems in other jurisdictions. A number of cities have begun to experiment with these analytic frameworks and have experienced some encouraging preliminary results. Consistent with the problem-solving approach, these cities have tailored the approach to fit their violence problems and operating environments.

Minneapolis, Minnesota

Homicide in Minneapolis, traditionally a city with a very low homicide rate, increased dramatically from 59 victims in 1994 to 97 victims in 1995. In 1996, the number of homicides remained unusually high at 83 victims. In response to these unprecedented increases, a group of community members, law enforcement officers, government officials, and corporate representatives retained Police Executive Research Forum (PERF) and Harvard University researchers to help analyze their homicide problem and develop appropriate preventive strategies (Kennedy & Braga, 1998). The Minneapolis problem-solving enterprise was organized as an integrated academic-practitioner partnership and involved a working group composed of Minneapolis Police Department officers, Hennepin County probation officers, local and federal prosecutors, ATF field agents, and other local, state, and federal criminal justice agency representatives.

Using a blend of quantitative and qualitative exercises, the research team closely examined all homicide incidents between January 1994 and May 1997. The problem analysis revealed that homicide victims and offenders tended to have criminal histories, often substantial ones, and committed a wide variety of crimes including drug offenses, property crimes, disorder offenses, weapons offenses, and violent crimes (Kennedy & Braga, 1998). Many homicide victims and offenders were under probation supervision, sometimes at the time of the homicide incident. Gang-related violence played an important role in Minneapolis homicides. Reviews with Minneapolis practitioners suggested that Minneapolis did indeed have both "native" and Chicago-style gangs, plus groups linked to other cities and to Native Americans. Nearly 45% of the homicide incidents were considered to be gang related (Kennedy & Braga, 1998). Of all homicide incidents during the period examined, 26% of the victims and slightly more than 45% of the offenders were gang members (Kennedy & Braga, 1998). Some 32 active gangs with about 2,650 members were identified as being central to gang violence in Minneapolis; these individuals represented less than 3.5% of Minneapolis residents between the ages of 14 and 24 (Kennedy & Braga, 1998). These gangs tended not to be territorial, but operated fluidly geographically across Minneapolis and other local jurisdictions.

The working group decided that the results of the problem analysis supported the use of a pulling-levers ceasefire-style intervention. The working group responded to outbreaks of gang violence with a wide variety of criminal justice activities focused on the gang or gangs in question, communicated this new policy directly to gangs and gang members as the implementation unfolded, and matched the criminal justice intervention with social service and community-based interventions wherever possible (Kennedy & Braga, 1998). A key element in the enforcement portfolio was the creation, in the Hennepin County Probation Department, of a small number of field probation officers dedicated to the project and detailed to conducting home visits, street enforcement, and the like, in the company of Minneapolis Police Department officers.

The enforcement phase of the operation was kicked off by selecting a particularly violent gang, the Bogus Boyz, that was ultimately largely dismantled through the use of federal weapons prosecutions. The Minneapolis working group pursued a wide variety of means to deliver the deterrence message to the target audience. The Mayor and the enforcement team held a press conference to announce the Bogus Boyz arrests and their antiviolence rationale; teams of police and probation officers made home visits to troublesome gang members and paid special visits to gang-involved victims of gang violence (often in the company of their friends) in the hospital where they would warn against retaliation; and posters detailing the city's new gang violence policy were displayed prominently in the Hennepin County jail for viewing by the arrestees.

Although a formal evaluation of this effort has not been conducted, preliminary findings suggest that the intervention had an impact on homicide. After the intervention was implemented in June 1997, monthly homicide counts during the summer of 1997 showed a sharp reduction compared to monthly counts of homicide over the previous two summers (1995, 28 victims; 1996, 41 victims; 1997, 8 victims; Kennedy & Braga, 1998). After the initial success of the operation, adherence to the core strategy by the agencies involved slackened, and homicide in the city increased, though not to the levels observed immediately prior to the initial intervention.

Baltimore, Maryland

Baltimore has long suffered from high yearly counts of homicides. During the 1990s, however, Baltimore experienced more than 300 homicides per year between 1990 and 1997, with a 30-year peak of 353 homicides in 1993 (Kennedy, Braga, & Thomson, 2000). In 1996 and 1997, Baltimore had the fourth highest homicide rate in the United States among cities with more than 250,000 residents (Pastore & Maguire, 1999). Beginning in 1998, with the support of the Baltimore Safe and Sound Campaign, a working group composed of Baltimore Police Department officers, Baltimore State's Attorney's Office and U.S. Attorney's Office prosecutors, probation and parole officers, juvenile corrections officers, federal law enforcement agencies (ATF, FBI, and DEA), and Harvard University researchers engaged in a problem-solving enterprise to unravel the dynamics underlying the homicide problem, develop a comprehensive violence

reduction strategy, and implement the strategy (Kennedy et al., 2000).

The research team began the homicide problem analysis by obtaining official data on 303 homicide victims and 211 homicide suspects from 1997. A close examination of the criminal history data revealed that 74% of the victims and 87% of the suspects had adult and/or juvenile charges filed against them in court (Kennedy et al., 2000). Some 53% of the victims and 68% of the offenders had been under either adult or juvenile court-ordered supervision. Among those with criminal records, victims averaged about 8 prior charges and offenders nearly 10 prior charges; these prior offenses include a wide range of violent, drug, and property offenses (Kennedy et al., 2000). Using semi-structured qualitative data collection techniques, the research team closely examined the circumstances of the homicide victimizations. About 20% of the homicide incidents involved an ongoing dispute that was not about drug business between individuals or groups. Disputes involving drug business were involved in 18% of the homicides, and street drug robberies characterized 10% of the homicides. The remaining incidents were characterized as the result of robberies (nonstreet drug, 10%), spontaneous arguments (9%), domestic violence (6%), other circumstances (4%), or unknown circumstances (22%). Some 59% of the incidents occurred in or near a street-level drug market, and about 46% of the suspects and 37% of the victims were members of a drug organization or some recognized neighborhood criminal network (Kennedy et al., 2000). The project research identified some 325 drug groups in Baltimore that ranged in nature from rather sophisticated drug organizations, to structured neighborhood groups or "gangs" that sold drugs, to loose neighborhood groups that sold drugs (Kennedy et al., 2000).

The overall picture that emerged from this research suggested that violent groups of chronic offenders immersed in Baltimore's drug markets were responsible for the bulk of the city's homicides. As such, the working group felt that a pulling-levers-focused deterrence strategy was a promising way to reduce the city's homicide problem. Unlike Boston and Minneapolis, the sheer number of groups, the high homicide rate—averaging nearly one a day—and the clear role of street drug activity as a driver of the violence made the idea of an operation focused solely on groups implausible. Instead, the Baltimore strategy took *violent street drug market areas* as the basic unit of work. The basic operational idea was to take these areas in turn, reaching out to the groups in a particular area, "calming" the violence, establishing a maintenance strategy for the area, and then expanding the operation to new areas.

The first application of Operation Safe Neighborhoods, as the operation was called, focused on a very violent drug market area in the Park Heights neighborhood (Kennedy et al., 2000). The strategy proceeded by delivering a benchmark intervention that focused a varied menu of criminal justice operations on the violent groups in the target area. Selected members of the violent groups, usually those members on probation or under some form of criminal justice supervision, were then required to attend a forum where the new strategy was explained to the offenders. The forum was supplemented by a variety of other communication strategies, including the posting of fliers in the area and direct one-on-one communications with offenders on the street. Beyond the communication of cause and effect between violent behavior and law enforcement actions, the offenders were also offered access to social intervention and opportunity provision programs organized by the Safe and Sound Campaign. The violence prevention strategy was designed to ensure compliance in the targeted area, and new violent areas were addressed until the strategy was implemented citywide. Although a formal evaluation of the strategy has not been completed, preliminary analyses suggest that the intervention was associated with a 74% reduction in shootings and a 22% reduction in homicides in Park Heights during the 5 months following the intervention relative to shootings and homicides in the target area during the same time period one year earlier (Kennedy et al., 2000).

Boyle Heights, City of Los Angeles, California

In March 1998, the National Institute of Justice (NIJ) funded RAND to develop and test strategies for reducing gun violence among youth in Los Angeles. In part, the goal was to determine which parts of the Boston Gun Project might be replicable in Los Angeles. In designing the replication, RAND drew a clear distinction between the process governing the design and implementation of the strategy (data-driven policy development, problem solving, working groups) and the elements and design (pulling levers, collective accountability, retailing the message) of the Boston model. Processes, in theory, can be sustained and adaptive, and as such can be utilized to address dynamic problems. By singling out process as an important component, the RAND team hoped to make clear that process can affect program effectiveness independently of the program elements or the merits of the actual design (see Tita, Riley, & Greenwood, 2003, for a detailed analysis of the project).

The Los Angeles replication is unique in several important ways. First, the implementation was not city wide, but only within a single neighborhood (Boyle Heights) within a single Los Angeles Police Department Division (Hollenbeck). The project site, Boyle Heights, also differs from other sites in that the population is relatively homogenous. Well over 80% of the residents are Latinos of Mexican origin. The same is true for the gangs, many of which were formed prior to the Second World War. These gangs are clearly "traditional" gangs, with memberships exceeding a hundred members. The gangs are strongly territorial, contain age-graded substructures, and are intergenerational in nature (Maxson & Klein, 1995).

Unlike the other cities where gang and group-involved violence is a rather recent phenomenon, Los Angeles represents an attempt to reduce gun violence in a "chronic gang city" with a long history of gang violence and an equally long history of gang reduction strategies. The research team first had to convince members of the local criminal justice and at-large community that the approach we were espousing differed in important ways from these previous efforts to combat gangs. In fact, it does—the RAND project was not about "doing something about gangs," but rather "doing something about gun violence" in a community where gang members committed an overwhelming proportion of the gun violence. The independent analysis of homicide files confirmed the perception held by police and community alike that gangs were highly overrepresented in homicidal acts. From 1995 to 1998, 57% of all homicides had a clear gang motivation. Another 25% of the homicides could be coded as "gang related" because they involved a gang member as a victim or offender but were motivated for reasons other than gang rivalries.

The analysis found very little evidence that drug dealing motivated much of the violence. Among the 90 gang-motivated homicides, less than 10% (8) also included a drug component. Law enforcement officials from the working group were skeptical and insisted, "These kids are . . . being killed because of [dope]." The group revisited the homicide files with the gang detective personally responsible for assembling the cases. In the end, 4 homicides out of the 90 were recoded: Three homicides that were originally coded "gang-motivated only" were changed to "gang-/drug-motivated" and 1 case was recoded from "gang-/drug-motivated" to "gang-motivated only" (Tita et al., 2003).

Given the social organization of violence in Boyle Heights, the multi-disciplinary working group fully embraced the pulling-levers-focused deterrence strategy developed in Boston. The processes of communicating the message have also been formally adopted, though to date this has been accomplished through personal contact rather than in a group setting. Police, probation, community advocates, street gang workers, a local hospital, and local clergy are all passing along the message of collective accountability for gangs continuing to commit gang violence.

It is too early to comment on any successes that the actual implementation of the strategy has had on reducing gun violence. However, participants are encouraged that in 2000, a year in which the citywide homicide rate in Los Angeles increased by 30% (and is being attributed to a rise in gang violence), homicide within the Hollenbeck area decreased by 15%. This at least suggests that the working group process and the collection and sharing of information among agencies may be responsible for some level of proactive responses to potential incidents of violence, as opposed to purely reactive responses.

Strategic Approaches to Community Safety Initiative in Five Cities

The Strategic Approaches to Community Safety Initiative (SACSI) is a U.S. Department of Justice pilot project that follows the Boston Gun Project's strong emphasis on partnerships, knowledge-driven decision making, and ongoing strategic assessment (Coleman, Holton, Olson, Robinson, & Stewart, 1999). The project is spearheaded by U.S. Attorneys and has been implemented in five cities—Indianapolis, Indiana; Memphis, Tennessee; New Haven, Connecticut; Portland, Oregon; and Winston-Salem, North Carolina. The crime problems addressed vary across the cities and range from gun violence (Indianapolis, Portland, and Winston-Salem), to community fear (New Haven), to sexual assault (Memphis). Several of the sites have adopted pulling-levers strategies that are well enough along to discuss here. In addition, although not formally part of SACSI, U.S. Attorneys have spearheaded pulling-levers operations in High Point, North Carolina, and in Omaha, Nebraska. We will discuss these operations as a group.

The Indianapolis project's working group is composed of Indiana University researchers and federal, state, and local law enforcement agencies (McGarrell & Chermak, 2003). During the problem analysis phase, the researchers examined 258 homicides from 1997 and the first 8 months of 1998 and found that a majority of homicide victims (63%) and offenders (75%) had criminal and/or juvenile records. Those with a prior record often had a substantial number of arrests. The working group members followed the structured qualitative data gathering exercises used in Boston to gain insight into the nature of homicide incidents. The qualitative exercise revealed that 59% of the incidents involved "groups of known chronic offenders" and 53% involved drug-related motives such as settling business and turf disputes (McGarrell & Chermak, 2003). It is worth noting that the terminology "groups of known chronic offenders" was used because there was not a consensual definition of *gang*, and the reality of much gang activity in Indianapolis is of a relatively loose structure (McGarrell & Chermak, 2003).

The working group developed two sets of overlapping strategies. First, the most violent chronic offenders in Indianapolis were identified and targeted for heightened arrest, prosecution, and incarceration (McGarrell & Chermak, 2003). Second, the working group engaged the pulling-levers approach to reduce violent behavior by groups of known chronic offenders (McGarrell & Chermak, 2003). The strategy implemented by the Indianapolis working group closely resembled the Boston version of pulling levers. The communications strategy, however, differed in an important way. The deterrence and social services message was delivered in meetings with high-risk probationers and parolees organized by neighborhoods. Similarly, home visits to probationers and parolees were generally organized by neighborhood. As the project progressed, when a homicide or series of homicides involved certain groups or gangs, the working group attempted to target meetings, enforcement activities, and home visits on the involved groups or gangs (McGarrell & Chermak, 2003). The research team has not yet completed a formal evaluation of the intervention. However, homicides citywide in Indianapolis fell from roughly 150 a year in the 2 years preceding the intervention to 100 in the year following implementation (Edmund F. McGarrell, personal communication, March 25, 2001). In addition, a preliminary analysis following an application of the pulling-levers approach in the Brightwood neighborhood suggests that the approach significantly reduced gun assaults and robbery incidents in the targeted area (McGarrell & Chermak, 2003).

High Point, North Carolina, is a city that began experiencing a quite severe street homicide problem in the mid-1990s. Working with Kennedy, U.S. Attorney Walter Holton, members of his staff, and members of the High Point police department determined that the problem fit the groups-of-chronic-offenders mold and instituted a pulling-levers strategy in late 1998. The High Point working group was quite robust and, in addition to the usual state and local actors, included very active participation by ATF, FBI, and DEA. As in Indianapolis, High Point followed a mixed strategy that focused both on repeat drug, gun, and violent offenders and on violent groups. The working group identified several hundred violent offenders and held a series of meetings with them; these meetings were formatted such that community representatives and service providers met privately with the offenders first, then enforcement representatives met with them subsequently. The operation was launched in the wake of the federal prosecution of a repeat gun offender, a prosecution that

was then heavily "marketed" to offenders through the meeting process. In addition, as violence occurred in the community, the groups involved were identified and targeted for enforcement.

Homicides in High Point had numbered 14 (5 firearm) in 1994; 11 (9 firearm) in 1995; 11 (8 firearm) in 1996; 16 (11 firearm) in 1997; and 14 (14 firearm) in 1998. After the operation began in late 1998, homicides fell to 5 (2 firearm) in 1999 and 9 (8 firearm) in 2000. According to High Point officials and the U.S. Attorney's office, none of the 1999 or 2000 homicides was the drug/gang type targeted by the strategy (Caren Johnson, personal communication, March 26, 2001).

The Winston-Salem operation is similar to High Point's, with an interesting elaboration. The Winston-Salem SACSI team was quite deeply focused on preventing juvenile offending. As the problem assessment proceeded, it became clear to the Winston-Salem team that juvenile offending, especially violent offending, was often the result of juveniles being incorporated into the criminal activity of older offenders, for instance as drug couriers and enforcers. Therefore, while maintaining its focus on juveniles and holding meetings with juvenile offenders, the Winston-Salem working group also sought to break this cycle by holding meetings with older offenders in which they were warned quite explicitly that incorporating juveniles into their illegal activity would result in focused state and federal enforcement attention (Coleman et al., 1999). In Winston-Salem, SACSI has focused on the four areas of the city that account for the vast majority of juvenile violent offenses. In these four areas, since the implementation of the SACSI strategy in September 1999, the city has seen a 36% reduction in juvenile violent offenses and a 60% reduction in the use of firearms by juveniles (Caren Johnson, personal communication, March 26, 2001).

Stockton, California

Beginning in mid-1997, criminal justice agencies in Stockton began experimenting with the pulling-levers approach to address a sudden increase in youth homicide. The Stockton Police Department and other local, state, and federal law enforcement agencies believed that most of the youth violence problem was driven by gang conflicts and that the pulling levers approach used in Boston might be effective in reducing Stockton's gang violence problem. The strategy was implemented by the Stockton Police Department's Gang Street Enforcement Team and grew into what is now known as Operation Peacekeeper as more agencies joined the partnership. The Peacekeeper intervention is managed by a working group of line-level criminal justice practitioners; social service providers also participate in the working group process as appropriate. As street gang violence erupts or when it comes to the attention of a working group member that gang violence is imminent, the working group follows the Boston model by sending a direct message that gang violence will not be tolerated and pulling all available enforcement levers to prevent violence while continuing communications and providing social services and opportunities to gang members who want them.

To better document the nature of youth homicide in Stockton, the working group retained Harvard University researchers to conduct an analysis of youth (age 24 and under) homicide incidents between 1997 and 1999 (see Braga, Thomson, & Wakeling, 2000). The research revealed that many offenders and victims involved in youth homicide incidents had noteworthy criminal histories and criminal justice system involvement. Following the same qualitative research methods used in Boston and elsewhere, gang-related conflicts were identified as the motive in 48% of the youth homicides. The research analysis also revealed that there were 44 active gangs with a total known membership of 2,100 individuals. Most conflicts among Stockton gangs fall into three broad categories: Asian gang beefs, Hispanic gang beefs, and African American gang beefs. Within each broad set of ethnic antagonisms, particular gangs form alliances with other gangs. Conflicts among Asian gangs were among clusters of different gangs composed mostly of Laotian and Cambodian youth. Conflicts among Hispanic gangs mainly involved a very violent rivalry between Norteño gangs from Northern California and Sureño gangs from Southern California. African American gangs tended to form fewer alliances and divided along well-known Blood and Crip lines. The research also suggested that Operation Peacekeeper was a promising approach to preventing gang violence as youth

homicides in Stockton dropped by 54% between 1997 (24) and 1998 (11) and remained low in 1999 (14).

Key Elements of the New Approaches

The available research evidence suggests that these new approaches to the strategic prevention of gang and group-involved violence have generated promising results. It is important to recognize that, with the exception of the Boston experience, rigorous evaluations of the interventions implemented in the various cities have not been completed. As such, these promising results should be interpreted with caution. Nevertheless, there are some core elements of this approach that seem to be the key ingredients in their apparent success. These key elements are worth delineating here.

Recognizing that violence problems are concentrated among groups of chronic offenders who are often, but not always, gang involved. Research has demonstrated that the character of criminal and disorderly youth gangs and groups varies widely both within cities and across cities (see, e.g., Curry, Ball, & Fox, 1994; Maxson & Klein, 1995). The diverse findings on the nature of criminally active groups and gangs in the jurisdictions described in this chapter certainly support this assertion. The research also suggests that the terminology used to describe the types of groups involved in urban violence matters less than their behavior. Gangs, their nature, and their behavior remain central questions for communities, police, and scholars. At the same time, where violence prevention and public safety are concerned, the gang question is not the central one (Kennedy, 2001). The more important observation is that urban violence problems are in large measure concentrated among groups of chronic offenders and the dynamics between and within these groups (Kennedy, 2001). This is an old observation in criminology, and is essentially well known among line law enforcement personnel, prosecutors, probation and parole officers, and the like. These new strategies offer a way of responding to this reality without setting the usually unattainable goals of eliminating chronic offending and/or eliminating criminal gangs and groups.

At the core of much group and gang vio-

lence is a dynamic or self-reinforcing positive feedback mechanism. The research findings indicate that groups of chronic offenders are locked in a self-sustaining dynamic of violence often driven by fear, "respect" issues, and vendettas. The promising reductions observed in the cities engaging these strategic crime prevention frameworks suggest that the "firebreak hypothesis" may be right. If this cycle of violence among these groups can be interrupted, perhaps a new equilibrium at a lower level of risk and violence can be established. This may be one explanation for the rather dramatic impacts apparently associated with what are in fact relatively modest interventions.

The utility of the pulling-levers approach. The pulling-levers deterrence strategy at the heart of these new approaches was designed to influence the behavior, and the environment, of the groups of chronic offenders that were identified as the core of the cities' violence problems. The pulling-levers approach attempted to prevent gang and group-involved violence by making these groups believe that consequences would follow violence and gun use and that they would, therefore, choose to change their behavior. A key element of the strategy was the delivery of a direct and explicit "retail deterrence" message to a relatively small target audience regarding what kind of behavior would provoke a special response and what that response would be.

Several of these sites have modified Boston's basic approach in interesting ways. Indianapolis and the North Carolina sites have incorporated a focus on individual dangerous offenders as well as on groups, and Indianapolis has a focus on neighborhoods as well. Indianapolis has also extended the strategy to felons returning from prison, warning them as part of the release process about the new enforcement regime to which they will be exposed. Winston-Salem has incorporated an intriguing attempt to prevent juveniles from being drawn into criminal activity. Those sites using Boston-style offender call-ins have developed their own variations on that theme, whereas Minneapolis and the Boyle Heights project in Los Angeles have relied on one-on-one outreach to their target populations. In addition, none of the sites have working groups or sets of partners that look exactly like Boston's or like each other's. This all fits with the original idea behind the Boston project and the pulling-levers idea, which was that the intervention and the logic behind the intervention were both flexible, open to adaptation according to local conditions, local preferences, and the strengths and weaknesses of variable sets of partners (Kennedy, 1997, 2001).

Drawing on practitioner knowledge to understand violence problems. The experiences, observations, local knowledge, and historical perspectives of police officers, street workers, and others with routine contact with offenders, communities, and criminal networks represent an underutilized resource for describing, understanding, and crafting interventions aimed at crime problems (Kennedy et al., 1997). The semi-structured qualitative research performed by the academics in these initiatives essentially refined and specified existing practitioner knowledge. Combining official data sources with street-level qualitative information helped to paint a dynamic, real-life picture of the violence problem.

Convening an interagency working group with a locus of responsibility. Criminal justice agencies work largely independent of each other, often at cross-purposes, often without coordination, and often in an atmosphere of distrust and dislike (Kennedy, 2001). This is also often true of different elements operating within agencies. The ability of the cities to deliver a meaningful violence prevention intervention was created by convening an interagency working group of line-level personnel with decision-making power that could assemble a wide range of incentives and disincentives. It was also important to place on the group a locus of responsibility for reducing violence. Prior to the creation of the working groups, no one in these cities was responsible for developing and implementing an overall strategy for reducing violence.

Researcher involvement in an action-oriented enterprise. The activities of the research partners in these initiatives depart from the traditional research and evaluation roles usually played by academics (see, e.g., Sherman, 1991). The integrated researcher/practitioner partnerships in the working group setting more closely resembled policy analysis exercises that blend research, policy design, action, and evaluation (Kennedy & Moore, 1995). Researchers have been important assets in all of the projects described above, providing what is essentially "real-time" social science aimed at refining the working group's understanding of the problem; creating information products for both strategic and tactical use; testing—often in a very elementary, but important, fashion—prospective intervention ideas; and maintaining a focus on clear outcomes and the evaluation of performance. They have begun to produce accounts both of basic findings and of intervention designs and implementation processes that will be helpful to other jurisdictions. In addition, in several sites, researchers played important roles in organizing the projects.

Conclusion

We have provided here an account of a number of related violence prevention efforts. We underscore, again, that none of these have been fully evaluated, nor have they used desirable controlled experimental designs. However, we interpret the cumulative experience described above as supportive, at this preliminary stage, of the proposition that the basic Boston approach has now been replicated, with promising results, in a number of disparate sites.

If this is true, it suggests that there was nothing particularly unique about either the implementation or the impact of Operation Ceasefire in Boston. It suggests further that the fundamental pulling-levers framework behind Ceasefire can be successfully applied in other jurisdictions; with other sets of partners; with different particular activities; and in the context of different basic types of gangs and groups. Further operational experience and more refined evaluation techniques will tell us more about these questions, as experience and analysis continue to accumulate. At the moment, however, there appears to be reason for continued optimism that serious violence by gangs and other groups is open to direct and powerful prevention strategies.

References

Braga, A. A., & Kennedy, D. M. (2001). Reducing gang violence in Boston. In *Responding to gangs: Research and evaluation.* Washington, DC: U.S. Department of Justice, National Institute of Justice.

Braga, A. A., Kennedy, D. M., Waring, E. J., & Piehl, A. M. (2001). Problem-oriented policing, deterrence, and youth violence: An evaluation of Boston's Operation Ceasefire. *Journal of Research in Crime and Delinquency*, 38, 195–225.

Braga, A. A., Thomson, G., & Wakeling, S. (2000). *The nature of youth homicide in Stockton, California.* Unpublished report. Cambridge, MA: Harvard University, John F. Kennedy School of Government.

Coleman, V., Holton, W. C., Olson, K., Robinson, S., & Stewart, J. (1999, October). Using knowledge and teamwork to reduce crime. *National Institute of Justice Journal*, pp. 16–23.

Curry, G. D., Ball, R. A., & Fox, R. J. (1994). *Gang crime and law enforcement recordkeeping* (NIJ Research in Brief No. NCJ148345). Washington, DC: U.S. Department of Justice.

Kennedy, D. M. (1997). Pulling levers: Chronic offenders, high-crime settings, and a theory of prevention. *Valparaiso University Law Review*, 31, 449–484.

———. (1998, July). Pulling levers: Getting deterrence right. *National Institute of Justice Journal*, pp. 2–8.

———. (2001). A tale of one city: Reflections on the Boston gun project. In G. Katzmann (Ed.), *Managing youth violence.* Washington, DC: Brookings Institution.

Kennedy, D. M., & Braga, A. A. (1998). Homicide in Minneapolis: Research for problem solving. *Homicide Studies*, 2(3), 263–290.

Kennedy, D. M., Braga, A. A., & Piehl, A. M. (1997). The (un)known universe: Mapping gangs and gang violence in Boston. In D. L. Weisburd & J. T. McEwen (Eds.), *Crime mapping and crime prevention.* New York: Criminal Justice Press.

Kennedy, D. M., Braga, A. A., & Thomson, G. (2000, November). *Problem solving for homicide prevention in Baltimore.* Paper presented at the annual meeting of the American Society of Criminology, San Francisco.

Kennedy, D. M., & Moore, M. H. (1995). Underwriting the risky investment in community policing: What social science should be doing to evaluate community policing. *The Justice System Journal*, 17, 271–290.

Kennedy, D. M., Piehl, A. M., & Braga, A. A. (1996). Youth violence in Boston: Gun markets, serious youth offenders, and a use-reduction strategy. *Law and Contemporary Problems*, 59(1), 147–196.

Maxson, C. L., & Klein, M. W. (1995). Investigating gang structures. *Journal of Gang Research*, 3, 33–40.

McGarrell, E. F., & Chermak, S. (2003). Problem solving to reduce gang and drug-related violence in Indianapolis. In S. H. Decker (Ed.),

Policing gangs and youth violence. Belmont, CA: Wadsworth.

Pastore, A. L., & Maguire, K. (Eds.). (1999). *Sourcebook of criminal justice statistics, 1998.* Washington, DC: U.S. Department of Justice, Bureau of Justice Statistics.

Sherman, L. (1991). Herman Goldstein: Problem-oriented policing. *Journal of Criminal Law and Criminology, 82,* 693–702.

Tita, G. E., Riley, K. J., & Greenwood, P. (2003). From Boston to Boyle Heights: The process and prospects of a "pulling levers" strategy in a Los Angeles barrio. In S. H. Decker (Ed.), *Policing gangs and youth violence.* Belmont, CA: Wadsworth. ✦

Chapter 29
A Study of Police Gang Units in Six Cities

Vincent J. Webb
and Charles M. Katz

The proliferation of street gangs throughout the nation has led understandably to a proliferation of gang-control programs, especially among law enforcement agencies. Prominent among these have been police gang units, elite groups of antigang police specialists. The "gang cop" is a new fixture in many departments. Webb and Katz have been at the forefront of efforts to understand and evaluate the place of gang units in gang-control efforts. In this chapter, the authors describe these units in a number of contrasting settings, including several different conceptions of why they developed as they did; there are different rationalities behind gang unit formation. The different functions that gang units serve are outlined; uniformity of approach is not found, suggesting a good deal of uncertainty about how gang units might best respond to gang problems.

The growth of gangs during the last two decades has been accompanied by the development and growth of specialized law enforcement responses to gangs. Traditionally, the police response to gangs and gang-related problems was to assign responsibility for gang control to existing units such as patrol, juvenile bureaus, community relations, investigations, and crime prevention (Huff, 1990; Needle and Staple-

ton, 1983). However, in the 1980s many police departments established specialized units for gang control, including what is commonly referred to as the police gang unit. By 1999 over 55 percent of all large American police departments reported that they had a specialized gang unit for addressing local gang problems (Bureau of Justice Statistics, 1999). A police gang unit is a "secondary or tertiary functional division within a police organization, which has at least one sworn officer whose sole function is to engage in gang control efforts" (Katz, Maguire, and Roncek, 2000: 14). Therefore, by their very nature police gang units are specialized, have unique administrative policies and procedures, often distinct from those of the rest of the department, and have a front line of "experts" who are uniquely trained and dedicated to perform specific and focused duties. . . .

[T]his chapter reviews the extant research on police gang control efforts and makes use of data obtained from several ongoing research projects designed to examine the police response to gangs. In particular, we rely heavily on data that we collected as part of three federally funded studies that examined the police response to gangs in six cities: Albuquerque, New Mexico; Inglewood, California; Junction City (a pseudonym); Las Vegas, Nevada; Mesa, Arizona; and Phoenix, Arizona (Katz, 1997; Katz, Webb, and Haar, 1998; Katz, Webb, and Schaefer, 2000).

These sites provide several opportunities to examine police gang control efforts. First, as seen in Table 29.1, the sites provide the opportunity to examine the police response to gangs in cities of varying size, with different-sized gang units and diverse gang problems. Second, the selected sites provide the opportunity to examine a variety of organizational configurations, allowing us to examine the implications of different configurations in shaping responses to the gang problem. Third, most of the sites studied are located in the Southwest region of the United States. While researchers have found that police departments across the country are claiming to have a gang problem, police departments in the Southwest have been found to be significantly more likely to respond to their gang problem by establishing specialized police gang units (Curry et al., 1992).

All of the studies involved a combination

Table 29.1
Site Characteristics

	Albuquerque	Inglewood	Junction City	Las Vegas	Mesa	Phoenix
Size of gang unit (sworn)	4	4	10	50	13	42
Size of city	431,027	113,015	351,745	929,940	350,592	1,172,538
UCR Part I crimes (per 1,000)	111.2	49.6	72.4	63.4	77.3	96.1
No. of gangs	100	33	15	201	25	336
No. of gang members	5,000	—	2,400	6,905	1,500	6,439

of observations of the gang unit officers and interviews with gang unit officers and key stakeholders from other parts of the police organization, the criminal justice system, and the community. Combined, these three studies involved a total of about 700 hours of observation, 62 interviews with gang unit officers, 21 interviews with police managers, and 120 interviews with stakeholders (for example, police agency personnel, other criminal justice officials, school administrators, and special interest group administrators). As part of these three studies we also reviewed official police documents and newspaper articles from local newspapers. In all, 237 official police documents and 349 newspaper articles were reviewed.

Our purpose in this chapter is to examine the nature, characteristics, and scope of police gang control efforts through a consideration of police gang units. The first section explores the establishment of police gang units and considers theoretical and policy rationales for police gang units as well as theoretical explanations of their growth. The second section reviews gang unit functions and patterns of functional specialization. . . .

Theoretical and Policy Rationales for the Establishment of Specialized Police Gang Units

Spergel and Curry (1993), from a survey of 254 professionals in 45 cities, identified five strategies that are used by communities to respond to gangs. They reported that suppression techniques employed by the police were the most commonly cited strategy. Some have noted that police gang units are perhaps the clearest embodiment of the gang suppression approach (Klein, 1995a: 161).

Under the suppression approach, Klein (1995a) argues, enforcement officials see their primary responsibility as responding to gang street crimes. In other words, officials are to deal with the crimes that are most likely to come to the attention of the public, such as assaults, drive-by shootings, drug sales, and graffiti. In turn, prevention and treatment strategies are not given high priority. In fact, police officials see these activities as outside the scope of their responsibility. Suppression strategy is based on deterrence theory. The idea is that swifter, severer, and more certain punishment will lead to a reduction of gang-related activity by those currently in gangs, as well as to a reduction in the number of individuals wishing to participate in gangs and gang behavior in the future. Accordingly, Klein argues that the "underlying assumption of all this is that the targets of suppression, the gang members and potential gang members, will respond 'rationally' to suppression efforts [and] will weigh the consequences of gang activity, redress the balance between cost and benefit, and withdraw from gang activity" (1995a: 160).

To understand the current response to the gang problem, it is helpful to first understand several developments that have shaped and justified the shift toward suppression-oriented strategies. First, policymakers no longer believe that the social intervention approaches of the 1960s and 1970s are a successful way to deal with the gang problem. Although this strategy took many forms, it was based on the assumption that gang membership is the by-product of a socially deprived community and that the values and norms of gang youths can be changed by reorienting the youths' attitudes, values, and expectations toward mainstream society. Social intervention approaches frequently relied on a detached worker who was assigned to work with gangs and gang members to steer youth away from delinquency and encourage them to pursue more socially acceptable activities such as athletic teams, club activities, and fund-raisers (President's Commission on Law Enforcement and Administration of Justice, 1967). However, many have argued that this approach did not lead to reduced delinquent activity and may in fact have led to increased group cohesiveness, which in turn may have led to increased delinquency. Additionally, some of these critics have claimed that the assignment of a caseworker increased the local reputation of particular gangs, which helped to attract new members and led to a growing gang problem in areas employing detached workers (Klein, 1971; Spergel, 1995).

Second, many believe that the scope and nature of the gang problem has dramatically changed over past years. In 1983 only 45 percent of cities with populations of 100,000 or more reported a gang problem (Needle and Stapleton, 1983), whereas by 1992 this figure had risen to over 90 percent (Curry, Ball, and Fox, 1994). These studies illustrate that gangs are no longer just a big-city problem but are also becoming prevalent in many small and medium-sized cities (Office of Juvenile Justice and Delinquency Prevention, 2000). A number of studies have also found that gang members are disproportionately responsible for delinquency, crime, drug use, and drug dealing when compared to non-gang members (Howell, 1999; Katz, Webb, and Schaefer, 2000; Klein, 1995a, b; Spergel, 1995). As a result, many local officials see the gang problem as only getting worse in the future, and believe that the only way to stop the gang problem is by removing gang members from society through the criminal justice system.

The third reason for the shift to suppression-oriented strategies follows from the disenchantment with social intervention strategies and the belief that the gang problem has grown. Surveys of the public have illustrated that residents are fearful of the growing gang problem (Katz, 1990). Citizen surveys have consistently shown that one of the top priorities of the police should be dealing with gang-related problems (Webb and Katz, 1997). As a result, state and federal legislators have responded to public demands by allocating additional dollars toward suppression-oriented interventions (Klein, 1995a; McCorkle and Miethe, 1998). For example, many municipal and state agencies have received additional funding—usually through federal grants for inter-agency task forces, information tracking systems, and overtime pay for the police—to target hard-core gang members. Additionally, with the implementation of community policing in many police agencies, public pressures to address gang problems have forced many departments to make gang control efforts a top priority.

The Growth and Development of Police Gang Units

In 1999, the Law Enforcement and Management Administrative Statistics (LEMAS) survey reported that among large agencies with 100 or more sworn officers, special gang units existed in 56 percent of all municipal police departments, 50 percent of all sheriffs' departments, 43 percent of all county police agencies, and 20 percent of all state law enforcement agencies (Bureau of Justice Statistics, 1999: Table C).[1] These findings lead to an estimate of approximately 360 police gang units in the country.[2] The recentness of this phenomenon can be further seen by the fact that over 85 percent of specialized gang units have been established in the past 10 years (Katz, Maguire, and Roncek, 2000). . . .

Research on the rise and development of specialized police gang units suggests that there are four theoretical explanations for their creation: contingency theory, constructionist theory, resource dependency theory, and institutional theory (see Katz, 2001; Katz, Maguire, and Roncek, 2000).

Contingency Theory: The Creation of Police Gang Units as a Result of Rational Considerations. Contingency theory is based on the notion that organizations are developed and structured to achieve specific goals (Lawrence and Lorsch, 1967; Mastrofski, 1998). It is believed that some organizational structures and operational strategies are more effective than others in achieving established goals. Successful organizations act purposely, continually adapting to varying contingencies in their environment in an effort to maximize effectiveness (Mastrofski and Ritti, 2000). Those organizations that do not adjust their structures and strategies to effectively address contingencies in their environment will fail to achieve their goals and eventually will not survive and will be replaced by another, more effective organization (Ogle, 1998: 45). Therefore, contingency theory holds that police organizational behavior is influenced by real problems to which a department must respond if it is to goals such as crime control.

From this perspective, police gang units are created as a rational response to the growth of gangs and gang-related crime. Many researchers, police officials, and policymakers have claimed that the relatively rapid development and growth of police gang units is more or less "natural," given the spread of gangs and gang members across America's communities (Burns and Deakin, 1989; Huff and McBride, 1990; Jackson and McBride, 1985; Weisel and Painter, 1997). They point out that by 1994, 88 percent of America's largest cities and 56 percent of medium-sized cities were described as having a gang crime problem (Curry, Ball, and Decker, 1996). As Huff (1990) explains, "Gangs pose a significant challenge to law enforcement agencies as well as to citizens, schools, and the quality of life in our communities" (p. 401).

Others have more specifically argued that special police gang units have been created as a consequence of the growing amount of gang crime, including drug trafficking, that has accompanied the rise in gangs and gang members (Burns and Deakin, 1989; Jackson and McBride, 1985; Weisel and Painter, 1997). In Chicago between 1987 and 1994 the number of gang-related homicides increased 500 percent, and in Los Angeles County they doubled over the same time period (Maxson, 1999). Likewise, Curry, Ball, and Decker (1996) estimated that nationally gang crime incidents increased eight- to twelvefold between 1991 and 1993. Some police officials maintain that the rise in gang-related crime was the result of gang members migrating to neighborhoods outside their usual "turf" for the purpose of selling drugs to increase profits, which in turn resulted in increased violent conflict between gangs (Brantley and DiRosa, 1994; Jackson and McBride, 1985; Weisel and Painter, 1997). Some researchers have also suggested that with the increase in gang drug sales, gangs have become more organized and have recruited more violent members in an effort to protect their marketplace (Skolnick, 1990; see also Fagan, 1996).

Accordingly, many police officials, policymakers, and researchers maintain that the emergence of specialized gang units is a police response (the gang unit) to an environmental contingency (the community gang problem) (Rush, 1996; Weisel and Painter, 1997). They explain that specialized police gang units have been created as a result of *rational considerations* on the part of police agencies, that their organizations are faced with *real* gang problems, and that, through specialization, they can more effectively and efficiently control gang-related crime.

Constructionist Theory: The Creation of Police Gang Units as a Result of Moral Panic. Much of the academic research (for example, Archibold and Meyer, 1999; McCorkle and Miethe, 1998; Zatz, 1987) that has examined the establishment of specialized police gang units has used a moral panic or a social constructionist perspective to understand the police response to gangs. Constructionist theory attempts to understand social problems through activities and assertions of claims makers who bring issues to the attention of a large number of people (Best, 1995). Advocates of the theory argue that when attempting to understand a response to a social problem, what is important is not the objective threat of the social problem, but rather what claims makers say about the threat (McCorkle and Miethe, 1998).

Claims makers present the existence of a social problem by creating and promoting images that are consistent with characteristics that are popularly associated with the social problem in an effort to validate that the problem actually exists. These images are often exaggerated for the purpose of gaining the recognition and attention of the public. Public concerns can be cemented by authority figures who lend their expertise to verify the existence of the social problem. Once this occurs, if the claims have been exaggerated, a moral panic can ensue in which the response to the problem far exceeds the objective threat of the problem (Jenkins, 1994).

Several researchers examining the police response to gangs have argued that the establishment of specialized police gang units has not been the consequence of police departments responding to contingencies in their environment. Rather, these researchers view the establishment of specialized police gang units as a response to a moral panic. For example, Zatz (1987) examined the police response to gangs in Phoenix, Arizona using a variety of data obtained from community members, media reports, and court records. She reported that there was not a serious gang problem in Phoenix at the time that the gang unit was established, but rather, police officials constructed the gang problem in an effort to obtain federal resources. She argued that the police department, along with the media, constructed an image of gang members as dangerous, crime-prone, Chicano youth—an image that fit with the Anglo community's notion of gang members. At the same time, police officials claimed that if they were not given the resources to address the gang problem, it was sure to escalate. Official court data and interviews with social service agents indicated that gang members did not pose a significant threat to the community, and that the police department's claims of a serious gang problem were exaggerated.

McCorkle and Miethe (1998) examined legislative records, media reports, and official crime data in Las Vegas, Nevada to assess whether the city's response to gangs was the consequence of a moral panic. After examining the objective threat posed by gangs, the authors reported gang members accounted for a relatively small proportion of arrests for violent crimes and an even smaller proportion of drug arrests in the city. When describing the factors that led to the moral panic, the authors reported that at the time the specialized police gang unit was established, the police department had a tarnished public image and was in desperate need of additional resources. Accordingly, McCorkle and Miethe suggest that police officials in the Las Vegas Police Department linked national reports of a growing gang problem to local concerns of increasing crime in order to divert public attention away from problems within the police department and to justify an infusion of additional financial resources into the department.

Institutional Theory: The Creation of Police Gang Units as a Result of Institutional Considerations. Institutional theory is based on the idea that organizations are created and shaped by their institutional environment. The institutional environment of an organization is composed of powerful actors, referred to as sovereigns, who have the capacity to influence organizational policies, decisions, and resources (Crank and Langworthy, 1992; DiMaggio and Powell, 1991; Meyer and Rowan, 1977). The ideas

and values shared by sovereigns in an organization's environment are referred to as myths. In this context, myths can be conceptualized as "an ideology made up of sets of interwoven beliefs that represent our agreed-upon meaning for things in the social world that we really do not empirically understand" (Ogle, 1998: 47). Accordingly, from the institutional perspective, organizational structures and operational activities do not necessarily reflect rationality. That is, organizations do not create structures or engage in operational activities because they are necessarily more effective. Rather, structures are adopted and strategies are embraced because they reflect the values and beliefs of the institutional environment (Meyer and Rowan, 1977).

Katz's recent (2001) study of the development of a police gang unit in a midwestern city relies heavily on institutional theory to explain the police response to gangs. In the police department studied, Katz found that the gang unit was created under pressure from important community stakeholders. The creation of the gang unit was an attempt to maintain the organization's legitimacy and communicate to its institutional environment that it was responding to the local gang problem. Furthermore, he found that once the gang unit was created it was often required to incorporate competing ideas and beliefs into its organizational structure and operational strategy to communicate an image of operational effectiveness when it otherwise was unable to demonstrate success.

Resource Dependency Theory: The Creation of Police Gang Units as a Result of Financial Considerations. At the core of resource dependency theory is the notion that organizations need resources to survive, and that to obtain resources they must actively engage in exchanges with other organizations (Oliver, 1990; Pfeffer and Salancik, 1978). To ensure survival and resources, organizations continually adapt strategically to their environment to guarantee the continued flow of resources. Organizations actively scan their environment, and, if an opportunity arises, they may make structural and/or operational changes in an effort to obtain resources and ensure survival (Banaszak-Holl, Zinn, and Mor, 1996). According to this theory, organizations are not simply passive actors, but rather they have the capacity to manipulate their environment to secure needed resources (Pfeffer and Salancik, 1978).

While resource dependency theory has played a minor role in understanding police organizations in general, and specialized police gang units specifically, there is some evidence that the theory might be helpful in understanding the creation of police gang units. In particular, some gang scholars have argued that police departments have created gang units to secure financial resources. In particular, they have pointed out that agencies that can demonstrate a gang problem are more likely to obtain federal grant dollars (Bursik and Grasmick, 1995). Likewise, other researchers have found that police agencies that claim a gang problem receive significantly higher levels of municipal funding than agencies that do not claim a gang problem. Thus, some gang researchers have argued that gang units have been created to signal to a community that it has a gang problem in order to justify additional resources (McCorkle and Miethe, 1998; Zatz, 1987).

Katz, Maguire, and Roncek (2000) found partial support for this claim in their macrolevel examination of the factors that influence police departments to create gang units. They analyzed survey data obtained from about 300 police agencies and controlled for both organizational and environmental factors. They reported that police departments that received funding for gang control efforts were significantly more likely to have established a specialized police gang unit than those agencies that did not receive funding. While noting that there might be a number of explanations for this finding, they posited that some of the gang units were created prior to receiving external funding for the purpose of justifying the need for more resources, as found by Zatz (1987) and McCorkle and Meithe (1998).

Police Gang Unit Functions and Specialization

Police gang units generally engage in one or more of four principal functions: intelligence, enforcement/suppression, investigations, and prevention (Huff and McBride, 1990). The relative emphasis placed on each of these functions varies from one department to the next. Some gang units are single-function units and engage in only one activity—for example, intelligence or sup-

pression. Other units engage in more than one of these functions, while others are very comprehensive and carry out all of these functions, which is the approach recommended by Huff and McBride (1990). How police agencies organize their resources to carry out these functions also varies from one department to the next. In some police departments the gang unit is a stand-alone bureau with status equivalent to other bureaus such as patrol and investigations, while in other departments the gang unit is a unit within a larger bureau such as the organized crime bureau. In the following section we briefly consider some of the different functions and organizational patterns characteristic of police gang units.

Intelligence Activities

Both police officials and researchers have identified intelligence gathering and the development and maintenance of gang tracking systems and databases as one of the most important functions carried out by specialized gang units (Bureau of Justice Assistance, 1997; Jackson and McBride, 1985; Katz, Webb, and Schaefer, 2000). Our research in the police departments of Albuquerque, Inglewood, Junction City, Las Vegas, Mesa, and Phoenix indicates that the gang units in each of these departments performed an intelligence function. This finding is consistent with that of Klein (1995b), who found that intelligence gathering, as opposed to enforcement, investigation, or prevention, was the primary function in 83 percent of the gang units across the country.

Although nearly every gang unit engages in some form of intelligence gathering, the importance of this function to the gang unit and to its respective department varies from one department to the next. For example, in Inglewood, purported to be the original home of the Bloods and Crips, intelligence gathering and dissemination is the sole activity performed by the department's gang unit. Key stakeholders in that department, such as detectives working in the robbery and burglary units, attribute substantial value to gang unit intelligence in supporting the investigative process. Information such as monikers (street names), legal names, addresses, known associates, photographs, and gang affiliation are useful in conducting investigations. Detectives are quick to cite instances in which intelligence from the gang unit was instrumental in solving a crime and leading to an arrest. On the other hand, the fact that a gang unit has an intelligence function does not necessarily mean that the function plays a central role within the unit. For example, in Las Vegas we found that a large gang unit carried out suppression, investigation, and intelligence functions. However, it was clear that in comparison to intelligence, suppression and investigation activities were given top priority and were thought to be of greater importance to the functioning of the gang unit by the gang unit's officers. Relatively little emphasis was placed on the unit's computerized gang intelligence database, in part because there were few officers who could actually use the database. That gang unit's stakeholders articulated the need for good intelligence, but in contrast to Inglewood, for example, they were critical of the general unavailability and lack of access to information thought to be contained in the intelligence system.

Gang unit stakeholders in Albuquerque reaffirmed the importance of the intelligence function when they tied their assessment of the gang unit's value directly to the amount of information that the unit provided to other units. Stakeholders in patrol and area command units recalled that, in the early days, the original gang unit was valuable to the department because it was a dependable source of intelligence on gangs and gang members. However, it appears that as the unit became more autonomous and institutionalized, it focused less on intelligence and more on suppression, and as a result stakeholders tended to devalue the unit's contribution to gang control efforts. For stakeholders in Albuquerque, like those in the other departments we have studied, the gang unit's most valuable commodity is information gathered and shared as part of its intelligence function.

Suppression/Enforcement Activities

Suppression and enforcement gang unit activities are those most likely to capture the imagination of the public and the media as well as of police officers looking for action on the streets. Whereas the intelligence function and the sharing of information gives value to gang unit activities and legitimizes the existence of the unit from the perspective of many departmental stakeholders, it is suppression/enforcement that legitimizes the unit in the eyes of the public and the media, and gives them confidence that the unit is actively engaging in enforcement efforts directed at gangs and gang crime.

Suppression activities in the cities studied were typically restricted to directed patrol in known gang areas—meaning minority public housing districts as well as parks and parking lots that gang members were believed to frequent. Many of the officers explained that patrolling gang areas allows them to keep an eye on gang members and gang activity, and at the same time provides them with the opportunity to develop personal relationships with gang members for the purpose of establishing a thorough intelligence network.

Suppression activities are of central value in the gang unit's work group culture, even though the amount of time actually spent on such activities can vary immensely from one gang unit to the next. The one exception to the centrality of suppression in gang unit ethos is the situation where the unit performs a single nonsuppression function such as intelligence, as we found in Inglewood. The gang units in Las Vegas, Mesa, and Phoenix stand in marked contrast to Inglewood. Although they have responsibility for intelligence, most of their resources are focused on enforcement activities. Compared to intelligence gathering, suppression activities are highly visible, and when covered by the media they demonstrate that the department is combating the local gang problem.

We found that while most of the gang units emphasized enforcement as a core function of the gang unit, the amount of time spent engaging in suppression activities varied across the departments. For example, we found that members of the gang unit in Albuquerque, Las Vegas, and Phoenix on average spent over two hours per eight-hour shift on enforcement activities and had a relatively high number of enforcement-related contacts (for example, over two per eight-hour shift). However, observations of the Junction City gang unit indicated that the officers spent relatively little time on enforcement activities and had few contacts with gang members. Specifically, we found that the gang unit officers averaged only about 60 minutes per shift on enforcement-related activities and averaged only one contact for every 16 hours of work.

Criminal Investigation Activities

The gang units that we studied devoted relatively few resources and little time carrying out criminal investigation activities. The most common involvement in criminal investigations tended to be indirect and performed largely as part of the intelligence function. As was previously mentioned, detectives in most of the sites studied were quick to point out the value and use of information provided by the gang intelligence unit in solving cases involving gang members. As a consequence, gang unit officers were occasionally found to be called in by other specialized investigative units to assist in the investigation of crimes involving gang members.

In two of the six sites, Las Vegas and Phoenix, the gang units had primary responsibility for investigating all "serious" gang-motivated crimes with the exception of homicide, kidnapping, and sexual assault. Gang unit officers in these units maintained that their expertise with gangs put them in a unique position to investigate and solve crimes. The officers also believed that it was essential for the unit to be involved in gang-related investigations in order to gather worthwhile and timely intelligence. For these reasons the Las Vegas Metropolitan Police Department's gang unit wanted investigative responsibility for gang-motivated homicides as well. However, the homicide bureau wanted to retain investigative responsibility, maintaining that their crime-specific expertise was required to investigate and solve homicides— gang motivated or not.

Interestingly, Klein, Gordon, and Maxson's (1985) study of gang and non-gang homicide investigations carried out by the Los Angeles County Sheriff's Department (LASD) and the Los Angeles Police Department (LAPD) bears directly on this issue. They found that in LASD cases investigative outcomes were enhanced when the gang unit was involved, but that in LAPD cases gang unit involvement made no difference in investigative outcomes.

Prevention Activities

Nearly all of the gang units that we have observed perform some prevention function, although, with the exception of Junction City, prevention received much less priority than intelligence, suppression, or investigations. In describing gang unit activity, prevention is probably at best a residual category that includes activities other than intelligence, suppression, or investigation. Prevention, when it does occur, frequently takes the form of public education. For example, in Junction City, a city with limited gang activity, the gang unit officers were directed by departmental order to spend 25 percent of their time on educational activities. Observations of Junction City's gang unit's educational activities, such as presentations to local schools and community groups about the local gang problem, indicated that they were largely performed in order to gain support and help legitimize the unit's existence. Public educational appearances increased awareness of the unit and "promoted an image of operational effectiveness" (Katz, 2001: 32). Public education activities were found to provide a forum for the gang unit to convince the unconvinced that there is a gang problem that justifies the establishment and maintenance of a specialized gang unit.

Interestingly, none of the gang units studied participated in the best-known prevention effort, the Gang Resistance Education and Training (GREAT) program. Instead, in the departments studied we found that the community relations unit or bureau conducted these types of formalized prevention efforts. When we asked officers in the gang units why their units were not responsible for these prevention efforts, they stated that while they believed that these activities were worthwhile and "should be performed by someone in the department," they should not be the responsibility of the gang unit. Officers in all of the units studied agreed that enforcement-related activities should be the primary focus of the unit and not prevention or education-related activities. Some of the officers pointed out that such activities conflict with expectations of the purpose of the gang unit, while others stated that the unit's resources were already strained and that they could not afford to be distracted from their "real job" of combating gang-related crime.

Patterns of Specialization in Police Gang Units

Police gang units generally can be placed along a continuum of complexity based on the number of different functions that a unit performs. At one end of the continuum is the single-function gang unit, which focuses on one activity such as intelligence. As was mentioned previously, the Inglewood, California gang unit is an example of this type. Inglewood's unit consists of four officers who are assigned to collect, maintain, and disseminate gang intelligence. Further along the continuum is a somewhat more complex pattern of specialization characteristic of multiple-function gang units. This type of gang unit tends to perform two or three different functions such as intelligence and suppression or intelligence and prevention, with one of the functions being primary and the other secondary. Here we define the primary function as the focal activity of the unit and the one on which most of the unit's efforts and resources are expended. The secondary function usually receives far less attention and resources and is viewed as being less important by gang unit officers. The Phoenix Police Department's gang unit is a good example of this type of unit. This unit engages in a combination of suppression, investigation, and intelligence activities, with emphasis placed on suppression. At the other end of the continuum, opposite the single-function gang unit, is the comprehensive unit, or a gang unit that performs intelligence, suppression/enforcement, investigation, and prevention, with each of these functions receiving differing levels of effort and resource investment. The Junction City unit is an example of a comprehensive gang unit.

This continuum of gang unit complexity based on specialization should be seen as a schematic, with different gang units placed at different points along the continuum. In reality, none of the gang units that we have studied fits one of the three points on the continuum perfectly; rather, each approximates a type. For example, although Inglewood's gang unit is considered to be a single-function unit, there are occasions when the unit will assist other units with suppression or investigative activity. Of all of the gang units observed, the Junction City unit came closest to approximating the comprehensive unit. Katz (2001) provides the following details on the formally assigned activities of that unit.

> Gang unit officers were instructed to allocate approximately 50 percent of their time toward intelligence activities, 25 percent toward enforcement activities, and 25 percent toward educational activities. The gang unit was also recon-

figured as a support unit, and was mandated to assist other units and organizations with gang-related problems and issues (e.g., gang investigations, patrolling known gang areas). (p. 33)

In observing Junction City's gang unit activities, we found that 42 percent of the unit's time was allocated for enforcement, 24 percent for investigation, 20 percent for education, and 13 percent for intelligence (Katz, 1997).

With the exception of Inglewood, the single-function unit with responsibility for intelligence, the other gang units studied tended to place the greatest value, but not necessarily the greatest amount of effort, on suppression activities. This was the case in those departments where there was a serious gang problem (for example, Albuquerque, Las Vegas, and Phoenix), as well as those with a less serious gang problem (for example, Mesa, Junction City). We found that communities with serious gang problems present gang units with the greatest opportunities to devise and engage in suppression activities, whereas communities with less serious gang problems (for example, Junction City) present fewer such opportunities. Nevertheless, suppression is the most highly valued function among gang unit officers even in those departments with few opportunities to execute suppression activities. . . .

Toward Improving the Effectiveness of Police Gang Units

Our observation of police gang units convinces us that police organizations need to carefully reassess the organization configuration of their response to gangs as well as the investment of resources in that response. The starting point is a thoughtful and careful assessment of the local gang problem and of whether or not it is of sufficient magnitude to warrant a specialized unit to address the problem. With the possible exception of Junction City, the gang units that we have observed were in communities with substantial gang problems, and specialized gang units were a reasonable response to the local problem. However, we suspect that a substantial number of police gang units developed during the last decade were formed not in response to local gang problems, but were the result of mimetic processes (DiMaggio and Powell, 1991).

Mimetic processes occur when organizations model themselves after other organizations. DiMaggio and Powell (1991: 67–68) explain that mimetic processes may occur when (1) there is little consensus as to which organizational structures and operational activities are most efficient and effective, (2) organizational goals are unclear, or (3) the "environment creates symbolic uncertainty" (for example, is there or is there not a gang problem in our community?). The authors argue that organizations mimic others in response to uncertainty. By adopting organizational structures and operational activities that are used by organizations that are considered successful, they themselves gain legitimacy. If anything, they argue, it illustrates to the organization's institutional environment that they are trying to do something to improve the (albeit ambiguous) situation.

In other words, we suspect that many police departments have created gang units for reasons related to institutional legitimacy rather than to respond to actual contingencies in their environment. Klein (1995a, b) alludes to this point in his discussion of Sergeant Wes McBride of the Los Angeles County Sheriff's Department (LASD). Many departments across the nation have adopted the structures and strategies recommended by McBride and the LASD because of their national reputation for gang control efforts, rather than because it is a model that is appropriate for a particular jurisdiction's gang problem.

While there is evidence that some police departments are eliminating their gang units (Katz, Maguire, and Roncek, 2000), it is unclear if this is in response to a diminished local gang problem, a growing awareness of problems stemming from the decoupling of gang units, or for other reasons. One would hope that it is a reflection of careful assessments of local gang problems that have in turn led to the elimination of police gang units. However, gangs remain a problem in jurisdictions throughout the country, and therefore warrant a continued response by the police. The challenge becomes one of the reassessing present patterns of response and adjusting them to improve their effectiveness.

Notes

1. For a discussion of validity problems relevant to specialized units and the LEMAS data, see Walker and Katz (1995).
2. The estimate of 360 gang units was determined as follows: 56 percent of the 454 police departments (254), 50 percent of the 167 sheriffs' offices (83), 43 percent of the 30 county police departments (13), and 20 percent of the 49 state law enforcement agencies (10). A specialized unit was defined in the survey as an organizational unit that has at least one person assigned on a full-time basis.

References

Archibold, Carol, and Michael Meyer. 1999. "Anatomy of a Gang Suppression Unit: The Social Construction of an Organizational Response to Gang Problems." *Police Quarterly* 2 (2): 201–224.

Banaszak-Holl, Jane, Jacqueline Zinn, and Vincent Mor. 1996. "The Impact of Market and Organizational Characteristics on Nursing Care Facility Service Innovation: A Resource Dependency Perspective." *Health Services Research* 31: 97–117.

Best, Joel, ed. 1995. *Images of Issues: Typifying Contemporary Social Problems*, 2d ed. New York: Aldine De Gruyter.

Brantley, Alan, and Andrew DiRosa. 1994. "Gangs: A National Perspective." *FBI Law Enforcement Bulletin*, May, 1–17.

Bureau of Justice Assistance. 1997. *Urban Street Gang Enforcement*. Washington, D.C.: Bureau of Justice Assistance.

Bureau of Justice Statistics. 1999. *Law Enforcement Management and Administrative Statistics, 1997: Data for Individual State and Local Agencies with 100 or More Officers*. Washington, D.C.: U.S. Government Printing Office.

Burns, Edward, and Thomas J. Deakin. 1989. "A New Investigative Approach to Youth Gangs." *FBI Law Enforcement Bulletin*, October, 20–24.

Bursik, Robert J., and Harold G. Grasmick. 1995. "Defining Gangs and Gang Behavior." In *The Modern Gang Reader*, edited by Malcolm W. Klein, Cheryl L. Maxson, and Jody Miller. Los Angeles: Roxbury.

Crank, John, and Robert Langworthy. 1992. "An Institutional Perspective of Policing." *Journal of Criminal Law and Criminology* 83: 338–363.

Curry, G. David, Richard A. Ball, and Scott H. Decker. 1996. *Estimating the National Scope of Gang Crime from Law Enforcement Data*. Washington, D.C.: National Institute of Justice.

Curry, G. David, Richard A. Ball, and Robert J. Fox. 1994. *Gang Crime and Law Enforcement*

Record Keeping. Washington, D.C.: National Institute of Justice.

Curry, G. David, Richard A. Ball, Robert J. Fox, and Darryl Stone. 1992. *National Assessment of Law Enforcement Anti-Gang Information Resources. Final Report.* Washington, D.C.: National Institute of Justice.

DiMaggio, Paul, and Walter Powell. 1991. "The Iron Cage Revisited: Institutional Isomorphism and Collective Rationality in Organizational Fields." In *The New Institutionalism in Organizational Analysis,* edited by Walter Powell and Paul DiMaggio. Chicago: University of Chicago Press.

Fagan, Jeffery. 1996. "Gangs, Drugs, and Neighborhood Change." In *Gangs in America,* 2d ed., edited by C. Ronald Huff, 39–74. Thousand Oaks, Calif.: Sage.

Howell, James. 1999. "Youth Gang Homicides: A Literature Review." *Crime and Delinquency* 45 (2): 208–241.

Huff, C. Ronald. 1990. *Gangs in America.* Newbury Park, Calif.: Sage.

Huff, C. Ronald, and Wesley D. McBride. 1990. "Gangs and the Police." In *Gangs in America,* edited by C. Ronald Huff. Newbury Park, Calif.: Sage.

Jackson, Robert K., and Wesley D. McBride. 1985. *Understanding Street Gangs.* Sacramento, Calif.: Custom Publishing.

Jenkins, Philip. 1994. *Using Murder: The Social Construction of Serial Homicide.* New York: Aldine De Gruyter.

Katz, Charles M. 1997. "Police and Gangs: A Study of a Police Gang Unit." Ph.D. diss., University of Nebraska at Omaha.

———. 2001. "The Establishment of a Police Gang Unit: An Examination of Organizational and Environmental Factors." *Criminology* 39 (1): 301–337.

Katz, Charles M., Edward R. Maguire, and Dennis Roncek. 2000. "A Macro-Level Analysis of the Creation of Specialized Police Gang Units: An Examination of Rational, Social, Threat, and Resource Dependency Perspectives." Unpublished manuscript.

Katz, Charles M., Vincent J. Webb, and Robin Haar. 1998. *The Police Response to Gangs: A Multi-Site Study.* NIJ Research in Brief submitted to the National Institute of Justice, Office of Justice Programs. Washington, D.C.: U.S. Department of Justice.

Katz, Charles M., Vincent J. Webb, and David R. Schaefer. 2000. "The Validity of Police Gang Intelligence Lists: Examining the Differences in Delinquency between Documented Gang Members and Non-documented Delinquent Youth." *Police Quarterly* 3 (4): 413–437.

Katz, Jesse. 1990. "Officers' Folksy Tactics Pay Off in Gang Domain." *Los Angeles Times,* 5 November, p. B5.

Klein, Malcolm W. 1971. *Street Gangs and Street Workers.* Englewood Cliffs, N.J.: Prentice Hall.

———. 1995a. "Attempting Gang Control by Suppression: The Misuse of Deterrence Principles." In *The Modern Gang Reader,* by Malcolm W. Klein, Cheryl L. Maxson, and Jody Miller. Los Angeles: Roxbury.

———. 1995b. *The American Street Gang.* New York: Oxford University Press.

Klein, Malcolm W., M. A. Gordon, and C. L. Maxson. 1985. Differences Between Gang and Nongang Homicides. *Criminology* 23: 209–222.

Lawrence, Paul R., and Jay W. Lorsch. 1967. *Organization and Environment: Managing Differentiation and Integration.* Boston: Harvard University.

Mastrofski, Stephen D. 1998. "Community Policing and Police Organizational Structure." In *How to Recognize Good Policing,* edited by Jean-Paul Brodeur, 161–189. Thousand Oaks, Calif.: Sage.

Mastrofski, Stephen D., and R. Richard Ritti. 2000. "Making Sense of Community Policing: A Theoretical Perspective." *Police Practice and Research* 1 (2): 183–210.

Maxson, Cheryl. 1999. "Gang Homicide." In *Homicide Studies: A Sourcebook of Social Research,* edited by Dwayne Smith and Margaret Zahn, 239–254. Newbury Park, Calif.: Sage.

McCorkle, Richard, and Terance Miethe. 1998. "The Political and Organizational Response to Gangs: An Examination of a 'Moral Panic' in Nevada." *Justice Quarterly* 15: 41–64.

Meyer, John, and Brian Rowan. 1977. "Institutionalized Organizations: Formal Structure as Myth and Ceremony." *American Journal of Sociology* 83: 340–348.

Needle, Jerome, and William Stapleton. 1983. *Police Handling of Youth Gangs. Reports of the National Juvenile Justice Assessment Centers.* Washington, D.C.: U.S. Government Printing Office.

Office of Juvenile Justice and Delinquency Prevention. 2000. *National Youth Gang Survey.* Washington, D.C.: Office of Juvenile Justice and Delinquency Prevention.

Ogle, Robin. 1998. "Theoretical Perspectives on Correctional Structure, Evaluation, and Change." *Criminal Justice Policy Review* 9: 43–51.

Oliver, C. 1990. "Determinants of Inter-organizational Relationships: Integration and Future Directions." *Academy of Management Review* 11: 241–265.

Pfeffer, Jeffery, and Gerald Salancik. 1978. *The External Control of Organizations.* New York: Harper & Row.

President's Commission on Law Enforcement and Administration of Justice. 1967. *The Chal-*

lenge of Crime in a Free Society. Washington, D.C.: U.S. Government Printing Office.

Rush, Jeffery P. 1996. "The Police Role in Dealing with Gangs." In *Gangs: A Criminal Justice Approach,* edited by J. Mitchell Miller and Jeffery P. Rush. Cincinnati: Anderson.

Skolnick, Jerome H. 1990. "The Social Structure of Street Drug Dealing." *American Journal of Police* 9: 1–41.

Spergel Irving A. 1995. *The Youth Gang Problem: A Community Approach.* New York: Oxford University Press.

Spergel, Irving A., and G. David Curry. 1993. "The National Youth Gang Survey: A Research and Development Process." In *The Gang Intervention Handbook,* edited by Arnold P. Gold-stein and C. Ronald Huff. Champaign, Ill.: Research Press.

Walker and Katz. 1995. "Less Than Meets the Eye: Police Department Bias-Crime Units." *American Journal of Police* 14: 29–47.

Webb, Vincent J., and Charles M. Katz. 1997. "Citizen Ratings of the Importance of Community Policing Activities." *Policing: An International Journal of Police Strategy and Management* 20: 7–23.

Weisel, Deborah, and Ellen Painter. 1997. *The Police Response to Gangs: Case Studies of Five Cities.* Washington, D.C.: Police Executive Research Forum.

Zatz, Marjorie S. 1987. "Chicano Youth Gangs and Crime: The Creation of a Moral Panic." *Contemporary Crises* 11: 129–158. ✦

Chapter 30
Gang Problems and Gang Programs in a National Sample of Schools

Summary

Gary D. Gottfredson
and Denise C. Gottfredson

Three primary contexts for understanding and affecting gangs are families, peers, and schools. Of these, schools have received by far the least attention in gang research. This chapter illustrates how useful such school-based research can be, especially when, as in this case, a comprehensive national sample of schools is employed. The authors present valuable data on gang member prevalence and their characteristics and behaviors. There are interesting indications that school officials may be in denial of or have inadequate recognition of gang problems in their schools. Prevention and intervention programs are widespread, but usually aim at problem behavior in general rather than at gang-specific issues. Most discouraging of all is the authors' reports of the low quality of these programs and their inadequate targeting of gang members or potential gang members.

The Survey of School-Based Gang Prevention and Intervention Programs is a study of

Reprinted from: Gary D. Gottfredson and Denise C. Gottfredson. (2001). Summary. In Gary D. Gottfredson and Denise C. Gottfredson, *Gang Problems and Gang Programs in a National Sample of Schools* (pp. ii–xi). Ellicott City, MD: Gottfredson Associates.

approaches used by schools to prevent or reduce gang involvement among schools. The study describes students' involvement with gangs, the characteristics of students who are involved with gangs (including their levels of involvement with drugs, weapons, and other forms of delinquent behavior), and the extent and correlates of gang problems in schools. The study also describes what and how much is being done in the nation's schools to prevent or reduce gang-related problems, and to assess how well these prevention and intervention activities are being done. The research identifies features of prevention and intervention activity that local schools and communities can consider to strengthen their programs.

Study Design

The study of gang prevention and intervention builds on a large-scale National Study of Delinquency Prevention in Schools (G. D. Gottfredson et al., 2000). It makes use of a national sample of schools and the activities they are undertaking to prevent problem behavior and promote safe and orderly school environments.

Five main kinds of information were collected.

1. Examples of prevention and intervention models being used in schools were collected, examined and classified to develop a comprehensive taxonomy of activities. The resulting taxonomy guided the development of other data collection instruments.

2. Principals in a national probability sample of schools were surveyed to identify activities their schools had in place to prevent or reduce gang involvement, delinquency, drug use, or other problem behavior or to promote a safe and orderly school environment. Principals also described features of their schools and reported on past experiences with the implementation of programs and on school staffing.

3. Individuals knowledgeable about prevention or intervention activities in each school (called "activity coordinators") were surveyed to obtain detailed descriptions of specific prevention activities and to describe certain features of their school. Activity coordinators

also reported about themselves and about school support and supervision for prevention activities.

4. Teachers and students in participating schools were surveyed to obtain their reports about victimization, safety, gang participation, delinquent behavior, school orderliness, and other aspects of school climate. Generally, all teachers in participating schools were sampled, and a sufficient number of students were sampled to produce an estimated 50 respondents per school.

5. Principals were surveyed for a second time. They reported about gang problems, schoolwide disciplinary policies and practices, crimes occurring in the school, and other characteristics of the school.

A sample of 1279 schools was designed to describe schools in the United States. Participation was obtained from principals in 66% of schools in the initial principal survey and 50% of the schools in the second principal survey. Of 847 secondary schools asked to participate in surveys of students, 37% did so—greater cooperation was obtained from middle schools than from high schools, and rural schools cooperated more often than urban schools. In participating schools the mean student response rate was 76%. Of 847 secondary schools asked to participate in teacher surveys, 48% did so. In participating schools the mean teacher response rate was 78%. When both school and coordinator participation are considered, a final 52% response rate was obtained in the survey of activity coordinators. Weights to take account of the sample design and survey non-response are applied in making tabulations.

Gang Participation

Overall, 7.6% of male and 3.8% of female secondary students reported that they had "belong[ed] to a gang that has a name and engages in fighting, stealing, or selling drugs" in the last 12 months. Because of the possibility that some students fail to take survey self-reports seriously, a Veridicality index was used to identify students who make inconsistent responses. When only responses from students with acceptable scores on the Veridicality index are examined, 7.1% of males and 3.6% of females reported gang participation.

Youths who participate in gangs have much lower educational expectations than do other students, and are very much more likely to be threatened or victimized in school. For example, 28% of gang-involved boys but only 5% of other boys reported that they had been threatened with a knife or a gun in the current year in school. Corresponding percentages for girls were 18% of gang-involved girls but only 2% of other girls. Gang-involved boys and girls are more often afraid of being hurt or bothered in school and away from the school than are other students.

Statistical models of the likelihood of gang participation imply that being male, not being non-Hispanic White or Asian; having low commitment to education, low belief in conventional rules, or delinquent peers; and feeling unsafe or fearful in school are associated with gang involvement. Low commitment, low belief, delinquent peers, and fear make substantial direct contributions to gang involvement. (Community and family variables were not examined by these models, and models based on cross sectional data may not reflect causal processes.)

Gang participants are very much more involved with drugs than are other students. For example, 54% of male gang participants versus 9% of non-participants sold marijuana or other drugs in the last 12 months (42% and 4% of females, respectively). For drugs that have lower base rates for use, the contrast between gang participants and others is even sharper; 18% of male gang participants and 1% of nonparticipants report using heroin (23% and .6% of girls) in the last 12 months.

Gang participants are much more likely than other students to have carried a hidden weapon other than a pocket knife (51% of gang involved boys versus 9% of others; 32% and 2% of girls). Gang participants of both sexes are much more involved in violence such as hitting teachers or other adults, robbery, and fighting. Carrying a concealed weapon is strongly associated not only with gang participation but also with use of crack, heroin, cocaine, and other drugs. Although carrying a concealed weapon is associated with fearfulness, the association is weak compared to its association with gang or drug involvement.

Gang Problems in Schools

Definitions of gang problems differ from one study to another. In the present research, principals were told that "a 'gang' is a somewhat organized group, sometimes having turf concerns, symbols, special dress or colors. A gang has a special interest in violence for status-providing purposes and is recognized as a gang by its members and by others." They were asked whether gangs are a problem in the school or in the community. Overall 5% of principals reported that gangs are a problem in their schools and 36% reported a gang problem in the community. Urban principals and principals of secondary schools were more likely to report school gang problems. Principals are also more likely to report gang problems when the school enrolls relatively many Hispanic students. Principals' reports of school gang problems do not show strong convergence with other measures of problem behavior in schools or with the percentage of schools' students who report that they participate in gangs. In the 10% of schools with the highest student gang participation rates (14.4% or more of students reporting gang participation), only 18% of principals report that gangs are a problem in the school. Nevertheless, principals' reports of school gang problems are associated with more victimization, less safety, and poorer administrator leadership according to teacher reports.

A statistical model of the extent to which schools have high rates of student self-reported gang participation implies that concentrated poverty and disorganization in the community, public school auspices, receiving students with behavior problems from various sources, and student perceptions that the school is unsafe (or fear) influence levels of student gang participation. The association of perceptions that the school is unsafe with gang participation rate is especially strong. The correlation between the square root of the percentage of students who reported gang participation and scores on a school Safety scale is –.49, and this correlation is scarcely reduced at all (to –.46) by the application of statistical controls. Although interpretation of these preliminary results should be tempered by the possibility that some of this association may be reciprocal in the sense that gang activity may lead to fear as well as fear leading to gang participation, the finding suggests that maintaining safe environments may be helpful in reducing gang participation.

School-Based Gang Prevention and Intervention Programs

We define a gang prevention activity as one that aims to reduce or prevent gang involvement. A gang intervention activity is defined as a program the activities of which are directed at youths who are gang members. From the survey of program providers we estimate that there are 781,800 gang prevention activities underway in the nation's schools, and 159,700 gang intervention activities. Most of these programs are not limited to a gang prevention focus but are also concerned with other forms of problem behavior.

The most common type of program intended to prevent or reduce gang involvement entails prevention curriculum, instruction, or training. About 15% of all gang prevention programs are of this type (about 115,400 such programs in U.S. schools). Naturally, many of these programs are also directed at other objectives such as reducing drug use or other problem behavior. About 11% of school based gang prevention programs involve efforts to create or maintain a distinctive school culture or climate for interpersonal exchanges; and about 8% involve recreation, enrichment, or leisure activities. Other types of prevention activities are less common. Fewer than 3% of gang prevention programs involve youth roles in regulating or responding to student conduct (e.g., conflict resolution, mediation, or youth courts), but there are so many schools and so many programs in the nation that this nevertheless amounts to about 20,500 such programs.

By far the most common type of gang intervention program involves counseling, social work, psychological or therapeutic intervention—with over 20% (or about 32,700) programs of this kind. About 13% of gang intervention activities in schools involve prevention curriculum, instruction or training, 12% involve services or programs for family members, 10% are behavioral interventions, 10% seek to influence school culture or climate, and 10% seek to improve intergroup relations or relations between the school and the community.

Quality of Gang Prevention and Intervention Programs

Like anything else done in schools, gang prevention or intervention programs may be well implemented or poorly implemented. They may employ practices that are found in programs that have been shown to be effective in prior research, or they may fail to use such practices. They may be transitory, or they may be implemented consistently over long periods of time. The typical participant may participate a great deal, or the dosage may be very small. The activity may be widely applied or be very limited in scope—involving a small percentage of students or school personnel.

The indicators of program quality developed for the National Study of Delinquency Prevention in Schools (Gottfredson et al., 2000) were applied to measure the quality of gang prevention and gang intervention activities. Data to describe the quality of prevention and intervention activities come from the reports of program coordinators in Activity Questionnaires asking about fourteen specific types of "discretionary" program activity.

Differences were observed among the average quality of implementation of activities of different types, and great variability was observed in the quality of implementation of activities of each type.

The average gang *prevention* program involving curriculum, instruction or training can be characterized as follows:

- One or more persons is conducting it *from time to time;*
- It employs 88% of the *content* elements identified as representing best practices;
- It employs 50% of the *methods* elements identified as representing best practices;
- It involves 28 sessions or lessons;
- It lasts about 23 weeks;
- Students participate once per week or slightly more often;

- 47% of the school's students participate or are exposed.

The average gang *prevention* program involving counseling, social work, psychological, or therapeutic activity can be characterized as follows:

- One or more persons is conducting it *from time to time;*
- It employs 35% of the *methods* elements identified as representing best practices;
- It involves 13 sessions or lessons;
- It lasts about 20 weeks;
- Students participate about 3 times a month;
- 29% of the school's students participate or are exposed.

Counseling, social work, psychological, or therapeutic activities constitute the most common gang *intervention* approach. The quality of counseling gang intervention activity resembles the quality of counseling prevention activity. For several types of activity, however, gang *intervention* activities are sometimes implemented with greater strength and fidelity to best practices than are the less targeted gang prevention activities. Curricular gang *intervention* programs can be characterized as follows:

- One or more persons is conducting it *from time to time,* but significantly more frequently than prevention programs are conducted;
- It employs 81% of the *content* elements identified as representing best practices;
- It employs 56% of the *methods* elements identified as representing best practices (significantly better than prevention programs);
- It involves 39 sessions or lessons;
- It lasts about 23 weeks;
- Students participate once per week or slightly more often;
- 42% of the school's students participate or are exposed.

In some respects the quality of gang intervention programs involving classroom organization and management, improvements to instructional methods, or the involvement of youths in school discipline is somewhat higher than gang prevention programs of the same type.

The typical gang prevention or intervention program implemented in schools does not compare favorably with the characteristics of effective programs—for those kinds of programs that have been the subject of research. An exception is classroom organization and management interventions directed at gang members, which make use of a high proportion of best practices and are sometimes used regularly by school personnel; but this type of intervention is relatively rarely used.

There is much room for improvement in the quality of gang prevention and intervention programs in the nation's schools.

Participation in Programs by Gang-Involved Youths

Gang-involved secondary school students are usually less likely to be involved in or exposed to most kinds of gang prevention or intervention programming. For example, in the current year 39% of gang-involved males received instruction in ways to avoid getting involved in problem behavior such as fighting, drug use, or risky behavior compared to 49% of other male students. Among females, 37% of the gang-involved and 57% of others received such instruction. Students who are gang participants are much less likely to participate in special events, recreation or activities inside or outside of the school and much less likely to report that teachers have engaged in sound classroom management procedures.

Gang participants—both boys and girls—are about twice as likely as other students to be referred or have their family referred by the school to another agency for some kind of help, and the school is somewhat more likely to have worked with the gang participants' families. Gang-involved girls are more likely than other girls to be advised by a school counselor, social worker or psychologist about ways to avoid involvement with drugs or violence than are other girls (42% versus 34%). In contrast, gang-involved boys are less likely than other boys to be advised by a school counselor, social worker or psychologist (29% versus 35%).

Quality of Gang Prevention or Intervention Activity, Perceptions of Gang Problems, and Formal Needs Assessment

Programs that were developed following a formal needs assessment are implemented in significantly stronger form than those not based on a needs assessment. Programs guided by a needs assessment are of higher overall quality, of longer duration, make more use of best practices with respect to the methods employed, involve a larger proportion of students, and achieve a higher level of use by school personnel. In all, 46% of gang prevention or intervention programs were guided by a formal needs assessment—which may have been perfunctory.

School gang prevention or intervention programs are somewhat more likely to have been developed following a formal needs assessment in schools in which the principal reports that gangs are a problem in the school than in schools in which the principal reports no problem. And the programs are more likely to target gang members (as opposed to being more general prevention efforts) in schools in which the principal reports that gangs are a problem in the school.

Limitations of the Research

The most important limitation of the research is that the assessment of program quality depends on judgments by the authors about the aspects of quality to measure. Guided by their understanding of the literature on the efficacy of problem-behavior-prevention programs, they emphasized measures of dosage and those aspects of interventions that appear to be associated with effectiveness in program research. They also emphasized the extent of coverage on the grounds that interventions reaching large portions of the population are likely to have more aggregate effect. This approach to assessing program quality is a limitation because when there has been little or no research on a type of prevention or intervention activity, there is little basis for assessing program quality.

A second limitation is that results are based on a sample survey involving the reports of program implementers, principals, teachers, and students. In all surveys, respondents' reports are of imperfect reliability and validity. The method depended upon the principals' identification of prevention and intervention activities in their schools—and the correct classification of those activities. Nonparticipation in surveys may also bias results in unknown ways.

The research incorporated steps to cope with these limitations. Nonresponse adjustments were made in producing estimates (and nonresponse adjustments as well as the complex sample design were taken into account in estimating standard errors). Student self-reports of gang involvement were examined for the potential of invalid reporting to bias estimates of gang participation upwards, and estimates excluding responses that appear to be invalid were made. Including or excluding student respondents with low scores on a Veridicality index has little effect on patterns of association of gang participation with other measures.

Despite these limitations, the results provide new information on the extent of youth participation in gangs, the relation of individual gang participation to personal characteristics and problem behaviors, and the kinds of schools that tend to have greater problems with gangs. Results also provide the first comprehensive description of the nature and extent of gang prevention and intervention activity in schools, and the extent of exposure of young people to those programs. Results indicate that it is possible to measure some aspects of program quality through questionnaire surveys.

Some Implications

Results imply that there is great variability in the quality of school-based gang prevention and intervention programs. Perhaps most importantly, they imply that there is much room for the improvement in the quality of programs in some straightforward ways. This includes increases in the use of practices with respect to program content and methods that are found in programs that have been evaluated and found to be effective. It includes increases in the intensity (duration and frequency) with which programs are operated, and it includes increases in extent of their application.

Results show that secondary school students who report being involved in gangs are less exposed to many prevention activities than are students who are not involved in gangs. This suggests the potential for including more of the highest risk youths by actively seeking ways to include them. An analysis of the forces that limit the participation of gang-involved youths from participation should be a part of the planning of any gang prevention or intervention program, with program design features or arrangements put in place to cope with or minimize the influence of these forces.

Fewer than half of gang prevention or intervention programs have been guided by a formal needs assessment. Goldstein and Kodluboy (1998) among others have emphasized the importance of a comprehensive assessment of problems, and the development of programs only after such assessment. Evidently, there is much room for the increased practice of needs assessment in program planning. Formal planning was associated with stronger programs in the present research. Other correlates of the quality of school-based prevention programs are described by G. D. Gottfredson et al. (2000).

Formal needs assessment may contribute to (or depend on) principals' willingness to identify problems related to gangs. The finding that principals usually reported that gangs are not a problem even in schools with a high percentage of students reporting that they participate in gangs suggests that lack of principal recognition of problems may be an obstacle to the development of effective prevention and intervention programs. At the very least, the results imply that principals' reports that gang activity is not a problem should be met with skepticism unless evidence from other sources confirms the reports.

In an earlier report (G. D. Gottfredson et al., 2000) we showed that principals' reports of school crime show little convergence with reports by students and teachers of school safety, problem behavior, victimization, or classroom order. When combined with the present observation that principals' accounts of school gang problems are of limited validity, those results suggest the possibility that school leaders are an obstacle to confronting problems of school safety—including gang problems.

The results extend those of earlier research on gangs in schools (Howell & Lynch, 2000) by including measures of individual gang participation and by allowing an examination of rates of gang participation in specific sampled schools. Individual gang participation—and rates of gang participation in schools—is strongly associated with fear (or perceptions that the school environment is not safe), drug involvement, and other forms of problem behavior. The analyses conducted do not allow a determination about the extent to which fear or unsafe school environments contribute to gang involvement versus the extent to which gang involvement produces fear or unsafe environments. The strong inverse link between perceptions of school safety and levels of gang involvement suggests that efforts to promote a safe environment and make all students feel safe may reduce the risk of youth gang involvement.

References

Goldstein, A. P., & Kodluboy, D. W. (1998). Gangs in schools. Champaign, IL: Research Press.

Gottfredson, G.D., Gottfredson, D.C., Czeh, E.R., Cantor, D., Crosse, S., & Hantman, I. (2000). National study of delinquency prevention in schools. Ellicott City, MD: Gottfredson Associates (available online at http://www.gottfredson.com).

Howell, J. C., & Lynch, J. P. (2000). Youth gangs in schools (Juvenile Justice Bulletin). Washington, DC: U.S. Department of Justice, Office of Juvenile Justice and Delinquency Prevention. ✦

Chapter 31
The National Evaluation of the Gang Resistance Education and Training (G.R.E.A.T.) Program[1]

Finn-Aage Esbensen

Public health practitioners embrace primary prevention strategies to reduce the frequency of unhealthy behaviors. Primary prevention efforts are directed toward a whole population rather than those at highest risk (secondary prevention) or those already involved in the behavior (tertiary prevention). The G.R.E.A.T. program is a primary prevention program that exposes eighth graders to a gang-prevention curriculum. In this chapter, Esbensen describes the results of two approaches to evaluating the program's impact. The findings of the cross-sectional study suggested the program was moderately successful in preventing youths from joining gangs. However, the more thorough, longitudinal research found the same percentage of gang members among youths who received G.R.E.A.T. and those who did not. The author offers several possible explanations for these divergent results and discusses the challenges that evaluators confront in assessing the effectiveness of gang-prevention programs. Not included in this chapter are the results from a four-year follow-up that revealed consistent but slight positive effects for G.R.E.A.T. subjects on most variables, but no effect whatsoever on delinquent behavior and gang membership.

Overview

Youth delinquent gangs received considerable academic and media attention during the 1990s. Much of this attention focused on the violence and drug dealing in which gang members are involved. Despite this widespread concern with gangs, there has been a paucity of research and evaluation of prevention and intervention programs. In this chapter, I report on a multiyear, multifaceted evaluation of one school-based gang prevention program in which uniformed law enforcement officers teach a nine-week curriculum to middle-school students.

The Gang Resistance Education and Training (G.R.E.A.T.) program was developed in 1991 by law enforcement agencies in the greater Phoenix area. The primary purpose of the G.R.E.A.T. program was to reduce gang activity and to educate a population of young people as to the consequences of gang involvement.

From October 1994 through September 2000, the National Institute of Justice (NIJ) funded a National Evaluation of the G.R.E.A.T. program. Two separate objectives guided the evaluation design. The first objective was to conduct a process evaluation, that is, to describe the program and its components, and to assess the program's fidelity. The second objective was to assess the effectiveness of G.R.E.A.T. in terms of attitudinal and behavioral consequences.

The process evaluation consisted of two different components: (1) assessment of the G.R.E.A.T. officer training, and (2) observation of officers actually delivering the program in school classrooms. For the outcome analysis, three different strategies were developed. First, a cross-sectional study was conducted in which 5,935 eighth-grade students in 11 different cities were surveyed to assess the effectiveness of the G.R.E.A.T. program. Second, a five-year longitudinal, quasi-experimental study was conducted in six different cities. Third, parents, teachers, and law enforcement officers were surveyed to determine their level of satisfaction with the program and its perceived effectiveness.

Problem Statement

In spite of years of research and years of suppression and intervention efforts, the American gang scene is poorly understood and far from being eliminated. There is a lack of consensus about the magnitude of the gang problem, the extent and level of organization of gangs, and most importantly, what should be done to address the gang issue. Some of the epidemiological and etiological confusion can be traced to different methodologies and different theoretical perspectives. Disagreement about policy can be attributed largely to political agendas and to a shortage of evaluations of strategies enacted to address the gang phenomenon. To address the latter issue, a number of gang-specific programs with evaluative components were implemented at both the local and national level during the 1990s.

With respect to knowledge about gangs, information has been derived from a variety of research methodologies and countless studies. Sections I–IV of this reader provide an overview of the multitude of issues involved in gang research. Of particular interest in this chapter is discussion of the extent to which a gang prevention program can be implemented in middle schools and with what degree of success.

The G.R.E.A.T. Program

The Gang Resistance Education and Training (G.R.E.A.T.) program is a school-based gang-prevention program taught by uniformed police officers. G.R.E.A.T. was developed in 1991 by Phoenix Police Department officers in cooperation with officers representing other Phoenix area police departments. The Bureau of Alcohol, Tobacco, and Firearms, the Federal Law Enforcement Training Center, and representatives from five local law enforcement agencies (Phoenix, AZ; Portland, OR; Philadelphia, PA; La Crosse, WI; and Orange County, FL) share responsibility for and oversight of the current program. Since its inception, G.R.E.A.T. has experienced rapid acceptance by both law enforcement and school personnel. Evidence for this is its adoption by numerous law enforcement agencies across the country; as of January 2000, more than 3,500 officers from all 50 states and the District of Columbia had completed G.R.E.A.T. training.

The stated objectives of the G.R.E.A.T. program are (1) "to reduce gang activity" and (2) "to educate a population of young people as to the consequences of gang involvement." The curriculum consists of nine lessons offered once a week to middle school students, primarily seventh graders. Officers are provided with detailed lesson plans containing clearly stated purposes and objectives. In order to achieve the program's objectives, the nine lessons cover such topics as conflict resolution, goal setting, and resisting peer pressure. Discussion about gangs and how they affect the quality of people's lives are also included. The nine lessons are listed below:

1. Introduction—Acquaint students with the G.R.E.A.T. program and presenting officer.

2. Crimes, Victims and Your Rights—Students learn about crimes, victims, and the impact on school and neighborhood.

3. Cultural Sensitivity/Prejudice—Students learn how cultural differences affect their school and neighborhood.

4/5. Conflict Resolution (2 lessons)—Students learn how to create an atmosphere of understanding that would enable all parties to better address problems and work on solutions together.

6. Meeting Basic Needs—Students learn how to meet their basic needs without joining a gang.

7. Drugs/Neighborhoods—Students learn how drugs affect their school and neighborhood.

8. Responsibility—Students learn about the diverse responsibilities of people in their school and neighborhood.

9. Goal Setting—Students learn the need for goal setting and how to establish short- and long-term goals.

Process Evaluation

Of primary importance in the process evaluation was determining if the program described in written documents was, in fact, the program delivered. In this section, I will briefly describe the procedures used to assess program fidelity. During the first year of the evaluation, members of the research staff observed five officer training sessions.

In addition to enhancing the researchers' understanding of the program, these observations allowed for assessment of the training program and the appropriateness of instructional techniques. The consensus of the evaluators was that these training sessions were well-organized and staffed by a dedicated group of officers (Esbensen and Osgood 1997).

Our next concern was to assess the extent to which the officers brought the materials learned at training to the classroom. A total of 87 lessons were observed by one or two trained observers in six different cities and 14 different schools. Each observer noted the extent to which the officers adhered to the lesson outline and conformed to the lesson content. As with the training sessions, the consensus was that the officers did a commendable job of presenting the materials as they were taught in the G.R.E.A.T. officer training. On the basis of these two observational components, we concluded that the program was delivered with a high degree of conformity to the written description (Sellers, Taylor, and Esbensen 1998).

Outcome Evaluation

Although the development of the G.R.E.A.T. curriculum was not theory driven, the design of the National Evaluation was. The theories judged to be most relevant to the program were social learning theory (Akers 1985) and self-control theory (Gottfredson and Hirschi 1990). The identification of relevant theoretical constructs is critical to the short-term evaluation of prevention programs because prevention necessarily takes place well before the outcome of major concern (gang membership) is likely to occur. Thus, the evaluation placed considerable emphasis on theoretical constructs that were logically related to the program's curriculum and that were both theoretically and empirically linked to gang membership and delinquency (Grasmick et al. 1993; Hawkins and Catalano 1993; Huizinga, Loeber, and Thornberry 1994; Winfree, Vigil-Backstrom, and Mays 1994). It was maintained that if the program had positive effects on those variables in the short term, then it held promise for long-term benefits of reducing serious gang delinquency. Decisions about the potential value of G.R.E.A.T. could not wait for research that would track program participants through their entire adolescence to determine whether they ever joined gangs or participated in serious delinquency. Nor would the expense of such research be justified without evidence of short-term effects.

Winfree, Esbensen, and Osgood (1996) elaborated on the relationship between the G.R.E.A.T. curriculum and the theoretical constructs included in this evaluation. For example, lesson 4/5 of G.R.E.A.T. (Conflict Resolution) deals with concepts closely linked to self-control theory's anger and coping strategies. Lesson 6 (Meeting Basic Needs) has conceptual ties to the risk-taking element of self-control theory. Lessons 7, 8, and 9 include elements addressing delayed gratification and impulsive behavior by attempting to teach responsibility and goal setting, including personal and career goals.

Elements of social learning theory appear in lessons 1, 3, and 4/5. These lessons introduce definitions of laws, values, norms, and rules supportive of law-abiding behavior. Tolerance and acceptance (lesson 3), for instance, are presented as values that reduce conflict and, subsequently, violence. Further, lesson 4/5 addresses conflict resolution and steps students can take to ward off negative peer influences.

Measures

The questionnaires administered to students participating in both the cross-sectional and longitudinal studies were identical. Measures included in the student questionnaires can be divided into three main categories: attitudinal, cognitive, and behavioral. Although the attitudinal measures included in these instruments can be classified as measures of five different theoretical perspectives (social learning, social control, social strain, labeling, and self-concept) and have been used for testing theoretical propositions in other publications (Deschenes and Esbensen 1999; Esbensen and Deschenes 1998; Winfree and Bernat 1998), they will be referred to as attitudinal variables in the subsequent discussion. The following questionnaire items are representative of the diversity of questions answered by the student respondents:

- There are gang fights at my school.
- My parents know who I am with if I am not at home.
- Sometimes I will take a risk just for the fun of it.

- Police officers are honest.
- If your group of friends were getting you into trouble at home, how likely is it that you would still hang out with them?
- I'll never have enough money to go to college.
- It's okay to tell a small lie if it doesn't hurt anyone.
- I try hard in school.
- Being in my gang makes me feel important.

In addition to attitudinal items, the students were requested to complete a self-report delinquency inventory. This technique has been used widely during the past 40 years and provides a good measure of actual behavior rather than a reactive measure of police response to behavior (e.g., Hindelang, Hirschi, and Weis 1981; Huizinga and Elliott 1986; Huizinga 1991). The types of behaviors comprising this 17-item inventory included status offenses (e.g., skipping classes without an excuse), crimes against property (e.g., purposely damaging or destroying property; stealing or trying to steal something worth more than $50), and crimes against persons (e.g., hitting people with the idea of hurting them; attacking someone with a weapon). Additionally, students were asked about drug use, including tobacco, alcohol, and marijuana. Given that the focus of the G.R.E.A.T. program was on gang prevention, a series of questions asked the students about their involvement in gangs and the types of gang activities in which they and their gang were involved.

Analysis Issues

Prior to a discussion of program effectiveness, several methodological issues need to be addressed. G.R.E.A.T. is a school-based program, delivered simultaneously to entire classrooms rather than separately to individual students. For analysis of program effectiveness, this poses a problem concerning the appropriate unit of analysis: individuals, classrooms, or schools. If students from the same classroom tend to be more similar to one another than to students from other classrooms, then treating individuals as the primary unit of analysis is likely to violate the standard statistical assumption of independence among observations (Judd and McClelland 1989:403–416). When this assumption does not hold, we risk the possi-

bility of concluding that there is a reliable treatment effect when it is, in fact, idiosyncratic to only a few classes, or we may fail to establish the statistical significance of a small but very consistent effect.

For the independence assumption to hold, *all* similarity within classes must be explained by the treatment effect and control variables. In most cases there are many other sources of similarity as well, such as which trainer delivered the program, the teacher's classroom management style, and all extraneous factors that determine which students end up in which classrooms. Though it is possible that an analysis would succeed in accounting for all such differences between classes, it is more prudent to assume that this may not be the case. Although it would be ideal to use an analysis strategy that allows for the possible nonindependence within classrooms by including classrooms as a unit of analysis, we could not do this with the cross-sectional data. It was not possible to reconstruct the seventh-grade class configuration with the available data. It was possible, however, to use *school* as a level of analysis and thus be able to control for school differences and, indirectly and in a more limited way, officer and teacher characteristics. In the longitudinal survey, we randomly assigned classrooms to G.R.E.A.T. or non-G.R.E.A.T. and were thus able to conduct those analyses using *classroom* as a unit of analysis.

Cross-Sectional Design—1995

The first outcome analysis was based on the cross-sectional survey completed in the spring of 1995. In this cross-sectional design, two *ex post facto* comparison groups were created to allow for assessment of the effectiveness of the G.R.E.A.T. program. Because the program was taught in seventh grade, eighth-grade students were surveyed to allow for a one-year follow-up while at the same time guaranteeing that none of the sample was currently enrolled in the program. Eleven cities met all the required conditions for participation in the National Evaluation: Las Cruces, NM; Omaha, NE; Phoenix, AZ; Philadelphia, PA; Kansas City, MO; Milwaukee, WI; Orlando, FL; Will County, IL; Providence, RI; Pocatello, ID; and Torrance, CA. These sites provide a diverse sample. One or more of the selected sites can be described by the following characteristics: large urban area, small city, racially and ethnically homogeneous, racially and ethnically heterogeneous, East Coast, West Coast, Midwest, inner-city, working class, or middle class (Esbensen and Winfree 1998).

Within the selected sites, schools that offered G.R.E.A.T. during the past two years were selected and questionnaires were administered to all eighth graders in attendance on the specified day. This resulted in a final sample of 5,935 eighth-grade students from 315 classrooms in 42 different schools. Passive parental consent procedures were approved in all but the Torrance site.[2] That is, parents had to sign a form indicating that they did not want their child to participate in the survey. The absence of such a form indicated "passive parental consent." The number of parental refusals at each school ranged from 0 to 2 percent. Thus, participation rates (the percentage of students in attendance on the day of administration actually completing questionnaires) varied between 98 and 100 percent at the passive consent sites.

Demographic Characteristics

Approximately half of the sample was female (52 percent) and most lived in intact homes (62 percent)—respondents indicated that both a mother and father were present in the home, including stepparents. The sample was ethnically diverse, with whites accounting for 40 percent of respondents, African-Americans 27 percent, Hispanics 19 percent, Asians 6 percent, and others 8 percent. As expected with an eighth-grade sample, most of the respondents were between 13 and 15 years of age, with 60 percent being 14 years old. The vast majority reported having parents with a minimum educational level of a high school diploma, with a sizable number having mothers and/or fathers with some college-level education. It is worth noting that approximately 25 percent of the respondents did not know their father's highest level of education and 20 percent did not know their mother's.

With respect to gang affiliation, some interesting insight to self-reported gang membership is revealed. As with most social phenomena, definitional issues arise. In the current research, two filter questions introduce the gang-specific section of the questionnaire: "Have you ever been a gang member?" and "Are you now in a gang?"

Given the current sample, with almost all the respondents under the age of 16, even affirmative responses to the first question followed by a negative response to the second may still have indicated a recent gang affiliation. Relying upon responses to the first question as an accurate reflection of the magnitude of the gang problem, fully 17 percent (994 youths) of the sample indicated that they had belonged to a gang at some point in their lives. This contrasts with 9 percent (522) indicating that they were currently gang members.

Comparison Group

A primary concern for assessing program impact was determination of whether the students who participated in the G.R.E.A.T. program were comparable to those who did not. The treatment group (G.R.E.A.T. participants) and the comparison group (nonparticipants) were defined through answers to the question "Did you complete the G.R.E.A.T. program?" Of the 5,836 respondents who answered the question (99 students did not respond), 2,629 (45 percent) reported they had completed the program. The 3,207 (55 percent) who did not became the comparison group.

However, the schools varied substantially in the number of students who reported they had or had not completed the G.R.E.A.T. program. Because the precision with which program impact can be established at each school depends on the number of students in *both* participant and nonparticipant groups, schools with few students in one of the groups could contribute relatively little to the evaluation. Therefore, analysis of the treatment and comparison groups was replicated using a restricted sample of 28 schools in which there were at least 15 students in each group, participants and nonparticipants.

Because data were gathered on only a single occasion, a year after completion of the program, it was necessary to compare the participants and nonparticipants using statistical controls to rule out the possibility that differences between them were attributable to various background characteristics. Questions were asked in the survey to determine background characteristics that could be associated with the outcome measures. The analysis controlled for five characteristics:

1. Sex.

2. Race (white, African American, Hispanic, Asian American, and other).

3. Age (because only eighth-grade students participated in the evaluation, there was little variation in age).

4. Family status (as reflected in the adults with whom the youths resided).

5. Parental education (defined as the highest level attained by either parent).

Background Characteristics

Not surprisingly, there were differences among the 42 schools in terms of racial composition and socioeconomic status (as reflected by family status and parental education). The analysis, which controlled for differences between schools, found a few small but statistically significant differences in background characteristics between the treatment and comparison groups.

Ideally, the treatment and comparison groups should have been matched, but this could not be expected in a *post hoc* evaluation, such as this study. The pattern of group differences in background characteristics was ambiguous, but it did not appear especially problematic to determining the impact of the G.R.E.A.T. program. Comparisons of the treatment and comparison groups revealed no systematic bias. Demographic characteristics indicating high or low risk for delinquency and/or gang membership were found in both groups. In the comparison group, 15-year-old students were overrepresented while in the treatment group African-American youths were overrepresented. Similarly, there were fewer females in the comparison group but more youths from single-parent homes. Given this inconsistent pattern and the small size of group differences, it was concluded that the outcome measures were not a product of preexisting differences between the G.R.E.A.T. and comparison students.

Outcome Results

Findings from the cross-sectional study indicated that G.R.E.A.T. appeared to be meeting its objectives of reducing gang affiliation and delinquent activity. The students who reported completing the G.R.E.A.T. program reported *lower* levels of gang affiliation (9.8 percent of G.R.E.A.T. students reported gang membership compared to 11.4 percent of the comparison group) and self-reported delinquency. These differences were small but statistically significant. Not only was the aggregate measure of delinquency lower for the G.R.E.A.T. group, but so were most of the subscales, for example, drug use, minor offending, property crimes, and crimes against persons. No differences between the groups were found for rates of victimization or selling drugs.

A number of differences also were found for attitudinal measures. As discussed above, G.R.E.A.T. lessons are aimed at reducing impulsive behavior, improving communication with parents and other adults, enhancing self-esteem, and encouraging students to make "better" choices. The cross-sectional survey results revealed that one year after completing G.R.E.A.T., the G.R.E.A.T. students reported better outcomes, that is, more positive attitudes and behaviors than students who did not complete the program (see Box 31.1).

Longitudinal Research Design

The cross-sectional evaluation of the G.R.E.A.T. program reported above contains several methodological limitations.

Box 31.1:
Cross-Sectional Design Outcomes

Students completing the G.R.E.A.T. program reported more positive attitudes and behaviors than did the comparison group of students. They reported:

- Lower rates of self-reported delinquency.
- Lower rates of gang affiliation.
- More positive attitudes toward the police.
- More negative attitudes about gangs.
- Having more friends involved in prosocial activities.
- Greater commitment to peers promoting prosocial behavior.
- Higher levels of perceived guilt at committing deviant acts.
- More commitment to school.
- Higher levels of attachment to both mothers and fathers.
- More communication with parents about their activities.
- Fewer friends involved in delinquent activity.
- Lower likelihood of acting impulsively.
- Lower likelihood of engaging in risky behavior.
- Lower levels of perceived blocks to academic success.

(*See* Esbensen and Osgood 1999 for further discussion of these results.)

That design lacked a pre-test measure and required the *ex post facto* creation of a comparison group. While statistical procedures were used to strengthen the validity of that design, it is generally considered a weak design (e.g., Sherman et al. 1997). The longitudinal research strategy implemented in the second phase of the National Evaluation, with a quasi-experimental research design and random assignment of classrooms to treatment, serves two very important functions. First, this assignment process should create groups of G.R.E.A.T. and non-G.R.E.A.T. students at equal risk for future delinquency and gang involvement. Second, the longitudinal research design greatly increased statistical power for detecting program effects by controlling for previous individual differences and examining change over time.

Site Selection

Six cities were selected for inclusion in the longitudinal phase of the National Evaluation. The first criterion was the existence of a viable G.R.E.A.T. program. A second criterion was geographical location. It was desired to include an East Coast city (Philadelphia, PA), a West Coast location (Portland, OR), the site of the program's inception (Phoenix, AZ), a Midwest city (Omaha, NE), a nongang city (Lincoln, NE), and a small "border town" with a chronic gang problem (Las Cruces, NM). Clearly, some consideration was given to proximity to the location of the research office (Lincoln). A third criterion was the cooperation of the school districts and the police departments in each site.

Quasi-Experimental Research Design

The longitudinal study includes relatively equal-sized groups of treatment (G.R.E.A.T.) and control (non-G.R.E.A.T.) students in the seventh grade at five of the sites and sixth-grade students in the sixth (Portland). Table 31.1 reports the number of schools, classrooms, and students at each of the sites. Because G.R.E.A.T. is a classroom-based program, assignment was implemented for classrooms rather than for individual students. When data were pooled across sites, there was a large enough sample of classrooms for confidence in our results, even when classrooms were used as the unit of analysis. The longitudinal sample consists of 22 schools, 153 classrooms, and more than 3,000 students (all students whose names appeared on class lists at the beginning of the school year).

The "random" assignment process was a critical feature of this research design. During late summer and early fall of 1995, procedures for assignment of classrooms to experimental and control conditions were developed at each of the 22 middle schools participating in the longitudinal study. Because the G.R.E.A.T. program was implemented differently at each site, unique solutions were required to implement random assignment at each site and, in some situations, at each school. The exact nature of the process was dependent on what was possible at each site, but in all cases the goal was to minimize the potential for differences between the sets of treatment and control classes. Working in conjunction with principals, teachers, and G.R.E.A.T. officers, "random" samples were derived at each site. These various procedures resulted in 76 G.R.E.A.T. classrooms representing 1,871 students and 77 control classrooms with 1,697 students.

Active Consent Procedures

The University of Nebraska Institutional Review Board approved a research design that allowed passive parental consent (students were included unless specifically prohibited by parents) during the pre- and post-test data collection. These surveys were conducted two weeks prior to and two weeks following completion of the G.R.E.A.T. program. Active parental consent (students were excluded unless written approval for participation was obtained from parents) was required for the subsequent annual surveys. These procedures were also approved by each of the participating school districts.

A modified Dillman (1978) total design method was utilized to obtain the active consent forms, although the specific procedures varied slightly in terms of timing and sequencing across the six sites. The following serves as an "ideal type" of the procedures that were followed. Three direct mailings were made to parents of survey participants. Included in the mailings were a cover letter (both English and Spanish versions were included in Phoenix and Las Cruces), two copies of the parent consent form for student participation, and a business reply envelope. All parents not re-

Table 31.1
National Evaluation of G.R.E.A.T. Completion Rates

Site	Total Sample Size	G.R.E.A.T.	Non-G.R.E.A.T.	Active Consent Sample Size	Consent Yes N (%)	No N (%)	No Return N (%)	Pre-Test	Post-Test	1 Yr	2 Yr
		Classroom / Student N						N (%)			
Las Cruces	626	11 / 280	17 / 346	301	301 (48)	71 (11)	254 (41)	518 (83)	519 (83)	275 (91)	242 (80)
Lincoln	653	13 / 324	13 / 329	425	425 (65)	79 (12)	149 (23)	595 (91)	351 (83)	388 (91)	366 (86)
Omaha	672	20 / 363	20 / 309	470	470 (70)	48 (7)	154 (23)	440 (94)	414 (88)	390 (83)	354 (75)
Philadelphia	465	9 / 286	6 / 179	228	228 (49)	28 (6)	209 (45)	388 (83)	317 (68)	174 (76)	147 (64)
Phoenix	569	11 / 316	10 / 253	300	300 (53)	54 (9)	215 (38)	493 (87)	434 (76)	250 (83)	195 (65)
Portland	583	12 / 302	11 / 281	321	321 (55)	58 (10)	204 (35)	502 (86)	468 (80)	281 (88)	246 (77)
Total	3568	76 / 1871	77 / 1697	2045	2045 (57)	338 (9)	1185 (33)	2936 (82)	2503 (80)	1758 (86)	1550 (76)

* Completion percentages based on Total Sample for Pre-Test and Post-Test, all sites except Omaha.
Completion percentages based on Active Consent Sample for 1 Year and 2 Year Follow-Ups.
Completion percentages for Omaha based on Active Consent Sample for Pre-Test, Post-Test, 1 Year and 2 Year Follow-Ups.

sponding after the second mailing were contacted by telephone. School personnel also cooperated by distributing consent forms and cover letters at school.

The results of the active consent process (see Table 31.1) led to an overall retention of 57 percent of the initial sample. (For a more detailed discussion of the active consent process and examination of the effects of active consent procedures on the representativeness of the sample, consult Esbensen et al. 1999). All together these efforts cost in excess of $60,000 in terms of supplies, personnel time, telephone, and mailing costs.

Questionnaire Completion Rates

The completion rates for the student survey were excellent. Of the 2,045 active consents obtained at the six sites, 1,758 (86 percent) surveys were completed during the one-year follow-up and 1,550 (76 percent) were competed in the two-year follow-up (see Table 31.1). Given the multisite, multischool sample, combined with the fact that respondents at five of the six sites made the transition from middle school to high school between the year-one and year-two surveys, this completion rate is commendable. Hansen and colleagues (1985) examined attrition in a meta-analysis of 85 longitudinal studies and reported an average completion rate of 72 percent for the 19 studies with a 24-month follow-up period. Few of these 19 studies included multisite samples. Tebes, Snow, and Arthur (1992) report on the attrition rates from middle school to high school. In their study examining differential attrition for different age groups, they report losing 41.3 percent of their sample between eighth and ninth grade!

For the year-two follow-up, considerable difficulty was introduced into the retention of the student sample. As the cohort moved from middle school to high school, combined with normal mobility patterns, we found students enrolled in more than 10 different high schools each in Omaha, Phoenix, and Philadelphia. It thus became necessary to contact school officials at these schools, whether fewer than 10 respondents or more than 100 were enrolled at the school. In some instances, these new schools were in different districts, which required approval from the necessary authorities to survey their students. In spite of these logistical concerns, we successfully obtained completed questionnaires from 76 percent during the 24-month follow-up survey.

Outcome Results

Of particular interest in the longitudinal design is assessment of within-individual change over time (for a detailed discussion of the longitudinal results, consult Esbensen et al., 2000). The results reported here are based on examination of immediate (post-test) and intermediate (one- and two-year follow-up surveys) program effects.

The longitudinal sample differs from the cross-sectional sample on some of the demographic characteristics. Those completing the pre-test are younger, representing sixth- and seventh-grade students with a modal age of 12 (60 percent); a higher percentage of students are white (46 percent), fewer are African American (17 percent), but there is approximately the same representation of Hispanics (19 percent) and others (16 percent). With respect to sex and family structure, the longitudinal sample is virtually identical to the cross-sectional, with 51 percent females and 61 percent living in two-parent households.

The assignment of classrooms to G.R.E.A.T. and non-G.R.E.A.T. was relatively successful in establishing comparable groups. Some differences were noted but the only statistically significant difference was for race; more white youths were in the comparison group while the treatment group consisted of proportionately more African-American and Hispanic youths. A review of attitudinal and behavioral measures collected in the pre-test indicated that the comparison group was slightly more prosocial than the G.R.E.A.T. group (e.g., more positive attitudes to police, more negative attitudes about gangs, more peers involved in prosocial activities, and lower rates of self-reported delinquency). The analysis strategy, however, controls for school, classroom, and preexisting differences between groups.

The longitudinal analysis failed to replicate the cross-sectional results. There were no consistent behavioral or attitudinal differences between those students who were assigned to G.R.E.A.T. and those who were assigned to the control classrooms. For instance, in both the year-one and year-two follow-up surveys, the same percentage (3 percent in both years—see Box 31.2 for a discussion of defining and measuring gang membership) of students in the G.R.E.A.T. and control groups reported being gang members.

The current analyses were restricted to the year-one and year-two follow-up surveys. Analyses incorporating the year-three and year-four follow-up surveys are in progress. Thus, unlike the cross-sectional study that found consistent differences between the G.R.E.A.T. and non-G.R.E.A.T. groups, the longitudinal study found no short-term or intermediate effects of the G.R.E.A.T. program on either attitudes or behavior. Of importance is assessing why these different research strategies (the cross-sectional versus the longitudinal) produced different results. Possible explanations for the different results are discussed in Conclusions and Policy Implications.

Two additional analysis strategies were conducted to more fully explore the possibility of finding programmatic effects. The first alternative strategy restricted the analysis to those cities in which both the G.R.E.A.T. program and the evaluation design were best implemented. The second approach examined program impact based on the classification of respondents into high- and low-risk categories.

In terms of the quality of program implementation, three of the six cities were categorized as having greater program fidelity to the G.R.E.A.T. program model than the other three sites (i.e., officer experience, strength of local organization of G.R.E.A.T.). With respect to the research design, we were more successful in some cities than in others in eliciting student participation in the evaluation. Thus, program effects were assessed in optimal circumstances by limiting the sample to the cities with the highest quality program implementation and the classrooms with most adequate participation rates. Results from the cross-sectional analysis of program impact suggested that G.R.E.A.T. is more effective for students who are at higher risk of future problems of delinquency and gang membership. Thus, in the longitudinal analysis, separate analyses contrasted program effectiveness for students displaying both high and low risk for involvement in delinquency and gang activity. Neither of these alternative strategies produced results that differed from the initial longitudinal results; we found no systematic differences

Box 31.2: Gang Definition and Gang Measurement

As discussed in Section I of this book, there is a lack of agreement about the definition of *gang* or *gang member*. To highlight this point, consider some of the issues involved. In the cross-sectional study, we classified respondents as gang members if they answered "yes" to the question "Have you ever been a gang member?" and also indicated that the gang was involved in at least one of four delinquent activities (gang fights, thefts, assaults, or robberies). In that study we used the "ever" question because the average respondent was 14 years of age and any gang affiliation would have been relatively recent. This produced a prevalence rate of 10.6 percent. However, had we chosen a different definition, we could have concluded that from 2.3 percent to 16.9 percent of the students were gang members! For example, if we had only used the single question "Have you ever been a gang member?" 16.9 percent of the responses were "yes." On the other hand, if we had limited our definition to students who were currently core members of an organized delinquent gang, then our gang members would be reduced to only 2.3 percent. Further, in the longitudinal study, we find that only 9 percent of the year-one respondents reported ever being a gang member, slightly more than half the findings in the cross-sectional study. And only 3 percent indicated that they were currently members of a delinquent gang. Why this difference? Is it because of sampling differences? The cross-sectional study included a more diverse sample of cities than did the longitudinal study. What about the fact that the cross-sectional surveys were anonymous (students did not provide their names) and the longitudinal surveys were confidential? Did the active consent process reduce the number of gang members in the sample? Remember that 33 percent of the parents failed to respond to the request for their children to participate in the evaluation. Does the fact that this was the third data collection point affect the responses? Was there a "testing effect"? From a policy standpoint, it is clear that which definition you choose can have serious implications not only for research but also for policy consideration. Does it make sense, for instance, to have a general prevention program when only 2 percent of the students are involved in the behavior you are trying to prevent?

between the G.R.E.A.T. students and the control group.

Conclusions and Policy Implications

The Gang Resistance Education and Training program is one of a myriad of gang prevention efforts being employed to reduce adolescent involvement in crime and gangs. As other programs await evaluation results, the preliminary findings of this study supported continuation of G.R.E.A.T. The process evaluation assessing the officer-training program as well as the observation of officers delivering the program indicated a high degree of program fidelity. Additionally, the results from the cross-sectional survey of 5,935 eighth-grade students conducted during spring 1995 suggested that students who participated in G.R.E.A.T. reported significantly more prosocial behaviors and attitudes, including less gang membership and less delinquency, than students who did not take part in the program. This one-year follow-up survey supported the idea that trained law enforcement personnel can serve as prevention agents as well as enforcers of the law.

These cross-sectional results, however, needed to be viewed with caution. Some differences existed between the two groups prior to the introduction of the program. Although most of these differences were controlled through available statistical techniques, an experimental design with random assignment would provide a stronger test of program effect.

The quasi-experimental longitudinal design was implemented in six cities and the current results rely on data obtained from the pre- and post-tests administered during the fall and winter of the 1995–96 academic year. One- and two-year follow-up surveys were obtained during the fall of 1996 and 1997. Additional surveys not yet ready for analysis were collected during 1998 and 1999, eventually allowing for assessment of long-term (four-year) effects. Contrary to the cross-sectional study, no programmatic effect was found. The two groups (G.R.E.A.T. and non-G.R.E.A.T.) were comparable on all measures, both before and after treatment.

This discrepancy in findings between the cross-sectional and longitudinal studies raises several methodological and conceptual issues:

- Were the cross-sectional results an artifact of the research design?
- Was the cross-sectional sample more diverse, especially with respect to the inclusion of more high-risk students?
- Is there an effect of analyzing cases grouped by official assignment to the program that produces different results than reliance upon subjects' self-reports of program completion?

- Is it possible that the mandated active parental consent process contributed to a more homogeneous sample in the longitudinal study?
- Is it possible that the schools experienced a saturation or contamination effect? That is, G.R.E.A.T. officers had been assigned to the schools for a number of years and had contributed to a school-wide change in attitudes and behaviors.
- Is it reasonable to expect a nine-lesson "canned" curriculum can have an effect on students' attitudes and behaviors?

Clearly, these methodological issues defy a firm response. I pose them merely to acknowledge that different samples and different research designs, even though utilizing the same method and survey instruments, may introduce unique effects that affect outcomes. We can address some of these issues. First, analyses examining the differential attrition possibility indicate that the active consent sample did not differ significantly from the initial sample (Esbensen et al. 1999).

Second, the analyses restricted to the three sites in which both the program and evaluation were best implemented included two sites in which the G.R.E.A.T. program was in the first year of implementation in the selected schools. Results from those sites did not differ from those for the entire sample. On the basis of comparison of the cross-sectional and longitudinal samples, it is evident that the cross-sectional sample included a more racially and ethnically diverse sample, as well as including a broader geographic representation. We attempted to address this concern by examining site-specific analyses for cities included in both studies. In three cities, there was considerable overlap between schools participating in the cross-sectional and longitudinal studies. In these cases, the same pattern of results persisted—significant program effects in the cross-sectional study but not in the longitudinal. To date, we have not analyzed the longitudinal data based on self-reported program completion, as this would defy the logic of random assignment. Methodological issues aside, is it reasonable to expect that a nine-hour program can measurably change student attitudes and behaviors? The majority of school-based prevention programs, even those with more intense and prolonged treatment dosages, do not produce measurable program effects (see, for example, Sherman et al. 1997). This is especially true for curriculum-based programs, such as G.R.E.A.T.

Where does this leave us with regard to policy? Can officers be effective providers of treatment? Given the lack of consistent findings for G.R.E.A.T., this is an important question. However, from a school safety perspective, and from a community policing perspective, it may be reasonable to continue this strategy. School administrators commented during both formal and informal interviews that the officers were welcome in the schools because their presence promoted a feeling of safety. Additionally, there has been a resurgence of interest in school resource officers and in proactive policing strategies. G.R.E.A.T. and other school-based prevention programs such as DARE and law-related education can possibly be integrated into the role of school resource officers. Teachers and parents appear to be quite satisfied with the G.R.E.A.T. program. According to surveys administered to these groups, the majority of teachers and parents were in favor of school-based prevention programs, in favor of officers instructing students, and generally supportive of the G.R.E.A.T. program.

A lingering question, however, remains. With the absence of a measurable program effect, is it reasonable to continue the program because people feel good about it? Unlike many other programs with no evaluation data or with evaluations that report no effect, G.R.E.A.T. administrators responded to the results of this evaluation. When the results (the lack of program effect) were conveyed to the G.R.E.A.T. administration, the reaction was "Well, what can we do to make it a successful program?" At their request, a group of G.R.E.A.T. representatives, members of the National Evaluation research team, and experts in school-based prevention programs undertook a critical review of the G.R.E.A.T. curriculum and the overall structure of the program. This group reviewed the curriculum within the context of the evaluation results and within the context of successful school-based prevention programs. The group provided the G.R.E.A.T. administration with a report detailing a number of recommended changes and modifications to the existing program. These suggestions are currently being reviewed by G.R.E.A.T.'s governing body members for possible implementation.

It remains to be seen whether these changes to the G.R.E.A.T. program will produce positive outcomes for future recipients of the program. While the G.R.E.A.T. program is in the process of developing a family component to supplement its school curricula, to what extent can such individual-based prevention programs affect gang involvement? A significant reduction in gang activity may be too much to expect from any program if the more fundamental causes and attractions of gangs (i.e., social, structural, community, and family conditions) are not simultaneously addressed.

Note

1. This chapter is a compilation of evaluation results published or presented in various venues. My sincere thanks and indebtedness are due to my colleagues, without whom this research would not have been possible: T. J. Taylor, Dana Lynskey, Adrienne Freng, Lesley Brandt, Wayne Osgood, Chris Sellers, Tom Winfree, Libby Deschenes, and Fran Bernat. Additionally, I would like to thank the numerous respondents (students, parents, teachers, and law enforcement officers) who provided their time and assistance in the completion of this evaluation. This research was supported under award #94-IJ-CX-0058 from the National Institute of Justice, Office of Justice Programs, U.S. Department of Justice. Points of view in this document are those of the author and do not necessarily represent the official position of the U.S. Department of Justice.

2. Active parental consent was required in the Torrance site. See Chapter 14, this volume, for a discussion.

References

Akers, Ronald L. 1985. *Deviant Behavior: A Social Learning Approach.* 3d ed. Belmont, CA: Wadsworth.

Deschenes, Elizabeth Piper, and Finn-Aage Esbensen. 1999. "Violence and Gangs: Gender Differences in Perceptions and Behavior." *Journal of Quantitative Criminology* 15: 53–96.

Dillman, Don A. 1978. *Mail and Telephone Surveys: The Total Design Method.* New York: Wiley.

Esbensen, Finn-Aage, and Elizabeth Piper Deschenes. 1998. "Boys and Girls in Gangs: Are There Gender Differences in Attitudes and Behavior?" *Criminology* 36: 799–828.

Esbensen, Finn-Aage, Michelle H. Miller, Terrance J. Taylor, Ni He, and Adrienne Freng.

1999. "Differential Attrition Rates and Active Parental Consent." *Evaluation Review* 23: 316–335.

Esbensen, Finn-Aage, and D. Wayne Osgood. 1997. *Research in Brief.* National Evaluation of G.R.E.A.T. Washington, D.C.: U.S. Department of Justice.

———. 1999. "Gang Resistance Education and Training (G.R.E.A.T.): Results from the National Evaluation." *Journal of Research in Crime and Delinquency* 36: 194–225.

Esbensen, Finn-Aage, D. Wayne Osgood, Terrance J. Taylor, Dana Peterson Lynskey, and Adrienne Freng. 2000. "Longitudinal Results from the National Evaluation of the Gang Resistance Education and Training (G.R.E.A.T.) Program." Washington, D.C.: National Institute of Justice.

Esbensen, Finn-Aage, and L. Thomas Winfree, Jr. 1998. "Race and Gender Differences Between Gang and Non-Gang Youth: Results from a Multi-Site Survey." *Justice Quarterly* 15: 505–526.

Gottfredson, Michael R., and Travis Hirschi. 1990. *A General Theory of Crime.* Stanford, CA: Stanford University Press.

Grasmick, Harold G., Charles R. Tittle, Robert J. Bursik, Jr., and Bruce J. Arneklev. 1993. "Testing the Core Empirical Implications of Gottfredson and Hirschi's General Theory of Crime." *Journal of Research in Crime Delinquency* 30: 5–29.

Hansen, William B., Linda M. Collins, C. Kevin Malotte, C. Anderson Johnson, and Jonathan E. Fielding. 1985. "Attrition in Prevention Research." *Journal of Behavioral Medicine* 8: 261–275.

Hawkins, J. David, and Richard F. Catalano. 1993. *Communities That Care: Risk-Focused Prevention Using the Social Developmental Model.* Seattle, WA: Developmental Research and Programs, Inc.

Hindelang, Michael J., Travis Hirschi, and Joseph G. Weis. 1981. *Measuring Delinquency.* Beverly Hills, CA: Sage Publications.

Huizinga, David. 1991. "Assessing Violent Behavior with Self-Reports." In Joel Milner (ed.) *Neuropsychology of Aggression.* Boston, MA: Kluwer.

Huizinga, David, and Delbert S. Elliott. 1986. "Reassessing the Reliability and Validity of Self-Report Delinquency Measures." *Journal of Quantitative Criminology* 2: 293–327.

Huizinga, David, Rolf Loeber, and Terence P. Thornberry. 1994. *Urban Delinquency and Substance Abuse.* Washington, D.C.: U.S. Department of Justice.

Judd, Charles M., and Gary H. McClelland. 1989. *Data Analysis: A Model-Comparison Approach.* New York: Harcourt Brace Jovanovich.

Sellers, Christine S., Terrance J. Taylor, and Finn-Aage Esbensen. 1998. "Reality Check: Evaluating a School-Based Gang Prevention Model." *Evaluation Review* 22: 590–608.

Sherman, Lawrence W., Denise Gottfredson, Doris MacKenzie, John Eck, Peter Reuter, and Shawn Bushway. 1997. *Preventing Crime: What Works, What Doesn't, What's Promising.* Washington, D.C.: National Institute of Justice.

Tebes, Jacob K., Davis L. Snow, and Michael W. Arthur. 1992. "Panel Attrition and External Validity in the Short-Term Follow-Up Study of Adolescent Substance Use." *Evaluation Review* 16: 151–170.

Winfree, L. Thomas, Jr., and Frances Bernat. 1998. "Social Learning, Self-Control, and the Illicit Drug Use Patterns of Eighth-Grade Students: A Tale of Two Cities." *Journal of Drug Issues* 28: 539–558.

Winfree, L. Thomas, Jr., Finn-Aage Esbensen, and D. Wayne Osgood. 1996. "Evaluating a School-Based Gang Prevention Program: A Theoretical Perspective." *Evaluation Review* 20: 181–203.

Winfree, L. Thomas, Jr., Teresa Vigil-Backstrom, and G. Larry Mays. 1994. "Social Learning Theory, Self-Reported Delinquency, and Youth Gangs: A New Twist on a General Theory of Crime and Delinquency." *Youth and Society* 26: 147–177. ✦

Chapter 32
Antigang Legislation and Its Potential Impact

The Promises and the Pitfalls

Beth Bjerregaard

Prior to the 1980s, many attempts to use gang membership itself as a charge that could lead to prosecution proved ineffective, and were often ruled by courts to be vague and ambiguous. With the advent of the California Street Terrorism Enforcement and Prevention (STEP) Act, this is no longer the case. This act, and its equivalents in many other states, has passed the test of legal acceptance and is now used to suppress gang crime as a special form of crime. In this chapter, Bjerregaard provides a fine overview of the STEP Act with its advantages and drawbacks. Although such legislation has been on the books since 1988 and is promoted by authorities as a major tool in gang crime suppression, it is remarkable that no research has been reported to address the effectiveness, good or bad, of this gang-specific legislation.

There is a growing perception that street gangs are becoming more powerful and aggressive and are infiltrating areas of the United States previously thought to be immune to the threat of gang activity. There is evidence that both the nature of gangs and their criminal activities have changed significantly in recent years (Quinn & Downs, 1993). Several theses have been advanced to explain these changes, such as the gangs' increased involvement in the drug trade, in-

creased access to firearms, and increased sophistication. In conjunction, media coverage of gangs began to intensify during the 1980s (McCorkle & Miethe, 2002, p. 4). There is little doubt that these changes have resulted in an increased awareness of the problems associated with gangs. As a result, law enforcement personnel and policy makers began to focus on strategies to solve the emerging gang problem. Communities, whose social lives have been negatively affected by gangs and their criminal activities, also began to search out ways to effectively deal with gang-related activities.

Review of Legislative Approaches

There are essentially three primary strategies that have been developed to deal with gangs: prevention, intervention, and suppression. Prevention programs have been designed to identify and amend the factors associated with gang membership. Intervention programs are designed to direct youth out of the gangs. Suppression strategies, on the other hand, emphasize the supervision, arrest, prosecution, and incarceration of known gang members. In recent years, the growing conservativism that has emerged in the United States, coupled with the perceived failure of rehabilitation as an effective approach to crime control, has resulted in an increased emphasis on suppression techniques (Klein, 1995). This approach has been best developed in areas with established gang problems and has resulted in a variety of inventive policies. Police departments, in mainly large urban areas, have created specialized gang units designed to conduct surveillance and gather information about both gangs and gang members operating in their jurisdictions. Other strategies have included such things as conducting police sweeps, establishing special gang prosecution units, and incarcerating serious known gang members (for a summary of these approaches, see Spergel, 1995). However, research has suggested that these approaches have not been particularly successful (Klein, 1995; Oehme, 1997).

In conjunction with these approaches, a number of innovative approaches have emerged in recent years including the creation of new legislation aimed specifically at prosecuting gang members. Some jurisdictions have relied on traditional tactics utiliz-

Reprinted from: Beth Bjerregaard, "Antigang Legislation and Its Potential Impact: The Promises and the Pitfalls." *Criminal Justice Policy Review* 14(2): 171–192. Copyright © 2003 by Sage Publications, Inc. Reprinted by permission of Sage Publications, Inc.

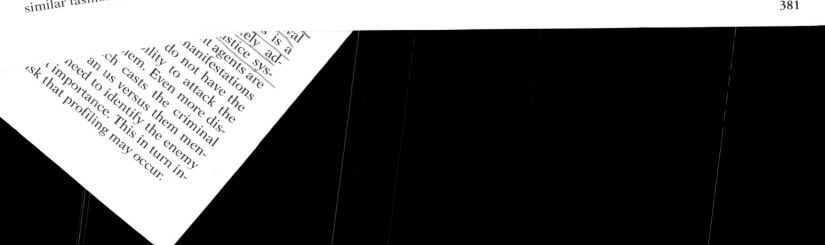

ing antiloitering, public nuisance, curfew, and parental responsibility statutes to prosecute gang members. Additionally, legislatures have criminalized a variety of gang activities such as gang solicitation and recruitment, witness intimidation, and drive-by shootings. One of the most comprehensive approaches was initiated in the state of California. In 1988, the state enacted the California Street Terrorism Enforcement and Prevention Act (STEP) (1997). The STEP Act makes it a substantive crime ⟨to⟩ participate in criminal gang activity. Th⟨e Act⟩ states that any person who

> actively participates in an⟨y⟩
> street gang with knowledge ⟨that its mem⟩
> bers engage in or have e⟨ngaged in a pat⟩
> tern of criminal gan⟨g activity, and who⟩
> willfully promotes
> any felonious cri⟨minal conduct by mem⟩
> bers of that g⟨ang⟩

is guilty of
several y
ifornia's
(for a rev
1999).

Most of
the Califor
common f
under these
number of el
onstrate the ex
gang. Although a
utilized by differen
states clarify that a ga
least three individuals, ⟨
mal or informal organiz
and include members who ⟨
a pattern of criminal activi⟨
Act, 1997). Once the state has pi
istence of a criminal street gang,
demonstrate that the defendant haq
edge that [the gang] members engage
have engaged in a pattern of criminal a⟨
ity" and that he or she had the specific ⟨
tent to "promote, further, or assist the criminal conduct of the gang" (e.g., STEP Act, 1997). Last, the state must demonstrate that the defendant is a member of that gang. There are a variety of definitions utilized by states to identify an individual as a gang member.

The purpose of this article is to examine these legislative responses by analyzing them in terms of their potential benefits and abuses. Particular emphasis will be placed

on the potential discri⟨min⟩ation of these legislative r⟨...⟩ tions for improvi⟨ng...⟩ offered.

Poter⟨...⟩

l.
an⟨d⟩
iors a⟨nd⟩
punish.
criminal
legislation
sense that so⟨...⟩
the problem.

There is ample evidence that minorities comprise the vast majority of all gang databases. In fact, in Orange County, California, 92% of those listed were youth of color; similarly, in Cook County, Illinois, the database was found to be two-thirds Black (Pintado-Vertner & Change, 2000, p. 5). These databases identify youth as "suspects" before any crime has been committed (Pintado-Vertner & Change, 2000, p. 4).

Leading gang experts caution that such labeling may serve to increase group cohesion by drawing attention to the gang and increasing the alienation that exists between the gang and the community (Conly, Kelly, Mahanna, & Warner, 1993; Klein & Maxson, 1989). Malcolm Klein (1995) points out that focusing on gangs and gang members also gives status and identity to the gang.

Practical Difficulties With the Statutory Construction of the Legislation

Although antigang legislation was enacted with ambitious objectives, it is unclear that such legislation has been or will be an effective tool to address gang-related problems. Existing statutes present a variety of issues, which need to be addressed to enhance their effectiveness and to reduce the chance that such legislation will be utilized inappropriately.

Constitutionality of Statutes

All of these statutes were designed to provide states with a tool to attack gangs and gang members directly instead of simply addressing the resultant criminal activities. Since their enactment, several of these statutes have faced constitutional challenges. The most common method of attacking this legislation has been to challenge it as unconstitutionally vague. Cases have questioned specific terminology contained within the statutes such as "actively participates," "criminal street gang," and "gang membership" (Bjerregaard, 1998). These statutes have also been attacked for being overbroad and infringing on constitutionally protected activities such as freedom of association. Thus far, state antigang legislation modeled after the California STEP Act has withstood these challenges and been upheld at the state appellate level. In upholding these statutes, the courts have rec-

ognized the importance of employing limiting elements. Specifically, the courts have emphasized the importance of requiring specific intent and knowledgeable active participation in the construction of these statutes. Similarly, they have applauded states for clearly defining key terminology within the statutes. All of these components operate to reduce discretion and act to ensure the fair and equitable application of the law.

In 1998, for the first time, the U.S. Supreme Court, in *City of Chicago v. Morales et al.* (1999), considered the constitutionality of a city ordinance prohibiting gang loitering. In response to citizen complaints, the city of Chicago enacted an ordinance, which stated that

> whenever a police officer observes a person whom he reasonably believes to be a criminal street gang member loitering in any public place with one or more other persons, he shall order all such persons to disperse and remove themselves from the area. Any person who does not promptly obey such an order is in violation of this section. (Chicago Municipal Code §8-4-015)

The key problem cited by the Supreme Court was the vagueness of the key terminology in the ordinance, which essentially gave the police officers the "absolute discretion to determine what activities constitute loitering" (*City of Chicago v. Morales et al.*, 1999, pp. 32–33) and therefore potentially enforce the law in an arbitrary and/or discriminatory fashion.

Thus far, almost all of these statutes have withstood constitutional challenges at the state appellate level. Having been held facially valid, we need to turn toward the application of such laws.

Definitional Issues

Social scientists have been grappling with definitional issues since they first started studying gangs (see Ball & Curry, 1995). Although a consensus seems to exist among the STEP legislation, not all antigang statutes employ similar definitions. Most states' statutes are patterned after California's STEP Act (1997) and define a gang as

> any ongoing organization, association or group of three or more persons, whether formal or informal, having as one of its primary activities the commission of one

or more of the criminal acts enumerated, having a common name or common identifying sign or symbol, and whose members individually or collectively engage in or have engaged in a pattern of criminal gang activity. (STEP Act, 1997)

Perhaps most troubling, in terms of providing guidance for enforcement of these statutes, are the definitions of gang membership. Under existing legislation, law enforcement officers must have probable cause to believe that the alleged offender either is a gang member or has knowledge that he or she is assisting known gang members. A gang member is typically defined as "a person who engages in a pattern of criminal street gang activity and who meets two or more of a list of enumerated criteria," most often including self-admission, identification by a parent/guardian, information from a reliable informant or an informant plus corroboration, physical evidence, photographs, tattoos, clothing style, colors, residence in an area frequented by gang members, use of hand signs, and being stopped in the company of or arrested with gang members a number of times (e.g., Arizona Rev. Stat. Ann., 1996).

Under Florida and South Dakota laws, a person could potentially meet the statutory definition of a gang member simply by living in a gang area, associating with known gang members, and being stopped in the company of gang members more than four times. (Truman, 1995, p. 717)

There are several problems inherent in this type of definition. First, social science researchers recognize that there are varying levels of participation in gangs and that membership in some types of gangs is evasive (Covey et al., 1997, p. 12). Researchers have found that gang membership is relatively unstable and that many individuals drift in and out of gang involvement (Esbensen & Huizinga, 1993; Thornberry, Krohn, Lizotte, & Chard-Wierschem, 1993). Additionally, leading gang scholars have recognized that there are several different types of gang members whose participation and commitment to the gang vary (Klein, 1995). Core members are much more actively involved in the gang than fringe members or "wannabees" who are not considered to be true gang members by their peers. Therefore, identification of an individual by a third party and even self-identification may not be reliable indicators of gang members without more objective criteria.

Second, and even more problematic, is the fact that several of the enumerated gang indicators are extremely open to interpretation and provide law enforcement officers with little guidance and broad discretion in enforcing these statutes. Herein lies the crux of the problem. The flexibility provided by such broad definitions gives law enforcement officers a fair amount of discretion in enforcing these statutes. In fact, a certain amount of discretion is necessary for officers to be able to do their jobs efficiently and effectively. However, discretion also opens the door to the possibility of abuse. Racism in the criminal justice system has frequently hidden behind the cloak of discretion (Herman, 1993).

The race of a suspect may influence an officer's decision to stop and potentially arrest in a number of different ways. First, because the majority of gangs are composed primarily of minority members and because law enforcement efforts to eradicate gangs are primarily conducted in inner-city minority communities, they are the individuals who are most likely to be subjected to this law. Whereas police officers, as well as judges, would agree that approaching and/or detaining a suspect solely on the basis of his or her race would be illegal, police also admit that race is often a factor that contributes to their decision to detain a suspect (S. L. Johnson, 1983). African Americans and other ethnic minorities frequently "reside and work in areas associated with criminal activity thereby increasing the likelihood of [police contact]" (Harris, 1994, pp. 677–678).

The definition is constructed in such a way that it allows officers to compose profiles of potential or likely gang members. Race and/or ethnicity would likely be one of the factors included in such a profile. This practice has already been noted with drug courier profiling (Allen-Bell, 1997). There is evidence that suggests many police officers believe that minority status correlates with a general propensity to commit crime and that this belief can influence their decisions to investigate and/or detain a suspect (S. L. Johnson, 1983). One commentator has argued that using race as a proxy for criminality "results from a self-fulfilling prophecy: racial stereotypes influence police to arrest

Improving Definitions

First and foremost, we must strive to ensure that these statutes are not written in such a fashion as to be vague or overbroad. Although the appellate courts have almost unanimously held that the terminology defined within the existing statutes is not unconstitutionally vague, this is an area in which legislatures would benefit from consulting social science research and experts in the study of gangs. As one commentator noted, "for a statute to have a reasonable expectation of achieving its intended goal, those crafting it must have knowledge of the behavior that they are attempting to alter" (Holland, 1995, p. 278). At this point in time, law enforcement agencies, legislatures, and sociologists often employ vastly different definitions of gangs and gang-related activity. Although it is beyond the scope of this article to create the perfect definition, there are several ways in which existing definitions can be improved.

Gang Membership

First, there should not be an overemphasis on the social ties of the individual or on his or her area of residence. Although both of these factors may be related to gang membership, they should not by themselves define an individual as a gang member. By identifying youth as gang members if they meet two or more of the enumerated criteria, one can be identified solely on the basis of these criteria.

Likewise, there should be a tempered focus on the juvenile's attire. The Portland Police Department employs a definition that both recognizes that attire can be a sign of gang membership and narrows the criteria so that sole reliance on basic attire is not acceptable. Their definition states that "an individual [must] display clothes, jewelry, hand signs and/or tattoos *unique* to gang affiliation; clothing color alone is *not sufficient* for designation" [italics added] (quoted in Mayer, 1993, p. 973).

Definitions should attempt to focus on hard-core, committed gang members. Additionally, laws should be aimed toward groups with clear criminal agendas. Legislatures should be careful to restrict their definitions of gang membership to include only individuals who are actively and not peripherally involved in the gangs, thereby excluding wannabees and fringe members from their statutes. There are several ways that

this could be accomplished. One is to examine factors such as the frequency of association. Commitment can also be demonstrated by emphasizing the individual's intent to further the criminal purpose of the group. Ensuring that the statute requires specific intent helps to ensure that only blameworthy individuals are targeted by the legislation. If legislatures are going to rely on an enumerated list of indicators, they should require the presence of at least three of these criteria so that no two factors such as clothing and area of residence are enough to identify someone as a gang member.

Gangs

In terms of defining a criminal gang, reconceptualizing the requirement of a "pattern of criminal activity" would help to ensure that the individual criminal behavior of one or two individuals does not become the shared responsibility of all youth who associate with them. This would reduce the risk of all members being treated as presumptively culpable. Furthermore, the enumerated offenses should be serious offenses. Similarly, to punish someone for his or her gang involvement, the enumerated offenses should be restricted to gang-related offenses. Finally, legislatures should clearly define this term to exclude concurrent activities and to require that this element can only be met by repeated violations of the law, demonstrated by at least two separate offenses.

The adoption of a narrower, more specific definition of gang membership is beneficial for a number of reasons. First, it ensures that the legislation is targeting serious, involved gang members. This will help preserve police-community relations as well as guard against such possibilities as increasing gang cohesion and/or inappropriately labeling juveniles as gang members and potentially increasing their criminal involvement and perhaps contributing to a breakdown in respect for the law. Finally, narrow definitions operate to curtail police discretion and therefore reduce the possibility that the laws will be applied in a discriminatory fashion.

Additionally, any time the possibility of discriminatory application of a law exists, we should strive to employ stricter standards of review to ensure that this will not occur. The U.S. Supreme Court recognized as far back as their decision in *Terry v. Ohio*

(1968) that certain investigative techniques resulted in tensions between urban citizens and the police. Whenever evidence exists that racial profiling might have occurred or that race played a significant role in the decision to label an individual as a gang member, courts should employ a heightened level of scrutiny to these cases. Judges should carefully screen these cases to ensure that independent evidence against the defendant exists. Kennedy (1997) suggests that race should be prohibited from entering into the decision-making process, except in those cases when the state can offer a compelling justification for its existence.

Antigang Legislation as an Effective Tool

Perhaps the biggest problem with these approaches is that they provide only temporary solutions and ignore the real problems that have contributed to the increase in both gangs and gang-related activity in our society. By focusing on gang suppression, we take the emphasis off of identifying and eradicating the ultimate causes of gang development and gang membership. Thus, these strategies fall short of offering meaningful solutions to the problem (Shelden, Tracy, & Brown, 1997). In many communities, gangs represent a survival strategy for some youth (Covey et al., 1997). Gangs are not created only to commit criminal acts. If gangs are eradicated in these neighborhoods, we need to think about what will replace the gang in these youths' lives. Likewise, gang suppression techniques may simply temporarily reduce membership in the gang. Without addressing the causes of gang involvement, other youth will be there to simply replace, or at least supplement, the incarcerated member.

Current gang initiatives should decrease the emphasis on suppression by increasing the commitment to prevention. It is vitally important to utilize research to identify the factors that place a juvenile at risk for gang involvement and to initiate programs to help control these factors. To effectively address the issue of gang membership, we need to focus on the root causes of gang membership rather than expending our efforts in trying to control gangs once they are formed. Inasmuch as the causes of gang membership are extensive and interrelated, dealing with gangs requires a comprehensive, multifaceted approach. We have a good deal of social science research to help guide policy in this regard. Although there is much that can be done at the individual level, such as providing youth with alternatives to gang involvement, strengthening of family ties, and educational commitment, to institute large-scale reforms, change must take place at the societal level. Hagedorn (1988) suggests deemphasizing the criminal justice system as a method of handling the gang problem. Instead, he suggests we should focus our efforts on providing meaningful employment opportunities and improving education. We need to develop programs that will address housing conditions in our inner cities, promote economic revitalization in minority communities, and primarily reduce economic and social inequality in our society (Joseph, 1997). McKenzie (1996) suggests that the best place to initiate these policies might be the inner suburban rings of metropolitan areas. Gang problems are not as well established in these areas and also these communities may have some of the features that would enhance successful implementation; these include substantial tax bases, a core group of residents with solid ties to the community and the proximity to the large city. These areas also have more heterogeneous populations that would allow for a multicultural approach.

To be successful, any intervention strategy will need to include systematic evaluation as a necessary component. A key problem is that there have been no real systematic evaluations of any of these strategies. What we currently know has been pieced together from a variety of sources. With appropriate evaluation, we can enhance and elaborate polices that are successfully meeting their goals, eliminate those that are not, and rework those that are struggling.

Programs designed to attack the root causes of gang membership are going to be complex and costly. Additionally, the results of these programs are not going to be realized immediately. Currently, there is a "deep-rooted reluctance to face up to the implications of the social context of gang life" (Covey et al., 1997, p. 313). In fact, Anonymous (1994, p. 1707) points out that by implementing our current strategies, we as a society have overreacted to the gang problem in what she also terms a moral panic. She feels that this panic is, at least in part, driven by our lack of empathy for the problems facing inner-city youth and our images of minorities as criminals. Moore (1993, pp. 28–29) also identifies some of the most common stereotypes concerning gangs. She states that these stereotypes contribute to our moral panic. These stereotypes, coupled with a lack of research to address their validity, contribute to our lack of ability to address the problem effectively. We should educate our law enforcement personnel so that they are not susceptible to these clichés and therefore not prone to typecast.

Prosecutors and police officers can also rely on existing legislation to attack the substantive crimes committed by gang members, deemphasizing the use of antigang legislation because its deterrent value is at the least questionable. This would move police officers away from the difficult and potentially dangerous task of having to identify gangs and gang members and would place the emphasis back on the substantive crime being committed by the individual, regardless of his or her status as a gang member. Most jurisdictions already have in place "three strikes you're out" legislation, which would allow prosecutors to attack offenders with subsequent offenses more harshly.

At a minimum, these issues should be taken seriously. We need to allocate the resources necessary to deal with these issues and be committed to developing and implementing long-term strategies that will benefit future generations. All of us, academicians, social science researchers, legislators, and practitioners alike should work together to address this issue. The gang problem needs to be addressed in a comprehensive and deliberate manner. For any solution to be ultimately effective, it must not only address the root causes of the problem, but it must also ensure that it operates in such a way as to protect the rights of innocent citizens. Although the task may seem overwhelming at first, it is one that we must tackle if we are to advance and improve our society.

Notes

1. McCorkle & Miethe (2002, pp. 11–12) point out that the claims makers are often sincere and convinced they are pursuing noble goals.
2. An important notable exception to this is the recent Supreme Court decision, *City of Chicago v. Morales et al.* (1999) where the Court held that the definition of loitering used by the city of Chicago was impermissibly vague.

References

Allen-Bell, A. A. (1997). The birth of the crime: Driving while Black (DWB). *Southern University Law Review*, 25, 195–225.

Anonymous. (1994). Juvenile curfews and gang violence: Exiled on main street. *Harvard Law Review*, 107, 1693–1710.

Ariz. Rev. Stat. Ann. § 13-105 (8) (West Supp. 1996).

Armor, J. D., & Jackson, V. K. (1995). Juvenile gang activity in Alabama. *The Journal of Gang Research*, 2, 29–35.

Austin, R. (1992). The Black community, its lawbreakers, and the politics of identification. *Southern California Law Review*, 65, 1769–1817.

Ball, R. A., & Curry, G. D. (1995). The logic of definition in criminology: Purposes and methods for defining "gangs." *Criminology*, 33, 225–245.

Bayley, D. H., & Mendelsohn, H. (1969). *Minorities and the police: Confrontation in America*. New York: Free Press.

Bjerregaard, B. (1998). The constitutionality of anti-gang legislation. *Campbell Law Review*, 27, 31–47.

———. (1999). The Supreme Court and antigang legislation: The potential impact of the Morales case. *The Criminal Law Bulletin*, 35, 27–41.

Browning, S. L., Cullen, F. T., Cao, L., Kopache, R., & Stevenson, T. J. (1994). Race and getting hassled by the police: A research note. *Police Studies*, 17, 1–10.

Burrell, S. L. (1990). Gang evidence: Issues for criminal defense. *Santa Clara Law Review*, 30, 739–790.

California Street Terrorism Enforcement and Prevention (STEP) Act, Cal. Penal Code § 186.20-28 (West, 1997).

Chicago gangs adopt Duke, UNC clothing as uniforms. (October 13, 1998). Daily News. Retrieved June 17, 1999, from http://www.jacksonville.com/stories/l998/10/13/hboh24.shtml.

Chicago Municipal Code § 8-4-015.

Chicago v. Morales, U.S. Briefs 1121 (1997).

City of Chicago v. Morales et al., U.S. LEXIS 4005 (1999).

Conly, C. H., Kelly, P., Mahanna, P., & Warner, L. (1993). *Street gangs: Current knowledge and strategies*. Washington, DC: National Institute of Justice.

Covey, H. C., Menard, S., & Franzese, R. J. (1997). *Juvenile gangs* (2nd ed.). Springfield, IL: Charles C Thomas.

Dahmann, J. (1995). An evaluation of Operation Hardcore: A prosecutorial response to violent gang criminality. In M. W. Klein, C. L. Maxson, & J. Miller (Eds.), *The modern gang reader* (pp. 301–303). Los Angeles: Roxbury.

Developments in the law—race and the criminal process. (1988). *Harvard Law Review*, 101, 1472–1641.

Esbensen, F. A., & Huizinga, D. (1993). Gangs, drugs, and delinquency in a survey of urban youth. *Criminology*, 31, 565–589.

Etter, G. W., Sr. (1998). Common characteristics of gangs: Examining the cultures of the new urban tribes. *Journal of Gang Research*, 5, 19–33.

Freed, D. (1995). Policing gangs: Case of contrasting styles. In M. W. Klein, C. L. Maxson, & J. Miller (Eds.), *The modern gang reader* (pp. 288–291). Los Angeles: Roxbury.

Hagedorn, J. (1988). *People and folks: Gangs, crime and the underclass in a rust belt city*. Chicago: Lake View Press.

Harris, D. A. (1994). Factors for reasonable suspicion: When Black and poor means stopped and frisked. *Indiana Law Journal*, 69, 659–688.

———. (1997). Driving while Black and all other traffic offenses: The Supreme Court and pretextual traffic stops. *Journal of Criminal Law and Criminology*, 87, 544–582.

Herman, S. N. (1993). Why the Court loves *Batson*: Representation, reinforcement, color-blindness, and the jury. *Tulane Law Review*, 67, 1807–1853.

Holland, L. (1995). Can gang recruitment be stopped? An analysis of the societal and legal factors affecting anti-gang legislation. *Journal of Contemporary Law*, 21, 259–305.

Howell, J. C. (April, 1994). *Gangs: Fact sheet #12*. Retrieved October 26, 1999, from http://www.ncjrs.org/txtfiles/gangsfs.txt.

Huff, C.R. (1989). Youth gangs and public policy. *Crime and Delinquency*, 35, 524–537.

In re Leland D., 272 Cal. Rptr. 709 (Cal. Ct App. 1990).

In re Lincoln J., 272 Cal. Rptr. 852 (Cal. Ct. App. 1990).

In re Nathaniel C., 279 Cal. Rptr. 236 (Cal. Ct. App. 1991).

Jackson, P. (1997). The police and social threat: Urban transition, youth gangs, and social control. In G. L. Mays (Ed.), *Gangs and gang behavior* (pp. 81–98). Chicago: Nelson-Hall Publishers.

Jackson, P., & Rudman, C. (1993). Moral panic and the response to gangs in California. In S. Cummings & D. J. Monti (Eds.), *Gangs: The origins and impact of contemporary youth gangs in the United States* (pp. 257–275). Albany: State University of New York Press.

Johnson, D. (1993, December 11). Two out of three young Black men in Denver listed by police as suspected gangsters. *The New York Times*, p. A-8.

Johnson, S. L. (1983). Race and the decision to detain a suspect. *Yale Law Journal*, 93, 214–258.

Joseph, J. (1997). Black youth gangs. *Journal of Gang Research*, 4, 1–12.

Kennedy, R. (1997). *Race, crime and law*. New York: Vintage.

Klein, M. W. (1995). *The American street gang: Its nature, prevalence, and control*. New York: Oxford University Press.

Klein, M. W., & Maxson, C. L. (1989). Street gang violence. In N. A. Weiner & M. E. Wolfgang (Eds.), *Violent crimes, violent criminals* (pp. 198–234). Newbury Park, CA: Sage.

L. A. City Attorney Gang Prosecution Section. (2001). Civil gang abatement: A community-based policing tool of the Office of the Los Angeles City Attorney. In J. Miller, C. L. Maxson, & M. W. Klein (Eds.), *The modern gang reader* (2nd ed., pp. 320–329). Los Angeles: Roxbury.

Maclin, T. (1998). *Race and the Fourth Amendment*. Vanderbilt Law Review, 51, 333–393.

Mayer, J. J. (1993). Individual moral responsibility and the criminalization of youth gangs. *Wake Forest Law Review*, 28, 943–998.

McCorkle, R. C., & Miethe, T. D. (1998). The political and organizational response to gangs: An examination of a "moral panic" in Nevada. *Justice Quarterly*, 15, 41–64.

———. (2002). *Panic: The social construction of the street gang problem*. Upper Saddle River, NJ: Prentice Hall.

McKenzie, E. (1996). Suburban youth gangs and public policy: An alternative to the war on violence. *Journal of Emotional and Behavioral Problems*, 5, 52–55.

Moore, J. (1993). Gangs, drugs, and violence. In S. Cummings & D. J. Monti (Eds.), *Gangs: The origins and impact of contemporary youth gangs in the United States* (pp. 27–46). Albany: State University of New York Press.

National Youth Gang Center (n.d.). *Analysis of gang-related legislation*. Retrieved August 25, 2002, from http://www.iir.com/nygc/gang-legis/analysix.htm.

Oehme, C. G., III. (1997). *Gangs, groups and crime: Perceptions and responses of community organizations*. Durham, NC: Carolina Academic Press.

People v. Gardeley, 927 P.2d 713 (Cal. 1996).

Pintado-Vertner, R., & Change, J. (2000). The war on youth. *Color Lines*. Retrieved August 25, 2002, from http://www.alternet.org/story.html?storyid=285.

Quinn, J. R, & Downs, B. (1993). Predictors of the severity of the gang problem at the local level: An analysis of police perceptions. *Gang Journal*, 1, 1–10.

Salt Lake City Sheriff's Department, (n.d.). *Gangster clothing*. Retrieved February 20, 2002, from http://www.slsheriff.org/html/org/metro gang/clothes.html.

Shelden, R. G., Tracy, S. K., & Brown, W. B. (1997). *Youth gangs in American society.* Belmont, CA: Wadsworth.

Skolnick, J., & Fyfe, J. (1993). *Above the law: Police and the excessive use of force.* New York: Free Press.

Spergel, I. (1990). Youth gangs: Continuity and change. In M. Tonry & N. Morris (Eds.), *Crime and justice: A review of the research* (pp. 171–275). Chicago: University of Chicago Press.

———. (1995). *The youth gang problem: A community approach.* New York: Oxford University Press.

Stover, D. (1986). A new breed of youth gangs is on the prowl and a bigger threat than ever. *American School Board Journal, 173,* 19–25.

Taylor-Greene, H. (1994). Black perspectives on police brutality. In A. T. Sulton (Ed.), *African-American perspectives on crime causation, criminal justice administration and crime prevention* (pp. 139–148). Englewood, CO: Sulton.

Terry v. Ohio, 392 U.S. 1 (1968).

Texas Youth Commission, (n.d.). *Gang related clothing.* Retrieved February 20, 2002, from http://www.tyc.state.tx.us/prevention/clothing.html.

Thornberry, T., Krohn, M. D., Lizotte, A., & Chard-Wierschem, D. (1993). The role of juvenile gangs in facilitating delinquent behavior. *Journal of Research in Crime and Delinquency, 30,* 55–87.

Truman, D. R. (1995). The Jets and Sharks are dead: State statutory responses to criminal street gangs. *Washington University Law Quarterly, 73,* 683–735.

An urban ethnology of Latino street gangs in Los Angeles and Ventura Counties. (n.d.). Retrieved October 26, 1999, from http://www.csun.edu/~hcchs006/table.html.

Wilson, W. J. (1987). *The truly disadvantaged: The inner city, the underclass, and public policy.* Chicago: University of Chicago Press.

Zatz, M. (1987). Chicago youth gangs and crime: The creation of a moral panic. *Contemporary Crisis, 11,* 129–158. ✦

Chapter 33
For the Sake of the Neighborhood?

Civil Gang Injunctions as a Gang Intervention Tool in Southern California

Cheryl L. Maxson,
Karen Hennigan,
and David C. Sloane

Civil gang injunctions are the newest form of antigang suppression employed by law enforcement and the courts. Pioneered in Southern California but now being seen elsewhere as well, gang injunctions have been widely praised for their capacity to reduce gang activity and bring needed relief to neighborhoods subjected to gang harassment and violence. Yet such claims have derived, at best, from selected anecdotal reports rather than from careful, independent research evaluations. The authors of this chapter provide useful background information for understanding this form of gang suppression activity, along with some indications of limited but promising measurable positive effects of injunctions. The legal issues involved remain ambiguous, but to date appellate courts have approved the use of gang injunctions, backing community rights to relief over individual civil rights of gang members.

Introduction

Civil gang injunctions (CGIs) are a legal tool for addressing the hold that entrenched gangs have on urban neighborhoods. Unlike some law enforcement gang intervention

Reprinted from: Scott H. Decker (ed.), *Policing Gangs and Violence,* 1st edition, pp. 239–263. Copyright © 2003. Reprinted with permission of Wadsworth, a division of Thomson Learning: www.thomsonrights.com. Fax: 800 730-2215.

strategies that focus on individuals or gangs without regard to place, CGIs are spatially based, neighborhood-level interventions intended to disrupt a gang's routine activities. As several police officers and attorneys have told us, CGIs are not simply ways to attack a gang problem, they are also for the sake of the neighborhood. The injunction targets specific individuals (and often other unnamed gang members) who affect the daily lives of residents through intimidation and public nuisances and restricts their activities within the boundaries of a defined geographic space.

The CGI asserts that as an unincorporated association, a gang has engaged in criminal and other activities that constitute a public nuisance. Specific members are liable for civil action as a consequence of their membership in the association. The use of injunctions against gangs was pioneered as early as 1980, but only since 1993 has the strategy become widespread in Los Angeles and Southern California. The accelerated use reflects the perceived successes of injunctions in disrupting gang activities as well as the continuing search by law enforcement for new tools to respond to gangs.

The region's law enforcement agencies have been national leaders in experimenting with gang suppression and intervention strategies. Southern California is the second largest metropolitan area in the nation with roughly 15 million residents. It has become known nationally as an incubator for gangs. The latest law enforcement estimates, as reported to the National Youth Gang Survey (NYGS) in 2000, totals 1,958 gangs and 165,078 gang members in the seven-county (Ventura, Los Angeles, Orange, Riverside, San Bernardino, San Diego, and Imperial) Southern California region.[1]

The city of Los Angeles and its suburbs have long garnered national media attention as the "gang capital" of the United States. Gang homicides in Los Angeles County have declined precipitously from the peak of about 800 incidents per year in the mid-1990s to 349 in 1999 (based on data provided by Los Angeles Sheriff's Department), but represented around 40 percent of all homicides in the region throughout the 1990s. In 2000, countywide gang homicide incidents increased to 520, or 55 percent of all homicides. Los Angeles city figures generally exceed those of the closest contender,

Chicago, by 50 percent (see Maxson, 1999, for a comparison of Los Angeles and Chicago gang homicide patterns and Maxson and Klein, 2002, for a more general discussion of the gang dynamics in these two cities).

Although the sheer numbers of Southern California gangs and gang members, as well as the violence and other criminal activity committed by gang participants, dwarf those of the nation's other regions, are its gangs unique? Multiple-city comparisons of gangs are becoming more common, but recent studies by Thornberry (1998), Miller (2001), and Huff (1996) omit cities in Southern California. Three recent comparative works include at least one Southern California gang site. Decker's (2001) comparison of organizational characteristics of selected gangs in San Diego, Chicago and St. Louis found Chicago to be the outlier (see also Decker, Bynum and Weisel, 1998). Maxson and Klein (2002) also report differences between Chicago and Los Angeles, confirming Decker's conclusion that the more organized character of Chicago gangs influences some aspects of gang migration from that city. Torrance, located just south of Los Angeles, is one of 11 cities studied by Esbensen and Lynskey (2001). These researchers found no striking differences in the patterns of gang organizational characteristics, reasons for joining gangs, and gang activities in Torrance as compared to the other 10 cities in their study. The evidence from these three studies suggests that street gangs in Southern California are not substantially different from gangs in many cities elsewhere in the nation, whereas the organizational qualities of some Chicago gangs are quite distinct.

Southern California has gangs of all types. The region encompasses both chronic and emergent gang cities (Spergel and Curry, 1993), a vast array of ethnic and national origins among its gang participants, drug gangs and taggers (individuals who spray paint a distinctive design on buildings), skinheads and prison gangs. Maxson and Klein (1995) identified five gang structures in a national sample. These ranged from the large, age-based or territorial-based clique structures of the traditional and neotraditional types, to the mid-sized compressed and amorphous collective types, to the small, crime-specialty type. They documented all five gang types in Southern California. This diversity makes it difficult to describe the gang situation here succinctly; it also presents a formidable challenge, as well as unique opportunities, for social service practitioners and law enforcement personnel to intervene.

The expanding use of CGIs may reflect a growing general interest in place-based policing. Although not all Southern California gangs have a strong impact on their communities, some are deeply entrenched. They view their street, block, or neighborhood as their territory, to be defended against all invaders. Computer technologies allow police forces to focus problem-oriented policing strategies not just on individual offenders but on specific places, including neighborhoods (Block and Block, 1993; Braga et al., 1999; Lasley, 1998). Most of these activities have centered on identifying and responding to "hot spots," and have been dependent on locating single buildings or businesses that are the site of greater than normal criminal activity. With the advent of community policing, a neighborhood focus is a common foundation in many contemporary law enforcement intervention programs (see Fearn, Decker, and Curry, 2001, for examples of such programs). The CGI not only identifies specific individuals to be enjoined but also a specific area in which their activities are proscribed. It gives officers a means for intervening in the routine activities that often are the core of a gang's intimidation of community residents and control of a neighborhood. By limiting their right to associate in public, their ability to conduct street-level drug sales, and their freedom to harass residents, the civil injunction attempts to abate gang members' influence and activities.

Although we have described the injunction strategy as a place-based, community-oriented intervention, alternative conceptual orientations, most notably deterrence, may also explain the perceived successes and popularity of injunctions. In the next section, we describe the various theoretical approaches that might be used to justify optimistic views of the impact of this strategy. For those readers who are not familiar with the injunction mechanism, we describe the injunction process in detail. We then move from policy to the practice arena, providing a brief history of the use of gang injunctions in Southern California. . . .

Southern California has been a laboratory for injunction implementation, although unfortunately, not for its systematic evaluation. We use several case studies to illustrate some important dimensions of injunctions, such as their flexibility and an emphasis on partnerships. We then review the available evidence of the impact of CGIs and the legal issues that have been raised. We conclude this chapter by addressing how this new intervention technology might be placed in several categories of the Spergel and Curry (1993) gang intervention typology. As shown in the following sections, the development and implementation of injunctions show considerable variation. This flexibility makes it difficult to reduce this strategy to any one dimension of the intervention typology.

Conceptual Underpinnings of Gang Injunctions

The theoretical basis for the use of injunctions is suggested by law enforcement documents and the statements of participants in injunction programs, but these are often vague and not developed sufficiently to provide testable conceptual models. In this section, we use documents and interview responses to illustrate program rationales and link these to three conceptual perspectives: social disorganization, deterrence, and de-individuation.

In the forward to the SAGE (Strategies Against Gang Environments) manual (Los Angeles County District Attorney, 1996), then district attorney Gil Garcetti distinguished the strategy from the traditional approach to prosecuting criminal street gang offenders:

> SAGE's approach has been: (1) to create an atmosphere in a local community that leads to cooperative conduct between residents in that community and the law enforcement components that are there to protect them; (2) in conjunction with the community, to identify those gang members who are problems; and (3) to stop those targeted criminal street gang members from committing acts that degrade the quality of life in that community, thus preventing an escalating scale of events that leads to violence. (p. i)

The SAGE approach is advanced as a model to combat the deterioration of neighborhoods:

> Instead of relying chiefly on arrests and convictions, community-based law enforcement (policing and prosecuting) is premised upon the fact that the quality of life of a neighborhood cannot improve unless residents actively participate with police and elected officials in the restoration of the neighborhood. (p. 2)

As these quotes illustrate, the SAGE manual frames the strategy of instituting injunctions against street gangs squarely within the tradition of community policing or problem-oriented policing perspectives. The manual is subtitled "A Handbook for Community Prosecution" and its first appendix is a reprint of the oft-cited "Broken Windows" article by Wilson and Kelling (1982).[2] The theoretical antecedents of such statements can be traced to the social disorganization model of neighborhood crime, which has a long tradition among gang researchers (Bursik and Grasmick, 1993). This theory postulates that gang activity arises in unstable, poor neighborhoods where institutional networks and mechanisms of informal social control are relatively weak. Gang injunctions can be seen as a strategy to engage community involvement in an overall effort to build informal social control, social capital (Short, 1997), and supportive organizational structures in deteriorated or deteriorating neighborhoods.

The development of gang injunctions must be firmly embedded in a community context to capitalize on the conceptual underpinnings of social disorganization theory (but see Buerger, 1994, for a discussion of the difficulties confronted in such efforts). Indicators of a community-based process might include resident involvement in the selection of the target gang and the nuisance behaviors to be enjoined, the willingness of residents or local business owners to provide declarations and testimony, and residents partnering with police officers to enforce the provision of the injunctions— for example by keeping records of graffiti they paint out and reporting violations.

Our observations of an injunction process in Inglewood, a suburb of Los Angeles, reinforced the priority placed on community involvement by the lead attorney, Henry Kerner. In a staff meeting he stated that "nothing is more important than community support. If there are no citizens to give their community back to, it [the injunction] doesn't do any good" (field notes, 23 May 1996). In a community meeting two weeks later, he described the injunction process as suing gangs like they were a polluting plant, dumping toxic chemicals. Gang members can stay, but they must stop the conduct that creates fear and hopelessness in neighborhood residents. He said he looked to residents to tell him what activities to restrict in the injunction (field notes, 5 June 1996).

An alternative rationale for employing gang injunctions draws from deterrence theory. Deterrence theory postulates that crime results from the offender's calculation that the probability of receiving punishment is outweighed by the anticipated benefits of committing the crime. As Klein (1993) notes, suppression approaches are loosely based on a deterrence perspective; one must look to explicit references by officials to recognize deterrence propositions because programs rarely articulate a theoretical paradigm. Our Inglewood field notes are rife with such comments: examples from one staff meeting with police, prosecutors and probation officers present include, "Stamp out the gang," "the gang feels under siege and they leave," and "we're putting them on the defensive." These comments suggest that deterrence goals are aimed primarily at the targeted gang, and range from specific deterrence (the impact of sanctions on those who are targeted) to general deterrence (the impact on the public at large, but defined here as the gang). Certainty and celerity (the speed with which a sanction is applied) are deterrence principles more aptly applied to injunctions than severity. Serving injunction papers to individual gang members makes clear they are intended targets. Fast hearings to prosecute injunction violations means that punishment is quick. The presumption is that few arrests will be required to send the message to the rest of the gang.

In contrast to community disorganization theory, deterrence perspectives suggest that the injunction's salutary effects result when targeted gang members perceive an ongoing threat of apprehension for enjoined behaviors. Serving legal papers alerts gang members that they are subject to sanctions, and learning about a fellow gang member's arrest and incarceration should increase perceptions of the probability of sanctions (see Braga et al., 1999, for a description of this process in Boston). Ongoing injunction enforcement would seem necessary to support the deterrent effect. In the absence of injunction program implementation guided by deterrence principles, one can expect that group processes that solidify gang identity could easily overwhelm any salutary effect realized by serving the papers alone.[3]

Gang researchers have noted the potential for gang suppression programs to backfire in the face of group processes that undermine deterrence messages through status enhancement, building cohesion within the gang, and invoking an oppositional culture, all of which lead to increased gang activity (Klein, 1995). A member of the 18th Street gang in Los Angeles makes the same point succinctly: " 'We're not taking it seriously.' . . . He said that the official attention being focused on the gang—which police say has up to 20,000 members in Southern California—united members and helping attract recruits. 'Other gangs are getting . . . into 18 Street,' he said. 'It's growing' " (Lopez and Connell, 1997). The potential for gang intervention efforts to unintentionally support group processes that solidify gang identity is a dynamic that could be examined empirically (see Klein, 1971, for one study that measured changes in gang cohesion resulting from a street worker program).

An alternative perspective within social psychological theory suggests that activities associated with injunctions might serve to decrease identification through individuation. The social identity and status conferred on individuals by virtue of membership in an admired group is particularly important in the adolescent stage of development (see Erikson, 1968) and is often cited as a primary reason for joining and maintaining gang ties (Curry and Decker, 1998; Decker and Van Winkle, 1996; Klein, 1995; Vigil, 1988). One way individuals reconcile committing extreme behaviors on behalf of the group with which they identify is to deindividuate (see Zimbardo, 1969)—that is, become less self-aware and feel less personally responsible for their behavior. Group attire, such as wearing gang colors, tattoos, or haircuts helps deemphasize the individual and emphasizes the group. Deindividuation may explain how street gang members comply with violent, ruthless group norms even if they have not fully internalized these values themselves. Gang members may engage in violent attacks or drive-by shootings as "group behavior"— that is, the individual is not acting out of personal malice toward the victim, but on behalf of the gang. Victims of gang homicides often are targeted for their gang affiliation rather than in retaliation for individual actions (Maxson, 1999).

We repeatedly heard from police and attorneys that the very act of presenting the injunction papers to the gang member had profound effects, including the person leaving the jurisdiction. We wondered how a piece of paper (that is, the injunction) stops gang members from participating in gang activities, when those same gang members have shown an utter indifference to other legal processes (for example, criminal laws, prosecutions, and jail time). Gang members are served with court papers that name them personally, describe in detail their individual actions, and state that they will be held personally accountable for actions they take. Members who have not fully internalized the gang norms and values may feel more inhibited about future participation in "group mode" behavior. In this respect, a CGI might decrease group cohesiveness and lessen deindividuation.

In other situations, gangs have responded defiantly as a group. We know of one enjoined gang, in an area where enforcement had been difficult, that set a palm tree on fire as a symbol of their defiance. This is a clear example of increased group cohesion rather than deindividuation. The period of time between serving the injunction papers notifying individual gang members and the first enforcement events appears to be crucial. The group's bond may be broken or at least weakened. Conversely, bonds may be strengthened as the group rallies in the face of an attack from the outside. As Decker (1996) found in his study of St. Louis gang members: "The key element [of gang violence] is the collective identification of threat, a process that unites the gang and overcomes the general lack of unity by increasing cohesion" (p. 261). These varied results undoubtedly depend on a wide variety of factors that bear further study.

Our interviews and review of injunction documents reflect a mixture of all these perspectives. When asked about the rationales for seeking injunctions and for explanations of how they achieve their perceived salutary effects, law enforcement officials often reply in terms recognizable as social disorganization, deterrence, or group process thinking. All three theoretical perspectives appear to be appropriate rationales for injunctions, but in the absence of theoretically based empirical research, we can only speculate as to how injunctions might work to reduce (or increase) gang activity in targeted neighborhoods. One clear avenue of needed research would focus on the social psychological impacts on gang members and the linkage between these and gang activity. CGIs may create a resurgence of informal social control by community residents. They may provide clearly articulated and enforced deterrence messages to gang members. The injunction process may individuate members and weaken essential group bonds. Conversely, CGIs may increase group cohesion and solidify gang identification, thereby strengthening individuals ties to gangs. This would lead to more gang crime, except if, as one prosecutor has proposed, peer pressure is used to enforce injunction restrictions within the group. Until these questions are addressed through systematic research, understanding why or how injunctions work will continue to elude us.

The Injunction Mechanism Described

The process used to obtain CGIs varies somewhat from jurisdiction to jurisdiction. The procedure commonly used in Southern California involves gathering evidence to support the claim that gang members create a public nuisance in a specified community and then applying to a civil court to require these individuals to refrain from continuing nuisance behavior. After the injunction is issued and targeted individuals are notified, they can be arrested for violating the conditions and prosecuted in either civil or criminal court.

The process of obtaining an injunction has been honed through the experience of prosecutors across the state and refined by a series of legal challenges since the first efforts in the early 1980s. The California District Attorneys Association provides workshops on CGIs for police and prosecutors. Nascent efforts are further informed by the SAGE manual (Los Angeles District Attorney, 1996) and by how-to articles published in practitioner journals (for example, Whitbread and Mazza, 1999). Figure 33.1, taken from law enforcement training materials, illustrates the major steps in the injunction process.

According to prosecutors, the primary

Figure 33.1
The Gang Injunction Process

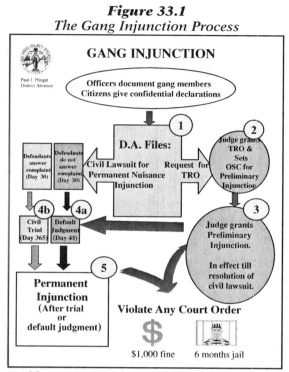

Used by permission of San Diego Deputy District Attorney Susan Mazza.

goal is usually to obtain a preliminary injunction with or without a temporary restraining order (TRO). The preliminary injunction is anticipated to have an immediate impact on the targeted gang's activities and stays in effect until the resolution of the lawsuit. If the defendants do not file an answer to the lawsuit, the injunction becomes permanent by default. If any defendant decides to take the suit to trial (see Mazza, 1999, for a description of such an instance in San Diego), the injunction remains in effect pending the outcome.

Typically, the application requests that the court find the targeted gang responsible for creating and maintaining a nuisance, in violation of California Civil Code section 3479, defined as follows: "Anything which is injurious to health, or is indecent or offensive to the senses, or an obstruction to the free use of property, so as to interfere with the comfortable enjoyment of life or property, or unlawfully obstructs the free passage or use, in the customary manner, of any navigable lake or river, bay, stream, canal, or basin, or any public park, square, street, or highway, is a nuisance."

A *public* nuisance is defined in Civil Code section 3480: "A public nuisance is one which affects at the same time an entire community or neighborhood, or any other considerable number of persons, although the extent of the annoyance or damage inflicted upon individuals may be unequal."

The nuisance is demonstrated in a "finding" submitted to the court. The evidence supporting the finding is a series of declarations which document that (1) the gang is an unincorporated association, (2) a public nuisance exists in the proposed area, and (3) the gang is responsible for creating and maintaining the public nuisance (Los Angeles County District Attorney, 1996:31).

The first requirement is met easily if the gang has already been found to be an illegal criminal street gang under the Street Terrorism Enforcement and Prevention (STEP) Act (California Criminal Code section 186.22). Enacted in 1989, this statute provides sentence enhancements for convicted individuals who have been previously notified that they are known to associate with a group engaged in criminal activity. This notification, referred to as "stepping" gangs, is statutorily distinct from CGIs. Most "stepped" gangs are not subjects of injunctions and, conversely, an injunction may be obtained against a gang that has not been "stepped."

Individuals' arrest records, field contacts, and, particularly, police and resident declarations are used to establish the existence of the public nuisance and the gang's responsibility for creating it. Typically, local police department gang experts will submit declarations detailing the gang's activities and the implied threat to community well-being. Sometimes, only police declarations are provided, but community resident declarations are viewed as especially persuasive:

> The citizen declarations have been the single most important piece of evidence in convincing the court to grant an injunction. This is not to say that everything else required is superfluous, but judges have placed a lot of weight on the declarations. Citizen declarations are also a way for the victims of gang oppression to reassert control over their neighborhood. It is empowering. (Whitbread and Mazza, 1999: 37)

However, obtaining community declarations can be difficult. Targeted communities by definition suffer from gang intimidation. Residents may fear reprisal. Prosecutors typically pull community declarations from the injunction papers if the judge refuses to grant permission to seal them. In addition, stressed police-community relationships may make it difficult to locate individuals willing to cooperate with the police. One jurisdiction circumvented these difficulties by designating an officer who had been raised in the community to gather these declarations.

Because of these concerns for resident safety, the contents of these declarations are not readily accessible to researchers. In Inglewood, we were permitted to read several declarations, but not allowed to make copies of them. The declarations seemed to provide compelling evidence of the deleterious impact of gang members in this neighborhood.

Our field notes recorded our best recollection of the declarations:

> A property owner in the Darby-Dixon area talked about how hard it was to rent out his units (because of the gang), and how he had lowered the price drastically—he doesn't even break even on the rent. He talked about drug dealing that he had witnessed, and his concern for the children in the area. He mentioned the fact that the gangsters drive the wrong way down the one-way streets in the area. (field notes, 17 October 1996)

Several days later, our field notes summarized five other declarations:

> Two civilians note seeing a pregnant woman getting beaten up by some members. Another man talked about two dead bodies that were found in the area. One woman recalled the gang members breaking into her car and setting it on fire because she had called the police about loud music. One property owner explained how he bought his tenant new tires because the gang members had slashed her tires. They all talk about blatant drug dealing that goes on in the area. (field notes, 28 October 1996)

The process of soliciting resident involvement in developing injunction evidence represents a substantial investment in time, but can be critical to establishing the public aspect of the nuisance. The community declarations lend validity to the need for law enforcement to take this extraordinary step in limiting otherwise legal activities. One repercussion of the LAPD Rampart CRASH officer scandal was suspension of an area CGI, because several officers who provided declarations became targets of investigation related to their misconduct, including fabrication of evidence and testimony in cases unrelated to the CGI. This Rampart CGI did not include resident declarations. During the period of the suspension, a prosecutor from a different jurisdiction noted to us: "It's unfortunate that they didn't get citizen declarations; they may have helped validate the officers' testimony."

After the declarations are gathered, the prosecutor prepares an application for the TRO and/or preliminary injunction that includes the list of restricted activities. The proscribed activities vary since the nature of the nuisance is specific to a particular community. Gang members are generally prohibited from congregating in certain locations, committing vandalism, harassing or intimidating residents, trespassing on private property, selling drugs, engaging in behaviors commonly associated with selling drugs (for example, possessing pagers or acting as a lookout), urinating in public, and clustering near certain locations, such as parks or schools. The prosecutor files the application with the superior court, civil division, and obtains a hearing date.[4] Specified gang members must be notified of the hearing several days in advance, but are not required to appear. The defendants may have legal representation, although because this action is a civil proceeding, they have no right to public defender services.

At the hearing, the judge may delete certain individuals' names from the application or change the restricted activities. If the TRO/preliminary injunction is issued at that time, targeted individuals must be served again with the amended papers before the conditions can be enforced. After individuals are served, they can be arrested for violating any of the injunction's conditions. If they are prosecuted, such action can be taken either in criminal court, where a misdemeanor has a maximum penalty of $1,000 fine and/or six months incarceration in county jail, or in civil court, where contempt has a maximum penalty of a $1,000 fine and five days in jail (Whitmer and Ancker, 1996). In California, either civil or criminal contempt for violation of a court order is a misdemeanor.

A Brief History of Gang Injunctions in Southern California

No official agency is mandated with tracking the use of injunctions against street gangs. The first reported use of a civil injunction for gang abatement was in Santa Ana, California, in 1980, although site abatements for other disorder problems like drugs or pornography were not uncommon. The Santa Ana city attorney obtained an injunction prohibiting youths from gathering and partying at a known gang hangout. Shortly thereafter, the Los Angeles County district attorney secured injunctions for specific addresses in Pomona (1981), West Covina (1982) and East Los Angeles (1986). In 1982, the Los Angeles City attorney obtained an injunction against three gangs. Castorena (1998) cites this injunction as the first to sue a gang, as well as individual gang members, as an unincorporated association. The four provisions were focused on graffiti.[5]

Much of this history seems to have escaped public attention, because the Los Angeles City Attorney's Office is generally credited with introducing the strategy in 1987, with the widely publicized injunction against the Playboy Gangster Crips. (See Los Angeles City Attorney Gang Prosecution Section, 1995, for a detailed description of this injunction.) Some publicity was due to the court challenge lodged by the American Civil Liberties Union (ACLU). The challenge was partially successful as an attorney was appointed to represent the gang and only illegal behaviors were included in the injunction issued in December of 1987. The ACLU has continued to play a role in the evolution of the injunction process by defending gang members, assisting in appeals, conducting a study of the Blythe Street injunction (ACLU, 1997), and expressing concerns in newspaper editorials (see Hoffman and Silverstein, 1995). The Playboy Gangster Crips injunction was also noteworthy in that, unlike most previous injunctions, the injunction had no neighborhood-defined geographic limits; it covered the entire city.

No new injunctions were issued for the next several years. In 1992, two gang shootings involving innocent bystanders spurred the Burbank City Attorney's Office to obtain an injunction against 34 members of the Barrio Elmwood Rifa. According to Castorena (1998), the Burbank injunction was the first to limit gang members from associating with one another, prohibiting them from "standing, sitting, walking, driving, gathering or appearing anywhere in public view with any other defendant from [the

gang] anywhere in the [target area]." The prohibition from associating has since been included in most injunctions.

From 1993 to 2000, at least 30 gang injunctions have been issued in Southern California (see Figure 33.2 for a map of a Southern California CGIs since 1980). Injunction activity accelerated in 1996. From 1996 to 1999, a Southern California gang was enjoined, on average, every two months. Although injunctions have been issued in San Diego, Orange, San Bernardino and Ventura counties, 23 of the 31 injunctions granted in the 1990s were in Los Angeles County. Four injunctions have also been obtained in Northern California counties and at least two in Texas. Local prosecutors report inquiries from jurisdictions across the United States, but it appears that most of the injunction activity takes place in Southern California. . . .

What Is the Evidence of Success?

The law enforcement agencies that have experimented with injunctions uniformly view their efforts as successful, as is typical of practitioners' assessments of their own programs. Such views are clearly evident in our interviews, in media accounts, and in policy documents. Success is variously defined as reductions in gang activity, the splintering of gang structures resulting from relocation of targeted gang members, decreases in violent crime rates and in calls for service, and in visible improvements in neighborhood disorder and in residents' sense of security. These success stories are often compelling, but are never buttressed with supporting evidence that meets minimal scientific standards of evaluation, such as equivalent area comparisons or addressing rival explanatory factors (see Whitbread and Mazza, 1999, for attribution of crime reductions to 10 separate injunctions). . . .

Three independent studies have reviewed crime statistics following the issuance of injunctions; two produced negative findings, but the most recent, and most thorough, assessment suggests that injunctions may produce at least a moderate reduction in violent crime.[6] Maxson and Allen (1997) found that Part I crime reports in Inglewood were substantially higher in the six months following issuance of the injunction (January–June 1997) than in the comparable six-month period in the prior year (January–

Figure 33.2
Gang Injunctions in Southern California, 1980 to 2000

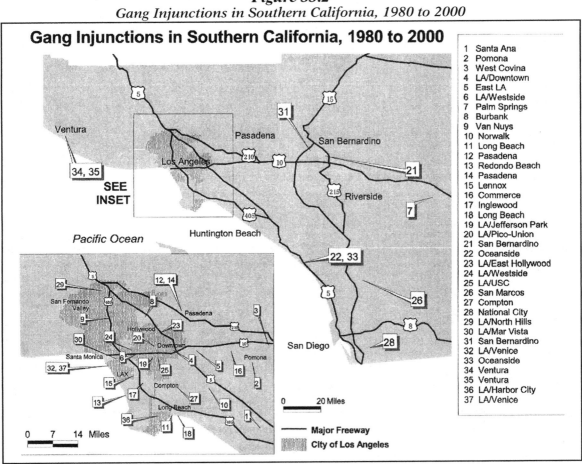

Source: Maxson, Hennigan & Sloane (2002), fn. 6
Map drawn by Geoffrey DeVerteuil, USC.

June 1996). Crime reports had risen during the six months immediately preceding the injunction (July–December 1996), so a negligible decrease in crime immediately following the issuance provided little support for a positive effect. As we have noted earlier, this injunction was not enforced because of the department's failure to provide resources when federal funds were depleted. Nevertheless, the Inglewood injunction is cited as a success in the practitioner literature (see Whitbread and Mazza, 1999).

The ACLU Foundation of Southern California conducted a statistical analysis of crime to assess the effectiveness of the Blythe Street injunction (ACLU, 1997). The foundation looked at crime trends in LAPD reporting districts adjacent to Blythe Street in Los Angeles's San Fernando Valley. Via the California Public Records Act, the foundation obtained monthly totals of serious violent felonies, total calls for police service, and felony drug arrests for the six-year period from 1991 through 1996 in the 19 reporting districts including and surrounding Blythe Street. The report concluded that the injunction

> was accompanied by a net increase in violent crime, even in the small reporting district most immediately effected by the injunction. . . . Violent crime and drug trafficking patterns for the 19 reporting district zones reflect significantly more pronounced increases in crime categories than citywide totals for the same offenses. . . . The implications of these findings for policymakers—including the Mayor, the City Council, the Office of the City Attorney, and the LAPD—are unmistakable. The Blythe Street gang injunction was preceded, and has been followed, by elaborate claims for its effectiveness in cutting crime and making

communities safer. According to statistical materials provided by the LAPD, the truth is precisely the opposite. (p. 44)

An LAPD gang expert challenged this report with a statement that the Blythe Street gang's activities have decreased in the last four years in response to the injunction and the city attorney's office's gang prosecutor director "questioned the organization's motives in preparing the report" (Tamaki, 1997). Although the ACLU study methods have been criticized (see Maxson and Allen, 1997 regarding selection of comparison areas and presentation of trend data), the report's assertion that there is little evidence that crime reductions are attributable to the injunction is worth noting.

In the most thorough and rigorous test to date, Grogger (2000) investigated changes in reported Part I violent and property crimes for 14 Los Angeles County injunctions imposed between 1993 and 1998. He compared crime trends in the five quarters preceding the injunctions with trends in the following year (including the quarter the injunction was imposed). He also looked at neighboring areas to detect spillover, or displacement effects, and at matched comparison areas to identify whether crime changes were attributable to injunctions. Looking at the effects of all 14 injunctions together, Grogger concluded that injunctions lead reported violent crime to fall somewhere between 1.4 and 3.0 crimes per quarter in the average target area. This translates to a decline of roughly 5 to 10 percent when compared with the preinjunction period. This effect was concentrated in reductions in assault, rather than robbery, and no positive effects were detected for property offenses. Finally, this study found no evidence of displacement, or the spillover of criminal activity into adjoining areas. Although Grogger was not able to assess the effect of individual injunctions due to data limitations, his study provides clear evidence of modest positive effects of injunctions on violent crime.

Unfortunately, implementation of injunctions in other sites has not been associated with comparable analyses of crime trends in the immediate and surrounding districts. Furthermore, program implementers or researchers have not used alternative data sources, such as community surveys, to assess the impact of injunctions empirically. The anecdotal reports show consistent, positive evidence of the effectiveness of injunctions in reducing gang activity and in improving deteriorating neighborhood conditions. These reports from program practitioners (that is, attorneys and police officers who develop and implement injunctions) and a few select neighborhood residents are clearly inadequate by scientific standards. Law enforcement and public officials will likely continue to respond to the promise of a quick fix to gang problems. . . .

Conclusion

We have argued that the paucity of independent, scholarly evaluation of the effect of injunctions should raise some concerns about their accelerated use. Each of the 32 injunctions issued in Southern California in the 1990s has offered an opportunity for a field test of some of the questions raised by this review. We have offered some theoretical perspectives that suggest this is a strategy with some promise; other perspectives would predict negative results. Do they "work" and in what ways? If so, how do they work? Among a variety of questions that remain unanswered, we can list the following:

- With what types of gang (for example, territorial, specialty, small, and so on) are injunctions most likely to be effective?

- How are gangs, gang members, and gang activity affected? Do the penalties have deterrent value, are neighbors empowered to exert social control, are gang ties increased or decreased? Do gangs dissolve or regenerate? Does activity simply get displaced to other neighborhoods? What is the impact on gang rivalries or on other gangs in the area? Do other gangs take over if a gang is handicapped by the injunction process?

- What are the optional collaborative arrangements, both among law enforcement agencies and with the community? What is the appropriate role of the community in developing and implementing injunctions? How much cooperation from the community is necessary or desirable?

- What is the effect of injunctions on neighborhood life? Do residents see less evidence of gang activity; do they feel safer and less fearful? Are they empowered to intervene to reverse physical or social disorder problems in their neighborhoods? How does the CGI fit into a constellation of place-based or community policing strategies?

- What is the most effective way to implement an injunction? Should there be a special unit assigned or department-wide enforcement? Should this be routinized or is enforcement through special operations such as sweeps or probation searches more effective? Is police visibility an effective deterrent, or are arrests and prosecution required? What are the most effective penalties?

Answering these questions would require various data collection strategies: assessment of official crime data, community resident (including gang members) surveys and interviews, block observations and ethnography. These should be replicated at several injunction test sites. Such a research venture would be costly, but would require far fewer funds than expended thus far on a strategy that has largely unexamined effects. Moreover, given the concerns regarding civil liberties and the appropriate reach of the law, such costs should be viewed as highly justified—for the sake of the neighborhood.[7]

Notes

1. We report these figures only to provide the reader with a general sense of the scope of gang participation. Because multiple agencies may report the same gangs and members as active in their jurisdictions, the National Youth Gang Center data set reflects an unknown degree of duplicate counts. Also, the reader should note that the NYGS does not provide a definition of gangs or membership for respondents, and this may result in inflated estimates. Finally, the validity and reliability of law enforcement gang counts is the subject of considerable debate (see Curry, Ball, and Decker, 1996, and Maxson, 1999, for further discussion). The authors acknowledge their appreciation for the data and assistance provided by the National Youth Gang Center and its director, John Moore.

2. For a similar statement by the L.A. City Attorney Gang Prosecution Section, see their description of civil gang abatement, 1995.

3. The Inglewood injunction was not fully implemented because resources for enforcement dwindled shortly after the injunction

was issued. Mr. Kerner's view is that the mere process of developing the injunction has a direct effect on gang activity through focusing attention on the gang. In particular, the service of legal documents to targeted gang members applies pressure to reduce criminal activity, and often to leave the area. According to Mr. Kerner, enforcement of the injunction is less important than the process that lets gang members know "we're looking at you" (phone conversation, 10 October 1997). The Boston Gun Project (Braga et al., 1999) also employed advance notice to gang members as part of that city's targeted deterrence strategy, Operation Ceasefire.

4. The civil injunction lawsuit is filed in this court because a violation of the Civil Code (for example, public nuisance) is alleged. Whitbread and Mazza (1999) provide a primer for peace officers unfamiliar with civil procedure. The plaintiffs are the "People," the defendants are the named gang members, and generally, the gang is "an unincorporated association." The court order (injunction) is sought as a remedy to the alleged public nuisance. Since money damages are not sought, the defendants do not have the right to a jury trial. Obtaining a TRO or preliminary injunction (under the argument that immediate and urgent attention is required) circumvents the long waiting period to trial that is typical in civil suits.

5. Our description of this history draws from documents prepared by Los Angeles prosecutors (Castorena, 1998; Los Angeles City Attorney Gang Prosecution Section, 1995; Whitmer and Ancker, 1996), a research proposal prepared by Allan (1999), newspaper articles, and more than two dozen interviews with police gang experts and other injunction practitioners.

6. Crime statistics have limited utility for assessing the short-term impact of injunctions. As in other community-based policing strategies, one goal may be to encourage residents' reports of crime. Increased patrolling and surveillance of gang members should increase arrests. Over the long term, reports of violence, drug sales, property crime, and nuisance crime (for example, graffiti and disorderly conduct) should decrease if the targeted gang commits a substantial proportion of these crimes in the area and if the injunction is successful in reducing crime. Preferred evaluation strategies would track crime trends over an extended period of time, include several areas for comparison, and investigate the potential displacement of the targeted gang's criminal activity from the targeted neighborhood to other areas.

7. Web sites with further information on civil gang injunctions:
   http://www.streetgangs.com/injunctions
   http://www.lacity.org/atty/atycb1c2g.htm.

References

Allan, Edward L. 1999. "Policing by Injunction: Problem-Oriented Dimensions of Civil Gang Abatement." Unpublished manuscript. State University of New York at Albany.

American Civil Liberties Union (ACLU). 1997. *False Premises, False Promises: The Blythe Street Injunction and Its Aftermath.* Los Angeles: ACLU Foundation of Southern California.

Block, Carolyn R., and Richard Block. 1993. *Street Gang Crime in Chicago.* Research in Brief. Washington, D.C.: National Institute of Justice.

Braga, Anthony A., David Weisburd, Elin J. Waring, Lorraine Green Mazerolle, William Spelman, and Francis Gajewski. 1999. "Problem-Oriented Policing in Violent Crime Places: A Randomized Controlled Experiment." *Criminology* 37(3):541–580.

Buerger, Michael. 1994. "The Limits of Community." In *The Challenge of Community Policing,* edited by Dennis Rosenbaum, 270–273. Thousand Oaks, Calif.: Sage.

Bursik, Robert J., and Harold G. Grasmick.1993. *Neighborhoods and Crime: Dimensions of Effective Community Control.* Lexington, Mass.: Lexington Books.

Castorena, Deanne. 1998. *The History of the Gang Injunction in California.* Los Angeles: Los Angeles Police Department Hardcore Gang Division.

Curry, G. David, Richard A. Ball, and Scott H. Decker. 1996. "Estimating the National Scope of Gang Crime from Law Enforcement Data." In *Gangs in America,* 2nd ed., edited by C. Ronald Huff, 21–36. Thousand Oaks, Calif.: Sage.

Curry, G. David, and Scott H. Decker. 1998. *Confronting Gangs: Crime and Community.* Los Angeles: Roxbury Press.

Decker, Scott. 1996. "Collective and Normative Features of Gang Violence." *Justice Quarterly* 13(2): 243–264.

———. 2001. "The Impact of Organizational Features on Gang Activities and Relationships." In *The Eurogang Paradox,* edited by Malcolm W. Klein, Hans-Jurgen Kerner, Cheryl L. Maxson, and Elmar Weitekamp, 21–39. Dordrecht, The Netherlands: Kluwer.

Decker, Scott, Tim Bynum, and Deborah Weisel. 1998. "A Tale of Two Cities: Gangs as Organized Crime Groups" *Justice Quarterly* 15: 395–425.

Decker, Scott, and Barrik Van Winkle. 1996. *Life in the Gang.* New York: Cambridge University Press.

Erikson, E.H. 1968. *Identity: Youth and Crisis.* New York: Norton.

Esbensen, Finn-Aage, and Dana Peterson Lynskey. 2001 . "Young Gang Members in a School Survey." In *The Eurogang Paradox,* edited by Malcolm W. Klein, Hans-Jurgen Kerner, Cheryl L. Maxson, and Elmar Weitekamp, 93–114. Dordrecht, The Netherlands: Kluwer.

Fearn, Noelle, Scott H. Decker, and G. David Curry. 2001. "Public Policy Responses to Gangs: Evaluating the Outcomes." In *The Modern Gang Reader,* 2d ed., edited by Jody Miller, Cheryl L. Maxson, and Malcolm W. Klein, 330–343. Los Angeles: Roxbury.

Grogger, Jeffrey. 2000. *The Effects of the Los Angeles County Gang Injunctions on Reported Crime.* Los Angeles: University of California, Department of Policy Studies.

Hoffman, Paul, and Mark Silverstein. 1995. "Safe Streets Don't Require Lifting Rights." In *The Modern Gang Reader,* edited by Malcolm W. Klein, Cheryl L. Maxson, and Jody Miller, 333. Los Angeles: Roxbury.

Huff, C. Ronald. 1996. "The Criminal Behavior of Gang Members and Nongang At-Risk Youth." In *Gangs in America,* 2nd ed., edited by C. Ronald Huff, 75–102. Thousand Oaks, Calif.: Sage.

Klein, Malcolm W. 1971. *Street Gangs and Street Workers.* Englewood Cliffs, N.J.: Prentice Hall.

———. 1993. "Attempting Gang Control by Suppression: The Misuse of Deterrence Principles." *Studies in Crime and Crime Prevention: Annual Review,* 2: 88–111.

———. 1995. *The American Street Gang.* New York: Oxford University Press.

Lasley, James. 1998. *"Designing Out" Gang Homicides and Street Assaults.* Research in Brief. Washington, D.C.: National Institute of Justice.

Lopez, Robert J. and Rich Connell. 1997. "Court Order Against LA Gang Expanded." *Los Angeles Times,* 30 August.

Los Angeles City Attorney Gang Prosecution Section. 1995. "Civil Gang Abatement: A Community Based Policy Tool of the Office of the Los Angeles City Attorney." In *The Modern Gang Reader,* edited by Malcolm W. Klein, Cheryl L. Maxson, and Jody Miller, 325–331. Los Angeles: Roxbury.

Los Angeles County District Attorney. 1996. *SAGE: A Handbook for Community Prosecution.* Los Angeles: Los Angeles County District Attorney.

Maxson, Cheryl. 1999. "Gang Homicide." In *Homicide Studies: A Sourcebook of Social Research,* edited by M. Dwayne Smith and Margaret A. Zahn, 239–254. Newbury Park, Calif.: Sage.

Maxson, Cheryl L. and Theresa L. Allen. 1997. *An Evaluation of the City of Inglewood's Youth Firearms Violence Initiative.* Los Angeles: Social Science Research Institute, University of Southern California.

Maxson, Cheryl L. and Malcolm W. Klein. 1995. "Investigating Gang Structures." *Journal of Gang Research* 3 (1): 33–40.

———. 2002. " 'Play Groups' No Longer: Urban Street Gangs in the Los Angeles Region. In *From Chicago to L.A.: Revisioning Urban Theory*, edited by Michael Dear, 239–266. Newbury Park, Calif.: Sage.

Mazza, Susan. 1999. "Gang Abatement. The San Diego Experience." *Law Enforcement Quarterly* 11 (spring): 288.

Miller, Jody. 2001. *One of the Guys: Girls, Gangs and Gender.* New York: Oxford University Press.

Short, James F., Jr. 1997. *Poverty, Ethnicity and Violent Crime.* Boulder, Colo.: Westview Press.

Spergel, Irving, and David Curry. 1993. "The National Youth Gang Survey." In *The Gang Intervention Handbook*, edited by Arnold P. Goldstein and C. Ronald Huff, 359–400. Champaign, Ill.: Research Press.

Tamaki, Julie. 1997. "Valley Gang Injunction Only Shifted Crime, ACLU Says," *Los Angeles Times*, 29 May, p. 3A.

Thornberry, Terence P. 1998. "Membership in Youth Gangs and Involvement in Serious and Violent Offending." In *Serious and Violent Juvenile Offenders: Risk Factors and Successful Interventions*, edited by Rolf Loeber and David P. Farrington, 147–166. Thousand Oaks, Calif.: Sage.

Vigil, J. Diego. 1988. *Barrio Gangs.* Austin: University of Texas Press.

Whitbread, Brian J., and Susan Mazza. 1999. "Utilizing Civil Injunction to Combat Gangs: Parts 1 and 2." *Law Enforcement Quarterly* 28 (1/2): 34–37.

Whitmer, John, and Deanne Ancker. 1996. "The History of the Injunction in California." Appendix M in LACDA's *SAGE: A Handbook for Community Prosecution.* Los Angeles: Los Angeles County District Attorney's Office.

Wilson, James Q., and George L. Kelling. 1982. "Broken Windows." *Atlantic Monthly*, March, 29–38.

Zimbardo, Philip G. 1969. "The Human Choice: Individuation, Reason, and Order Versus Deindividuation, Impulse and Chaos." In *Nebraska Symposium on Motivation*, vol.17, edited by William J. Arnold and Donald Levine. Lincoln: University of Nebraska Press. ✦

Recommended Readings

Battin, Sara R., Karl G. Hill, Robert D. Abbott, Richard F. Catalano, and J. David Hawkins. 1998. "The Contribution of Gang Membership to Delinquency Beyond Delinquent Friends." *Criminology* 36:93–115.

Chesney-Lind, Meda, and John M. Hagedorn. 1999. *Female Gangs in America: Essays on Girls, Gangs, and Gender.* Chicago: Lakeview Press.

Chin, Ko-Lin. 1996. *Chinatown Gangs: Extortion, Enterprise, & Ethnicity.* New York: Oxford University Press.

Covey, Herbert C., Scott Menard, and Robert J. Franzere. 1997. *Juvenile Gangs,* 2nd Edition. Springfield, IL: Charles C. Thomas.

Curry, G. David. 2000. "Self-Reported Gang Involvement and Officially Recorded Delinquency." *Criminology* 38:1253–1274.

Curry, G. David, and Scott H. Decker. 1998. *Confronting Gangs: Crime and Community.* Los Angeles: Roxbury Publishing.

Decker, Scott H. 1996. "Collective and Normative Features of Gang Violence." *Justice Quarterly* 13(2):243–264.

Decker, Scott H., and Barrik Van Winkle. 1996. *Life in the Gang.* Cambridge: Cambridge University Press.

Decker, Scott H., ed. 2003. *Policing Gangs and Youth Violence.* Belmont, CA: Wadsworth/Thomson Learning.

Esbensen, Finn-Aage, Stephen G. Tibbetts, and Larry Gaines, eds. 2004. *American Youth Gangs at the Millennium.* Long Grove, IL: Waveland Press.

Fleisher, Mark S. 1998. *Dead End Kids: Gang Girls and the Boys They Know.* Madison: Wisconsin University Press.

Gordon, Rachel A., Benjamin B. Lahey, Eriko Kawai, Rolf Loeber, Magda Stouthamer-Loeber, and David P. Farrington. 2004. "Antisocial Behavior and Youth Gang Membership: Selection and Socialization." *Criminology* 42:55–87.

Hagedorn, John M. 1998. *People and Folks: Gangs, Crime, and the Underclass in a Rustbelt City,* 2nd Edition. Chicago: Lakeview Press.

Horowitz, Ruth. 1983. *Honor and the American Dream.* New Brunswick, NJ: Rutgers University Press.

Huff, C. Ronald, ed. 1990. *Gangs in America.* Newbury Park, CA: Sage.

———. 1996. *Gangs in America,* 2nd Edition. Thousand Oaks, CA: Sage.

———. 2002. *Gangs in America,* 3rd Edition. Thousand Oaks, CA: Sage.

Klein, Malcolm W. 1995. *The American Street Gang: Its Nature, Prevalence and Control.* New York: Oxford University Press.

———. 2004. *Gang Cop: The Words and Ways of Officer Paco Domingo.* Walnut Creek, CA: AltaMira Press.

Klein, Malcolm W., Hans-Jurgen Kerner, Cheryl L. Maxson, and Elmar E. M. Weitekamp, eds. 2000. *The Eurogang Paradox: Youth Groups and Gangs in Europe and America.* The Hague: Kluwer.

Maxson, Cheryl L., Monica L. Whitlock, and Malcolm W. Klein. 1998. "Vulnerability to Street Gang Membership: Implications for Practice." *Social Service Review* (March):70–91.

Miller, Jody. 2001. *One of the Guys: Girls, Gangs and Gender.* New York: Oxford University Press.

Miller, Walter B. 1958. "Lower Class Culture as a Generating Milieu of Gang Delinquency." *Journal of Social Issues* 14:5–19.

Moore, Joan. 1991. *Going Down to the Barrio: Homeboys and Homegirls in Change.* Philadelphia: Temple University Press.

Peterson, Dana, Terrance J. Taylor, and Finn-Aage Esbensen. 2004. "Gang Membership and Violent Victimization." *Justice Quarterly* 21:793–815.

Rodriguez, Luis J. 1993. *Always Running: La Vida Loca*. Willimantic, CT: Curbstone Press.

Short, Jr., James F., ed. 2005. "Why Study Youth Gangs?" *Journal of Contemporary Criminal Justice,* special issue, volume 21.

Short, James F., and Fred L. Strodtbeck. 1965. *Group Process and Gang Delinquency*. Chicago: University of Chicago Press.

Spergel, Irving. 1995. *The Youth Gang Problem: A Community Approach*. New York: Oxford University Press.

Thornberry, Terence P., Marvin D. Krohn, Alan J. Lizotte, and Deborah Chard-Wierschem. 1993. "The Role of Juvenile Gangs in Facilitating Delinquent Behavior." *Journal of Research in Crime and Delinquency* 30:75–85.

Thornberry, Terence P., Marvin D. Krohn, Alan J. Lizotte, Carolyn A. Smith, and Kimberly Tobin. 2003. *Gangs and Delinquency in Developmental Perspective*. New York: Cambridge University Press.

Thrasher, Frederic. 1927/1963. *The Gang: A Study of 1,313 Gangs in Chicago*. Chicago: University of Chicago Press.

Vigil, James Diego. 1988. *Barrio Gangs: Street Life and Identity in Southern California*. Austin: University of Texas Press.

———. 2002. *A Rainbow of Gangs: Street Cultures in the Mega-City*. Austin: University of Texas Press.

Zatz, Marjorie S. 1987. "Chicano Youth Gangs and Crime: The Creation of a Moral Panic." *Contemporary Crises* 11:129–158. ◆